INFORMATION SYSTEMS
A Management Perspective

THIRD EDITION

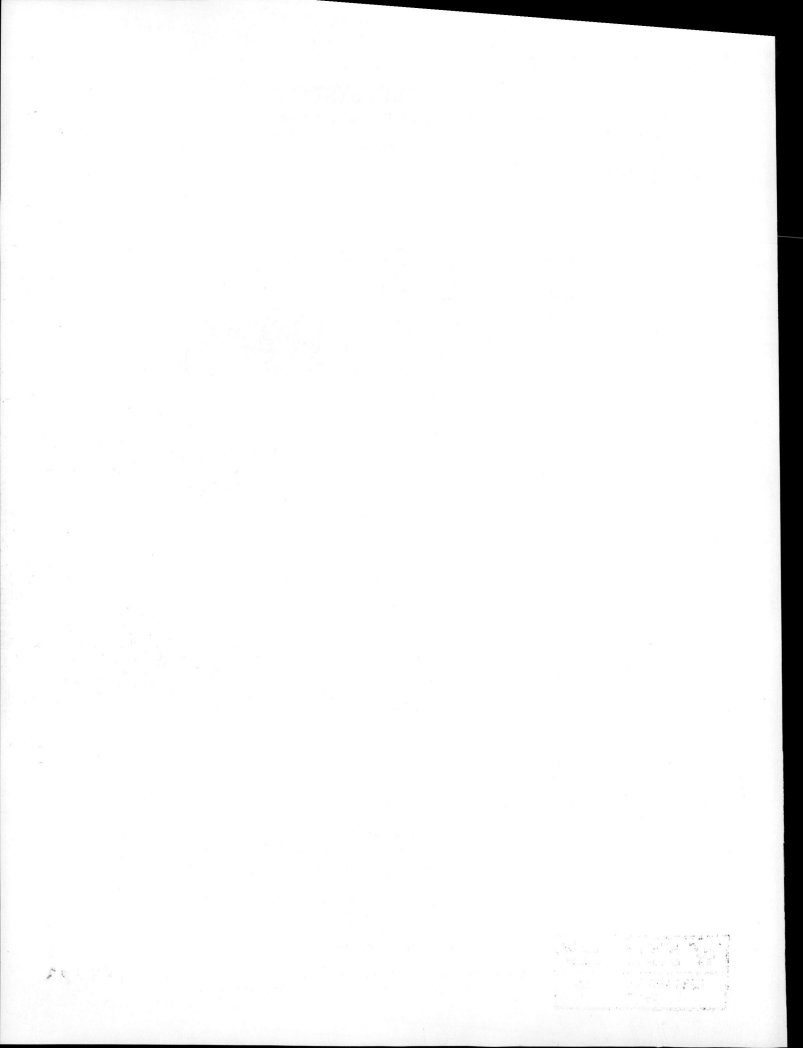

INFORMATION SYSTEMS

A Management Perspective

Third Edition

Steven Alter
University of San Francisco

ADDISON-WESLEY

An imprint of Addison Wesley Longman, Inc.

Reading, Massachusetts • Menlo Park, California • New York • Harlow, England
Don Mills, Ontario • Sydney • Mexico City • Madrid • Amsterdam

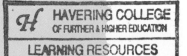

Executive Editor: Michael Roche
Associate Editor: Ruth Berry
Editorial Assistant: Adam Hamel
Development Editor: Maxine Effenson Chuck
Marketing Manager: Tom Ziolkowski
Senior Marketing Coordinator: Deanna Storey
Project Coordination and Text Design: Electronic Publishing Services Inc., NYC
Cover Designer: Regina Hagen
Cover Photo: © Don Bishop for Artville
Photo Researcher: Electronic Publishing Services Inc., NYC
Manufacturing Manager: Sheila Spinney
Electronic Page Makeup: Electronic Publishing Services, NYC
Printer and Binder: World Color Book Services

Library of Congress Cataloging-in-Publication Data
Alter, Steven.
Information systems : a management perspective / Steven Alter. —
3rd ed.
p. cm.
Includes bibliographical references and index.
ISBN 0-201-35109-9 (hc.)
1. Management information systems. I. Title.
T58.6.A44 1999 98-36555
658.4'038'011—dc21 CIP

Please visit our Web site at http://hepg.awl.com

ISBN 0-201-35109-9

12345678910ptr—RNV—01009998

PREFACE

Tomorrow's successful business professionals need more than the ability to do personal work on a computer and general familiarity with business and technical terms. Contributing fully to current organizations requires an ability to participate in systems, evaluate them, and contribute to system development efforts. This requires an organized approach for thinking about systems, an approach that can be used successfully today and will still be valid five or ten years from now when today's technical and business terms are no longer at the cutting edge.

This third edition of *Information Systems: A Management Perspective* is built around a practical, widely applicable approach for analyzing IT-enabled systems from a business viewpoint. Its ambitions go far beyond merely covering current vocabulary for talking about information systems and technology. It couches its entire coverage in terms of a systems analysis approach developed with the help of students who used these ideas to write papers about information systems in real business settings. This approach is called the work-centered analysis (WCA) method. It is based on the WCA framework, which provides a way to summarize a system in terms of six elements. To emphasize this integrating concept, each chapter opening case is accompanied by a tabular "system snapshot" that summarizes the elements in that situation.

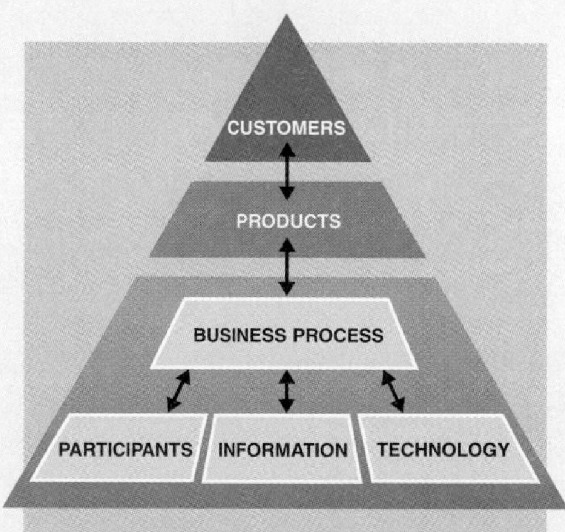

Chapter 2 explains how to use these elements to analyze virtually any system from a business viewpoint. The rest of the book explores each topic in more depth. Table P.1 shows the part of the framework that each chapter emphasizes. It also shows how each chapter contributes to the ideas any business professional can use for thinking about any information system or any work system it supports.

TABLE P.1 How Each Chapter Contributes to an Understanding of Systems

Primary emphasis	Chapter
	• Chapter 1, *The Challenge of Applying IT for Business Advantage,* starts by summarizing the process of building a system and the technical advances that made today's IT-enabled systems possible. It gives examples of IT-enabled improvements in every functional area of business. It closes by citing challenges such as embracing technology without succumbing to hype and overselling and while accepting the difficulty of anticipating how technology will be adapted in practice. • Chapter 2, *Basic Concepts for Understanding Systems,* explains the WCA framework and shows how it can be used from five different perspectives when examining a work system in more depth. It emphasizes the importance of understanding both an information system and the work system it supports.
	• Chapter 3, *Business Processes,* shows how to examine a business process. It starts with graphical methods for summarizing processes. Then it discusses alternative process rationales, major characteristics that determine how well processes perform, and performance variables themselves.
	• Chapter 4, *Information and Databases,* starts by explaining data modeling, a general technique for understanding information requirements. It then discusses database management systems that store and control databases. It also talks about evaluating information and about the use of models.
	• Chapter 5, *Communication, Decision Making, and Different Types of Information Systems,* presents basic ideas about communication and decision making and shows how these ideas are related to different types of information systems. Current techniques newly introduced in the chapter include intranets, extranets, knowledge management, OLAP, and data mining.
	• Chapter 6, *Product, Customer, and Competitive Advantage,* looks at the two elements at the top of the framework and explains why the criteria customers use to evaluate the product of a work system are usually different from the criteria for evaluating the internal operation of the work system. It goes on to look at competitive uses of information systems.
	• Chapter 7, *Human and Ethical Issues,* focuses on positive and negative impacts of work systems and information systems on people at work. It points out that the success of any system in business depends on its participants. It closes by discussing ethical issues such as privacy, accuracy, property, and access.
	• Chapter 8, *Computer Hardware,* starts with measures of performance for technology, provides an overview of different types of computer systems, and presents some of the technical choices for capturing data, storing and retrieving data, and displaying data. • Chapter 9, *Software, Programming, and Artificial Intelligence,* discusses the evolution of programming languages and operating systems. It then looks at steps toward machine intelligence such as expert systems and neural networks. • Chapter 10, *Networks and Telecommunications,* looks at different types of networks that link communication devices and computers. It closes by discussing standards and policy issues that affect the future of telecommunications.
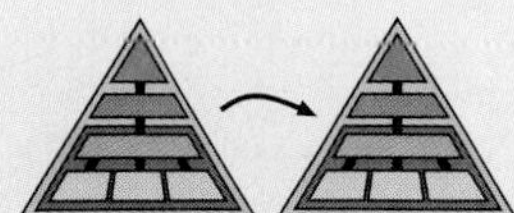	• Chapter 11, *Information Systems Planning,* looks at the strategic and practical issues when deciding how to incorporate IT into a firm's business strategy. It covers a series of strategic issues, methods for selecting among proposed information system investments, and issues related to project management. • Chapter 12, *Building and Maintaining Information Systems,* identifies the phases of any information system project, and shows how these phases are performed in four different approaches for building information systems.
	• Chapter 13, *Information System Security and Control,* discusses risks related to project failure, accidents and malfunctions, and computer crime. It then explains some of the methods for minimizing these risks.

WHAT'S NEW?

The improvements in this new edition include streamlining, improved representation of the framework, new real world cases, and more extensive coverage of electronic commerce, hypertext, Java, and other current topics.

Streamlining. This third edition continues a theme of streamlining that began in the second edition. This edition added more focus instead of more chapters and the text has now gone from 20 to 15 to 13 chapters in successive editions. The sequence of the chapters is basically unchanged. The two chapters that were removed are Chapter 6, Increasing Efficiency and Effectiveness of Internal Operations, and Chapter 12, Steps Toward Computer Intelligence. Material from Chapter 6 was moved into the new introductory chapter and also into Chapter 3. Material from Chapter 12 was merged into the chapter on Software and Programming (Chapter 9). Material from the four part openers in the second edition were incorporated into the body of various chapters.

Improved visual representation of the framework. The new triangular representation of the WCA framework makes it somewhat easier to visualize the basic ideas the framework conveys. It shows more clearly that six elements should be considered when summarizing or analyzing any system in a business, that four of those elements are within the system, and that the product and customer are outside of the system but need to be considered.

New real world cases. Each chapter ends with two real world cases based on sources through mid-1998. Additional real world cases for subsequent years will be available through the third edition's greatly expanded Web site.

Chapter by chapter changes. In addition to substantial updating of the real world examples throughout all the chapters, many of the chapters were changed in significant ways:

- Chapter 1, *The Challenge of Applying IT Successfully,* was completely rewritten to highlight leading edge IT applications in each functional area of business. To provide balance between the promise of technological breakthroughs and the reality of slow adoption and unexpected consequences, the chapter ends with a section on obstacles that occur when applying IT in the real world.
- Chapter 2, *Basic Concepts for Understanding Systems,* incorporates material from a part opener in the second edition and provides greater clarity on the difference between an information system and the work system it supports. It also explains more about how to use the WCA method to analyze a system from a business professional's viewpoint.
- Chapter 3, *Business Processes,* now includes material on management work that was in Chapter 6 of the second edition.
- Chapter 4, *Information and Databases,* includes a new section on text databases and hypertext.
- Chapter 5, *Communication, Decision Making, and Different Types of Information Systems,* identifies six types of information systems instead of eight identified in the second edition. MIS and EIS are combined into a single category; groupware is treated as a type of communication system.
- Chapter 6, *Product, Customer, and Competitive Advantage,* incorporates a new section on electronic commerce and a clearer explanation of mission-critical versus strategic information systems. In addition, the product positioning map from the second edition was reformatted to illustrate more clearly that products can be improved by changing the way they combine information, service, and physical things.
- Chapter 7, *Human and Ethical Issues,* contains updated examples.
- Chapter 8, *Computer Hardware,* starts with a section on measuring technology performance that was previously in a part opener.
- Chapter 9, *Software Programming and Artificial Intelligence,* ends with material on artificial intelligence that was previously part of Chapter 12 in the second edition. This clarifies the chapter's overarching themes concerning long-term improvements in software and programming that are gradually moving toward making software "smarter." The section on object oriented programming was moved near

the beginning of the chapter to reflect its increasing importance. Java is covered in the section on programming languages.

- Chapter 10, *Networks and Telecommunications,* incorporates increased coverage of virtual private networks and TCP/IP, along with updates related to telecommunications standards and policy.
- Chapter 11, *Information Systems Planning,* incorporates material previously in a part opener and adds new material on Broadbent and Weill's business and IT maxims.
- Chapter 12, *Building and Maintaining Information Systems,* adds an explanation of the capability maturity model.
- Chapter 13, *Information System Security and Control,* adds many new examples plus new coverage of firewalls and public key encryption.

PEDAGOGICAL FEATURES

This book's pedagogical features start with typical pedagogical features of a good current textbook. Each chapter contains study questions, a chapter summary, keywords, review questions, and discussion questions. Pedagogical features that help differentiate this book include the following:

Unifying framework. This book's most unique pedagogical feature is its use of a unifying framework that is reflected in the book's outline and is the core of a systems analysis approach that any business professional can use. All good books in this field provide a thorough coverage of terminology. This book keeps the big picture visible and shows how current terminology is related to a simple set of ideas that the students can use long after a new generation of business and technical practices emerges.

Real world cases. Another key pedagogical feature is the inclusion of real world cases. Some students learn best by focusing on examples and seeing how they are related to concepts and theories. Many others learn best by focusing on theory and seeing how examples validate it. This book is designed to serve both groups well. Each chapter starts with an interesting, current, real world case and ends with two more. Most chapters contain many real world examples that are integrated into the explanation of the concepts rather than being thrown in as an afterthought. To provide a balanced representation of the real world, the cases include both successes and failures.

Debate topics and reality checks. The debate topic following each chapter-opening case is designed to encourage active interest and participation by students. The reality checks following major sections within the chapters serve a similar purpose.

Web site. This book's Web site is designed to supplement the coverage in the book and will be updated periodically to make sure it provides links to the most current case material. The Web site is designed to go far beyond just listing Web sites of companies mentioned in the text. For each chapter, the Web site links to additional recent case material that is readily available through the Web. Included with many of these examples are several questions for discussion. This book's Web site also contains a list of longer cases that are available through a variety of sources, thereby increasing the choices available to instructors and making it unnecessary to lengthen the book with long cases. The book's Web site also provides direct access to cases and application scenarios from the first and second edition that remain valuable even though they are several years old. In addition, it provides a list of Web sites that delve more deeply into major issues discussed in the chapters.

TEACHING SUPPLEMENTS

A complete set of teaching supplements is available for instructors who adopt this book. These supplements are designed to enhance the accessibility, versatility, and teachability of the text material.

Instructor's Manual & Test Bank. This supplement was prepared by Professor Errol Martin of the University of Canberra in Australia. The Instructor's Manual portion contains alternative syllabi and approaches to teaching with this text, lecture outlines for each chapter, teaching suggestions for specific points, additional study questions, and answers to end-of-chapter questions and cases. The Test Bank portion contains 75–100 multiple choice questions per chapter. Each question is labeled as conceptual, definitional, or applied. Each question is also labeled in terms of level of difficulty.

Computerized Test Bank. The Test Bank is available in Addison Wesley Longman's TestGen-EQ test generating software. TestGen-EQ's friendly graphical interface enables instructors to view, edit, and add questions, transfer questions to tests, and print tests in a variety of fonts and forms. Search and sort features let the instructor quickly locate questions and arrange them in a preferred order. Graphics and equations can also be imported into TestGen-EQ. The network testing component—QuizMaster-EQ—is fully networkable and automatically grades quizzes, stores results, and allows the instructor to view or print a variety of grading reports. Both of these programs are components of the Instructor's CD-ROM.

FastFax Testing. As an additional service for instructors using this text, FastFax testing is available through our Glenview Software Products and Services Group. This group will create tests based on guidelines from the instructor and send out a hard copy of the test via fax or mail within two days of receipt of the guidelines. To receive more information or forms for requesting tests, please contact your local Addison Wesley Longman sales consultant.

Instructor's CD-ROM with PowerPoint Slides. All the book's diagrams have been assembled in the form of PowerPoint slide presentations and placed on CD-ROM. Instead of making transparencies from transparency masters, all you need to do is hook up a computer to a projector. If desired, you may also print the slides and use the printed output as transparency masters. The Instructor's CD-ROM also contains the Computerized Test Bank.

Web site. An enhanced Web site for the third edition includes a variety of cases, relevant news updates, chapter-specific links, interactive exercises, and links to numerous online resources for instructors and students. Also included is a model transaction processing system, which contains sample transactions, standard inquiries, and management reports related to the cumulative Custom T-Shirt, Inc. case (also on the Web). The system uses Microsoft Access 2.0, and it can be examined and enhanced in many ways to provide students with a hands-on view of what a transaction processing system is and how transaction processing and database queries are supported by a relational DBMS.

Videos. The Addison Wesley Longman library of information systems videotapes is available to adopters of this text. Instructors may select from "Computer Concepts," "Computers in Business, Part I,"and "Computers in Business, Part II."

ACKNOWLEDGMENTS

Many individuals and organizations have contributed to this book, either directly or indirectly. I especially want to thank students in undergraduate, MBA, and executive MBA classes at the University of San Francisco who provided an excellent testing ground for both the ideas in this book and the approach for conveying those ideas.

This book benefited greatly from the efforts of many reviewers, who identified strengths that could be amplified and shortcomings that could be eliminated or minimized. Although it is impossible to respond to every request and answer every criticism (in both books and information systems), and although I am responsible for any confusions or misunderstandings that remain, I did my best to incorporate the many insightful ideas and criticisms provided by the following reviewers:

Cynthia M. Beath
Southern Methodist University

Robert Behling
Bryant College

Linda J. Behrens
University of Central Oklahoma

Harry Benham
Montana State University, Bozeman

Elia V. Chepaitis
Fairfield University

William Cummings
University of Illinois

Donald L. Davis
University of Southern Mississippi

David Fickbohm
Golden Gate University

Mary Beth Fritz
University of Florida

Jonathan L. Gifford
George Mason University

Ernest A. Kallman
Bentley College

Edward M. Kaplan
Bentley College

William Leigh
University of Central Florida

Michael D. Myers
University of Auckland, New Zealand

Leah R. Pietron
University of Nebraska at Omaha

Erik Rolland
University of California

Samuel A. Rebelsky
Grinnell College

Roger Smith
Yale University

Louise L. Soe
California State Polytechnic University, Pomona

Brian A. Yahn
Northern Alberta Institute of Technology

The task of producing this third edition involves a lot of work beyond writing the chapters. Mike Roche, editor and publisher, showed exceptional knowledge and commitment to both publishing and information systems. Maxine Effenson Chuck, developmental editor, analyzed reviews and provided many valuable comments about details of the chapters. This book was produced by Electronic Publishing Services, Inc., whose production editor Jodi Isman coordinated a talented team including book designer JoAnne Chernow, illustrator Stephanie McWilliams, photo researcher Francis Hogan, and copy editor Eileen Smith. Patty Mahtani, the production supervisor for Addison-Wesley maintained effective communication with EPS and made sure the book was completed on time.

Finally, I would like to thank my daughter Emily, whose gentle but telling comments and criticisms reveal a fine writer in the making. Heaven help her.

CONTENTS

ABOUT THE AUTHOR

Steven Alter is Professor of Information Systems at the University of San Francisco. He holds a B.S. in Mathematics and a Ph.D. in Management Science, both from MIT. While on the faculty of the University of Southern California, he revised his Ph.D. thesis and published it as *Decision Support Systems: Current Practice and Continuing Challenges,* one of the first books on this important type of information system. Professor Alter's journal articles have appeared in *Harvard Business Review, Sloan Management Review, MIS Quarterly, Communications of the ACM, TIMS Studies in Management Sciences, Interfaces, Data Processing, Futures,* and *The Futurist.*

Prior to joining the University of San Francisco, he served for eight years as a founding vice president of Consilium, Inc. (CSIM on the NASDAQ stock exchange). His many roles included starting departments for customer service, documentation and training, technical support, and product management. He participated in building and implementing early versions of manufacturing software currently used by major semiconductor and electronics manufacturers in the United States, Europe, and Asia.

Upon returning to academia he decided to work on a problem he observed in industry, the difficulty business people have in articulating what they expect from computerized systems and how these systems can or should change the way work is done. His initial efforts in this area led to the 1992 publication of the first edition of this text. The second edition and this new third edition benefit from additional research on how business professionals understand information systems.

When not working, he indulges his love of music by playing cello-piano duets and string quartets with friends and by stumbling through Chopin's easier piano pieces when no one else is within earshot. His other hobbies include hiking, skiing, and international travel. The photo is from a hike in Yosemite during a beard-growing experiment.

INFORMATION SYSTEMS
A Management Perspective

THIRD EDITION

The Challenge of Applying IT Successfully

1

Study Questions

- What are the phases in building and maintaining systems?
- What are some of the areas in which IT-based innovations have affected the major functional areas of business?
- What technology trends have enabled IT-based innovation in business?
- What obstacles and real world limitations have slowed the pace of implementation for IT-based innovations?

Outline

Opening Case

AMAZON.COM: AN ONLINE BOOKSTORE

Amazon.com operates quite differently from a traditional bookstore. When you enter a traditional bookstore, you may ask for help, but it is more likely that you will stroll around browsing the shelves. Even if you are looking for a specific book, as you make your way to the part of the store where you hope to find the book, you may find something else of interest to you that you had not considered. When you find the book you've been looking for, you may pick it up and discover that you like it more or less than you had anticipated. Depending on the bookstore, you might talk to a staff member who can discuss the book with you or can steer you to another book of interest. In many bookstores you can stop for a cup of coffee as you browse through some books, or even meet an acquaintance.

Amazon.com, which was launched in 1995 as the first major bookseller on the World Wide Web, touts itself as the earth's biggest bookstore. To shop at Amazon.com, you log on to the Web, type its uniform resource locator (URL), which is *www.* plus its name, and find yourself at its Web site. You have now entered a virtual bookstore that can sell you any of 2.5 million books, even though it has no apparent physical location and actually stocks very little inventory. If you know the book you want, you can find information about it immediately. If you are not sure which book you want, you can enter an author's name or a title and receive a response that helps you find what you might want. In some cases, you can look at a book review or even a sample chapter to make sure that you are ordering what you want.

The way Amazon.com provides value for its customers is quite different from the approach of traditional stores. The number of books in its online catalog is more than ten times larger than the number of books at the largest chain store, and the readily available information about those books may be more detailed. It gives discounts on some items, just as most chain stores do, but it charges a shipping fee and always has a delay for shipping. It keeps its costs low by carrying little inventory, and fills orders by obtaining the books from several wholesalers, packing them, and shipping them to customers from a central facility. Although Amazon.com started out as an innovator, it soon faced growing competition as other booksellers responded by creating their own online bookstores. In May 1997 Barnes & Noble opened its own online bookstore and sued Amazon.com over its assertion about being the earth's biggest bookstore. Barnes & Noble argued that Amazon's assertion amounted to false advertising because it keeps only a few hundred titles in stock at any given time. "[Amazon] isn't a bookstore at all," Barnes & Noble claimed. "It is a book broker making use of the Internet exclusively to generate sales to the public." Barnes & Noble's new Web site trumpeted itself as "The World's Largest Bookseller Online."[1]

Wide access to online stores has only existed for several years, so the ramifications of this type of commerce are not yet clear. What is clear, however, is that online stores can provide information that may not be readily available from typical bookstores and can also replace the social aspect of going to a bookstore with the convenience of shopping at home. In the mid-1990s, there was growing concern that Wal-Mart and other superstores would overwhelm small merchants in small-town shopping areas. Today, traditional merchants of many types face a similar threat through the new options online commerce provides for consumers.

Debate Topic

Will online bookstores ultimately have a negative effect on city life by wiping out most smaller local bookstores other than those in niche locations such as vacation areas?

This text has a very practical purpose, namely, to help you understand and analyze information systems from the viewpoint of a **business professional,** a person in a business or government organization who manages other people or works as a professional in fields such as engineering, sales, manufacturing, consulting, and accounting. Understanding information systems from this viewpoint is important to you because you will inevitably encounter information systems in today's business world. Many of you will not only use information systems extensively, but will also be called upon to analyze systems by identifying their strengths and weaknesses, recommending changes, and helping to implement these changes as well as fostering ongoing improvements.

The opening case about Amazon.com illustrates the challenge business professionals face in trying to seize opportunities while warding off competitors' threats related to information technology (IT). Although the Internet originated in the late 1960s as a government-funded research project, businesses such as Amazon.com are relatively new and depend on IT advances that only recently have made the Internet powerful enough to support this type of business. The part of the Internet called the World Wide Web (WWW, or the Web) was not even created until 1992; yet within five years, it provided an enormous opportunity for the founders of Amazon.com and a corresponding threat to conventional bookstores. While technological innovations are an essential part of the story, from a business viewpoint, the story of Amazon.com is not about technology. Rather, it is about applying IT in order to do business differently.

Table 1.1 accompanying the case illustrates this book's approach for making sense of IT applications. Subsequent chapters will explain the elements of this table in much more detail. For now, we will simply look at the way the table summarizes the system that originally made Amazon.com unique, namely, its system of providing information about books and permitting customers to enter orders through the World Wide Web. The *system* we are considering is not the World Wide Web, but rather a **work system,** a system that produces products for internal and external customers through a business process performed by human participants with the help of information and technology. This book emphasizes a particular class of work systems called information systems. (As Chapter 2 will discuss in

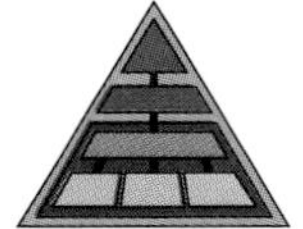

TABLE 1.1 Amazon.com Provides a New Way to Shop for Books

CUSTOMER

- Person who purchases books
- Wholesalers that supply the books
- Amazon.com's shipping department

PRODUCT

- Information about books that might be purchased
- Information describing each book order
- Books that are eventually delivered

BUSINESS PROCESS

Major steps:

- Purchaser logs on to www.amazon.com
- Purchaser identifies desired book or gives search criteria
- Purchaser looks at book-related information and decides what to order
- Purchaser enters order
- Amazon.com orders book from wholesaler
- Wholesaler sends book to Amazon.com
- Shipping department packages order and sends it to the purchaser

Rationale:

- Instead of forcing book buyers to go to typical bookstores, permit them to use online access from home or from work.

PARTICIPANTS

- People interested in purchasing books
- Order fulfillment department of wholesaler
- Shipping department of Amazon.com

INFORMATION

- Orders for books
- Price and other information about each book

TECHNOLOGY

- Personal computer used by purchaser
- Computers and networks used by Amazon.com for order processing

depth, an **information system** is a work system that uses information technology to capture, transmit, store, retrieve, manipulate, or display information, thereby supporting other work systems.)

It would be perfectly reasonable for you to argue that the summary in Table 1.1 does not represent the situation adequately. You might say that the table is too sketchy to be useful or that important issues are missing in its current form, such as how well the system performs, how satisfied most customers are, and how the firm's competition will respond. You might also be concerned about the process of building such a system and about how to manage the risks of owning such a system.

Questions such as these arise whenever systems are being discussed and analyzed; the responses to these questions lead to improvements in these systems. This book provides information and analysis methods business professionals can use to delve deeply into these and many other questions. It goes beyond merely covering the current vocabulary for discussing information systems and technology. In this book, we look at information systems using a systems analysis approach. This approach was developed with the help of MBA and EMBA students who applied their knowledge and understanding of information systems in real business settings. Each chapter presents ideas that you, or any business professional, can use when applying information technology to a work system, whether the system is a business or governmental organization.

This introductory chapter is called "The Challenge of Applying IT Successfully" because attaining business advantage through IT is a genuine challenge today. Every large firm in a modern economy uses IT extensively; in fact, most small firms have begun to incorporate it into their operations as well. Attaining advantage means not only using IT as well as everyone else does, but using it better. This requires an in-depth understanding of how to apply IT in basic work systems and in the products they produce.

This chapter is organized in a way that introduces this book's three main themes:

1. Business professionals participate in all the major phases of building and maintaining IT-enabled systems, and therefore need knowledge and skills necessary for that participation.
2. Advances in IT have been and continue to be driving factors in business innovation.
3. The success of IT-enabled systems is in no way guaranteed even when the latest technology is used.

This chapter starts with the first theme by summarizing the process of building and maintaining systems and noting that business professionals play important roles throughout. It then moves to the second theme by looking at some of the business innovations that have emerged during the last decade as a result of advances in IT and at the amazing technological progress that made these advances possible. The chapter conclusion emphasizes the third theme by showing that even though technical progress has been astounding, a number of real world limitations and uncertainties often make it difficult to use IT effectively in organizations. As you read this book, your challenge is to appreciate the enormous potential in this area while also cultivating a practical way to think about any system that uses IT in business.

PHASES IN BUILDING AND MAINTAINING SYSTEMS

The challenge of applying IT successfully falls as much on business professionals as on IT professionals. This is clear when one looks at the phases in building and maintaining systems. Figure 1.1 shows that both work systems and information systems that support them go through four phases: initiation, development, implementation, and operation and maintenance. Highly technical work such as programming usually takes up less than 20% of this effort.

Initiation is the process of defining the need to change an existing work system, identifying the people who should be involved in deciding what to do, and describing

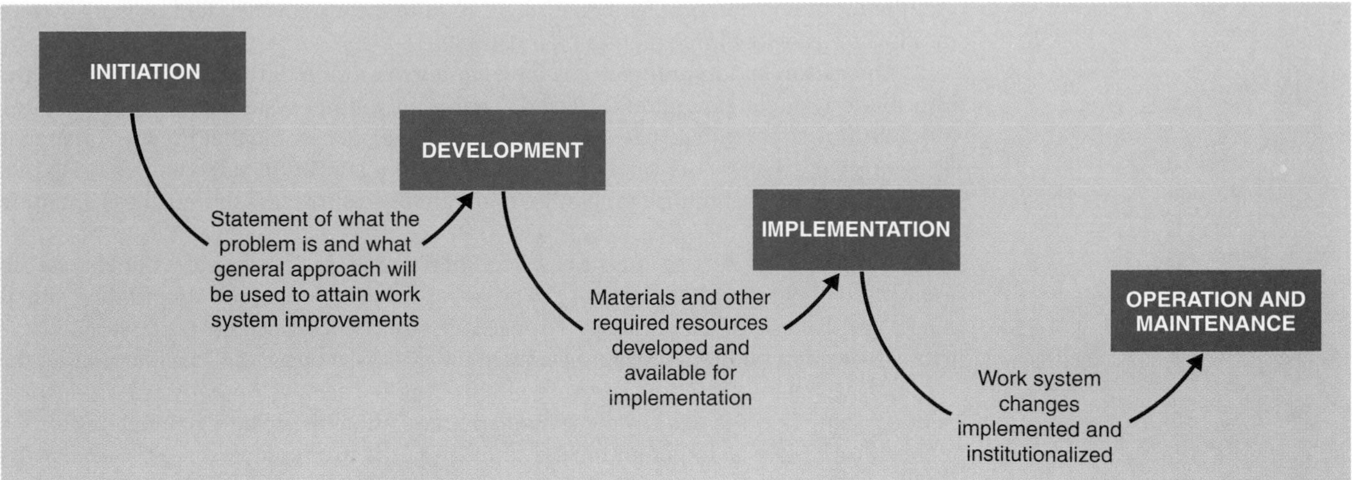

Figure 1.1
Four phases of a system

The business process of building and maintaining a work system or an information system that supports it has four phases. These phases apply to all systems in business even though the details of the individual phases may be quite different for different systems.

in general terms how the work system should operate differently and how any information system that supports it should operate differently. This phase may occur in response to recognized problems, such as data that cannot be found and used effectively, or high error rates in data. In other cases it is part of a planning process in which the organization is searching for ways to improve and innovate, even if current systems pose no overt problems. This phase concludes with a verbal or written agreement about the directions in which the work system and information system should change, plus a shared understanding that the proposed changes are technically and organizationally feasible.

Development is the process of acquiring and configuring hardware, software, and other resources needed to perform both the required IT-related functions and the required functions not related to IT. This phase starts by deciding exactly how the computerized and manual parts of the work system will operate. It then goes on to acquire the needed resources. If the hardware isn't already in place, development includes purchasing and installing the hardware. If the software isn't in place, it includes purchasing the software, producing it from scratch, or modifying existing software. Regardless of how the hardware and software are acquired, this phase includes creating documentation explaining how both the work system and the information system are supposed to operate. The development phase concludes with thorough testing of the entire information system to identify and correct misunderstandings and programming errors. Completion of development does not mean "the system works." Rather, it only means that the computerized parts of the work system operate on a computer. Whether or not the "system works" will be determined by how it is actually used in the organization.

Implementation is the process of making a new work system operational in the organization. This phase starts from the point when the software runs on the computer and has been tested. Activities in implementation include planning, user training, conversion to the new information system and work system, and follow-up to make sure the entire system is operating effectively. The implementation phase may involve major changes in the way organizations or individuals operate. Conversion from the old to the new must be planned and executed carefully to prevent errors or even chaos. For information systems that keep track of transactions such as invoices and customer orders, the conversion process requires some users to do double work during a pilot test, operating simultaneously with the old and new systems. Running two information systems in parallel helps identify unanticipated problems that might require information system or work system modifications before implementation is complete.

Operation and maintenance is the ongoing operation of the work system and the information system, plus efforts directed at enhancing either system and correcting bugs. At minimum, this requires that someone be in charge of ensuring that the work system is operating well, that the information system is providing the anticipated benefits, and that the work system and information system are changed further if the business situation calls for it.

Regardless of how the four phases are performed, business professionals play an important role in all four of the phases. For example, regardless of whether the software is developed from scratch or purchased from a software vendor, business professionals have to be involved throughout the four phases. In the initiation phase they decide whether the system is worth building from a business viewpoint. In the development phase they help define exactly how the work system should operate, thereby providing guidelines for the technical staff that is programming the software in the information system. Because the implementation phase is the process of changing from the old way of doing work to the new way, it is clearly the responsibility of the business professionals and their managers. Similarly, the wholehearted support and commitment of business professionals is usually necessary for successful operation and maintenance.

Contributing effectively to these four phases calls for a strong background in how IT-based innovations have changed business practices. We will look at this area next.

Reality Check

PHASES IN BUILDING AND MAINTAINING SYSTEMS

This section identified four phases in building and maintaining systems.

1. Use the phases to describe a project of any type that you have done.
2. Identify the important challenges in each phase and explain whether these challenges are related to the discussion of the phases above.

IT-BASED INNOVATIONS IN EVERY BUSINESS FUNCTION

Applications of computer and communications technology have revolutionized the way most business professionals work and play essential roles in the way businesses compete. The personal impacts start with the personal productivity tools such as word processors and spreadsheets that have become essential for everyday office work. Communication tools such as voice mail, electronic mail, cellular telephones, and pagers have made communication so much more immediate that people in fast-moving firms sometimes feel overwhelmed with the amount of communication they receive.

IT applications have changed the nature of the workplace. Tasks ranging from taking orders to analyzing business plans are done using computers rather than paper and pencil. Where people once relied on the corporate office or factory as their workplace, much more of the work is being done wherever and whenever it is most convenient. **Telecommuting,** using telecommunications technology as a substitute for travel, is one part of a trend of bringing the work to the workers rather than the workers to the work. In the same general vein, the phrase "any place, any time" increasingly summarizes the customer's expectation that businesses will provide what the customer wants, when and where the customer wants it.

The role of IT in organizational business processes such as manufacturing and selling has expanded greatly. The first generations of computer technology were primarily used for recordkeeping and monitoring performance by telling managers today what happened yesterday and last week. Advances leading to online processing made it possible to capture and use information virtually from the moment it was generated. Much previously manual recordkeeping has been automated by capturing information as a byproduct of doing work rather than as a separate clerical step. Computerized systems can now help monitor the work as it is being done, thereby warning workers about obvious or likely errors before those errors cascade to create additional problems elsewhere. Many previously manual processes have been automated completely. In some cases this eliminated jobs; in other cases it allowed people who previously performed manual steps to work more like programmers specifying what machines should do.

Not only has the impact of technology affected the nature of work and the workplace; there has also been significant change in the way firms compete. IT has helped firms improve their internal operations, thereby reducing internal costs and developing products more quickly. Lower internal costs make profits possible even at lower selling prices. The sooner a product is on the market, the sooner it can generate profits. Quicker time to market is especially important for technology products in which prices drop rapidly as soon as many similar products become available. IT also supports sales and marketing processes in many ways. It provides salespeople better information about prospective customers; it helps salespeople identify and demonstrate the right product choices; it helps companies calculate individualized prices based on the needs and resources of specific customers. IT applications also make the actual purchase transactions simpler and faster.

The role of IT does not end once the customer has purchased the product. IT can support customer service activities by keeping track of both general information about each customer and information related to specific customer interactions, such as repairs or warranty claims. IT can also be built into products and services as an important component of what the customer is buying. For example, we may think of automobiles as physical objects, but they are increasingly served and controlled using IT-based devices such as antilock brakes.

A common way to think about IT's competitive impact across a firm's entire scope is to look at its **value chain,** the set of processes a firm uses to create value for its customers. The core of the value chain is the primary processes that directly create the value the firm's customers perceive, such as product design, purchasing, manufacturing, sales, distribution, and customer service. Also essential for the value chain are support processes, such as finance, human resources, and management. Chapters 2 and 6 will discuss the value chain concept in more depth. For now, we will simply look at representative examples of IT applications that have important competitive impacts.

Product Design Systems

The first step in creating value for the customer is designing the product based on a combination of the customer's desires, the designer's imagination, and the firm's goals and capabilities. **Computer aided design (CAD)** software has helped change the nature of design processes once the basic concept of the new product has been envisioned. CAD software accepts coded descriptions of components or processes and can display the resulting product specification graphically. CAD starts with the ability to draw the shape of an object but extends much further. It includes the ability to create photo-realistic representations that allow a designer to see exactly what an object will look like without ever producing a physical model. Many types of CAD also include the ability to evaluate the object being designed. For example, an electrical engineer might test a circuit or an architect might verify that a building is strong enough before it is built. CAD software can also perform calculations such as the area of the rooms and the amount of paint required. By automating both drawings and calculations, it is easy to evaluate the cost and acceptability of design alternatives. Taking this a step further, systems for designing mechanical objects can use the laws of geometry and physics to check for design flaws such as two objects occupying the same space, moving parts that will interfere with each other, or excessive physical stresses that may cause structural failure. Systems for designing electrical circuits and semiconductor chips can run exhaustive simulations to determine whether correct outputs will be produced under all foreseeable conditions.

One of the most fascinating things about CAD is the wide range of applications for which it has been used. When CAD was originally conceived, it was used as a tool comparable to a word processor for engineering drawings. CAD has moved out of the engineer's domain and has become an important part of the organizational process of creating and approving products and product modifications. The visualization capabilities in advanced CAD systems permit the customer to have a simulated walk-through of a building that has never been built or to view how a washing machine works even though it has not yet been manufactured. Boeing used a CAD system to design the Boeing 777 airliner without ever creating a physical scale model. Although most CAD applications are used for electronic, mechanical, and architectural design, CAD has also moved into a broad range of activities that use two- or three-dimensional representations. Orthopedic surgeons and plastic surgeons use CAD to design operations; clothes designers use CAD to design clothes; even hairdressers can use a form of CAD to try out alternative hairstyles before they cut hair. (See Figure 1.2.)

Procurement Systems

Regardless of whether the firm is a manufacturer or a retailer, its system for procuring raw materials and components should help the company acquire what it needs at comparatively low costs. For a manufacturer, all necessary materials should arrive just before the manufacturing schedule calls for its use. If it arrives too late, manufacturing will be disrupted. If it arrives too early, money and warehouse space will be tied up in unused inventory for too long, and the material may even become obsolete if the product changes. The challenge is similar for retailers. If the merchandise arrives too early it will tie up money while it sits on shelves or racks. If it arrives too late the customer will have already gone somewhere else and it may be necessary to sell the merchandise at deep discounts before the next product season.

Figure 1.2
CAD in unexpected places

CAD has been used for a wide range of applications, some of which might seem surprising.

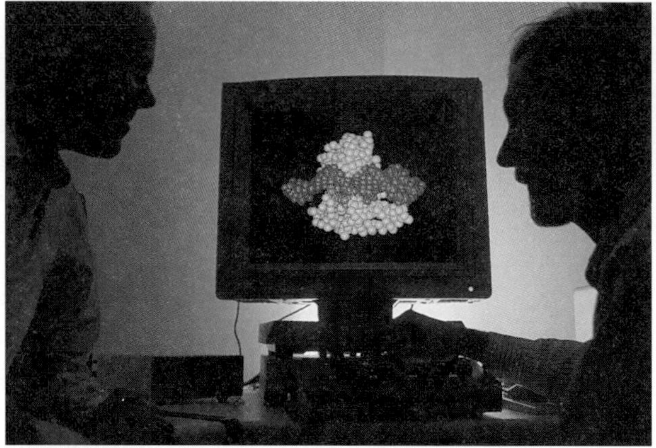

Procurement systems start with information about what inventory is available, when previously ordered material will arrive, and when material will probably be needed based on manufacturing schedules or sales forecasts. This information is used to:

- determine material requirements for future weeks or months
- generate new orders
- send the orders to suppliers
- obtain commitment dates for likely receipt, and eventually
- verify that the ordered material actually arrived

Delays between any of these steps may significantly reduce procurement system efficiency. The slower the system operates, the more likely it is that demand will change before the material arrives. If demand increases, the material will be insufficient and customers will be inconvenienced or will go elsewhere. If demand decreases, the excess material will tie up money and may become obsolete before it is ever used.

The view of procurement as a largely internal process of ordering the right material at the right time became outdated for many large distributors and manufacturers when networks made it possible to transmit data between companies. A more current viewpoint emphasizes **supply chain management (SCM),** which is the overall system of coordinating closely with suppliers so that both the firm and its suppliers reap the benefits of smaller inventories, smoother production, and less waste. Standardizing and automating both internal data processing and the data transfer between suppliers and customers is the fundamental tool of SCM because it makes procurement systems faster and more effective.

Links between suppliers and their customers have become much more effective in the last decade with the widespread use of **electronic data interchange (EDI),** the electronic transmission of business data such as purchase orders and invoices from one firm's computerized information system to that of another firm. Since EDI transmission is virtually instantaneous, the supplier's information system can check for availability and respond quickly with a confirmation. Some of the advantages of EDI are apparent when you look at the traditional way of transmitting data such as purchase orders between firms that use computers. Traditionally, the firm uses a computer to generate a printed purchase order, puts the purchase order in an envelope, and mails the envelope to the supplier. The supplier receives the envelope, sends it to the order processing department, and enters the data on the purchase order into an internal computer system. Thus, data from one computerized system is printed on paper, mailed, and reentered into another computer. In terms of dollars, a company typically spends $55 to process a paper purchase order, whereas EDI can reduce that amount to $2.50.[2] (See Figure 1.3.)

SCM and EDI are essential ingredients in a trend toward integration between suppliers and their customers. The more integrated they are, the quicker suppliers respond to customer requests and the quicker customers respond to schedule changes at the supplier. This trend toward integration applies if the supplier and customer are separate firms or if they are departments within a single firm. This tighter integration has even occurred across several

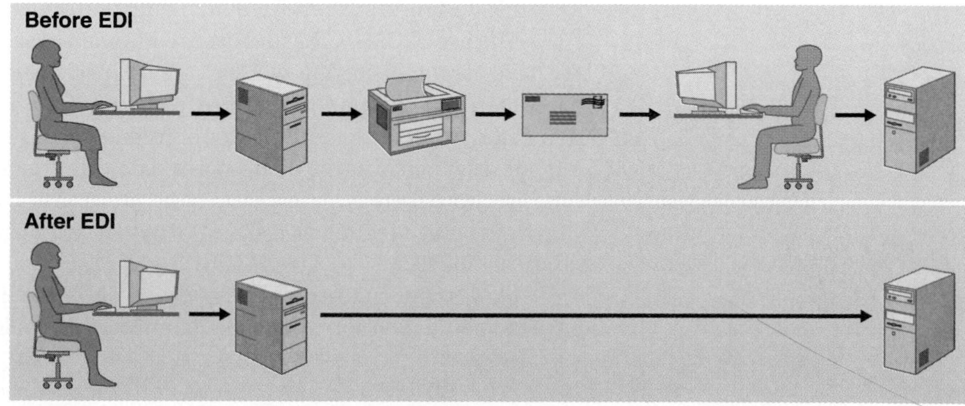

Figure 1.3
Customers link to suppliers using EDI

Before EDI, purchase orders and many other communications between customers and suppliers were generated by computer, mailed, and then manually reentered into another computer. EDI eliminates delays and increases accuracy by providing electronic transmission of data between the customer's computer and the supplier's computer.

consecutive stages of a product's value chain. A case in point is the links between Dillard's Department Stores, the apparel manufacturer Haggar, and the textile manufacturer Burlington Industries. When Dillard's inventory of a pants style goes below a specified level, it automatically sends an electronic message to Haggar. In turn, Haggar electronically notifies Burlington Industries if it doesn't have enough cloth to manufacture the pants Dillard's requested.[3]

Manufacturing Systems

A manufacturing system is a firm's system of producing physical products that it sells. The impact of IT on manufacturing systems came in several waves. The first uses were in keeping track of inventory and work-in-process and in performing recordkeeping about who did what work, when they did it, and how well they did it. Separate manual recordkeeping has gradually been replaced through the use of bar codes and automatic sensors. In addition, computerized controls have been built into the manufacturing equipment itself. The most highly automated factories operate under conditions that once seemed like science fiction. For example, as early as 1983 a Fanuc factory in Japan producing 10,000 electric motors a month operated with people doing maintenance during the day and only robots working at night. The factory contained 60 machining cells and 101 robots and produced 900 types and sizes of motor parts in lots ranging from 20 to 1,000.[4] Automated machinery is actually only one type of component of an automated factory. In totally automated factories, all production is scheduled and performed automatically. This requires extensive information systems that integrate automatic material movement, automatic scheduling of all work steps, automatic execution of work steps, and automatic sensing of quality.

Despite progress in automating manufacturing systems, most current factories are only partially automated because it is possible to get better results by automating some functions and leaving others to the flexibility, common sense, and ingenuity of human workers. General Motors' failed attempt to reap rewards from spending over $40 billion building highly automated factories in the 1980s is a cautionary tale about overemphasizing machines and underemphasizing people. Many of the robots never worked properly due to a variety of technical, social, and political circumstances. The fallacy of viewing automation as a silver bullet was demonstrated again by the subsequent NUMMI joint venture involving GM and Toyota, whose market value in the 1980s was less than $40 billion. The plant used comparatively little automation and had many of the same workers as a previous GM plant at the same location, but attained higher productivity mostly by changing the expectations for both labor and management.

Even when work steps are only partially automated, IT has often had a major impact in manufacturing through various degrees of **computer integrated manufacturing (CIM),** which includes computerized data collection and integrated information flows between design, manufacturing, planning, accounting, and other business functions. When people in one department complete their tasks, the data produced are immediately available for use by people in other departments. Technical advances in the last decade that have made CIM more of a reality include increased computer power at much lower cost, better data management capabilities, and distributed computing and telecommunications. Reasons for adopting CIM include reduced cost, better quality, better customer service, greater flexibility in responding to customer requirements, and quicker time to market with new products.

The use of CAD, CIM, and other computer-based techniques has gradually changed the logic of manufacturing, which is increasingly divided between two phases that involve computerized information. First is a design phase, which creates a computerized description of the product including the options that customers can select. Next is a manufacturing phase, which uses the computerized description directly. As manufacturing moves in this direction, there is an increase in the **information content of products,** the degree to which the value of products resides in product specification information rather than in just physical objects.

Many manufacturers trying to exploit the increasing information content of products have created tighter links between their factories, their sales efforts, and their customers.

Consider how this idea can be applied in the automobile industry to implement a build-to-order strategy instead of building thousands of cars in a variety of styles and shipping them to dealers who will then try to sell them. With a build-to-order strategy, the factory builds the car only when a dealer has taken an order from a specific customer. Going beyond simply selecting color and style options, heightened customer expectations by customers have made more extensive customization a key competitive issue for many products. The ability to link CAD systems to order entry systems and to transmit order details directly into the factory is making it more practical to tailor anything from clothes to machines based on the customer's requirements or wishes. Today many firms are moving toward **mass customization,** the use of mass production techniques to produce customized products or services. Mass customization is an attempt to retain the advantages of mass production while providing value related to customization. From the manufacturer's viewpoint, the product or service is mass produced. From the consumer's viewpoint, the product or service is customized. Figure 1.4 shows an example of mass customization. Matsushita's National Bicycle increased its share of the Japanese sports bicycle market from 5 percent to 29 percent by moving from inexpensive, non-customized bicycles to customized bicycles that start from measurements determining the exact size of frame the rider needs.[5]

Sales and Marketing Systems

The previous sections on product design and manufacturing show how IT makes it easier to provide the product the customer wants, when and where the customer wants it. In fact, IT also enables companies to use radically different sales and marketing approaches than were possible when IT applications were less developed. One way to summarize a firm's sales and marketing approach is through what are often called the four P's of marketing: product, price, place, and promotion. Table 1.2 shows how Amazon.com uses IT in addressing the four P's. In terms of product, it simulates having millions of books in stock by providing information about these books and by directing its customers' electronic orders to publishers or other book distributors. Its prices are higher because of delivery charges, but the customer can order from home or from a work site (place) and does not have to absorb the cost of actually going to a bookstore. Amazon.com and other online bookstores can also handle promotion in nontraditional ways by providing online information about each book including reviews, background information, and even excerpts.

Figure 1.4
Building a customized bicycle

A subsidiary of Matsushita uses an information system to build customized bicycles in Japan. The photo on the left shows the session in which the customized dimensions of the bicycle are determined. These measurements are entered into a special computer aided design (CAD) system that creates a diagram (shown on right) that is transmitted directly to the factory.

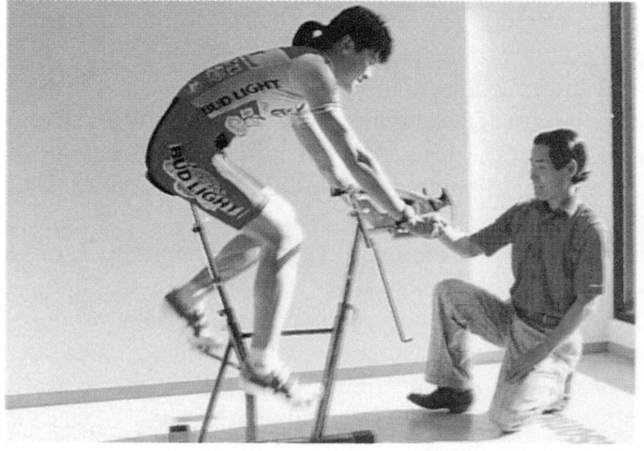

(a)

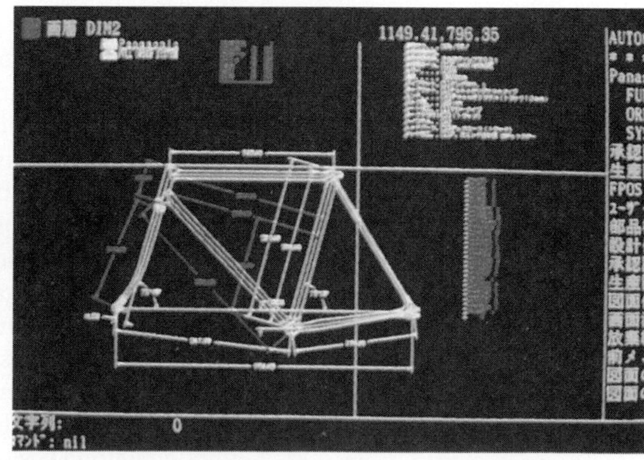

(b)

TABLE 1.2	The Four P's of Marketing at Amazon.com
Product	Amazon.com offers 2.5 million books for sale.
Price	Although Amazon.com charges for delivery, it can offer deep discounts for some books because it does not have to pay for rent for retail stores and because its inventory costs are low.
Place	Customers buy books from their homes or offices instead of going to a book store.
Promotion	Amazon.com provides extensive background information about some books. It promotes its business by advertising on other Web sites and through traditional media such as radio.

Amazon.com is an example of electronic commerce opportunities that have become a reality since the World Wide Web was established in 1992. **Electronic commerce** refers to using the Web and other electronic means to:

- inform a customer of a product's existence
- provide in-depth information about the product
- establish the customer's requirements
- perform the purchase transaction
- deliver the product electronically if the product happens to be software or information

As with traditional markets, electronic commerce provides many alternatives for linking the buyer and the seller. In some cases, a manufacturer sets up a Web site and sells directly to customers. In other cases, a retailer or distributor like Amazon.com uses a Web site to sell products produced by many different firms. In yet other situations, a Web site may be designed as an auction or clearinghouse that permits different possible buyers to bid for merchandise that is offered for sale. In all these examples, the use of a Web site is only one of several possible ways to handle the interactions. For example, electronic commerce activities directed at a limited set of prequalified customers might control access to a Web site using passwords or might bypass the Web altogether by using a private network that might or might not have a Web-like interface.

There is a lot more to electronic commerce than just setting up a Web page. Consider the following example. After performing a 1997 survey of costs related to using electronic commerce, the Gartner Group warned its clients that many firms had unrealistic expectations. Around 90% of the firms expected at least 15% of their revenue would come from electronic commerce within several years, yet less than half the firms surveyed had a separate electronic commerce group with the responsibility of designing and operating the Web site and linking the Web transactions to other information systems in the company. Although Gartner estimated the cost of developing a complete Web site for electronic commerce can exceed $3 million, 74% of the firms surveyed had allocated less than $1 million.[6] There was a clear tendency to underestimate the scope and cost of engaging in electronic commerce successfully.

Even without electronic links to customers, IT has had a major impact on traditional sales activities such as keeping track of customers or taking orders. One of the most important innovations in keeping track of customers occurred as a by-product of **point-of-sale (POS)** systems that use bar codes to generate customer bills at checkout counters. Many supermarkets now give their repeat customers an ID card for check cashing and for rewarding customer loyalty with discounts on selected items. Using the ID cards in conjunction with POS systems provides the extra benefit to the store, namely, a cumulative history of every item the repeat customer purchased on each trip to the store. This type of history provides customer profiles that reveal individual customer's preferences and buying patterns. Von's, a Southern California grocery chain, has used this data aggressively by sending customized promotions to specific customers based on their past purchases. This is an example of **addressability,** the ability to direct specific marketing messages to specific individuals or groups instead of broadcasting them by radio or through advertising flyers. The Von's card has been so successful that Von's has established a subsidiary called Von's Direct Marketing, which provides data to market research and consumer products companies.[7]

IT's influence on traditional sales work has also been great. Consider the traditional problems of salespeople who travel to customer sites to sell products ranging from perishable farm produce to life insurance to heavy equipment. In each case, salespeople participating in traditional sales processes couldn't respond immediately to questions such as whether a desired product is actually available for shipment or what the final price will be when complicated discounts are applied. Many types of communication and computer technology make it easier for salespeople to answer questions such as these. Cellular phones, e-mail, voice mail, and even networked database access all make it easier to get messages from an office without interrupting anyone else. Laptop computers support computing needs of mobile salespeople by making it easier for them to demonstrate options and to provide accurate pricing information because the same rules that might be used at the office can be programmed into the laptop.

Delivery Systems

Delivery systems, also called logistics systems, are responsible for transporting materials to where they are needed. The requirement for accurate, accessible information in delivery systems is illustrated by the U.S. Army's experience during the 1991 Persian Gulf War. The Army had sent 40,000 tractor-trailer-sized containers to Saudi Arabia with no identifying information. It was necessary to open each container to find out whether it contained tires, generators, or something else. In addition, there were many overshipments because, according to *Fortune*, supply sergeants traditionally ordered everything three times in the expectation that two requisitions will go astray in unmarked containers. A review of logistics operations following the war led to a vastly improved approach in which bar codes on the containers are used to access a database listing their contents and global positioning satellites are used to signal their location.[8]

Another example of a delivery system is FedEx, the delivery parcel business. FedEx's emergence illustrates the importance of timely, reliable delivery in the everyday commercial world. FedEx's founder, Frederick Smith, had originally written about a national overnight delivery service while still a student at Yale in the 1970s, but he received a "C" on his paper because the professor thought the idea was impractical. As the company developed, one of its key selling points was the way it tracked each package as it went through each successive step from the time the company picked up the package from a customer or drop-off box to the time it was delivered to its destination. Any customer wondering about the location of a package could call a help line to find out where it was. More recently, customers have been able to obtain the same information by going to the FedEx Web site and simply entering the package number. United Parcel Service (UPS), one of FedEx's main competitors, later extended the tracking idea to even include storing the signature of the person who received the package at its destination.

In both examples just cited, the Army example and the FedEx example, information that tracked objects from their origin to their destination was key to the success of the delivery system. When the delivery system involves delivering actual information as opposed to physical objects, the options may change. Information can often be delivered immediately over a data network, thereby avoiding the delays and extra work of printing it, packaging it, and delivering the physical package to the destination the next day, at the earliest. The U.S. Internal Revenue Service has taken many strides in this area. Until several years ago, for example, the way to order an infrequently used U.S. tax form was to call the IRS, stay on hold until someone answered, request the form, and then wait five days or more until it arrived. The new approach is much faster. Simply log onto the IRS Web site, download the form, and print it on a laser printer. Many organizations have used the Web in a similar way because this method of information distribution is faster and cheaper for all concerned. Similar processes are also used frequently for downloading software.

Customer Service Systems

The main principles of good customer service include knowing who the customer is and being aware of the customer's status and past interactions with the firm. Good customer service also requires being able to handle customer requests, questions, and complaints quickly and efficiently. USAA, a major insurance company based in San Antonio, Texas, is one of the leaders in this area. Like most of its competitors, it once stored most of its customer contact information on paper in a warehouse, which meant that finding a particular document, such as a letter from a customer, often took a day or more. (See Figure 1.5.) However, in the 1980s USAA began working with IBM on what was then an innovative IT application that got rid of the paper altogether. Using this system, all incoming mail containing more than a check is scanned and stored on an optical disk. On receiving a phone call and entering a customer's account number at a terminal, any customer service agent can have immediate access to all the recent transactions and correspondence with the customer. This allowed USAA to complete over 90% of all requests and transactions at the first point of contact with customers, without talking to multiple agents or waiting until the files can be located.[9]

Progressive Insurance, an automobile insurance agency, used IT in a different way as part of its customer service strategy. It established an immediate response service in which agents go to the scene of automobile accidents in vans and communicate the extent of the damage directly to a central office, which estimates the amount that should be paid on the claim. Checks can be prepared in the van and given to the customer within an hour of the accident. The agent also helps arrange towing to a repair shop on Progressive's approved list of shops that have committed to meeting quality and turnaround time goals. These shops also have EDI links with Progressive to minimize transaction costs and delays.[10] Cutting total settlement time from 18 days to 11 meant less paperwork, fewer hours spent by claim adjusters, and involvement of fewer lawyers.[11]

Finance Systems

The field of finance includes the business of finance as well as the finance departments within all firms, regardless of what those firms produce. Firms in the business of finance include banks, credit card companies, stock brokerages, home mortgage companies,

Figure 1.5
Connecticut Mutual and its sea of paper

In 1990, Connecticut Mutual Life Insurance used this warehouse, which is the size of a football field, to store paper files. Vans stuffed with paper shuttled between the office and warehouse hourly. Simple changes in an insurance policy could take a week.

currency traders, and suppliers of financial information. The "products" in the business of finance include bank accounts, money market funds, credit cards, loans, and buying and selling of stocks, bonds, foreign currencies, real estate, and even entire businesses. The finance function within a typical business is a support activity that handles transactions involving money, produces financial statements, and pays taxes. These are all essentially information system functions, and they have been computerized for decades. The difference in the 1990s, however, is that this information has been integrated more effectively and made more readily available for decision making in matters ranging from how to treat slow paying customers to how to invest the firm's working capital so that it generates revenue even when it is not being used immediately.

To better understand the impact of IT on finance systems, consider the changing form and use of money, which was first invented because people found that bartering for everything was inconvenient. Using money made it possible to exchange value without possessing the specific commodity the trading partner wanted. Money had its own problems, however. What if you wanted to buy something but didn't have your cash at hand? Or what if you wanted to pay a bill without traveling to the merchant's place of business and handing over cash? Or what if you simply didn't want to carry large amounts of cash? Information systems are the basis of a number of alternatives that were developed or are still being developed:

- *Checking accounts* are basically information systems that keep track of account balances and permit people to write checks if they have enough money in their bank accounts. But checking accounts operate using paper checks that take days to clear through a complex settlement process.
- *Credit cards* permit users to make payments through short-term loans. Credit cards require large-scale information systems for approving transactions as the customer waits, consolidating monthly customer statements, and paying merchants.
- *Debit cards* are based on a similar idea, but operate differently. Instead of providing credit to be paid off later, **debit cards** move money immediately from the cardholder's account to the merchant's account.
- *Smart cards,* such as prepaid phone cards, copy cards, and electronic meal tickets, provide another card-based option in which a person transfers an amount such as $10 or $20 onto a card containing a memory chip. The **smart card** is used via simple vending machines that deduct the amount of a purchase from the stored amount on the card and add that amount to an account that is receiving the payment.
- *Electronic cash* is currently being promoted in a variety of implementations as a way to make small payments for access to information on the World Wide Web or for other small transactions for which credit card systems are prohibitively expensive. The basic idea is similar to that of a smart card except that the recordkeeping takes place on a personal computer instead of a smart card. A person acquires the **electronic cash** by transferring funds to a company that issues electronic cash; that company updates information on the purchaser's personal computer; the electronic cash is used by transferring it to an account on another computer when making a small purchase.

IT has also been essential for the operation of stock and commodity markets. These finance systems simply could not operate at their current scale without computerized systems for entering buy and sell orders, transmitting them to the traders, recording the transactions, and making payment within three days. This reliance on computerized systems became highly visible during the stock market crash on October 19, 1987, when over 500,000,000 shares were traded on the New York Stock Exchange. This was more than twice the previous high volume. Because of this unprecedented data processing load, the online information about stock prices lagged as much as two hours behind the trading on the floor of the stock market, contributing to the panic during the crash. Subsequent IT investments increased capacity to well over a billion shares per day, over twice the volume on the previous peak day.

Real time (immediate) access to the latest stock, bond, and commodity price information has also permitted large firms to make some buy and sell decisions automatically using a technique called **program trading.** An approach to program trading that exploits the availability of real time information is using the speed of computers to search for temporary discrepancies between prices of large groups of stocks and options to buy or sell these stocks in the future. On finding such discrepancies, the system can lock in a guaranteed profit by buying stocks in one market and selling options in the other. A fundamentally different approach to program trading uses statistical analysis and models to identify price conditions under which specific buy or sell orders have a high probability of making money. Some observers believe this form of program trading tends to reinforce instability when market values are changing rapidly. In response, the New York Stock Exchange has created rules called "circuit breakers," which disallow program trading if aggregate price indicators, such as the Dow Jones Industrial Average, have changed more than a particular amount in any day.

Even individual investors with small portfolios are benefiting from IT. Until the mid-1990s, it was necessary to buy and sell stocks through licensed stockbrokers working for brokerage firms. Brokerage firms used computers to perform transactions and generate monthly reports and trade confirmations, but the information individual investors received was all on paper. In the 1990s Charles Schwab started giving 10% discounts on commissions for using a telebroker service that permitted customers to enter buy or sell orders by touch-tone telephone. The advent of the Web permitted even small individual investors to obtain investment information and to enter buy or sell orders directly from their homes without ever talking to stockbrokers or paying their higher commission rates. Between 1996 and early 1998 the average commission for the ten leading online brokerage firms dropped from $53 to $16, leading some observers to wonder whether individual investors will discard the standard long-term "buy and hold" strategy in favor of a riskier, active trading approach because the transaction costs are so low.[12] The long-term effect of greater independence by individual investors is not known. It may affect their personal success in the stock market and will certainly affect the strategy and ultimate success of firms in the brokerage industry.

The preceding examples of IT-related innovations barely scratch the surface, but they certainly support the claim that IT is playing an increasingly important role in the way business is conducted. The purpose of this book is to help you understand information systems so that you can be an effective business professional in today's business environment. Part of that understanding includes recognizing the major technical changes that have occurred and appreciating that technical progress is not a panacea that automatically solves all the world's problems.

Reality Check

IT-BASED INNOVATIONS IN EVERY BUSINESS FUNCTION

This section mentioned a few IT-based innovations in a number of business functions.

1. Give examples of how some of these IT-based innovations have affected you directly.
2. Identify other IT-based innovations that have affected one or more business functions in important ways.

DRAMATIC PROGRESS IN PROCESSING DATA

A first step in understanding the role of IT in business is to recognize that everything IT does can be boiled down to six basic data processing functions: capturing, transmitting, storing, retrieving, manipulating, and displaying data. Consider a grocery store's customer checkout system:

1. It *captures* information using the bar code.
2. It *transmits* information to a computer that looks up the item's price and description.
3. It *stores* information about the item for calculating the bill.
4. It *retrieves* price and description information from the computer.
5. It *manipulates* the information when it adds up the bill.
6. It *displays* information when it shows each price it calculates and prints the receipt.

Table 1.3 defines the six functions and shows some of the technologies that focus on each of them. Some of these technologies have been used and improved for decades, while others have appeared only recently. The entire history of computing in this century has been about performing these six functions faster and more efficiently through an amazing sequence of technological breakthroughs. Since the 1960s, key characteristics of computer hardware technologies such as price, reliability, and density have been improving at a rate of 30% to 50% per year. Even at a rate of 20%, the equivalent of hardware capabilities costing $100 in 1960 would have cost $10.74 in 1970, $1.15 in 1980, $0.12 in 1990, and little more than a penny in 2000. To put this in perspective, if automotive technology had improved at that rate since 1960, a new car would cost less than a movie ticket, and we could drive across the United States on several ounces of gasoline.

TABLE 1.3 **Six Data Processing Functions Performed by Information Technology**

Function	Definition	Example of devices or technologies used to perform this function
Capture	Obtain a representation of information in a form permitting it to be transmitted or stored	Keyboard, bar code scanner, document scanner, optical character recognition, sound recorder, video camera, voice recognition software
Transmit	Move information from one place to another	Broadcast radio, broadcast television via regional transmitters, cable TV, satellite broadcasts, telephone networks, data transmission networks for moving business data, fiber optic cable, fax machine, electronic mail, voice mail, Internet
Store	Move information to a specific place for later retrieval	Paper, computer tape, floppy disk, hard disk, optical disk, CD-ROM, flash memory
Retrieve	Find the specific information that is currently needed	Paper, computer tape, floppy disk, hard disk, optical disk, CD-ROM, flash memory
Manipulate	Create new information from existing information through summarizing, sorting, rearranging, reformatting, or other types of calculations	Computer (plus software)
Display	Show information to a person	Laser printer, computer screen

Most experts believe the current rate of improvement will continue for at least another decade, extending trends that have operated for years. Major directions for these improvements include:

- greater miniaturization, speed, and portability
- greater connectivity and continuing convergence of computing and communications
- greater use of digitized information and multimedia
- better software techniques and interfaces with people

Each of these trends continues to have important implications for business operations.

Greater Miniaturization, Speed, and Portability

The increasing speed and power of electronic components is the force underlying the immense progress to date in computers and telecommunications. These enhancements result directly from **miniaturization,** the process of creating smaller electronic components with greater capabilities. Miniaturization of computers started when the solid-state transistor (an off-on device that can represent a 0 or 1) superseded the vacuum tube (an older off-on device). It started to increase exponentially with the 1959 invention of the **integrated circuit,** a device incorporating multiple transistors on a single silicon chip the size of a fingernail. Integrated circuits were smaller, used less electricity, and were more reliable because they replaced many separate parts that previously had to be wired together. (See Figure 1.6.)

The degree of progress that has occurred through miniaturization of electronic components is difficult to imagine because it defies our typical experience. Back-to-back improvements of 10% or 15% starting from a respectable base are viewed as significant achievements. In contrast, Table 1.4 shows that the capacity of computer memory chips has increased at a rate predicted in the early 1970s by Gordon Moore, a cofounder of Intel. Consistent with this prediction, which is often called **Moore's Law,** chip capacities have doubled approximately every 18 months for over 20 years, and will probably continue to do so for years to come. Sixteen-megabit memory chips containing the equivalent of over 16 million transistors are commonplace now, with 256-megabit chips likely to be available by the year 2000. This is just one of many aspects of the technical progress that has occurred.

Figure 1.6
Comparison of a vacuum tube and an integrated circuit

The first general purpose computers contained thousands of vacuum tubes, each of which represented a single off-on switch. The Pentium II microprocessor, shown in its plastic package, is the size of a fingernail but contains complex logical circuitry along with the equivalent of 7.5 million transistors.

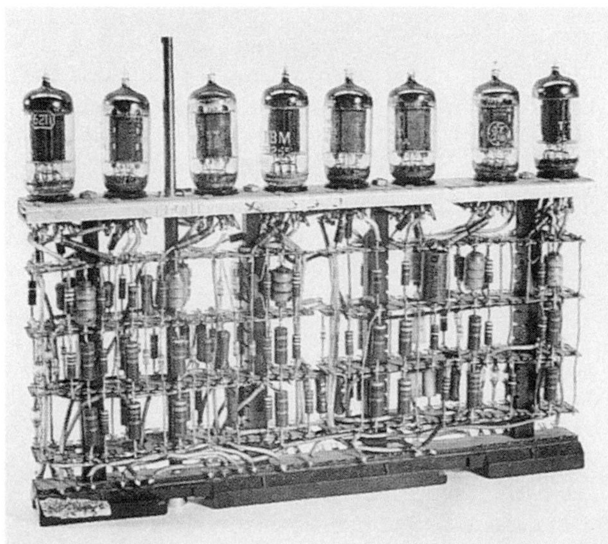

(a)

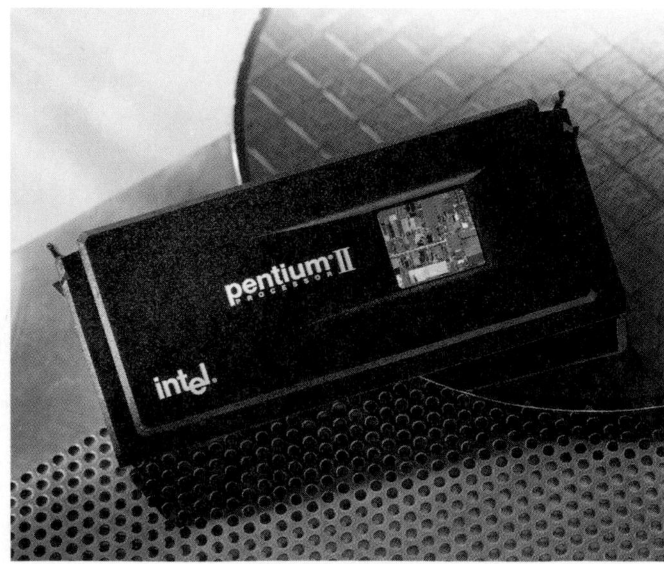

(b)

TABLE 1.4 **Progress in Memory Chip Capacity Since 1973**

This table shows that the storage capacity of computer memory chips has been doubling approximately every 18 months. For each type of chip up to 1997 the date given is one or two years after its first commercial introduction, but before its sales peaked and started to decline as the next generation came into use. The date was estimated by combining data on product introductions and product sales patterns.[13,14] (The term *kilobit* refers to approximately one thousand bits since a kilobit chip actually contains 1,024 off-on units. Similarly, a megabit chip actually contains 1,024 times 1,024 bits.)

Approximate date of widespread commercial availability	Type of chip	Capacity in number of bits
1973	1 kilobit	1,024
1976	4 kilobit	4,096
1979	16 kilobit	16,384
1982	64 kilobit	65,536
1985	256 kilobit	262,144
1988	1 megabit	1,048,576
1991	4 megabit	4,194,304
1994	16 megabit	16,777,216
1997	64 megabit	67,108,864
2000	256 megabit	268,435,456

The increase in speed and reliability due to miniaturization has paved the way toward the development of computers, VCRs, fax machines, bar code scanners, cellular phones, telephone switches, fiber optic phone cables, and many other types of information technology. The current rate of progress implies that raw computing power in the year 2000 could be 100 times cheaper than it was in 1990.

The miniaturization of electronic components plus advances in communication technology has also led to much greater **portability** of computer and communications devices; devices are considered portable when their users can carry them around conveniently. Previous generations of computers and telephones were far from portable. Early computers required specially air-conditioned rooms, and telephones were anchored in place by wire connections. Just being able to store hundreds of pages of data on a pocket-sized diskette was an important step toward portability, even if the computer remained anchored in place. Today, the equivalent of 70 diskettes can be stored on a portable, pocket-sized 100-megabyte disk that costs under $10.

Although large computers and major telephone installations are still in fixed locations, today's individual users have many choices of portable devices. The popularity of portable cellular phones has clearly demonstrated that telephones no longer must be anchored by wires. The first common portable computers were laptops, which business professionals could carry conveniently for use on airplanes and other locations away from the office. Pen computers, which look like tablets and have no keyboards, are another type of portable computer used for specific tasks performed by people who are continually on the move. Examples include the computers used by police officers to give parking tickets and the computers used by field technicians to record residential usage of gas and electric. (See Figure 1.7.)

While portable computers are more convenient for users, the downside is that portability makes it much more difficult to control the flow of information. A single diskette in a person's pocket can contain a company's entire customer list; the hard disk in a laptop computer can store over 1,000 times that amount of information. The risks created by carrying around this much confidential information are evident from what happened when someone stole a laptop computer from a car parked for five minutes in downtown London in late 1990. The car belonged to a wing commander in Great Britain's Royal Air Force. The laptop contained some of General Schwartzkopf's plans for attacking Iraq. (The commander was court-martialed, demoted, and fined. The computer was returned anonymously a week later.)[15]

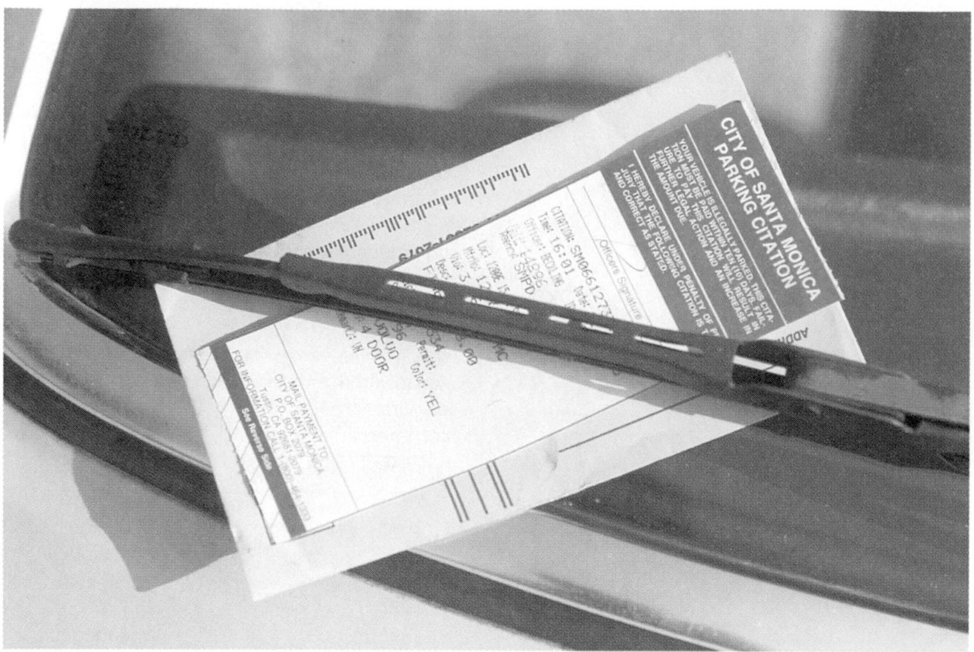

Figure 1.7
Using a portable computer to give parking tickets

A portable computer was used to generate this parking ticket. Advantages of producing parking tickets this way include legibility of the parking ticket itself plus automatic updating of the city's database of unpaid tickets.

Greater Connectivity and Continuing Convergence of Computing and Communications

Connectivity is the ability to transmit data between electronic devices at different locations. Increasingly, computerized data can be transmitted almost instantaneously nearly anywhere in the world. The scope of connectivity includes interactive communication between people, electronic mail, transmittal of faxes, and transmission of business data between computers. Connectivity is important to businesses because it reduces some of the disadvantages of being separated geographically. It also makes it easier to obtain important business information, much of which comes from outside sources, such as customers and suppliers.

Connectivity means more than just transmitting a signal from one place to another, however. Because many organizations own hardware and software purchased from a variety of vendors, true connectivity often depends on the ability of these heterogeneous components to work together conveniently and inexpensively. This is often called **interoperability.** Software products that perform the same or complementary functions are often rated in terms of interoperability. For example, the interoperability of two word processing programs is determined by the extent to which a document produced using one word processor looks the same and is handled the same way when it is displayed by another word processor, perhaps on a different type of computer. In this case, interoperability requires compatible internal coding of data, compatible program logic, compatible user interfaces, and compatible communication with storage devices and printers.

The need for connectivity and interoperability has generated customer demand for **open systems,** which are technical systems that use clearly described, nonproprietary industry standards available to anyone. Hardware and software buyers insisted on the movement toward open systems in order to make it easier to switch hardware or software brands without a complete technical overhaul. Deploying open systems supports a range of opportunities to compete more effectively. Within the firm, these trends make it easier and cheaper to build information systems and transmit data. Reducing these costs makes it more practical to use information systems to help people work together and to link more effectively with customers. On the other hand, open systems are not always a boon to hardware and software suppliers. Many of them have tried to resist an open systems approach because they see open systems as a direct threat to a strategy of providing unique, incompatible capabilities which lock in customers by making brand switching difficult.

Greater connectivity supports the continuing **convergence of computing and communications** whereby communication capabilities have become essential to many computer systems, and computing capabilities have become essential to communication systems. (See Figure 1.8.) Consider the way salespeople at many firms use touch-tone telephones to obtain pricing information and enter orders. In these systems, a telephone becomes a data entry terminal for an information system. Similarly, companies deploying computers in branch offices often require communication networks to perform company-wide computing tasks such as consolidating results and sharing data. Even within a single building, wireless data transmission between computers can make work more effective. As the overlaps between computing and communications became more apparent, companies combined their previously separate computer and communications staffs to manage this convergence. This convergence has also affected individuals. (See Figure 1.9.)

Greater Use of Digitized Information and Multimedia

Information exists in five different forms—predefined data items, text, pictures, sounds, and video (sequences of pictures and sound), each of which can be digitized. **Digitization** involves coding the data as an equivalent or approximately equivalent set of numbers. For example, the letters in the word "cab" might be coded 33-31-32 if the coding rule were to add 30 to the position of each letter in the alphabet. Likewise, a picture can be digitized by dividing it into tiny dots on a grid and assigning a number to represent the color and intensity of the dot. Because any type of data can be digitized, any type of data can be stored, manipulated, and transmitted by computerized systems.

The method used to digitize pictures and sounds originally limited the feasibility of processing these types of data on computers. The problem was that digitized pictures and sounds require much more storage and transmission capability than pure text. For example, all the paragraphs of straight text in this book can be stored on several pocket-sized

Figure 1.8
Convergence of computing and communications

The convergence of computing and telecommunications sprang from separate innovations related to telegraphs (1794), telephones (1876), radio broadcasting (1906), television broadcasting (1925), and computers (around 1945). Existing combinations of computers and telecommunications will continue to evolve into new applications in the future.

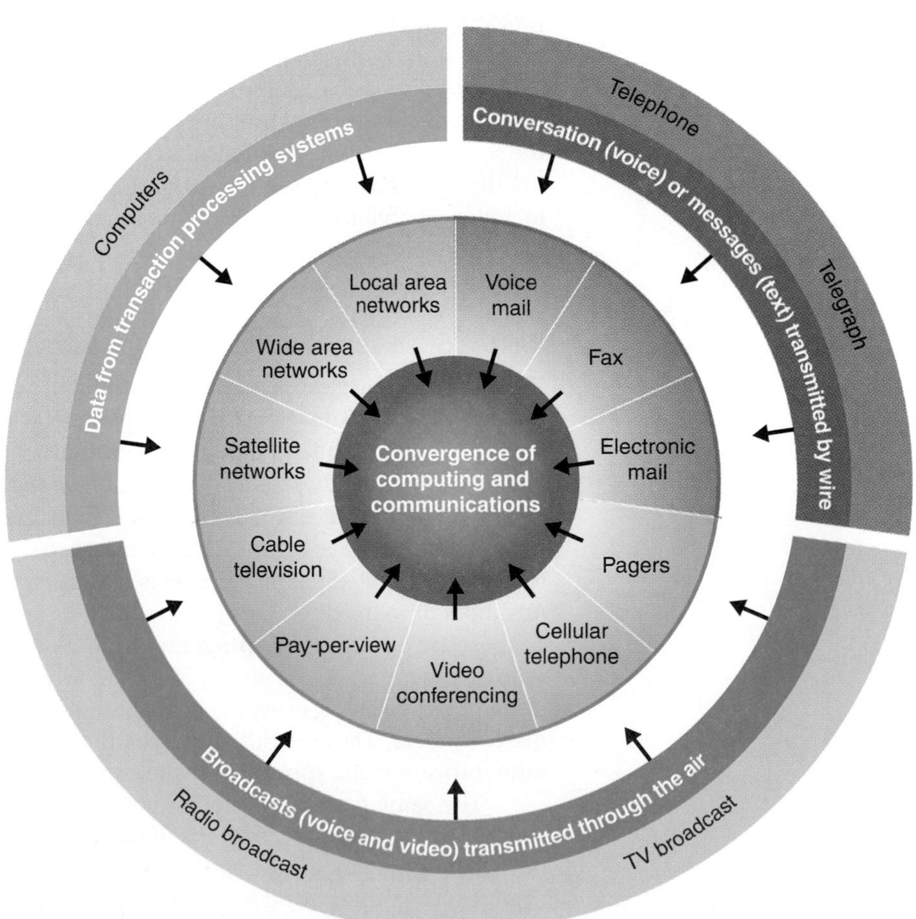

Figure 1.9
Example of the convergence of computing and communications

A computer in this car converts a signal from a global positioning satellite (GPS) into precise coordinates on Earth, and then displays that location on a map so that the driver can decide how to drive to the destination.

diskettes, but a single high-resolution photograph could require a similar amount of storage as all of that text.

Fortunately, advances in miniaturization and speed of electronic components made large-scale use of digitized data affordable. These advances started solving the problem by providing processing speeds and storage capacities needed to store, manipulate, and transmit pictures and sounds. This made widespread use of fax machines and videoconferencing economically feasible. These advances also made the extensive use of multimedia feasible. **Multimedia** is the use of multiple types of data, such as text, pictures, and sounds, within the same application. The first steps toward multimedia involved things such as combining drawing software with word processors. Software for creating presentations now includes capabilities to handle photographs, sound clips, and video clips. Anyone who uses the World Wide Web sees that multimedia has emerged from its infancy and can be used extensively in education, entertainment, and business applications.

Better Software Techniques and Interfaces with People

The first computerized systems were difficult to develop and use. People who created these systems used development methods and programming languages that are primitive in comparison to today's methods. They had to share computers that were often overloaded and frequently produced results after substantial delays. They had to use computer terminals that were small, somewhat indistinct, and unable to handle different font sizes or graphics. (See Figure 1.10.) They lacked database management systems and other tools that separated technical aspects of data handling from the logic of the application. Advances in many directions have made it easier to define how the computer system is supposed to operate and to program it and debug it. These advances generally involve permitting programmers (or users) to specify what they want the computer to accomplish rather than specifying every detail of how the computer should store, retrieve, and manipulate the data. The software advances themselves were made possible by advances in miniaturization and speed that made computers much more powerful.

The same types of advances that made programming easier also made the use of computers easier. Today, millions of workers use desktop computers interactively, even though they may know little about computer technology. Computer monitors designed to display text, graphics, and even photographic images have replaced early computer terminals with limited ability to handle graphics. Interactive techniques for requesting,

Figure 1.10
A leading edge flat panel monitor and a computer terminal from the 1980s

Comparison of the powerful flat panel monitor with the older computer monitor illustrates how far display technology has come since the 1980s.

filtering, and displaying information have replaced earlier methods of delivering management data using inflexible computer-generated listings that only programmers could specify. Users of current computer systems can often specify what they need by pointing and filling in blanks instead of mastering complicated computer languages and remembering awkward command codes. Computer users have ready access to word processors, spreadsheets, and presentation tools that personal computers could not handle a decade ago. Even though we don't know exactly how computers will be used in the future, ongoing advances in both hardware and software make it safe to predict that they will be even easier to use than they are today.

Reality Check

PROGRESS IN PROCESSING DATA

This section identified four important trends in processing data.

1. Explain how these trends have affected you directly.
2. Identify areas where you wish the trends had affected you but you have not yet felt any impact.

OBSTACLES WHEN APPLYING IT IN THE REAL WORLD

One of this book's central goals is to help you see information technology and information systems for what they really are—powerful, valuable tools, but not magic. When applied thoughtfully, these tools can bring important benefits for individuals, organizations, and customers. When misapplied, they can waste tremendous amounts of time, effort, and money. We will close this introductory chapter by identifying some of the obstacles to applying IT successfully in the real world of business. These obstacles include unrealistic expectations, difficulty building and modifying information systems, difficulty integrating systems that are built for different purposes, organizational inertia and problems of dealing with change, and genuine difficulty anticipating what will happen.

Unrealistic Expectations and Techno-hype

Computer technology has always received more than its share of speculation and hype. In 1952 an early Univac computer used simple statistical methods to "predict" the winner of the Presidential election. The day following the election, a newspaper headline read: "Big Electronic Gadget Proves Machines Smarter Than Men."[16] What might have seemed like a giant brain at the time had considerably less computing power than a personal computer you can put in a shopping cart at an office supply store today.

In today's business world, computer mystique has expanded to encompass business and social environments that use computers extensively. Many books and articles have described what businesses must do to succeed in the information age—the age of smart machines, of intelligent corporations, of total quality, of globalization, and of continual change and reengineering. Separating hype from reality in these discussions is sometimes difficult, especially when the message is conveyed in a loosely disguised infomercial for technology vendors or consulting firms.

Hardware and software vendors often add to the confusion by claiming that they "sell solutions." Real business problems usually require much more than changing computer hardware and software. The solution to most business problems is for the organization to do something in a different way. This may involve better use of IT, but other factors may be much more important. For example, a company may invest in a top-of-the-line computer system with the most current software on the market, but if the right people aren't in place to operate the software, or if the people working on the computer aren't properly trained, the investment may be wasted.

Even when they have no reason to express a bias, people often exaggerate or misstate the role of technology. "Auto screws up" might seem a strange headline for an article about a traffic accident, but the business magazine *Forbes* used "When machines screw up" as the title of an article about an ill-fated decision to use computers to grant mortgage loans in as little as 15 minutes. According to the article, the problem had much less to do with computers than with an overly aggressive business decision to sidestep basic loan qualification procedures.[17] In another example, a *Business Week* article about the German company SAP and its highly integrated enterprise software package said that its interwoven programs "can speed decision making, slash costs, and give managers control over global empires at the click of a mouse."[18] Although this software certainly can help in speeding decision making and slashing costs, it cannot perform the magic trick of giving managers control over global empires with a click of a mouse. Exaggerations or poetic license of this type might seem a trivial matter, except that we often hear that computers made errors, were slow and inaccurate, or were responsible for problems. A careful look usually reveals that the real problems were human business decisions related to the design or execution of business processes. Confusions about what computers can and cannot do make it more difficult to use IT to the fullest.

Difficulty Building and Modifying IT-Based Systems

Today it is much easier to build IT-based systems than it ever has been, but the task is still difficult. The fact that IT still has a long way to go is illustrated by the enormous effort going into the **Year 2000 (Y2K) problem,** which is related to the way many information systems use just two digits to identify the year portion of a date. Coding dates as mm/dd/yy is fine if the year is 1988 and a computer is calculating how many more years of payments will occur for a loan that will be paid off in 1992. The calculation is "92–88 = 4." However, if the same program performs the same calculation ten years later for a loan to be paid off in 2002, the result is nonsense because the calculation is "02–98 = –96," in other words, that the mortgage will be paid off 96 years ago. Any subsequent calculations that use this result will generate more nonsense. Because almost all business data processing systems use date calculations, and because errors in these calculations can create a cascade of erroneous results, finding and correcting computer programs that contain 2-digit year codes or use calculations based on those codes will cost industry and government a huge amount of money, by one estimate $300 to $600 billion.[19]

Business and government organizations are spending so much money on this problem because some Y2K-related errors could be disastrous. For example, the 10- to 25-year-old IBM 3083 computers used by air traffic control facilities might refuse to accept flight plans for planes taking off late on Dec. 31, 1999, because the calculated landing time would be 99 years in the past. The computers are no longer being produced. The Federal Aviation Administration cannot simply switch to a different computer because the date functions are written in the machine language of the 3083 computer, and most of the experts in that machine language have retired. A letter from IBM to an FAA contractor said, "IBM remains convinced that the appropriate skills and tools do not exist to conduct a complete Year 2000 assessment of the 3083 computers."[20]

Even with technological problems such as difficulty undoing the 2-digit year codes, much of the difficulty in building and maintaining business systems is elsewhere. We can see this by referring back to the four phases of a system's life cycle (see Figure 1.1). It would be convenient if there were some "correct," guaranteed method for performing these phases either for work systems or information systems that support them. Unfortunately it is generally agreed that no best method exists. To the contrary, different situations call for different processes that will be explained later in the book. Regardless of which method is used, the likelihood of success is highest when the system is small, self-contained, and easily understood. As the situation becomes more complicated, people analyzing both the work system and the information system have to contend with more details, more complexity, and a higher likelihood that the stakeholders will not agree wholeheartedly about what should happen.

These generalizations are consistent with the findings of surveys concerning the success rate for information systems even with the advanced technology available in the mid-1990s. A study by the Standish Group obtained data about 8380 systems from 365 respondents across a spectrum of large and small organizations. The summary result was that only16.2% of the information systems were completed on schedule and within budget; 52.7% were late, went over budget, or produced fewer functions than planned, and 31.1% were canceled before completion. The factors most strongly associated with success were user involvement, executive support, clear statement of requirements, proper planning, and realistic expectations. None of these are technical matters. The factors most strongly associated with cancellation were incomplete requirements, lack of user involvement, lack of resources, and unrealistic expectations.[21] A 1997 survey by the Meta Group produced similar findings, with over 30% of new software projects canceled before completion and more than 50% of projects at least 80% over budget.

Difficulty Integrating IT-Based Systems

One of the most difficult issues related to building and maintaining IT-based systems is the requirement that these systems be integrated with the organization's other systems. This issue arises frequently when hardware and software best suited for one purpose must be used in conjunction with hardware and software acquired for a different purpose. For example, two separate factories within the same firm may have purchased different factory management software because their products and processes are different. If the firm subsequently decides to develop a new enterprise-wide management reporting system, one of the factories or possibly both may have to scrap a system designed around local problems in order to address an issue for the entire organization. In effect, each factory may have deployed its resources in what seemed the best way, only to find that that best way was not the best way for the entire firm.

An attempt to create an effective information system for handling Medicare insurance claims demonstrates how difficult integration problems can be. In 1994, the Clinton administration initiated a project that was to provide for timely payment of Medicare claims and to reduce fraudulent claims. The U.S. Secretary of Health and Human Services declared, "We're going to move from the era of the quill pen to the era of the superelectronic highway." The ultimate goal was to create a single national system for paying doctors, hospitals, nursing homes, HMOs, and others who provide care for Medicare patients. The system would pay one billion bills a year and would help reduce fraud by detecting suspicious billing patterns, including unnecessary services and submission of multiple claims for the same services. GTE was hired as the main contractor; however, as the project team got deeper into the analysis of the project, they discovered that a unified Medicare information system would have to integrate 72 separate systems built and operated by different insurance companies. Integrating these systems would require team members to develop an understanding of how each of the 72 systems worked and then to define commonalities that would unify all of them. In 1997, the administration canceled the project, which was behind schedule and over budget, and told GTE to stop work. A GTE spokesman said that the project had been far more complex than anyone anticipated. Around $100 million had been spent.[22]

The year 2000 problem may create a different type of integration problem for supply chain management systems mentioned earlier. Those systems enforce consistent transactions and communication links throughout a supply chain, thereby minimizing costs and delays in ordering materials from suppliers. Initiatives in this area have been very effective, but what happens if a supplier's information system generates incorrect information due to Y2K problems? Even firms that have solved their own internal Y2K problems are concerned that their supply chain systems will fail as the year 2000 approaches because their suppliers will not have solved the problem themselves.[23] Seeing the possibility of enormous lawsuits because this problem has been known for many years, some law firms have geared up for a lot of business in this area.

Organizational Inertia and Problems of Change

A distressing reality for those who are enthusiastic about any particular technology-based innovation is that it is simply difficult to change the way an organization operates. Here is one observer's way of summarizing this issue:

- All technical progress exacts a price; while it adds something on the one hand, it subtracts something on the other.
- All technical progress raises more problems than it solves, tempts us to see the consequent problems as technical in nature, and prods us to seek technical solutions to them.
- The negative effects of technological innovation are inseparable from the positive. It is naive to say that technology is neutral, that it may be used for good or bad ends; the good and bad effects are, in fact, simultaneous and inseparable.
- All technological innovations have unforeseeable effects.[24]

Restated in terms of systems within organizations, this says that any particular change that has positive consequences in some areas may have negative consequences in other areas. For example, new efficiencies may mean that fewer employees are needed or that hard-earned skills are no longer important. (See Figure 1.11.) Differences of opinion and uncertainties about the positive and negative impacts of proposed changes often contribute to **organizational inertia,** the tendency to continue doing things in the same way, and therefore to resist change. Inertia related to information systems starts with the fact that formal systems are only a component of organizational operations and decision processes. Just changing an information system may not have much impact unless other things are changed, such as the way work is organized and the incentives that are established for the participants.

Unless a business problem is both evident and painful to all concerned, overcoming inertia often takes a lot of work across all four phases of the system life cycle summarized in Figure 1.1. During the initiation phase, this effort is related to identifying stakeholders, understanding their views of the situation, and considering those views in deciding on the focus and scope of the project. Extensive involvement of work system participants in the development phase helps ensure that the work system details are specified appropriately and that work system participants feel ownership of the way the system eventually operates. During the implementation phase, people who were initially uninvolved or only marginally involved must be educated about why the problem is important, how the system changes address the problem, and how the system will affect them. Unless all the phases are handled well, the time and effort spent overcoming inertia may exceed the time and effort spent in the computer-related parts of system development.

Figure 1.11
Example of the positive and negative impacts of technical change

In telephone systems of the 1930s, switchboard operators at telephone company offices and customer offices plugged in wires to connect telephone calls. Automating this task had a positive impact by making it much more convenient to use telephones, but it also had the negative impact of eliminating jobs that some switchboard operators relied on.

Genuine Difficulty Anticipating What Will Happen

A final aspect of real world limitations to IT-based innovation is that no one really knows how any particular innovation will develop or will be adapted over time. For example, the electronic transfer of money seemed like a good idea and has had numerous advantages for legitimate businesses; however, it also allows criminals to move drug money surreptitiously.

Even inventors, business leaders, and major researchers often have great difficulty foreseeing the development and potential application of their inventions. Table 1.5 presents many examples of this phenomenon. What might now seem like an inevitable unfolding of technical advances in each of these areas was not at all obvious at the time. Many technologies have succeeded when other technologies with the same initial potential failed for various business and technical reasons. Many currently commonplace technologies such as fax machines and the use of a mouse in computing languished for years before becoming commercially important. Today's researchers and business managers know some of the technical capabilities that will come out of the lab three to five years from now, but even in that short time frame, there will probably be surprises, especially in the ways the new technical capabilities are combined in new, unanticipated applications. The brief and incredible history of the World Wide Web is a case in point. The WWW was invented in 1992; within five years it became a phenomenon that has had an impact on most large businesses and universities. If you look back at what was written in 1991 and 1992, however, you would see that these developments were quite unexpected.

Reality Check

OBSTACLES TO APPLYING IT IN THE REAL WORLD

This section identified five obstacles to applying IT.

1. Identify examples of techno-hype that you have encountered and explain whether you think these were accidentally or intentionally misleading in any important way.
2. Describe several situations in which you have encountered any of the other four obstacles to applying IT in the real world.

TABLE 1.5 **Technology Predictions or Business Assessments That Missed the Mark**

These predictions or assessments show how difficult it is even for experts to predict the development and application of technology.

Expert and topic	Expert's prediction or comment
Alexander Graham Bell, inventor of the telephone, around 1876	He thought the telephone network would be primarily an entertainment instrument, transmitting concerts and operas to homes.[25]
Chairman of Western Union when offered exclusive patent rights to the telephone in 1876	"What use would this company have for an electrical toy?"[26]
Mercedes Benz, 1900, on the future demand for cars	"In 1900 Mercedes Benz did a study that estimated that the worldwide demand for cars would not exceed one million, primarily because of the limitation of available chauffeurs."[27]
General Electric, RCA, IBM, Remington Rand, refusing a chance to develop the basic patent for copy machines	Chester Carlson invented xerography in 1938 but spent years trying to find a corporate sponsor for his invention. Only after a long series of refusals did he persuade Battelle Memorial Institute in Ohio to continue the research.[28]
Thomas Watson, Sr., CEO of IBM, in the early 1950s	The worldwide demand for data-processing computers is less than 50 machines.[29]
Xerox Corporation, on funding early development work on the laser printer	Garry Starkweather of Xerox invented the laser printer in 1971 by modifying existing copier technology. Before he built a prototype he was instructed to stop working on the project. He might have had to leave the company to pursue the project if he had not learned of the new Xerox research lab in California where other researchers were interested in being able to print computer screen images.[30]
Herbert Simon and Allen Newell, early researchers in artificial intelligence, in 1958	Within ten years, a digital computer will be the world's chess champion unless the rules bar it from competition.[31]
Ken Olson, CEO of Digital Equipment Corporation, 1977	"There is no reason for any individual to have a computer in their home" (attributed to Ken Olson, at a convention of the World Future Society in Boston, 1977).[32]
IBM's view of the MS-DOS operating system in the early 1980s	The DOS operating system was first purchased by Microsoft for $50,000. IBM did not realize the significance of the operating system and did not insist on owning it. Eventually, ownership and future development of the operating system became more important and profitable than the hardware it ran on.
Microsoft's view of Lotus Notes in 1988	Lotus Development Corporation started developing this system in 1984. In 1988 it tried to sell it to Microsoft for $12 million, but Microsoft would go no higher than $4 million. In 1993, Lotus Notes generated $100 million in revenue and was central to Lotus Development Corporation's strategy. In 1995, IBM purchased Lotus Development Corporation for $3.5 billion, largely because of the possibilities presented by Notes.[33]
IT executives' view of personal computers and Microsoft Windows	At the Gartner Group's Symposium/Expo 95, a survey of 600 IT executives revealed that less than 20% had anticipated in 1985 that personal computers would become dominant desktop devices. Similarly, less than 20% had anticipated in 1990 that Microsoft Windows would become the dominant operating system.[34]

CHAPTER CONCLUSION

Summary

What are the phases in building and maintaining systems?
Both work systems and information systems that support them go through four phases: initiation, development, implementation, and operation and maintenance. Initiation is the process of defining the need to change an existing work system, identifying the people who should be involved in deciding what to do, and describing in general terms how the work system should operate differently and how any information system that supports it should operate differently. Development is the process of acquiring and configuring hardware, software, and other resources needed to perform both the required IT-related functions and the required functions not related to IT. Implementation is the process of making a new work system operational in the organization. Operation and maintenance is the ongoing operation of the work system and the information system, plus efforts directed at enhancing either system and correcting bugs.

What are some of the areas in which IT-based innovations have affected the major functional areas of business?
In design systems, CAD software accepts coded descriptions of components or processes and can display the resulting product specification graphically and in many cases can identify design flaws. In procurement systems, supply chain management systems and electronic data interchange are essential ingredients of a trend toward integration between suppliers and their customers. In manufacturing systems, computer integrated manufacturing supports computerized data collection and integrated information flows between design, manufacturing, planning, accounting, and other business functions. Many firms are moving toward mass customization, the use of mass production techniques to produce customized products or services. In sales and marketing, electronic commerce uses the Web and other networks to provide product information, establish the customer's requirements, perform the purchase transactions, and deliver software or information products electronically. POS systems provide the data needed for addressability applications that direct specific marketing messages to specific individuals. Delivery systems use IT to provide accurate, accessible information throughout delivery processes. Customer service systems use IT to inform agents about the customer's identity and past interactions with the firm and to respond quickly to customer service requests. Accounting and finance functions integrate information more effectively for decision making. IT supports new ways to handle money transfers, such as smart cards and electronic cash. In stock and bond markets, IT-based innovations support higher levels of trading and also new business approaches such as program trading.

What technology trends have enabled IT-based innovation in business?
Major directions for these improvements include greater miniaturization, speed, and portability, greater connectivity and continuing convergence of computing and communications, greater use of digitized information and multimedia, and better software techniques and interfaces with people.

What obstacles and real world limitations have slowed the pace of implementation for IT-based innovations?
Implementation of IT-based innovations has been delayed by a combination of unrealistic expectations, difficulty building and modifying information systems, difficulty integrating systems that are built for different purposes, organizational inertia and problems of dealing with change, and genuine difficulty anticipating what will happen.

Key Terms

business professional
work system
information system
initiation
development
implementation
operation and maintenance
telecommuting
value chain
computer aided design (CAD)
supply chain management (SCM)
electronic data interchange (EDI)

computer integrated manufacturing (CIM)
information content of products
mass customization
electronic commerce
point-of-sale (POS)
addressability
debit card
smart card
electronic cash
real time
program trading
capture data
transmit data
store data
retrieve data
manipulate data
display data
miniaturization
integrated circuit
Moore's Law
portability
interoperability
open systems
convergence of computing and communications
multimedia
year 2000 (Y2K) problem
organizational inertia

Review Questions

1. What are the facets of a work system, such as the way Amazon.com sells books?
2. What are the phases of building and maintaining a system?
3. Why is it important for business professionals to be involved throughout the four phases of building and maintaining a system?
4. How has the role of IT in manufacturing and selling evolved beyond recordkeeping and performance monitoring?
5. Describe how computer aided design involves more than capturing line drawings.
6. What is the relationship between electronic data interchange and supply chain management?
7. How is the information content of products related to mass customization?
8. How are point-of-sales systems related to the trend toward addressability in marketing?
9. What was the progression of IT-applications in handling money?
10. How does program trading rely on advances in IT over the years?
11. What are the six basic data processing functions?
12. Why does Moore's Law describe a phenomenon unlike other things in the history of business?
13. How does portability of computers make it difficult to control the flow of information?
14. Why can open systems be viewed as both an opportunity and a threat?
15. How do continuing trends toward connectivity and interoperability provide opportunities to compete more effectively?
16. What is the year 2000 problem?
17. What factors are most strongly associated with information system success?
18. How is organizational inertia related to information systems?
19. How does the history of past business and technology predictions explain how the growth of the World Wide Web was a major surprise?

Discussion Topics

1. Competition between individuals, organizations, cities, and countries has existed for centuries. Do you believe that computerized information systems are changing the nature of global competition? Why or why not?
2. It is possible that computer systems for air traffic control and other essential functions may not work properly as the year 2000 approaches. Someone has proposed that the commercial airline industry simply cancel all Dec. 31, 1999 flights that are scheduled to land or that could possibly land on Jan. 1, 2000. Explain why you agree or disagree with this proposal.
3. A quote in the section on the difficulty of handling organizational change says that technological change always creates new problems and has both positive and negative consequences. Explain how this might affect you personally in your career.
4. Someone has argued that there is nothing special about techno-hype because it is discounted just like other forms of advertising and exaggeration that we hear every day. Explain why you agree or disagree.

CASE

Dell Computer: Profiting from Mass Customization

In 13 years the computer business Michael Dell started while still a student at the University of Texas grew to a $12 billion enterprise. A central insight that guided much of this incredible story was that Dell Computer could bypass computer dealers and could sell directly to customers, who range from individuals to large companies buying thousands of computers. Accordingly, some of its sales occurred through an 800-telephone number and a Web site that attained $3 million of sales per day by 1998, whereas sales to large companies occurred through more traditional industrial sales relationships. Many of Dell's large competitors built personal computers starting from estimates of demand and contracts with distributors that sold the computers to individuals or businesses. They decided how many computers to assemble based on these demand estimates, shipped them to distributors, and hoped they would be sold before they became outdated. Dell used a different approach. It could eliminate markups charged by dealers and vastly reduce the risks of carrying large inventories by taking orders directly from the customers and building computers with the specific options individual customers wanted. Dell implemented this strategy through a combination of outsourcing and mass customization.

As an aggressive outsourcer, Dell has been a leader in permitting partners and suppliers to do work that might otherwise be done by company employees. At each stage in its value chain, Dell asks whether there is any reason to do the work internally. Dell does not manufacture the semiconductor chips used in its computers and does not attach the chips to the computer motherboards. Instead, it buys computer motherboards from suppliers with which it has long-term contracts. Similarly, it does not make monitors but purchases them from suppliers such as Sony. Because there is no advantage in receiving a shipment of Sony monitors, repackaging them, and shipping them to the customers, Dell asks Airborne Express or UPS to pick up computers at the Dell plant in Austin, match the computers with monitors from the Sony plant in Texas, and ship both to the customer at the same time. In a similar fashion, most of the 10,000 technicians who service Dell computers in the field are actually employees of other firms operating under contract with Dell. Furthermore, because there is no special value in insisting that only Dell employees have access to Dell's help-desk tools and information, people from major customers such as MCI can access this information directly through www.dell.com.

Dell's approach to mass customization is to create an efficient order fulfillment process that provides rapid delivery and low prices while also providing important options related to computer power, storage, the type of monitor, and other features. Because many customers wanted specific software installed on the computers before delivery, Dell created a network within its factory that made it possible to select one of many possible configurations and load it efficiently.

The internal processes that make this mass customization approach possible start with estimates of demand and long-term contracts with component suppliers. Dell maintains electronic links to its suppliers that tell them exactly when the parts are needed. These electronic links help make sure that Dell uses only the most current parts and does not have to store large inventories. Dell tracks inventory velocity and related measures closely and has reduced its inventory to 11 days, meaning that its risk of holding obsolete inventory is minimal. When its inventory balance is not quite right, it can use its direct sales model to steer customers toward products that can be built with the available inventory.

QUESTIONS

1. Describe the role of information technology in running Dell's business.
2. Dell has moved toward what is called a "virtual value chain," because many value-adding steps are outsourced. What are some of the advantages and disadvantages of this approach?

Sources:

Dell Computer Corporation. "The Dell Online Store," June 4, 1998 (http://commerce.us.dell.com/welcome/welcome.asp).

Magretta, Joan. "The Power of Virtual Integration: An Interview with Dell Computer's Michael Dell," *Harvard Business Review,* Mar.–Apr. 1998, pp. 72–84.

Pixar: Creating Computerized Animations

Pixar Animation Studios is a leader in three-dimensional computer animation. In 1995 it produced the first fully computer animated feature film, *Toy Story,* which won an Academy Award. That entire film was produced using RenderMan, Pixar's software tool kit for creating realistic visual effects. The process of creating an animation using software of this type differs vastly from the highly manual process that was used to create traditional cartoons and Disney features. The traditional animation process involved a huge number of individual drawings created by animation artists. It started with a story board providing a visual outline of the action and dialog, but required artists to fill in enough pictures to create the illusion of smooth action when the pictures were projected on a screen at 24 frames per second.

Computerized animation also starts with storyboard sketches and dialog but proceeds with the creation of computerized models. The 112,000 frames in *Toy Story* contained more than 400 separate three-dimensional models of characters, props, and sets. These models describe the shape of the object as well as the motion controls that animators use to create movement and expressions. *Toy Story's* characters were animated using more than 700 controls, such as separate controls for moving different parts of a character's eyebrow. Next is the animation step, in which choreographers place the models in key frames or poses and the computer uses interpolation methods to create the frames between the poses that make the animation seem smooth. If necessary, an animator can modify the computer generated frames. Next comes the shading step, in which the computer adds colors, finishes, and textures to the surface of every object in the scene. The computer programs that do this are called shaders. The 112,000 complex, realistic frames in *Toy Story* contained more than 400 models, more than 1,500 RenderMan shaders, and over 2,000 texture maps. Part of Pixar's animation tool kit is a library of surface appearances including wood, metal, fabric, glass, hair, and skin. The next step is lighting. Creating a photorealistic appearance requires the ability to identify, locate, and control a series of light sources throughout any scene. The treatment of light includes simulating the reflection and absorption of light by the various types of surfaces in the scene. The final step is rendering, in which software creates a finished image by computing every pixel in each frame. Even with today's workstations, the computations for just one frame take an average of three hours to produce the incredible detail that gives Pixar's films a unique three-dimensional appearance. Final images can be stored on film or on CD-ROM.

A key aspect of computerized animation is the impact it has on the people doing the work. Previously, animation was done through a laborious totally manual process of drawing each frame. Now, the same work can be done much faster using a computer, but some of the people who always did the drawings have not accommodated to computerization. Very few of the old-time animators do computerized animation, and every animator or technical director who joins Pixar starts with a three-month training course in its methods and technology. The animators even take acting lessons to help them breathe life into the movable characters they create.

QUESTIONS

1. Use the WCA framework to summarize the situation.
2. How is the switch from manual animation to computerized animation related to the ideas in each section of this chapter?
3. Explain why you do or do not believe computerized animation permits production of high-quality works of art by people who are less artistically talented than traditional animation artists.

Sources:

Hodkins, Jessica K. "Animating Human Motion," *Scientific American,* March 1998.

Jobs, Steve. "Letter from Steve Jobs," June 1997. May 30, 1998 (http://www.pixar.com/aboutpixar/sj_letter.html).

Pixar Corporation. "The Animation Process," May 30, 1998 (http://www.pixar.com/funstuff/how-its-done.html).

Basic Concepts for Understanding Systems

2

Study Questions

- Why is it important to have a framework for analyzing information systems?
- What six elements can be used for summarizing any work system?
- What is the relationship between information systems and work systems?
- What five perspectives can be used for thinking about work systems?
- What is the relationship between process architecture, process performance, and product performance?
- What are the steps in systems analysis and how can business professionals apply these steps?

Outline

Opening Case

RESUMIX: PROCESSING RÉSUMÉS WITHOUT PAPER

Did you ever wonder what happens when a job applicant sends a résumé to a large company that has placed an advertisement in a newspaper? Who actually looks at it? If 100 résumés arrive on the same day, how do they decide which applicants to interview? And if a similar job opens three months later, how does the company find the many applicants who are probably still interested, regardless of whether they have seen the company's next newspaper advertisement?

While an engineering manager at TRW's artificial intelligence research center in northern California, Steve Leung grappled with issues relating to hiring practices at his company. He was totally frustrated by what happened when he called job applicants who had responded to TRW's advertised job openings. The best applicants were no longer available by the time he called them. When he went to the human resources department to complain, he found four people reading through piles of résumés that had been accumulating for weeks. A year later, he founded Resumix, a software company devoted to solving problems related to the processing of résumés.

What Steve Leung saw at TRW was typical. The traditional large company approach for processing résumés and matching them to requisitions for new employees was slow and paper-intensive. The human resources department received and processed résumés submitted by job applicants, mostly in response to requisitions or newspaper ads. The résumés were date-stamped and passed on to internal recruiters who coded the résumés, categorized them by job grouping, and filed up to several hundred résumés in a day. The paper-intensive steps in matching the résumés to job requisitions included identifying the résumés that seemed appropriate for a particular job requisition, copying those résumés, and forwarding them to the hiring managers for review. Recruiters then tracked each forwarded résumé manually to make sure the applicant received an appropriate letter, either setting up an interview or saying the résumé will be kept on file.

An HR department using Resumix software handles résumés quite differently. First, the résumé is captured in electronic form using a scanner if it has come in by mail or by fax. Next, an optical character recognition program finds and catalogues the text in these images regardless of the résumé's format, font, or style. A patented program analyzes the text to extract key résumé information and then transfers that information into an applicant database. The information in the résumé summary includes name, addresses, telephone numbers, degrees, schools, grade point averages, and work history including dates, companies, job titles, and up to 80 skills. The software does this using a knowledge base of over 85,000 rules and concepts defining skill terms and phrases, abbreviations, acronyms, and even common misspellings. With high-volume optical scanners it is possible to scan and process up to 2,000 pages a day per scanner.

Computerizing the résumés transforms the initial screening for eligible applicants. The recruiter or manager simply identifies skill and experience criteria and clicks on a search button. Resumix responds with a prioritized list of qualified candidates for review. Instead of looking through a large number of résumés, the recruiter or manager examines only the résumés of the applicants who fit reasonably well based on the selection criteria entered into Resumix. No one needs to examine the large number of résumés that are an obvious mismatch. Storing the résumé data in a database also makes it more likely that an unsuccessful respondent to this month's newspaper ad might be contacted three months from now when another job opening arises. With paper-based résumé processing, finding that résumé again would often be difficult, regardless of what the rejection letter says about "keeping your application on file." Having a computerized record of each application also makes it easier to track the status of all résumés, to send out rejection letters efficiently, and to compile statistics about the efficiency and turnaround time of the hiring process. Where equal opportunity goals apply, having computerized information makes it easier to submit reports to the government and to justify that hiring was consistent with guidelines.

Debate Topic

The technology in Resumix is designed to convert a résumé into a series of fields in a database regardless of what the initial résumé looked like. Statements that don't match these specific data fields aren't recognized. Does the use of this technology imply that a company does not care very much about the individuality of the applicants?

Like the Amazon.com case at the beginning of Chapter 1, this case about a human resources department that uses Resumix demonstrates how progress in IT has enabled work practices fundamentally different from those of even the recent past. Both cases also demonstrate that IT is just part of the story. Merely having the hardware and software installed on a computer does not mean that anything different will happen. The benefits of IT investments are felt only when the technology is integrated into work systems.

The purpose of this chapter is to introduce the basic ideas that you need in order to analyze an IT-enabled system from a business professional's viewpoint. These ideas start with basic awareness of concepts such as *framework, system,* and *value chain,* but quickly move to an approach for thinking about any business system regardless of whether IT plays an important role. This approach is called *work-centered analysis* because it focuses on systems dedicated to doing specific types of work in specific business settings. Examples of such systems include systems by which a particular company hires new employees, designs new products, contacts new customers, or does any of the myriad of things that must be done systematically in order for the business to compete effectively. The starting point for work-centered analysis is a more detailed version of the system snapshot you see in Table 2.1, which summarizes the work system in terms of human participants performing a business process using information and technology to produce a product for an internal or external customer. (Internal customers are people within the same firm; external customers are outside the firm.) This way of viewing a system is especially useful when business professionals deal with software and hardware companies that talk about "selling

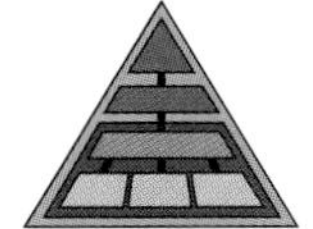

TABLE 2.1 **Processing Résumés Using Resumix**

CUSTOMER
- Manager who needs to hire an employee
- Applicant who receives responses about a job application
- Government agency that receives reports about compliance to equal opportunity guidelines

PRODUCT
- List of applicants who fit the criteria
- Selected data items about each applicant
- Automatically generated rejection letters

BUSINESS PROCESS

Major steps:
- Define the criteria for selecting applicants
- Receive résumés
- Scan résumés and extract data
- Select applicants meeting criteria and forward their résumés to the hiring manager
- Send out rejection letters
- Track the hiring process
- Store applicant data for future searches

Rationale:
- Instead of finding appropriate candidates by searching through paper résumés, extract the information on the résumés and do the search automatically.

PARTICIPANTS	INFORMATION	TECHNOLOGY
• Human resources employees • Manager doing the hiring	• Description of job opening • Scanned résumés converted into a database format • List of qualified applicants	• Resumix software • Scanner • Unidentified computers

systems." Hardware and software are important, but these are clearly just a part of what business professionals really care about—a system of doing work in their organization.

As the chapter unfolds, you will see how any business professional can understand a lot about even a technically complex information system by starting with the work system that the information system supports. By the end of the chapter, you will have a general approach that you can apply to start the analysis of any system in a business. You will be able to use this method to think about how a video store keeps track of its videos, how a stock market operates, or how a marketing manager decides where to advertise. Like any general method for studying or designing systems, the ideas presented here and developed throughout the rest of the book are not a cookbook. You cannot just follow a recipe or fill in the blanks. Studying these ideas will not make you an expert in information systems, but it will improve your ability to recognize information systems, understand their role in businesses, and participate in their development and use.

THE NEED FOR FRAMEWORKS AND MODELS

This book's goal is to teach you how to analyze information systems from a business professional's viewpoint. It presents many ideas and examples related within a framework that helps you create models as part of your systems analysis process. To clarify the basic approach, we will start by defining the terms *framework* and *model.*

A **framework** is a brief set of ideas for organizing a thought process about a particular type of thing or situation. It identifies topics that should be considered and shows how the topics are related. Here are some frameworks you have probably encountered:

- in economics, the concept of supply and demand as an explanation for how markets operate and how people make buying and selling decisions
- in biology, the classification into species, which helps biologists understand relationships between different types of animals
- in sports such as football, the rules that determine how to play the game and what types of actions are permitted

A **model** is a useful representation of a specific situation or thing. Models are useful because they describe or mimic reality without dealing with every detail of it. They typically help people analyze a situation by combining a framework's ideas with information about the specific situation being studied. Figure 2.1 shows examples of how a model can be used. The dummy represents a person in a crash test, permitting testing that would otherwise be impractical or unsafe. Other types of models frequently used in conjunction with automobiles include computerized drawings, wind-tunnel models, and simulators for training drivers. A less dramatic example in Figure 2.1 is a spreadsheet model used to decide whether a planned sales effort will probably meet profit goals by month. This model supports the decision by providing an organized way to combine past results and assumptions about the future.

Models always emphasize some features of reality and downplay or ignore others. For example, a scale model of a car could illustrate what it would look like, but would be useless for understanding how the car's shape affects its handling during rainstorms. Likewise, the spreadsheet model might emphasize the company president's assumptions about next year's sales, but might totally ignore the sales manager's unannounced plan to leave the firm next month.

The entire history of science can be viewed as the development and testing of frameworks and models for understanding the world. When people believed that the sun rotated around the earth, they interpreted their observations of the sun, moon, planets, and stars in terms of models based on this framework. Shifting the framework so that the earth rotated around the sun made it easier to understand their observations and led people to examine things they might have never considered otherwise.

Frameworks and models are important in business and society as well as science because they help us make sense of the world's complexity. For example, Table 2.1 was a simple descriptive model of a typical Resumix application. It summarized in a single table a

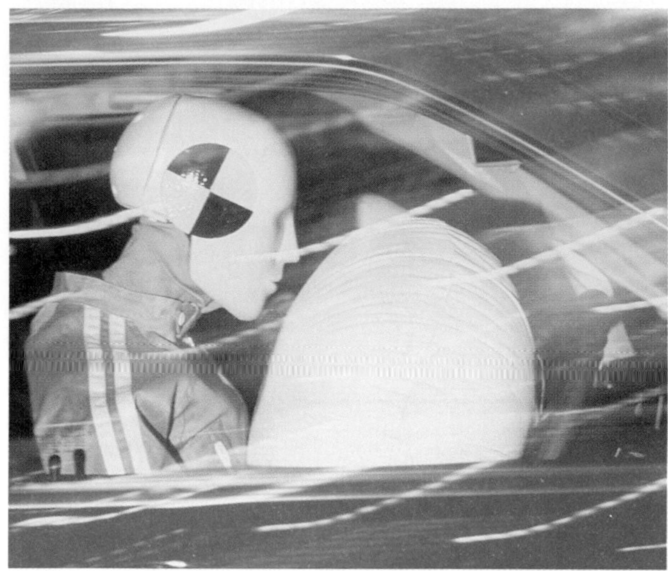

(a)

	A	B	C	D	E	F
1		Jan	Feb	Mar	Apr	
2						
3	# of sales people	3	3	4	4	
4	est. unit sales	30	35	42	48	
5	projected revenue	14100	16450	19740	22560	
6						
7	projected expenses:					
8	- salary + benefits	3000	3000	4000	4000	
9	- commission	6000	7000	8400	9600	
10	- cost of goods sold	3000	3500	4200	4800	
11	- overhead	2750	2750	2750	2750	
12	total expenses	14750	16250	19350	21150	
13	pretax profit	-650	200	390	1410	
14						
15						
16						

(b)

Figure 2.1
Examples of models

The mechanical dummy is a model used for testing the safety of automobile designs in crash situations. The spreadsheet is a model managers use to plan for the coming year.

complex situation for which a detailed description could have been 100 pages long. This chapter will explain why this type of summary is a useful starting point for analyzing a system.

Reality Check

WHY ARE FRAMEWORKS IMPORTANT?

A framework is a set of ideas that helps in thinking about a particular type of situation. While everyone generalizes from personal experience, the idea of using a framework to think about particular types of situations may not be as obvious.

1. Identify some of the frameworks you have studied or used in areas such as government, languages, history, literature, music, sports, or everyday life.
2. Identify situations in which you have disagreed with someone about either the framework that should be used for resolving an issue or the way to use a particular framework.

VIEWING BUSINESSES AS SYSTEMS

A **system** is a set of interacting components that operate together to accomplish a purpose. Systems that play a role in our everyday lives include our bodies' circulatory and digestive systems as well as society's transportation and communications systems. In this book we are concerned with systems that perform work in business and government organizations (with the help of IT). A **subsystem** is a component of a system, even though it can also be considered a system in its own right. The systems we are concerned with are always subsystems of a larger system and typically have subsystems that perform different parts of the work.

Understanding the significance of any particular system usually requires at least some understanding of the larger system it serves. To demonstrate this, Figure 2.2 represents a manufacturing firm as a system consisting of five subsystems: product design, production, sales, delivery, and service. Each of these subsystems can be subdivided further

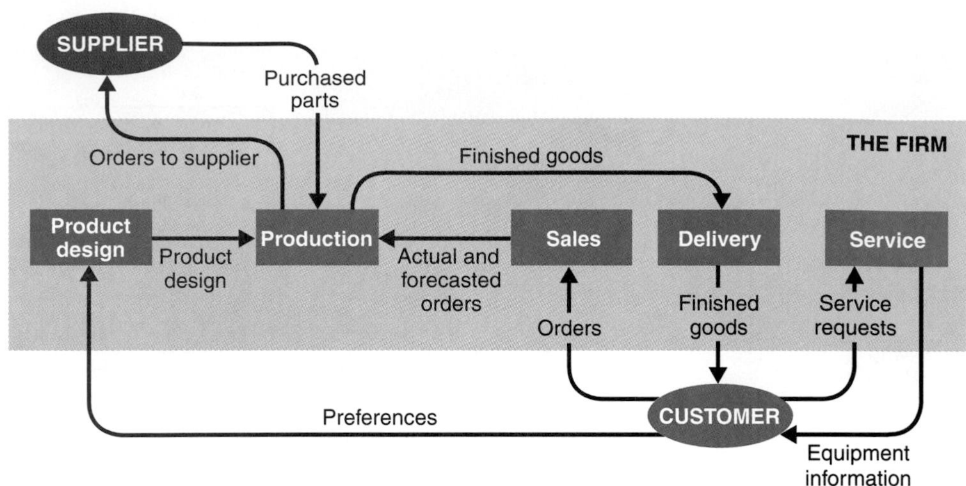

Figure 2.2
Viewing a firm as a system

This diagram represents a firm as a system consisting of five subsystems: product design, production, sales, delivery, and service.

into smaller subsystems that are not shown in the figure. Some of those smaller subsystems are information systems that help people perform the work and that reinforce the division of labor within the larger system by helping to coordinate tasks.

Other terms frequently used when discussing systems include the system's purpose, boundary, environment, input, and output:

- A system's **purpose** is the reason for its existence and the reference point for measuring its success. For example, the purpose of a résumé processing system that uses Resumix software is to facilitate a hiring process.
- A system's **boundary** defines what is inside the system and what is outside. For example, Table 2.1 included sending out rejection letters as part of the system. A different organization that used the Resumix software might have defined the boundary differently.
- A system's **environment** is everything pertinent to the system that is outside of its boundaries. The environment for the Resumix example might have included the company's unusually high salaries or the sterling reputation of its major local competitor.
- A system's **inputs** are the physical objects and information that cross the boundary to enter it from its environment. The incoming résumés are the main input in the Resumix case.
- A system's **outputs** are the physical objects and information that go from the system into its environment.

Figure 2.2 illustrates four of the five terms that define a system. The box around the five subsystems shows the *boundary* between the system (the firm) and its *environment*. The environment is everything outside the boundary, such as the suppliers and customers. The suppliers and customers are shown explicitly because they provide *inputs* and receive *outputs*. The inputs into the firm include parts purchased from suppliers and information such as preferences, orders, and service requests from customers. The outputs to the customers include finished goods and information such as warranties and advice about how to use the product.

Businesses as Systems Consisting of Business Processes

If you asked people to say more about the five subsystems in Figure 2.2, some would probably describe the subsystems as functional areas of business and would focus on the management structure within each subsystem. Others would probably describe the subsystems as business processes and would focus on how each successive step adds value for customers. For now we will take the latter view and will focus on business processes.

When we talk about analyzing systems later in this chapter, we will step back a notch and view the unit of analysis as a work system, which includes a business process, participants, and other elements.

A **business process** is a related group of steps or activities that use people, information, and other resources to create value for internal or external customers. These steps are related in time and place, have a beginning and end, and have inputs and outputs.[1, 2] Figure 2.2 shows that the design process creates the product design for an internal customer, the process of producing the product. In turn, the production process creates finished goods for another internal customer, the delivery process. The delivery process provides finished goods to an external customer.

The **scope** of a business process is the specific set of subprocesses and activities it includes. **Subprocesses** are parts of a process that are processes in their own right because they consist of well defined steps related in time and place, have a beginning and end, and have inputs and outputs. For example, the process of producing a textbook includes subprocesses such as writing the manuscript, revising the manuscript, designing the book's layout, producing the artwork, and printing the book. In contrast to the term subprocess, however, we will use the term *activity* to denote more general, often less well defined things that people do in businesses, such as communicating with others, motivating employees, and analyzing data. In some cases, an important role of IT is to convert a poorly defined activity into a better defined subprocess that is done in a predictable way and produces consistent outputs. For example, this happens when voice mail is installed to improve message taking.

A process's **value added** is the amount of value it creates for its internal or external customer. For example, the process "assemble an automobile" starts with the automobile's component parts and ends with a completely assembled automobile. From the internal or external customer's viewpoint, the value added is the difference between the value of the components (for the customer) and the value of the assembled automobile.

Scope and value added present a number of immediate design issues for any process. If its scope is too small, it doesn't add as much value as it might. If its scope is too large, it may be too difficult to understand or manage, and may be more effective if separated into subprocesses.

The most obvious question to ask about any business process or step within a business process is whether it adds any value at all. Consider what happened when the employees at a General Electric plant met to identify ways to improve internal processes. The editor of an award-winning plant newsletter complained that seven approvals were needed before each monthly edition could be released. The plant manager's public response: "This is crazy. I didn't know that was the case. From now on, no more signatures." Producing the newspaper added value for internal customers, but getting signatures added nothing but delay and wasted effort.[3]

Next we will discuss the value chain and the functional areas of business. Both were mentioned in the discussion of IT-based innovations in Chapter 1, but they need to be revisited here as a facet of understanding business systems.

The Value Chain

The set of processes a firm uses to create value for its customers is often called its **value chain**.[4] The value chain includes **primary processes** that directly create the value the firm's customer perceives and **support processes** that add value indirectly by making it easier for others to perform the primary processes. The idea of the value chain is important because the way work is organized within a firm should be related to the way the firm provides value for its customers.

Figure 2.3 identifies some of the processes in a hypothetical restaurant's value chain. These primary processes include purchasing, taking orders, and serving food. Essential support processes not mentioned in the figure include cleaning the kitchen, hiring employees, paying taxes, and managing the restaurant. Managing can be viewed as a support process because it is not directly involved with doing the work that provides value for customers. This particular value chain probably does not belong to a fast food restaurant.

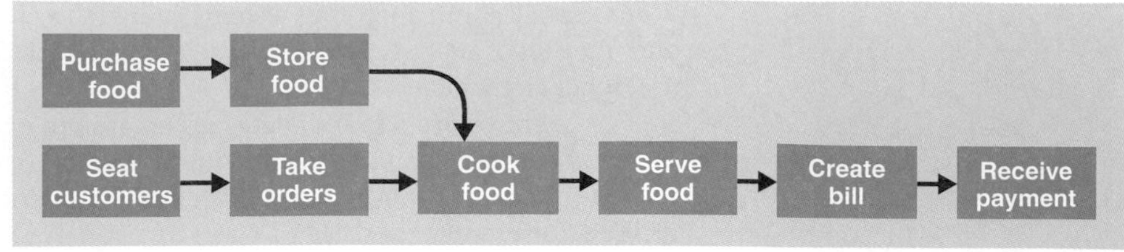

Figure 2.3
Primary processes for a hypothetical restaurant

Based on the primary processes shown, this probably is not the value chain for the type of fast food restaurant that cooks the food before taking orders.

In most fast food restaurants, the customers seat themselves instead of waiting to be seated. In addition, many fast food restaurants cook the food before receiving the orders and receive payment before serving the food.

Attaining agreement about a useful view of any firm's value chain is an important step in improving its effectiveness. Although a value chain may seem obvious after a useful view of it is produced, that view is often far from obvious in advance. For example, the value chain in Figure 2.3 leaves out deciding what menu to serve and developing recipes. For some purposes, these might have been the heart of the issue. Deciding what to include and what to exclude requires judgment and careful attention to the purpose of the analysis.

Business Processes and Functional Areas of Business

Businesses have traditionally organized around **functional areas of business,** which are large subsystems of a firm related to specific business disciplines, such as Production, Sales and Marketing, and Finance. Chapter 1 surveyed IT-based innovations in these functional areas and in several others. Most businesses are organized around the functional areas because this provides a focus for work and because it promotes professionalism and expertise. Unfortunately, organizing in terms of business functions sometimes reinforces an inward-looking orientation. This tendency to focus inward at the organization instead of outward at the customer is sometimes called managing in terms of **functional silos.** This means that while careful attention is paid to what happens within the functional area (the "silo"), comparatively little attention is given to maximizing value for the customer by coordinating across the functional areas. After recognizing the disadvantages of functional silos, many have moved a bit closer to organizing around customer-oriented processes. For example, some parts of AT&T have started doing annual budgets based not on functions or departments, but on processes such as maintenance of a worldwide network. Its Network Systems Division identified 13 core processes, each of which has an "owner" who focuses on day-to-day operations, and a "champion" who makes sure the process remains linked with overall strategies and goals.[5]

Figure 2.4 shows why functional areas are important in many practical situations but are ineffective as a basis for studying information systems. Three types of processes are shown:

- *Processes that cross functional areas:* Essential processes such as creating a new product, creating a coordinated plan for an entire business, and fulfilling customer orders usually span multiple functional areas. Seeing these processes from the viewpoint of just one functional area is often misleading and contrary to the way today's business leaders want their organizations to operate.
- *Processes related to a specific functional area:* Other essential processes such as manufacturing products, identifying potential customers, and paying taxes are typically viewed as belonging to a particular functional area. The best way to learn about these processes and the information systems that support them is by learning about the functional area rather than by learning about information systems per se.
- *Activities and subprocesses occurring in every functional area:* These common activities and subprocesses include communicating with other people, analyzing data, planning the work that will be done, and providing feedback to employees. These activities often use information systems in one way or another, and are not at all unique to a particular functional area.

Business processes requiring coordinated work from many functional areas

- Creating a new product
- Creating a coordinated plan for an entire business
- Fulfilling customer orders

Business processes typically within a functional area

Engineering

- Performing research about new methods
- Determining how to produce products
- Determining how to improve production processes

Sales and Marketing

- Identifying potential customers
- Defining customer wants and needs
- Identifying market opportunities
- Making customers aware of the product
- Persuading customers to buy the product
- Performing the sales transaction

Production

- Purchasing materials
- Assembling or fabricating the product
- Delivering the product
- Servicing the product and supporting the customer

Accounting and Finance

- Performing financial transactions
- Creating financial statements
- Paying taxes
- Investing cash
- Financing operations

Human Resources

- Determining hiring requirements
- Hiring people
- Introducing employees to the way the company operates
- Paying employees
- Administering employee benefits
- Administering disciplinary actions and terminations

Subprocesses and activities occurring in all functional areas

- Communicating with other people
- Analyzing data
- Motivating employees
- Planning the work that will be done
- Keeping track of work being done
- Providing feedback to employees

Figure 2.4
Business processes and functional areas of business

At the top of the figure are business processes that require coordinated effort involving several functional areas. The center shows business processes that typically occur within a particular functional area. The bottom of the figure shows business processes and activities that occur in all functional areas.

All three groups of processes and activities rely heavily on IT, yet only one of the three groups tends to be unique within the functional silos. This shows that even specialists in one functional area may spend much of their careers involved in work that is not unique to that area. It also shows why devoting individual chapters to information systems in each of the functional areas would be repetitive and possibly misleading. To present as realistic a picture as possible, this book contains many examples from different functional areas but doesn't make functional areas a key emphasis. Instead, it focuses on analyzing information systems from a business professional's viewpoint regardless of the area involved.

Reality Check

DESCRIBING A BUSINESS AS A SYSTEM

The text states that ideas pertaining to systems, in general, can be used for thinking about how a business operates.

1. Summarize your understanding of the inputs, outputs, and major subsystems of any business with which you are familiar.
2. Explain your view of the advantages and disadvantages of dividing any business or government organization into specialized functional areas.

INFORMATION SYSTEMS AND WORK SYSTEMS

Before we present an approach for analyzing IT-enabled systems, the difference between information technology, information systems, and work systems needs to be clarified. People may use the term *system* to refer to any of these three levels, and they sometimes switch back and forth between them without realizing they are doing so. In the case of Resumix, for example, people in the HR department might refer to "the system" as the department's entire cycle of handling résumés. A Resumix salesperson participating in this conversation might refer to "the system" as the hardware and software being sold. A member of the in-house IT staff, who is trying to support the HR department, might view "the system" as an information system that includes Resumix and other tools such as electronic mail. Although none of these viewpoints is incorrect, they cause confusion when used together. Because we want a way to analyze IT-enabled systems, we need to clarify our terms.

Which "System" Are We Talking About?

As just described, confusion results when the concept of "system" is simultaneously used with different meanings. Figure 2.5 shows several possible levels people with different responsibilities might use for defining "the system" being discussed in any particular situation. This "system" might actually be the information technology, the information system that uses the technology, the work system that contains or is supported by the information system, or even an entire firm that consists of multiple work systems. Each of these terms will now be defined.

- **Information technology** is the hardware and software used by information systems. **Hardware** refers to the devices and other physical objects involved in processing information, such as computers, workstations, physical networks, and data storage and transmission devices. **Software** refers to the computer programs that interpret user inputs and tell the hardware what to do. Software includes operating systems, end user software such as word processors, and application software related to specialized business tasks such as recording credit card transactions or designing automobiles. (Although "pencil and paper" and chalkboards are also forms of information technology, our definition is stated in terms of hardware and software because we are primarily concerned with computerized systems.)
- An **information system** is a particular type of work system that uses information technology to capture, transmit, store, retrieve, manipulate, or display information, thereby supporting one or more other work systems. Software products such as spreadsheets and word processing software are not information systems because they are not work systems in their own right.
- A **work system** is a system in which human participants perform a business process using information, technology, and other resources to produce products for internal or external customers. The core of a work system is a business process consisting of steps related in time and place, having a beginning and end, and having inputs and outputs. This concept of work has nothing to do with paying people to be present at a particular place during a particular part of the day. **Work** is the application of human and physical resources such as people, equipment, time, effort, and money to generate outputs used by internal or external customers. Work occurs only if products are generated for use by internal or external customers.
- A firm (or government organization) consists of interrelated work systems that operate together to generate products or services for external customers in a business environment. Although many of the ideas discussed here might be used for thinking about how an entire firm operates, this book focuses on how to understand and analyze specific IT-enabled work systems within a firm.
- The **business environment** includes the firm itself and everything that affects its success, such as competitors, suppliers, customers, regulatory agencies, and demographic, social, and economic conditions.

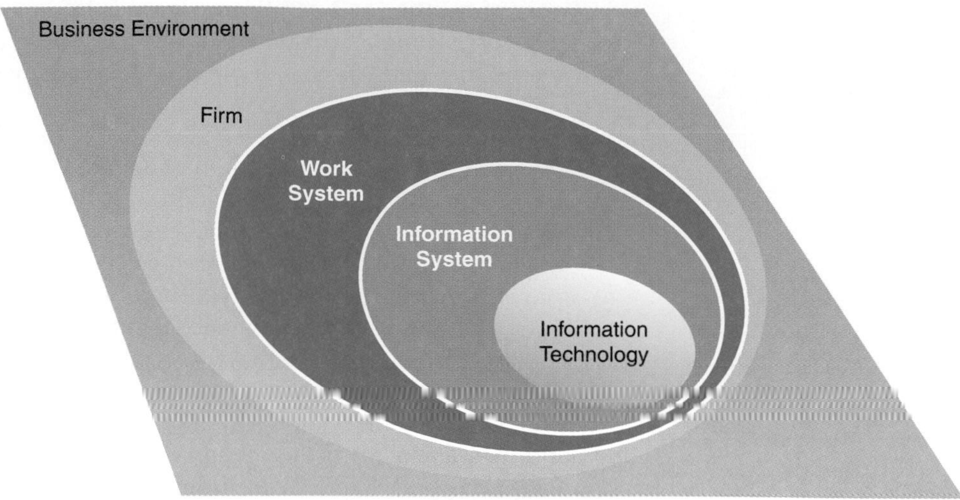

Figure 2.5
Information technology, information systems, and work systems

Information systems are work systems that use information technology to capture, transmit, store, retrieve, manipulate, or display information used work systems they support. Firms consist of interrelated work systems and compete in a business environment.

Examples in Table 2.2 illustrate the distinction between a work system and a related information system. In each case, the information system plays an important role in a work system, but does not directly affect other aspects of it.

Increasing Overlap between Information Systems and Work Systems

The distinction between the information system and the work system used to be simpler because the work occurred in the work system and the information system observed and recorded what happened. This is basically what happens in farming even today. In an apple orchard, for instance, the main work system involves cultivating the apples; the information systems, if any, help with decisions about irrigation and picking schedules. In other situations the work system and the information system overlap significantly and the distinction between them is unclear. In a bank's student loan program, for example, the

TABLE 2.2 **Roles of Information Systems within Work Systems**

The table shows that each of the information systems listed supports some, but not all, of the important aspects of a work system.

Information system	Work system supported by the information system	Aspects of the work system not included in the information system
Bar code scanners and computers identify the items sold and calculate the bill	Performing customer checkout	Establishing personal contact with customers, putting the groceries in bags
University registration system permits students to sign up for specific class sections	Registering for classes	Deciding which classes to take and which sections to sign up for in order to have a good weekly schedule
Word processing system used for typing and revising chapters	Writing a book	Deciding what to say in the book and how to say it
Interactive system top managers use to monitor their organization's performance	Keeping track of organizational performance	Talking to people to understand their views about what is happening
System that identifies people by scanning and analyzing voice prints	Preventing unauthorized access to restricted areas	Human guards, cameras, and other security measures

work of granting and monitoring loans is information-intensive because it is mostly about processing information such as identification, qualifications, references, payments, and balance due. Whether or not computers are involved, the work system is mostly an information system.

Increasing overlap between the work system and the information system appeared in every one of the IT-based innovations mentioned in Chapter 1. The evolution of manufacturing information systems illustrates how this trend developed over time. The earliest of these systems used paper log sheets to record events in the work system (such as items completed at each step or items scrapped) and later compiled that information and reported it to accountants and management for subsequent use. These information systems collected information about the work being done but did not directly help production workers perform manufacturing operations. Subsequent developments in interactive computing made it possible for the information system to help manufacturing workers by immediately checking data input for detectable errors and by making up-to-the-second information available whenever workers or managers needed it for current decisions. Highly automated manufacturing takes this a step further by automatically collecting data whenever a work step is completed, automatically making decisions about what item to work on next, and automatically downloading the correct machine recipe. In these situations, the information system and the work system overlap so much that the manufacturing is largely controlled by the information system. Turn off the information system and this type of manufacturing grinds to a halt.

FRAMEWORK FOR THINKING ABOUT ANY SYSTEM IN BUSINESS

The general framework in Figure 2.6 is a starting point for thinking about a specific work system and information systems that support it. This is called the **work-centered analysis (WCA) framework** because it emphasizes a business professional's need to understand a work system in order to decide whether an information system needs to be created or improved. This framework combines ideas from sources including total quality management, business process reengineering, and general systems theory. It consists of six linked elements:

- the internal or external customers of the work system
- the products (or services) produced by the work system
- the steps in the business process
- the participants in the work system
- the information the work system uses or creates
- the technology the work system uses

The large box surrounding the business process, participants, information, and technology defines the boundaries of the work system that produces the outputs (products) customers receive. Since the work system's purpose is to generate the product for the customer, analyzing only things within the boundary would be too inward looking because it would ignore the customer's view. If processing data plays any role in performing the work, which is almost always true, part of the system is an information system.

Making the work system the unit of analysis does not diminish the importance of the business process, which is pictured as the core of the work system and which is usually viewed as the fundamental element of a value chain. We will view a work system as the unit of analysis because the same business process can be performed with drastically different levels of efficiency and effectiveness depending on who does the work and what information and technology they use. In other words, just looking at the steps in a business process often reveals only part of the story about whether performance is adequate and what could be done to improve it.

All the links in the WCA framework are represented as two-headed arrows because all six elements should be in balance and because a change in one area can affect any of the

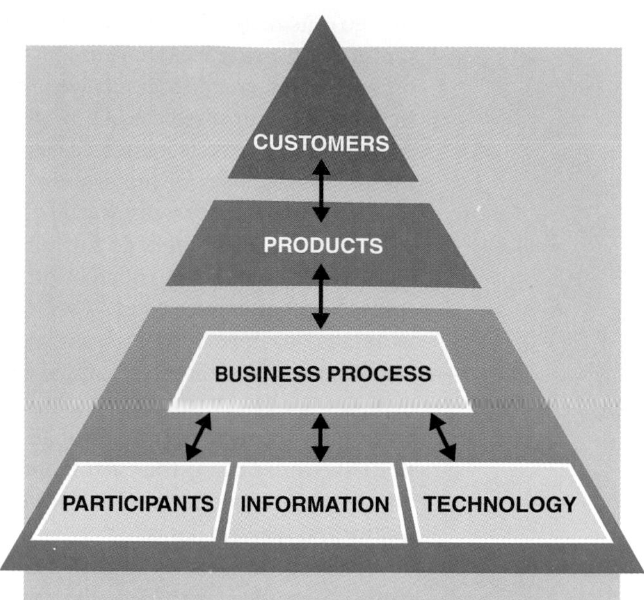

Figure 2.6
The WCA framework for thinking about any system in business

The WCA framework consists of six linked elements that can be used for thinking about any information system or work system.

others. Consider what happened when Mutual Benefit Life (MBL) switched to a new process for deciding whether to issue a policy, setting the price, and issuing the policy. Previously this process involved 40 steps, 12 functions, and an average of 22 days. By assigning each policy application to a case team consisting of a case manager and two assistants, MBL reduced cycle time to two to six days, reduced costs 40%, and provided more responsiveness to customer concerns. The new process called for greater employee responsibility than the previous assembly line approach because each case manager had to deal directly with customer issues instead of repeatedly asking for approvals from senior managers or technical experts. The new process was successful in many ways, but it led to significant personnel problems. MBL had made a major commitment to hiring and training local, disadvantaged employees, many of whom could not master case management skills and felt betrayed. Some of these employees picketed the firm's headquarters to show their frustration.[6]

Although the previous process had many shortcomings, moving to this new process created a new imbalance between two crucial elements: participants and the business process. In general, changing any of the six elements may affect any of the other elements and may lead to changes, for better or worse, in those areas. For example, availability of more powerful technology could affect every other element within a framework. By making more information accessible, the new technology could permit business process changes, which in turn would affect the types of skills required of participants and ultimately the quality of the product that the customer receives. If customers want a product that is cheap and if they don't care about customization, a process capable of producing a highly customized product may be too expensive. Similarly, if the process is designed to check and double-check the work of unskilled participants with lackadaisical attitudes, highly committed individuals will probably regard it as an insult. We will now look at each of the elements of the WCA framework in turn.

Customers

The internal and external customers of a work system are the people who receive and use its outputs. **Internal customers** are people within the same firm who participate in other work systems that create additional value before the firm's product or service goes to the external customer. **External customers** are people who receive and use work system outputs that go outside the firm. These outputs include the products or services that are the reason for the firm's existence. They may also include outputs that go to governmental agencies or other external groups that receive taxes or information required by law or by membership in industry groups. Table 2.1 showed that the Resumix example involves both internal and external customers. The internal customers are the hiring managers and the external customers are the job applicants, and possibly government agencies if any of the data is used for equal opportunity reporting.

External customers do not typically participate in the work system itself, although some work systems have been improved by making customers participants. For example, this is how banks have used ATMs to improve the convenience and efficiency of processes related to depositing and withdrawing money. Health product distributors such as McKesson and Baxter International were once considered pioneers for permitting external customers to perform the data input for their internal order entry systems. Electronic commerce through EDI and through the Web has now made this approach commonplace. Benefits from making the customers direct participants in these systems include not only eliminating data entry clerks, but also providing quicker response about product availability and delivery dates.

Trying to identify a work system's customer sometimes leads to surprises. For example, one might think that the customers of a toy company's manufacturing process are the children who use the toys; however, Figure 2.7 shows there is actually a chain of customer relationships between the manufacturing line and the children. For purposes of scheduling and balancing work inside the factory, the immediate customer of the manufacturing process is an internal customer, the shipping department, which is trying to meet its shipping schedule while using its staff efficiently. In turn, the direct customer of the shipping is an external customer, the distributor, which is concerned with receiving the toys around the time they can be sold. The distributor's direct customer is the person who makes the purchase rather than the child who will eventually use the toy directly. This example shows that a work system may have many different customers and that the customers to consider when analyzing a system depend on the purpose of the analysis.

When identifying customers, it is also useful to distinguish between customers and stakeholders. Customers make direct use of whatever the work system produces; therefore, they are in the best position to evaluate the product. Stakeholders such as the vice president

Figure 2.7
Who is a toy factory's customer?

The product produced by a toy factory goes to a series of internal and external customers.

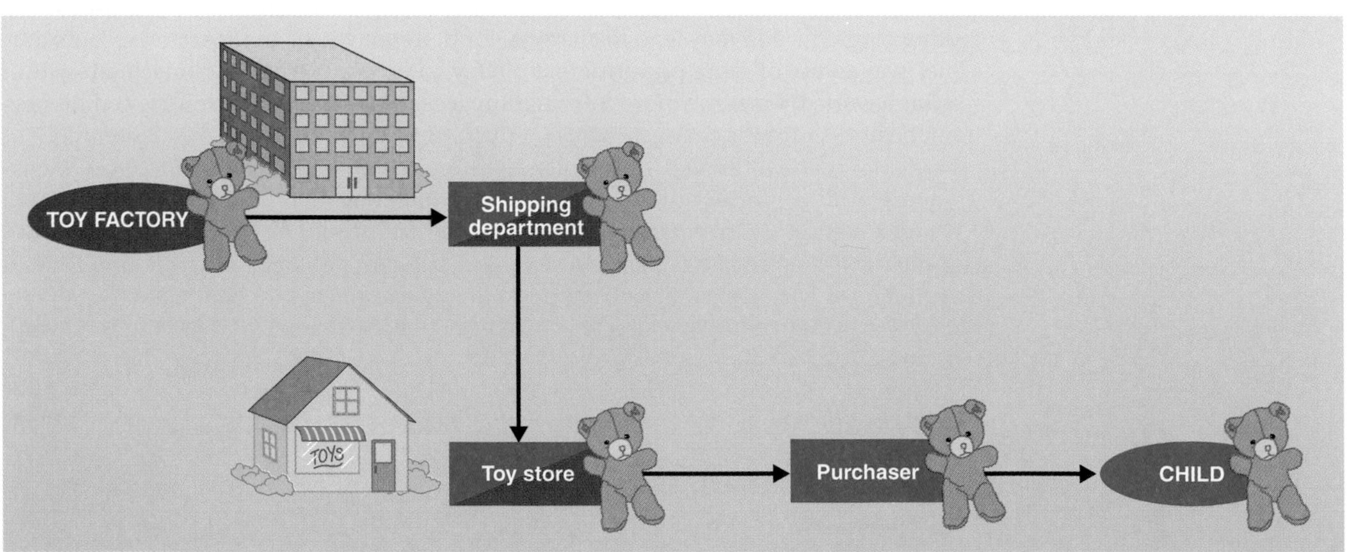

of human resources might care greatly about the results produced using a tool such as Resumix, and might gain power or prestige by introducing such a tool, but they are not direct customers of the work system it supports.

Having multiple customers with different concerns is often a complicating factor when the work involves building an information system. The most obvious customers are the people who will use the information system, but the IT staff is also a customer because it will have to maintain and improve the resulting information system over time. Because an information system that might satisfy all the end users' wishes might also be a nightmare to maintain, the process of building systems must often reconcile the differing needs of these two sets of customers.

Product

The product is the output of a work system. It usually contains a mix of information and physical and service components, although one or two of these components usually comprise most of the value the customer receives. For example, a custom tailor shop produces the clothing (a physical thing), measures the client and customizes patterns for the client's needs (a service), and may provide information about related products. In contrast, an online bank performs banking services and provides information but does not produce physical things for the customer.

Quality experts frequently assert that the work system's customer should evaluate its product because the work system exists to produce that product or service for the customer. Customers evaluate products in terms of characteristics such as the total cost they bear and the quality, responsiveness, reliability, and conformance to standards or regulations they perceive. Although one or two of these characteristics are often more important than the others in specific situations, separate consideration of each often helps in thinking about ways to improve the product from the customer's viewpoint.

Business Process

As defined earlier, a business process is a related group of steps or activities that uses people, information, and other resources to create value for internal or external customers. Business processes consist of steps related in time and place, have a beginning and end, and have inputs and outputs. Business processes are at least somewhat formalized, but they need not be totally structured. For example, some auto dealerships require that salespeople sell cars at a pre-specified price, whereas others permit salespeople to negotiate on price. An automobile is being sold in both cases, but one process is somewhat more structured when the price is fixed in advance. A common way to improve work system performance is to change the business process by adding, combining or eliminating steps or by changing the methods used in the steps. For example, incorporating Resumix into the handling of résumés improved performance by eliminating manual work and by automating the initial screening efforts.

Table 2.1 summarized the business process in the Resumix example by naming the major steps and by identifying its rationale for adding value. The major steps in the process include defining criteria, receiving résumés, scanning them to extract data, selecting the most eligible candidates, responding to candidates, and saving information for later use. The rationale for this process is to eliminate paper-based résumé processing by scanning résumés, storing information, and then taking maximum advantage of the computerized database. The major steps and rationale of a bank's ATM system can be described in a similar fashion. The steps might include reloading the cash and paper supplies, removing the deposits, obtaining instructions from customers, performing transactions, and performing nightly updates to accounts. The rationale might be described as automating tasks the teller would otherwise perform by providing a network of geographically distributed terminals customers can use directly. This type of summary is just a first step in understanding a business process. A complete analysis of a work system would necessarily document the business processes in much greater detail. This could be done verbally or using diagramming tools such as such as the ones explained in Chapter 3.

Participants

Participants in a work system are the people who do the work. Even highly automated systems typically include human participants, such as the human attendants who can sometimes be reached when none of the options in an automated voice mail system suffices. Although information systems are often viewed as computer systems, human participants in these systems typically play essential roles such as entering, processing, or using the information in the system. The importance of human participants in information system success and failure is often underplayed. There is a tendency to attribute success to the wonders of the computer. Simultaneously, human errors such as entering incorrect data or failing to follow required procedures are often reported as a "computer glitch."

Work systems depend on participants' skills, interest, and involvement. They also affect participants personally even though many systems are designed as if these impacts were irrelevant or unimportant. A typical symptom of this problem is when a clerk or other system participant knows what to fill out on a form but doesn't know why the information is needed or how it will be used. Traditional education of engineers may have contributed to this problem by sanctioning the design of complex, technical systems without regard to participants. A study of over 100 engineering textbooks and books on equipment design in the Boston University Library (all published between 1938 and 1989) found only 42 that made any mention of workers' roles. Even the 42 that mentioned workers' roles all view "the role of people in production as subordinate, if not marginal." Some presented an antagonistic tone toward participants, such as the 1968 text that said, "The engineer must never forget that whatever he designs is meant to be used by human beings.... Unless the designer goes to apparently absurd lengths to prevent it, people will operate the device incorrectly." [7]

Just as participants play a key role in a work system, the work system also has an impact on its participants. The nature of this impact depends on a participant's individual characteristics because people bring vastly different capabilities and backgrounds to their work. Highly structured, repetitive systems may be fine for some participants but unsatisfying for others with different skills or personality traits. Applying technology to change a work system may foster personal learning and growth by instilling jobs with a more appropriate degree of engagement and challenge. To the contrary, however, it may devalue job skills and make jobs tedious or even obsolete. One way to think about impacts on participants is to ask whether system participants are being treated as **secondary customers,** namely, people who receive some benefits from the work system even if they don't receive and use its outputs directly.

Information

The information in a work system can potentially take a variety of forms including numbers, text, sounds, pictures, and even video. Some of the information in a work system may be created or modified with the system while other information may be received from other work systems.

The distinction between data, information, and knowledge is important for deciding whether providing better information would have any effect on the results a work system produces. Figure 2.8 shows that data form the basis of information and that knowledge is needed to use information. **Data** are facts, images, or sounds that may or may not be pertinent or useful for a particular task. In our everyday lives, we absorb data from newspapers and television, from billboards, and from other people. We receive so much data every minute that our conscious minds can't possibly pay attention to all of it. **Information** is data whose form and content are appropriate for a particular use. Converting data into information by formatting, filtering, and summarizing is a key role of information systems.

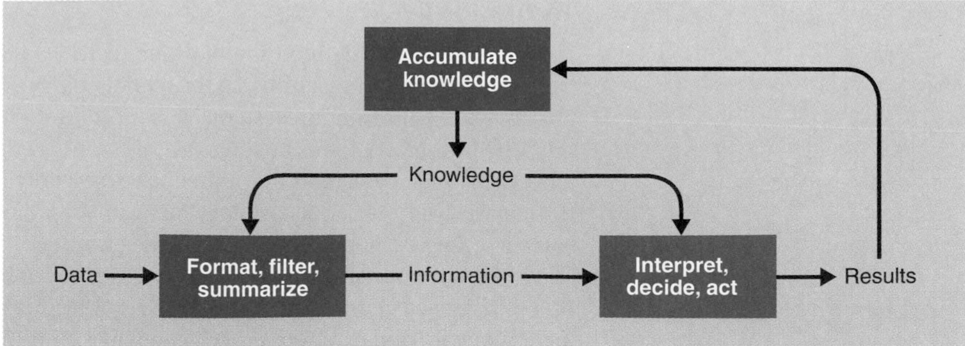

Figure 2.8
Relationship between data, information, and knowledge

People use knowledge about how to format, filter, and summarize data as part of the process of converting data into information useful in a situation. They interpret that information, make decisions, and take actions. The results of these decisions help in accumulating knowledge for use in later decisions.

People need knowledge to use information effectively. **Knowledge** is a combination of instincts, ideas, rules, and procedures that guide actions and decisions.

The distinction between data and information is easy to remember. It is cited frequently in explaining why systems that collect vast amounts of data often fail to satisfy managerial information needs. These data constitute information for people performing day-to-day operational tasks such as processing orders, but are not useful for managers, who need the data converted into information for management decision making. There are many ways to do this. Some examples include:

- selecting the data pertinent to the situation and removing the irrelevant data
- combining the data to bring it to a useful level of summarization
- highlighting exceptions that may bias the results, or explaining more clearly what the data really say
- displaying the data in an understandable way
- developing models that convert data and assumptions into explanations of past results or projections of future results

In addition to showing the conversion of data into information, Figure 2.8 shows the process of accumulating knowledge and using that knowledge. It says that people act based on their information about the current situation plus their accumulated knowledge about using information. The results of action feed into the process of accumulating more knowledge, which in turn makes people more able to process data into information and more able to use that information in the future. For example, this is the process by which medical students become expert doctors. As medical students examine patients, treat them, and observe the results, their medical knowledge deepens.

Systems with human participants use both hard and soft data. **Hard data,** clearly defined data generated by formal systems, must often be balanced with **soft data,** intuitive or subjective data obtained by informal means such as talking to people or interpreting stories and opinions. Although hard data are factual and explicit, soft data are often essential for understanding what really happened in a situation, or whether proposed actions will probably encounter resistance within an organization. The distinction between hard and soft information explains why existing methods for identifying and defining the information in formal, computerized systems usually miss some of the information that is important in any situation. The simple fact is that some information in any work system will never be formalized. Furthermore, even in business processes that are formalized, unanticipated situations sometimes make it necessary to create workarounds, situation-dependent steps that bypass the formal process because it doesn't fit the situation. In these instances, the problem may not be the methods for building information systems, but rather the human inability to anticipate everything that can possibly happen, even in relatively small systems. Information system designers primed to define information requirements for computerized systems often seem to find this realization disappointing.

Technology

Technology can be defined many different ways. For sociologists, technology includes both tools and methods for using those tools, such as a region's "agricultural technology." For analyzing information systems, it is more useful to separate the tools from the methods. The framework treats business processes as methods and procedures for doing work; it treats technology as tools that either perform work directly or are used to help people perform work. Information technology mentioned in the Resumix case includes the Resumix software, the scanners, and unidentified computers.

The key point about technology in a work system is that it has no impact whatsoever unless it is used within a business process. A business professional's view of information technology is primarily concerned with whether the technology can support the desired work system and with long- and short-term costs, risks, and other business implications. A business professional's work system analysis must include technology but should emphasize technology use in the work system rather than the internal details of the technology.

Reality Check

ELEMENTS OF THE FRAMEWORK

The WCA framework identifies six elements needed to understand a work system.

1. Identify each of these elements in a work system with which you are familiar, such as registering for classes, renting a video, or ordering a meal at a restaurant.
2. From a customer's viewpoint, identify the product of the work system and explain how you would evaluate that product.

FIVE PERSPECTIVES FOR VIEWING A WORK SYSTEM

The six elements in the WCA framework provide a comparatively easy way to summarize any work system, including an information system that supports it. To gain a better understanding of an IT-enabled system, it is useful to view the system from five distinct perspectives: architecture, performance, infrastructure, context, and risks. Table 2.3 summarizes the key issues each of the five perspectives raises for business and IT professionals analyzing any system. The five perspectives are defined as follows:

1. **Architecture** specifies how the current or proposed system operates mechanically by summarizing its components, the way the components are linked, and the way the components operate together. Although the term "architecture" may sound technical, it applies equally to processes, information, technology, and organizations. For example, *information architecture* refers to how information is organized within a system, whereas *organizational architecture* refers to how the people and departments are organized.
2. **Performance** describes how well the work system, its components, or its products operate. Each of the six elements in the framework can be described and monitored quantitatively or qualitatively to provide guidance for process and product improvement. Because system performance depends on the balance and alignment between system components, improving the performance of just a part of the system may not affect the results if the other parts are left unchanged.
3. **Infrastructure** is the human and technical resources the work system depends on and shares with other systems. Infrastructure is typically not under control of the systems it serves, yet it plays an essential role in those systems. For information systems, the technical infrastructure typically includes computer networks, telephone systems, and software for building and operating these systems. The human infrastructure for these systems is the support staff that keeps them operating effectively. Examining

TABLE 2.3 **Issues Raised by Five Perspectives for Understanding a Work System**

Five perspectives each raise a set of questions that should be considered when analyzing a system from a business or IT professional's viewpoint.

Perspective	Key issues
Architecture	• What are the components of the system that performs the work and who uses the work product? • How are the components linked? • How do the components operate together?
Performance	• How well do the components operate individually? • How well does the system operate? (How well is the work performed?) • How well should the system operate?
Infrastructure	• What technical and human infrastructure does the work rely on? • In what ways does infrastructure present opportunities or obstacles?
Context	• What are the impacts of the organizational and technical context? • In what ways does the context present opportunities or obstacles?
Risks	• What foreseeable things can prevent the work from happening, can make the work inefficient, or can cause defects in the work product? • What are the likely responses to these problems?

infrastructure may reveal untapped opportunities to use available resources, but may also reveal constraints limiting the changes that can occur.

4. **Context** is the organizational, competitive, technical, and regulatory realm within which the work system operates, including external stakeholders, the organization's policies, practices, and culture, and competitive and regulatory issues that affect the system. The context may create incentives and even urgency for change but may also create obstacles.
5. **Risks** consist of the foreseeable events whose occurrence could cause system degradation or failure. Because every business situation has some risks, any effort to build or change a system should include identifying foreseeable risks and deciding on either countermeasures or acceptance of the risks.

Figure 2.9 shows how links between the architecture and performance perspectives are at the core of any attempt to improve a work system. Starting at the top, it shows that customer satisfaction is largely determined by product performance, which the customer evaluates in terms of criteria such as cost, quality, and responsiveness. Next, product performance is shown as being determined largely by a combination of product architecture (the form and extent of the product) and internal work system performance, which is described in terms of variables such as consistency, productivity, and cycle time. In turn, work system performance is based primarily on work system architecture but is also affected by human and technical infrastructure, organizational, competitive, and regulatory context, and foreseeable risks.

The distinction between external and internal performance deserves special emphasis because work system changes can affect both internal and external performance, either of them, or neither. Any proposed change that affects neither external nor

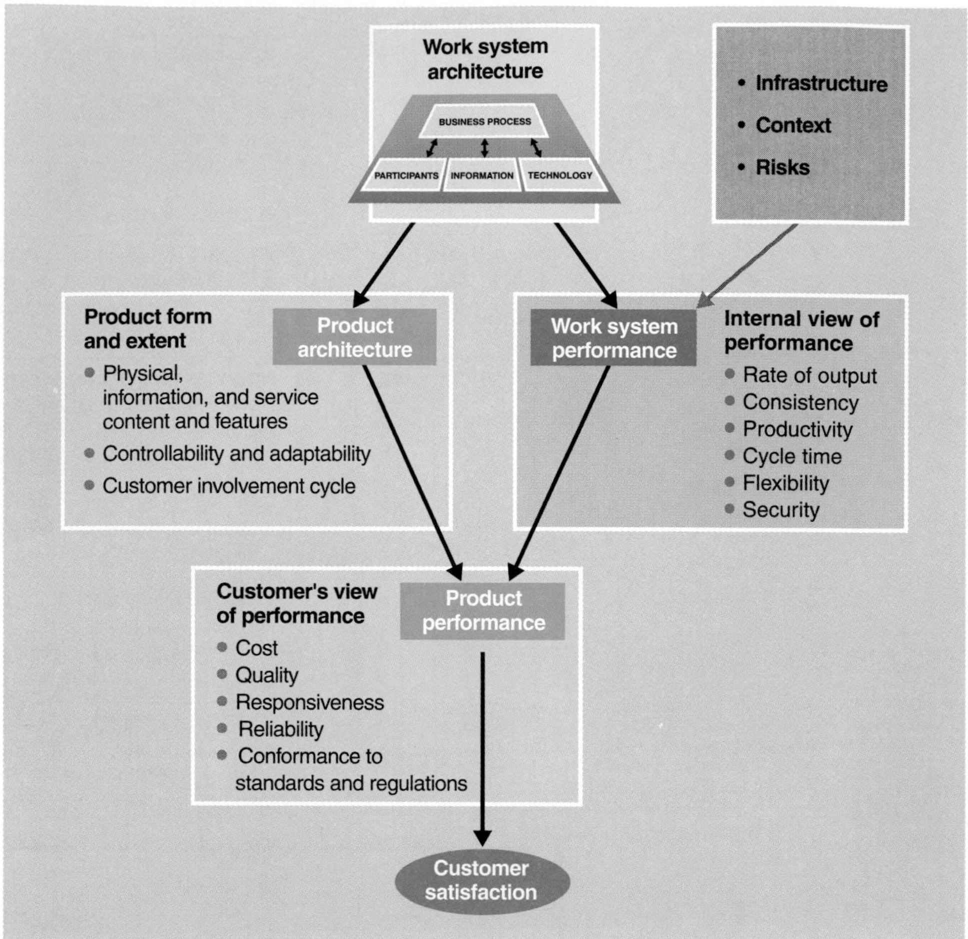

Figure 2.9
From work system architecture to customer satisfaction

This diagram shows how customer satisfaction for the product of a work system is related to all five of the WCA perspectives. Notice how work system architecture determines product architecture and work system performance, which affect product perfomance and customer satisfaction.

internal performance is usually not worth pursuing unless infrastructure, context, or risk provide a compelling rationale.

The distinction between external and internal performance parallels the common distinction between effectiveness and efficiency. **Effectiveness** involves doing the right things, whereas **efficiency** involves doing things in the right way. Effectiveness represents an external view related to whether the product is what the customer really wants. It is measured in terms of things the customer perceives directly, such as the product's cost, quality, and responsiveness. Efficiency represents an internal view related to the use of resources within the work system that produces a particular output. Typical internal performance measures include consistency, productivity, and cycle time. The links between work system performance and product performance illustrated in Figure 2.9 imply that effectiveness is usually related to efficiency even though each should be considered separately. We will now look at each of the five perspectives in more depth.

Architecture: System Components and How They Operate Together

Although the term *architecture* often connotes technical topics, we use this idea in a general way as a summary of how a work system operates. It focuses on the components of the work system, how those components are linked, and how they operate together mechanically to produce work system outputs. It is impossible to build an information system without a detailed specification of at least the information and technology portions of the architecture. The basic approach for documenting and summarizing architecture is **successive decomposition,** which is the process of dividing things into their components, and subdividing the components further until the person doing the analysis understands the architecture well enough for his or her purposes.

Table 2.4 identifies aspects of architecture that business professionals should consider for each of the six elements in the WCA framework. Work system architecture is not just a technical issue; IT professionals involved with a work system need to know how it operates. This starts with what the product is, how the customer uses it, and how the customer's entire cycle of involvement with the product operates (discussed in Chapter 6).

Notice how Table 2.4 divides architecture for business processes into two separate parts: **process operation** and **process characteristics.** Summarizing process operation means identifying the major subprocesses and the links between them. This is the beginning of the successive decomposition mentioned previously. Describing process characteristics means using conceptual terms such as degree of structure, range of involvement, and integration to think about the nature of the process. The purpose of assessing these characteristics is to rise above detailed documentation by asking questions such as whether the process has the right degree of structure, the right range of involvement, the right integration, and so on. These ideas will be explained in greater depth in Chapter 3.

TABLE 2.4 Architecture, Perspective #1

CUSTOMER

Customer's entire cycle of involvement with the product:
- Requirements
- Acquisition
- Use
- Maintenance
- Retirement

PRODUCT

Components:
- Information content
- Physical content
- Service content

BUSINESS PROCESS

Process operation:
- Processes providing inputs
- Sequence and scheduling of major steps
- Processes receiving the outputs

Process characteristics:
- Degree of structure
- Range of involvement
- Level of integration
- Complexity
- Degree of reliance on machines
- Linkage of planning, execution, and control
- Attention to exceptions, errors, and malfunctions

PARTICIPANTS

Formal and informal organization:
- Job responsibilities
- Organization chart

INFORMATION

Major data files in the database:
- Data organization and access

TECHNOLOGY

Major components:
- Hardware
- Software

Performance: How Well the System Operates

A complete analysis of a system involves more than learning about how it operates mechanically. It also includes qualitative or quantitative measurements evaluating how well the system operates. Table 2.5 shows how the framework supports this step by identifying performance variables that can be measured and evaluated for each element. For example, quality, accessibility, presentation, and prevention of unauthorized access are important for information, whereas skills, involvement, commitment, and job satisfaction are important for participants. Later chapters use many examples to explain these terms further.

The variables listed in Table 2.5 were chosen because they often have direct or indirect impact on work system operation and results. Inadequate performance or an improvement goal in terms of these variables is a typical starting point for the analysis of a system. Recognizing these variables is also important because of issues raised in natural conflicts between some of them. For example, increasing the reliability of a product might require a reduction in business process flexibility. In turn, this might decrease the responsiveness that a customer perceives when requesting a customized version of the product.

"More is better" almost always applies for some performance variables such as customer satisfaction and information quality. For others, however, more may not be better. The right levels of performance variables such as rate of output, security, and flexibility are a compromise between problems of excess and problems of deficiency. For example, too much consistency may mean participants cannot use their creativity to respond to changes, while too little makes the business process inefficient and the results chaotic. Even in today's harried business world, shorter cycle times may not always be beneficial. A good example of this is Xerox Corporation's conclusion that its business process for delivering products was sometimes too fast. It observed that customers cared much less about rapid delivery of a copier than about having the delivery occur on a committed delivery date when they are prepared to receive and install the new equipment. [8]

You might wonder why cost is listed with the product, whereas productivity (which is related to internal costs) is listed with the business process. Similarly, reliability is listed with the product whereas security is listed with the process. Things are broken out this way

TABLE 2.5 Performance, Perspective #2

CUSTOMER
- Customer satisfaction

PRODUCT
- Cost
- Quality
- Responsiveness
- Reliability
- Conformance to standards and regulations

BUSINESS PROCESS
- Rate of output
- Consistency
- Productivity
- Cycle time
- Flexibility
- Security

PARTICIPANTS
- Skills
- Involvement
- Commitment
- Job satisfaction

INFORMATION
- Quality
- Accessibility
- Presentation
- Prevention of unauthorized access

TECHNOLOGY
- Functional capabilities
- Ease of use
- Compatibility
- Maintainability

because the customer often does not care about the productivity of the business process that produced the product but is concerned with the total cost of ownership, the total amount of resources the customer must expend in acquiring, using, and maintaining the product. Likewise, the customer is concerned with the reliability of the product but may not feel a direct stake in the security of the business process.

Separately evaluating the performance of different elements is important because changes or improvements in one area may or may not generate better work system results. For example, substantial amounts of time, money, and effort are sometimes wasted improving the quality, accessibility, or presentation of information in ways that have little impact on work system results. This is what happens when someone uses a word processor to edit a document extensively, often with the net effect of improving the document's appearance much more than its substance. Similarly, people sometimes use spreadsheets on personal computers to run a model under numerous scenarios without ever thinking about whether those scenarios lead to genuine insight. In the same way, managers sometimes fund information systems that provide enormous amounts of information with little or no impact on decisions. These examples show why it is important to focus on overall work system performance before upgrading any particular component.

Finally, notice how each of the performance variables can be described or measured at different levels of clarity. Quality experts are adamant that measurement is essential for process improvement. Table 2.6 illustrates the nature of such measurements by comparing them with vague descriptions and interpretations for a few characteristics. Notice how the measurements are stated more precisely and quantitatively than the vague descriptions.

Infrastructure: Essential Resources Shared with Other Systems

Table 2.7 shows some of the major facets of infrastructure, essential resources shared among many otherwise independent applications. It is useful to compare the IT-infrastructure

TABLE 2.6 Comparing Vague Descriptions, Measurements, and Interpretations

Performance variables can be expressed at different levels of detail and precision, ranging from vague descriptions to careful measurements and interpretations. Here are examples showing vague descriptions, measurements, and interpretations for several performance variables related to work systems.

Performance variable	Vague description related to this variable	Measurement related to this variable	Interpretation related to this variable
Accuracy of information	The information doesn't seem very accurate.	97.5% of the readings are correct within 5%.	This is (or is not) accurate enough, given the way the information will be used.
Skills of participants	The sales people are very experienced.	Every salesperson has 5 or more years of experience; 60% have more than 10 years.	This system is (or is not) appropriate for such experienced people.
Cycle time of a business process	This business process seems to take a long time.	The three major steps take an average of 1.3 days each, but the waiting time between the steps is around 5 days.	This is (or is not) better than the average for this industry, but we can (or cannot) improve by eliminating some of the waiting time.
Quality of the work system output	We produce top quality frozen food, but our customers aren't enthusiastic.	65% of our customers rate it average or good even though our factory defect rate is only .003%.	Our manufacturing process does (or doesn't) seem OK, but we do (or don't) need to improve customer satisfaction.

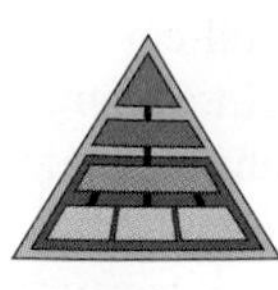

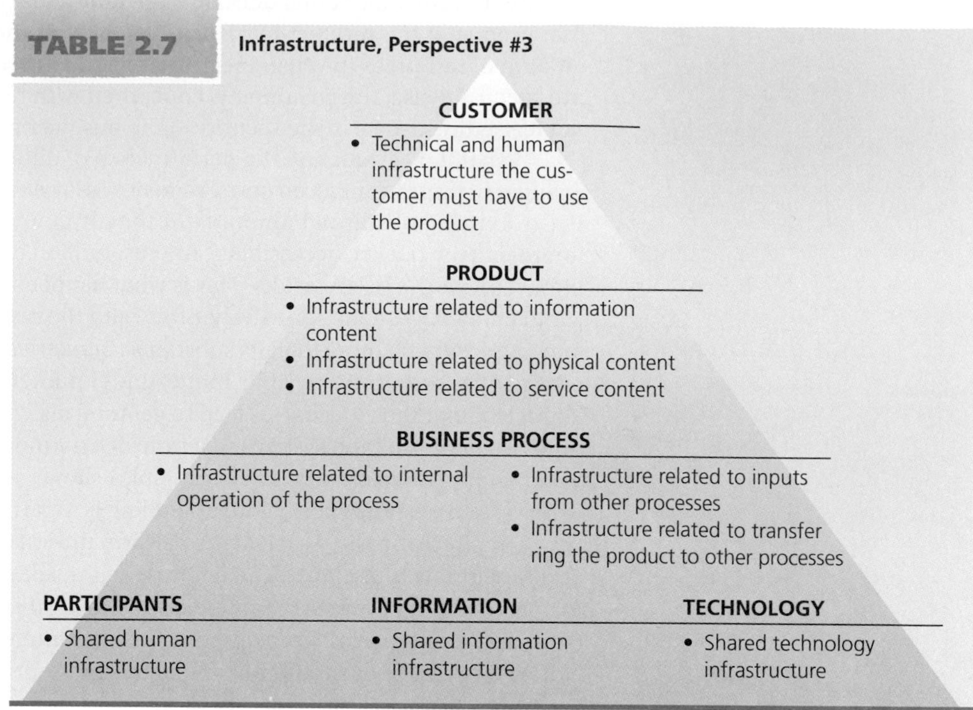

TABLE 2.7 Infrastructure, Perspective #3

CUSTOMER
- Technical and human infrastructure the customer must have to use the product

PRODUCT
- Infrastructure related to information content
- Infrastructure related to physical content
- Infrastructure related to service content

BUSINESS PROCESS
- Infrastructure related to internal operation of the process
- Infrastructure related to inputs from other processes
- Infrastructure related to transferring the product to other processes

PARTICIPANTS	INFORMATION	TECHNOLOGY
• Shared human infrastructure	• Shared information infrastructure	• Shared technology infrastructure

that supports a work system with the public infrastructure that supports a city's residential, commercial, and civic activities. Part of a city's infrastructure is physical things, such as streets, public buildings, electric lines, and water lines. Also essential is the human side of infrastructure, shared services such as police, fire fighting, education, and public health. In a similar way, a firm's IT infrastructure includes both technical and human components. Equally applicable to cities and to work systems, infrastructure itself is at least partially beyond the control of people who rely on it. This is demonstrated by infrastructure failures, such as telephone or electricity outages, and by work stoppages by public employees such as police officers or bus drivers. This lack of control sometimes tempts business professionals to think of infrastructure as someone else's problem, but its essential nature demands that it not be ignored.

The distinction between technology and infrastructure is often blurry. For example, consider the way insurance salespeople use laptops during personal sales presentations. These computers can be viewed as the technology used within a sales work system, or alternatively as a part of the firm's technical infrastructure for receiving e-mail, linking to the Internet, and performing other general communication and data processing activities. We will use the following guidelines to distinguish between a work system's technology and the infrastructure that supports it. Technology is part of the infrastructure if it is viewed as outside a work system, if it is shared among many work systems, if it is owned and managed by a centralized authority in charge of infrastructure, and if its details are generally hidden from users and seem inconsequential to them. Technology is not included in infrastructure if it is dedicated to a particular work system, if it is owned and controlled within the work system, if it is managed by whoever manages the work system, and if its hands-on users need to understand its technical details.

This book discusses both the infrastructure needed by an organization's value chain and the infrastructure used by IT professionals for information system development and operation. Typical elements of information system infrastructure include telecommunications networks for transmitting voice and computerized data, messaging services for handling e-mail and voice mail, centralized computers for large-scale data processing, database management systems (DBMSs) that permit sharing of data across application areas, and computer aided software engineering (CASE) systems used for building information systems. Deficiencies in any element of the hardware, software, or human and service infrastructure can cripple an information system. Conversely, a well managed infrastructure with sufficient power makes it much easier to maximize business benefits from these systems. Evaluating infrastructure is often difficult because the same infrastructure may support some applications excessively and others insufficiently. For example, a telephone network that is fine for voice conversations may be inadequate for video conferencing or data transfer. Likewise, a DBMS that is adequate for small information systems developed by end users may be totally inadequate for larger systems with stringent performance requirements.

Human and service infrastructure is often less noticed than the hardware and software components of infrastructure, but it is equally essential for successful information system development and maintenance. Responsibilities of human and service infrastructure include managing IT facilities, managing technical operation of hardware and software, helping business professionals use technology effectively, performing IT-related training, managing relationships with IT suppliers, recommending and enforcing IT standards, identifying and testing new technologies, establishing IT security, and planning for disaster recovery.[9]

This human infrastructure is often underfunded and underappreciated. Business professionals are often surprised at the amount of effort and expense absorbed by the human infrastructure needed to keep information systems operating technically and to train and counsel users. The tendency toward organizational decentralization and outsourcing of many system-related functions make it even more important to include human infrastructure in the analysis of new systems.

Context: Organizational, Competitive, and Regulatory Environment Surrounding the System

The context within which a work system operates is important to consider because the environment surrounding the system may create incentives and even urgency for change, but may also create obstacles that make those changes infeasible. Table 2.8 identifies important aspects of the context surrounding the system, such as external stakeholders, organizational policies and practices, personal incentives, organizational culture, resource availability, business pressures, and laws and regulations.

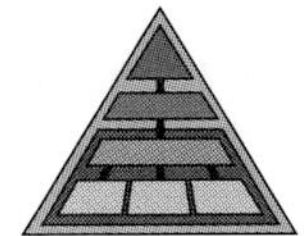

TABLE 2.8 **Context, Perspective #4**

CUSTOMER

- Issues in the customer's environment that may affect satisfaction or use
- Business and competitive climate

PRODUCT

- Substitute products
- Ways the customer might bypass this type of product altogether

BUSINESS PROCESS

- Organizational culture
- Concerns of stakeholders
- Organizational policies and initiatives
- Government regulations and industry standards

PARTICIPANTS	INFORMATION	TECHNOLOGY
• Incentives • Other responsibilities and job pressures	• Policies and practices regarding information sharing, privacy, etc.	• Technology policies and practices • Technology that may become available soon

The personal, organizational, and economic aspects of the context have direct impact on the work system success. Work systems that address external competitive threats and opportunities receive much greater attention than other systems along with a disproportionate share of human and monetary resources. Simultaneously, unavailability or diversion of the resources needed to build a system or operate it effectively reduces its likelihood of success. Even if the firm has the necessary monetary resources, context factors ranging from historical precedents and budget cycles to internal politics and culture can be stumbling blocks. We will say a bit more about three aspects of the context: incentives, organizational culture, and nonparticipant stakeholders.

Incentives

Personal incentives of system participants are often a key determinant of whether a system will succeed. Regardless of how well designed a system appears to be, system participants tend to put little energy into a system that is unrelated to or inconsistent with their personal incentives. Medical care systems are notorious in terms of conflicting incentives. Their idealized goal is to keep people healthy, but the traditional monetary incentives for health care providers was based on the number of procedures and patient visits, rather than on health-related outcomes. With monetary incentives structured this way, the doctors make less if the system succeeds in keeping people healthy and they make more the worse it performs. The recent move toward HMOs and other arrangements based on a fixed fee for each person enrolled have shifted the nature of conflicting incentives. Paying medical care providers a fixed amount per person while forcing them to absorb the incremental cost of each unit of medical care gives providers a monetary incentive to limit medical care as much as possible without making patients too angry. The incentives in the old system drove the providers to perform additional visits, tests, and procedures, regardless of whether they were genuinely needed. The new system motivates them to provide fewer, even if they might be needed. Both approaches suffer from internal incentive conflicts and neither brings about an ideal alignment of participant goals with customer goals.

As though conflicting or misdirected incentives weren't bad enough, some systems contain counterproductive incentives and may even encourage participants to cheat. Consider the way arbitrary date cutoffs in budget systems create counterproductive incentives. Ideally these systems should assure proper resource allocation and use, but departments trying to avoid future budget cuts often feel pressure to consume whatever is left in the budget before the next cycle begins. A clear example was the admission by a former Air Force pilot that he had been directed to fly out over the ocean and drop a load of jet fuel because the budget year was almost over and his group had not yet used up its fuel allotment. The incentives in that control system motivated the opposite of the desired careful stewardship of resources.

Organizational Culture

Discussions of systems often focus on formal procedures for performing tasks, but the organization's culture is often just as important as the system's official rationale in determining system success. **Organizational culture** is the shared understandings about relationships and work practices that determine how things are done in a workplace. Culture is subtle because it is a combination of written and unwritten rules and practices that govern the way people behave. It covers issues such as the importance of status symbols, the degree to which decisions are made based on organizational hierarchy, the extent to which people show respect to each other, the degree to which dissent is considered acceptable, and the extent to which the organization treats employees as family members or as contractors for hire.

One of the difficulties in dealing with organizational culture is that discussing important cultural issues is virtually taboo in many organizations. Defining procedures and measuring activities or results is much easier than showing how the organization's managers don't "walk the walk" even if they "talk the talk." Yes, the organization espouses its desire to balance home and work life, but it requires that everyone arrive just before schools open. Yes, the organization espouses the value of everyone's contribution, but the only way to get an idea accepted is to convince the boss that she invented it. Yes, the organization espouses customer focus, but its engineers are more motivated by doing sophisticated engineering than by solving simple customer problems. Cultural contradictions such as these may be readily apparent to people who work in the setting, but people rarely want to be the messenger who makes the announcement.

Stakeholders

Also part of the work system context are **stakeholders,** people with a personal stake in the system and its outputs even if they are neither its participants nor its customers. Managers who have high visibility roles as system sponsors or champions are key stakeholders in many strategically important systems because they work toward the system's success and ultimately receive some of the credit or blame. Other stakeholders may be affected less directly if a system shifts the balance of power in an organization or works contrary to their personal goals. Information systems that create new communication patterns are likely to have a wide range of stakeholders. For example, new voice mail or e-mail systems sometimes enhance the visibility and status of individuals with expert knowledge about specific activities; easy access to these experts often reduces the power of some support staff positions, middle managers, and others who formerly served as information conduits.

Information System (IS) staff members are important stakeholders of most information systems because they are responsible for system operation and enhancement. As professionals in the field, they have a deeper understanding than most business professionals about what it takes to build and maintain solid information systems. They also have a clearer view of technical relationships between different systems and of policies and practices related to systems. Business professionals shouldn't ignore the technical infrastructure and context issues identified in Table 2.7 and Table 2.8, but they should realize that the IS staff is usually much more aware of the technical structure and rationale in both areas.

Risks: Foreseeable Things That Can Go Wrong

While automated systems offer many advantages, they also create vulnerability. Table 2.9 identifies common risks related to each element in the WCA framework. We will look at risks in three areas: accidents and malfunctions, computer crime, and project failure. (Chapter 13 will discuss these and related topics along with some of the countermeasures that can reduce IT-related risks.)

Accidents and Malfunctions

Every computerized system has flaws. Some of these involve shortcomings in system design; others are programming errors called bugs. It is impossible to guarantee bug-free systems because even the best programmers cannot think of every possible state a system can enter. Consequently, even carefully tested systems may have flaws that cause catastrophic system failures.

Software bugs in computerized systems have proven to be inconvenient and costly; a few have even caused death. A tragic example is the enormous overdoses of radiation several patients received due to a bug in the software that controlled a type of x-ray machine.[10] Although the possibility of bugs must be considered in any project involving software, the danger from software bugs is especially serious in systems controlling processes whose failure could be disastrous. Systems with potential for software disaster include air traffic control, missile defense systems, electrical networks, communication systems, and electronic funds transfer systems.

Although bug-related risks are important, the majority of system failures are caused by human inattention, incorrect data, and failure to follow system procedures. The 1986 Chernobyl nuclear accident that contaminated a large area near the city Kiev

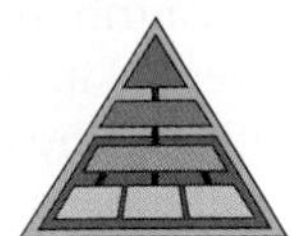

TABLE 2.9 Risk, Perspective #5

CUSTOMER
- Customer dissatisfaction
- Interference by other stakeholders

PRODUCT
- Inadequate or unreliable products
- Fraudulent products

BUSINESS PROCESS
- Operator error
- Sloppy procedures
- Inadequate backup and recovery
- Mismatch between process requirements and participant's abilities
- Unauthorized access to computers, programs, data

PARTICIPANTS	INFORMATION	TECHNOLOGY
• Crime by insiders or outsiders • Inattention by participants • Failure to follow procedures • Inadequate training	• Data errors • Fraudulent data • Data theft	• Equipment failure • Software bugs • Inadequate performance • Inability to build common sense into information systems

in the Ukraine illustrates this type of problem. A direct cause of the accident was that the plant operators turned off the nuclear reactor's safety system to test the reactor's response under certain low power conditions during which reactors of that type tend to be unstable.

Natural disasters such as floods and earthquakes and infrastructure outside the control of work system participants are also important causes of accidents and malfunctions. The use of computerized networks has created situations in which even distant infrastructure problems can prevent local work systems operation. For example, 5,000 ATMs across the nation shut down for a week because a snowstorm collapsed the roof of an Electronic Data Systems data center in New Jersey.

Computer Crime

Damage can also occur when someone uses computers for criminal activity. Frequently in the news are stories about computer hackers, viruses, forgeries, and unauthorized transfers of funds to overseas bank accounts. Computer crime costs businesses hundreds of millions of dollars every year. Most of this crime is related to fraudulent transactions generated inside a company rather than break-ins from outside. The threat of large-scale computer crime is increasing however. A report by the National Academy of Sciences noted increasing dependence on computers throughout society and cited the future possibility of a systematic attempt to subvert critical computer systems.[11] Clearly, any organization that relies on computerized systems should ensure that they are designed and managed properly.

Project Failures

A section of Chapter 1 on the difficulty of building and modifying IT-based systems demonstrated that project failure is a significant risk. In the study that was cited, only 16.2% of the projects were completed on schedule and within budget; 52.7% were late, went over budget, or produced fewer functions than planned; and 31.1% were canceled before completion. These problems occur in many different forms. Some system development projects never succeed. Some projects end when the original sponsors fail to resolve issues about what problem should really be addressed and how the system should operate. Other projects end when the analysis and programming work fails to produce a set of programs that operate efficiently and reliably on the computer. Some systems are implemented in organizations only to be rejected by users. Like inadequately serviced automobiles, systems may even fail after going into operation due to insufficient effort to keep them running efficiently and effectively.

ANALYZING AN IT-ENABLED SYSTEM FROM A BUSINESS PROFESSIONAL'S VIEWPOINT

This book's purpose is to teach you how to think about IT-enabled work systems from a business professional's viewpoint, which differs in an important way from the viewpoint of an IT professional. Since a business professional's primary role is in an area such as marketing, finance, manufacturing, accounting, or customer service, it is only natural for a business professional to focus on the operation and performance of work systems in these areas. In contrast, IT professionals are typically more concerned with the technical, interpersonal, and managerial tasks required for developing and maintaining information systems. To succeed, they must pay attention to the work systems they are supporting, but their day-to-day work is building and maintaining information systems.

Despite the differences in these viewpoints, building and maintaining successful information systems requires ongoing collaboration between business professionals who understand the business needs and IT professionals who understand how to create and maintain information systems. The remainder of this chapter presents an organized way to analyze a work system from a business viewpoint. Doing this type of analysis can help business professionals do a much better job of understanding a business situation, identifying the desired work system changes, and understanding how to explain those needs to IT professionals who make the information system changes. A business professional's ability to analyze systems in this way will become even more important as database and data analysis tools for nonprogrammers become more effective at the same time that organizations continue to downsize.

The General Idea of Systems Analysis

Systems analysis is a very general process of defining a problem, gathering pertinent information, developing alternative solutions, and choosing among those solutions. When stated in its most general form, systems analysis can be applied to almost any problem involving people, resources, and action. This chapter (and the remainder of the book) explains how the general concept of systems analysis can be expressed in a way that provides a lot of guidance in analyzing work systems and information systems. Many of the same ideas also apply when thinking about physical systems, social systems, and business organizations as a whole, but those areas are not the focus of this book. Although different authors express it differently, systems analysis is basically a four-step decision making process (shown in Figure 2.10):

- defining the problem
- describing the situation in enough depth
- designing potential improvements
- deciding what to do

The steps in the figure are presented as though they apply to a single system. If the situation being analyzed contains several major subsystems, the steps can be used to examine each subsystem separately, and then to examine the overall system. The fact that each step uses the WCA framework helps keep the analysis coherent and helps avoid excessive attention to tangential issues. The figure also shows that the process is iterative; that is, the cycle of steps can be repeated if necessary. This is consistent with the way people typically identify a problem they want to think about and then redefine the problem after gathering information that helps them understand it. We will now look at each of the four steps, with particular emphasis on the first.

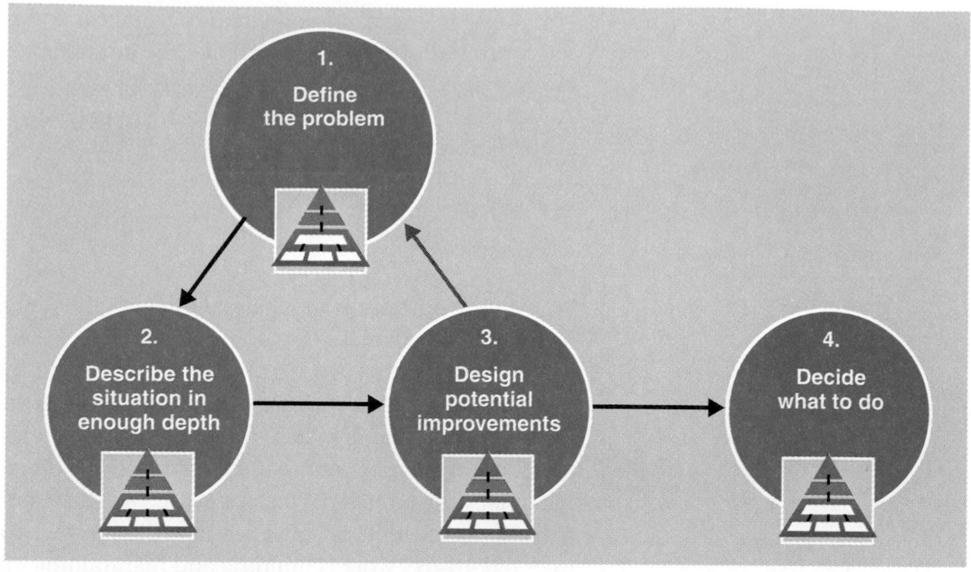

Figure 2.10
Steps in systems analysis for business professionals

Systems analysis iterates between defining the problem, describing the current situation, and designing potential improvements. The final step is deciding what to do. The WCA icon at each stage emphasizes that the framework can be used throughout the analysis process.

1. *Defining the problem:* The first step in analyzing a system is to define the problem by identifying the purpose of an analysis and the scope of the work system that is being analyzed. The purpose is typically to accomplish a goal; for the Resumix case, that goal was to increase the speed and efficiency of résumé processing. The scope of the work system is not fixed before the analysis starts, but rather, is a conscious choice based on the purpose of the analysis and a practical tradeoff between making the topic too broad and complex versus making it too narrow and insignificant. An overly broad problem definition may make the work system scope so large that even completing the analysis could prove impractical, no less implementing any necessary changes. Conversely, an overly restrictive definition may mean that the major problems are not addressed. For example, assume that the purpose of analyzing a work system is to improve sales results. The work system might be defined narrowly in terms of how a sales person interacts with a customer. This definition of the work system might be too restrictive. Defining the work system in terms of the entire process from identifying potential customers through closing the sale might reveal that any problems related to customer interactions are minor compared to problems about finding the right potential customers.

Another important part of the problem definition is identifying constraints and priorities that affect the way the analysis will be done. **Constraints** refer to limitations that make particular changes infeasible even though they might otherwise seem beneficial. Typical constraints that apply in some situations include budgetary limits, restrictions in shifting personnel, the organization's technology standards, and policies related to privacy. **Priorities** are statements about the relative importance of different goals. Because many different types of improvements are typically at least conceivable in most situations, the analysis process tends to be more successful if a small number of high priority issues are addressed directly.

This initial step of defining the problem is surprisingly difficult because people may not reach consensus about what the problem is. Sometimes the disagreements are conscious, but in many other cases, different people simply make different assumptions about what the system includes. For example, a business professional might believe that the system being analyzed is a work system for manufacturing air conditioners, whereas a software vendor or programmer might believe the system is a software product used to keep track of manufacturing work. These topics overlap, but they certainly aren't identical, and comments about one may not apply to the other.

Table 2.10 provides a way to avoid these confusions by clarifying the scope of a work system. For each of the six WCA elements, this table defines several topics that help in clarifying a work system's scope. We will call such a table a **system snapshot** because it summarizes a particular work system's scope on a single page. The summary table at the beginning of each chapter is a simplified system snapshot that focuses mostly on identifying the six elements and ignores distinctions that are important for analyzing a system, such as internal versus external information and participants versus human infrastructure the participants depend on. Summaries like the one at the beginning of the chapters or the slightly more extensive form in Table 2.10 are simplifications of reality that leave out many features essential for understanding the situation. They are nevertheless useful because

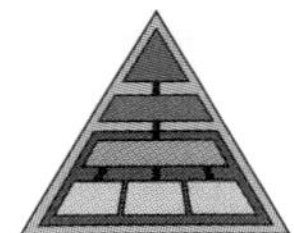

TABLE 2.10 Definitions of Topics in a System Snapshot

CUSTOMER

Product used by: Internal or external customers who use or receive direct benefit from the product

Other stakeholders: People who have a significant stake in the work system or its product even though they do not use the product directly and do not participate directly in the work system

Infrastructure requirements: Infrastructure the customer should have to use the product effectively

PRODUCT

Information content: The aspects of the product that consist of information

Physical content: The aspects of the product that consist of physical things

Service content: The aspects of the product that consist of services performed for specific customers

BUSINESS PROCESS

Major steps:
Listing the major steps in this business process

Rationale:
The overriding idea or approach that determined the process would be performed using the current approach rather than another

Processes providing inputs:
External processes outside the work system that produce inputs of information, physical things, or services needed in order for this business process to operate

Processes receiving the product:
The customer's processes that receive and use the product of this work system

PARTICIPANTS	INFORMATION	TECHNOLOGY
People who perform the work: The people directly involved in performing the steps in the business process	**Created or modified within this system:** Information that is created or modified by the steps in the business process	**Technology within the system:** Technology dedicated to this system and controlled within it
Shared human infrastructure: People engaged in other work systems that provide support for people working in this system	**Received from other work systems:** Information generated by other work systems and provided as an input to this work system	**Shared technology infrastructure:** Technology this work system uses that is shared with other work systems and is viewed as belonging to other, external work systems

they provide a balanced view of topics anyone can start learning about in just a few minutes. As the analysis proceeds, other approaches and ideas are explored in more depth.

2. *Describe the current situation in enough depth:* Describing the current situation in enough depth means much more than documenting the business process or the database. It also means more than creating a one-page system snapshot. The current situation can be described in terms of five perspectives including the way the system currently operates (its architecture), how well it operates (its performance), what infrastructure it relies on, what context it operates in, and what risks affect it. The appropriate depth for thinking about a situation depends on an individual's purposes. For example, a business professional might be expected to look at a business process in more depth whereas an IT professional might look at technical details in more depth.

3. *Design potential improvements:* Potential improvements are changes in the architecture of one or more of the six elements in the WCA framework. The links between the various elements show why changes in any of them may require changes in any of the others. The validity of any architecture change depends on the way it is reflected in the other perspectives, namely, performance, infrastructure, context, and risks. Because changes that improve one element of the framework may cause problems in other elements of the framework, no change should be recommended until a variety of potential improvements have been considered. For example, although switching to more current technology might improve the results for a particular work system, this might cause problems due to inconsistencies with other work systems. A better overall approach might involve adding a step to a business process or providing better training.

4. *Decide what to do:* Analyzing a system is a fruitless exercise unless the understanding developed by performing the first three steps is used to set a course of action. Ideally, this decision should be based on clearly stated decision criteria that help resolve tradeoffs and uncertainties related to constraints, priorities, and implementation capabilities. Typical tradeoffs involve conflicting needs of different work systems, conflicts between technical purity and business requirements, and choices between performance and price. The uncertainties encompass issues such as the direction of future technology and uncertainty about what is best for the business. Design decisions cannot be based on a formula because so many different considerations don't fit well into that approach.

Work-Centered Analysis Method

Up to this point, we have introduced the basic ideas any business professional can use for thinking about an information system or work system. These ideas include the six elements of the WCA framework, the five perspectives for viewing that framework, and the four steps in a general systems analysis process. Next, we will combine these ideas into the **work-centered analysis method,** a practical approach business professionals can use for analyzing systems at whatever level of depth is appropriate in the situation. This method can be used in a number of ways:

- As an organizing principle when business professionals must build their own small information systems using end-user tools.
- As a way to create an initial understanding of a situation and even a tentative recommendation before starting a collaboration with IT professionals.
- As a way to make sure that an ongoing collaboration between business and IT professionals balances business issues and computer system details. Maintaining this balance is especially important during discussions with software vendors, who often view the system as the software they sell rather than as the work system their customer is attempting to improve.
- As a way IT professionals can make sure they have an adequate understanding of the business situation.

Table 2.11 shows how the WCA method combines the ideas in the WCA framework, the perspectives, and the systems analysis steps into ten issues that anyone can use when thinking about how to improve a work system. Issue #1 is also step #1 in the systems

TABLE 2.11 The 10 Issues in the Work-Centered Analysis Method

The WCA method is based on ten issues that summarize major topics related to the six elements of the WCA framework and the five perspectives. Each issue can be discussed at various levels of depth, depending on the goal.

Systems analysis step	Corresponding issues for thinking about any system
1. Define the problem	Issue 1: Problem definition
2. Describe the current work system in enough depth and 3. Design potential improvements	Issue 2: Improvements from product changes Issue 3: Improvements from process changes Issue 4: Improvements related to work system participants Issue 5: Improvements from better information Issue 6: Improvements from better technology Issue 7: Improvements from shared infrastructure Issue 8: Improvements related to the business context Issue 9: Improvements from risk reduction
4. Decide what to do	Issue 10: Recommendation

analysis process in Figure 2.10. It asks the person analyzing the system to define the problem. A cursory answer would be something like: "The problem is slow response to customer requests." A more organized and detailed response to issue #1 would clarify the purpose of the analysis, the scope of the system (by creating a system snapshot outlined in Table 2.10), and the constraints and priorities in the situation.

The next systems analysis step after defining the problem involves looking at different facets of the system and trying to find potential improvements. Because people typically go back and forth between exploring an existing system and identifying possible improvements, it is simplest and most practical to combine these two questions in the WCA method. Table 2.11 shows that issues #2 through #9 provide an organized way to cover all six elements of the WCA framework and all five perspectives by trying to identify improvements in different facets of the system. Issues #2 through #6 look at how each element of the WCA framework is deployed and how well it is performing, thereby covering both architecture and performance. Issues #7 through #9 cover the remaining perspectives, namely, infrastructure, context, and risk. The most summarized way to inquire about each issue is to ask a broad question such as "How can we improve the business process?" or "How can we improve the information?" A more detailed look at each issue can be organized in terms of the various topics listed in Tables 2.4 through 2.9 which outline the perspectives in detail.

Issue #10 completes the analysis by asking for a recommendation that corresponds to systems analysis step #4—deciding what to do. As with the other issues, it is possible to simply ask what the recommendation is, or it is possible to examine the issue in more depth by covering separate topics, including:

- recommended changes in each element of the system
- a justification of the overall recommendation in terms of priority and feasibility
- a discussion of how the project would be done and what resources it would require
- a tentative project plan including timing and deliverables

Unlike highly constrained methods that require particular outputs in a particular format, the WCA method is designed to be adapted to the needs of a range of people who use it in different ways. Just looking briefly at the ten issues while thinking about a system-related problem or proposed improvement is often sufficient for identifying important questions that need to be answered. An overview of this type meets the needs of people who want to visualize the problem but don't want to study it in depth. For the business and IT professionals who actually have to build or modify the system, the ten issues are just a starting point, however, because each issue leads to deeper questions that should be examined carefully.

Realistically, most business professionals cannot answer all questions related to the way work should be done, and they usually need help with questions related to technical topics. Nonetheless, doing their own analysis using the WCA method clarifies what they would like and leaves them more able to communicate and negotiate effectively both with other business professionals and with the IT professionals responsible for filling in the technical details and operating the resulting computer system.

Reality Check

USING SYSTEMS ANALYSIS IN EVERYDAY LIFE

The systems analysis process described here is very general. Much of it can be applied to everyday life, even though we don't often think of everyday issues in terms of architecture, performance, infrastructure, context, and risks.

1. Identify any nontrivial problem you have had to deal with in your everyday life (not a problem assigned in a course) that required you to think about a situation and develop a plan of action. Describe the way you performed each of the four systems analysis steps in solving this problem.
2. What you really did in your situation may or may not have fallen neatly into these four steps. Explain why it did or did not.

Limitations and Pitfalls

Although the WCA method has many uses, it still has limitations. Like any general problem solving approach, it is not a formula or cookbook. Regardless of whether you are analyzing a work system or an information system that supports it, you have to use your own judgment to use the WCA method effectively. It applies most directly when the business process in the work system or information system consists of identifiable steps occurring over time and producing a recognizable output. It is not as effective when applied to activities such as "management" or "communication" unless the steps in a specific management or communication process are being explored.

The WCA method is a compromise between complexity and completeness. The six elements in the WCA framework were selected to be as understandable and broadly useful as possible. Other elements that could have received more emphasis include facilities, management, and organization. Facilities, such as computer rooms and wiring closets, were not treated as a separate topic because related questions are tangential to a business professional's understanding of systems. Instead of treating management as a separate element, the WCA method handles it either as the planning and control part of a work system or as a separate work system. Likewise, organization is not in the framework but is related to how the work is organized and the context surrounding the system. In similar fashion, the ten issues in the WCA method were chosen as the simplest way to incorporate the six elements and the five perspectives into a set of steps that could lead to useful insights at many different levels of detail.

The two major pitfalls in using the WCA method are inadequate problem definition and confusion about the difference between the information system and the work system. These pitfalls are often related because the confusion about the information system versus the work system often results in confusion about how to define the problem. A typical symptom of this type of confusion is when a statement like "The system is easy to use" occurs in the middle of a discussion of a work system. The term "easy to use" applies to technology, but not to work systems. Specific pitfalls related to the six elements and the five perspectives are shown in Table 2.12 and Table 2.13 respectively. Entries in these two tables provide hints about how to use the WCA method carefully.

This chapter has described a method that any business professional can use for thinking about work systems and the information systems that support them. Unlike systems analysis methods for IT professionals, this method makes no attempt to create a rigorous specification of a desired system. Instead, it is designed to help people think about different facets of a system so that discussions with other business professionals and with IT professionals will be more effective. Unlike a dogmatic statement of exactly how systems must be analyzed, the WCA method is meant as a set of guidelines that encourage consideration of issues business professionals understand and care about. The rest of this book presents a more in-depth view of the areas discussed in this chapter, presenting both ideas and examples that help business professionals understand both information systems and work systems.

TABLE 2.12 **Common Systems Analysis Pitfalls Related to Elements of the WCA Framework**

CUSTOMER

- Ignoring the customer and the fact that the customer should evaluate the product
- Treating managers as customers even though they don't use the system's product directly

PRODUCT

- Forgetting that the purpose of a system is to produce a product for a customer
- Forgetting that the product of a work system is often not the product of the organization

BUSINESS PROCESS

- Defining the business process so narrowly that an improvement has little consequence
- Defining the business process so broadly that it involves a wide range of products and customers and is difficult to analyze coherently; in particular, defining the business process as the firm's entire value chain (which usually contains a number of separate business processes)
- Confusing business process measures (such as consistency and productivity) with product measures (such as cost to the customer and quality perceived by the customer)
- Thinking about the business process as a theoretical set of steps and ignoring whether it is adequately supported by participants, information, and technology

PARTICIPANTS

- Ignoring the incentives felt by participants and ignoring other pressures on them
- Focusing on "users" rather than participants, thereby overemphasizing IT and underemphasizing how the work system operates and what it produces

INFORMATION

- Assuming that better information will generate better results
- Downplaying the importance of soft information not captured by formal systems

TECHNOLOGY

- Assuming that better technology will generate better results
- Focusing on technology without thinking about whether it makes a difference in the work system

TABLE 2.13 Common Pitfalls Related to the Five Perspectives

Perspective	Common pitfalls
Architecture	Overemphasis on tiny architectural details: While details are always important, trying to implement improvements often requires a basic rethinking of how the process is done, not just tweaking the details. Confusion related to people's roles: One pitfall is viewing managers or even participants as customers, even though they do not use work system outputs directly. Also, forgetting that customers may also be participants in some work systems and that participants may be treated as secondary customers.
Performance	Tendency to ignore performance: Describing how a system performs is usually easier to do and less controversial than explaining how well it performs. Tendency to exaggerate the scope of work system performance, especially by confusing measures of the firm's performance (such as profitability and market share) with measures of the business process (such as productivity and consistency) or measures of the work system's product (such as cost and quality).
Infrastructure	Tendency to ignore infrastructure issues: Business professionals sometimes underplay the essential nature of infrastructure because they view it as outside of their control. Even when they recognize the importance of technical infrastructure, they often overlook and under-fund human infrastructure.
Context	Tendency to ignore incentives, organizational culture, and nonparticipant stakeholders when designing systems: These factors may degrade system performance even though they play no direct role in the theoretical logic of most systems.
Risks	Tendency to assume systems will operate as planned: It is tempting to ignore the possibility that things could go wrong within the system or that it could be derailed from outside.

CHAPTER CONCLUSION

Summary

Why is it important to have a framework for analyzing information systems?
A framework is a brief set of ideas for organizing a thought process about a particular type of thing or situation. A framework helps people by identifying topics that should be considered and by showing how the topics are related. When studying information systems or other topics, a good framework helps people make sense of the world's complexity.

What six elements can be used for summarizing any work system?
A work system can be summarized as a system whose participants perform a business process using information, technology, and other resources to produce products for internal or external customers. The six elements are the customer, product, business process, participants, information, and technology.

What is the relationship between information systems and work systems?
An information system is a particular type of work system that uses information technology to capture, transmit, store, retrieve, manipulate, or display information used by one or more work systems. Information systems often play crucial roles in the work systems they support, but some

aspects of those work systems are usually unrelated to information systems. The more information-intensive the work system is, the larger the role the information system plays.

What five perspectives can be used for thinking about work systems?
The five perspectives include architecture, performance, infrastructure, context, and risk. Architecture specifies how the current or proposed system operates mechanically by summarizing its components, the way the components are linked, and the way the components operate together. Performance describes how well the work system, its components, or its products operate. Infrastructure is the human and technical resources the system depends upon and shares with other systems. Context is the organizational, competitive, technical, and regulatory realm within which the work system operates. Risks consist of the foreseeable events whose occurrence could cause system degradation or failure.

What is the relationship between process architecture, process performance, and product performance?
Process architecture is a key determinant of process performance, which in turn is a key determinant of product performance. Inward-looking process performance variables include rate of output, consistency, productivity, cycle time, flexibility, and security. Outward-looking product performance variables perceived directly by customers include cost, quality, responsiveness, reliability, and conformance to standards and regulations. Each of these performance variables can be measured in terms of various measures of performance, depending on the nature of the business process.

What are the steps in systems analysis, and how can business professionals apply these steps?
Systems analysis is a general process of defining a problem, gathering pertinent information, developing alternative solutions, and choosing among those solutions. These four steps can be fleshed out in many ways. The work-centered analysis method is a systems analysis approach designed to help business professionals analyze work systems and information systems. It restates the systems analysis steps as ten issues. Issue #1 is defining the problem. Issues #2 through #6 cover both architecture and performance by looking for improvements related to (#2) the customer and product, (#3) the business process, (#4) the participants, (#5) the information, and (#6) the technology. Issues #7 through #9 cover the remaining perspectives, (#7) infrastructure, (#8) context, and (#9) risk. Issue #10 is deciding what to do. The WCA method is not a cookbook and does not require a particular procedure. Its goal is to provide a way of thinking about systems that can be adapted to any practical situation.

Key Terms

framework
model
system
subsystem
purpose
boundary
environment
inputs
outputs
business process
scope
subprocess
value added
value chain
primary processes
support processes
functional areas of business
functional silos
information technology
hardware
software
information system
work system
work
business environment
work-centered analysis (WCA) framework
internal customers
external customers
secondary customers
data
information
knowledge
hard data
soft data
architecture
performance
infrastructure
context
risks
effectiveness
efficiency
successive decomposition
process operation
process characteristics
organizational culture
stakeholders
systems analysis
constraints
priorities
system snapshot
work-centered analysis method

Review Questions

1. What is the difference between a framework and model?
2. What is the difference between a system and a subsystem?
3. What is a business process?
4. Distinguish between business processes that cross functional areas of business and those that are specific to functional areas.
5. Explain the concepts of scope and value-added as they relate to business processes.
6. Explain whether there is a difference between an information system and a work system.
7. Provide examples of information systems that support aspects of a work system but not necessarily all of it.
8. In what situations would it be advantageous to transform customers of a business process into participants?
9. What is the relationship between data, information, and knowledge?
10. How does the business process affect participants, and how do participants affect the business process?
11. What five perspectives are necessary for understanding an existing or proposed system? Briefly describe each of them.
12. What is the difference between efficiency and effectiveness, and how is this related to the WCA framework?
13. What is the difference between summarizing process operation and describing process characteristics?
14. What are some of the performance characteristics associated with each element of the framework?
15. Explain why "more is better" is not always true for some performance characteristics.
16. What are the steps in a systems analysis process?
17. How can the WCA framework be used to identify the scope of the analysis?
18. What are some of the common pitfalls in analyzing systems?

Discussion Topics

1. When anthropologists working in Xerox's Palo Alto Research Center asked clerks how they did their jobs, the descriptions corresponded to the formal procedures in the job manual. But when they observed clerks at work they discovered that the clerks weren't really following the procedures at all. Instead they relied on a rich variety of informal practices that weren't in any manual but were crucial to getting work done.[12] How is this finding related to the topics in this chapter?
2. In 1973 an official of the United Auto Workers (UAW) asked that the following notice be posted on the union's in-plant bulletin boards in General Motors plants: "Quality products are our concern too." A General Motors executive called him to complain that quality is solely management's responsibility and demanded that the bulletins be taken down.[13] Explain why this story is related to ideas in this chapter.
3. Explain why you believe it is or is not important for managers and system participants to be able to analyze information systems.
4. Explain why you do or do not believe that the study of information systems is basically a study of how information technology operates.
5. Explain how the following passage from Machiavelli's *The Prince*, written in 1513, is related to the WCA method for analyzing information systems: "It must be remembered that there is nothing more difficult to plan, more doubtful of success, nor more dangerous to manage than the creation of a new system. For the initiator has the enmity of the old institution and merely lukewarm defenders in those who would gain by the new ones."[14]

CASE

Wake Forest University: Integrating Computers into a College Curriculum

In 1995 Wake Forest University came to a decision that affected every student on campus and every faculty member. The university decided to require each undergraduate student to have a laptop computer that could be used in any class. Based on a plan endorsed by the college faculty, the student legislature, and the board of trustees, each incoming freshman would receive a current laptop computer from the university. On becoming a junior, each student would return that computer and receive a new laptop to be kept after graduation. Tuition would be increased to pay for the computers and computer-related services.

To make it as easy as possible for computer ownership to have a meaningful impact on a Wake Forest education, the university adopted a standardization policy. For example, each member of the class of 2001 received a ThinkPad 380D computer with 32 MB of RAM, a 1.3 GB hard drive, a 150 MHz Pentium processor, an ethernet card, a 33.6 Kbs modem, and 8X CD-ROM drive, a 12.1-inch display, and an internal 3.5 inch diskette drive. Standard software included Windows 95, Microsoft Office 97, Lotus Notes groupware and mail, and other software as well. To facilitate collaboration among students and faculty, all computers were equipped with a custom-designed Lotus Notes–based course and project-filing system referred to as the Wake Forest template. The template served as an alternative to a Web environment and permitted students to post essays, comment on each other's work, and carry on discussions. The same type of template could be used for faculty purposes such as collaborative research and committee work.

Effective use of the laptops required substantial effort in infrastructure. Before laptops were distributed to incoming freshmen in the fall of 1996, network jacks were installed in all dorm rooms and faculty offices, as well as many classrooms. By the time all undergraduates would have laptops in the year 2000, the initial network would have to be upgraded to support the additional traffic, including multimedia. Human infrastructure was also addressed. Four major support groups included training provided by the library, a help desk to answer technical questions, 20 student resident technical advisors in the residence halls, and 14 academic specialists hired by department chairs to help the faculty. To help reach late adopters among the faculty, student technical advisors were paired with specific faculty members to provide assistance.

Within a few years the computers were used across many disciplines. Applications in sciences included data acquisition and analysis, use of simulation software for experiments, and use of visualization and computational software in mathematics. The arts and humanities also found many uses, including multimedia presentations, digitizing and archiving of artworks, use of MIDI keyboards in music, introduction of new cultural material, and practice techniques in languages.

The first several years brought many useful lessons. First, start with educational goals rather than by asking, "What can we do with computers?" Standardization of hardware and software was important to minimize costs and simplify training. The tuition increase did not hurt enrollment because education improved. Network traffic increased greatly; e-mail was quickly overloaded and had to be controlled. Training, procedures, and adequate staffing for the help desk were essential. Some computer vandalism and incivility did occur. Overall, a campus-wide commitment of time and energy was needed.

QUESTIONS

1. What are some of the business processes in this situation?
2. Explain how the perspectives of infrastructure, context, and risk apply to this situation.
3. Many elementary school classrooms now have one or several computers that are linked to the Internet. Based on this case, explain your view of what will probably determine whether this technology investment will be successful.

Sources:

Brown, David G., Jennifer J. Burg, and Jay L. Dominick. "A Strategic Plan for Ubiquitous Laptop Computing," *Communications of the ACM,* Jan. 1998, pp. 26–35.

Yip, Ching-Wan. "WFU Computing Overview 97," May 28, 1998 (http://www.wfu.edu/~yipcw/WFUcmp97/).

Armstrong World Industries: Adopting Sales Force Automation

Armstrong World Industries is a leader in vinyl flooring, ceilings, adhesives, insulation, ceramic tile, and installation materials used in homes and commercial buildings. Its CEO decided that the company's culture was too inward-looking and needed to move toward "fact-based" management, with emphasis on satisfying customers, who included architects, contractors, and distributors. One part of that effort involved improving customer satisfaction by formalizing and automating parts of the sales process. Traditionally, salespeople had maintained their own customer records in thick binders. There had been little consistency in the pricing negotiated for orders, and many orders had been accepted at barely profitable prices. Sales bonuses had been based on volume rather than on profitability. Because prices often changed during competitive bidding processes, customers often disputed bills. In many cases customers found errors in invoices and were annoyed by the need to complain about basic information that Armstrong should be able to get right the first time. Furthermore, Armstrong's internal management was starved for useful information about what customers really wanted and why they did or did not place certain orders.

To help improve customer satisfaction, to increase sales efficiency, and to collect better information, Armstrong decided to implement a salesforce automation system called HEAT, high-efficiency Armstrong technology. The salespeople would all have laptop computers that permitted entry of data about the customer's specific building project along with data about customer likes and dislikes. HEAT contained a "price is right" model that calculated the sales bonus based on job size, shipping dates, product specifications, and pricing. Consistent with a change in the bonus formula to recognize both volume and price, this model was designed to motivate salespeople to maintain company profits while doing well for themselves. The salespeople would be able to negotiate prices, but they would always be able to see how any discounts affected the bonuses they received.

In a previous attempt to give PCs to salespeople in the early 1990s, around 50% never took the PCs out of the box. This time, however, Armstrong executives decided that information system usage would be mandatory. Every order would be negotiated using the new software, and salespeople would also be obligated to use the information system to collect and maintain additional information about the customers and their product needs. The system was defined over the course of eight months with significant input from the salesforce. To ensure successful implementation, top executives devoted part of a year to showing salespeople how to profit from using HEAT.

The new system brought benefits but still left many salespeople displeased about the extra work it required. Sales grew 9% and 13% in the two years after the implementation, and prices increased 10%. Customer disputes decreased 48%, and customer satisfaction increased 15%. One customer noted that the error rate on invoices dropped from almost 40% to almost zero within a year. Despite these benefits, a number of salespeople complained that excessive data collection requirements ate into private time. Many were unhappy with the complex sequence of screens provided for data entry, and the salesforce satisfaction rating for the system was only 6 out of 10. Marketing did not get the strategic information it needed because salespeople complained of becoming data entry operators and resisted filling in so many data fields.

QUESTIONS

1. How did the use of the salesforce automation software change the work systems in sales?
2. Explain how the business process, participants, information, and technology were all considered in the process of implementing the salesforce automation software.

Sources:

Armstrong World Industries. "Our Corporate Mission," May 11, 1998 (http://www.armstrong.com/profile/mission.html).

Bresnahan, Jennifer, "Hard Sell: Sales Force Automation," *CIO Magazine*, Mar. 15, 1998. May 11, 1998 (http://www.cio.com/archive/enterprise/031598 sales content.htm).

Zerega, Blaise. "Armstrong Automates Under Y2K Spotlight," *Infoworld*, Mar. 9, 1998, p. 110.

3

Business Processes

Study Questions

- What is the role of data flow diagrams in process modeling?
- What business process characteristics can be used to describe system design choices impacting business process success?
- What is the difference between structured, semistructured, and unstructured tasks?
- What are the five possible levels of integration of business processes?
- Why are planning and control important elements of many business processes?
- In what ways do information systems support the various management roles?

Outline

Opening Case

FORD: REEINGINEERING A PAYMENT PROCESS

In the early 1980s Ford Motor Company initiated a project to reduce its Accounts Payable staff from 500 to 400 people whose main function was to pay suppliers for products and services they provide. Before paying a supplier, the Accounts Payable staff had to verify that invoices from suppliers were consistent with what Ford's Purchasing Department ordered and with what Ford's Receiving Department actually received. Looking for fresh ideas, Ford representatives visited Mazda, a Japanese auto company affiliated with Ford. To say the least, the representatives were amazed to find that only five people performed Mazda's Accounts Payable function. Even though Mazda was a much smaller company, it had to be doing something totally different to account for the staffing difference.

The main difference was related to the business process Mazda used. When a shipment arrived at Mazda, the Receiving Department staff looked up the purchase order that had originally been sent to the supplier. If the material matched the purchase order completely, the Receiving Department would enter a receipt confirmation into the database. The Accounts Payable Department now had a very simple job: Mazda had ordered the material, the supplier had delivered it, and Mazda should now pay. If the material received did not match the purchase order completely, the shipment was simply returned. Because Mazda would not accept an incorrect shipment, the Accounts Payable Department never had to figure out how to reconcile inconsistencies between the purchase order, material delivered, and the invoice sent by the supplier.

Ford had used a very different method. The Purchasing Department would send a purchase order to the supplier. The Receiving Department would accept some orders even if they did not match the purchase order exactly. Later the arrival of an invoice triggered action by the Accounts Payable Department, which verified that the material had been ordered and had arrived in the appropriate quantity. Much of the Department's time was spent on cases where the material received didn't match the purchase order. These cases required looking in several places and possibly making phone calls to figure out what to do.

Comparing their version and Mazda's version of the same business process, Ford decided to change the logic of its process. In the new system, the Purchasing Department puts the purchase order on a database that the Receiving Department and Accounts Payable Department can access. When material arrives, the Receiving Department finds the purchase order and verifies the quantity. If the purchase order and the material don't match, the material is returned. Now the Accounts Payable Department can pay the bill immediately without ever receiving an invoice. Suppliers appreciate this because it reduces their paperwork and pays them sooner. Ford benefits because it can reduce overhead by eliminating work that does not contribute to producing automobiles efficiently. In 1986 Ford employed 500 people paying bills in the old way. By 1990 only 125 were needed.[1, 2, 3] Notice how the new information system was only part of the solution and succeeded only because of the reorganized workflow. Before changing its information systems, Ford fixed its business process by eliminating steps that did not add value.

Debate Topic

Many large firms have payables systems similar to Ford's original system. Do the enormous productivity increases from the new method show that managers in these other large firms used poor judgment in designing these systems?

The Ford case is commonly cited as an example of **business process reengineering (BPR),** the complete redesign of a business process using information technology. Table 3.1 shows that reengineering affects the entire work system and the product it produces, and therefore involves much more than just changing the idealized steps in the business process. Regardless of whether the term "work system reengineering" might be more accurate than the established term business process reengineering, the important general point is the significance of analyzing business processes before changing the information systems that support them. By doing this type of analysis Ford attained much better results than it

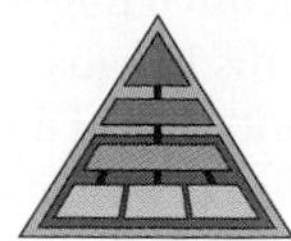

TABLE 3.1 Ford's New Payables System

CUSTOMER

- Ford's suppliers
- Ford's manufacturing and purchasing departments

PRODUCT

- Verification that the order was fulfilled correctly by the supplier
- Payment to the supplier

BUSINESS PROCESS

Major steps:	Rationale:
• Order material • Receive shipments • Reconcile receipts with purchase orders • Pay suppliers	• store purchase orders in a shared database • accept shipments only if they match the purchase order • pay on receipt, not invoice

PARTICIPANTS	INFORMATION	TECHNOLOGY
• Purchasing department • Receiving department • Accounts payable department	• Purchase order • Receipt confirmation • Payment to supplier	• Computer system supporting a shared database

might have attained by leaving the process unchanged and just trying to make the information system more effective.

This chapter explains a series of ideas that help you describe and analyze business processes within a work system. The chapter's organization reflects the relationship between process architecture and process performance. First it explains process modeling, a method of documenting process architecture by identifying major processes and dividing them into linked subprocesses. Next it looks at major architectural characteristics, such as degree of structure, range of involvement, and level of integration. These are business terms used to describe process architecture. Process performance is described in terms of inward-looking performance variables including rate of output, consistency, productivity, cycle time, flexibility, and security. These variables focus on the process rather than the product, and therefore differ from the outward-looking product performance variables introduced in Chapter 2.

Because most of the architectural characteristics and performance variables are familiar from everyday life, you might wonder why they are discussed in a book on information systems. The reason is that these terms provide many ways to think about business processes and how these processes can be improved using information systems. In fact, most of these terms discussed are equally applicable when thinking about the application of information technology to the process of building information systems.

PROCESS MODELING: DOCUMENTING BUSINESS PROCESS ARCHITECTURE

Process modeling is itself a business process. It is the business process of naming business processes and subdividing them into their basic elements so that they can be studied and improved. Process modeling is an essential part of information system development because it helps clarify the problem the information system attempts to solve and the way it goes about solving that problem.

If this were a systems analysis text for IT professionals, we would cover a number of different process modeling techniques in some depth. Because this is an information systems text for business professionals, we will look carefully at one process modeling technique, the data flow diagram, and will also mention flowcharts and structured English in less detail. Data flow diagrams are valuable for building information systems because they show how the structure of the business process depends on the storage and flow of data. Flowcharts are a technique for representing the flow of calculations, especially when sequence of calculations varies depending on results of intermediate calculations. Other process modeling techniques based on mathematical models can be used for other purposes, such as determining the time and resources a process will use under different circumstances.

Data Flow Diagrams

Data flow diagrams (DFDs) represent the flows of data between different processes within a system. They provide a simple, intuitive method for describing business processes without focusing on the details of computer systems. Virtually anyone who works in a business can understand a carefully designed DFD and can point out errors or omissions. DFDs are an attractive technique because they describe what users do rather than what computers do and involve only four symbols: the process, data flow, data store, and external entity (see Figure 3.1).

The four DFD symbols focus the analysis on flows of data between subprocesses, rather than on the information technology used. This approach makes sense to business professionals, whose main concern is to make sure the information system supports or enforces a specific set of activities performed using specific methods.

An important limitation of DFDs is that they focus only on flows of information. There is no symbol for flows of material such as the physical things actually ordered by Ford using its Purchasing system. In addition, DFDs do not include the symbols used in flowcharts for expressing decision points, sequences of operations, and other things that must be clarified before writing a computer program. The advantages of DFDs mirror their limitations. The fact that so few symbols are included makes it easy for users to understand DFDs and helps them focus on the business process. Other techniques such as flowcharts are used later to document decision criteria, timing of subprocesses, and other details not handled by DFDs.

Describing Business Process Organization and Hierarchy

Figure 3.2 shows that the starting point in using DFDs is to create a **context diagram,** which verifies the scope of the system by showing the sources and destinations of data used and generated by the system being modeled. At the center of the context diagram, the Purchasing system is represented as a single process. Surrounding that process are boxes

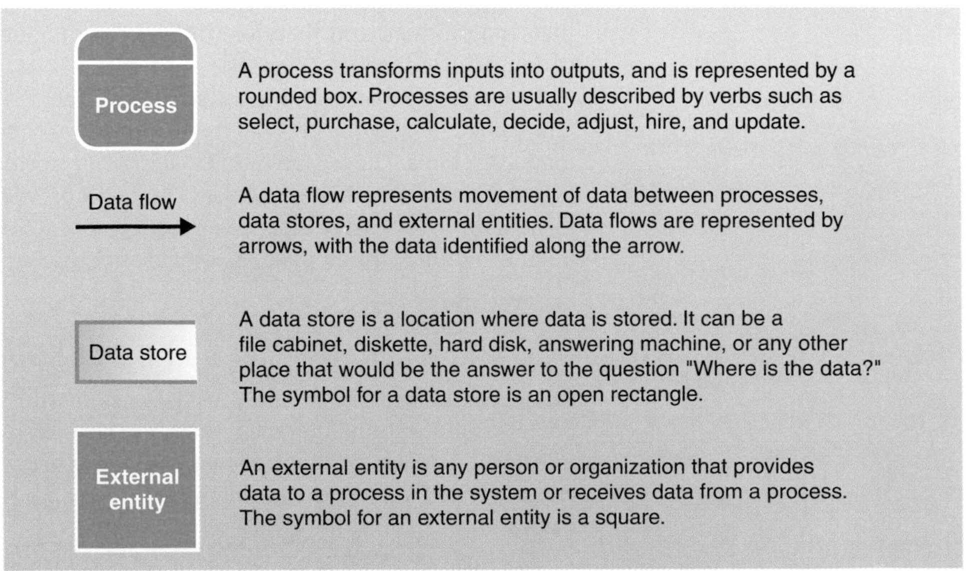

Process
A process transforms inputs into outputs, and is represented by a rounded box. Processes are usually described by verbs such as select, purchase, calculate, decide, adjust, hire, and update.
Data flow
A data flow represents movement of data between processes, data stores, and external entities. Data flows are represented by arrows, with the data identified along the arrow.
Data store
A data store is a location where data is stored. It can be a file cabinet, diskette, hard disk, answering machine, or any other place that would be the answer to the question "Where is the data?" The symbol for a data store is an open rectangle.
External entity
An external entity is any person or organization that provides data to a process in the system or receives data from a process. The symbol for an external entity is a square.

Figure 3.1
Symbols used in data flow diagrams

Data flow diagrams use only four symbols but can be applied to aid in understanding how the structure of a business process depends on the storage and flow of data.

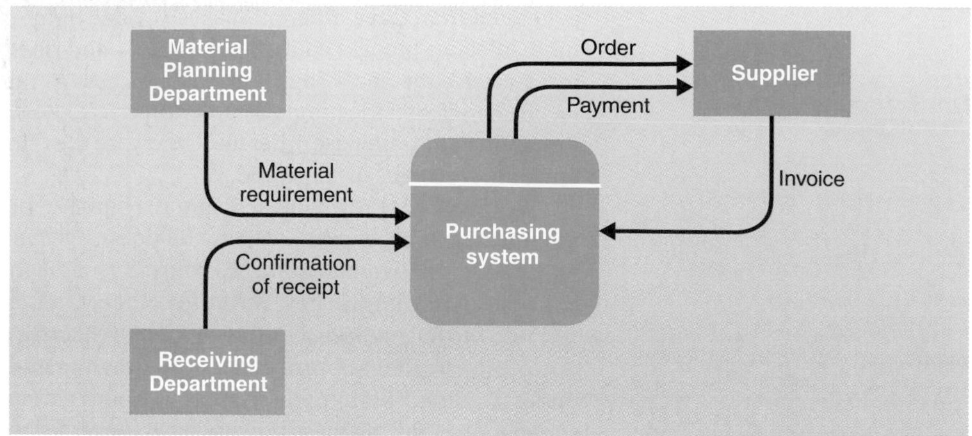

Figure 3.2
Context diagram for the Ford purchasing system

This context diagram says that the system we are considering is the purchasing system, and that external entities include the supplier and two internal departments.

representing the external entities that provide data for the Purchasing system or receive data from it. The external entities in this case are the Material Planning Department and the supplier. They are considered external to the business process because we are focusing on the flows of information related to ordering material, receiving it, and paying the supplier. System boundaries would be different for a different analysis.

In addition to bounding the system and summarizing flows of data, the context diagram might convey significant organizational issues and even surprises for some of the participants. For example, it says that the material requirement comes from only one source, the Material Planning Department. People reviewing it might object that other groups should be able to submit orders. This example shows how using data flow diagrams helps in identifying and resolving issues about responsibility and authority before the technical system design begins.

After using the context diagram to establish the scope of the system, the next step is to identify processes and break them down into subprocesses to describe exactly how work is done. DFDs make it possible to look at business processes at any level of detail by breaking them down into successively finer subprocesses. This type of analysis is needed to understand what an information system should do in this situation.

Figure 3.3 shows what might have been the first step toward breaking down the original Purchasing system into its constituent processes. The original Purchasing system might be divided into three major processes: PCH 1, order the material; PCH 2, decide what to pay; PCH 3, pay the vendor. Notice how the second process involves reconciling data

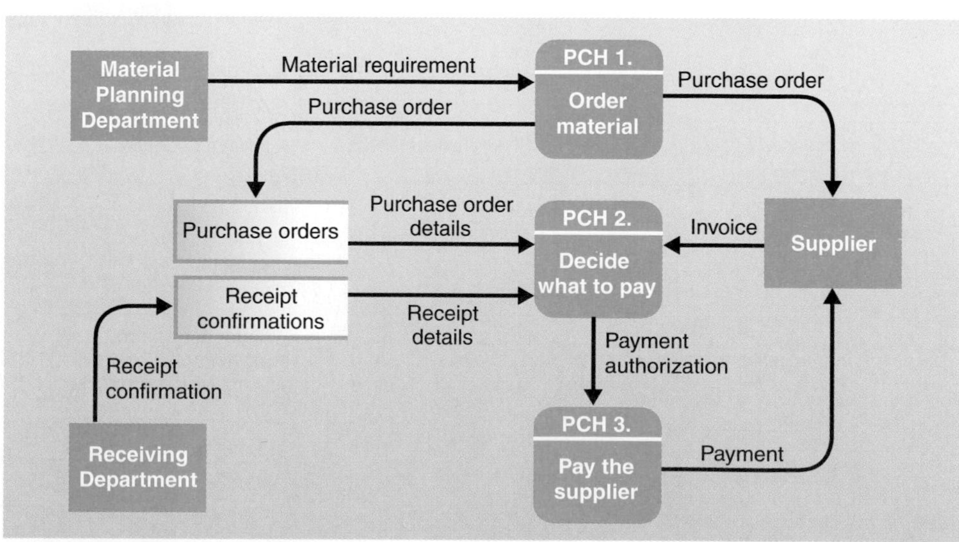

Figure 3.3
Data flow diagram showing the main processes in Ford's original purchasing system

This top-level data flow diagram breaks the business process into three separate processes: PCH 1, order the material; PCH 2, decide what to pay; PCH 3, pay the vendor. (PCH is an abbreviation for "purchasing.")

generated from three different places at three different times. This might be a hint that a more effective process could be used. As is described in the Ford case, the new business process gave the Receiving Department access to the purchase order file. If the material received matched the purchase order precisely, they accepted it and added a receipt confirmation to the purchase order file. Otherwise they simply returned it and the complex reconciliation process disappeared.

Compared to the context diagram, Figure 3.3 provides more information about how the business process operates but still doesn't give enough information to understand it fully. Doing that would require breaking each of the three processes into subprocesses. For example, depending on how Ford truly ordered material, the process PCH 1 might be broken into the four subprocesses in Figure 3.4. Each of these subprocesses could be broken down into smaller subprocesses until drawing additional diagrams added no further understanding. The completed analysis would cover many pages but would permit a person to look at the business process in whatever level of detail was important for thinking about a particular issue.

You might wonder whether all this detail is necessary, especially for a manager or end user. In fact, it is absolutely necessary because managers and users are the ones who understand how processes operate in the organization. For example, Ford's managers would certainly find fault with Figure 3.4 because much of Ford's purchasing is done through long-term agreements. However, this is the point. Much of the value in developing DFDs results from resolving disagreements about how work is done currently or how it should be done in the future. If users and managers cannot or will not describe things at this level of detail, any attempt to build a new information system will probably fail due to disagreements about what it should do.

The data flow diagram is only one of many process modeling techniques. This technique is easily understood by both system users and system developers, and it is used widely during the initial phases of information system development to clarify the boundaries and

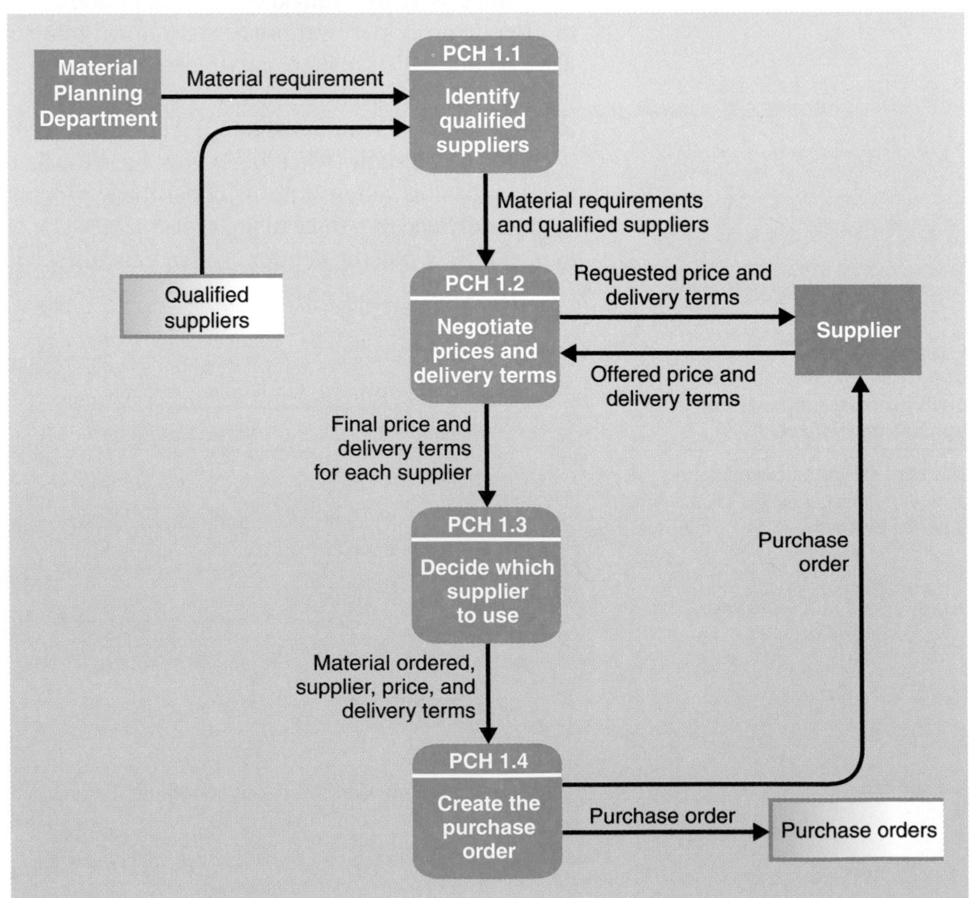

Figure 3.4
Data flow diagram dividing PCH 1 into four subprocesses

This DFD divides business process PCH 1 into four possible subprocesses: PCH 1.1, identify qualified vendors; PCH 1.2, negotiate prices and delivery terms; PCH 1.3, decide what vendor to use; PCH 1.4, create the purchase order.

internal operation of the business process being studied. It is also incorporated directly into most computer aided software engineering (CASE) systems discussed in Chapter 9.

Flowcharts and Structured English

Even when DFDs are used extensively, other techniques are often used to fill in the details not adequately expressed by DFDs. For example, although they express data flows between processes, DFDs express neither the sequence and timing of processes nor the detailed logic of processes, such as the precise rules for selecting among alternative actions such as accept or reject. Furthermore, they do not represent the physical devices used by the data processing system. Flowcharts and structured English are two techniques used to document these essential details.

Flowcharts are diagrams expressing the sequence and logic of procedures using standardized symbols to represent different types of input/output, processing, and data storage. Figure 3.5 shows some of the many standard flowcharting symbols used to represent both the logical flow of a process and the physical devices that capture, store, and display the data. Flowcharts were once the primary diagramming tool used for documenting systems. They are still used in many ways but have often been replaced by DFDs as tools for discussing information system logic with users and for documenting the flow of data between business processes.

Figure 3.6 shows an example of the type of flowchart you might use directly to document business rules and calculations within a subprocess after the data flows between processes have been clarified using DFDs. The diamond shaped decision box in Figure 3.6 exemplifies the type of procedural detail that DFDs do not capture but that flowcharts represent effectively. As with DFDs, flowcharts can be represented on many hierarchical levels and spread across many pages.

For specifying exactly how a procedure operates, pictures may not be as terse and precise as a carefully constructed set of declarative sentences. **Structured English** is a way to represent the precise logic of a procedure by writing out that logic using a few limited forms such as sequence, iteration, and selection using if-then or if-then-else formats. As an example, look at the following specification of how to decide whether the material received is equivalent to the material in an order.

Retrieve the purchase order

For each item on the purchase order

    if quantity received = quantity ordered

    then item code is "match"

If item code = "match" for all items in the purchase order

    then purchase order receipt code is "match"

If purchase order receipt is "match"

    then approve payment for order

    else return material received.

Figure 3.5
Standard flowchart symbols

These are some of the standard flowchart symbols. The punched card symbol is one of many that have become obsolete due to changes in storage technology.

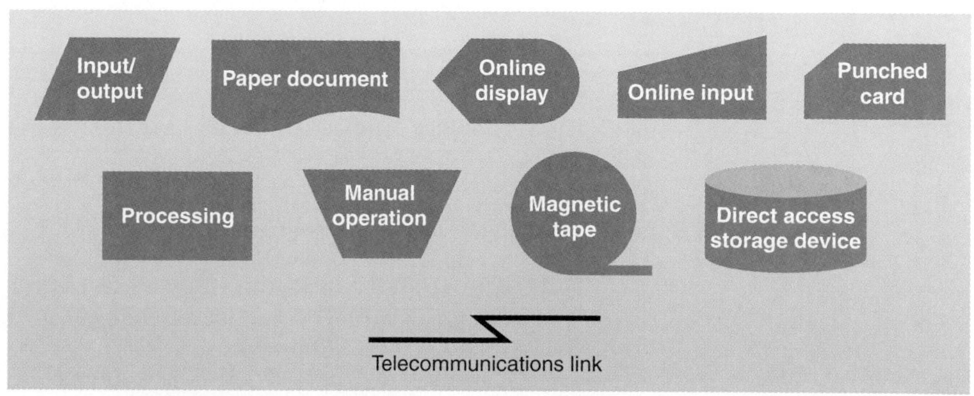

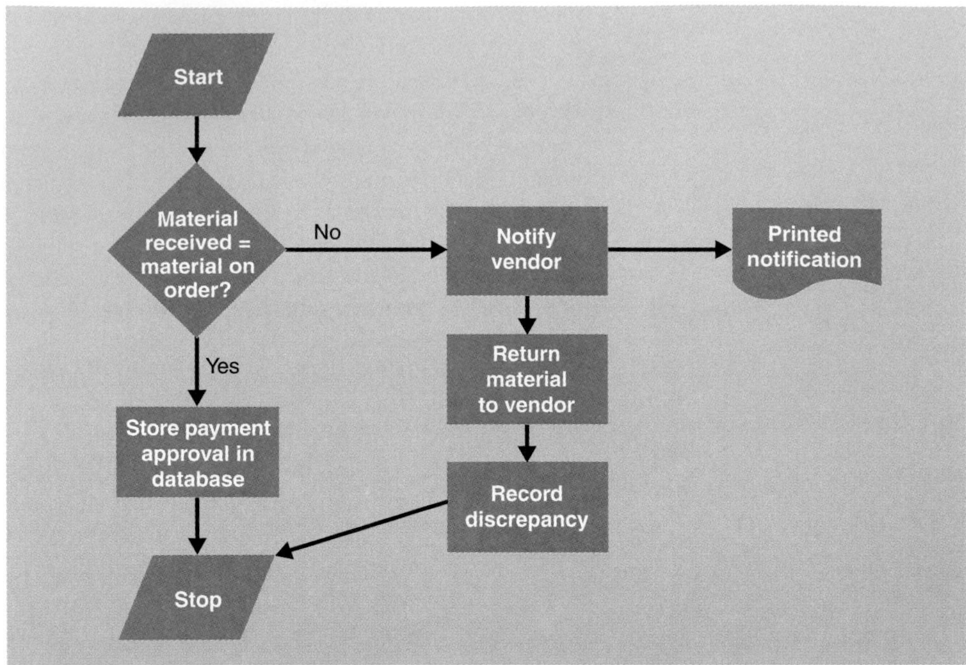

Figure 3.6
Flowchart showing the rules governing a procedure

This flowchart demonstrates something data flow diagrams cannot do. It shows different paths depending on conditions such as whether the material received is equal to the material on order.

Structured English is sometimes called pseudocode because it resembles the code in a computer program except that it ignores the grammar or peculiarities of any particular programming language. This level of description is so detailed that it requires careful scrutiny. For example, many people might read the nine lines of structured English on the previous page without realizing that they ignore the possibility of receiving merchandise that was not on the purchase order at all. If those nine lines were converted directly to a computer program, the program would contain a bug that would eventually cause problems.

This section has illustrated three techniques that are used to document business processes. DFDs are a primary tool for process modeling, which includes naming business processes and subdividing them into their basic elements so that they can be studied and improved. Flowcharts and structured English are used to fill out the details that cannot be expressed well using DFDs.

You might be surprised that defining the architecture of an existing or proposed system is largely about giving names to subprocesses and data. The naming process is surprisingly difficult and often raises controversy. For example, an item on an invoice might be called an item, line item, stock item, or something else. Likewise, commitment date might refer to when a product will be completed, when it will be shipped, or when the customer will receive it. Such distinctions might seem like nitpicking, but are absolutely essential for building systems regardless of whether computers are involved. Clarifying data definitions is especially important for avoiding confusion if people working in different departments could use the same term in different ways.

Reality Check

USING DATA FLOW DIAGRAMS TO DOCUMENT PROCESS ARCHITECTURE

This section has emphasized DFDs as a method for summarizing process architecture.

1. Write a one-level DFD (similar to Figure 3.3) for a process that you are familiar with, such as registering for classes, renting a video, or using an ATM to withdraw money from a bank account. Include at least two subprocesses.

2. Write a DFD for one of the subprocesses (as is done in Figure 3.4) and explain how you could keep track of everything if you needed to produce DFDs for subprocesses of the subprocesses.

ARCHITECTURAL CHARACTERISTICS OF A BUSINESS PROCESS

The previous section explained process modeling as a way to document subprocesses within a business process and the flows of information between the subprocesses. Although looking at a process in detail is essential, it is also important to look at the big picture in terms of architectural characteristics that summarize the way the process operates. This section discusses seven architectural characteristics that often affect business process performance. Table 3.2 lists the characteristics and shows how too little or too much of each can affect system performance. Instead of just covering the characteristics in general, the discussion of each characteristic emphasizes the way it is related to the role and value of the use of information systems.

Degree of Structure

The term *information system* implies that the purpose of these systems is to provide information. This is often true, although the purpose of many information systems could be described more accurately as "to systematize and structure business processes through information."

The **degree of structure** of a task or a business process is the degree of predetermined correspondence between its inputs and its outputs. For example, an ATM system is highly

TABLE 3.2 **Impacts of Architectural Characteristics of Business Processes**

Architectural characteristic	Problem if the level is too high	Problem if the level is too low
Degree of structure	• People doing the work are prevented from using their judgment. • People doing the work feel like cogs in a machine because they have too little autonomy.	• Easily foreseeable errors occur because well-understood rules are not applied consistently. • Outputs are inconsistent.
Range of involvement	• Work is slowed down because too many people get involved before steps are completed.	• Work is performed based on narrow or personal considerations, resulting in decisions that may not be the best for the overall organization.
Level of integration	• Steps in the process are too intertwined. Participants in different business processes get in each other's way. To change one step it is necessary to analyze too many other steps or processes.	• Steps in the processes are too independent. The process needs greater integration to produce better results.
Complexity	• Participants, managers, and programmers have difficulty understanding how the system operates or what will happen if it is changed.	• The system cannot handle the different cases that it should be able to handle.
Degree of reliance on machines	• People become disengaged from their work. • People's skills may decrease. • Mistakes occur because people overestimate what the computers are programmed to handle.	• Productivity and consistency decrease as bored people perform repetitive work that computers could do more efficiently.
Attention to planning, execution, and control	• Too much effort goes into planning and controlling within the process, and not enough goes into execution.	• Insufficient effort in planning and control leaves the business process inconsistent and unresponsive to customer requirements.
Treatment of exceptions, errors, and malfunctions	• The process focuses on exceptions and becomes inefficient and inconsistent.	• The process fails altogether or handles exceptions incorrectly, resulting in low productivity or poor quality and responsiveness perceived by customers.

structured because it is completely governed by rules stating how it will respond to each possible input. In contrast, the process of creating a perfume advertisement is quite unstructured. Because most tasks and decisions are neither totally structured nor totally unstructured, it is useful to compare structured, semistructured, and unstructured tasks.

Structured, Semistructured, and Unstructured Tasks

A totally **structured task** is so well understood that it is possible to say exactly how to perform it and how to evaluate whether it has been performed well. For example, totaling the previous month's invoices is a typical structured task. Specific characteristics of a highly structured task include:

- Information requirements are known precisely.
- Methods for processing the information are known precisely.
- Desired format of the information is known precisely.
- Decisions or steps within the task are clearly defined and repetitive.
- Criteria for making decisions are understood precisely.
- Success in executing the task can be measured precisely.

In a **semistructured task,** the information requirements and procedures are generally known, although some aspects of the task still rely on the judgment of the person doing the task. The way a doctor diagnoses an illness is often a semistructured task. It contains some structure because the physician understands common medical facts and diagnosis methods; on the other hand, it is not totally structured because many medical situations are ambiguous and require judgment and intuition.

An **unstructured task** is so poorly understood that the information to be used, the method of using the information, and the criteria for deciding whether the task is being done well cannot be specified. Unstructured decisions tend to be performed based on experience, intuition, trial and error, rules of thumb, and vague qualitative information. Examples include the selection of a company president or the choice of a picture for the cover of a fashion magazine. The decision about the president involves intangible factors such as how well the candidate gets along with people in the organization and the likelihood that the candidate would find the job challenging but not overwhelming. The magazine decision is based on artistic issues such as taste and intuition about what magazine readers would enjoy.

Using Information Systems to Impose Structure

Successful information systems impose the amount of structure that is appropriate for the activity being supported. Imposing too much structure stifles creativity and makes the participants in the process feel as though they have no responsibility for the outcome. Imposing too little structure results in inefficiencies and errors.

Table 3.3 shows how information systems can impose different degrees of structure on business processes. The extent to which a system structures a task can be divided into three broad categories, each of which has a number of gradations. Information systems that provide information and tools impose the least structure. This is consistent with the typical approach to personal computing, allowing people to do whatever computing they want to do, however they want to do it. Systems that enforce rules and guidelines impose more structure. This idea is consistent with parts of the total quality movement, which maintains that quality depends on using consistent methods and achieving consistent results. Systems that substitute technology for people automate tasks totally and impose the most structure. Substituting technology for people is a basic reason for using most machines.

Going in order from imposing the most structure to imposing the least structure, Table 3.3 lists the alternative approaches along with related examples. Notice that the table says nothing about whether imposing more structure is better or worse in general. Imposing a minimal amount of structure on well-understood tasks may permit excessive variability in results. Imposing too much structure on poorly understood tasks may prevent

TABLE 3.3 **Different Levels of Imposing Structure on Work**

Degree to which structure is imposed	Approach for imposing structure	Example
Highest: Substitution of technology for people	Replace the person with technology.	An automatic teller machine performs work that a teller would otherwise perform.
	Automate much of the work.	A construction company uses a program to generate bids for construction contracts. The computerized bids are usually changed only slightly.
High: Enforcement of rules or procedures	Control each step in the work.	A bank's loan approval system is based on a formula using data from a fill-in-the-blanks form.
	Provide real time guidance for work steps performed by people.	An interactive shop-floor control system tells workers what machine settings to use and warns them when exceptions occur.
Low: Access to information or tools	Use a model to evaluate or optimize a potential decision.	A pharmaceutical company uses a model to help allocate funds among research proposals. People make the decision.
	Provide specialized tools that help people do their work.	An architecture firm uses a computer-aided design system to help design buildings.
	Provide information that is filtered, formatted, and summarized to make it useful.	A management information system provides performance information for managers.
	Provide a general purpose tool to help people do work.	Provide a telephone, spreadsheet, or word processor.

people from using their intelligence to produce good results and may generate problems when unanticipated circumstances occur.

The different degrees of structure apply in different situations. Automating tasks by substituting technology for people is pertinent for parts of business processes that handle information in a totally structured way. Enforcement of rules and procedures applies to process steps that are largely repetitious but involve some degree of judgment. Providing tools and information applies to process steps that are truly novel or unstructured. Providing tools and information in unstructured situations may be ineffective, however, because most potential users may have no idea how to apply tools and information successfully in inherently unstructured situations. Despite the best efforts of software vendors, an information and tools strategy often fails unless it is reasonably apparent how work system participants will use the tools and information to perform their work.

The concept of structure can also be used to identify mismatches between an information system's goal and the way it tries to accomplish its goal. If its goal is to enforce consistency, providing access to information may not be powerful enough. If its purpose is to help people do their work, a system that enforces procedures may be overly restrictive or counterproductive. Looking at information systems this way also highlights a common problem in implementing systems. In some cases, the developer sees the system as a way to provide access to information, whereas the potential users see it as a personal threat because it may automate their work.

Finally, notice that it is often misleading to try to generalize about the degree of structure in a type of business process, such as granting automobile loans. Different businesses performing the same process may do it differently based on their business strategy or skills. One bank might use precise formulas and procedures to make automobile loan decisions and leave little discretion to the loan officer. Other banks might use formulas and procedures only as guidelines, leaving the task semistructured; yet other banks might leave the decision to the loan officer's discretion.

Range of Involvement

It sounds simple to say too many cooks spoil the broth, but the right range of involvement in business processes is often elusive. **Range of involvement** is the organizational span of people involved in a business process. When the range of involvement is too narrow, decisions are made from an excessively local viewpoint, often missing opportunities for the overall enterprise. When the range of involvement is too great, business processes seem to move at a glacial pace. For example when IBM's laser printer and typewriter division was spun off as Lexmark Corporation, management pledged to avoid IBM's bureaucratic ways, such as the contention system that pitted line managers against corporate staff analysts whenever important decisions had to be made. They communicated the spirit of the new firm by encasing the old IBM operations manual in a transparent block of lucite in the middle of the plant floor. This allowed everyone to see the book that turned one-year projects into three-year projects, but no one could ever open it again.[4]

Too Many Participants or Too Few

The IBM-Lexmark example illustrated the problem of business processes bogged down by too many participants and not enough authority and responsibility. Many state and local governments feel this issue acutely in business complaints about the large number of different permits and approvals that are needed to open a new business or modify a building. Even many small organizations have the same problem, such as when the owner feels obliged to be involved in every decision.

Too few cooks in the kitchen can also be a problem, however, when it is necessary to enforce organizational standards and quality expectations. This is why some large programming groups try to maintain quality and prevent unwarranted software modifications through a process called software change control. One person checks out a program and changes it, another person checks the program and its documentation, and yet another person replaces the program in the program library and records the fact that a change took place. A smaller range of involvement might seem more efficient, but it would not enforce quality or security standards as effectively. The individual work might proceed more quickly and might be more fun, but the software produced might contain more errors and might not be as maintainable over the long term.

Role of Information Systems

Information systems can be designed in ways that broaden or constrict the range of involvement in a business process. Information systems that provide upper management with daily access to detailed operational data give them the ability to examine data and ask questions they would not be able to ask if less information were available. Such systems broaden the range of involvement by allowing managers to get involved in the details of work their subordinates are managing. If done well, this may support the subordinates' performance. If done poorly, subordinates may feel intruded upon and unable to manage their own work.

In contrast, information systems may reduce the range of involvement by supporting a **case manager approach,** in which a single individual does different information-related tasks that many individuals might have done in the past. Pacific Bell moved in this direction when it redesigned its process of signing up business customers for Centrex telephone service. Previously this involved 11 separate jobs and more than 5 business days. Service representatives had to switch back and forth between 9 separate information systems involving things such as equipment inventory, customer requirements, and installation schedules. They often made mistakes requiring rework, and often had to consult customers several times. Service coordinators in the groups that adopted the changes handle all interfaces with customers and use workstations providing a consolidated view of the nine information systems. Service is installed on the day of the order 80% of the time, and within 2.3 days for more complicated situations.[5]

Doers Versus Checkers

A way to be more specific about the range of involvement in a business process is to categorize participants as *doers,* the people who perform the value added tasks, and *checkers,* the people who check to make sure the tasks were done or will be done properly by others. The Pacific Bell example was about reducing the number of doers in a process by providing a case manager the necessary information in an actionable form. The Lexmark-IBM example was about reducing the number of checkers. Trying to categorize participants as doers versus checkers also raises interesting questions about how to categorize specific contributions to a process. For example, individuals playing management and quality assurance roles probably see themselves as doers whose contribution adds value. Other participants in the same processes may view those roles as nothing more than checking the work and creating delays.

As with the degree of structure in a process, decisions about the proper range of involvement include a variety of issues. The total quality management (TQM) movement generally pushes for reducing the range of involvement in processes by insisting that work system participants have the knowledge to do their work and the responsibility for checking it. Successful TQM efforts have improved quality and reduced cycle times by providing more of a feeling of ownership and by eliminating unnecessary quality control inspections. In contrast, financial auditors insist on the segregation of duties to reduce the likelihood of financial fraud. Having one person create a purchase order, another approve it, and a third approve the payment makes it less likely that people will collude, but also means that three people are involved in the work that one or two might do.

Level of Integration

It is often unclear what people mean when they use the terms "integration" and "integrated system" because these terms are used in many different ways, sometimes in relation to technology and databases and sometimes in relation to business processes. As with degree of structure and range of involvement, the right level of integration in a business process is often not obvious. Insufficiently integrated systems are disorganized and unproductive, but overly integrated systems are complex and hard to control. We will start with a single general definition but will then look at five separate levels of integration, each of which may provide a clue about the right level of integration in a system being analyzed.

Integration is mutual responsiveness and collaboration between distinct activities or processes. The extent of integration between two processes or activities is related to the speed with which one responds to events in the other. This speed depends on both the immediacy of communication and the degree to which the processes respond to the information communicated. Information systems can play roles in both aspects of integration, first by supporting the communication, and second by making it easier for each business process to use the information to respond effectively.

As an example, consider the way integration between the sales effort and the production effort has become a major competitive issue in many industries. The more integrated these processes are, the faster the production process responds to new orders from sales. Motorola saw this form of integration as an important issue and cut the factory cycle time for building customized electronic pagers from two weeks to two hours. Highly automated production of the pager starts within 17 minutes of placing an order from the field.[6] Integration with suppliers has also become an important trend in manufacturing. (See Figure 3.7.) For example, a computer in a Nissan factory in Great Britain looks at the cars currently on the assembly line and sends orders to Akeda-Hoover, which supplies its seats. Akeda-Hoover schedules its daily production for seats with the specific color and style ordered by Nissan. The seats move directly from Akeda-Hoover to an automobile on Nissan's assembly line.[7] Information systems play a crucial role in integration because they convey the information and process it.

Figure 3.7
McKesson integrates inventory tracking and ordering

McKesson has extended the scope of its value chain by permitting its customers to enter data directly into its computerized inventory system. On the other side of the integrated system, workers within McKesson's distribution warehouses use specially designed "strap-on" computers and bar code readers to perform internal inventory tracking.

Five Levels of Integration

A basic question in business process redesign involves the desired level of integration between different business processes. Figure 3.8 summarizes five different levels of integration. The first two levels are conditions that make it easier to work together but are not inherently related to responsiveness and typically exist for reasons totally outside of any particular business process. Long-time employees of dissimilar organizations that have merged are painfully aware that cultural differences make it more difficult to communicate and work together. Similarly, the lack of common standards such as using the same word processing software, same database definitions, or even the same business vocabulary creates obstacles that make it more difficult to maintain processes and technologies, whether or not they are directly related.

Sharing information, the third level of coordination, is the least obtrusive way to attain responsiveness between processes. Information sharing occurs when all the lawyers working on a large legal case can use Lotus Notes to access any document about the case, or when the sales force can access a manufacturing database to know what capacity is still available for additional orders. Information sharing is comparatively unobtrusive because the people who produced the information do not have to take additional action to make the information useful to others. This approach to integration sounds easier than it really is because personal and political incentives in the organization often motivate people not to share.

Coordination, the fourth level of integration, can be defined as managing dependencies among activities. These dependencies might involve the synchronization of inputs and outputs among activities, such as not starting manufacturing steps until the materials have arrived. They might involve the sharing of resources, such as machines or people who can't do two things at once. They also might involve the fit between outputs, such as when several engineers are designing different parts of the same product.[8] Coordination is more obtrusive than information sharing because it calls for negotiations or two-way information flows that provide mutual responsiveness even though the processes operate separately.

By attaining collaboration, the fifth level of integration, interdependence between processes is so strong that their unique identity begins to disappear. To develop products more quickly and to make them easier to manufacture, for example, many firms have moved toward product development processes that involve close collaboration between marketing, engineering, and manufacturing. These highly collaborative processes try to minimize the problems of less integrated approaches in which marketing handed requirements to engineering, which then produced a product design that could not be manufactured economically.

Figure 3.8
Five levels of integration between business processes

Groups of business processes in a firm can be totally unrelated to each other or can be integrated at any of these five levels.

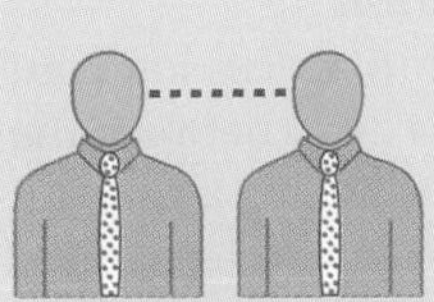

Common culture: *shared understandings and beliefs*

People involved in two independent processes share the same general beliefs and expectations about how people communicate and work together. These shared beliefs make it easier to work together and resolve conflicts whenever necessary.

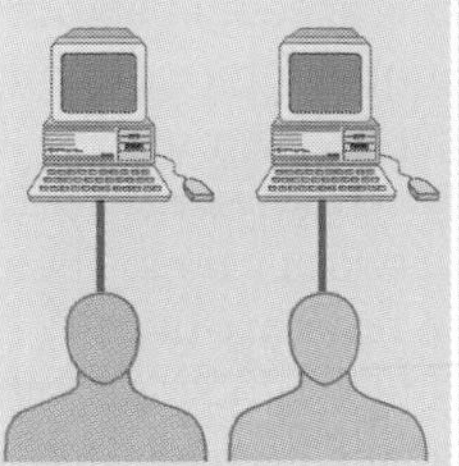

Common standards: *using consistent terminology and procedures to make business processes easier to maintain and interface*

Two different business processes use the same standards but otherwise operate independently. For example, two different departments may use the same type of personal computer or the same word processing software. Operating with agreed upon standards of this type may create economies of scale for the technical staff, who may be able to learn and service a smaller number of technical options. It also may enhance the possibility of other forms of integration in the future.

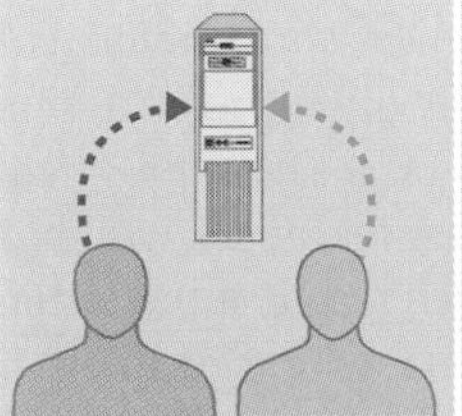

Information sharing: *access to each other's data by business processes that operate independently.*

Two different business processes share some of the same information even though the information sharing does not directly involve mutual responsiveness. For example, a sales department and a manufacturing department might share the manufacturing database so that sales would know what capacity was still available for additional orders.

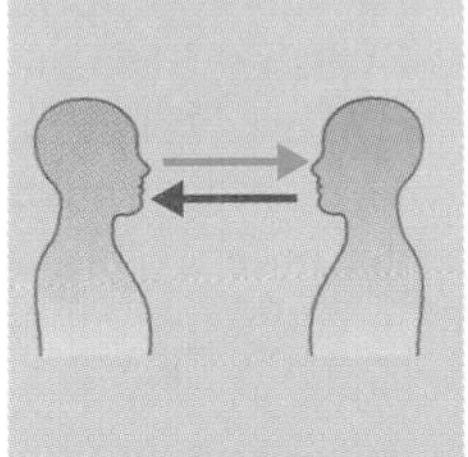

Coordination: *negotiation and exchange of messages permitting separate but interdependent processes to respond to each other's needs and limitations*

Different business processes maintain their own unique function and identity, but pass information back and forth to coordinate their efforts toward a common objective. For example, sales tells manufacturing what they can sell; manufacturing responds with a tentative output schedule; they negotiate to come up with a mutually feasible plan and then go about their individual work.

Collaboration: *such strong interdependence that the unique identity of separate processes begins to disappear*

Two different business processes merge part or all of their identity to accomplish larger objectives of the firm. For example, based on the need to get more easily manufacturable products to market sooner, many firms have moved toward product development processes that involve close collaboration between marketing, engineering, and manufacturing.

The difference between information sharing, coordination, and collaboration is especially important for thinking about potential benefits of information system investments. Although often touted as a major benefit of IT investments, information sharing does not necessarily imply that genuine coordination or collaboration will occur. Technology can provide access to information, but coordination and collaboration require commitment and action by the participants. Information system designers should therefore be careful about finding the level of integration that people in the organization are willing to commit to.

On the other hand, many forms of information sharing provide significant benefits without requiring responsiveness between business processes. Consider two business processes in libraries, the cataloguing process that keeps track of what the library owns, and the circulation process that keeps track of what has been checked out. If these are totally separate systems, you can learn that the library owns something but then find it is not on the shelves because it is checked out or missing. If the two systems are integrated using computers, the computer display that identifies catalogued items can also indicate whether they are checked out. This information sharing between the systems saves a lot of time for library users.

Problems with Tight Integration

Notice how some systems seem to be less integrated than they should be. For example, most current ATM systems have a delay between the time an ATM deposit is made and the time it is recognized as money available for use. This is especially apparent on weekends, when a Friday night deposit may not be recognized until Monday, the next working day. This time lag shows that the process of making deposits is not tightly integrated with the process of accounting for checking account balances.

Although the tight integration of processes might seem desirable, forcing processes to respond to each other too frequently may make it difficult for each process to get its work done. This is one of the reasons why many factories that produce noncustomized products "freeze" their schedules a week or two at a time. Their managers believe that changing production schedules continually in response to daily events in the sales department causes too much chaos and inefficiency in production. The difficulty in responding rapidly while also maintaining high production quality and efficiency is one of the reasons why responsiveness to customers is a genuine competitive issue.

Information system designers sometimes avoid highly integrated information systems for their own reasons. They often prefer to build two separate information systems plus an interface that operates on a schedule, such as daily or weekly. This approach is often far simpler than real time integration, which would assure that any event recorded by either system is immediately reflected in the other. Thinking of the connection between two systems as an interface divides a large problem into two smaller problems that can be solved individually. Often this means that a usable information system will be available sooner. Building an interface is especially appropriate where the desired capabilities of a new system are open to debate or when the business situation is changing rapidly. The lower level of integration that results may have negative consequences, however. For example, there might be a long delay in the interface between a customer returns system and the inventory system used for customer orders. This delay could result in situations when material returned by one customer could be shipped for another order except that the inventory system does not yet recognize the return has occurred.

Tightly integrated (also called tightly coupled) systems are also more prone to catastrophic failure than less integrated systems. Tightly coupled systems have little slack, require that things happen in a particular order, and depend on all components to operate within particular ranges. When one component fails, the others may also fail immediately. The most tightly coupled systems in our society include aircraft, nuclear power plants, power grids, and automated warfare systems.[9] In contrast, loosely coupled systems are decentralized, have slack resources and redundancies, permit delays and substitutions, and allow things to be done in different orders. Failures tend to be localized and therefore can be isolated, diagnosed, and fixed quickly. Thus, high levels of integration have both advantages and disadvantages that should be analyzed carefully.

Complexity

The U.S. federal income tax system demonstrates the issue of complexity. A simple system might just collect a fixed or sliding percentage of personal income and leave it at that. Such a system, however, would not explicitly address additional social, political, and economic goals, such as making it easier to own a house, making it easier to send children to day care, recognizing the depletion on oil wells, or granting special favors to major political contributors. Each additional tax code feature recognizes another goal, for better or for worse, but also adds to the number of differentiated components and creates a wider range of interactions between components. The resulting complexity has become virtually unmanageable, as was demonstrated by the 39% error rate in the advice the IRS tax hotline gave to taxpayers on 1986 changes in tax laws. Subsequently the IRS has issued statements saying, in effect, that the taxpayer, not the IRS, is responsible for any taxpayer errors resulting from incorrect information the IRS provides. A decade later, things had become even worse. The *Wall Street Journal* introduced the July 29, 1997 budget deal by saying the "mind-numbing complexity of the budget pact is good news for tax advisers. Even veteran tax lawyers are astonished by how tricky many of the new provisions are."[10,11,12]

Remove all the references to the tax system in this story and we are left with the fundamental tradeoff about complexity. Systems that are too simple don't handle the complexity of the problem (much like a word processor that can't number pages automatically). Systems that are too complex are hard to understand and hard to fix. Each additional function or feature shifts the balance away from simplicity and toward complexity.

Managing Complexity

A system's **complexity** is a combination of how many types of elements it contains and the number and nature of their interactions. As complexity increases, systems are more difficult to develop and manage because more factors and interactions must be considered, evaluated, and tested. Complexity also makes it more difficult to understand what is going on and even more difficult to anticipate the consequences of changes throughout the system.

The most direct strategy for reducing complexity is to eliminate low value variations. For example, Du Pont once printed paychecks over 3,300 times a year. Some plants and divisions paid on the first and 15th of the month, others in the middle and end of the month, and yet others every other Monday. Seeing little advantage in this way of doing things, Du Pont converted most of its payroll to the same bimonthly cycle, and consolidated to 36 payrolls. This eliminated over 100 jobs and saved $12 million annually.[13] Eliminating low value variations was a key factor in the adoption of electronic data interchange by most large companies. Part of the $55 that large companies like General Motors had to spend to process a paper invoice was related to deciphering data and formatting inconsistencies between invoices and other forms sent by suppliers. These inconsistencies added to costs and typically provided no value. Many industry groups have responded to these problems by banding together to create industry-wide EDI formats and then telling their suppliers that the use of EDI is a requirement for doing business.

Another approach for managing complexity is to recognize variations explicitly and treat them differently instead of trying to treat different problems using a fundamentally similar process. A business process might have a single name, such as "approve building permit," but that doesn't mean it has to be performed the same way in every instance. Consider, for example, why minor home improvement projects sometimes have to wait six months for a public hearing because they have to go through the same process as an application for a multimillion dollar office complex.[14] The sensible thing to do in such cases is to recognize that one size does not fit all and that complex requests with major ramifications call for a more complex process than small requests.

Degree of Reliance on Machines

Like other architectural characteristics of business processes, the degree of reliance on machines is a design decision. As is apparent when shopping at a store with a noncomputerized inventory system, doing things manually that could be done by computers is slow and inefficient and often makes it difficult to provide excellent service for customers. On the other hand, over-reliance on machines makes systems inflexible and may also lead to disengagement by human participants.

The general approach for the division of labor between people and machines is to assign tasks in a way that emphasizes the strengths and de-emphasizes the weaknesses of each. In general, tasks assigned to computers are totally structured, can be described completely, and may require a combination of great speed, accuracy, and endurance. Tasks with relatively little processing (such as keeping track of orders and invoices) can also be assigned to computers to assure organized and predictable execution. In contrast, tasks people must perform are those requiring common sense, intelligence, judgment, or creativity. People handle these tasks better than computers because they are flexible and can identify and resolve situations never encountered before.

Not a Silver Bullet

Although computers and other machines enable business processes that might have seemed unbelievable in the past, people have often relied too heavily on automation to solve problems machines alone cannot solve. For example, Chapter 1 mentioned the way the NUMMI joint venture between General Motors and Toyota used comparatively little automation but still achieved much higher productivity than highly automated GM plants.

In addition to not being a solution in many cases, excessive reliance on machines can be inefficient, ineffective, or even dangerous due to a shortcoming in the technology or in the way the technology affects system participants. An example of this type of problem occurred when the autopilot in a Boeing 747 began to malfunction as the plane was flying over Thunder Bay, Canada, on a dark night. The autopilot gradually began banking the plane to the right, but the motion was so gentle that the pilots did not notice the problem until too late. The plane banked 90 degrees, a position in which the wings provided no lift, and it began to dive toward earth. It fell two miles before the pilots could pull out of the dive. After more than a year of investigation, engineers could not agree on the cause. Airplane manufacturers and many pilots believe autopilot systems are safer and less error prone than human pilots under most circumstances; however, the question certainly remains about how much the pilots should rely on machines that were designed to assist and supplement the pilot's capabilities but not replace them.[15]

Even if the software and human procedures in a work system operate perfectly relative to its design specifications, over-reliance on machines may cause problems or even disasters because there is no guarantee that the system will operate correctly under unanticipated circumstances. A potentially apocalyptic example illustrates why major decisions should not be automated completely. On October 5, 1960, a missile warning system indicated that the United States was under a massive attack by Soviet missiles with probability exceeding 99.9%. Fortunately, human decision makers concluded that something must be wrong with the information they were receiving. In fact, the early warning radar at Thule, Greenland, had spotted the rising moon,[16] but nobody had thought about the moon when specifying how the information system should operate.

Attention to Planning, Execution, and Control

Participants in a business process need to know what to do, when to do it, and how to make sure work is being done properly. We can think of this as a cycle of planning, execution, and control. **Planning** is the process of deciding what work to do and what outputs to produce when. **Executing** is the process of doing the work. **Controlling** is the process of using information about past work performance to assure that goals are attained and plans carried out.

Planning, execution, and control occur wherever people do work. For example, a carpenter making a bookcase plans the work, performs the work, and uses carpentry techniques to ensure that the work is being done correctly. A manager implementing an organizational change goes through the same three steps. The manager's plan outlines the process of explaining the change, training the people, and converting from the old method to the new method. The execution is the explanation, training, and conversion. The control is the collection and use of information to make sure that the change is occurring.

Figure 3.9 shows flows of information between planning, execution, and control. Planning determines both work standards and what work will be done when. As work is executed, it generates information that is used in control processes. A control system feeds information back to execution to keep the execution on track and also to the planning process to ensure that future plans use realistic assumptions. To keep execution on track, recent performance is compared with work standards or work schedules and actions are taken to compensate for any deviations. Planning and control are information-intensive activities because a plan is information and because control involves the use of information to check how well the plan is being met and to take any necessary corrective action.

There are many ways to improve the cycle of planning, execution, and control. Planning for individual work can be supported by creating a standard planning format and then supplying information such as customer specifications or machine availability in a computerized form so that planning calculations can be automated. Organizational planning can be improved by creating standard formats and processing procedures for the structured parts of planning, such as transmitting and distributing plans, calculating planned results, and merging numbers from different organizations.

Figure 3.9
Planning, execution, and control

Planning, execution, and control are separate activities. Execution receives the output of planning and provides information inputs into the control process.

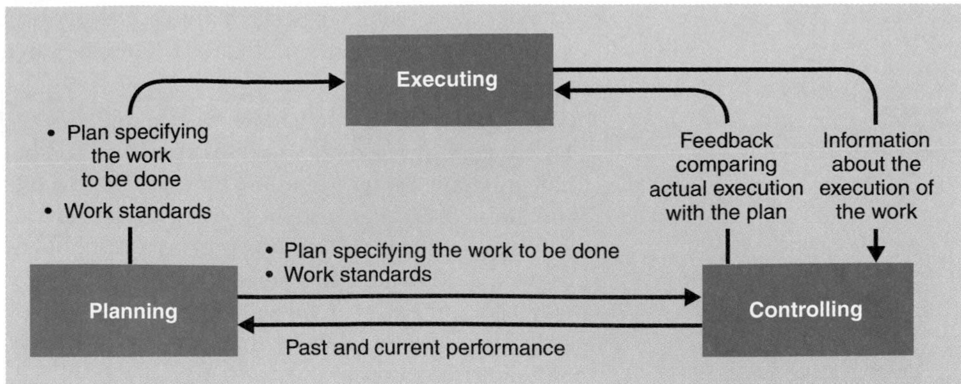

Execution can be improved by focusing information systems on execution per se, rather than mostly on planning or control activities. The emergence of powerful interactive computing makes this much more feasible today than it was even ten years ago, although its practicality depends on the nature of the work. Information-intensive processes such as designing a product or creating customer bills focus on information and require some type of information system. In contrast, information systems are less central for processes such as making a violin or training people to work effectively with peers.

Control processes can be improved in a number of ways using information systems, such as by making the collection of control data an automatic by-product of doing the work. Beyond combining data collection with work tasks, it is also possible to integrate control activities into the work itself. For example, instead of having a historically oriented control system that tells what went wrong lost week or last month, it is sometimes possible to use information systems to provide immediate feedback to the people doing the work.

Table 3.4 shows how information requirements for planning, execution, and control are different. Planning is about the future, whereas execution is about the present and control is about learning from the past. The differences in information requirements for these activities explain why some information systems are not helpful for particular decisions. The information system supporting a business process may be useful for control decisions but ineffective for execution or planning decisions. For example, an information system for

TABLE 3.4 **Comparison of Planning, Execution, and Control**

Step in the cycle	Time focus	Important issues related to information
Planning	Future	• Having reliable methods of projecting into the future by combining models, assumptions, and data about the past and present
Execution	Present	• Providing information that tells people what to do now to meet the plan and adjust for any problems that have occurred recently • Using current information to identify problems or errors in current work • Collecting information without getting in the way of doing the work
Control	Past	• Having reliable methods of using data about the past to develop or adjust plans, and to motivate employees • Provide information current enough that it can be used to guide current actions

managers may summarize last month's sales performance effectively but still not address crucial questions about how to proceed into new markets.

Treatment of Exceptions, Errors, and Malfunctions

Discussions of business processes often focus on how they are supposed to work in typical situations rather than how they should respond when an error, exception, or malfunction occurs. Because these things happen in all real business processes, part of the process architecture is the way the process should respond to these conditions. Focusing on what to do about likely errors, exceptions, and malfunctions is especially important when computers are involved because computerized business processes are often more structured and less flexible than manual processes and therefore have more difficulty handling exceptions.

As an example consider an order processing system built under the assumption that incomplete orders cannot be processed and that a complete order includes the customer's shipping address. What if the customer wants to order a product that takes a long time to build but has not decided where it should be shipped? Should the order be accepted without the shipping address? Regardless of the system developer's original intention, many real world order takers would treat this as an exception and would try to trick the information system by entering a "temporary" shipping address so that the computer system would accept the order. The fact that the shipping address was actually a workaround would probably be long forgotten by the time the material was ready to ship, perhaps to a fictitious location.

The approach for handling exceptions, errors, and malfunctions in any situation is a tradeoff between wasting time and resources by being unsystematic versus diverting energy away from the work system's major goals through excessive formalization of exception handling. Consider the question of how an accounts receivable process should handle adjustments to customer bills for reasons such as incorrect shipments, incorrect bills, and unsatisfactory merchandise. A highly informal process might give inconsistent responses to similar situations and would not accumulate useful information about the reasons for adjustments. An overly formalized process might have so many categories and cross checks that it would become a bottleneck in the process.

Inadequacies of Safety Systems

Unfortunately, subsystems for detecting and correcting errors are just as prone to errors as any other part of a work system. Chapter 2 mentioned an example well known to software developers, namely, a bug in the software that reset Therac-25 x-ray machines when the operator tried to correct an incorrectly entered setting. Several patients received fatal doses of radiation because of this bug.[17] More recently, the safety systems in a Lufthansa Airbus 320 caused a crash landing in Warsaw. The airplane had received faulty wind-speed information and came in too fast, creating a lift that lightened the load on the landing gear. The flight control software concluded the plane was not on the ground and prevented the jets from braking the aircraft by reversing thrust. The resulting crash killed two people and injured 45.[18]

Although automation-related malfunctions such as these are often dramatic, inattention and carelessness by human participants is probably a far more significant factor in the failure of safety systems. On an everyday level, look at the number of people who don't wear automobile seat belts or bicycle helmets. The National Transportation Safety Board says that 68% of people in cars use seat belts. Increasing that to 85% would save 4,200 deaths per year and $7 billion in medical and other costs, yet 36 states that require seat belt use explicitly forbid the police to stop drivers because they or their front seat passengers are not wearing one.[19] At a professional level, think of the many times you have read newspaper accounts of managers and other business professionals ignoring safety guidelines for investments or employee safety. The Chernobyl meltdown occurred when operators broke many essential safety rules, including the one about not shutting down the safety system. The fact that most safety systems seem to work most of the time is reassuring, but examples such as these show that procedures for handling exceptions, errors, and malfunctions are an important part of any work system that involves substantial resources or risks.

Reality Check

ARCHITECTURAL CHARACTERISTICS

The text has discussed seven architectural characteristics of business processes and has explained how these are related to choices about information systems.

1. Think about a business process with which you are familiar, such as registering for classes, borrowing books from a library, or voting in an election. Based on your personal experience, describe that business process in terms of the seven characteristics.
2. Explain differences in the process if each characteristic were increased or decreased.

EVALUATING BUSINESS PROCESS PERFORMANCE

We have now seen how to describe a business process in detail through process modeling and how to summarize its operation in terms of seven architectural characteristics. Concepts for evaluating process performance are the next part of the picture. We will focus on six of many possible performance variables that can be used.

Tables 3.5 and 3.6 illustrate the need to look at each of these six ideas separately. Table 3.5 shows that each performance variable involves genuine choices, with too much often as bad as too little along any of the dimensions. Business process participants and managers should be involved in designing and evaluating information systems because they have the most direct insight about the advantages and disadvantages of different levels of process performance. Table 3.6 lists common performance measures for each process performance variable and identifies some of the ways information systems can be used to improve performance in regard to that variable. Looking at each variable in turn helps in understanding most information system applications.

Rate of Output

The **rate of output** for a business process is the amount of output it actually produces in a given time period. Like other performance variables, rate of output is determined by a

TABLE 3.5 Finding the Right Level for Each Process Performance Variable

Process performance variable	Problem if the level is too high	Problem if the level is too low
Rate of output	• Lower productivity and consistency due to increasing rates of errors and rework	• Lower productivity due to the cost of unused capacity
Productivity	• Too much emphasis on cost per unit and too little emphasis on quality of the output	• Output unnecessarily expensive to produce
Consistency	• Inflexibility, making it difficult to produce what the customer wants	• Too much variability in the output, reducing quality perceived by the customer
Cycle time	• Lack of responsiveness to customer • Excess costs and waste due to delays	• Product produced too soon is damaged or compromised before the customer needs it • Delivery before the customer is ready
Flexibility	• Too much variability in the output, reducing quality perceived by the customer	• Inflexibility, making it difficult to produce what the customer wants or to modify the process over time
Security	• Excess attention to security gets in the way of doing work	• Insufficient attention to security permits security breaches

TABLE 3.6 Process Performance Variables and Related Roles of Information Systems

Process performance variable	Typical measures	Common information system role
Rate of output	• Average units per hour or week • Peak load units per hour or week	• Increase rate of output by performing some of the work automatically • Increase rate of output by systematizing the work
Productivity	• Output per labor hour or machine hour • Ratio of outputs to inputs (in dollars) • Scrap rate • Cost of rework	• Help people produce more output with the same effort • Automate data processing functions people perform inefficiently • Systematize work to reduce waste • Schedule work to improve resource utilization
Consistency	• Defect rate • Percentage variation • Rework rate	• Systematize work to reduce variability of the product • Provide immediate feedback to identify and correct errors • Help process participants analyze the causes of defects
Cycle time	• Elapsed time from start to finish • Total work-in-process inventory divided by weekly output (a useful approximation in some situations)	• Perform data processing work more quickly • Make it possible to combine steps, thereby eliminating delays • Make it possible to perform steps in parallel, thereby eliminating delays • Systematize work to reduce waste
Flexibility	• Number of possible product variations • Ease of customizing to customer specifications	• Systematize the form and content of product specifications to make it easier to handle variations • Make it possible to control the process based on specifications that can be entered through a computer
Security	• Number of process breaches in a time interval • Seriousness of process breaches in a time interval	• Systematize recordkeeping about the business process • Systematize recordkeeping about computer access and usage • Track all nonstandard transactions such as changes to completed transactions

combination of the way the business process is designed, the preparation and enthusiasm of the participants, the quality of the available information, and the operation of the technology. Rate of output differs from **capacity,** which is the theoretical limit of the output a system can produce in a given time period. When the stock market plunged temporarily on Oct. 27, 1997, the stock trading capacity of the NASDAQ exchange was around two billion shares per day and it actually traded 1.37 billion shares of stock without major problems. NASDAQ officials decided to double capacity within 18 months to be sure the exchange could keep up with expected volume increases.[20]

Variability in the rate of output is an important issue in designing business processes and in controlling how they operate. Most processes operate at maximum efficiency when they produce the same type of output at a consistent rate. In contrast, the demand for output varies in many situations. Information systems can reduce the related inefficiencies in a number of ways. They can be used to help smooth demand by increasing the cost borne by the customer as demand increases. This is how some electric utilities charge more for electricity during the day in order to shift demand toward low usage times at night. They can also be used to minimize the impact of demand variations by smoothing flows between intermediate steps in production.

Establishing an appropriate capacity and rate of output for a business process is a challenge because excess capacity is also a problem. Every unit of excess capacity typically has some monetary cost. In addition, excess capacity often permits sloppiness in the system, as was demonstrated repeatedly when downsized companies increased output and responsiveness to customers despite cutting layers of management and other staff. Similar effects apply when the excess capacity involves equipment or inventory. For example, a major advantage of minimizing the amount of the idle inventory sitting in warehouses or on factory floors is that nonexistent inventory cannot be broken, lost, stolen, or obsoleted. Minimizing inventory buffers also helps in identifying production problems, which become apparent quickly because they cannot hide behind excess inventory.

An important related characteristic of both business processes and the information systems that support them is **scalability,** the ability to significantly increase or decrease capacity without major disruption or excessive costs. The least scalable processes involve huge capital outlays for individual units of production, such as power plants or airports. Increased scalability is one of the important benefits of the client-server computer architectures explained in Chapter 8.

Consistency

Consistency in a business process means applying the same techniques in the same way to obtain the same desired results. Because one of the TQM movement's main tenets is that unwarranted variation destroys quality, TQM calls for careful specification of exactly how a process should be performed and careful monitoring to insure that it is being performed consistent with those specifications.

One of the main benefits of some information systems is that they force the organization to do things consistently. For example, companies in the air freight business such as Federal Express and United Parcel Service do very detailed tracking of each package as it passes each step. Part of the value of this tracking is that it enforces consistency in the way work is done. System participants know that if they deviate from the rules in their handling of a package, the information system will be able to show it was handled in a proper way until it got to them.

Other information systems are designed to provide information that helps people perform business processes in a consistent manner. Figure 3.10 shows a control chart, a device used widely to monitor business process consistency. The control chart graphs a process measurement such as the average width of a sample of machined parts or the average length of time customers had to wait on hold. The process is considered "in control" if it stays within limits, has expected variability, and has no trend toward going out of limits. The pattern of measurements over time helps in identifying problems before they have significant impacts on quality or productivity.

Productivity

Productivity is the relationship between the amount of output produced by a business process and the amount of money, time, and effort it consumes. As a firm's overall productivity

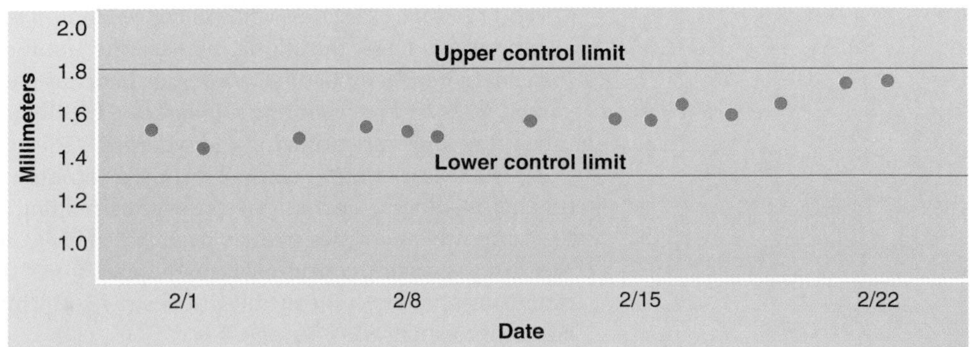

Figure 3.10
Control chart for monitoring consistency of a business process

This control chart shows data for a manufacturing process that is going out of control even though it has not yet exceeded a control limit. Machine operators looking at this control chart should stop the process and fix it before the output of their production step must be scrapped or reworked.

improves, it can make a profit at lower selling prices. Business process productivity can be improved by changing the process to produce more output from the same level of inputs or to produce the same output from lower levels of inputs. One approach to improving productivity is to increase the rate of work, thereby reducing the labor time and inventory costs related to a particular level of output.

Eliminating waste and rework is another approach to improving productivity, and it is surprisingly important. Quality experts often estimate that 20% to 30% of costs are actually just **waste,** which can be defined as any activity that uses resources without adding value. Taaichi Ohno, a Toyota executive who was a pioneer in lean production methods, identified seven causes of waste:

1. defects in products
2. overproduction of goods not needed
3. inventories of goods awaiting further processing or consumption
4. unnecessary processing
5. unnecessary movement of people
6. unnecessary transport of goods
7. time spent waiting for process equipment to finish its work, or for an upstream activity[21]

Looking at a list like this sometimes helps people realize that waste is built into the way many processes operate. This was certainly the case for the Ford example at the beginning of the chapter. Built-in waste is also present when the steps that customize a product to the requirements of different customers are performed too early in the process. At minimum, the customized units will remain in inventory longer. At worst, demand will change and unnecessarily customized units will have to be scrapped or reworked.

Most early computerized information systems supported productivity improvement by collecting detailed information and summarizing what happened yesterday, last week, or last month. More recently, information systems have attempted to increase productivity by supporting automation and by providing interactive tools used directly by professionals in their work.

Perhaps surprisingly, there is substantial question about whether information technology investments actually increase productivity. Looking at just computers, statistical studies relating computer investments to company performance have found little discernible impact on aggregate productivity, although recent research has started to find more positive results.[22, 23] Part of the question here is that computer investments involve many costs beyond the purchase price. For example, think of the total cost of a personal computer during the first year you own it. This includes the purchase price plus costs related to deciding what computer to buy, going to the store and buying the computer, installing it, buying software, and getting training on how to use it. In businesses, hidden or unobserved costs related to support, training, facilities, maintenance, administration, and time spent by end users doing programming can push total spending over $10,000 per PC according to many studies.

Computers can also reduce productivity by tempting people to waste time making endless refinements in documents and spreadsheets. For example, a study of Internal Revenue Service examiners who were given laptop computers found that they performed examinations faster but didn't increase the number of examinations they performed. Instead they spent more time writing aesthetically pleasing reports and sometimes playing games. A survey by accounting software maker SBT Corp. asked customers to estimate how much time they spent "futzing with your PC." They came up with 5.1 hours a week doing things such as waiting for computer runs, printouts, or help, checking and formatting documents, loading and learning new programs, helping coworkers, organizing and erasing old files, and other activities such as playing games.[24] Citing this estimate, a consultant with McKinsey, a leading consulting firm, quipped that if the estimate is correct, personal computers may have become the biggest destroyer of white-collar productivity since the management meeting was invented.[25]

Cycle Time

It is easy to say time is a scarce resource, but many business processes operate as though time barely matters. For example, in conventional batch manufacturing the time during which value is actually being added usually constitutes less than 5% of total manufacturing cycle time. Over 95% of the time, the product is either sitting in batches awaiting processing or being moved to another work center.[26] Delays of this type can be just as important in information-based processes, such as the processing of insurance or loan applications. Consider what happened with IBM Credit, which provides customers with financing for IBM products.

Before a reengineering project, the process for analyzing equipment loan requests and responding to the customer averaged six days and sometimes took up to two weeks. Salespeople hated the delays because this gave the customers six extra days to change their minds. When two managers walked a financing request through the steps while asking people to do the work immediately, they were amazed to find the actual work took only 90 minutes. During most of the six days, the requests simply sat on people's desks waiting for action.

The existing process operated like an assembly line. Its steps included logging the salesperson's loan request on a slip of paper, entering the request into a computerized system, checking for creditworthiness, modifying the standard loan document based on customer requests, determining the interest rate for the loan, and producing a quotation letter sent to the sales representative by overnight courier. IBM Credit moved to a case manager approach in which a single individual, the "deal structurer" in this instance, is in charge of the entire processing of a case. Instead of specializing in a small aspect of the task, the deal structurer is more of a generalist. With the new process, the deal structurer has direct access to all the standard information required, and uses discretion to call on specialists in other departments for more complex cases. The new system cut the turnaround to four hours with no staffing increase. It also increased the number of deals handled by the staff, reduced the error rate, and increased flexibility through adoption of three variations on the process to handle cases of different complexity.[27]

The use of time in a business process can be summarized as **cycle time,** the length of time between the start of the process and its completion. Cycle time is determined by a combination of the processing time for performing each step in the process, the waiting time between completing one step and starting another, and the dependencies between steps. Waiting time when no value is being added is often a major problem in back office processes such as the one at IBM Credit and in factories that produce physical goods.

Bottlenecks are another important source of delays and excessive cycle times. A **bottleneck** is an essential work step where a temporary or long term capacity shortage delays work on most of the items being produced or processed. In these situations, maximizing utilization of the bottleneck may be the key to reducing total cycle time. Information systems can help in these situations by helping people decide on the right order of work to improve flow through the bottleneck.

Self-imposed and legally imposed deadlines are another important aspect of time in business processes. Concerns about the freshness of packaged foods and pharmaceuticals leads manufacturers to stamp expiration dates on packages and remove stale product. Time is also a regulatory issue, such as the way the Securities and Exchange Commission decreed that settlement time, the time between stock or bond purchases and payment, should be reduced from five days to three days in 1995. Some observers believed conformance to this deadline would reduce the risks. Others believed the settlement deadline would simply be a bonanza for overnight delivery companies.[28]

Just drawing a picture like the one in Figure 3.11 can often help in identifying bottlenecks and unnecessary steps that expand total cycle times. In this example steps 2 and 3 can overlap in time but cannot begin until step 1 completes. In turn, step 4 cannot start until both 2 and 3 complete. Part of the analysis for reducing delays in business processes involves drawing this type of diagram and examining the processing time, waiting time, and dependencies for each step. Sometimes the delays jump out at you. For example, if step 3 is a meeting involving people from different groups, there may be a two-week delay

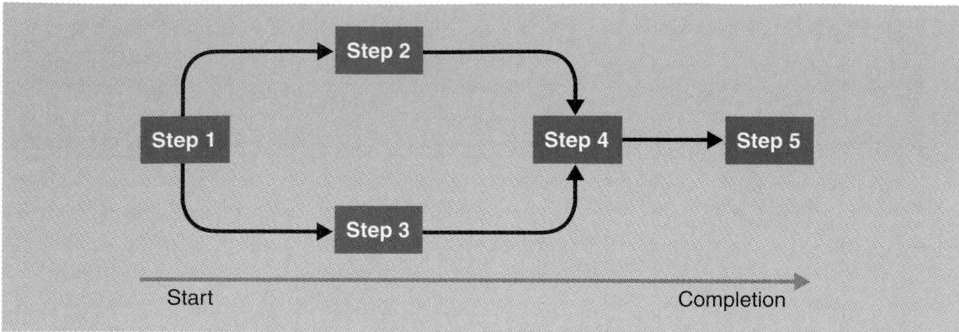

Figure 3.11
Identifying the causes of long cycle times

Five steps must occur before this process is complete. The total cycle time depends on factors including the elapsed time for each step, the amount of waiting time before each step begins, and the dependencies preventing one step from starting until several other steps are finished.

before any work on step 4 can begin. An attempt to reduce the process's cycle time would probably include an analysis of whether it is possible to eliminate the meeting, handle it by phone, or identify work that does not need to wait for the meeting to happen.

Flexibility

The **flexibility** of a business process is the ease with which it can be adjusted to meet immediate customer needs and adapted over the long term as business conditions change. The competitive advantages of flexibility are apparent: Customers prefer the product features they really want, rather than the product features suppliers think they want. It is also possible to make business processes too flexible, however. Excessive flexibility in a business process leads to chaos because process participants need reference points for keeping themselves organized and productive. In addition, flexibility can be the enemy of consistency, a performance variable discussed earlier.

There are a number of approaches for using information systems to make business processes flexible. One general principle is to avoid restricting things about the process that can be left to the judgment of the process participants. For example, don't force the participants to fill out computerized forms in a particular order unless the sequence really matters. Another principle is to delay as long as possible those choices that convert information into a physical result that is hard to change. According to this principle, installation of physical customer options should be delayed as long as possible if those options would make a customized product hard to sell to another customer. A third principle is to perform the business process using technical tools and methods that are flexible themselves. For example, use programming methods that generate programs that are comparatively easy to change. In an example of making processes flexible, Allen-Bradley built a highly automated factory that can produce 1,025 different electronic contractors and relays with zero defects in lot sizes as low as one.[29] The time from order placement to completion is one day. This type of flexibility relies on information systems to transmit orders to the factory and control the machines within the factory. (See Figure 3.12.)

Unfortunately systems can be an obstacle to flexibility and innovation. They may force people to do things a particular way, thereby creating a straitjacket that prevents them from handling exceptions well or even doing their work effectively. Consider the description by a reform-minded undersecretary of defense about what happened when the Department of Defense (DOD) wanted to buy mobile radios during the Persian Gulf War. The best available radio was a commercial product from Motorola, but DOD rules required the contractor to have a DOD-approved system in place for justifying the selling price. Motorola did not have such a system and DOD would not change its rules, even in time of war. The situation was resolved when Japan bought the radios and donated them to the United States.[30]

The time and effort required to change large information systems might also generate costs and delays that hinder process innovation. This problem is especially important when information systems related to production, sales, and finance are poorly designed and maintained. These systems do not age gracefully and often become very difficult to upgrade as business requirements change. Such systems are an obstacle to innovation because they make it much harder to implement innovative ideas.

Figure 3.12
Automation versus flexibility

A high degree of automation does not necessarily imply a high degree of flexibility. This highly automated frame welding process in a Range Rover factory in England is not designed to be as flexible as the Allen-Bradley production process mentioned on the previous page.

Security

The **security** of a business process is the likelihood that it is not vulnerable to unauthorized uses, sabotage, or criminal activity. Although companies avoid discussing security issues publicly, a number of security problems are well known. One of these involves telephone fraud, in which someone steals another person's telephone credit card number and then uses it illegally. In another form of telephone fraud, the criminal penetrates a company's internal telephone system and then uses it to make outgoing calls. Telephone fraud costs at least several billion dollars per year.

The security of a business process depends on procedures that insure accuracy and prevent unauthorized access. (See Figure 3.13.) Although preventing unauthorized access to computerized systems is obviously essential, even systems with adequate control over computer access may have insufficient controls over clerical procedures that surround the system. While accuracy is also obviously important, many systems contain insufficient methods for checking the accuracy of input data, identifying errors in the data in the system, and correcting those errors.

Information systems can improve security or can weaken it. They improve security when they contain effective safeguards against unauthorized access and use. They weaken security when they remove control from people and lead the people in the system to become complacent about security concerns and "trust the computer." Chapter 13 will discuss both the problems and the safeguards in some detail.

Vigilance of the participants is perhaps the most general characteristic leading to system security. Many system- and organization-related disasters prove the point. In 1987 a Pacific Southwest Airlines jet crashed because a recently fired employee brought a gun onto the airplane and shot the pilot and co-pilot. Unaware that he had been fired, airport security personnel had waved him past the security checkpoints even though regulations required that he show an ID card. Even security agencies can show insufficient vigilance. In 1994 the director of the U.S. Central Intelligence Agency (CIA) issued a scalding assessment of the failure to catch Aldrich Ames, a spy whose actions in exchange for more than $2 million between 1985 to 1994 had destroyed the CIA's network of spies inside the Soviet Union and caused the deaths of 10 double agents. Though the CIA knew Ames was an alcoholic who repeatedly flouted its rules, it promoted him to run the counterintelligence branch within the Soviet division. The

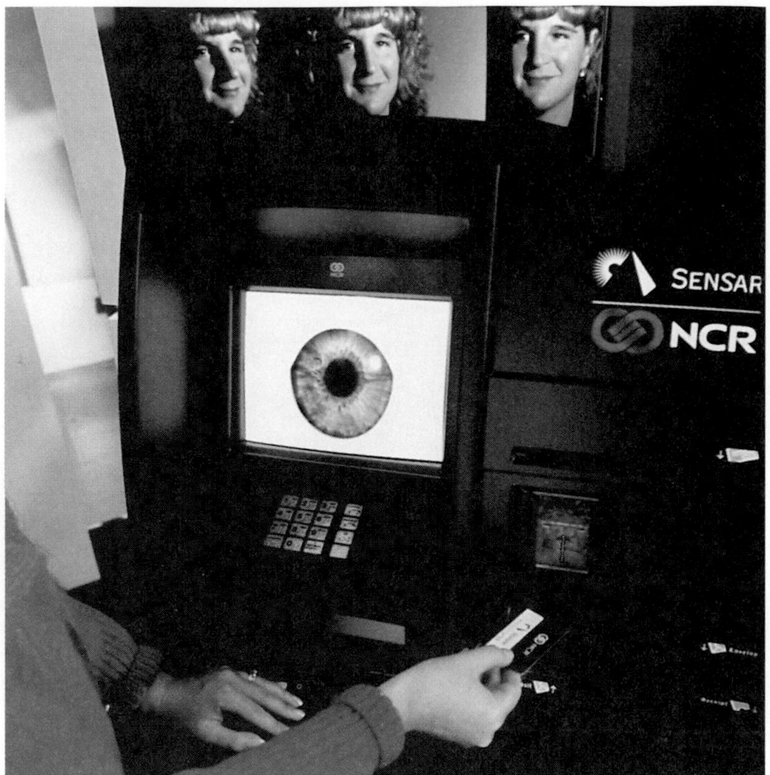

Figure 3.13
Using an eye scanner for controlling access

This eye scanner identifies people using the features of the iris of the eye.

CIA director said the inattention of senior officials was almost universal and went on for years. "One could almost conclude not only that no one was watching, but that no one cared."[31]

Reality Check

EVALUATING PROCESS PERFORMANCE

This section has discussed a number of variables used to evaluate process performance.

1. Consider the business process you selected earlier. Identify the process performance variables that seem most important and least important in this situation. Explain how you might measure those variables.
2. Assume someone actually measured each variable. Make an estimate of what the person would find currently and what the person might find if the business process were revamped to operate as well as is conceivable.

IS MANAGEMENT A BUSINESS PROCESS?

Thus far we have emphasized business processes that have a clear beginning and end and that use specific resources to produce specific outputs. We close this chapter by asking whether management, which is clearly an important activity, should also be characterized as a business process. We will see there is no general answer, even though some management activities are sufficiently systematized that they can be considered processes. Whether and how information systems can support management work in any particular situation depends on how this work is being done.

What Do Managers Do?

Different managers have very different types of responsibilities. First-line managers are deeply involved in the technical details of how work is done. Higher-level managers are more concerned with making an entire organization operate effectively. Top managers are also concerned with developing and instilling a long-range vision of where the organization is going. Most introductory management texts start discussing what managers do by identifying the classical management functions, such as planning, organizing, leading, and controlling. After identifying these functions, many texts point out that these functions do not adequately describe what managers actually do.

In an attempt to characterize what managers do, Mintzberg spent a week observing each of five CEOs. Although CEOs have broader jobs than most managers and although this research was done over 20 years ago, the resulting characterization of managerial work[32] is still used frequently.

Figure 3.14 identifies Mintzberg's list of managerial roles along with the types of formal information systems that support these roles. The roles are grouped into three categories: interpersonal, informational, and decisional. Even though the mix of roles would differ greatly between the CEO of General Motors and a branch accounting manager, most managers perform most of these roles to some extent. For example, as part of organizing a department, a manager could play interpersonal roles such as figurehead for the organizational effort, leader for meetings, and liaison to other departments. Informational roles in the process could include monitoring activities, disseminating the principles behind the new organization, and serving as organizational spokesperson. Decisional roles could include the entrepreneur defining the new goals, the negotiator resolving conflicts, and the disturbance handler.

The figure shows that different types of information systems support the different management roles. The relevance of communication systems to all of the management roles illustrates an important point about the nature of management. Management is a highly interactive job. As Mintzberg learned, typical managers spend little time doing detailed analytical work. To the contrary, brevity, variety, and fragmentation characterize managerial work. Many managers prefer verbal media rather than written media and work through their network of personal contacts.

If brevity, variety, fragmentation, verbal media, and working through personal contacts characterize managerial work, the information managers use must be consistent with this work style. Therefore, it is not surprising that much of the information managers use does *not* come from formalized information processing systems. Rather, managers get their information from their network of contacts inside and outside the organization and gather information related to particular issues or problems of current importance. They also get information from being present in an organization and observing what is happening, or from "management by walking around."[33] The discussion of information in the next chapter will summarize these ideas by pointing out that management information includes not only "objective" data generated by formal systems, but also information meant to be persuasive, such as suggestions, warnings, and detailed proposals.

Figure 3.14
Information systems related to Mintzberg's management roles

Different types of information systems support different types of management roles.

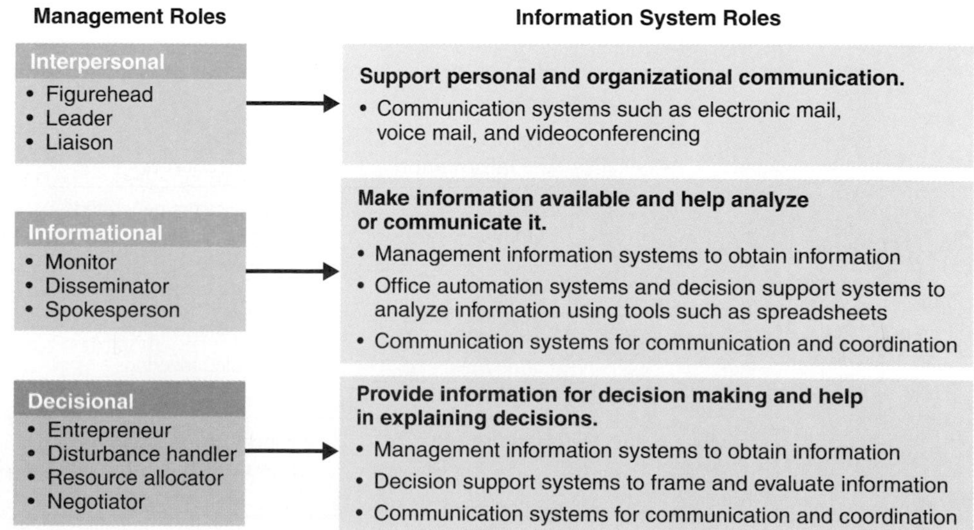

Management Roles
Information System Roles
Interpersonal
• Figurehead
• Leader
• Liaison
Support personal and organizational communication.
• Communication systems such as electronic mail, voice mail, and videoconferencing
Informational
• Monitor
• Disseminator
• Spokesperson
Make information available and help analyze or communicate it.
• Management information systems to obtain information
• Office automation systems and decision support systems to analyze information using tools such as spreadsheets
• Communication systems for communication and coordination
Decisional
• Entrepreneur
• Disturbance handler
• Resource allocator
• Negotiator
Provide information for decision making and help in explaining decisions.
• Management information systems to obtain information
• Decision support systems to frame and evaluate information
• Communication systems for communication and coordination

What Types of Information Do Managers Need?

Table 3.7 extends this theme by summarizing common sources of management information and categorizing them as formal or informal and internal or external. Formal information may come from computer-based data processing systems, written documents, or scheduled meetings. Informal information comes from a range of sources such as lunchtime gossip, trade shows, and what managers learn while walking around.

Recognizing this range of information sources helps clarify the managerial uses of formal information systems. Formal information systems contain much essential management information and much more information that could be very useful if it could be accessed effectively. However, these systems can provide managers with only part of the information they need. The high degree of variety and action in managerial work implies that information systems used by managers should be flexible and easy to use. Because managers often deal with exceptions and nonroutine situations, the particular information they need tomorrow may not be the same as the information they need today. If a formal information system does not readily support tomorrow's needs, an action-oriented manager will simply bypass it and find some other source of information.

Is Management Really a Process?

Whether or not ideas about processes can be used to describe management activities in any particular situation depends on what the organization needs and its managers want. Informal management styles often succeed if the organization is small and personalized enough that it is easy to see what is happening just by being present and talking to people. Even with informal systems for managing people, however, these organizations still need formal systems to track essential business information, such as what has been ordered and what customers owe. In contrast, as organizations grow and become geographically dispersed, formal management processes become more important.

The need to create formal management processes is apparent in the rationale of an information system used by Mrs. Fields Cookies, which created carefully defined methods for performing management tasks such as scheduling employees and deciding what to produce on a given day. As it grew from a single store to over 600 stores within a decade, it faced the problem of training and motivating relatively inexperienced store managers to use the standards and procedures that Mrs. Debbi Fields developed when she operated her first store in California. Years of experimentation and development work led to a unique information system used to systematize repetitive management activities while encouraging store personnel to focus on pleasing customers rather than doing paperwork. Each store manager starts the day using a computer program called a "Day Planner," which uses the store's history for similar days to suggest how many batches

TABLE 3.7 **Common Sources of Management Information**

Character of the information	Internal sources	External sources
Formal, computer-based	Key indicators generated by internal tracking systems	Public databases
Formal, document-based	Planning reports, internal audits	Industry reports, books, magazines
Formal, verbal	Scheduled meetings	Industry forums
Informal	Lunch conversations, gossip, management-by-walking-around	Trade shows, personal contacts

of what type of cookies to bake at what times during the day. At the end of each hour the cash register automatically transmits to the central computer the details of every sale that has occurred. A computer program uses this information to revise earlier projections. If sales are unexpectedly slow, the information system might suggest that someone stand outside the store and give away samples. Aside from systematizing selected store management activities, the Mrs. Fields system permits headquarters to monitor and control day-to-day operations at each store, thereby supporting central management as well as store management.

Reality Check

SUPPORTING MANAGEMENT

The text identifies different roles of managers, identifies how different types of information systems can support management work, and explains that management can be done with varying degrees of formality.

1. Identify several situations you have encountered personally in which management was important, such as in jobs, in clubs, or in group projects. What types of information were used to support management in these situations?
2. For each situation explain the extent to which that information was used in a formal management process and the alternatives for making the process more or less formal.

CHAPTER CONCLUSION

Summary

What is the role of data flow diagrams in process modeling?

Process modeling is a method of defining business process architecture by identifying major processes and dividing them into linked subprocesses. Data flow diagrams (DFDs) represent the flows of data between different processes in a business. They provide a simple, intuitive method for describing business processes without focusing on the details of computer systems. DFDs make it possible to look at business processes at any level of detail by breaking them down into successively finer subprocesses. The four symbols used in DFDs are the process, data flow, data store, and external entity.

What architectural characteristics can be used to describe system design choices impacting business process success?

Seven characteristics determined by system design include degree of structure, range of involvement, level of integration, complexity, degree of reliance on machines, attention to planning, execution, and control, and the treatment of exceptions, errors, and malfunctions.

What is the difference between structured, semistructured, and unstructured tasks?

The degree of structure of a task or a business process is the degree of predetermined correspondence between its inputs and its outputs. A totally structured task is so well understood that it is possible to say exactly how to perform it and how to evaluate whether it has been performed well. In a semistructured task, the information requirements and procedures are generally known, although some aspects of the task still rely on the judgment of the person doing the task. An unstructured task is so poorly understood that the information to be used, the method of using the information, and the criteria for deciding whether the task is being done well cannot be specified.

What are the five possible levels of integration of business processes?
Integration is mutual responsiveness and collaboration between distinct activities or processes. The five levels of integration include common culture, common standards, information sharing, coordination, and collaboration.

Why are planning and control important elements of many business processes?
Participants in a business process need to know what to do, when to do it, and how to make sure the work was done properly. Planning is the process of deciding what work to do and what outputs to produce when. Executing is the process of doing the work. Controlling is the process of using information about past work performance to assure that goals are attained and plans carried out. Planning and control activities provide the direction and coordination needed to attain the objectives of an entire organization or any of its business processes.

In what ways do information systems support the various management roles?
Management roles can be grouped into three categories: interpersonal, informational, and decisional. For interpersonal roles, information systems support personal and interpersonal communication. For informational roles, information systems make information available and help in analyzing it or communicating it. For decisional roles, information systems provide information for decision making and help in explaining decisions.

Key Terms

business process reengineering
process modeling
data flow diagram (DFD)
context diagram
flowchart
structured English
degree of structure
structured task
semistructured task
unstructured task
range of involvement
case manager approach
integration
common culture
common standards
information sharing
coordination
collaboration
complexity
planning
executing
controlling
rate of output
capacity
scalability
consistency
productivity
waste
cycle time
bottleneck
flexibility
security

Review Questions

1. What is process modeling?
2. What four symbols comprise a DFD, and what does each symbol represent?
3. What is a context diagram?
4. Why is it important to describe business processes at different levels of detail?
5. Why would a user of DFDs ever want to see information expressed in flowcharts or structured English?
6. Describe differences between structured, semistructured, and unstructured tasks.
7. How is the case manager approach related to range of involvement?
8. Define each of the five levels of integration.
9. What kinds of problems sometimes result from tight integration?
10. Will information sharing always result in coordination or collaboration between business processes?
11. In what ways can planning, execution, and control be improved?
12. Why is it important to discuss treatment of exceptions, errors, and malfunctions as part of the analysis of a business process?
13. Define each of the process performance variables. Describe how an information system can improve performance relative to each of them.
14. Identify some of the common forms of waste in business processes.
15. How can information systems support the various roles of managers?
16. Under what circumstances do formal management processes become more important?

Discussion Topics

1. General Electric once had 34 different payroll systems but reduced that number to one by 1994. It went from five financial processing centers to one. These moves allowed it to cut finance operation payroll by 40% and from 1,000 to 600 people over a decade.[34] Explain whether these productivity-related changes could raise any ethical issues for General Electric.
2. Federal Express charges incurred by the New York office of a financial services firm soared during a three-month period. People in the firm had discovered that sending a memo or file from the thirteenth floor to the fifth was slower using the company's interoffice mail system than using Federal Express. With the faster option, Federal Express picked up the package, transported it to Memphis, Tennessee, sorted it, and sent it back to the same building for delivery.[35] How is this example related to ideas in this chapter?
3. Great Western Bank in Chatsworth, California, started using a computerized 20-minute job interview in which the interviewee performs tasks ranging from making change to responding via microphone to video clips involving tense customer service situations. Bank managers say the system helps weed out the four out of ten candidates who would be a waste of time to interview in person. Some weary job hunters find that being interviewed by a computer is even more depersonalizing than a normal job interview.[36] Explain your view of the tradeoff, if any, between productivity issues and ethical issues in this situation.
4. Assume you are a manager in a company where a computerized calendar system has been installed. The system requires that you specify the times you are available for meetings, thereby making it possible for people you work with to set up a meeting without a lot of phone calls and delays. Explain why this increase in integration may affect you personally in some positive ways and some negative ways.
5. Consider the following claim: "Most information systems seem to be designed specifically to structure work and to eliminate judgment on the part of workers." Cite examples and explain whether you believe this claim about the purpose of most information systems is true. Explain the circumstances under which you believe it is best to structure work even if that reduces workers' ability to exercise judgment.

AUCNET: Auctioning Used Cars Electronically in Japan

Although www.aucnet.com is an online website for used car auctions in the United States, a version of AUCNET was created by a used car dealer in Japan in 1985 long before the Web existed. Due to complications in inspection and licensing, car owners wanting to sell used cars in Japan typically sell them to car dealers rather than to individuals. New car dealers typically do not sell used cars to customers, and therefore sell them to used car dealers. Auctions provide an efficient way to perform these sales.

Traditional used car auctions required the seller to transport the car to the auction site. The buyers went to the auction site, inspected the cars, and then bid for them. A buyer who wanted to buy only several cars might have to spend a day at the auction. Sellers whose cars did not sell because no bid was as high as the minimum reserve price they declared would then have to transport the unsold cars to other locations. AUCNET was designed to broaden the market and make it more convenient for both buyers and sellers. Sellers must have their cars inspected by AUCNET mechanics, who summarize their quality on a scale from 1 to 10. The cars are presented to sellers in an electronic catalog that includes a list of features and interior and exterior photos plus a specific time when the item will be sold. The auction is carried out electronically, meaning that buyers can participate without traveling and can log in only when they are actually interested in a particular car. Cars that are sold are transported from the seller's car lot to the buyer's car lot. AUCNET carved out a niche at the top end of the wholesale used car market and sold more than one million cars in its first ten years. By 1995 it was the largest of 144 used car auctions in Japan and had 4,150 dealer members.

It is commonly believed that sales prices in electronic auctions should be lower than sales prices in traditional auctions because the buyer's costs of searching for better alternatives will be lower. Contrary to this belief, prices for cars sold through AUCNET were substantially higher than prices for comparable cars sold in face-to-face used car auctions in Japan. Several reasons explain the higher prices. First, the sellers feel free to hold out for higher prices because a larger number of potential bidders might bid on their cars. Furthermore, they do not have to absorb the cost of moving the unsold car from the auction lot back to their car lot or to another auction. Instead, it can simply stay at their lot until the next auction. On the buyers' side, a slightly higher price might be acceptable because the buyers do not have to absorb the opportunity cost of traveling to the auction site and spending a day there instead of selling cars at their own lots. In 1998 U.S. dealers and wholesalers used www.aucnet.com to buy and sell 6,000 cars per month. For the same reasons as in the Japanese case, the sellers obtain a higher price than they might obtain on a physical lot.

QUESTIONS

1. Use the WCA framework to summarize the situation.
2. Compare the traditional auctions with the electronic auctions in terms of whichever business process characteristics and performance variables seem pertinent.
3. Identify products that might be sold by Internet auction to private individuals or to businesses belonging to industry associations. Explain any differences in auction operation that might result from differences between the types of customers.

Sources:

Aucnet Japan. "Welcome to Aucnet On-line," June 20, 1998 (www.aucnet.co.jp/index.html).

Cortese, Amy E. "Good-Bye to Fixed Pricing?" *Business Week*, May 4, 1998, pp. 71–84.

Lee, Ho Geun. "Do Electronic Marketplaces Lower the Price of Goods?" *Communications of the ACM*, Jan. 1998, pp. 73–80.

CASE

Chrysler and Daimler Benz: Integrating Systems in an International Merger

Even after the theme of globalization had been trumpeted for years, the merger of the German automaker Daimler Benz with the U.S. automaker Chrysler was one of the major business stories of 1998. In the press release, Chrysler Chairman Robert J. Eaton said: "Both companies have...world class brands that complement each other perfectly. We will continue to maintain the current brands and their distinct identities. What is more important for success: our companies share a common culture and mission. We are both clearly focused on serving the customer by building world class cars and trucks, we both have a reputation for innovation and quality, and we are both committed to increasing value for our shareholders. Daimler Chrysler has the most skilled and innovative workforce in the industry and we are committed to making their future as bright as the new company's. By realizing synergies and with our combined financial and strategic strengths, we will be ideally positioned in tomorrow's marketplace." The press release went on to say: "There will be immediate growth opportunities by using each other's facilities, capacities and infrastructure. Product strategies will be developed to enhance growth in mature markets as well as in Asia and other emerging markets. In 1999, the first year of merged operations, Daimler Chrysler expects to realize benefits of $1.4 billion through the exchange of components and technologies, combined purchasing power, and shared distribution logistics. These synergies do not involve plant closures or lay-offs."

Hidden behind the headlines were a number of challenges in working out the details of operating the newly merged company. Language was an obvious issue because few Americans know German even though most educated Germans know English. Corporate culture might also be an issue. Daimler produced conservative products and seemed to operate as an engineering-driven bureaucracy based on a top-down, command and control model. In contrast, Chrysler's brush with bankruptcy in the 1980s forged a culture dedicated to speedy product development, lean operations, and flashy design. Basic business practices and tenets of employee relations also differ between Germany and the United States. For example, German law requires substantial representation of labor on the board of large companies, whereas the boards of publicly traded U.S. companies primarily represent investors and management.

Important potential benefits of the merger might be delayed or even prevented by difficulties in integrating major information systems or at least sharing information effectively. Even assuming the language incompatibilities between German and American information systems could be addressed easily, the fundamental incompatibility of information system databases and operations would present significant stumbling blocks. For example, Chrysler built its cars using a set of CAD systems that were incompatible with the CAD systems Daimler used to build its cars. Moving to a single common CAD system would be a lengthy process. One observer estimated it would take five to ten years to design and implement common engineering and manufacturing systems. Similarly, inconsistencies between the supply chain systems used by the two firms could delay some of the added efficiencies of coordinated global sourcing.

QUESTIONS

1. Think about what needs to happen to attain maximum benefit from the merger. Explain how the five different levels of integration apply to key processes such as designing cars, ordering materials, building cars, and entering customer orders.
2. Identify possible measures of performance for the business processes mentioned in the previous question.

Sources:

Chrysler Corporation. "Merger Agreement Signed," Undated Press Release, May 27, 1998 (http://www.chrysler.com/daimlerchrysler/index.html).

Vlasic, Bill. "The First Global Car Colossus," *Business Week*, May 18, 1998, pp. 40–43.

Wallace, Bob, and Randy Weston. "Detroit, Autobahn Merge," *Computerworld*, May 11, 1998, p. 1.

4

Information and Databases

Study Questions

- What is the role of entity-relationship diagrams in data modeling?
- What are the different types of data, and when is each type particularly useful?
- What is the difference between a database and a database management system?
- Why is a single file often insufficient for storing the data in an information system?
- What is the difference between relational, multidimensional, and text databases?
- What are the purposes of a DBMS, and what functions does a DBMS perform?
- How is the World Wide Web different from a typical pre-structured database?
- What characteristics determine the usefulness of information?
- What is the purpose of building and using mathematical models?

Outline

Opening Case

BOEING: A DATABASE FOR PAPERLESS DESIGN

Boeing began designing its new 777 airliner by working with eight airlines for a year to obtain consensus about design issues such as the width of the fuselage, the shape of the overhead compartments, and the use of folding wing-tips so that a larger plane would fit into existing airport gates. Completing this work required Boeing to design 130,000 unique parts. By including rivets and fasteners Boeing engineers could say that the airplane they were producing would be "3 million parts flying in very close formation." The traditional approach to designing an airplane was to produce drawings for each part and assembly, manually check the drawings for compatibility and placement, build a scale model, and discover and fix the mismatches. Boeing decided to move to a paperless design process using CATIA, a mainframe-based CAD tool originally developed by the French aircraft manufacturer Dassault.

The basis of the new paperless design process was a CAD specification of the precise shape and location of every component. (See Table 4.1.) The CATIA system could use data to generate realistic pictures of individual components or combinations of adjacent components. Creating these specifications and making sure they were compatible was the principal work product of 238 engineering teams of up to 40 engineers. The data storage capacity for the system was 3.5 terabytes (trillion bytes), and the data was made available to 7,000 terminals spread around the world. Online access to the database of CAD specifications permitted an engineer working on any part to access the specifications, and hence electronic drawings, of any related part. Traditional delays in finding, copying, and moving paper drawings were eliminated.

A crucial CAD function was an electronic preassembly program called CLASH, which created flashing red zones whenever two separate components were designated to be in the same location, such as when one engineering team planned to run an electric cable through a location reserved for ductwork by another team. To test whether maintenance technicians could actually reach every location that required maintenance, the CAD team created simulated human forms that could be put into any location in the position needed to do the work. Physical mockups were constructed for some aircraft subsystems, but the CLASH program was so effective at detecting interference between parts that further mockups were not used. The completed CAD specifications were fed into computer-controlled fabrication equipment, whose error rate in a fuselage 20.33 feet in diameter was less than one part in 10,000.[1,2]

Debate Topic

There is a trend toward using CAD and linking it to computer-controlled fabrication equipment. Is this a major threat to both product designers and factory workers?

The Boeing case illustrates why maximizing the benefits of information within business processes almost always requires careful data organization and convenient access methods. The paperless design process for the Boeing 777 depended on creating a CAD specification of the precise size, location, and function of each component. In effect, this was a huge database that had to be accessible to engineers at Boeing's headquarters in Washington and to contractors and partners around the world. Operating in the background, and not even mentioned in the case above, was a group of people devoted to defining the database structure, making data access efficient, and assuring database integrity. The paperless process could not have been used without the database and without the human infrastructure that kept it operational.

Given the essential role information plays in business processes, business professionals must know how to identify the information they want, decide whether it is adequate, and explain their suggestions for improvements to programmers and system designers. If you are unable to do these things, it is less likely that you will receive the information you need to do your job well.

This chapter presents ideas that will help you describe and analyze information in an information system. Its ideas are directed at business professionals thinking about

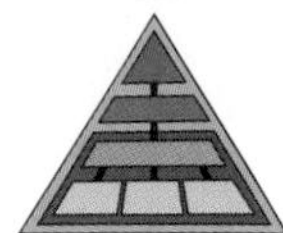

TABLE 4.1 Using a CAD System to Design the Boeing 777

CUSTOMER

- Boeing's manufacturing department
- Airline maintenance departments

PRODUCT

- Specification of the precise function, shape, and location of each component
- Verification that the components are physically compatible

BUSINESS PROCESS

Major steps:	Rationale:
• Decide on major features of airplane • Design individual components • Test for compatibility with other components and other subsystems • Transmit the specifications to manufacturing	• Use a paperless design process to avoid delays related to copying and moving paper, and to use the design data directly to test for interference between components.

PARTICIPANTS	INFORMATION	TECHNOLOGY
• Representatives of airlines • Boeing engineers	• General design goals • CAD specification of the shape, location, materials, and function of each component	• CAD database and computer for storing the data • Terminals and data network

information and computerized databases. Focusing on the architecture perspective, the first section shows a method for identifying and summarizing the information in an information system. Following a discussion of traditional databases, database management systems, and text databases, the topic changes to the performance perspective and the determinants of information usefulness. The last section looks at the role of models in turning data into information.

DATA MODELING: DOCUMENTING INFORMATION ARCHITECTURE

From a user's viewpoint, most issues about organizing and accessing information in an information system boil down to just three questions:

- What information is in the information system?
- How is the information organized?
- How can users obtain whatever information they need?

In the chapter-opening Boeing case, the information was CAD specifications for all Boeing 777 components. Information organization was not discussed in the case, but the engineers using the CAD system certainly needed to understand how the information was organized and how they could obtain what they needed.

Consistent with current system development ideas, the general discussion of these questions is introduced through **data modeling,** the process of identifying the types of entities in a situation, relationships between those entities, and the relevant attributes of those entities. Data modeling goes hand in hand with the process modeling introduced in Chapter 3. The basic tool for data modeling is called an entity-relationship diagram.

Entity-Relationship Diagrams

Assume you were designing a registration system for a university. What information should such a system contain? This question can be broken into three parts:

What kinds of things does this information system collect information about? The specific things it collects information about are **entities.** The kinds of things it collects information about are called **entity types.** In a registration system, the entity types usually include courses, professors, students, course sections, classrooms, and perhaps many others. Specific entities of each type might include Economics 101, Professor Jones, Dana Watts, the Monday night section of Economics 101, and classroom E324.

What is the relationship between these entities? The **relationship** between two entities is the way one of the entities is associated with the other. For example, a student can be enrolled in several courses, and a course section must meet in a particular classroom.

What specific information does it collect about each of those things? The specific information about the entities is called the **attributes** of the entity type. For example, attributes of the entity type "student" may include address, telephone number, and whether or not fees have been paid. The attributes of the entity type "classroom" may include its location and the number of seats it contains.

These questions are the basis of **entity-relationship diagrams (ERDs),** a technique for identifying the entity types in a situation and diagramming the relationships between those entity types. ERDs help in identifying the information in a system and making sure it is represented properly. They help create a shared understanding of the basic ideas underlying the specific information in the system. This technique forces people involved in the analysis to focus on the business situation instead of just listing every relevant item they can think of.

Figure 4.1 contains an entity-relationship diagram for part of a registration system. It uses one of several common notations for expressing the same ideas. This diagram identifies six entity types and the relationships between those entity types. For example, it says that a course may have no sections or may have one or more, and that each section has a single professor and one or more students.

The relationships in Figure 4.1 apply at some universities, but they aren't true in others. Looking at the ERD raises questions such as:

Does each professor really belong to exactly one department? Is it possible for a professor to belong to several departments or none?

Figure 4.1
Entity-relationship diagram for part of a university registration system

This entity-relationship diagram (ERD) identifies six entity types and shows relationships among them. The different types of relationships in ERDs are explained in Figure 4.2.

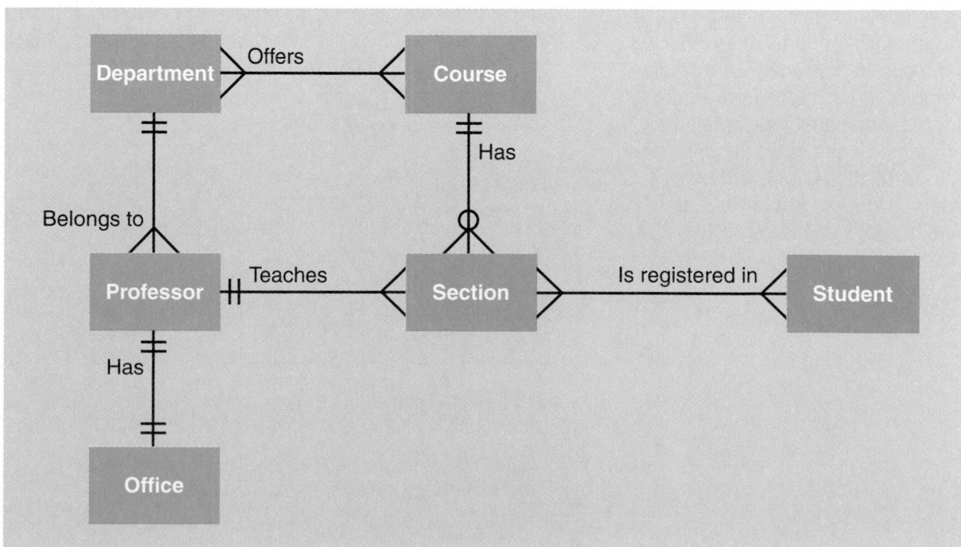

Is it possible to have several professors assigned to the same section? This would be the case for a team-taught course.

Does each section really have a professor, or is the more appropriate term "instructor," since people teaching some courses may not be professors?

Is it permissible for a course to have no sections? This would be permissible if a course in the catalogue is not offered during a particular semester, but the rules of the school would determine whether that is allowed.

Is it permissible for a section to have no students? This would certainly be true until the first student signed up for it, but a section that had no students would make no sense after the semester started.

Asking questions such as these is essential in building information systems. They help determine what information will be included and excluded, how the database will be structured, and some of the ways the system will eventually detect errors. In addition, they provide an excellent communication medium for system participants who often have trouble explaining the current and desired situation to the technical staff building the system. The term *entity-relationship diagram* sounds very technical, but these diagrams are actually used for the nontechnical purpose of identifying the types of things within the system's scope and the relationships among these types of things. (See Figure 4.2.)

Identifying the Data in Information Systems

After identifying the entity types and their relationships, it is much easier to identify the information that should be in the system. For each entity type, this information is the attributes that are significant in the situation. Table 4.2 lists some of the possible attributes that might be included in the registration system for each entity type in Figure 4.1. As the analysis of the system continued, these attributes might be renamed or modified, and many other attributes would surely be added.

Believe it or not, the innocuous looking list in Table 4.2 could create a lot of debate among the users and designers analyzing the system. Here are some possible issues:

- Is any information missing about each entity type? For example, should the system include course prerequisites or the average grades given by this professor in this course in previous years? Including the prerequisites would be necessary if the

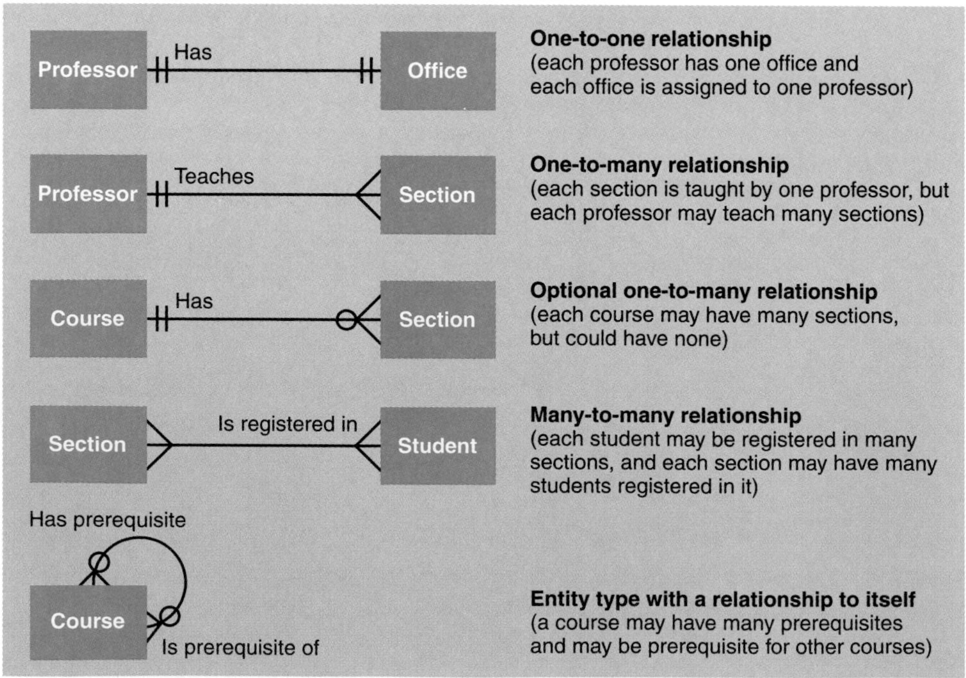

Figure 4.2
Types of relationships in entity-relationship

The ERD in Figure 4.1 includes four types of relationships: one-to-one, one-to-many, optional one-to-many, and many-to-many. Shown here are examples of each type from Figure 4.1 plus one additional type of relationship not included in that figure. Other types of relationships not shown include either-or relationships and relationships between entity types and subentity types.

TABLE 4.2 **Possible Attributes for the Entity Types in Figure 4.1**

Entity type	Possible attributes
Department	• Department identifier • College • Department head • Scheduling coordinator
Course	• Course number • Department • Required of department major (y/n) • Course description
Section	• Section identification number • Semester • Year • Classroom • Start time • End time • Days of week for class meetings
Professor	• Employee identification number • Name • Address • Birthdate • Office telephone • Social security number
Student	• Student identification number • Name • Address • Birthdate • Telephone • Gender • Ethnic group • Social security number
Office	• Office number • Building • Telephone extension

system is supposed to check automatically that the student has taken all prerequisites. Including the average grades given by the professor might help students decide which section to attend but would also raise many contentious issues.

- Are some attributes unnecessary or inappropriate? For example, do we want to use the professor or student's social security number, birthdate, gender, or ethnicity? Attributes such as these might be needed, might be extraneous, or might be improper or illegal to use or divulge.
- Is there any ambiguity in what the various attributes mean? For example, does the professor's address refer to home or office? To avoid mistakes, separate attributes might be named "office address" and "home address." Even seemingly obvious terms often have different meanings to different people. For example, the *Wall Street Journal* reported that EuroDollar, the European arm of Chrysler's Dollar Rent A Car gave one week specials but considered a week to be five days. A traveler who kept a car for seven days was surprised to receive a bill for one week plus two days.[3]
- Do the same attributes appear in two places? Notice how office telephone is an attribute of professor and telephone extension is an attribute of office. This kind of thing causes confusion for two reasons. First there are two different terms for the

same thing, and second, the information system needs to have each item in one place to make sure it is updated correctly. Telephone extension should be either as an attribute of the professor or an attribute of the office, but not both.

It would be easy to generate many more questions about the details of how things are named and what attributes of which entities should be included in the system. This type of analysis can be tedious and requires great attention to detail. Notice, however, that the main questions at this point are about how the logic of the registration process should operate, not about the details of computer technology. Answering these questions incorrectly could result in work wasted developing an information system ill-suited to the situation.

Data modeling is a comparatively new idea in building information systems. The first paper on the entity-relationship diagram was published in 1976,[4] but the need for this step is now widely accepted and has been incorporated into system development methods because it summarizes the business view of the information represented by the database.

Reality Check

DATA MODELING

We have introduced the idea of data modeling and have explained how entity relationship diagrams work.

1. Study Figure 4.1 and modify it to make it more consistent with your understanding of how your university's registration system operates. Add or remove entities and relationships as is necessary.
2. Study Table 4.2 and modify it to include other attributes you think might be important in the registration process. Include attributes of any entities you added in question #1.

USER'S VIEW OF A COMPUTERIZED DATABASE

Data modeling helps identify the definable information required by the work system. (It does not address soft information such as one-time situations, problems, exceptions, and opportunities.) The next step after data modeling is deciding how to structure the information in the computerized information system. Although users are typically shielded from much of the internal complexity of computerized databases, they need to know about types of data, logical versus physical views of data, and other topics that help them understand what information the system contains and how they can access it.

Types of Data

The five primary types of data in today's information systems include predefined data items, text, images, audio, and video. Traditional business information systems contained only predefined data items and text. More recent advances in technology have made it practical to process pictures and sounds using techniques such as digitization, voice messaging, and teleconferencing.

Predefined data items include numerical or alphabetical items whose meaning and format are specified explicitly and then used to control calculations that use the data. For example, credit card number, transaction date, purchase amount, and merchant ID are predefined data items in information systems that authorize and record credit card transactions. Most of the data in transaction-oriented business systems is of this type, and the operation of these systems is programmed based on the meaning and precise format of these data items. An extremely costly example of the importance of format is the Y2K problem mentioned in Chapter 1. This problem would have never occurred if the data item *year* had been defined as a four-digit number in all information systems.

Text is a series of letters, numbers, and other characters whose combined meaning does not depend on a prespecified format or definition of individual items. For example, word processors operate on text without relying on prespecified meanings or definitions of items in the text; rather, the meaning of text is determined by reading it and interpreting it. We will discuss text databases in a separate section later in the chapter.

Images are data in the form of pictures, which may be photographs, hand-drawn pictures, or graphs generated from numerical data. Images can be stored, modified, and transmitted in many of the same ways as text. Editing of images provides many other possibilities, however, such as changing the size of an object, changing its transparency or shading, changing its orientation on the page, and even moving it from one part of a picture to another. Figure 4.3 shows images that were produced by different types of information systems. Like text and unlike predefined data items, the meaning of an image is determined by looking at the image and interpreting it.

Audio is data in the form of sounds. Voice messages are the kind of audio data encountered most frequently in business. Other examples include the sounds a doctor hears through a stethoscope and the sounds an expert mechanic hears when working on

Figure 4.3
Images produced by information systems

Different types of information systems produced these three images. The pie chart summarizes network utilization data in an easily understood format. The MRI image of a patient's brain provides diagnostic information for a radiologist. The MRI combines multiple images into a form providing the clearest, most usable information. The satellite photograph shows crop growth and wetlands in South Florida.

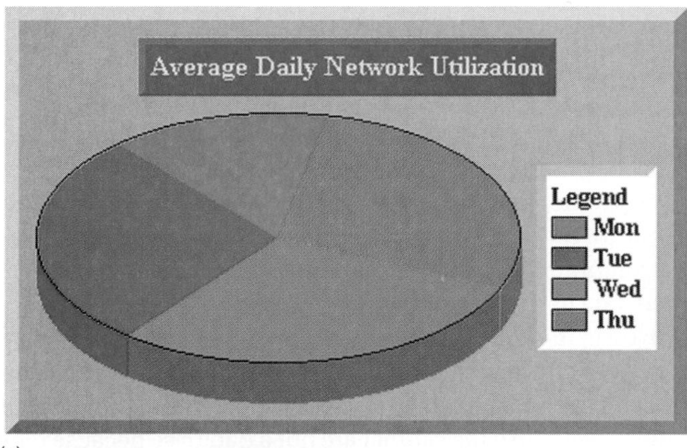

(a)

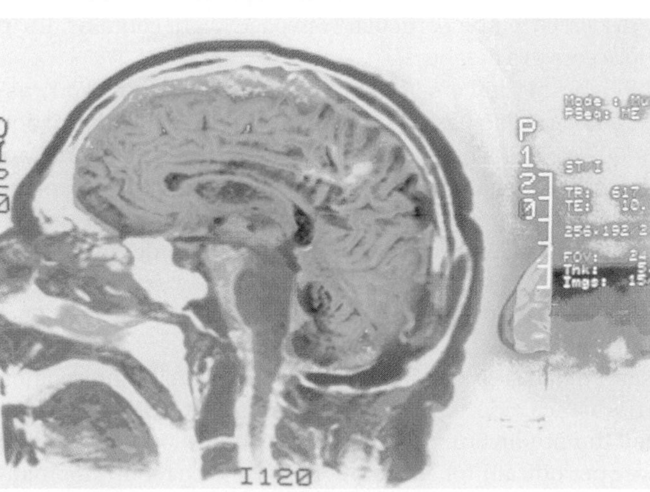

(b)

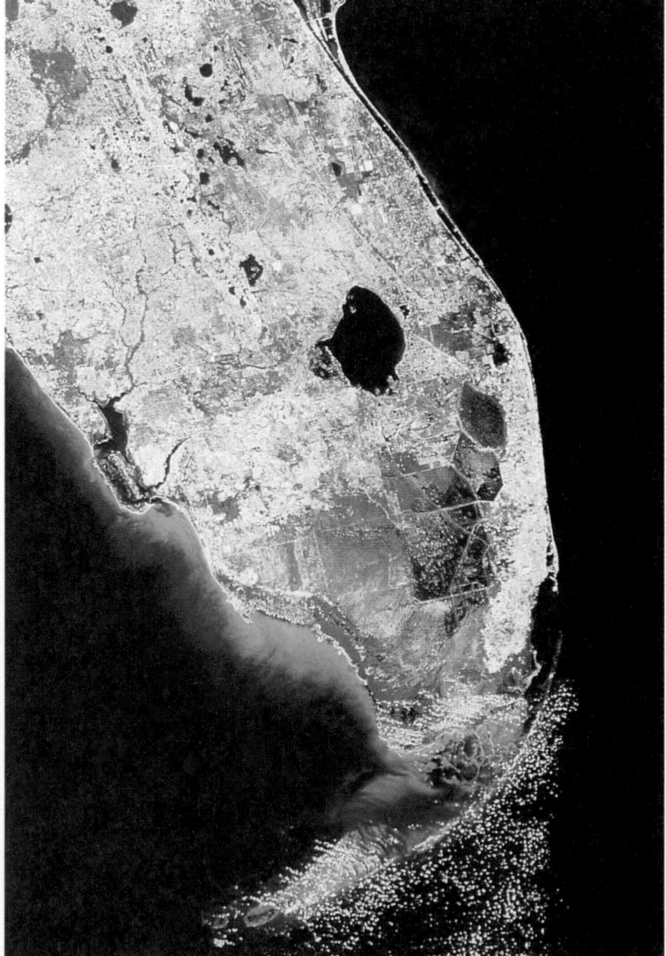

(c)

a machine. The meaning of audio data is determined by listening to the sounds and interpreting them.

Video combines pictures and sounds displayed over time. The term *video* is used here because it is becoming the catch-phrase for multiple types of data display that involve both sound and pictures, such as a videoconference. The meaning of video data is determined by viewing and listening over a length of time.

Although this book discusses these five types of data extensively, other types of data can be important in certain situations as well. For example, taste and smell are important in the restaurant and wine businesses, and the development of a fine sense of touch for robots is a key technical challenge in that area.

The five primary types of data serve different purposes and have different advantages and disadvantages. Predefined data items provide a terse, coded description of some event or object, but lack the richness of text, images, audio, or video. When Nissan truck designers commissioned a photographer to take pictures of small trucks in use as commuter and family cars, they were startled to discover how little their trucks were actually being used for the purposes being advertised and reported in market surveys. One surprise was how many people were eating in trucks, "not just drinks, but whole spaghetti dinners!" They also noticed how much people resembled their vehicles and how scuffed up some of the vehicles were, leading them to wonder whether vehicles could be more like denim and look better the more worn they became.[5]

Richer information is not necessarily better, however, and it can be worse. For example, a car dealer's accountants just want to know how much the car was sold for; they have no desire to read a story, listen to a tape, or watch a video. Predefined data items help them by reducing the sale of a car to a few facts they need to do their jobs. Such data might also be fine for a manager who needs to know whether weekly sales targets have been met. If the manager wants to understand why salespeople are having trouble meeting their goals, it might be more useful to observe their work.

What Is a Database?

The information in a computerized system is often called a database, although the term is used in many ways. For example, people sometimes refer to the World Wide Web as a text database even though the structure of the data is not defined in any independent way. This discussion of a user's view of a computerized database assumes the database consists of one or more tables of predefined data items. Text databases will be discussed separately.

Excluding text databases, we can think of a **database** as a structured collection of data items stored, controlled, and accessed through a computer based on predefined relationships between predefined types of data items related to a specific business, situation, or problem. By this definition, paper memos in a file cabinet are not a database because they are not accessed through a computer. Similarly, the entire World Wide Web is not a database of this type because it lacks predefined relationships between predefined types of data items (even though, as will be discussed later, a particular Web page might contain links to other pages and might provide access to a database).

Databases come in different forms and are used in many different ways. Work systems discussed thus far in this book use databases for storing and retrieving information needed for day-to-day operation of firms. The databases in these systems contain data about things such as inventory, orders, shipments, customers, and employees. Some of the everyday use focuses on retrieving and updating specific items of information, such as adjusting the units on hand of a product after each sale, or recording an order from a customer. Other everyday uses of databases produce summaries of current status or recent performance. Examples include a listing showing the total units on hand for each product group, or a listing showing total sales last week broken out by state.

In some situations the same database is used for both updating specific information and generating status and performance reports. In other situations, it is more practical to use one database (often called the production database) for real time updating and to generate a copy of that database periodically for status and performance reports for management. If this is done, the copy will be up to one shift or one day out of date, depending on how frequently the downloads occur, but that is usually current enough for purposes related to reporting.

Notice the difference between the term database and **database management system (DBMS).** A DBMS is an integrated set of programs used to define, update, and control databases. We are looking at databases first, and will discuss DBMS capabilities later.

Logical Versus Physical Views of Data

The basic idea about data organization in computerized information systems is that the person using the data does *not* need to know exactly where or how the data are stored in the computer. For example, a real estate agent wanting a list of all 3-bedroom apartments rented in the last two weeks should ideally be able to say, "List all 3-bedroom apartments rented in the last two weeks." Even if the information system only accepts coded questions in special formats, the user should not have to know the computer-related details of data storage.

Even most programmers do not need to know exactly where each item resides in the database. Instead, users and programmers need a model of how the database is stored. The technical workings of the computer system then translate between the model of the database and the way the database is actually handled technically. Hiding unnecessary details in this way is totally consistent with the way many things happen in everyday life. For example, people can drive a car without knowing exactly how its electrical system operates.

The terms *logical view of data* and *physical view of data* are often used to describe the difference between the way a user thinks about the data and the way computers actually handle the data. A **logical view of data** expresses the way the user or programmer thinks about the data. It is posed in terms of a **data model,** a sufficiently detailed description of the structure of the data to help the user or programmer think about the data. This data model may reveal little about exactly how or where each item of data is stored.

The technical aspects of the information system (the programming language, database management system, and operating system) then work together to convert this logical view into a **physical view of data,** that is, exactly what the machine has to do to find and retrieve the data. The physical view is stated in terms of specific locations in storage devices plus internal techniques used to find the data. Because this book is directed at business professionals rather than programmers, it emphasizes logical views of data.

Files

The file is the simplest form of data organization used in business data processing. A **file** is a set of related records. A **record** is a set of fields, each of which is related to the same thing, person, or event. A **field** is a group of characters that have a predefined meaning. A **key** is a field that uniquely identifies which person, thing, or event is described by the record. Table 4.3 illustrates the meaning of these terms. It is an excerpt from a hypothetical student file that contains one record for each student. Each record contains a set of fields, such as social security number, last name, and birthdate. Social security number is

TABLE 4.3 Excerpt from a Hypothetical Student File

Social security number	Last name	First name	Street address	City	State	ZIP code	Date of birth
044-34-5542	Bates	Alvin	243 Third St.	Middleton	MA	02137	05/07/78
434-98-8832	Chang	Brenda	87 Palm Ave.	Oakdale	MA	02143	09/30/80
888-23-9038	Schmidt	Dieter	663 Cress Way	Cresston	MA	02184	12/17/79
334-59-3087	Toliver	Gail	743 First St.	Middleton	MA	02137	07/02/78

the key field because two students will have different social security numbers even if they have the same name.

These basic terms about files correspond to the entities, relationships and attributes discussed in the previous section. The file contains data about a type of entity (student). Each record is the data for a particular entity (such as Alvin Bates). The key in the record identifies the entity. The other fields are attributes of that entity.

This example shows that a file can be seen as a table. Each row of the table corresponds to a different record. Each column represents a different field. The importance of thinking of a file as a table will become clear when the relational data model is discussed. The representation of the data in Table 4.3 shows that the fields appear in the same order and format in each record in a file. The data in the file is organized consistently. This consistency is the fundamental characteristic of computerized files and databases that makes it possible to write programs that use the data.

The order of records in a file also matters. The four records in the table are sorted by last name. Their order would have been different if they had been sorted by social security number. Sorting the data by social security number might be more appropriate for other applications, such as submitting payroll taxes. Some database management systems make it possible to maintain multiple sorts of the same data so that it can be accessed in multiple ways.

The general description of a file uses just a few terms (file, record, field, and key) that are widely applicable and easily understood. When data are in the form of a file, users or programmers can easily specify the subset of the data they need. They can select the records based on the values in individual fields. For example, they can say they want all the students who live in Oakdale or all students born before 1979. They can also identify the specific fields they want. For example, for a mailing list they can select the names and addresses, but not social security number.

Organizing data as a file works well when the information needed for the situation is limited to the attributes of a single type of entity. For example, if the business problem involved finding information about individual students, an expanded version of the student file in Table 4.3 might have been a good solution. The entity is the student (identified by social security number), and the attributes include name, address, and date of birth.

Unfortunately, organizing all the data in a situation as a single file is often impractical. The registration system example in Figure 4.1 showed why. Many situations involve data about different types of entities and therefore require use of multiple files. The highly simplified registration example identified six different entity types. If you were using a paper and pencil system to keep track of this information, you would probably organize it into six separate file folders related to each of these types of entities. You would do this because it would be easier to keep track of the data that way.

Organizing the data as totally separate files for each of the six entity types is usually inadequate, however, because the entity types are related. Otherwise there would be no reason to think of them as parts of the same system. The registration system requires combining data from different files and therefore needs to maintain links between entities of different types.

Relational Databases

The relational data model is the predominant logical view of data used in current information systems because it provides an easily understood way to combine and manipulate data in multiple files in a database. Posed in terms of this model, a **relational database** is a set of two-dimensional tables in which one or more key-fields in each table are associated with corresponding key or non-key fields in other tables. (The term "relational" comes from the fact that relational databases use the term *relation* instead of the term *file*. A **relation** is a keyed table consisting of records.)

Relational databases have the advantage of meshing with the data modeling techniques mentioned earlier. Entity-relationship diagrams provide a simple starting point for thinking about the tables in a relational database. The starting point includes a table for each entity type and for each relationship in the diagram. Figure 4.4 shows how Microsoft Access represents the entity-relationship diagram for a sample database supporting a retail

Figure 4.4
Entity-relationship diagram from a relational database

This entity-relationship diagram was generated from a sample database in Microsoft Access.

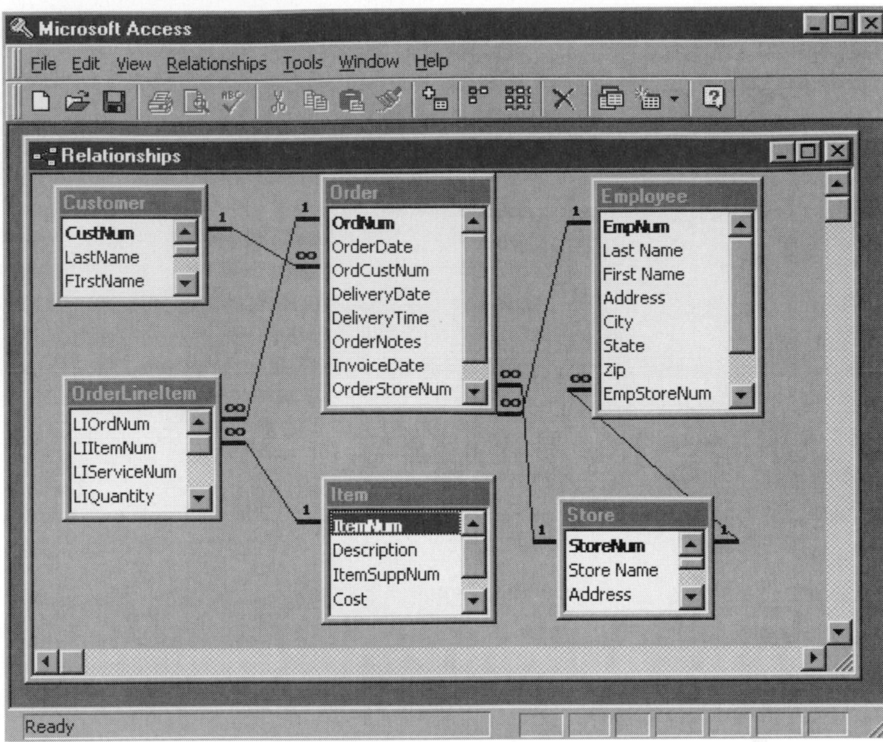

chain's order entry system. Notice how each order is linked to a customer, a store, and an employee, and how an order can contain multiple line items, each of which must be a legitimate item in the item table. The representation of each table was adjusted to show only a few of the attributes for each entity type.

Designing a database for efficiency requires a technique called **normalization,** which eliminates redundancies from the tables in the database and pares them down to their simplest form. Going beyond just normalization, database designers must also organize the database to achieve internal efficiency by reflecting the way the users will access the data. For a small database, this may be a simple question. For a large database with stringent response time requirements, this optimization process may stretch the knowledge of database experts.

Although the internal structure of a relational database may be quite complicated, its straightforward appearance to users makes it comparatively easy to work with by combining and manipulating tables to create new tables. The industry standard programming language for expressing data access and manipulation in relational databases is called **SQL (Structured Query Language),** but it is often possible to pose straightforward database queries without using SQL. Figure 4.5 shows how links between several tables are the starting point for specifying the query without requiring the use of arcane computer languages. Figure 4.6 shows an alternative approach in which a natural language query system uses a situation-specific dictionary to translate a natural language query into SQL.

Relational databases have become popular because they are easier to understand and work with than other forms of database organization. Early implementations of relational databases were slow and inefficient, but faster computers and better software have reduced these shortcomings. For example, some relational DBMSs contain optimization methods that determine the most efficient order for performing the steps in a particular query. Most new information systems for processing transactions in business are developed using relational databases even though many existing systems still use older data models called the hierarchical data model and the network data model. Because users are shielded from the details of these older data models, we will treat them as specialized concerns of the technical system staff and will not discuss them here.

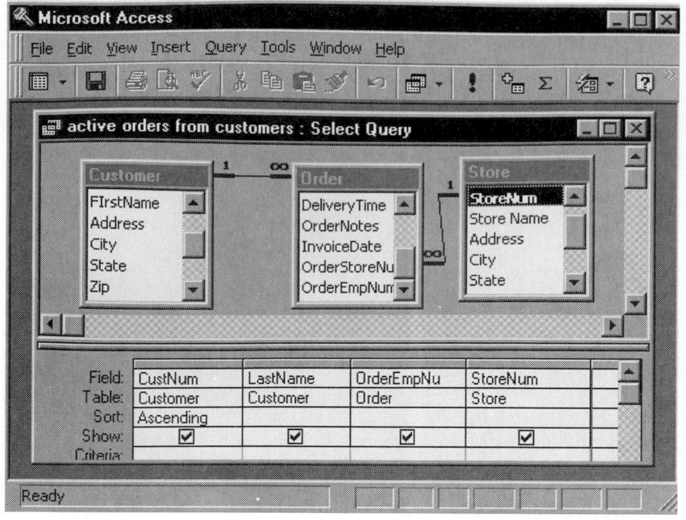

(a)

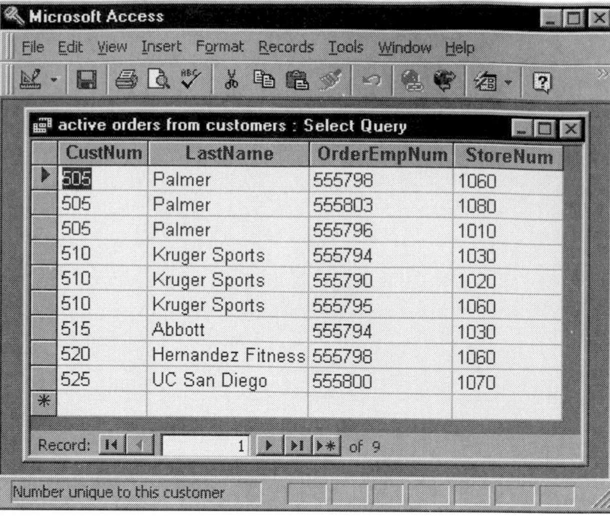

CustNum	LastName	OrderEmpNum	StoreNum
505	Palmer	555798	1060
505	Palmer	555803	1080
505	Palmer	555796	1010
510	Kruger Sports	555794	1030
510	Kruger Sports	555790	1020
510	Kruger Sports	555795	1060
515	Abbott	555794	1030
520	Hernandez Fitness	555798	1060
525	UC San Diego	555800	1070

(b)

Figure 4.5
Posing a query in Microsoft Access

This shows a query that lists the employee number and store number for each order from each customer.

Multidimensional Databases

Although relational databases bring the advantages mentioned above, they still have some shortcomings when the situation requires frequent analysis of massive databases. In many situations data are collected in a relational database or other type of database designed for transaction processing and are periodically downloaded into a separate database designed for data analysis. The database used for data analysis is often a **multidimensional database** consisting of a single file, each of whose keys can be viewed as a separate dimension.

Figure 4.7 shows an example of a multidimensional database of the type that might be used when a national market research organization collects weekly data about sales of

Figure 4.6
Using a natural language query

The user in this example has asked a question in English. Using a dictionary of terms developed for this particular database, a query program called English Wizard translates the question into an SQL query and produces the answer.

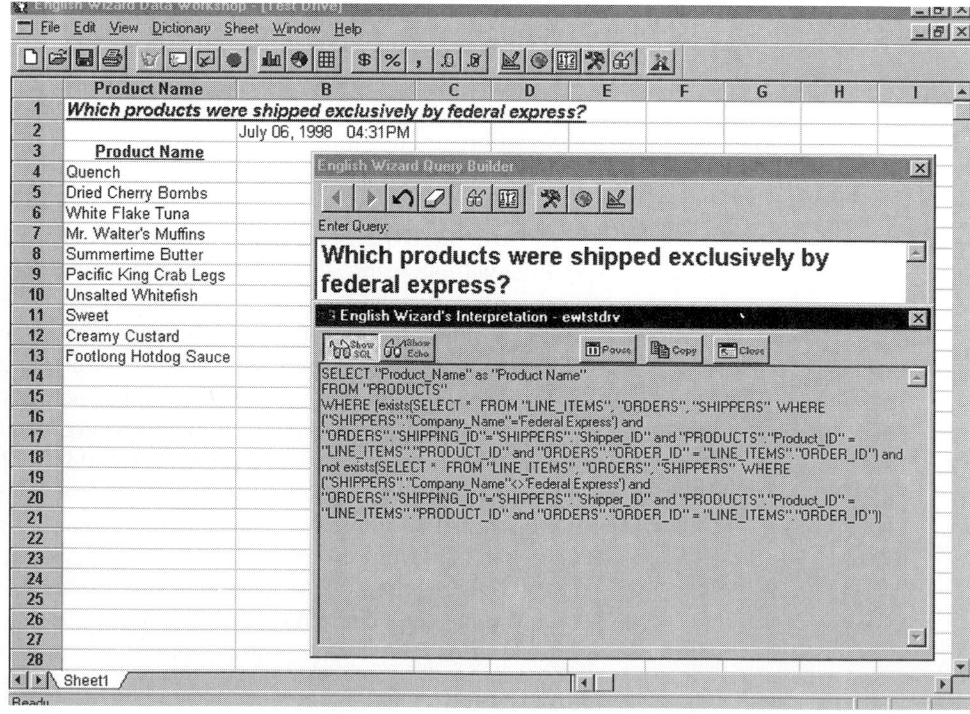

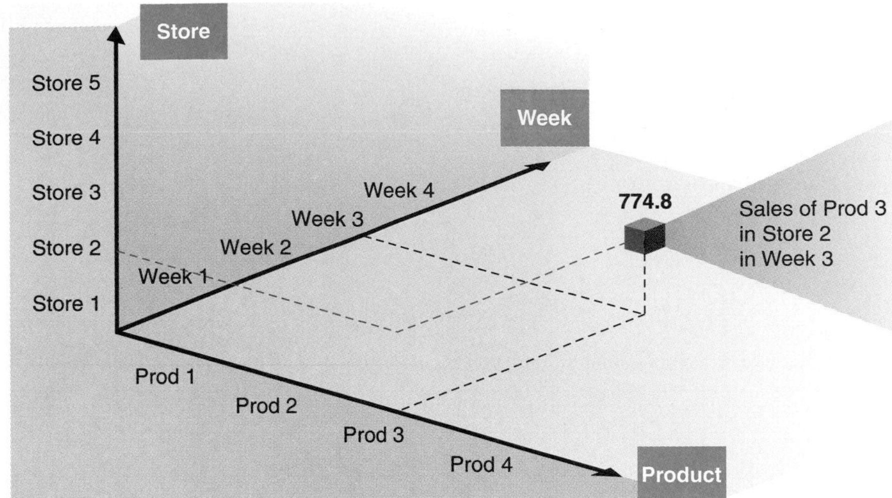

Figure 4.7
A multidimensional database

This multidimensional database contains three dimensions: product, store, and time. The valuable data in the database is the sales of each product in each store for each week.

thousands of products in thousands of stores across the United States. This database is a single table, each of whose records is a particular week's sales of a particular product in a particular store. This data can be analyzed from many different viewpoints to find trends and correlations involving individual products, groups of products, individual stores, and groups of stores. Much more important than relational data structures in this case is simply the ability to perform the calculations efficiently.

Frito-Lay's information system for tracking and analyzing store sales shows how these databases can be used. Frito-Lay outfitted its 10,000-person direct sales force with handheld terminals used while calling on the 400,000 stores that sell its 100 products. Salespeople save 4 or 5 hours of paperwork per week by using the terminals to enter replenishment orders and record the number of "stales" removed after their 35-day shelf life. Salespeople hook the terminals to telephone lines to transfer each day's data to the company's mainframe computers in Dallas, providing the marketing department up-to-date data for studying sales by any combination of product, store, and time period. Research about an unexpected drop in the sales of Tostitos tortilla chips in south Texas indicated that a small competitor had launched a white-corn tortilla chip. Frito-Lay developed a competitive white corn product within three months and regained market share.[6]

Geographical Information Systems

Organizing data so that it can be accessed by pointing at a region on a map has become useful in a wide variety of applications. Information systems that support this type of application are often called **geographic information systems (GIS)** because they permit a user to access data based on spatial or geographic coordinates. A GIS therefore includes both a database in the traditional sense and a way to retrieve or manipulate subsets of the data based on its location on a map or other spatial representation. Many marketing and planning applications use GIS to visualize the density of current and potential customers or users in particular areas. (See Figure 4.8.) GIS can be used by police departments to visualize the relationship between crime frequency and police coverage in different precincts. They can also be used to control mobile resources such as trucks or emergency vehicles. The important difference between GIS and other types of information systems is not in the database per se, but in the way users access the data through maps.

The Process of Accessing Data

Given a logical view of what the data is and how it is organized, the next part of a user's view involves data access. Concepts related to data access include push versus pull and preprogrammed versus ad hoc.

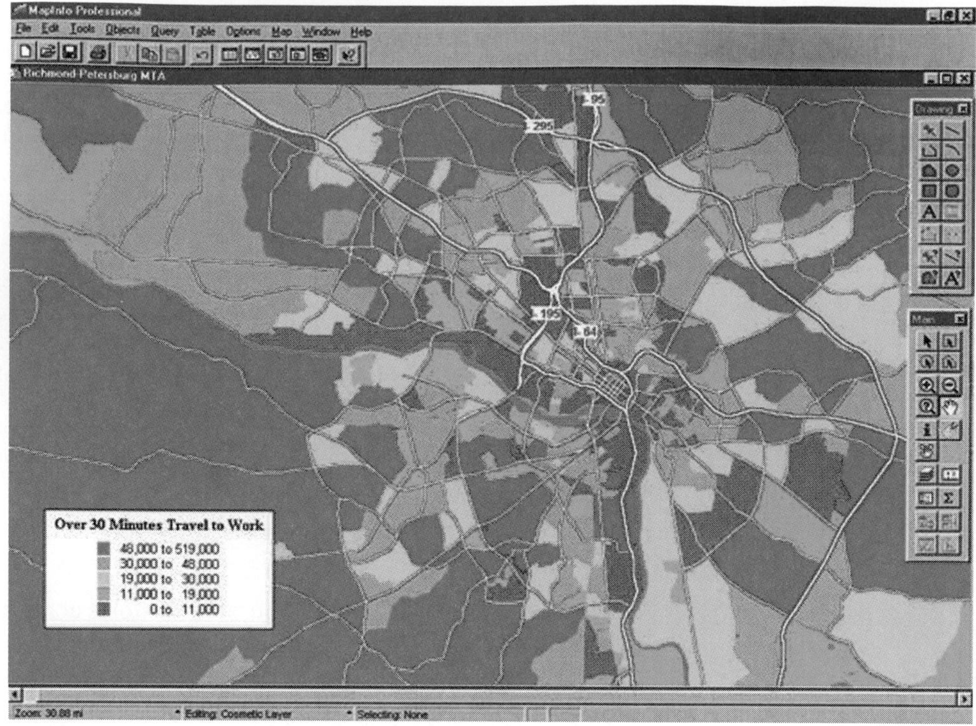

Figure 4.8
Using a geographical information system

This output of a GIS is used by radio stations trying to sell advertising time and by businesses trying to use radio to sell to customers from particular areas.

Push Versus Pull

A basic choice in designing many information systems involves the difference between push and pull systems. In a **push system,** the information is provided to the user automatically. In a **pull system,** the user must request the information explicitly each time it is to be used. Each of these approaches has been used extensively. Early information systems were typically set up as push systems in which people received lengthy printed reports daily or weekly. Such systems were the butt of many jokes because the reports often went into the trash without ever being opened. The advent of interactive computing in the 1970s and 1980s made it more possible to use pull systems because the users now had a means to ask for specific listings or queries directly.

Pull versus push is an important question for many users of the Internet. Regardless of whether they often use the Internet in pull mode to obtain information they need for a novel purpose, some users also like using it in a push mode to obtain specific information that they want updated on a daily basis, such as news reports and stock prices.

Preprogrammed Versus Ad Hoc

To provide preprogrammed access to data, programmers speak with users and identify a small set of queries that can be programmed and used repetitively. To permit ad hoc access, the users must have data access tools that allow them to specify individual queries that will generate the information they want at any particular time. According to this distinction, push systems are preprogrammed because the user identifies the specific information that will be provided on a schedule or whenever a triggering event occurs, such as a large swing in a company's stock price. Information requests in pull systems are ad hoc because they are specified for a current information need that may never recur. Providing easy ways to specify ad hoc queries was one of the major breakthroughs in information systems. Before ad hoc query capability was available, users often had to ask programmers to produce special programs whenever they needed information not included in existing preprogrammed reports.

We have now discussed basic ideas about a user's view of data. Next we will look at how database management systems provide capabilities for processing data.

DATABASE MANAGEMENT SYSTEMS

A database management system (DBMS) is an integrated set of programs used to define databases, perform transactions that update databases, retrieve data from databases, and establish database efficiency. Some DBMSs for personal computers can be used directly by end users to set up applications. Other DBMSs are much more complex and require programmers to set up applications. DBMSs include a query language that allows end users to retrieve data. DBMSs make data more of a resource and facilitate programming work, thereby making access to data more reliable and robust.

Making Data More of a Resource

DBMSs provide many capabilities that help in treating data as a resource. DBMSs improve data access by providing effective ways to organize data. They improve data accuracy by checking for identifiable errors during data collection and by discouraging data redundancy. They encourage efficiency by providing different ways to organize the computerized database. They encourage flexibility by providing ways to change the scope and organization of the database as business conditions change. They support data security by helping control access to data and by supporting recovery procedures when problems arise. They support data manageability by providing information needed to monitor the database.

Making Programming More Efficient

DBMSs also contain numerous capabilities that make programming more efficient. They provide consistent, centralized methods for defining the database. Also, they provide standard subroutines that programmers use within application programs for storing and retrieving data in the database. DBMSs free the programmer or end user from having to reinvent these complex capabilities.

DBMSs for different purposes provide vastly different features. A DBMS for a personal computer contains far fewer capabilities than a DBMS for a mainframe or complex network. The following discussion focuses on the range of DBMS functions rather than on the capabilities in any one DBMS. Business professionals unaware of these issues do not appreciate what it takes to use a DBMS successfully.

Defining the Database and Access to Data

DBMS applications start with a **data definition,** the identification of all the fields in the database, how they are formatted, how they are combined into different types of records, and how the record types are interrelated. A central tool for defining data in a DBMS is a repository called a **data dictionary.** For each data item the data dictionary typically includes:

- name of the data item
- definition of the data item
- name of the file the data item is stored in
- abbreviation that can be used as a column heading for reports
- typical format for output (for example, $X,XXX.XX or MM-DD-YY)
- range of reasonable values (for example, the codes used for months)
- identification of data flow diagrams where it appears in system documentation
- identification of user input screens and output reports where it appears

Data dictionaries can be used throughout the system development process. In the early stages they serve as a repository of terms. This is especially useful for coordination when many people are working on the project at the same time. In the example in Table 4.2, the data dictionary might have helped identify the confusion between office telephone as an attribute of the professor and telephone extension as an attribute of the office. During programming, data dictionaries make it unnecessary to write the same information multiple times and help check for errors and inconsistencies. Instead of cluttering programs with subroutines that check input data, equivalent data checks can be inserted automatically from the data dictionary when the program is compiled. This is an example of setting something up once and reusing it so that the programmer doesn't have to recreate it repeatedly.

A data dictionary consists of **metadata,** information defining data in the information system. Aside from defining the data in an information system, metadata helps in linking computer equipment from different vendors. This can be done by using interfaces that include two types of data, the application data (such as the information about courses and sections) and metadata defining the meaning and format of the application data.

The data definition for a database is often called a **schema.** Because some users may not be allowed access to part of the data in the database, many DBMSs support the use of subschemas. A **subschema** is a subset of a schema and therefore defines a particular portion of a database. Figure 4.9 shows how a system of schemas and subschemas can be used to identify the subset of a database that any particular group of users may access. The system of schemas and subschemas supports data independence because schemas and subschemas can be defined outside of the programs that access the data. Data independence permits modifications of the format or content of part of a database without having to retest every program that accesses the data. This is a major convenience for programmers, especially in large systems with many programs that access the same database.

Although schemas and subschemas are logical views of how the database is organized, in order to store or retrieve data DBMSs also need a physical definition of exactly where the files reside in the computer system. This physical definition can be quite complicated if the database contains many different files or is spread across multiple storage devices in multiple locations. A DBMS must reserve the areas in physical storage where the data will reside. It must also organize the data for efficient retrieval. Because the number of records in any file in a database can grow or shrink over time, a DBMS must provide ways to change the amount of space reserved for each file in the database. After the database is defined, a DBMS plays a role in processing transactions that create or modify data in the database.

Methods for Accessing Data in a Computer System

A computer system finds stored data either by knowing the exact location or by searching for the data. Different DBMSs contain different internal methods for storing and retrieving data. This section looks at three methods that could be used: sequential access, direct access, and indexed access. Programmers set up DBMSs to use whatever method is appropriate for the situation, while also shielding users from technical details of data access.

Sequential Access

The earliest computerized data processing used **sequential access** in which individual records within a single file are processed in sequence until all records have been processed or until the processing is terminated for some other reason. Sequential access is the only method for data stored on tape, but it can also be used for data on a direct access device such

Figure 4.9
Use of schemas and subschemas

Even though they need some information about each employee, the payroll and company telephone directory application do not need and should not have access to all the information about the employee.

Schema	Payroll Department's Subschema	Company Telephone Directory's Subschema
Name	Name	Name
Home Address	Home Address	....
Home Telephone #	....	....
Office Telephone Ext.	....	Office Telephone Ext.
Office #	Office #	Office #
Department	Department	Department
Date Hired	....	....
Employee Grade	Employee Grade	....
Tax Withholding Info.	Tax Withholding Info.	....
Pension Plan Info.	Pension Plan Info.	....
Health Info.	....	....

as a disk. Sequential processing makes it unnecessary to know the exact location of each data item because data are processed according to the order in which they are stored.

Although sequential processing is useful for many types of scheduled periodic processing, it has the same drawback as a tape cassette containing a number of songs. If you want to hear the song at the end of the tape, you have to pass through everything that comes before it. Imagine a telephone directory that is stored alphabetically on a tape. To find the phone number of a person named Adams, you would mount the tape and search until the name Adams was encountered or passed. If the name were Zwicky, you would need to search past almost every name in the directory before you could find the phone number you needed. On the average, you would have to read past half of the names in the directory. As if this weren't bad enough, you would also need to rewind the tape. These characteristics of sequential access make it impractical to use when immediate processing of the data is required.

Direct Access

Processing events as they occur requires **direct access,** the ability to find an individual item in a file immediately. Magnetic disk storage was developed to provide this capability. Optical storage is another physical implementation of the same logical approach for finding data. To understand how direct access works, imagine that the phone directory described earlier is stored on a hard disk. As illustrated in Figure 4.10, a user needing Sam Patterson's telephone number enters that name into the computer system. A program uses a mathematical procedure to calculate the approximate location on the hard disk where Sam Patterson's phone number is stored. Another program instructs the read head to move to that location to find the data. Using the same logic to change George Butler's phone number, one program calculates a location for the phone number, and another program directs the read head to store the new data in that location.

Finding data on disk is not as simple as this example implies because procedures for calculating where a specific data item should reside on a disk sometimes calculate the same location for two different data items. This result is called a **collision.** For example, assume that the procedure calculates that the phone numbers for both Liz Parelli and Joe Ramirez should be stored in location 45521 on a disk. If neither phone number is on the disk and the user wishes to store Joe's number, it will be stored in location 45521. If the user stores Liz's number later, the computer will attempt to store it in location 45521, but will find that this location is already occupied. It will then store Liz's phone number in

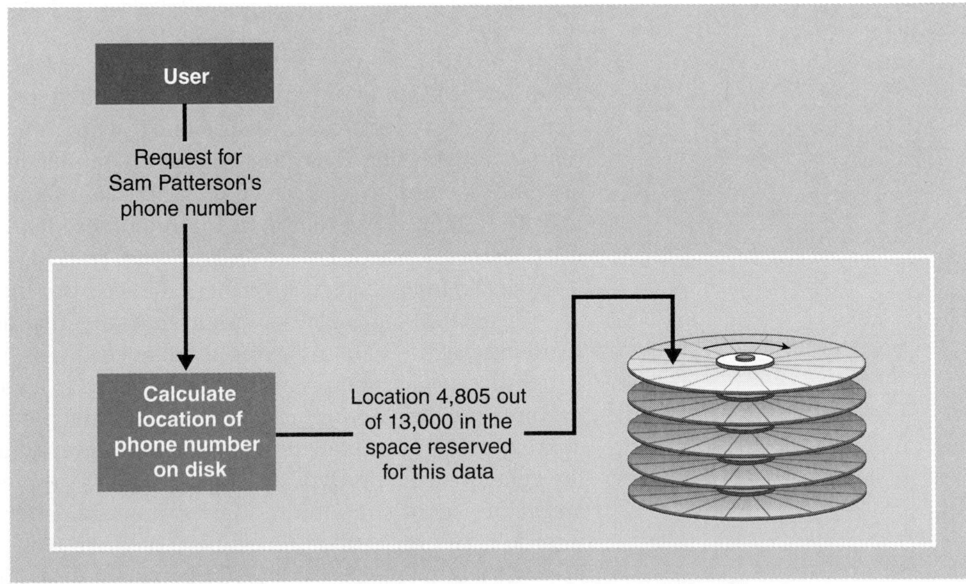

Figure 4.10
Locating data using direct access

With direct access, the computer calculates the approximate location of specific data in a direct access device such as a hard disk.

location 45522 if that location is not occupied. If it is occupied, the computer will look at successive locations until it finds an empty one. When Liz's number is retrieved at some later time, the computer will look for it first in location 45521. Observing that the number in this location is not Liz's, it will then search through successive locations until it finds her number.

Because users just want to get a telephone number and don't care about how and where it is stored on a hard disk, the DBMS shields them from these details. Someone in the organization has to know about these details, however, because ignoring them can cause serious problems. When direct access databases are more than 60% to 70% full, the collisions start to compound, and response time degrades rapidly. To keep storage and retrieval times acceptable, the amount of disk space available for the database must be increased. Someone must unload the database onto another disk or a tape and then reload it so that it is more evenly distributed across the allocated disk space. Maintaining the performance of large databases with multiple users and frequent updating requires fine-tuning by experts.

Indexed Access

A third method for finding data is to use **indexed access.** An *index* is a table used to find the location of data. The example in Figure 4.11 shows how indexed access to data operates. The index indicates where alphabetical groups of names are stored. For instance, the index contains the information that the names from Palla to Pearson are on track 53. The user enters the name Sam Patterson. The program uses the index to decide where to start searching for the phone number.

Using indexes makes it possible to perform both sequential processing and direct access efficiently. Therefore, access to data using such indexes is often called the **indexed sequential access method (ISAM).** To perform a sequential processing task, such as listing the phone directory in alphabetical order, a program reads each index entry in turn and then reads all of the data pointed to by that index entry. If the index entries and the data pointed to by the index entries are in alphabetical order, the listing will also be in alphabetical order.

Although they solve many problems, using indexes also causes complications. Assume that all the space on a track of a disk is used up and that another telephone number needs to be stored that belongs on that track. This situation is called an overflow. ISAM will put the data in a special overflow area but then may have to look in two places when it needs to retrieve a telephone number. Database performance degrades as more data goes into the overflow area. As a result, it is occasionally necessary to unload the data, store it again, and revise the indexes. Once again, these are the details the DBMS and technical staff take care of because most users have neither the desire nor the need to think about them.

Processing Transactions

When a DBMS stores or retrieves a particular item of data, it performs part of the translation from a query or program instruction in a program into machine language instructions. A programmer using a DBMS uses its data manipulation language to write commands such as "Find the next inventory record." In this command, the term *next inventory record* is a logical reference to the data. A **logical reference** identifies the data the programmer wants but doesn't say exactly how to find the data. The DBMS converts the logical reference into a physical reference, such as "retrieve the record at location 8452 on hard disk #5."

The DBMS also plays an important role in controlling access to data items when many transactions are occurring simultaneously, as happens in many business systems. Suppose that two concurrent transactions need to use or update the same data item. What prevents one transaction from reading the data, performing some other operations, and coming back to complete the transaction unaware that another transaction has changed the data? To avoid this type of problem DBMSs support **record locking,** the ability to lock a specific record temporarily, thereby preventing access by any other process until it is unlocked. In transaction processing, a program locks a record when the transaction first accesses it and unlocks the record when the transaction is finished.

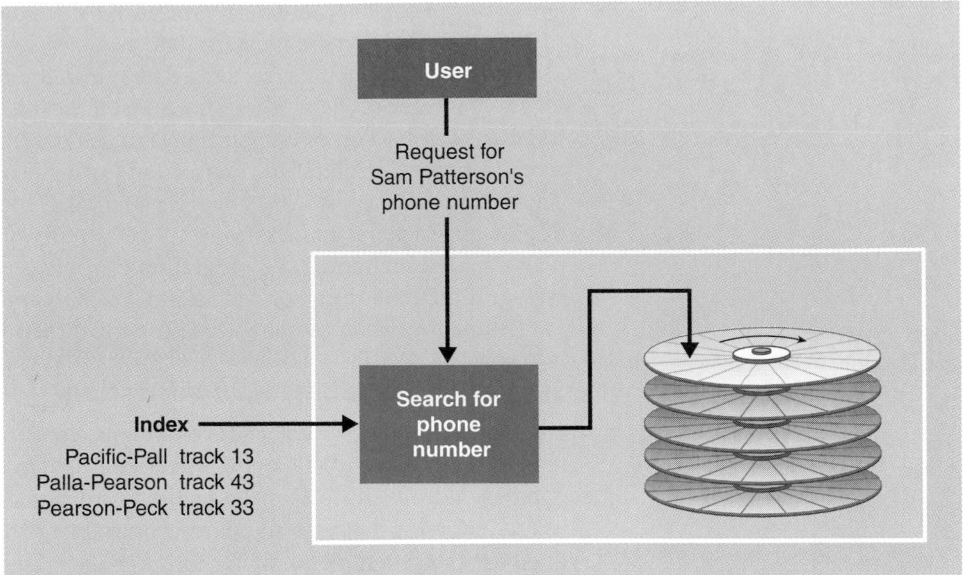

Figure 4.11
Locating data using indexes

With indexed access, the computer uses an index that stores the location of ranges of data such as an alphabetical subset of a telephone directory.

Controlling Distributed Databases

Ideally, a database should exist in one location and should always be updated there to maximize data integrity. Unfortunately this is not always feasible because many organizations are dispersed nationally or internationally. If the database is completely centralized in one location, each data update or retrieval from remote locations incurs data transmission costs. These costs led to the development of **distributed databases,** parts of which exist in different locations. Distributed databases have their own challenges, however, because decentralizing parts of the database to remote locations makes it more difficult to obtain a complete view of the entire database. General tradeoffs between centralized and distributed database architectures include issues such as the cost of data transmission, the costs of synchronizing distributed parts of the database, and the degree to which the entire database must be current at all times.

A common alternative to distributed databases is database **replication,** in which the DBMS permits programmers to define complete or partial copies (called *replicas*) of the same master database at remote locations. Transactions performed using any of the remote copies are later transmitted to the other databases so that the entire database stays consistent enough to avoid confusion. For example, Nashville-based Tractor Supply Co. uses Oracle's replication technology to update a central database every five minutes with transactions from 206 stores. The company believes this has cut a day out of its supply chain.[7]

A more rigorous and resource-intensive approach to synchronizing distributed databases is to keep them up-to-date at all times. Consider a database in which sales offices maintain billing data and warehouses maintain product availability data. When an order is shipped, data in both places must be updated. If something goes wrong while the transaction is being processed, it is possible that the billing data would be updated, but not the product availability data. This would make the database inconsistent. To maintain consistency across distributed databases, DBMSs use a **two-phase commit,** in which the DBMS first makes sure that the local parts of the database are ready for the transaction, and then it performs the transaction. If a network failure occurs during the transaction, the database rolls back to its previous state and the transaction is attempted again.

Backup and Recovery

Downtime in crucial transaction processing systems can virtually shut down a company. Therefore, the capability of a DBMS to recover rapidly and continue database operations after a computer or database goes down is essential. DBMSs contain backup and recovery capabilities for this purpose. **Backup** is storing additional copies of data in case something goes wrong. For example, if mechanical failure of a disk destroys the data it contains, backup data stored elsewhere prevents data loss.

Recovery capabilities restore a database to the state it was in when a problem stopped further database processing. As shown in Figure 4.12, the recovery process starts with the last complete backup plus a journal listing all the transactions since the last backup. The recovery process reruns all the transactions up to the one when the system crashed. That last transaction may be lost if it is not in the journal. Once the recovery is complete, processing of new transactions can continue. As with many other DBMS capabilities, backup and recovery are functions that a programmer would have to reinvent with each information system if a DBMS didn't provide them. DBMS capabilities for backup and recovery are successful only when they are used properly by people who administer the database.

Supporting Database Administration

Like an automobile, a database is a valuable resource that must be monitored and maintained. The process of managing a database is often called **database administration.** The database administrator is responsible for things such as planning for future database usage, enforcing database standards, controlling access to data, and maintaining efficient database operation. Planning for future usage starts with monitoring trends in database size and activity. Along with user comments, this data helps in deciding what resources will be necessary to support future database use. Enforcement of database standards includes procedures for ensuring data accuracy and proper backups. Control of database access is accomplished by defining subschemas and monitoring data access. Maintaining efficient database operation involves monitoring the database and making sure that response times

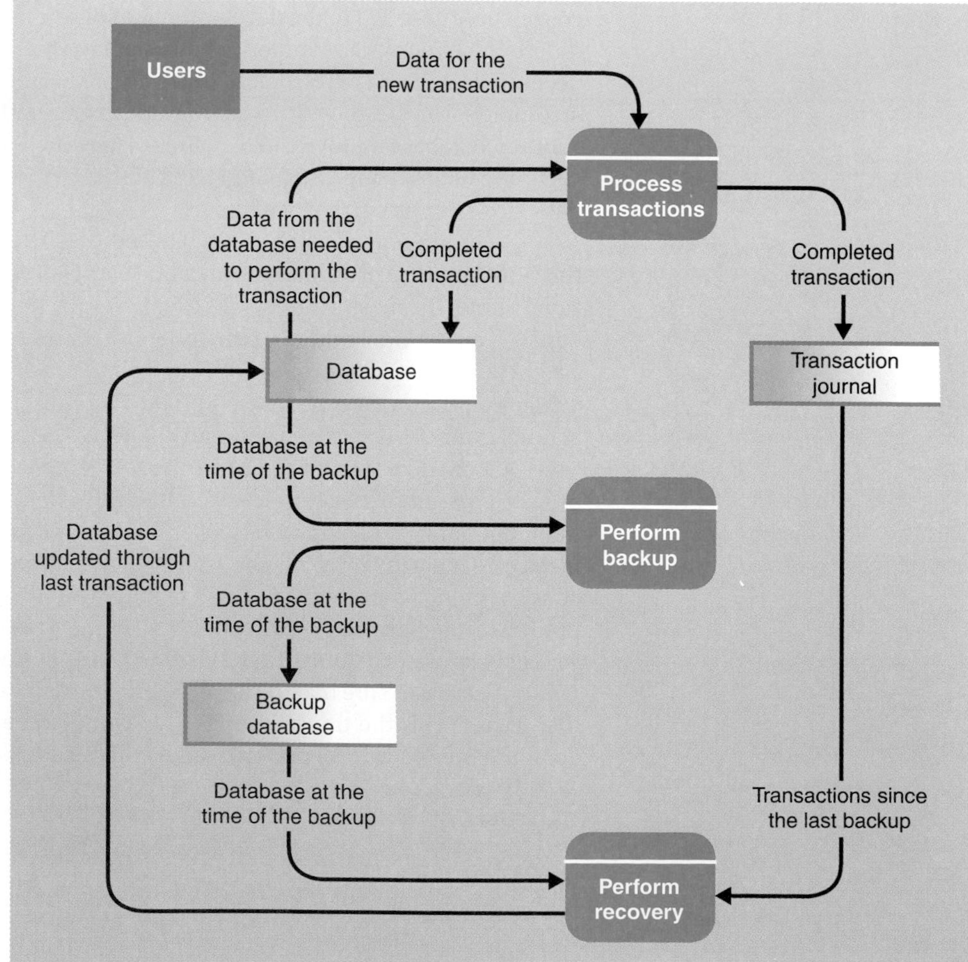

Figure 4.12
Backup and recovery

The normal processing of transactions uses the database and updates it. The backup process creates a separate backup copy of the database as of a specific time. If the transaction processing system goes down, the recovery process reruns transactions to bring the database back to its status at the time when processing stopped.

and other key indicators are acceptable. The internal record-keeping by the DBMS supplies much of the data needed for these functions.

Reality Check

DATABASE MANAGEMENT SYSTEMS

Roles of DBMSs include database definition, data access, transaction processing, control of distributed databases, backup and recovery, and database administration.

1. Think of a situation in which you have used a database or probably will use a database in the future. In what ways are these DBMS roles important in that situation?
2. The six roles are basically about formalizing rules and methods for handling data. Explain when this type of formalization is or is not advantageous.

TEXT DATABASES AND HYPERTEXT

Traditional databases of the type we have discussed so far are often viewed as the basis of business information systems, but text databases are increasingly important as computers and searching techniques have become fast enough to find information within text documents. A **text database** is a set of documents stored on a computer so that individual documents and information within the documents can be retrieved. It is typically possible to search for particular words or groups of words within the documents, and to retrieve documents based on keywords that categorize the document. An example of a text database is the LEXIS database of legal information, which was initially available through proprietary software but was revamped for access through the World Wide Web starting in 1998. This database includes documents from more than 4,800 national, state, and local jurisdictions.

Hypertext

It is possible for a text database to consist of completely independent documents, but the ability to link any point in a document to another related document is valuable in many situations. **Hypertext** documents are used online and contain interactive links that a user may select in order to move immediately to other parts of the current document or to other documents that provide related information. The existence of a link is indicated by underlining a word or providing an icon that can be clicked. The author of the hypertext document completes the linkage information by identifying the location of the related information. When the user of the document clicks on the link, the related information is retrieved and displayed. Use of the Web has focused attention on this type of access because the information on the Web is organized as a set of hypertext documents that can be downloaded on request from computers around the world. The Web is often described as a **hypermedia** system because hypertext documents on the Web may contain text, images, and other types of information such as data files, audio, video, and executable computer programs.

Browsers

The World Wide Web is accessed using software called a **browser,** which provides the user's interface to the Web and displays Web pages to the user. Common browsers include Netscape and Internet Explorer. A **Web page** is a hypertext document directly accessible via the Internet through its **uniform resource locator (URL),** which is an address that defines the route to obtain the page from a specific server. For example, a Web user wanting to access the Web site for Addison Wesley Longman, this book's publisher, would type http://www.awl.com. This is actually only part of the full URL, but it is enough to access the first page in the Web site. The full URL includes the protocol prefix (http), port address (a series of numbers that identify the server), domain name (www.awl.com), and subdirectory names separated by slashes (that would show a hierarchy of pages leading to a specific page within the Web site).

Browsers provide several methods for retrieving a Web page. The first method is to type a URL into a designated field on the screen and press *enter*. The second method is to click on a hypertext link within a document. That link may be presented to the user in the form of a URL or it may just be an underlined word or phrase that the author of the Web page associated with a particular URL when the Web page was created. Other possibilities involve selecting a URL previously recorded in a file on the user's computer when the corresponding Web page was visited in the past. URLs for these sites may have been recorded automatically in a history file or the user may have designated these sites as "favorites" in order to revisit them without searching for them.

Regardless of how the URL is selected, the following sequence occurs (see Figure 4.13): (1) The browser sends the textual domain name such as www.awl.com to a domain name server to determine the port address for the host computer that will supply the Web page. (2) The browser builds a request for the page that includes the port address of the server, a description of what is requested, and a return address. (3) The computer that is running the browser transmits this message onto the Internet, which routes it to the server that will supply the information. (4) The server processes the request, sometimes returning an existing page and sometimes building a new page in response to information the user provided by filling out an interactive form. (5) The server sends the information back to the user's computer via the Internet. (6) The browser displays the Web page.

Interoperability between many different types of computers is achieved by coding the Web pages using an agreed upon standard called **hypertext markup language (HTML).** The browser that receives the HTML automatically uses this data to display the page on the screen in an appropriate format. Included with the HTML may be **applets,** small programs that operate on part of the data transmitted to the user's computer as part of the Web page. For example, an applet might cause a logo to rotate as part of the appearance of the Web page, or it might perform calculations based on data the user enters.

Indexes and Search Engines

Query tools provided by a relational DBMS express the query in terms of predefined data items and relationships, and therefore make it possible to specify exactly what information is needed for a particular query. In contrast, query tools for a text database must operate in a different way because the documents in the text database lack predefined data definitions. Aside from the hypertext links mentioned earlier, methods for finding information in text databases include indexes, search engines, and keywords.

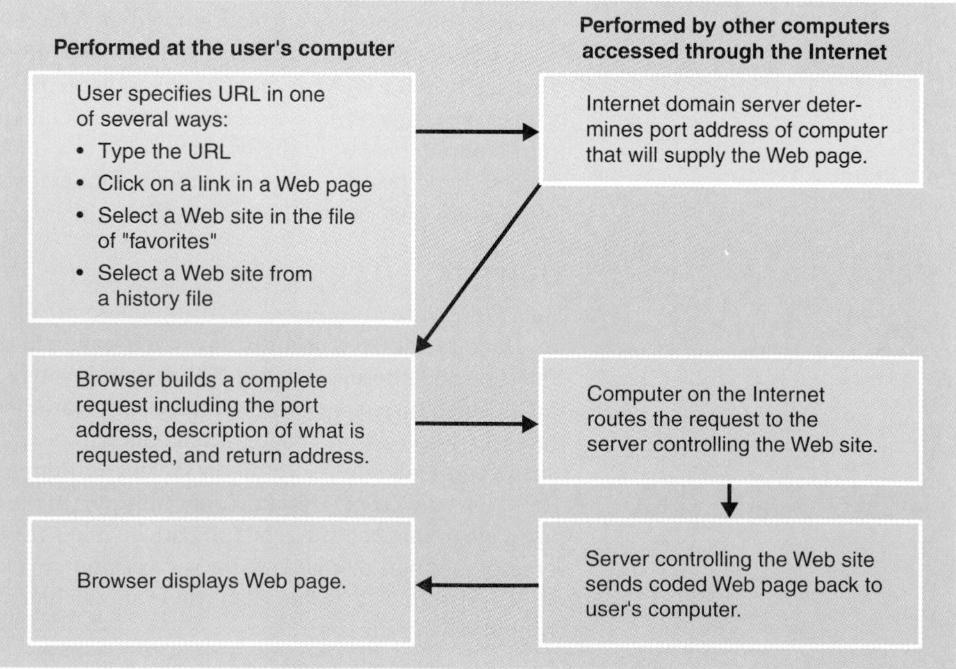

Figure 4.13
Retrieving a Web page

Retrieval of a Web page requires passing messages between computers in different locations.

An **index** is a list structure organized to identify and locate documents or portions of documents related to specific topics. The index at the end of this book identifies and locates references to all the key terms in the book and many other terms. A multilayer index such as the one used in the Yahoo! index tries to divide all topics on the Web into a hierarchy of successively finer topics and subtopics. At any level of subtopics Yahoo! can identify finer subtopics or Web pages related to the current subtopic. Building and maintaining this type of index of the Web is enormously more ambitious than creating the index of a book because the Web's vast content changes continually.

A **search engine** is a program that finds documents or Web pages that seem to be related to groups of words or phrases supplied by the user. A user who wants to find out about vacations in Alaska can simply type "Alaska vacation" in a search engine's query box and click enter. The search engine looks at a special alphabetical index created for each site on the Web. It identifies every site that contains Alaska and vacation and lists those sites. Unfortunately the AltaVista search engine yielded 137,779 sites in response to this query in 1998. The first 100 of the responses included things ranging from kayaking trips to apartments for rent. Identifying exactly what is needed is clearly a problem in a search of this type. Different search engines provide different means for specifying the search, such as saying that certain words must be included and that others may be included. Other search engines provide the capability to look for other sites that contain the same type of vocabulary as any particular site found by an initial search.

Search engines are usually designed to give extra weight to keywords associated with a particular site. **Keywords** are terms that describe a general area of information in which a document or Web site may be classified. Keywords are used in subject indexes in libraries. Keywords are often useful, but they may be somewhat unreliable because the keyword may not be stated in exactly the same terms the user might express. For example, a book on information systems might be listed only under the traditional heading of management information systems. Another problem with keywords is that the mere presence of a particular word does not prove that a document is pertinent to the user's inquiry. Consider the topics *apple, jaguar,* and *shark.* A search engine's response to the word *shark* might include documents about sea creatures, hockey teams (the San Jose Sharks), seafood prices (price of shark in fish markets), and even criminal activities (loan sharking). This is why search engines permit users to enter combinations of words and phrases to help eliminate the documents that use key terms in an irrelevant sense.

Compared with a traditional prestructured database, the World Wide Web's techniques of hypertext, browsing, and search engines have created a very different metaphor for dealing with collections of information. Table 4.4 shows some of the differences between a hypertext/search metaphor and a relational database metaphor.

Reality Check

FINDING DATA IN DATABASES AND THROUGH THE WORLD WIDE WEB

The comparison between databases and the World Wide Web emphasized the way the structure of a database makes it easier to retrieve and control information.

1. Identify a database you are familiar with or have at least encountered in some way. Assuming it is a relational database, identify the tables you think it contains and the types of questions it can answer for users.
2. Think about how you have used the World Wide Web to search for information. Explain how that process was different and how the process related to the quality of the results you obtained.

EVALUATING INFORMATION USED IN BUSINESS PROCESSES

We now turn from an architecture perspective to a performance perspective by looking at how to evaluate the information in a system. The usefulness of information is determined partially by factors related to the information itself, and partially by the knowledge of the

TABLE 4.4 Differences between Using a Relational Database and Using the World Wide Web

	Traditional database	The World Wide Web
Basic structural elements	Tables, records, fields, keys	Web pages and hyperlinks
Basic organizing principle	Predefined tables and relationships that have a specific meaning in a specific business context	Author-defined links from any location in a Web page to any other location on the same Web page or to another Web page
Finding specific information	Identify specific records or fields in those records and the DBMS will find them	Identify a specific Web address (URL) and the browser will find and display the page if it is available
Finding information related to the information most recently accessed	No typical method	Click on a hypertext link
Method for identifying data required in a query	State selection criteria in terms of specific values of specific data items in specific tables	Identify words or terms that should appear in the Web pages selected by the search engine
How the computer finds the data by searching	DBMS finds the pertinent tables in the database and selects the appropriate data from the records that meet the criteria	Search engine finds every Web page containing each word or phrase in the query, then prioritizes these based on the priorities in the query
Treatment of impossible or ridiculous queries	DBMS rejects queries not phrased in terms of tables, fields, and relationships in the database	The search engine performs whatever search is requested
Likelihood that a query will produce usable results	DBMS returns exactly what is requested; if the user asks the wrong question, the result may not be useful	Many of the Web pages found by a search engine may be unrelated to what the user wanted
Methods for controlling data quality	During data entry DBMS checks for obvious errors such as missing values, out-of-range values, etc.	The Web has no organized method of controlling quality of information in Web pages

user and the way business processes are organized. The three main factors related to information usefulness are:

information quality: how good the information is, based on its accuracy, precision, completeness, timeliness, and source.

information accessibility: how easy it is to obtain and manipulate the information, regardless of how good it is.

information presentation: the level of summarization and format for presentation to the user, regardless of how good the information is and how accessible it is.

Because preventing inappropriate or unauthorized use of information is also crucial, a fourth area for evaluating information is **information security,** the extent to which information is controlled and protected from inappropriate, unauthorized, or illegal access and use.

Table 4.5 shows that each factor can be subdivided into more detailed characteristics and that information systems can support improvements in each area. Some characteristics such as accuracy can be measured without regard to the way the information is used. Others such as timeliness and completeness depend on how the information is used and sometimes on the user's personal work style. For example, some managers feel comfortable making decisions with much less information than other managers might say they need. All of these characteristics involve tradeoffs between cost and usefulness. For example, keeping data more current generally means increasing data costs.

TABLE 4.5 **Determinants of Information Usefulness and Related Roles of Information Systems**

Characteristic	Definition	Related information system roles
Information quality		
• Accuracy	Extent to which the information represents what it is supposed to represent	Control data to insure accuracy; identify likely errors
• Precision	Fineness of detail in the portrayal	Provide information with adequate precision
• Completeness	Extent to which the available information is adequate for the task	Provide information that is complete enough for the user and situation; avoid swamping the user with excessive information
• Age	Amount of time that has passed since the data were produced	Update information more frequently and transmit it to user more quickly
• Timeliness	Extent to which the age of the data is appropriate for the task and user	Provide information quickly enough that it is useful
• Source	The person or organization that produced the data	Verify source of information; provide information from preferred sources; analyze information for bias
Information accessibility		
• Availability	Extent to which the necessary information exists and can be accessed effectively by people who need it	Make information available with minimum effort
• Admissibility	Whether or not use of the information is legal or culturally appropriate in this situation	No automatic approach even though it is possible to provide legal guidelines in an organized form
Information presentation		
• Level of summarization	Comparison between number of items in the original data and number of items displayed	Manipulate the data to the desired level of summarization
• Format	Form in which information is displayed to the user	Manipulate the data to the desired format
Information security		
• Access restriction	Procedures and techniques controlling who can access what information under what circumstances	Use passwords or other schemes to prevent unauthorized users from accessing data or systems that process data
• Encryption	Converting data to a coded form that unauthorized users cannot decode	Encrypt and decrypt the data

Because the characteristics related to the four factors involve very different issues, it should not be surprising that information usefulness itself is difficult to measure. For example, although it is easy to say that a particular fact, graph, or newspaper article seems useful, it is difficult to evaluate its use without discussing other available information. Decision theorists have developed what is probably the best formulation of this issue, but their approach is more elegant than practical. Their concept of the **value of information** assumes that reducing uncertainty about a particular decision is the purpose of acquiring information. If the decision would be the same with or without the information, it has no value for that decision because it does not reduce the uncertainty about what to do. It follows that the monetary value of information can be estimated by comparing the expected monetary value of the decision with the information and without it. Although it is difficult to assess the value of information in these terms, the underlying idea is still helpful for thinking about information systems. Whether or not it can be measured easily, the usefulness of the information in a system is related to the extent to which it influences decisions.

Information Quality

Information quality is related to a combination of characteristics including accuracy, precision, completeness, age, timeliness, and source.

Accuracy and Precision

The extent to which information represents what it is supposed to represent is its **accuracy.** Increasing accuracy is an important purpose of information systems. For example, the scanner systems used in supermarkets and department stores provide more accurate information about what has been received, what has been sold, and therefore what inventory is currently on hand. Accurate information of this type makes it possible to provide the same level of customer satisfaction with lower costs for inventory. Figure 4.14 shows that accuracy is an issue whenever information is used.

The related term *precision* is sometimes confused with accuracy. Whereas accuracy is the extent to which information represents what it is supposed to represent, **precision** is the fineness of detail in the portrayal. Assume that you had $5,121.68 in the bank. A statement that you had around $5,000 would be accurate but not as precise as the figure on your bank statement. On the other hand, a statement that you had $512,168.47 might appear to be very precise, but would actually be inaccurate, to say the least.

It is possible to measure both accuracy and precision, although the measures depend on the type of data and the situation. The typical measure of accuracy is error rate, the number of errors compared to the number of items. The measure of precision for numerical data is the number of significant digits. Figure 4.15 shows how the precision of an image can be measured as the number of dots per inch. The more dots per inch, the more precise the picture. This measurement is commonly used to describe the precision of printers, computer screens, scanners, and other image and print-related devices.

The two components of inaccuracy are bias and random error. **Bias** is systematic inaccuracy due to methods used for collecting, processing, or presenting data. An example of bias with far-reaching consequences is the way the U.S. consumer price index (CPI) is calculated. A study by the economic analysis firm DRI/McGraw-Hill concluded that the CPI overstates inflation by 1.2 points and therefore causes excessive cost-of-living-adjustments (COLAs) in social security and other federal programs calibrated to the CPI. Many

Figure 4.14
Data accuracy: an issue that occurs everywhere

Inscribed on the Vietnam War Monument in Washington, DC, are the names of 58,513 soldiers who died in that war. At least 14 are the names of survivors who were included mistakenly because of clerical errors and other problems.[8] Many other collections of data have much higher error rates because they are not checked as carefully.

Figure 4.15
Illustration of the precision of images

The precision of images can be measured in dots per inch. The image on the left contains 72 dots per inch. The same image is presented on the right at 2470 dots per inch, the standard precision for reproducing photos in books. Laser printers typically produce images at 300 to 600 dots per inch.

economists agree that the CPI is biased and believe retirees have reaped a windfall as a result, but changing the calculation would have major political ramifications.[9]

Figure 4.16 looks at bias in a different way. It uses different degrees of "intended truthfulness" to show the range of bias that may occur in business information. Bias is rarely an issue in the raw data from transaction processing systems (such as point-of-sale

Figure 4.16
Do managers expect the truth?

The transaction data produced by formal information systems is only part of the important information people encounter in business. Raw data can be aggregated into key indicators. Data can be interpreted. Project proposals are produced based on personal goals and beliefs. Each of these cases involves a different form of expected bias in important information.

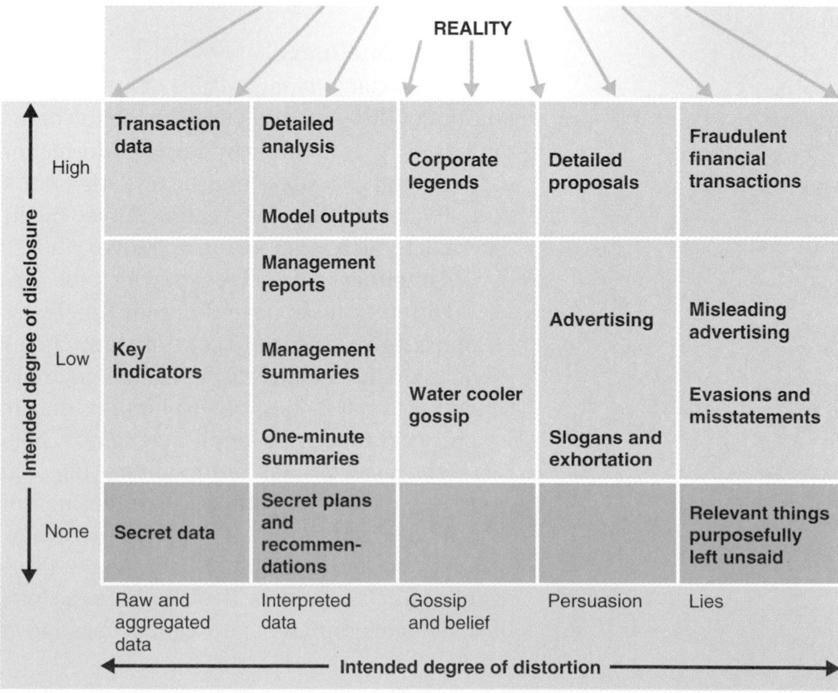

and purchasing) which are built and documented carefully and scrutinized in many ways. However, as with the CPI, data from these systems can be presented in a biased way using graphs and models. Bias also pervades informal systems in many organizations, especially in the way verbal information and recommendations are repeatedly filtered and sanitized until their meaning changes. Extreme cases of bias are various forms of lying, such as distortions, misleading advertising, and fraud.

A key point revealed by Figure 4.16 is that bias is expected, and in many cases even desired, in much important business information. For example, executives trying to decide which manager's proposal to adopt are not always looking for impartiality. Rather, they often are looking for a combination of integrity, persuasion, and the passion to follow through and implement the proposal. The implied challenge is to be clear about whether interpretations and suggestions are meant to be unbiased, or whether they are meant to persuade and therefore stress some points and leave out others that might also be important.

The other component of inaccuracy, **random error,** also called noise, is inaccuracy due to inherent variability in whatever is being measured or the way it is being measured. The concept of random error is important for interpreting fluctuations in measures of performance reported by information systems. Consider a repair shop monitoring its work quality based on the percentage of customers who return with complaints. The average complaint percentage last year was 3%, but last week just 1% of the customers complained. This change may indicate that quality is going up or may just be part of the inherent variability in the percentage. Part of the random error in the data in an information system often results from inadequate data entry controls and procedures for correcting mistakes. Difficulty enforcing controls on data collected from numerous sources is a major reason for the widely publicized errors in commercial credit databases that landlords and merchants sometimes use to check on a tenant or customer's creditworthiness.

Completeness

Completeness is the extent to which the available information seems adequate for the task. Except for totally structured tasks, it is often impossible to have totally complete information because some other factor might always be considered. In a practical sense, information is seen as complete if the user feels it is unnecessary to obtain more information before finishing the task or making a decision. Like it or not, people must often work with incomplete information. For example, doctors at a drop-in clinic often need to diagnose and treat seriously ill patients without having access to their patients' full medical history. Similarly, business managers are often confronted with crises that need some kind of resolution immediately, even if more information might lead to a better or more comfortable decision.

Age and Timeliness

Other important characteristics of information are related to time. The **age** of data is the amount of time that has passed since the data were produced. The age of data produced daily, weekly, or monthly by a firm's information systems is easy to determine. The age of data from other sources may be less apparent. For example, population data used in creating the sample for a marketing survey might be based on the last census or on more recent data such as population changes since the census.

Timeliness is the extent to which the age of the data is appropriate for the task and user. Different tasks have different timeliness requirements. For example, up-to-the-second data are needed to control many chemical processes, whereas marketing departments tracking an advertising campaign are generally satisfied with week-old data. For other tasks such as long-range planning, data from months or even years ago may be satisfactory because some long-range trends change slowly and predictably.

The recall of 1,800 Saturn automobiles illustrates the importance of timely information. These cars were shipped containing defective cooling liquid. Information from Saturn's dealer information network revealed a sudden increase in water pump changes within three days of the initial occurrence. All affected cars were recalled within two weeks, avoiding a calamity in the field. Without the information system, the defect would not have been detected until warranty claims began to arrive.[10]

Source

The **source** of data is the person or organization that produced the data. The source is often a tip-off about bias, for example when one economic forecaster tends to be more optimistic than another. Data sources may be internal or external to the firm. Most computerized information systems focus on internal data, although external data is really needed for many purposes. This is why market research firms gather and sell data related to supermarket sales and advertising by the major competitors in a local market. Combining and reconciling data from internal and external sources is crucial in analyzing the business environment.

Sources of data can also be formal or informal. Formal sources include information systems, progress reports, published documents, and official statements from company officers. Informal sources include personal communications such as meetings and conversations during and outside of work, conversations with customers and competitors, and personal observations of work habits, work environments, and work relationships. Interpreting data from informal sources often involves much more intuition and experience than interpreting data from well-defined formal sources. Even inaccurate data from formal sources is usually organized and reasonably clear. In contrast, data from informal sources is often disorganized. When a manager hears a tense confrontation between two employees, the data may be fragmented, incomplete, and hard to understand. Yet that data may be important if those two individuals need to work together to accomplish the organization's goals. In such situations, managers must use intuition and experience to fill in gaps and decide what to do.

Information Accessibility

Information accessibility involves two issues, whether the information is available and, in some cases, whether it is legally admissible. **Availability** of information is the extent to which the necessary information exists in an information system and can be accessed effectively by people who need it. For example, data on a corporate mainframe computer may not be available in a timely fashion if a potential user cannot download it to a personal computer. Similarly, even information that can be derived from paper documents in a file cabinet in the user's own office may be unavailable if the analysis process will take too long because the information is on paper.

Information availability is an important determinant of how effectively business processes operate. As was mentioned in Chapter 1, a search for improvements following the successful military effort in the 1991 Persian Gulf War found that 40,000 tractor-trailer-sized containers had arrived in Saudi Arabia with no identifying information. Because this information was not available when the containers arrived it was necessary to open each container just to find out whether it contained tires, generators, or something else. In addition, there were many overshipments because supply sergeants traditionally order everything three times in the expectation that two requisitions will go astray in unmarked containers. No more. From now on containers are bar coded to list their contents, and sensors signal their location using satellites.[11]

Admissibility of information depends on whether laws, regulations, or culture require or prohibit its use. This is an important factor when the use of age, gender, marital status, ethnicity, or medical condition might be viewed as relevant by some people and totally inappropriate by others. Such situations occur frequently in the course of business decisions such as hiring and promotion, assigning work tasks, determining insurance rates, and making loans. Issues related to admissibility of information are sometimes confusing because the use or reporting of such information is required in some cases and prohibited in others. Consider the idea of not discriminating against people based on age. How does this fit with the refusal of some rental car companies to rent to licensed drivers less than 25 years old? Similarly, U.S. law prohibits price fixing in the trucking and airline industries but gives an exemption to the international shipping cartel that fixes prices. People who build information systems need to recognize the issue of admissibility to make sure systems match both the law and the organization's culture.

Information Presentation

Information may be difficult to absorb and understand if it is presented in the wrong format or if it contains too many details. This is why graphs are sometimes used instead of tables of numbers, and why items of data are summarized into a smaller number of items. There are always alternative ways to present information to users, and the alternatives often have some advantages and some disadvantages. Graphs often make it easier to see general patterns, but they may hide particular items that are important exceptions. A similar thing can be said about summarized data presented in tables. For example, the fact that sales of a 600 product company increased 5% might be interpreted differently if you knew that sales of 10 new products had actually gone down. This is why it is important to look for exceptions and other unusual conditions.

Terms used to describe data presentation include level of summarization and format. **Level of summarization** is a comparison between the number of individual items on which data are based and the number of items in the data presented. For example, a report combining 600 products into 4 product groups is more summarized (and less detailed) than a report combining the 600 products into 23 product groups. From a user's viewpoint, **format** is the way information is organized and expressed. Format involves things ranging from the number of decimal places displayed in numbers through the different ways to present the same material graphically.

Differences between individuals are also important to consider when thinking about summarization and format of information. For example, given the same information, some people will understand it more completely if it is presented graphically, while others will understand it better in tabular form. Fortunately, current information technology makes it much easier for users to look at information in whatever form is most valuable for them personally.

Information Security

Because information used by the wrong people or in the wrong way can cause harm, it is necessary to round out the picture by mentioning information security, the extent to which information is controlled and protected from inappropriate, unauthorized, or illegal access and use.

Access restriction refers to the procedures and techniques used for controlling who can access what information under what circumstances. Although information systems are typically considered a means of providing data, many of their important capabilities involve access restrictions. The most obvious access restriction method is using passwords and other schemes for preventing unauthorized access to computers or specific data. Data **encryption** means converting data into a coded form that unauthorized users cannot decode. (Passwords, encryption, and related topics are explained in Chapter 13.)

Access restrictions in most businesses are related to management choices about how to run a business with maximum effectiveness and minimum friction. For example, many organizations consider employee salaries privileged information even though top management salaries are reported for publicly traded companies. Yet other access restrictions are attempts to conceal information because it is embarrassing or counterproductive. Consider the 1998 release of internal memos showing that strategies and advertising campaigns of the R. J. Reynolds Tobacco Company had specifically targeted smokers as young as 13. A 1985 internal report on pretests of the Joe Camel ad campaign said these ads were well received by youngsters "due to the fun/humor aspects of the cartoons." A 1987 memo stamped "RJR secret" spoke of a new brand aimed at "primarily 13–24-year-old male Marlboro smokers." The congressman who released these documents and also forwarded them to the Justice Department had presided over a 1994 congressional hearing in which the chairman of R. J. Reynolds denied that the company had ever conducted market research aimed at children.[12]

One of the ironies of the information age is that information technology cuts both ways in the area of access restriction. Passwords and other techniques can be used to restrict access, but the mere fact that so much information is recorded makes it much more difficult to keep embarrassing information hidden. U.S. presidents have certainly not been immune. Richard Nixon's Oval Office tapes played a major role in the investigation of the Watergate cover-up. Internal White House e-mail during the Reagan administration was important evidence during the investigation of illegal arms sales to Iran. The e-mail had been erased, but not before it had been stored on backup tapes. More recently, videotapes of 1996 fundraisers showed President Clinton seeming to acknowledge that some in the audience were foreigners, and then saying "I thank you for your financial contributions."[13] Because it is illegal for foreigners to contribute to federal election campaigns, the videotapes fueled an ongoing controversy about White House fundraising.

Reality Check

EVALUATING INFORMATION

Information usefulness is discussed in terms of information quality, accessibility, and presentation.

1. Identify a systematic use of information that you have encountered, such as the use of standardized test grades to determine class placement, the use of medical records, or the use of teacher evaluations. Based on your experience, evaluate that information in terms of the various determinants of usefulness.
2. Considering the same information, explain how you might measure each of the characteristics discussed in this section.

MODELS AS COMPONENTS OF INFORMATION SYSTEMS

When managers and other business professionals need to make decisions, even accurate, timely, and complete data obtained through information systems and other sources may not provide the kind of coherent picture needed to make the decision comfortably. The person may need a model for converting the data into estimates or tentative conclusions directly related to the decision.

Recall from Chapter 2 that a model is a useful representation of something. Figure 2.1 showed examples of models. The dummy in the figure represents a person in a crash test. This example is an ideal use of a model because it permits testing that would otherwise be impractical or unsafe. The spreadsheet in the figure is a model that represents a situation mathematically rather than physically. Models stress some features of reality and downplay or ignore others. They are useful because they mimic reality without dealing with every detail of it.

Many information systems are actually models. Consider an information system that collects and reports sales results for a large company. Monitoring the company's sales by observing every sale would create an overwhelming amount of information. Instead, sales can be monitored by looking at a simple model such as the number of new customers and dollar volume for each salesperson. This model misses some of the richness of reality but contains enough information to support parts of an effective management process.

Mental Models and Mathematical Models

Two types of models are especially important in information systems: mental models and mathematical models. **Mental models** are the unwritten assumptions and beliefs that people use when they think about a topic. A sales manager's mental model might say that no salesperson with less than two years of experience can be trusted fully, or that repeat customers are more important than new customers. Figure 4.17 uses a diagram to show some of the interrelated variables in a manager's mental model of a marketing decision involving a new line of imported motorcycles. Because the motorcycle is produced elsewhere, the analysis focuses on advertising and hiring salespeople.

Mental models determine what information we use and how we interpret it. If our mental models don't include a particular type of information, we tend to ignore that information.

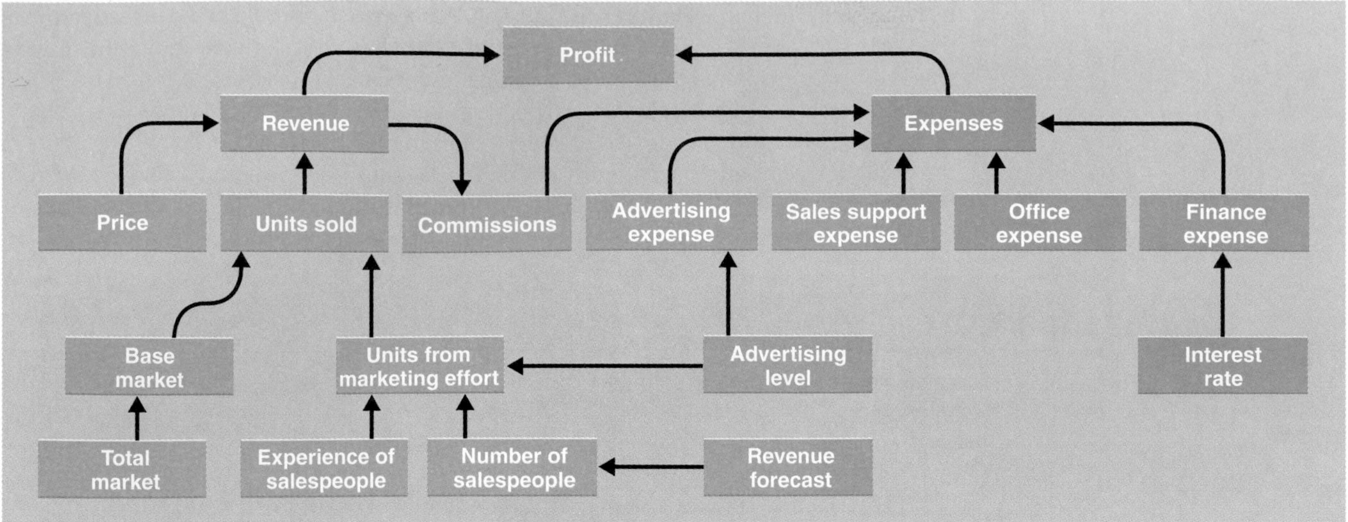

Figure 4.17
Diagram representing a mental model

This influence diagram represents a manager's mental model of a new product marketing decision. Some aspects of this mental model might seem surprising, such as the belief that the number of units sold depends on the base market and additional units from marketing effort but doesn't depend on price. To produce monetary estimates of revenues and profits, it would be necessary to describe each relationship precisely as part of a mathematical model.

The relationship between mental models and information usage affects information systems. For example, the sales manager who is very concerned about new prospects will find an information system inadequate unless it includes information about new prospects.

Although mental models are essential for organizing and interpreting information, they are often inconsistent. For example, a senator's mental models might include a series of ideas about the burden of excess debt plus a set of other ideas about the necessity of using debt to finance business growth. Such inconsistencies between vague mental models often make it difficult to think through the consequences of decisions. This is one of the advantages of mathematical models.

A **mathematical model** is a series of equations or graphs that describe precise relationships between variables. The explicit nature of a mathematical model forces people to say exactly what they mean, which clarifies and organizes various mental models that may be pertinent to a decision.

Both mental and mathematical models provide ways to distill the meaning of information for a particular situation. Mental models identify the factors that are important and the general way the factors interact. Mathematical models express these ideas precisely and produce more precise conclusions.

More important, mathematical models compensate for our inability to pay attention to hundreds of things at the same time. Putting a large number of tiny models into a single mathematical model helps organize an analysis and ensures that many factors have been considered, even if a person cannot think about all of these factors at the same time. Keeping track of which factors have been considered, and in what way, is especially important when a group discusses a decision. Because each individual has different mental models, a mathematical model helps everyone focus on the same issues and visualize what has or has not been included.

What-If Questions

Mathematical models convert data into information by performing calculations that combine many elements, by evaluating tentative decisions, and by responding to what-if questions. Tentative decisions are possible decisions that users try out as part of a decision making process. Users try these out by setting values of decision variables in the model. In a planning model for a bank, these decisions might include the number of people hired and the prices to be charged for services such as checking accounts. The model might start with tentative decisions and then calculate the value of other variables, such as expenses, profit, and estimated market share. These calculated variables could be used to think about whether the tentative decisions are wise.

Mathematical models also make it easy to ask **what-if questions** that explore the effect of alternative assumptions about key variables. For example, a bank's planning model may contain the assumption that it will be able to make loans next year at 9% interest. Bank managers might want to see whether the bank will still be profitable if the interest rate drops to 8% or if it takes six extra months to roll out a new service.

Using an organized sequence of what-if questions to study the model's outputs under different circumstances is called **sensitivity analysis.** A sensitivity analysis determines how much the results of the model change when a decision or important assumption changes by a small amount or a progression of amounts. If a large change in a variable generates a small change in the results, that variable probably doesn't affect the decision very much. If a small change in a variable generates a disproportionate change in the results, this indicates that something is wrong either with the model or with the user's understanding of the model.

Virtual Reality: The Ultimate Interactive Model?

Virtual reality is a special type of model that is becoming important in entertainment and may become important in business. **Virtual reality** is a simulation of reality that engages the participant's senses and intellect by permitting the participant to interact with the simulated environment. The person wearing the helmet in Figure 4.18 is controlling a robot by using a data glove. Flight training for pilots is one of the most extensive uses of virtual reality. It can also be used to support telepresence, the ability to view and manipulate things in a distant, dangerous, or unreachable environment such as the surface of the moon, the part of a chemical plant where a dangerous spill has just occurred, or the interior of a blood vessel. In one of the first uses of virtual reality in entertainment, VR movie theaters that appeared in a Los Angeles and Las Vegas in 1993 used sight, sound, and motion to simulate

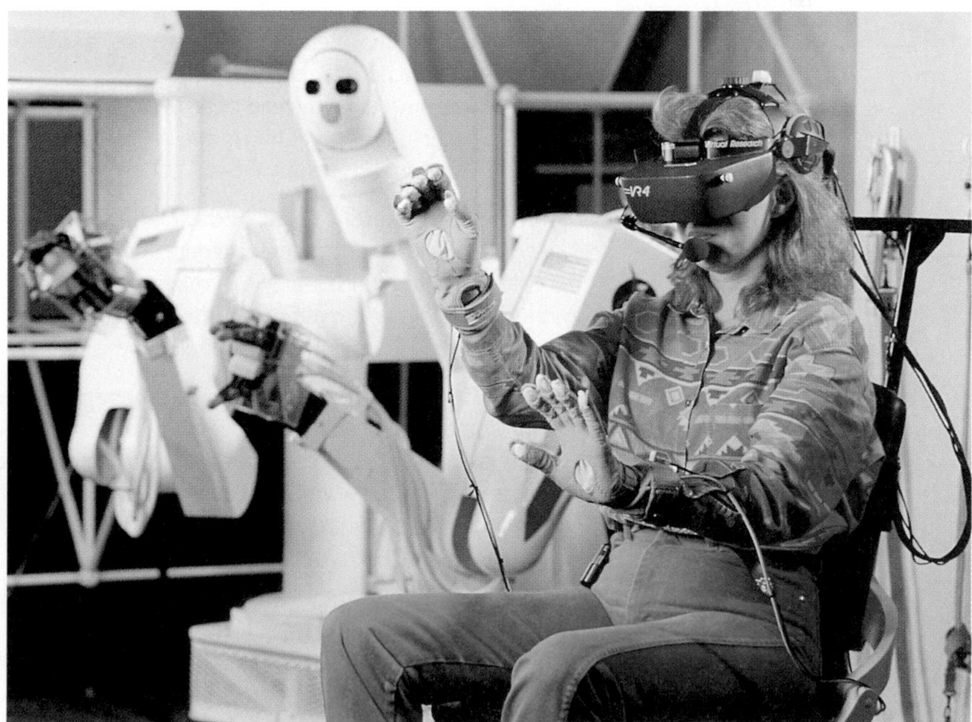

Figure 4.18
A virtual reality simulation

Hand movements by the engineer in the foreground are controlling the movements of the white robot in the background. NASA developed this VR robot for use in dangerous environments such as planetary exploration or work in the presence of radioactivity.

a flight through an adventure environment. Instead of feeling like people sitting in a theater seat munching popcorn, audience members feel like participants because of the intense, coordinated sensations of movement, light, and sound.

The idea of virtual reality clarifies the breadth and scope of information systems. Most systems covered in this book provide useful information because they model reality as a small number of specific types of data, such as orders, customers, and schedules. They purposely filter out huge amounts of extraneous information that might have been captured. Virtual reality goes in the opposite direction by bombarding the user with sensory information, sometimes to the point of overload. A challenge for future information systems is to enhance the scope and richness of information while remaining coherent and understandable.

Reality Check

MODELS AS COMPONENTS OF INFORMATION SYSTEMS

This section explained why models are often needed to convert data into information.

1. Think about the information needs of the president of a university or coach of a football team. In what ways might models be important to draw conclusions from information that is probably available from transaction databases, from external text databases, and from informal sources?

2. Assume you were helping the president or dean analyze the possible impact of a sequence of tuition increases over the next several years. What factors would you include in the model, and what potentially relevant factors do you think you would leave out?

CHAPTER CONCLUSION

Summary

What is the role of entity-relationship diagrams in data modeling?
Data modeling is the process of creating a graphical model identifying the types of entities in a situation, relationships between those entities, and the relevant attributes of those entities. It helps create a shared understanding of the information in the system and forces users to focus on the business situation instead of just listing relevant data items. The entity-relationship diagram is a technique for identifying the entity types in a situation and diagramming the relationships between those entity types.

What are the different types of data, and when is each type particularly useful?
The types of data include predefined data items, text, images, audio, and video. Predefined data items are used to reduce reality to a manageable number of salient facts that can be recorded and retrieved for performing specific tasks. Text can convey more information about unique circumstances of a situation. Images, audio, and video add more richness.

What is the difference between a database and a database management system?
The information in a computerized system is often called a database, although the term is used in many ways. For our purposes, a database is a structured collection of data stored, controlled, and accessed through a computer based on predefined, situation-specific relationships between the data items. A database management system (DBMS) is an integrated set of programs used to define, update, and control databases.

Why is a single file often insufficient for storing the data in an information system?
A file is a set of related records. In data modeling terms, a file contains data about the entities of the same entity type. It is often impractical to identify all the data in a situation using a single file because many situations involve relationships between entities of different types.

What is the difference between relational, multidimensional, and text databases?
A relational database is a set of two-dimensional tables in which one or more key-fields in each table are associated with corresponding key or non-key fields in other tables. Relational databases have become popular because they are easier to understand and use than other forms of database organization. A multidimensional database consists of a single file each of whose keys can be viewed as a separate dimension. These databases are typically used for analyzing data and are typically updated through downloads from transaction databases. A text database is a set of documents stored on a computer so that individual documents and information within the documents can be retrieved.

What are the purposes of a DBMS, and what functions does a DBMS perform?
The two major purposes of a DBMS are making data more of a resource for an organization and making programming work more effective and efficient. A DBMS is used by programmers and end users to perform a variety of functions, including defining the database, providing data access, performing the transactions updating the database, controlling distributed databases, performing backup and recovery, and supporting database administration.

How is the World Wide Web different from a typical prestructured database?
Instead of predefined tables, relationships, fields, and keys, the structural elements of the WWW are hypertext Web pages and hyperlinks. Its organizing principle is author-defined links to any location on the WWW. Specific information is located through a URL rather than through identifying data items in a structured database. Instead of selecting data from prestructured database records that meet the user's criteria, WWW search engines search for Web pages containing the desired words or phrases.

What characteristics determine the usefulness of information?
Information quality is based on accuracy, precision, completeness, age, timeliness, and source. Information accessibility is related to how easy it is to obtain and manipulate the information, regardless of its quality. Information presentation is related to the level of summarization and format for presentation to the user, regardless of information quality and accessibility. A fourth characteristic is information security, the extent to which information is controlled and protected from inappropriate, unauthorized, or illegal access and use.

What is the purpose of building and using mathematical models?
Models are useful because they mimic reality without dealing with every detail of it. Mathematical models are sets of equations or graphs that describe precise relationships between variables. They compensate for our inability to pay attention to hundreds of things at the same time and help organize an analysis. They also create information by evaluating tentative decisions and responding to what-ifs.

Key Terms

data modeling
entity
entity type
relationship
attribute
entity-relationship diagram (ERD)
predefined data items
text
images
audio
video
database
database management system (DBMS)
logical view of data
data model
physical view of data
file
record
field
key
relational database
relation
normalization
SQL (Structured Query Language)
multidimensional database
geographical information system
push system
pull system
data definition
data dictionary
metadata
schema
subschema
sequential access
direct access
collision
indexed access
indexed sequential access method (ISAM)
logical reference
record locking
distributed database
replication
two-phase commit
backup
recovery
database administration

text database
hypertext
hypermedia
browser
Web page
uniform resource locator (URL)
hypertext markup language (HTML)
applets
index
search engine
keyword
information quality
information accessibility
information presentation
information security
value of information
accuracy
precision
bias
random error
completeness
age
timeliness
source
availability
admissibility
level of summarization
format
access restriction
encryption
mental model
mathematical model
what-if questions
sensitivity analysis
virtual reality

Review Questions

1. What is data modeling?
2. What is the difference between an entity and an entity type?
3. Describe some typical attributes of the entity type *patient.*
4. What is an entity-relationship diagram, and why is this technique important?
5. What is the difference between a database and a database management system?
6. Why does defining the data in a database sometimes generate debate?
7. What is the difference between a logical and physical view of data?
8. What is metadata?
9. Explain why it is often impractical to organize all data in a given situation as an individual file.
10. What is a relational database?
11. What five types of data are found in information systems?
12. What is the difference between a conventional paper document and a hypertext document?
13. Explain the difference between a schema and a subschema, and why this is important.
14. Define backup and recovery, and explain why these capabilities are needed in a DBMS.
15. Identify characteristics that constitute information quality, accessibility, and presentation of information.
16. Explain how bias is a component of inaccuracy and whether total objectivity is always desired.
17. Describe the difference between mental and mathematical models.
18. What are the advantages of asking what-if questions?

Discussion Topics

1. The chapter's discussion of accuracy raised the issue that people may intentionally shade or distort the truth. A survey published in the British medical journal *Lancet* asked doctors in Europe how they would break bad news about a cancer diagnosis. The survey found that doctors in Scandinavia, Great Britain, and the Netherlands would be the frankest with their patients, while doctors in southern and eastern Europe generally said they would be evasive even if asked directly by their patients.[14] Explain why this is or is not related to truthfulness of management explanations and recommendations.
2. Virginia Senator John Warner, ranking Republican on the Intelligence Subcommittee, said "I was astonished at the magnitude of the site." The Clinton administration had just declassified information about a $310 million project to create a 70-acre office complex for the National Reconnaissance Office, which procures the nation's space-satellite systems. Senator Warner said that the full scope of the project, which had been approved and started during the Bush administration, hadn't been authorized or appropriated by Congress, as is required by law.[15] How are ideas in this chapter related to this situation? What does this situation imply about information systems in general?

3. Explain how models might be used in making the following decisions:
   a. deciding how much to pay for an apartment building
   b. deciding whether to build a nuclear or fossil fuel power plant
   c. deciding which products to carry in a grocery store
   d. deciding whom to marry
   e. deciding how to allocate a stock portfolio
   f. deciding what to eat for lunch
4. Identify some of the important databases the following individuals might encounter in their work. Identify some of the files in these databases, and the important fields in each file.
   a. factory manager
   b. owner of a construction company
   c. mechanic working in a large automobile repair shop
   d. loan officer in a bank
   e. newspaper reporter
   f. lawyer
   g. marketing analyst in a frozen foods company
5. A distributor of building supplies for contractors has a database involving three types of entities: suppliers, products, and customers. Identify some of the important attributes of each type of entity. Based on your own background and intuition, try to sketch out an entity-relationship diagram and a set of relations that might be applicable in this case.
6. A family uses a database to identify all of its belongings. Assuming the database consists of a single file, identify ten fields that might appear in the database. Explain advantages and disadvantages of having different files for different types of belongings. Show the structure of a database that has different types of records for different types of belongings. Think about how you would include things such as the person in the family who owned the item, what room in the house it was in, and when it was purchased.

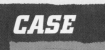

Whirlpool and Thomas & Betts: Managing Price and Product Information Effectively

Maintaining and distributing complete information about product prices is a surprisingly complicated matter for a major manufacturer such as Whirlpool, which manufactures clothes washers, dryers, refrigerators, and other home appliances. Whirlpool sells over 2,000 models, given its many variations of function, size, and color. The quarterly process of revising these prices previously took 110 days and was highly error prone because it was done by updating 180,000 cells in spreadsheets. The spreadsheets were used because pricing was based on separate pricing models and order entry systems for each division of Whirlpool. Unfortunately, a change in a formula in one part of a spreadsheet might have unexpected effects elsewhere. Overall, the quarterly pricing process included calculating the prices, checking them, reviewing the results, inputting the prices into a mainframe, and then distributing the prices to customers and sales reps. The old system also resulted in many pricing discrepancies in which customers were quoted one price but billed at another price when the merchandise arrived.

This pricing system was revamped as part of an effort to make Whirlpool easier to do business with and as a way to respond quickly to pricing decisions by competitors. Starting in mid-1998 the new centralized pricing system would use consistent pricing models that would permit marketing managers to try out price changes, do a profitability analysis, and then distribute the new prices to sales reps immediately. A single pricing administrator would then put that price in effect for the next time the product is ordered.

Thomas & Betts faced a similar problem. It is a worldwide producer of connectors and components for worldwide electrical and electronics markets, with manufacturing facilities throughout North America, in Europe, and in the Far East. Each time it changed a product specification or price for any of its 130,000 products, it had to send a message to each of its 650 distributors. The cost of sending all these messages through electronic data interchange (EDI) was excessive.

Because every major player in this market faced similar problems, 40 of the largest got together to create a centralized, industry-wide repository of product information that any distributor could access at any time. Creating this repository required that all parts manufacturers format their product and pricing data according to the same agreed upon standard. The initial work on the repository identified more than 125 data fields for each part, ranging from the product's name and component parts to the dimensions of its packaging. The plan was to fund the repository via transaction fees paid by users.

QUESTIONS

1. What are the similarities and differences between these situations?
2. Explain why the 41st electrical parts supplier might or might not want to store its product data in the central repository. Explain why the original 40 might or might not want to allow others to join.

Sources:

King, Julia. "Dismantling a Tower of Babel," *Computerworld*, Apr. 27, 1998, p. 1.

Thomas & Betts. "Thomas & Betts Home Page," June 15, 1998 (www.thomasandbetts.com).

Weston, Randy. "Appliance Firm Gives Pricing System a Whirl," *Computerworld*, Mar. 23, 1998, p. 1.

Centerville Home Care Registry: Finding Home Care Workers

Like many urban areas, Centerville (a disguised name) has a Personal Assistance Services Agency (PASA) whose many responsibilities include maintaining a registry of home care workers who provide in-home services for low-income, mostly elderly individuals with significant physical or cognitive disabilities. These services include help in dressing and bathing, reading services for blind people, and a variety of services for people with cognitive disabilities. About 7,000 home care workers perform this work in the Centerville area, and about 300 are included in the registry at any given time. They are paid slightly more than the minimum wage by the state and receive no benefits such as medical coverage or vacation pay. The workers are recruited by six separate nonprofit agencies operating on a contract basis at different sites. Acceptance into the home care registry occurs only after a background check including whether the applicant has a criminal record or other potentially disqualifying problems. The agencies also inform the clients about workers who live nearby and whose qualifications and scheduled availability meet client needs. The payroll process is based on semi-monthly timesheets signed by the workers and clients and sent through county offices to the state for payment. Unlike most home care programs, which provide the client little choice in who provides the services, in Centerville each client (or in some cases, the client's guardian) has the authority to hire specific individuals to do specific tasks. About half the clients hire workers who are family members. The other half hire people who may have been strangers before the agencies helped them make contact.

A small information system was developed by a consultant to keep track of information about the home service providers and to facilitate matches between clients and workers. The original intention was that people at each of the six agencies could enter data into the information system when they received it from applicants. Unfortunately, the information system never worked properly. Several months after the initial installation, the PASA staff discovered that updating the database from multiple sites was generating data errors due to a lack of error checking and other design problems. In one case, for example, a serious complaint against a worker was recorded and inadvertently erased when other data was entered after the worker reapplied at a second agency. The second update apparently erased the first. Due to these problems, PASA had to adopt an awkward workaround in which the six separate agencies collected the data manually and then sent it to the PASA staff, which entered it into the computer and then downloaded the updated database to the six agencies each night. In addition to basic operational problems, the information system could not provide useable management information.

After recognizing these problems, PASA performed a thorough review of its information needs. It wanted a database that could keep track of home care workers and clients, and that could be updated at each of the six agencies. It wanted a more effective way to match workers and clients. It wanted to maintain adequate security for sensitive information. It wanted useful management information. It wanted an information system that could be used by contract agency staff members who had disabilities themselves.

QUESTIONS

1. Use the WCA framework to summarize the situation.
2. Produce an entity-relationship diagram summarizing the information that might appear in the new database.
3. Explain how this case illustrates the applicability of ideas in this chapter.

Source:

Cooper, Michael, Deborah Doctor, Ellen Lacayo, and Brid Sarazin, "Analysis of the Centerville Help Registry," Executive Masters in Rehabilitation Administration Program, University of San Francisco, Apr. 21, 1998.

Communication, Decision Making, and Different Types of Information Systems

5

Study Questions

- How are social context and nonverbal communication important when communication technologies are used?
- What are the phases of decision making?
- What are some of the common limitations and problems in decision making?
- What are the different approaches for improving decision making using information systems?
- What are the general differences between the types of information systems?
- How are features of one type of information system transferable to systems of other types?

Outline

Opening Case

LEVI STRAUSS: PRODUCING JEANS THAT FIT

The Levi Strauss Personal Pair product brought customization to the casual clothing industry by producing customized jeans designed to fit better than off-the-shelf jeans. To purchase these jeans the customer willing to pay an extra $10 must go to a properly equipped Levi's retailer where a salesperson takes four measurements, inseam, waist, hips, and rise. The salesperson enters these numbers into a computer, which identifies one of over 400 pairs of nonadjustable "fitting jeans" that are only for try-on use. The customer tries on the fitting jeans and tells the salesperson about any adjustments that would improve the fit. The salesperson uses these suggestions to produce the precise measurements for the customized jeans. In effect, these are a manufacturing specification for a factory in Tennessee. A computer network transmits the specification to the factory, where the customized jeans are assembled and mailed directly to the customer or to the store within three weeks. Sewed into the waistband is a barcode with an individual customer reference number. The customer can order another pair easily because the personal measurement information is saved in a database.

The gradual introduction of the Personal Pair product began in 1995. Despite its success, it does have shortcomings. A properly equipped store must use some of its valuable space for over 400 pairs of nonsaleable jeans, and even these may not be sufficient to insure that a customer will find a perfect match. The fitting process is more work for the salesperson. It is also less efficient at the factory because the fabric for each pair of jeans must be cut just for that pair by a specially adapted cutting machine. In contrast, most machines cutting cloth for regular jeans can cut 60 layers of denim simultaneously. Other factory problems include complicated scheduling and the need for additional inspections.[1]

Debate Topic

Within five or ten years most clothing products sold by high-quality retailers will be manufactured by using information systems as part of a customization process.

The previous chapters showed how to think about systems, business processes, and information from a business professional's viewpoint. This chapter shows the range of possibilities for using information systems to improve communication, decision making, and execution within a system. The introductory case showed how customization and production of Levi Strauss Personal Pair jeans depends on a series of information systems that support communication and decision making functions. These systems store information about the customer, record the sales transaction, suggest which sample pair to try on, store the precise measurements, transmit the measurements to the factory, and support the scheduling, inspection, and delivery. (See Table 5.1.)

This chapter serves two purposes. First, it explains basic ideas about communication and decision making, crucial aspects of executing almost any business processes. Table 5.2 shows that information systems can improve communication and decision making in terms of each of the internal business process performance variables identified by the WCA method (Table 2.5). Second, the chapter summarizes six basic types of information systems, each of which uses a different approach for supporting business processes. As you will see, the process of providing customized jeans uses features of most of these types of information systems. These two purposes are combined in a single chapter because the major differences between the types of information systems are related to the different ways they support communication, decision making, and execution.

This chapter starts with basic communication concepts, such as social context, the time, place, and direction of communication, and different approaches for improving communication. It covers ideas about decision making, such as steps in decision making, rationality, common flaws in decision making, and approaches for improving decision making. The last half discusses the ways various types of information systems support communication and decision making. The types of systems discussed include office automation systems,

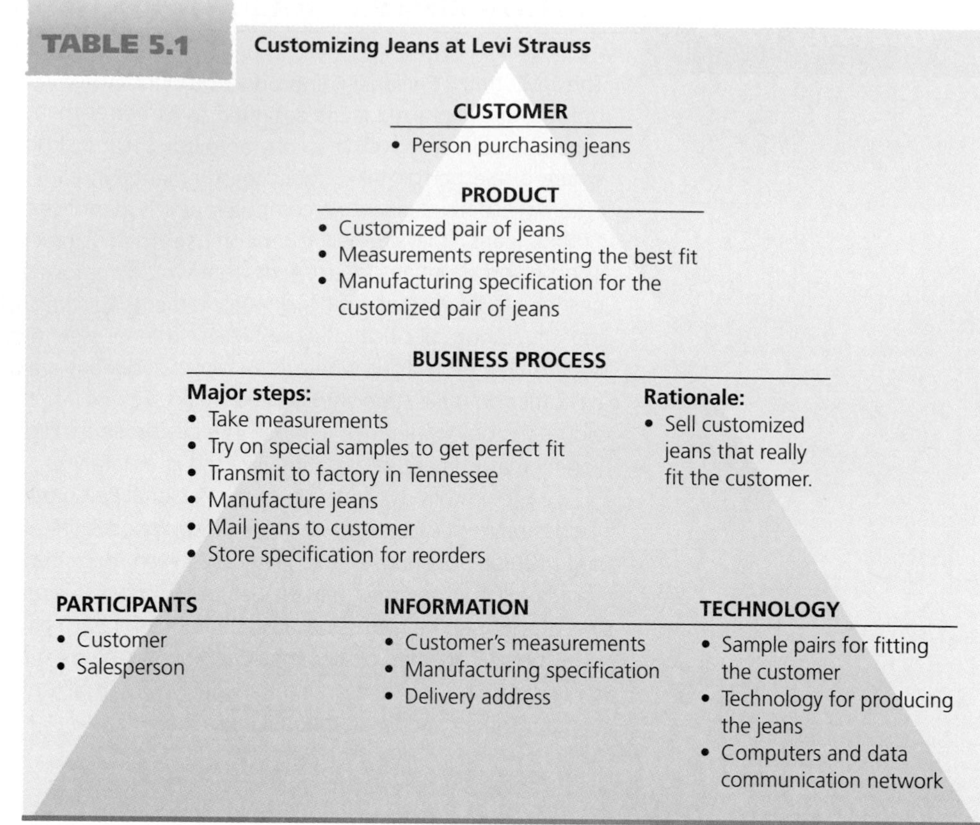

TABLE 5.1 **Customizing Jeans at Levi Strauss**

CUSTOMER

- Person purchasing jeans

PRODUCT

- Customized pair of jeans
- Measurements representing the best fit
- Manufacturing specification for the customized pair of jeans

BUSINESS PROCESS

Major steps:

- Take measurements
- Try on special samples to get perfect fit
- Transmit to factory in Tennessee
- Manufacture jeans
- Mail jeans to customer
- Store specification for reorders

Rationale:

- Sell customized jeans that really fit the customer.

PARTICIPANTS

- Customer
- Salesperson

INFORMATION

- Customer's measurements
- Manufacturing specification
- Delivery address

TECHNOLOGY

- Sample pairs for fitting the customer
- Technology for producing the jeans
- Computers and data communication network

communication systems, transaction processing systems, management and executive information systems, decision support systems, and execution systems.

BASIC COMMUNICATION CONCEPTS

Basic concepts about communication are a necessary starting point for analyzing many types of IT applications. Where there is a mismatch between the technology and the situation's needs, communication technology may hinder rather than help communication.

Social Context

Social context, the situation and relationships within which communication takes place, includes social presence, organizational position, relationships, cultural norms, age, gender, and the topic being discussed. The first component, social presence, is the extent to which the recipient of communication perceives it as personal interaction with another person. We feel social presence strongly because we all learn how to communicate in face-to-face situations where social presence is powerful.

Much of what is communicated in face-to-face situations is communicated through **nonverbal communication,** such as facial expressions, eye contact, gestures, and body language. This is why two different people saying exactly the same words may communicate different thoughts and feelings. This is also why different degrees of social presence are desirable in different communication situations. In some situations, getting the message across requires a strong feeling of social presence. In others, such as communication of orders and bills between companies, social presence is unimportant.

Different communication technologies filter out nonverbal information and decrease social context cues to varying extents. A face-to-face meeting provides richer communication than a telephone call because the telephone filters out body language, eye contact, and facial expressions. Similarly, a telephone call provides richer communication than a computerized text message because text filters out voice inflection and intensity.

TABLE 5.2 **Ways Information Systems Can Improve Communication and Decision Making Performance within Business Processes**

This table is organized in terms of the internal performance variables for business processes (Table 2.5 in Chapter 2).

Business process performance variable	How information systems can improve communication	How information systems can improve decision making
Rate of output	Communicate more information or more types to more people	Make more decisions using better, more complete information
Consistency	Make sure different people receive the same communication	Make sure repetitive decisions are made in the same way
Productivity	Achieve more communication with less effort	Make better decisions with less effort
Cycle time	Eliminate undesirable delays in communication	Eliminate unnecessary delays in decision making
Flexibility	Permit communication in many different forms	Maintain decision quality across a wider range of situations
Security	Make sure communications go only to the intended recipients	Make sure decisions are controlled only by those authorized to make the decisions

Personal, Impersonal, and Anonymous Communication

The form and content of communication vary depending on whether communication is personal, impersonal, or anonymous. In **personal communication** the personal relationship between the sender and receiver affects both form and content even in business situations. Even though an employee's performance review conveys factual information in a business setting, it is based in a personal relationship and therefore is an example of personal communication. In **impersonal communication** the specific identity and personality of the sender and recipient affect the communication less, if at all, because the sender and receiver act as agents implementing the policies and tactics of business organizations. Impersonal communication occurs when you pay a credit card bill because what matters most is receipt of the payment before the deadline. The sender's identity is purposely hidden in **anonymous communication,** which is used in situations ranging from the suggestion box to crime tips for the police.

IT can make communication more personal or more impersonal. For example, using an automated voice messaging system makes parts of communication more impersonal because the caller leaves a message without speaking to a person. In contrast, IT has been used in customer service to create the appearance of personal service by making customer information readily available to customer service agents as soon as they answer a call.

Time, Place, and Direction of Communication

Communication can be described in terms of whether the sender and recipient are present at the same time, whether they are present at the same place, and whether the communication is inherently one-way or two-way. *Same-time* (also called synchronous) communication occurs when both sender and recipient are available simultaneously. *Different-time* (also called asynchronous) communication occurs when the participants are not available simultaneously, and therefore requires recording of a message. As electronic communication technologies advanced, the first step was often same-time transmission, such as telephone, live radio, and live television. Different-time communication became possible as cost-effective recording technologies appeared, ranging from taping TV programs to recording phone messages.

Table 5.3 shows how common communication technologies can be categorized by the time and place of communication. Technologies that link people across a distance

TABLE 5.3 **Communication Technologies Classified by Time and Place of Communication**

This table classifies communication technologies based on the time/place relationship between the sender and recipient. Notice that electronic mail and voice mail can be used when the sender and recipient are in the same place (such as in the same office) or in different places.

	Same time	Different time
Same place	• Presentation systems • Group decision support systems (GDSS)	• Transaction databases • World Wide Web • Electronic mail • Voice mail
Different place	• Typical telephones • Computer conferencing • Video telephones and conferencing • Nonrecorded radio or TV broadcast	• Transaction databases • World Wide Web • Electronic data interchange (EDI) • Electronic mail • Voice mail • Fax • Prerecorded radio or TV broadcast

are commonly thought of as communication technology, but IT can support communication in other ways as well. As described later, presentation systems and group decision support systems help people in face-to-face meetings communicate more effectively. Even online databases from data processing systems, such as inventory and reservations systems, serve a role in communication by substituting computer queries for unnecessary person-to-person communication when all that is needed is data.

The direction of communication is also important because one-way and two-way communications are different. Typical radio and television broadcasting involves one-way communication. In contrast, video conferencing systems support two-way communication needed for interactive business meetings. An important issue in planning for the future of telecommunications infrastructure for voice, computerized data, and video is about which parts of the infrastructure will be one-way or two-way.

Approaches for Improving Communication

The ways information systems can help improve communication include making face-to-face communication more effective, eliminating unnecessary person-to-person communication, making communication systematic, and combining and extending electronic communication functions.

Making Face-to-Face Communication More Effective

Face-to-face communication is a starting point for thinking about using technology to improve communication. **Presentation technologies** are devices and techniques used to help present ideas more effectively in same-time, same-place meetings. The simplest of these technologies include chalkboards and overhead projectors. More complex technologies use computer-controlled multimedia combining audio and video.

Different presentation technologies can be compared in terms of cost-effectiveness, degree of preparation required, and availability. Although least expensive, the chalkboard is probably the least effective because people have trouble writing clearly while saying something interesting and because the audience must split its attention between listening and taking notes. However, chalkboards are readily available and can be used with little preparation. Computer-controlled multimedia presentations require more preparation but can communicate more effectively than a speaker with a chalkboard. Similar advantages and disadvantages should be considered when comparing any computerized or noncomputerized techniques for improving communication or decision making.

Eliminating Unnecessary Person-to-Person Communication

Substituting online data access for person-to-person communication has been essential for keeping costs under control while firms expand. For example, this permits a salesperson at a customer site to find out about product availability without disturbing someone else's work. Obtaining data is important in these situations, but personal communication is not. This same approach has been used to improve links with both suppliers and customers. After negotiating long-term commitments with suppliers, firms transmit daily production schedules to their suppliers, who time their shipments so that components arrive when needed. Similarly, firms ranging from airlines to stock brokerages improve customer service by permitting purchases using computerized systems to bypass unnecessary person-to-person communication.

Whether or not person-to-person communication is necessary is especially important when external customers are involved. Replacing human contact with an automated system sometimes conveys a less personal and more machine-like appearance to customers. Bank customers seem to accept "talking to" ATMs instead of bank clerks but sometimes wish a person would answer the telephone instead of an automated attendant with the message "Hello, this is Intergalactic Savings. Press 1 to obtain account information. Press 2 for customer service. Press 3 for the personnel department."

Making Communication Systematic

Communication between people tends to be unstructured. Usually there is little or no effort to make the individual messages conform to a pre-conceived format, such as saying this is a formal request from a specific *sender* to a specific *recipient* about doing a specific *task* by a specific *date*. Instead, people tend to say things in whatever way strikes their fancy, consistent with the social context. In contrast, recordkeeping practices long before computers showed that structuring information is essential for handling it systematically. At minimum, having structure reduces the effort required to figure out how the information is defined.

As communication systems became more automated, users found more advantages in structuring parts of these systems. The greatest structuring goes into impersonal or anonymous communications between departments in a business, or between separate businesses. For example, systems using computers to communicate orders between suppliers and customers must conform to strict data formats and definitions. Otherwise people on both sides of the transaction would have to communicate directly to clarify what it meant. Even with communication between groups of people rather than computers, it is often more efficient to systematize the repetitive steps. For example, repetitive approval cycles for expenses or projects typically use a prescribed format so that the people involved don't have to waste time deciding on the format each time a similar situation arises.

Combining and Extending Electronic Communication Functions

Early electronic communications came from several different directions. The telegraph transmitted a coded text message across a wire. The telephone supported a same-time, different-place voice conversation between two people using wired telephones connected by a human telephone operator. Radio and television broadcasting transmitted audio and video signals through space. Figure 1.8 in Chapter 1 showed how these original ideas have been combined and expanded through the convergence of computing and communications. Clearly, point-to-point communication over a distance can now be much more than a two-person conversation over a wire. The caller or receiver could be a person or a computer; the data transmitted might be voice, computerized data, pictures, or video; the data might be stored when received; the device used for sending or receiving might be portable; the addressing information for locating the receiver might be used in many ways.

The basic communication concepts just covered are essential for understanding why different types of information systems may be effective or ineffective in the different types of things they do. A set of ideas about decision making are also needed as background before we look at different types of information systems.

Reality Check

EFFECTS OF COMMUNICATION SITUATIONS

The text differentiates between different degrees of social presence in communication (personal, impersonal, and anonymous) and between different combinations of time, place, and direction of communication (same-time versus different-time, same-place versus different-place, and one-way versus two-way).

1. Thinking about things you have done at work or in school, give examples of communication illustrating each variation on these two aspects of the communication situation.
2. For each example identify ways it might have been possible to improve the communication by changing these aspects of the communication situation in some way.

BASIC DECISION MAKING CONCEPTS

An understanding of decision making is essential because information systems are designed to support decision making in one way or another. The phases of decision making are covered first, followed by rationality, common flaws in decision making, and approaches for improving decision making.

Steps in a Decision Process

Figure 5.1 combines several models researchers have proposed for describing decision processes. Decision making is represented as a problem solving process preceded by a separate problem finding process. **Problem finding** is the process of identifying and formulating problems that should be solved.[2] Although often overlooked, problem finding is the key to effective decision making because a seemingly good solution to the wrong problem may miss the point. For example, we might come up with many solutions to the problem of how to expand our airports, but it might be better to formulate the problem as "How can we avoid expanding our airports by using transportation substitutes such as video conferencing?"

Problem solving is the process of using information, knowledge, and intuition to solve a problem that has been defined previously. The problem solving portion of Figure 5.1 says that most decision processes can be divided into four phases: intelligence, design, choice, and implementation.

- **Intelligence** includes the collection and analysis of data related to the problem identified in the problem finding stage. Key challenges in the intelligence phase include obtaining complete and accurate data and figuring out what the data imply for the decision at hand.
- **Design** includes systematic study of the problem, creation of alternatives, and evaluation of outcomes. Key challenges in this phase include bounding the problem to make it manageable, creating real alternatives, and developing criteria and models for evaluating the alternatives.
- **Choice** is the selection of the preferred alternative. Key challenges here include reconciling conflicting objectives and interests, incorporating uncertainty, and managing group decision processes.
- **Implementation** is the process of putting the decision into effect. This includes explaining the decision to the appropriate people, building consensus that the decision makes sense, and creating the commitment to follow through. Key challenges involve

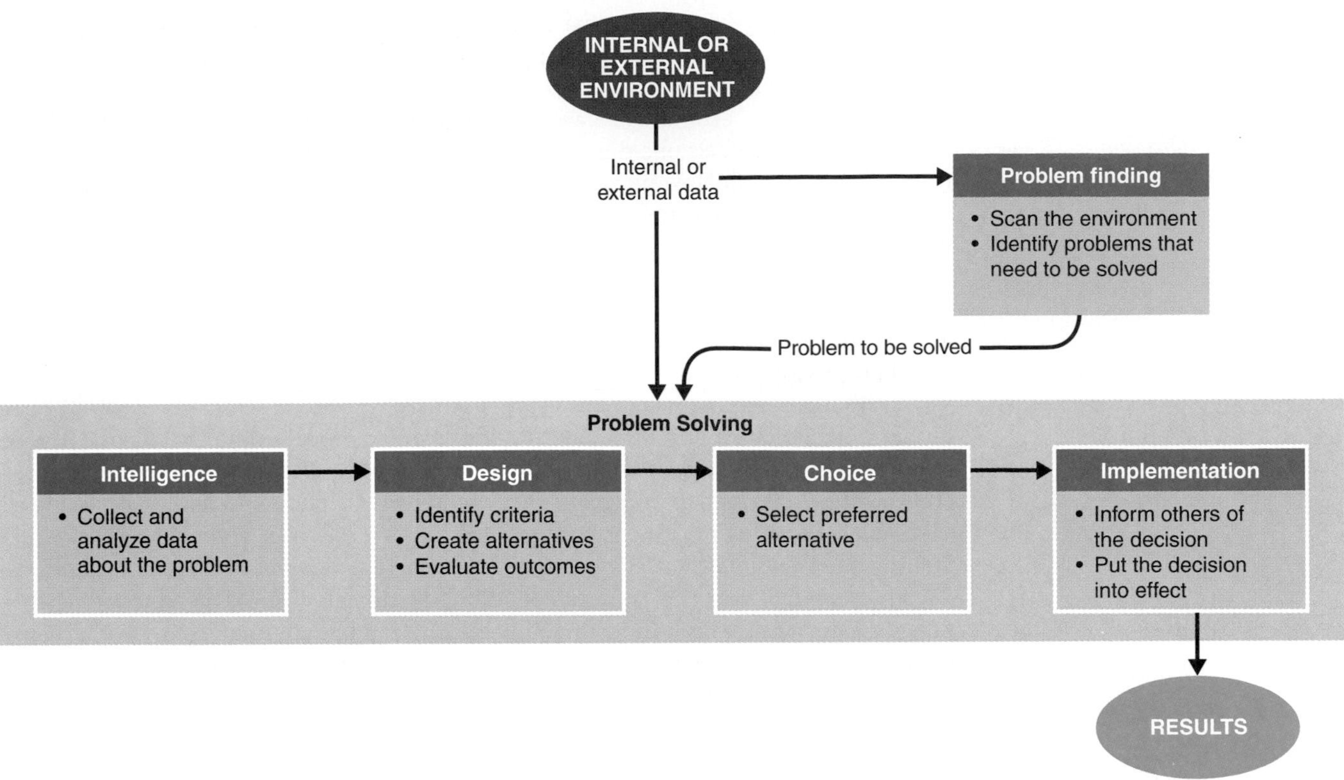

Figure 5.1
Steps in decision making

The diagram shows decision making as a four-phase problem solving process preceded by a problem finding process.

ensuring that the decision and its implications are understood and that others in the organization will follow through, whether or not their preferred alternative is chosen.

The first three phases of the problem solving process are Simon's classic model of decision making.[3] The intelligence phase converts data into information for designing alternatives. The design phase creates the alternatives, one of which is selected during the choice phase. Implementation is the fourth phase because the problem is not solved until the decision is put into operation. Perhaps surprisingly, many information systems designed to support decision making have their greatest impact not in making decisions, but in implementation activities such as explaining and justifying decisions.

The model is an idealization that separates decision making into separate phases, but real decision processes are iterative and return to previous phases. This can happen if the intelligence phase determines that the problem was not defined properly, or if the design phase determines that more information is needed. In similar fashion, the choice or implementation phases might identify needs for additional information or issues requiring the development of additional alternatives.

Rationality and Satisficing

Describing the phases in decision making is a starting point for explaining how people make decisions, but it raises questions as well, such as whether people are rational decision makers and what that means.

Rationality is a common model for explaining how people should make decisions. Classical economic theory says that rational decision makers maximize their welfare by performing the first three phases of problem solving thoroughly. First, they gather all pertinent information and interpret it. Second, they identify all feasible alternatives and evaluate them based on criteria that maximize the good of the individual or organization. Third, they choose among the alternatives based on consistent and explicit tradeoffs between the criteria.

For centuries economists have argued about whether people show rationality by making economic decisions that maximize their own welfare and whether the sum of these decisions ultimately maximizes society's welfare. Consider two situations. In the first, Pat is an unmarried employee who has decided to move to a new apartment in a different area of town and has plenty of time to look for a good apartment. In the second situation, Pat has volunteered to move temporarily to another city to work on an important project that will last eight months. Pat can stay in a hotel for a few weeks but needs to find an apartment for the remainder of the time. The project has been underway for over a year, and there is a lot of work to catch up on.

Although the process of renting an apartment involves the phases of intelligence, design, and choice in both situations, the phases would proceed differently. In the first situation, Pat would have more time to look around, identify alternatives, and select the best choice within a budget. In the second, Pat would have to make a decision quickly, even if the available apartments weren't very good. As is often the case, it would be necessary to identify a few feasible alternatives and choose one. The fact that Pat would not optimize doesn't mean that the decision would be irrational. Rather, it would mean that this situation called for a fast decision after finding several acceptable alternatives. In another sense, the problem being solved is not just finding an apartment, but a combination of which apartment to rent and how much time to spend looking. Under the circumstances, spending much more time to get a slightly better apartment wouldn't be feasible.

Choosing a satisfactory alternative rather than searching for an optimal alternative is called **satisficing.** The concept of satisficing came from Simon's attempt to describe the way people actually behave rather than the way they should behave if they optimized all or even most decisions. Satisficing is consistent with a theory of **bounded rationality,** whereby people make decisions in a limited amount of time, based on limited information, and with limited ability to process that information. Think about any decision you made recently: where to live or what to do next weekend. As you examine the way you made the decision, you will probably conclude that you could not obtain all relevant information. In fact, you probably couldn't even define all possible alternatives, much less consider them seriously. You may also have had difficulty defining the criteria to use in choosing the desired alternative.

Information systems have value in decision making because they reduce some of the bounds on rationality by providing more information, helping generate and evaluate alternatives, and helping select among them. Except in extremely structured decisions, however, you might still feel that you don't have all the information you would like to have and that you aren't totally sure how to create and evaluate the alternatives.

Common Flaws in Decision Making

Both business professionals and psychologists have observed common flaws in the way people make decisions. To supplement the examples that follow, Table 5.4 defines each problem and mentions some of the ways information systems might be used to avoid the related errors. Although few information systems are designed specifically to counter these problems, recognizing them helps in understanding what information systems can and cannot do for us.

- *Poor framing:* Decision makers often allow a decision to be "framed" by the language or context in which it is presented. In one experiment, two groups of students were given identical information about a business strategy. One group was told that the strategy had an 80% probability of success; the other was told that it had a 20% probability of failure. The majority of the "80% success" group gave the go-ahead, whereas the majority of the "20% failure" group did not. The only difference was the way the issue was framed.[4]

TABLE 5.4 How Information Systems Might Help Counteract Common Flaws in Decision Making

Common flaw	Description	How an information system might help
Poor framing	Allowing a decision to be influenced excessively by the language used for describing the decision	Provide information encouraging different ways to think about the definition of the issue
Recency effects	Giving undue weight to the most recent information	Provide information showing how the most recent information might not be representative
Primacy effects	Giving undue weight to the first information received	Show how some information is inconsistent with the first information received
Poor probability estimation	Overestimating the probability of familiar or dramatic events; underestimating the probability of negative events	Make it easier to estimate probabilities based on pertinent data
Overconfidence	Believing too strongly in one's own knowledge	Provide counterexamples or models showing that other conclusions might also make sense
Escalation phenomena	Unwillingness to abandon courses of action decided upon previously	Provide information or models showing how the current approach might give poor results
Association bias	Reusing strategies that were successful in the past, regardless of whether they fit the current situation	Provide information showing how the current situation differs from past situations
Groupthink	Bowing to group consensus and cohesiveness instead of bringing out unpopular ideas	Provide information inconsistent with the current consensus and prove its relevance

- *Recency effects:* People frequently make decisions based on information received most recently. This is why an indecisive executive's advisers sometimes jockey to be the last person to give advice. This effect is sometimes called availability bias, meaning that the most easily visualized or most readily available information has the greatest weight in the decision.
- *Primacy effects:* It is often difficult for people to change an opinion or position about an issue once they have defined it. Because they are stuck on that spot, this effect is sometimes called anchoring. Negotiators sometimes exploit this idea by establishing a bargaining position and gradually giving in just a little.
- *Poor probability estimation:* People tend to overestimate the probability of familiar, dramatic, or beneficial events and greatly underestimate the probability of negative events. This is why people overestimate the frequency of deaths from causes such as accidents, homicides, and cancer and underestimate the frequency of deaths from unspectacular causes and diseases that are common in nonfatal form such as diabetes, stroke, tuberculosis, and asthma.[5]
- *Overconfidence:* Both experts and the general public tend to be overconfident about the accuracy of what they know. As they think about an issue and reach initial conclusions, they tend to remember supporting facts and ignore contrary ones. This may be one reason why one year before the space shuttle Challenger disaster, NASA estimated the probability of such an accident as one in 100,000, even though the historical proportion of booster rockets blowing up is 1 in 57.[6] (See Figure 5.2.)
- *Escalation phenomena:* Decision makers often find it difficult to abandon courses of action that have already been adopted and therefore ignore feedback indicating the course of action is failing. Decision makers who are not caught in escalation phenomena cut their losses by changing strategies and do not throw good money after bad.

Figure 5.2
How likely was this tragedy?

NASA demonstrated overconfidence when it ignored history when estimating the probability of this type of accident.

- *Association bias:* Decision makers trying to repeat their past successes may choose strategies more related to a past situation than the current one.
- *Groupthink:* This is what happens when the need to maintain group consensus and cohesiveness overpowers the group's desire to make the best decision. A famous example is the acceptance of faulty assumptions by President Kennedy and his advisors during the disastrous decision to support the Bay of Pigs invasion of Cuba. They assumed a force outnumbered 140 to 1 could prevail because the Cuban people would immediately join invaders trying to overthrow the government.[7]

Although Table 5.4 lists some possible ways information systems could be used to counteract these flaws, few information systems are designed specifically for this purpose. A much more general way to think about the role of information systems is to look at different approaches information systems use for improving decision making.

Approaches for Improving Decision Making

Because communication and decision making are tightly intertwined, any of the approaches mentioned earlier for improving communication can have an impact in improving decision making. This section focuses on ideas specifically related to decision making.

Much of an information system's impact is determined by the extent to which it imposes structure on decisions or other tasks. Chapter 3 explained three broad categories describing the degree to which a task or decision is structured. An information system imposes a small degree of structure if it provides tools or information a person can use, but does not dictate how the tools or information should be used in making the decision. It imparts more structure if it enforces rules and procedures but still permits the decision maker some leeway. It imposes the most structure when it automates the decision. Selecting the approach for structuring decisions is a basic design choice in using information systems to improve decision making. This choice is important because decision quality can be reduced by imposing too little structure or too much. Each category will be discussed, starting with the lower degrees of structure.

Providing Access to Tools and Information

Access to tools or information makes them available but does not force the user to perform the task or make the decision in a particular way. The gradations within this category start with providing general-purpose tools such as telephones, word processors, and spreadsheets, which make work more efficient but have little or no impact on the content of the information being used. Raw data in a marketing database supports a brand manager's analysis but doesn't determine exactly how the analysis will be done. The filtered and summarized information in a management report provides structure by focusing on pertinent performance measures and leaving out irrelevant detail; again, it doesn't tell the manager what to do.

Specialized tools such as computer aided design (CAD) systems for architects add more structure because they determine parts of the architect's design and problem solving process. Nonetheless, they determine neither the function nor features of the building being designed. Finally, simulation or optimization models may structure parts of an investment analysis, even though the planner's recommendations will be based on other factors as well, including organizational history, politics, and personal ambitions. This shows that even use of an optimization model doesn't guarantee that the information system determines the final decision.

Enforcing Rules and Procedures

Many situations involve repetitive decisions for which the information requirements are known along with rules or methods for making the decisions most of the time. In such cases, major parts of the decision process can be structured to improve the consistency and quality of the outcome. Decisions of this type occur in everyday tasks such as authorizing, assigning, scheduling, pricing, buying, and diagnosing.

An information system that enforces rules and procedures exerts more control over the process and substance of work than a system that just provides tools or information. A minimal level of enforcement occurs when the system identifies exceptions or provides warnings that corrective action may be needed. Providing active guidelines for each step imposes more structure by dictating what information will be used and how it will be combined in making the decision. Finally, a system that controls work, such as a short order chef's system that beeps when a hamburger should be done, monitors a business process and tells someone what to do.

An example of structuring repetitive decisions is the use of standardized procedures by banks to authorize car loans and other types of credit. The basic approach is to obtain particular data about the loan applicant, assign a weight for each item, and then calculate a total score. (See Figure 5.3.) The data include things such as salary, available collateral, and length of time at the current address and job. The system in such situations tries to make sure decisions are made consistently and do not overlook key factors.

Typical of information systems that structure repetitive work, the example in Figure 5.3 uses an explicit model for making or evaluating a decision. Models in such systems may be as simple as rules and formulas on pencil and paper worksheets. They may also be computerized simulation or optimization models. The significance of using a computer involves much more than adding up the numbers. Using a computer allows storage of data for later analysis and use of more complex rules and procedures than might be possible on a paper and pencil worksheet. Computerized systems also store data that regulators can use to decide whether loans have been allocated fairly among different ethnic and income groups.

Automating Decisions

Information systems that impose the most structure automate most or all of a task by dictating the rules or procedures that will be used rather than relying on human judgment in each case. Automating decisions can have important advantages if a great deal of information must be processed or if small time delays affect the outcome. For example, automatic collision avoidance systems in airplanes perform high-speed evasive actions more reliably than human pilots. In the very different realm of finance, brokerage firms use computerized

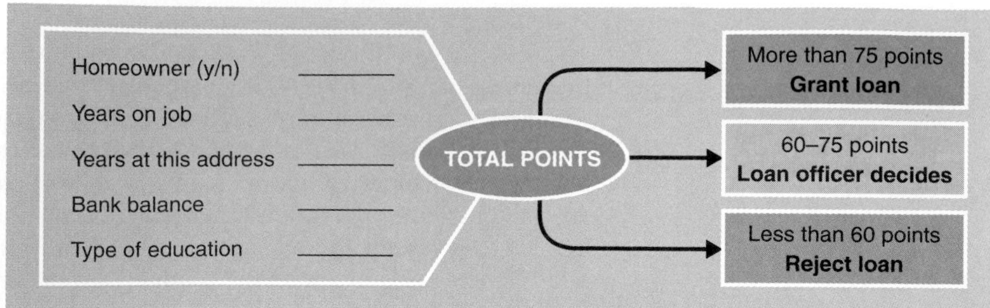

Figure 5.3
Structuring loan authorizations

One way to structure loan authorizations is to assign a certain number of points for each response on a loan application. If the application scores more than a high cutoff amount, the loan is automatically granted. Applications with less than a low cutoff are automatically rejected. Applications between the high and low cutoffs are in a gray area and the loan officer makes the decision based on judgment.

program trading systems to find short-term discrepancies between prices of large groups of stocks and options to buy or sell these groups of stocks in the future. On finding such discrepancies, the system can lock in a guaranteed profit by buying stocks in one market and selling options in the other. Another reason to automate decisions is to improve consistency or efficiency and make errors less likely. Systems for automating inventory reordering are of this type. Some automated systems such as ATMs are simply cheaper and more convenient than having a person perform similar work.

Automating a decision can be seen as a two-step process. First, decide exactly how the decision should be made. Second, create an automatic system for making the decision that way. A computer may play an important role in this second step or may simply automate exactly what a person might do. Consider a college admissions office deciding whom to admit. The dean has decided to divide applicants into two groups, those whose College Board scores exceed a cutoff and those whose scores are lower. Anyone below the cutoff will receive a rejection letter. Regardless of whether this process is carried out by a computer or by a clerk, the dean has eliminated any discretion the admissions office had. Although a person receiving a computer-generated rejection letter might feel that a computer made the decision, the real decision was whether to use a fixed rule as part of the admissions process and exactly what rule to use. In other words, the key issues in automating decisions are often not about computers, but about advantages and disadvantages of delegating a decision to an automatic process instead of human judgment.

Automatic decision making is acceptable only when every aspect of the decision is so well understood that any mistakes will be minor. For example, an automatic inspection machine on a canning line in a food-processing factory may incorrectly designate some good fruit as bad. As long as the percentage of error is tolerably small, this automated system may be cheaper and just as reliable as a system using human inspectors. Automatic decision making is inadvisable when the consequences of errors are large and when important errors are likely due to the possibility of erroneous data or of unanticipated factors that need to be considered. For example, dirt on sensors can cause data errors that affect critical systems such as automatic flight or traffic control.

In contrast, even repetitive business decisions may be difficult to automate without risking too many mistakes. Consider the automated reordering of inventory based on recent usage. If a store sells 1,000 different items, think of the time saved if a computer could automatically reorder an item whenever a corresponding item was sold. But this automatic method would make poor decisions for many fad or fashion items. A totally automated approach might also have difficulty with factors such as quantity discounts, the need to supply an entire product line, and the importance of cooperating with suppliers to maintain business relationships. Except where occasional mistakes are unimportant, human judgment and intuition should be part of any decision process.

Reality Check

DECISION MAKING CONCEPTS

The text names the phases of decision making, discusses the idea of rationality, identifies common flaws in decision making, and explains different ways to improve it.

1. Identify several decisions you have made recently and explain how well or poorly these ideas fit with what happened.
2. Identify aspects of these decisions that seemed easier or more difficult, and explain how the ideas in this section are related to what was easy and what was difficult.

ROLES OF DIFFERENT TYPES OF INFORMATION SYSTEMS IN COMMUNICATION AND DECISION MAKING

This section identifies the different types of information systems and summarizes the way each type supports communication and decision making. Any discussion of types of information systems faces a difficult problem because the categories simply won't hold still. This section will look at six types of information systems used in all the functional areas of business. Previous editions of this book used slightly different categories because real world applications have expanded into many new areas. The first computerized systems were used to collect and summarize data about financial transactions or work that had been done in the past. The advent of real time computing made it possible to integrate computers into the process of doing the work itself. The advent of personal computers made it possible to provide personal tools individuals could use to keep track of their own information, independent of what the rest of the organization was doing. Moreover, the vast expansion of communication capabilities and computer networks made new types of team-oriented systems possible.

Perhaps more problematic from a purist's viewpoint, the categories are not mutually exclusive. Information system categories differ in this regard from categories used in the natural sciences, where there is often detailed agreement about minute differences between biological species or chemical compounds. In contrast, information system categories often overlap and change as new applications combine new capabilities with old ones.

Despite this classification problem, general categories must be discussed because the terms are used frequently in business and because each category supports communication and decision making from a different and important viewpoint. Table 5.5 summarizes the basic idea of each type of system along with the ways each type supports communication and decision making. Table 5.6 gives a brief example of each in the functional areas of sales, manufacturing, and finance. After introducing each system type, the chapter concludes with general issues related to all the system types.

Office Automation Systems: Supporting General Office Work

An **office automation system (OAS)** facilitates everyday information processing tasks in offices and business organizations. These systems include a wide range of tools such as spreadsheets, word processors, and presentation packages. Although telephones, e-mail, v-mail, and fax can be included in this category, we will treat communication systems as a separate category.

OASs help people perform personal recordkeeping, writing, and calculation chores efficiently. Of all the system types, OASs and communication systems are the most familiar to students. Tools generally grouped within the OAS category include:

Spreadsheets are an efficient method for performing calculations that can be visualized in terms of the cells of a spreadsheet. Although spreadsheet programs seem second nature today, the first spreadsheet program was VisiCalc, which helped create the demand for the first personal computers in the late 1970s.

TABLE 5.5 **Typical Ways Each Type of Information System Supports Communication and Decision Making**

Although people often think of information systems as tools for decision making, each type of information system supports both communication and decision making in a number of ways.

System type	Typical user	Impact on communication	Impact on decision making
Office automation system: provides individuals effective ways to process personal and organizational business data, to perform calculations, and to create documents	• Anyone who stores personal data, creates documents, or performs calculations	• Provides tools for creating documents and presentations, such as word processors and presentation systems	• Provides spreadsheets and other tools for analyzing information • Communication tools also help in implementing decisions
Communication system: helps people work together by sharing information in many different forms	• Anyone who communicates with others, including office workers, managers, and professionals	• Telephones and teleconferencing for communication • E-mail, v-mail, fax, for communicating using messages and documents • Access to memos and other shared information • Scheduling meetings • Controlling flow of work	• Telephones and teleconferencing for decision making • E-mail, v-mail, fax, other tools for obtaining information • Supports sharing information related to making joint decisions
Transaction processing system (TPS): collects and stores information about transactions; controls some aspects of transactions	• People whose work involves performing transactions	• Creates a database that can be accessed directly, thereby making some person-to-person communication unnecessary	• Gives immediate feedback on decisions made while processing transactions • Provides information for planning and management decisions
Management information system (MIS) and executive information system (EIS): converts TPS data into information for monitoring performance and managing an organization; provides executives information in a readily accessible interactive format	• Managers, executives, and people who receive feedback about their work	• Provides a basis of facts rather than opinions for explaining problems and their solutions • May incorporate e-mail and other communication methods with presentation of computerized data	• Provides summary information and measures of performance for monitoring results • May provide easy ways to analyze the types of information provided in less flexible form by older MIS
Decision support system (DSS): helps people make decisions by providing information, models, or analysis tools	• Analysts, managers, and other professionals	• Analysis using DSS helps provide a clear rationale for explaining a decision	• Provides tools for analyzing data and building models • Analysis using a DSS helps define and evaluate alternatives
Execution system: directly supports the organization's value added work (e.g., helps sales people sell, helps doctors practice medicine, or helps architects design buildings)	• People who do an organization's value added work, especially if that work involves special skills or knowledge	• May support communication or information sharing between people doing different parts of the task • May help explain the result of the task to customers	• May provide tools, information, or structured methods for making decisions • May store and provide expert knowledge to support decisions in specific areas

Text and image processing systems store, revise, and print documents containing text or image data. These systems started with simple word processors but have evolved to include desktop publishing systems for creating complex documents ranging from brochures to book chapters.

Presentation packages help managers develop presentations independently, instead of working with typists and technical artists. These products automatically

TABLE 5.6 **Examples of Each Type of Information System in Three Functional Areas of Business**

One of the reasons the various categories are mentioned frequently is that each is used in every functional area of business.

System type	Sales examples	Manufacturing examples	Finance examples
Office automation systems	• Spreadsheet to analyze different possible prices • Word processor to create sales contract	• Spreadsheet to analyze a production schedule • Word processor to write a memo about how to fix a machine	• Spreadsheet to compare several loan arrangements • Word processor to write a memo about new financial procedures
Communication systems	• E-mail and fax used to contact customer • Video conference to present new sales materials to sales force • Work flow system to make sure all sales steps are completed • System to coordinate all work on a complex sales contract	• E-mail and v-mail used to discuss a problem with a new machine • Video conference to coordinate manufacturing and sales efforts • Work flow system to make sure engineering changes are approved	• V-mail and fax to communicate with bank about loan arrangements • Video conference to explain effect of financing on factory investments • Work flow system to make sure invoice approval precedes payment • System for exchanging the latest information related to lawsuit
Transaction processing system (TPS)	• Point of sale system for sales transactions • Keeping track of customer contacts during a sales cycle	• Tracking movement of work in process in a factory • Tracking receipts of materials from suppliers	• Processing credit card payments • Payment of stock dividends and bond interest
Management information system (MIS) and executive information system (EIS)	• Weekly sales report by product and region • Consolidation of sales projections by product and region • Flexible access to sales data by product and region	• Weekly production report by production and operation • Determination of planned purchases based on a production schedule • Flexible access to production data by product and operation	• Receivables report showing invoices and payments • Monthly financial plan consolidation • Flexible access to corporate financial plan by line item
Decision support system (DSS)	• System helping insurance salespeople test alternatives • Marketing data and models to analyze sales	• System displaying current priorities for machine operator • Production data and models to analyze production results • Use of a GDSS to identify production problems	• System analyzing characteristics of customers who pay bills promptly • Stock database and models to help in selecting stocks to buy or sell
Execution system	• System to generate competitive bids • System to help salespeople suggest the best choice for the customer	• System to diagnose machine failures • System to transfer customer requirements to an automated machine cell	• System to support a loan approval process • System to find price inconsistencies between different equity markets

convert outlines into printed pages containing appropriately spaced titles and subtitles. These pages can be copied directly onto transparencies or slides used in presentations.

Personal database systems and *note-taking systems* help people keep track of their own personal data (rather than the organization's shared data.) Typical applications include an appointment book and calendar, a to-do list, and a notepad.

When using these tools for personal productivity purposes, users can apply any approach they want because the work is unstructured. In these situations, some individuals use them extensively and enjoy major efficiency benefits, whereas others do not use them at all. The same tools can also be used for broader purposes, however, in which they are incorporated into larger systems that organizations use to structure and routinize tasks. For example, a corporate planning system may require each department manager to fill in and forward a pre-formatted spreadsheet whose uniformity will facilitate the corporation's planning process.

Communication Systems: Making Communication Effective and Efficient

Electronic **communication systems** help people work together by exchanging or sharing information in many different forms. New communication capabilities have changed the way many businesses operate by making it possible to do many things at a distance that previously required being present in a specific location. This section groups these tools into four general categories. Teleconferencing systems make it possible to hold same-time, different-place meetings. Messaging systems make it possible to transmit specific messages to specific individuals or groups of individuals. Groupware systems start with messaging but go further by facilitating access to documents and controlling team-related work flow. Knowledge management systems facilitate the sharing of knowledge rather than just information.

Teleconferencing

The use of electronic transmission to permit same-time, different-place meetings is called **teleconferencing.** We can think of a traditional telephone call as a minimal teleconference, but the term is normally applied to other options including audio conferencing, audiographic conferencing, and video conferencing. (We will include computer conferencing in the discussion of groupware.)

The distinction between these approaches is related to the type of information that is shared. **Audio conferencing** is a single telephone call involving three or more people participating from at least two locations. If several people on the call are in the same office, they can all participate using a speakerphone, which includes a high-sensitivity microphone and a loudspeaker that can be heard by anyone in a room. **Audiographic conferencing** is an extension of audio conferencing permitting dispersed participants to see pictures or graphical material at the same time. This is especially useful when the purpose of the meeting is to share information that is difficult to describe, organize, or visualize, such as a spreadsheet or model used to perform calculations under different assumptions. (See Figure 5.4.) **Video conferencing** is an interactive meeting involving two or more groups of people who can see each other using television screens. The least expensive forms of video conferencing are tiny cameras and 4-inch screens added to telephones or separate video conferencing windows displayed on computer screens. In typical business video conferencing, remote participants appear on a television screen.

Video conferencing simulates a face-to-face meeting without requiring unnecessary travel, which absorbs time and energy, not to speak of the cost of airplane and hotel bills. However, the effectiveness of video conferences decreases if the participants lack a prior social bond. For example, doing sales calls via video conference might seem tempting but might not foster the personal relationship needed to succeed in many sales situations. On the other hand, Citibank and other banks have begun to experiment with stripped-down branch offices that have no tellers but permit customers to open accounts by video conferencing with multilingual staffers in another state.[8]

Messaging Systems

Different-time, different-place communication has been used for centuries in the form of books and letters. Messaging systems make it possible to transmit specific messages to specific individuals or groups of individuals. They use technologies such as electronic mail, voice mail, and fax to make different-time, different-place communication more effective.

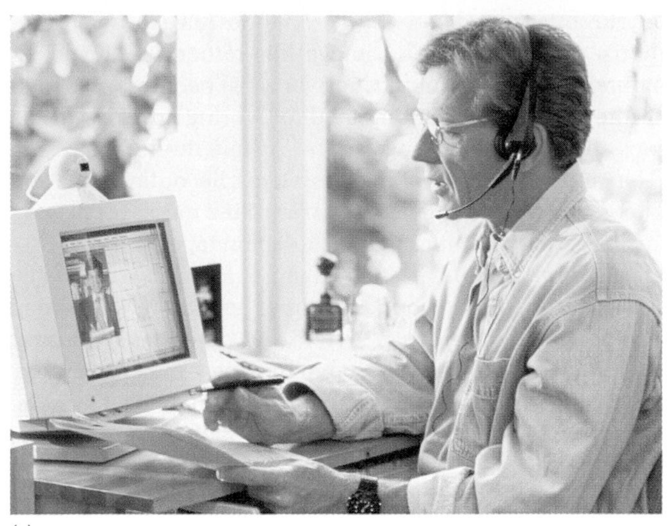
(a)

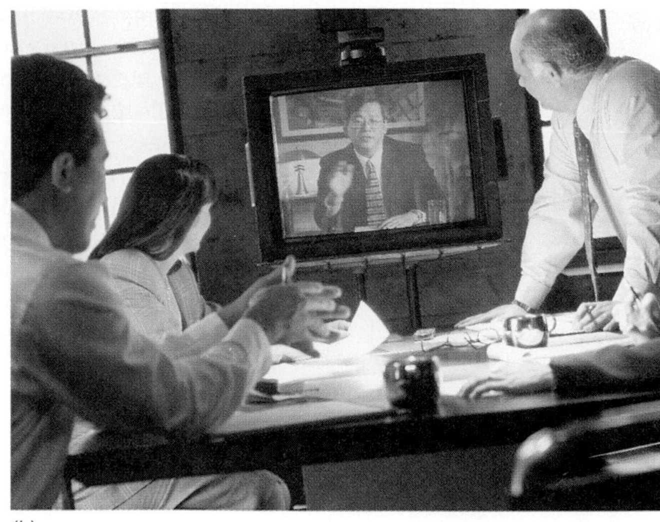
(b)

Figure 5.4
Options for teleconferencing

These photos show examples of two extensions of the original idea of the telephone. The first shows an audiographic conference in which financial analysts in different cities are working together on the same spreadsheet model. The second shows how a video conference provides more social presence than a regular phone call and costs much less than getting on an airplane.

The use of computers to send and retrieve text messages or documents addressed to individual people or locations is called **electronic mail (e-mail).** Each user is identified by an individual account name entered when logging onto the computer. That account name is usually based on the person's name and also serves as the person's e-mail address. The sender uses a word processor to create a message and then addresses it to a distribution list. The distribution list might be an individual account name or a group of names, such as those for the sales department or everyone working on a particular project. The recipient can read the message immediately or can wait until it is convenient. The recipient of an e-mail message can save it, print it, erase it, or forward it to someone else. The recipient can also edit the message to extract parts to be saved, printed, or passed on.

E-mail is effective in many situations, such as permitting you to leave a message without going through an additional person who might garble it. With e-mail you can send a message to a person traveling away from the office who can log onto a network using a laptop computer. If you are working on a memo or other document and want to get feedback from someone before you distribute it, you can use e-mail to send it to the person for a quick response. E-mail also allows you to send the same message to many individuals without having to contact them individually. For example, a product designer can send a request for product ideas to 100 salespeople simultaneously. If even one of them responds with a good idea, the minimal effort of distributing the request is worth it.

There have been many innovative uses of e-mail to improve communication. People in large organizations have used it to bypass bureaucratic structures. For example, top managers sometimes bypass intermediate management levels by obtaining specific information directly from people throughout the organization. Some organizations have replaced the majority of their formal memos with informal e-mail that gets to the point directly. As happened at IBM's Europe headquarters in Paris, e-mail has also been used as a communication tool for people who are not fluent in the language in which business is conducted. E-mail removes accents and permits nonfluent speakers to read a message several times that otherwise might be misunderstood in a phone conversation. It also helps them express their ideas more effectively than they might by using a telephone.[9]

Although e-mail has many advantages and potential uses, it does have the major disadvantage of being a computerized text (or text plus image) file rather than a spoken message, which is the most natural form of communication for most people. **Voice mail (v-mail)** fills this need by providing a computerized method for storing and forwarding spoken messages. It combines the voice recording feature of telephone answering machines with the editing and forwarding concepts of e-mail systems. Recording v-mail on a direct access device makes it possible to access, edit, and forward the messages in ways that were impossible on earlier answering machines that recorded on tape.

In corporate settings v-mail automates the message taking that was once done by telephone attendants who wrote out the message but sometimes garbled it. The v-mail recipient retrieves messages by dialing into the v-mail system and entering an account number and password. This telephone can be anywhere, often making v-mail more practical than e-mail for sending and receiving brief messages in most situations. Once the recipient learns that a v-mail message is waiting, v-mail operates much like e-mail. The recipient can listen to the message, erase it, save it, or forward it. As with an e-mail system, a message can be sent to an individual or to a distribution list.

Voice mail has been used in many innovative ways. Instead of sending notes home with students, teachers in a Connecticut school use voice mail to record messages for parents. The parents call a special telephone number, key in their identification number, and receive the messages. They also use the system to leave messages for the teachers. One teacher who formerly talked to parents once a year at parents night now receives up to ten messages every day.[10] In another innovation, some pharmacies use v-mail for prescription refill orders. Instead of having to talk to a pharmacist, a person with a prescription on file can just call a special voice mail number and leave a voice mail message indicating the patient's name, prescription number, and doctor.

V-mail has several advantages over e-mail. The most important is that telephones are much more commonly available than computers linked to networks. V-mail can be installed in an organization that makes minimal use of computers. Another advantage is that v-mail can convey more emotion and social context than e-mail. However, e-mail has advantages over v-mail in certain areas. For example, e-mail is much better than v-mail systems for conveying details and complex technical information, whereas v-mail is effective for short, nontechnical messages.

Fax is a third electronic form of communication to a different place. It is the transmission of a picture of a page to create a facsimile of the page at a different location. A fax machine scans a piece of paper, digitizes its image, and then transmits this image to another location, where it is printed or stored on a computer for later use. Technical advances commercialized in the early 1980s transformed fax from a decades-old but impracticably slow technology to an everyday tool used in millions of offices. It is possible to send a fax on the day a contract or engineering drawing is due and have it arrive on time, even if the sender is in Minneapolis and the recipient is in Hong Kong. A fax sent late at night (when transmission costs are lowest) can cost less to send than a first class letter.

It is ironic that many faxed documents start as word processing documents and are converted to a less usable digitized form before being transmitted. Regardless of whether the digitized image is produced within the computer or by printing and scanning, ideally it would be more efficient to simply transmit the word processing document by e-mail as an attached file. Current incompatibility problems between e-mail systems and word processors that make this awkward in many cases are gradually disappearing, and e-mail should eventually replace fax for this type of application.

Issues Related to E-mail, V-mail, and Fax

As with any technology, e-mail, v-mail, and fax all have strengths and weaknesses, some of which limit their effectiveness and generate unanticipated consequences.

- *Social context:* E-mail, v-mail, and fax all filter out some of the social context. Ideas communicated using these tools may seem less forceful or caring compared to the same ideas communicated personally. These tools should be used only when social presence is unimportant for understanding the message.

- *Danger of misinterpretation:* The meaning of speech is conveyed partly in the inflection of a voice. Consider the sentences, "That really helped" and "I think you made a mistake." Depending on the context and inflection of the speaker's voice, the first comment could be complimentary or sarcastic. The second could be anything from a mild observation to a reason for firing someone. E-mail and fax provide no clue about inflection, and v-mail filters out body language. People using these tools need to be especially careful not to say things that could be misconstrued, such as jokes.
- *Power relationships:* Use of e-mail and v-mail may create new communication patterns, sometimes involving people who have never communicated previously. With these tools, high-level managers find it easy to obtain information directly from people lower in the organization without going through intermediate managers and chains of command. People in the middle may find themselves out of the loop, as happens with assistants who formerly served as conduits to their bosses.
- *Privacy and confidentiality:* Confidentiality problems may arise because fax outputs can be read by whoever is near the machine, which is often in a clerical work area. The issue of privacy took a bizarre turn in the Iran-gate investigation of illegal arms sales to Iran. Government officials who sold the arms had communicated with each other using e-mail but carefully covered their tracks by erasing the messages. Investigators found backup tapes that had been produced before many of the messages were erased. In this way, the use of e-mail left a trail that eventually aided the investigation.
- *Electronic junk mail:* All three technologies can distribute messages that waste the recipient's time. Users may find that half their e-mail messages are something like "Has anyone seen a green sweater left in room 10-250?" This might seem trivial except that many people receive 50 or more mail messages daily. Junk fax may tie up fax machines when important faxes should be arriving or may use up all the paper in the machine. Some states have considered legislation against it. Companies sending these faxes argue that prohibiting this practice would violate their right to free speech.
- *Information overload:* Common use of e-mail, v-mail, and fax means that people receive more information faster than they ever did before. Sometimes there is an expectation that people will respond quickly and thoroughly, even from home. For managers and professionals already overloaded with information and work, this is not always a welcome development. Some complain that e-mail, v-mail, and fax have generated higher workloads, more stress, and an inability to get away from work.

E-mail, v-mail, and fax have been described as separate technologies but have begun to merge in some ways. The first e-mail systems transmitted text only, but the use of attachments supports images within e-mail messages, thereby adding a capability of fax. How e-mail, v-mail, and fax features will be combined in future products remains to be seen.

We will now turn to communication technologies that became far more visible on the corporate scene in the late 1990s. These technologies include groupware, intranets and extranets, and knowledge management.

Groupware

A relatively new and still somewhat unshaped category, **groupware** helps teams work together by sharing information and by controlling internal workflows. Coined in the late 1980s,[11] the term groupware has attained wide recognition due to the increasing need for groups to work together more effectively at a distance as a result of downsizing and rapid organizational change. Products viewed as groupware are still new enough that their long-term direction is unclear even though the competitive need to work effectively in dispersed teams is greater than ever.

Groupware goes beyond messaging by facilitating access to documents and controlling team-related workflow. Many groupware products are related to specific group-related tasks such as project management, scheduling meetings ("calendaring"), and retrieving data from shared databases. Lotus Notes, a prominent product in this category, is designed for sharing text and images and contains a data structure that is a cross between a table-oriented database and an outline. For example, a law firm in Seattle uses Lotus Notes to permit everyone working on a particular case to have access to the most current memos and other information about that case, even if they are traveling. Other companies use Lotus Notes to store and revise product information for salespeople selling industrial products, thereby replacing the massive three-ring binders they formerly lugged around.

Yet other groupware functions are performed through **computer conferencing,** the exchange of text messages typed into computers from various locations to discuss a particular issue. When done through the Internet this is sometimes called a **newsgroup.** A computer conference permits people in dispersed locations to combine their ideas in useful ways even though they cannot speak to each other face-to-face. Any conference participant may be able to add new ideas, attach comments to existing messages, or direct comments to specific individuals or groups. Proponents of computer conferencing recognize some disadvantages of working through computers but emphasize major advantages, such as preventing a single forceful individual from dominating a meeting. Also, because everything is done through a computer, a record of how ideas developed is automatically generated.

A different type of groupware product focuses primarily on the flow of work in office settings. These products provide tools for structuring the process by which information for a particular multistep task is managed, transferred, and routed. A typical example is the approval of a travel expenditure. In this case, one person must propose the expenditure and someone else must approve it. The workflow application is set up to make the approval process simple and complete. In effect, groupware is being used as a small transaction processing system for multistep transactions. (See the section on transaction processing.)

Intranets and Extranets

The widespread use of the World Wide Web has led many firms to apply the information sharing concepts of groupware on a much larger scale by creating an additional type of communication system, intranets and extranets. **Intranets** are private communication networks that use the type of interface popularized by the Web but are accessible only by authorized employees, contractors, and customers. They are typically used to communicate nonsensitive but broadly useful information such as recent corporate news, general product information, employee manuals, corporate policies, telephone directories, details of health insurance and other employee benefits, and calendars. In some cases employees can use intranets to access and change their personal choices regarding health insurance and other benefits. Once security issues are addressed adequately, intranets for accessing general-purpose corporate data may lead to widespread use of intranets as a front end to transaction processing systems and management information systems described in the following sections.

Extranets are private networks that operate similarly to intranets but are directed at customers rather than at employees. Extranets provide information customers need, such as detailed product descriptions, frequently asked questions about different products, maintenance information, warranties, and how to contact customer service and sales offices. Much of this information was formerly difficult for customers to access because paper versions of it at the customer site became scattered and outdated. By using extranets, companies are making this type of information increasingly available at a single interactive site that is easy to navigate.

Knowledge Management

A final type of communication system is very different from systems that support real time communication or provide access to information. Today's leading businesses are increasingly aware that their employees' knowledge is one of their primary assets. In consulting companies and other organizations that rely heavily on unique competencies and methods, knowledge has more competitive significance than physical assets because the physical assets can be replaced or replenished more easily.

Knowledge management systems are communication systems designed to facilitate the sharing of knowledge rather than just information. As with groupware, the idea of knowledge management is still emerging and is applied in many different ways in different firms. The computer applications underlying knowledge management systems are often built on technologies such as intranets, electronic mail, groupware, databases, and search engines. Functions supported by these technologies include codifying knowledge (such as best practices), organizing it in repositories for later access, finding knowledge (using search engines and other schemes), and providing organized ways to find people who have needed knowledge.[12,13]

The human element is paramount in knowledge management. The companies with the best results to date stitch technologies together into a system that operates effectively and that is genuinely supported by the culture. For example, employee reviews in many consulting companies give significant weight to demonstrated contribution to internal knowledge management systems. This type of recognition is especially important if the firm's culture otherwise encourages hoarding of knowledge for personal advancement. In many cases, the most effective use of knowledge requires involvement of the person who is the expert. When a British Petroleum drilling ship in the North Sea encountered an equipment failure, it put the equipment in front of a video camera and used a satellite link to contact a drilling expert in Scotland. His rapid diagnosis of the problem prevented delays and a possible shutdown.[14]

Transaction Processing Systems: Structuring Repetitive Communication and Decision Processes

A **transaction processing system (TPS)** collects and stores data about transactions and sometimes controls decisions made as part of a transaction. A transaction is a business event that generates or modifies data stored in an information system. TPSs were the first computerized information systems. We encounter computerized TPSs frequently, including every time we write a check, use a credit card, or pay a bill sent by a company. A TPS used to record a sale and generate a receipt is primarily concerned with collecting and storing data. If the TPS validates a credit card or helps a clerk determine whether to accept a personal check, it also controls decisions made within the transaction. Figure 5.5 contains a TPS data entry screen.

TPSs are designed based on detailed specifications for how the transaction should be performed and how to control the collection of specific data in specific data formats and in accordance with rules, policies, and goals of the organization. Most contain enough structure to enforce rules and procedures for work done by clerks or customer service agents. Some TPSs bypass clerks and totally automate transactions, such as the way ATMs automate deposits and cash withdrawals. A well-designed TPS checks each transaction for easily detectable errors such as missing data, data values that are obviously too high or too low, data values that are inconsistent with other data in the database, and data in the wrong format. It may check for required authorizations for the transaction. Certain TPSs such as airline reservation systems may automate decision making functions such as finding the flight that best meets the customer's needs. Finally, when all the information for the transaction has been collected and validated, the TPS stores it in a standard format for later access by others.

As anyone knows who has tried to make a reservation when a computerized reservation system is down, organizations rely heavily on their TPSs. Breakdowns disrupt operations and may even bring business to a complete halt. As a result, a well-designed TPS has backup and recovery procedures that minimize disruptions resulting from computer outages.

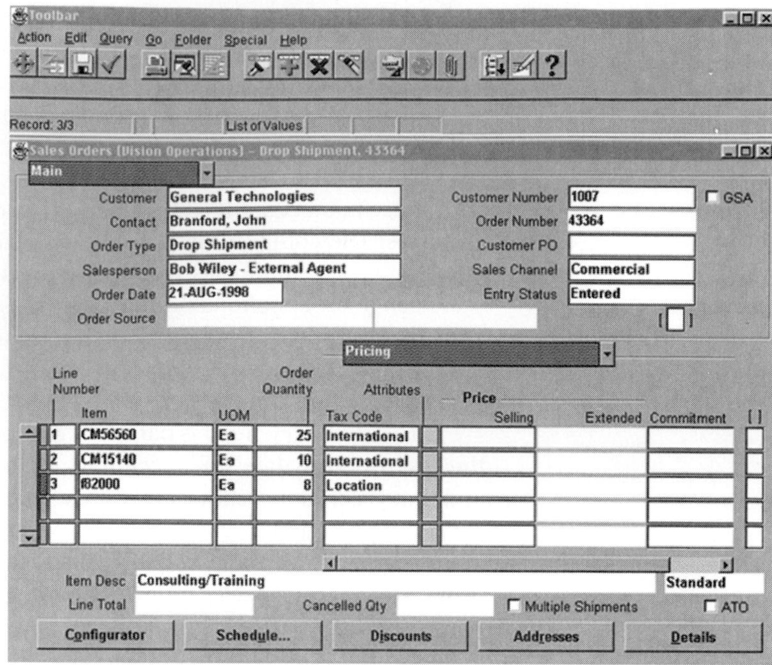

Figure 5.5
Data entry screen from a transaction processing system

This is a data entry screen from a TPS used to enter customer orders. A well-designed TPS can minimize data entry errors by automatically filling in data such as customer address or unit price once the user has entered the customer or product number.

Batch Versus Real Time Processing

The two types of transaction processing are batch processing and real time processing. With **batch processing,** information for individual transactions is gathered and stored but isn't processed immediately. Later, either on a schedule or when a sufficient number of transactions have accumulated, the transactions are processed to update the database. With **real time processing,** each transaction is processed immediately. The person providing the information is typically available to help with error correction and receives confirmation of transaction completion. Batch processing was the only feasible form of transaction processing when data were stored only on punched cards or tapes. Real time transaction processing requires immediate access to an online database.

Batch processing is currently used in some situations where the transaction data comes in on paper, such as in processing checks and airline ticket stubs. A batch approach is also used for generating paychecks and other forms of paper output that will be distributed after a delay. Unfortunately time delays inherent in batch processing may cause significant disadvantages. The central database may never be completely current because of transactions received while the batch was being processed. Worse yet, batching the transactions creates built-in delays, with transactions not completed until the next day in some cases. Even systems with interactive user interfaces may include lengthy delays before transactions are completed. For example, weekend deposits into many ATMs are not posted to the depositor's account until Monday. Even though the ATM's user interface is interactive, the system in a larger sense doesn't perform real time processing.

Compared to batch processing, real time processing has more stringent requirements for computer response and computer uptime. As is obvious when a travel agent says "Sorry, the computer is down," the jobs and work methods of the people in the real time TPS are designed under the assumption that the system will be up and available.

Enterprise Information Systems

Many firms have tried to take transaction processing to a higher level by creating enterprise information systems that encompass the transaction processing done in the various functional silos described in Chapter 2. The idea of these efforts is to create unified databases that permit any authorized individual to obtain whatever information would be helpful in making decisions across the organization. In theory at least, having all this information in a unified database should improve decision making. Enterprise information systems are quite controversial because the effort to create them is enormous. They involve much more than changing the format of databases. Often it is necessary to change business processes to suit the needs of the information system instead of vice versa. Nonetheless, many organizations have found that the integration resulting from this large investment seems to be worthwhile. The last section of this chapter explains why these information systems are usually called enterprise resource planning (ERP) systems even though planning is not their main focus.

Management and Executive Information Systems: Providing Information for Management

A **management information system (MIS)** provides information for an organization's managers. The idea of MIS predates the computer age. For example, as long ago as the middle 1500s, the Fugger family in Augsberg, Germany, had business interests throughout Europe and even into China and Peru. To keep in touch, they set up a worldwide news reporting service through which their agents wrote letters about critical political and economic events in their areas of responsibility. These letters were collected, interpreted, analyzed, and summarized in Augsberg and answered through instructions sent to the family's agents. This paper-based system encompassing planning, execution, and control helped the family move more rapidly in the mercantile world than their rivals.[15] Instructions went out to the agents; the agents executed their work; and the agents reported their results.

Computerized MISs generate information for monitoring performance, maintaining coordination, and providing background information about the organization's operation. Users include both managers and the employees who receive feedback about performance indicators such as productivity. Figure 5.6 shows a sample report generated by an MIS. Notice how it provides summary information rather than the details of individual sales transactions.

The concept of MIS emerged partly as a response to the shortcomings of the first computerized TPSs, which often improved transaction processing but provided little information

Figure 5.6
A management report from an MIS

This figure represents a management report showing last month's sales results for an office supplies company that is expanding out of its major Midwest markets into the Southeast and Far West.

Division/ Branch	Sales	Plan	Perf vs. Plan	Sales Per Rep.	% Repeat Sales
Southeast					
Atlanta	1217	1189	1.02	112	51
Miami	1643	1734	0.95	137	34
New Orleans	1373	1399	0.98	108	44
Tampa	2300	2106	1.09	145	53
Total	6533	6428	1.02	129	46
Midwest					
Chicago	6323	6523	0.97	144	66
Detroit	6845	6448	1.06	137	53
Minneapolis	5783	6300	0.92	150	71
St. Louis	5345	5318	1.01	129	55
Total	24296	24589	0.99	140	61
Far West					
Phoenix	2337	2445	0.96	104	44
Portland	3426	3276	1.05	120	52

for management. Computerized MISs typically extract and summarize data from TPSs to allow managers to monitor and direct the organization and to provide employees accurate feedback about easily measured aspects of their work. For example, a listing of every sale during a day or week would be extremely difficult to use in monitoring a hardware store's performance. However, the same data could be summarized in measures of performance, such as total sales for each type of item, for each salesperson, and for each hour of the day. The transaction data remains indispensable, and the MIS focuses it for management.

As part of an organization's formal control mechanisms, an MIS provides some structure for the comparatively unstructured task of management by identifying important measures of performance. The fact that everyone knows how performance is measured helps in making decisions and helps managers motivate workers. For example, in a sales group expecting $1,000 per day of evenly distributed sales, the MIS might report that a salesperson met weekly and monthly sales targets but usually did poorly on one group of products. In this typical situation, the MIS reports information but leaves it to the people to decide how to improve performance.

From MIS to EIS

An **executive information system (EIS)** is a highly interactive system that provides managers and executives flexible access to information for monitoring operating results and general business conditions. These systems are sometimes called *executive support systems (ESS)*. EIS attempts to take over where the traditional MIS approach falls short. Although sometimes acceptable for monitoring the same indicators over time, the traditional MIS approach of providing prespecified reports on a scheduled basis is too inflexible for many questions executives really care about, such as understanding problems and new situations.

EISs provide executives with internal and competitive information through user-friendly interfaces that can be used by someone with little computer-related knowledge. EISs are designed to help executives find the information they need whenever they need it and in whatever form is most useful. Typically, users can choose among numerous tabular or graphical formats. They can also control the level of detail, the triggers for exception conditions, and other aspects of the information displayed. Most EISs focus on providing executives with the background information they need, as well as help in understanding the causes of exceptions and surprises. This leaves executives better prepared to discuss issues with their subordinates.

A typical sequence of EIS use is shown in Figure 5.7. The EIS user starts with a menu listing available types of information, such as sales results, manufacturing results, competitive performance, and e-mail messages. The categories are customized for individual executives. The user selects a category from the menu and receives an additional menu identifying available subcategories plus the specific online reports that can be obtained. The executive can often customize these reports by choosing options, such as selecting a subset of the data, sorting, or providing more detail. For example, while looking at last month's sales results, a user might select the branches with less than 2% improvement, sort these sales branches from highest to lowest percentage improvement, and obtain more detail for these branches by looking at results for individual departments within these branches. In addition, users can generate graphical displays such as trend charts and pie charts to make it easier to visualize what is happening.

For an EIS to operate, technical staff members must ensure that the right data are available and are downloaded to the EIS from other systems in a timely manner. The data in EISs are usually replenished periodically from internal company databases and external databases. Although technical advances in data display and networking capabilities have made EISs much easier to maintain, EISs continually modified to keep up with current business issues still require major efforts and substantial technical maintenance. An extensive EIS at Lockheed-Georgia had a staff of nine people: a manager, six information analysts, and two computer analysts.[16]

While EIS users are executives and managers, ideally anyone in a business should be able to get the right information in the right format. Even when commercial EIS software

Profit before tax report for September, 1999

	Actual	% of total	Budget	% of total	Variance	% Variance
Microwave	2248	48.63	2197	0.46	51	2.3
Mixers	1337	28.92	1390	0.29	-53	-3.8
Coffee ma	590	12.76	630	0.13	-40	-6.3
Toasters	448	9.69	550	0.12	-102	-18.5
	4623	100.00	4767	100.00	-144	-3.0

(a)

Profit summary for Microwave Ovens, September 1999

	Actual	% of total	Budget	% of total	Variance	% Variance
Net sales	14014	100.00	13167	100.00	847	6.4
Cost of sal	-7987	-1.33	-7367	-1.27	-620	8.4
Gross mar	6027	100.00	5800	100.00	227	3.9
Product D	1635	0.46	1223	0.37	412	33.7
Selling	1449	0.40	1675	0.51	-226	-13.5
Gen. & Ad	494	0.14	406	0.12	88	21.7
Expenses	3578	100.00	3304	100.00	274	8.3
Net profit	2449	0.17	2496	0.19	-47	-0.1

(b)

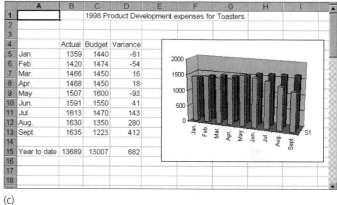

1998 Product Development expenses for Toasters

	Actual	Budget	Variance
Jan.	1359	1440	-81
Feb.	1420	1474	-54
Mar.	1466	1450	16
Apr.	1468	1450	18
May	1507	1600	-93
Jun.	1591	1550	41
Jul.	1613	1470	143
Aug.	1630	1350	280
Sept.	1635	1223	412
Year to date	13689	13007	682

(c)

Figure 5.7
Use of an executive information system

This sequence, using a spreadsheet, demonstrates how an executive can use an EIS to study a firm's financial results by "drilling down" to understand specific items in more detail. (a) The executive scans the firm's standard financial report summarizing actual versus budgeted revenues and expenses for the month of September. The executive wants to look at the Microwave division in more detail and with an EIS would use a mouse or touch screen to identify the area where more detailed data is needed. (b) The more detailed data for the Microwave division shows that product development expenses are 33.7% over budget for the month. This variance calls for a deeper look. (c) The executive looks at monthly actual versus budget for this category and sees that expenses have not fallen as they were supposed to. This background information will help the executive ask probing questions when discussing the situation with the managers in charge of product development.

is used, the time and effort to customize and maintain an EIS limits use to high-level managers. Ideally, the flexibility and ease of access built into EIS should also be built into other information systems. Ten years ago, it was much more expensive to provide EIS capabilities to executives. Ten years from now, the interfaces in information systems at all organizational levels may mimic or exceed those in today's EIS.

Decision Support Systems: Providing Information and Tools for Analytical Work

A **decision support system (DSS)** is an interactive information system that provides information, models, and data manipulation tools to help make decisions in semistructured and unstructured situations where no one knows exactly how the decision should be made. The traditional DSS approach includes interactive problem solving, direct use of models, and user-controllable methods for displaying and analyzing data and formulating and evaluating alternative decisions. This approach grew out of dissatisfaction with the traditional limitations of TPS and MIS. TPS focused on record keeping and control of repetitive clerical processes. MIS provided reports for management but were often inflexible and unable to produce the information in a form in which managers could use it effectively. In contrast, DSSs were intended to support managers and professionals doing largely analytical work in less structured situations with unclear criteria for success. DSSs are typically designed to solve the structured parts of the problem and help isolate places where judgment and experience are required.

DSSs may support repetitive or nonrepetitive decision making. They support repetitive decision making by defining procedures and formats, but they still permit the users to decide how and when to use the system's capabilities. They support nonrepetitive decision making by providing data, models, and interface methods that can be used however the user wants. The broad spectrum of information systems with the DSS label range from general tools such as spreadsheets, data analysis, and graphics packages to highly customized simulation or optimization models focusing on a specific business situation. Figure 5.8 shows an output of one particular DSS.

Many of the originally innovative DSS concepts have now become commonplace in the way people use personal computers as interactive tools. Nonetheless, there are still many applications with a distinct DSS flavor. Consider two examples reflecting common approaches for using DSS today: helping people make a repetitive decision by structuring that decision to some extent and helping analysts by providing information, models, and analytical tools.

Figure 5.8
Graphical output from a decision support system

This is the output from a decision support system used by the San Francisco Police Department to schedule police officers. This three-dimensional graph shows the average requirement for police officers for each hour in each day of the week.

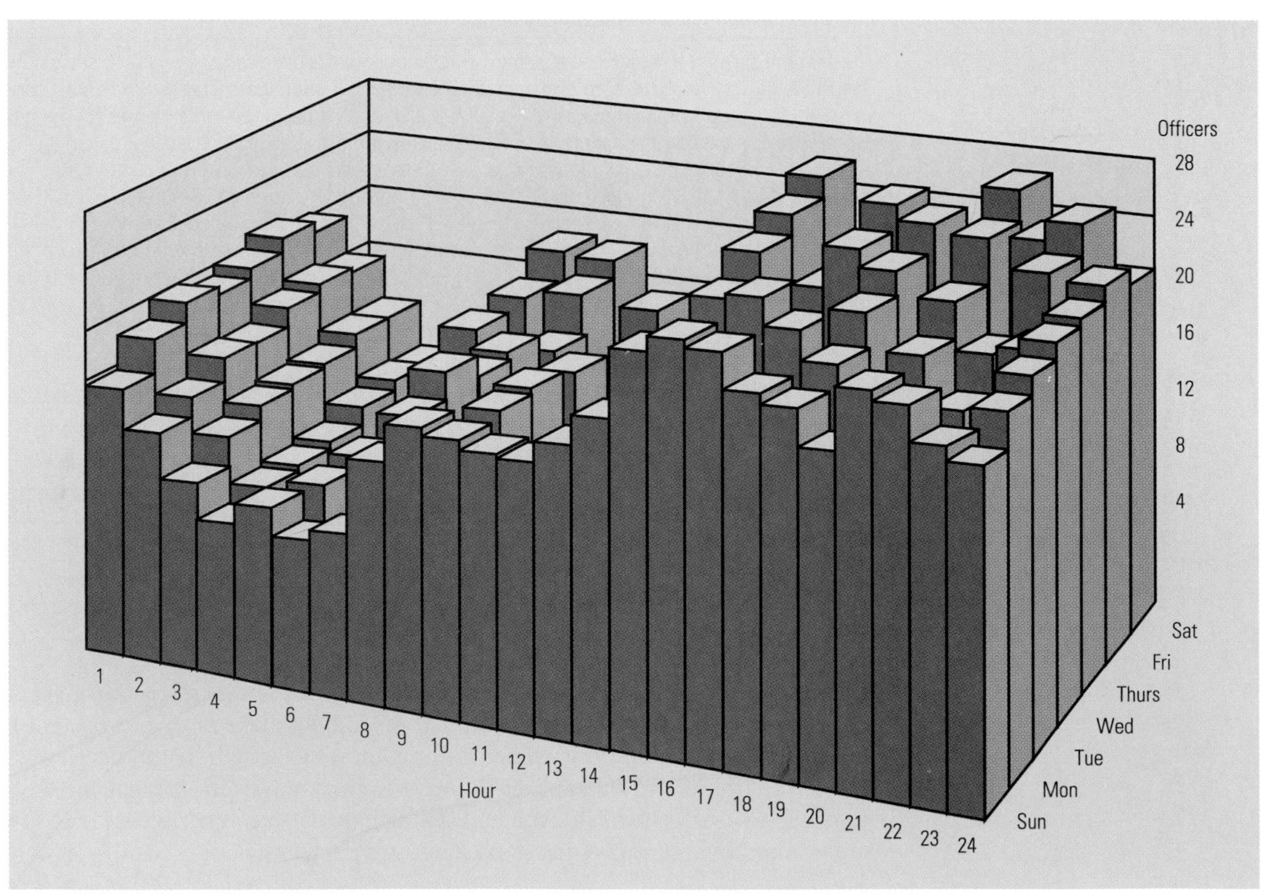

In an example of repetitive use, many insurance agents apply a DSS to help customers choose the insurance policy options that they would prefer. The DSS operates on a laptop computer the insurance agent brings to the customer's business or home. Insurance agents are trained to use these flexible tools to structure sales situations. After surveying the available options, the insurance agent and customer identify a few possible choices. The agent enters the appropriate data and the DSS responds with a report showing costs and benefits. After reviewing this report, the agent and customer try other options. Using this approach, the insurance agent can do a better job of selling insurance.

In an example of nonrepetitive use, marketing managers in a consumer products company use DSS as an analytical tool consisting of a set of models and databases. The data include internal sales results and databases purchased from market research firms. These external databases provide weekly data about sales of all brands in the industry, advertising in various media, and supermarket shelf space devoted to various brands. The models focus on issues such as advertising effectiveness, consumer perceptions of product features, and strategies of competitors. The DSS helps marketing managers evaluate alternative marketing plans and then helps them track the results and recalibrate if the results deviate from their expectations.

The second example shows how DSS may overlap with EIS to some extent, even though they support a different type of usage. Most DSS users do a lot of analytical work and feel comfortable working with models, data analysis, and statistics. Executives who use EIS often receive the results of analyses done by others but rarely spend time doing analytical work themselves. Consequently, EISs are much more concerned with providing information in an easy-to-use format rather than providing sophisticated analytical capabilities such as statistical tests or model building.

As the original DSS concepts became absorbed into typical patterns of personal computing, a number of new approaches were developed for supporting decision making. These include online analytical processing, data mining, and group decision support systems.

OLAP and Data Mining

The use of online data analysis tools to explore large databases of transaction data is called **online analytical processing (OLAP).** The idea of OLAP grew out of difficulties analyzing the data in databases that were being updated continually by online transaction processing systems. When the analytical processes accessed large slices of the transaction database, they slowed down transaction processing critical to customer relationships. The solution was periodic downloads of data from the active transaction processing database into a separate database designed specifically to support analysis work. This separate database often resides on a different computer, which together with its specialized software is called a **data warehouse.** Downloading data to a data warehouse makes it possible to perform both transaction processing and analytical processing efficiently without mutual interference.

Data mining is the use of data analysis tools to try to find the patterns in large transaction databases such as the customer receipts generated in a large sample of grocery stores across the United States. Careful analysis of this data might reveal patterns that could be used for marketing promotions, such as a correlation between diaper sales and beer sales during the evening hours. For example, MCI used data mining to identify customers who were likely to switch to other carriers. It analyzed data on 140 million households and looked at as many as 10,000 characteristics, such as income, lifestyle, and details of past calling patterns. Eventually it found 22 statistical profiles of customers who are likely to switch. An MCI executive said that these highly confidential profiles could not have been developed without data mining.[17] In another example, Chase Manhattan Bank discovered that a lot of customers with multiple accounts were actually unprofitable. This finding helped the bank refocus its approach to selling products.[18]

The problem with data mining is that many patterns occur strictly by chance and have no value in making business decisions. For example, a data mining program might find many valid patterns but might also discover that sales of ice cream in Iowa are correlated with sales of rice in Bangladesh. This type of correlation is simply a low probability accident. Unlike what would usually happen with a meaningful pattern, a spurious pattern such as this would probably disappear if the same data were gathered next year.

Group Decision Support Systems

A form of groupware called a **group decision support system (GDSS)** provides decision support by expediting meetings. In its original concept, a GDSS was a specially outfitted conference room containing hardware and software that facilitates meetings. (See Figure 5.9.) This technology may include advanced presentation devices, computer access to databases, and capabilities for the participants in a meeting to communicate electronically. These rooms improve same-time, same-place communication by a group of people working together in a meeting. The meeting's purpose could be anything from brainstorming about possible new product features to reviewing business operations or responding to an emergency. Typical GDSS capabilities include: [19]

- *Display.* A workstation screen or previously prepared presentation material is displayed to the entire group.
- *Electronic brainstorming.* Participants enter and share comments anonymously through their computer screens.
- *Topic commenting.* Participants add comments to ideas previously generated by themselves or others.
- *Issue analysis.* Participants identify and consolidate key items generated during electronic brainstorming.
- *Voting.* Participants use the computer to vote on topics, with a choice of prioritization methods.
- *Alternative evaluation.* The computer ranks alternative decisions based on preferences entered by users.

GDSS has been more of a research topic than common practice in business, although experience to date suggests GDSS has significant potential for improving both the efficiency and effectiveness of certain types of decision making. Typical meetings in a pilot study of GDSS for internal problem solving at IBM generated a large number of high-quality ideas. The meetings took about half as long as participants' estimates of the

Figure 5.9
A GDSS

This computerized conference room has been used for research and pilot studies of group decision making. It combines carefully designed physical space with extensive software capabilities for recording and processing ideas, votes, and other data generated by meeting participants.

length of regular meetings on the same topics.[20] An important GDSS phenomenon is the impact of entering and transmitting ideas anonymously. Unlike typical meetings, little crosstalk occurs during anonymous brainstorming sessions, and participants tend to comment on the topic at hand. Anonymity encourages participation by all members of the group, independent of their status. It tends to reduce groupthink, pressures for conformity, and dominance of forceful individuals. It also tends to heighten conflict because people's comments in this context are more assertive and less polite than spoken comments. It remains to be seen whether or not this type of decision support will become commonplace.

Execution Systems: Helping People Do the Work That Provides Value for Customers

The information system categories discussed so far are primarily oriented toward planning and control activities or toward general office and communication activities. What about systems designed to directly support people doing the value added work that customers care about, such as practicing medicine, designing buildings, or selling investments? Some people call these systems "functional area systems," but Table 5.6 showed that name is not very helpful because the same types of systems (OAS, TPS, MIS, DSS) are used in every functional area. Some people calls these systems "knowledge-based systems," but that term is often used to refer specifically to expert systems, a subcategory mentioned below as a particular type of execution system.

Because there is no generally accepted term for information systems that support value added work, we will call them **execution systems.** These systems have become much more important in the last decade as advances in computer speed, memory capacity, and portability made it increasingly possible to use computerized systems directly while doing value added work. Such systems help plastic surgeons design operations and show the likely results to their patients, help lawyers find precedents relevant to lawsuits, and help maintenance engineers keep machines running. (See Figure 5.10.) Some of these systems focus on retrieving information from external databases, some focus on storing

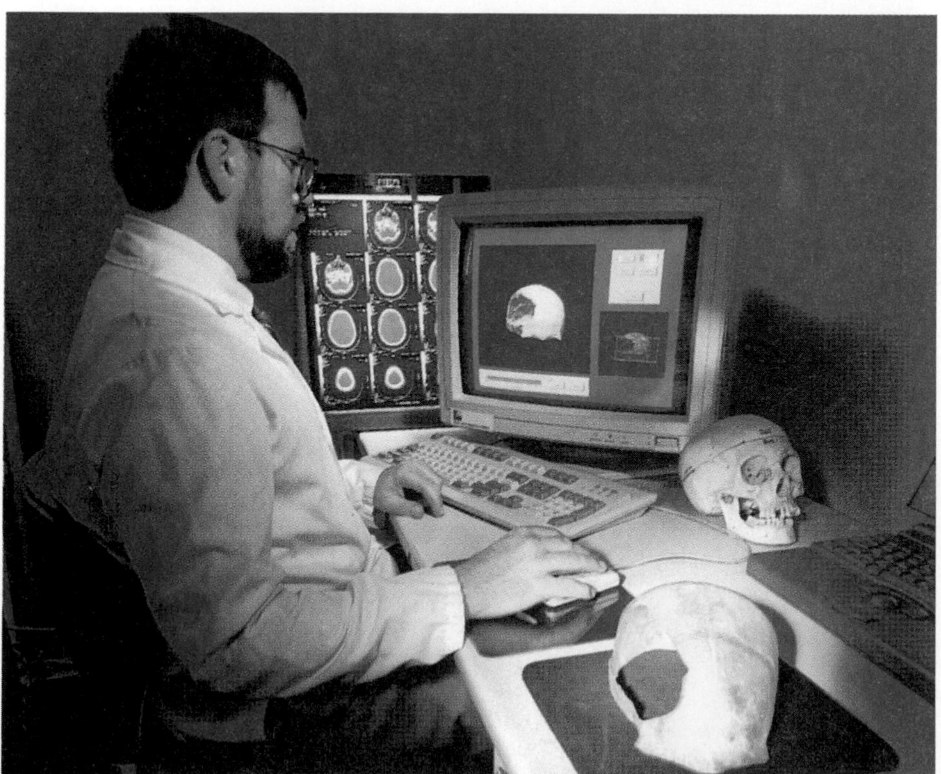

Figure 5.10
Execution system that helps a surgeon plan an operation

The photo shows how a surgeon can use an interactive simulation to plan the steps in an operation before lifting a scalpel.

and displaying design data, and yet others focus on using transaction data to help people do their work instead of just looking back at how well they performed in the past.

Expert systems are a type of execution system that has received attention as an offshoot of artificial intelligence research. An **expert system** supports the intellectual work of professionals engaged in design, diagnosis, or evaluation of complex situations requiring expert knowledge in a well-defined area. Expert systems have been used to diagnose diseases, configure computers, analyze chemicals, interpret geological data, and support many other problem solving processes. This type of work requires expert knowledge of the process of performing particular tasks. Although these tasks may have some repetitive elements, many situations have unique characteristics that must be considered based on expert knowledge. Intellectual work even in narrowly defined areas is typically much less repetitive than transaction processing or general office work.

Despite the designation "expert system," these systems are not true experts because they lack common sense and only contain some of the knowledge of a human expert. Instead, these systems use techniques developed in "artificial intelligence" research to capture some of the special knowledge of experts and make it available to others who have less knowledge or experience. The knowledge is captured not only as facts but also in the form of reasoning processes that the expert would go through in solving a problem.

The common reasons for developing expert systems include preserving an expert's knowledge, improving the performance of less experienced people doing similar tasks, and enforcing some consistency in the way people do particular types of work. These were among the reasons Campbell's Soup developed a commonly cited expert system to capture the knowledge of Aldo Cimino, a long-time plant engineer who was about to retire. He was the company's best expert on soup sterilizers. The system preserved some of his knowledge in the form of 151 rules built into an interactive system used by other engineers to diagnose problems with the sterilizers.

Reality Check

TYPES OF INFORMATION SYSTEMS

The text identifies six different types of information systems, each of which can have an impact on both communication and decision making.

1. For each type of system either identify an example that you have encountered or explain when you think you will first encounter an example.
2. In each of the situations explain how the system affects communication and decision making.

GOING BEYOND THE INFORMATION SYSTEM CATEGORIES

The field of IT moves so rapidly that terminology often fails to keep pace with innovation. This may be why the stiff 3.5-inch diskettes used with personal computers today are still called floppy disks. The 5.25-inch diskettes from an earlier generation were called floppies because they came in flexible casings. The physical characteristic changed, but the name stuck. Similarly strange examples include "writeable CD-ROMs" (ROM means read-only memory) and "wireless cable" (which means using wireless transmission to accomplish the function previously performed by cable television).

The same problem occurs with information system classifications. People identify a new type of system, such as DSS or EIS, and describe its characteristics. Ten years later, the name still exists but some of the original characteristics are no longer as important or have become commonplace. Eventually many information systems contain characteristics from several system categories. Furthermore, a system that fits in a category today may not fit once new features are added.

Information systems that contain characteristics of several different categories can be called **hybrid information systems.** The Levi Strauss system in the chapter opening case is a hybrid. At one level, it is a TPS that collects and uses information about individual sales transactions. At another level it is a communication system. It is also an execution system that supports a manufacturing process. Not mentioned in the case but surely in the background are MISs or EISs that help managers and executives monitor the market, and DSSs that help in deciding what the price should be and in evaluating the effectiveness of advertising.

In the mid-1990s the widespread adoption of a form of hybrid information system called an **enterprise resource planning (ERP)** system became highly visible and somewhat controversial. Resource planning actually describes only a small part of why ERP systems exist. As with many IT terms, the term ERP evolved out of an early form of DSS called material requirements planning (MRP). These systems provide an integrated view necessary to coordinate purchasing and production scheduling activities. They start with a firm's output requirement by week or other period and work backward to calculate a schedule of how many units must be started, when the units must be started, and when the necessary materials must be ordered. They also permit user adjustments in case lead times are inadequate or in case capacity is insufficient. The need for an integrated view of different activities led to MRP II systems that were broader in scope, and eventually led to the name ERP even though ERP systems focus elsewhere.

ERP systems try to create an integrated database that spans the major activities in a company. Ideally, having production, sales, human resources, and finance data in the same database should make it easier to analyze the business and to coordinate decision making. ERP software is currently sold by software vendors such as SAP, Baan, Peoplesoft, and Oracle. These vendors analyzed basic business processes such as purchasing and manufacturing in many firms and then created database structures that incorporate many of the process variations they found. This design strategy makes their products enormously complicated. Just figuring out which of the many options to use often takes several hundred person-months of time. In many situations, departments must give up existing customized systems that address their unique problems in order to use the more general software and its integrated database. When Owens Corning acquired a number of other companies and needed to integrate its sales and manufacturing efforts, a large ERP project addressed a pressing need and was successful. In other situations where the need for integration within the firm is not as pressing and where the ERP system may force departments to change their processes in order to fit the software, ERP projects sometimes become enormous drains of effort with little reward. Some companies such as Dell Computer looked at ERP and decided their business was changing too rapidly to implement information systems that were so large and monolithic.[21] In other cases only one or two modules are implemented, resulting in systems that may be called ERP because the software was sold by an ERP vendor, but which don't accomplish the integration they may have set out to accomplish.

Combining Features of Different System Types

In spite of the shortcomings of information system classification schemes, they still do have a practical use. Even though there is overlap, each system category emphasizes certain features that may be relevant in many situations. The practical use of system classifications is in identifying a number of widely usable features that are typically associated with particular system types.

Table 5.7 identifies some of these features and suggests questions about any information system. For example, the absence of DSS-like features in a TPS might indicate a direction for future improvement. Conversely, the controls typically built into a TPS might be the model for building similar controls into a DSS or even an MIS. As the trend toward hybrid information systems continues, it will be more difficult to classify real information systems using current categories, a small price to pay for more powerful and usable systems.

TABLE 5.7 **Transferable Features of Particular Types of Information Systems**

Certain features and characteristics are usually associated with each of the types of information systems. This table identifies some of these features that can be transferred to systems of other types.

Type of system	Transferable features
Office automation systems	• Multiple forms of information, sometimes used in combination • Immediacy and interactivity of communication • Avoidance of unproductive work
Communication systems	• Emphasis on communication in addition to data processing • Consideration of social presence and other communication characteristics when building systems • Recognition of the need to handle different combinations of same or different time or place • Sharing information between different people working on different parts of a task • Controlling work flows and approval loops within a group • Incorporating efficient methods of scheduling meetings
Transaction processing systems	• Control • Procedures and rules • Repetition
Management and executive information systems	• Emphasis on measures of performance • Use of standard formats and measures by people in different departments • User friendly interface • User friendly methods for analyzing data
Decision support systems	• User-controlled interaction with computers • Use of models and data • Information systems applied to semistructured tasks
Execution systems	• Integrating computerized systems into doing the organization's value added work • Bringing knowledge in active form to people doing the work

CHAPTER CONCLUSION

Summary

How are social context and nonverbal communication important when communication technologies are used?
Social context is the situation and relationships within which communication takes place. Much of what is communicated in face-to-face situations is communicated through nonverbal communication, such as facial expressions, eye contact, gestures, and body language. Technologies that filter out nonverbal information decrease social context cues and therefore limit communication. Technology may hinder communication if it is mismatched with the needs of the situation.

What are the phases of decision making?
Decision making is a problem solving process preceded by a problem finding process. The four phases of decision making are intelligence, design, choice, and implementation.

What are some of the common limitations and problems in decision making?
In the real world, rationality is always bounded by the amount of time available to make the decision and the limited ability of people to process information. Additionally, many common flaws in decision making have been observed, such as poor framing, recency and primacy effects, poor probability estimation, overconfidence, and groupthink.

What are the different approaches for improving decision making using information systems?
Because communication and decision making are intertwined, different ways to improve communication often improve decision making in turn. Much of an information system's direct impact on decision making is determined by the extent to which it imposes structure on decisions or other tasks. This can be divided into three broad categories. An information system imposes a small degree of structure if it provides tools or information a person can use but does not dictate how they should be used in making the decision. It imparts more structure if it enforces rules and procedures but still permits the decision maker some leeway. It imposes the most structure when it automates the decision.

What are the general differences between the types of information systems?
Office automation systems (OAS) provide tools supporting general office work such as performing calculations, creating documents, scheduling meetings, and controlling the flow of office work. Communication systems help people work together by exchanging or sharing information. General categories of these systems include teleconferencing systems, messaging systems, groupware, and knowledge management systems. Transaction processing systems (TPSs) collect and store data about transactions and control aspects of transaction processing and related decision making. Management and executive information systems (MISs and EISs) summarize data from transaction processing systems and other data sources to convert them into information useful for managing an organization, monitoring performance, and planning. Decision support systems (DSSs) help people make decisions by providing information, models, or tools for analyzing information. They provide methods and formats for portions of a decision process but leave the users with substantial discretion in using the system and making decisions. Execution systems directly support people doing the value added work internal or external customers care about, such as practicing medicine, designing buildings, or selling investments. One type of execution system is an expert system, which captures expert knowledge to make it available to others.

How are features of one type of information system transferable to systems of other types?
Each category emphasizes certain features that may be relevant in many situations. For example, the absence of DSS-like features in a TPS might indicate a direction for future improvement.

Key Terms

social context
social presence
nonverbal communication
personal communication
impersonal communication
anonymous communication
presentation technologies
problem finding
problem solving
intelligence
design
choice
implementation
rationality
satisficing
bounded rationality
office automation system (OAS)
communication systems
teleconferencing
audio conferencing
audiographic conferencing
video conferencing
electronic mail (e-mail)
voice mail (v-mail)
fax
groupware
computer conferencing
newsgroup
intranet
extranet
knowledge management system
transaction processing system (TPS)
batch processing
real time processing
management information system (MIS)
executive information system (EIS)
decision support system (DSS)
online analytical processing (OLAP)
data warehouse
data mining
group decision support system (GDSS)
execution system
expert system (ES)
hybrid information system
enterprise resource planning (ERP)

Review Questions

1. Why is it important to differentiate between personal, impersonal, and anonymous communication?
2. Why is the distinction between same or different time or place important when discussing communication technology?
3. Why is it sometimes important to make communication systematic?
4. How is problem finding related to problem solving?
5. What is the relationship between rationality and satisficing?
6. What are the different degrees of structuring decisions?
7. What are examples of tools typically grouped with office automation systems?
8. Compare the different forms of teleconferencing.
9. Describe the similarities and differences between e-mail, v-mail, and fax.
10. What is the difference between MIS, DSS, and EIS?
11. Why is it difficult to keep EISs current?
12. How is data mining related to DSS?
13. What kinds of functions do group decision support systems (GDSSs) contain?
14. What is an expert system?
15. Why are many information systems hybrids?
16. What is an enterprise resource planning system?
17. What typical features of particular types of information systems are often transferable?

Discussion Topics

1. Alana Shoars, the e-mail administrator for Epson computer company in Torrance, California, trained 700 employees to create and send e-mail messages to coworkers. She assured them that e-mail communications would be totally private but later discovered that her boss was copying and reading employees' e-mail. When she was fired after complaining, she sued her former employer on behalf of the employees whose e-mail had been opened. Epson argued that state privacy statutes make no mention of e-mail. The judge agreed and dismissed the case.[22] What ethical issues does this case and the legal finding raise?
2. Although executives are typically described as people who work on long-term, strategic issues, the discussion of EIS emphasizes the use of these systems to monitor recent organizational performance. Assuming you were an executive concerned with long-term issues, explain why you would or would not find this type of EIS useful. Explain some of the things an EIS would have to do if it were to focus specifically on long-term strategic issues.
3. Some people believe that e-mail, v-mail, and fax have reduced the quality of work life for many professionals by making it difficult to escape work for an evening or weekend. These observers believe any-time, any-place may be a fine goal for serving customers but may not be appropriate as an expectation of company employees. Discuss the pros and cons of this issue.
4. You are a manager looking for a secretary. You place an ad in a newspaper and receive 500 résumés. Use ideas about decision making to describe the process of deciding whom to hire. Assume that 400 of the 500 meet all objective criteria you can think of, such as typing speed, business experience, and education.
5. Why is there a distinction between management information systems and decision support systems? After all, one of the basic purposes of management information systems is to provide information that is used for decision making.
6. Assume that all current telephones were replaced with picture phones that could transmit both audio and video and could operate as video extensions of v-mail. Explain whether this would have any important impact on you personally.

CASE

U.S. House of Representatives: Patients' Bill of Rights Act of 1998

The rapid growth of health maintenance organizations (HMOs) and managed care was a hot button issue because it involved contradictory goals. On one side, people wanted to be able to choose their own doctors and to receive convenient, high-quality medical care. On the other side, reducing medical costs was a key issue for anyone paying medical insurance premiums, primarily businesses and government organizations, but also self-employed individuals who pay for themselves. Doctors, hospitals, and HMOs were caught in the middle because greater patient choice and higher quality care are more expensive to deliver. The resulting tug of war left many stakeholders unhappy. Patients complained that the insurance companies or HMOs used by their employers forced them to switch doctors or use inconvenient hospitals or accept inadequate treatment. They also complained they could not obtain outcome data to help in choosing a physician. The doctors complained they wasted inordinate amounts of time trying to convince insurers that particular treatments were necessary. The insurers and HMOs complained they couldn't make a profit.

H.R. 3605, the Patients' Bill of Rights Act of 1998, was introduced in the House of Representatives on March 31, 1998, to address some aspects of these issues. It contained provisions related to access to medical care, quality assurance, patient information, and grievance and appeals procedures. Section 112 (one of 19 sections of the bill) concerned the collection of standardized data about medical care. It started by saying, "A group health plan and a health insurance issuer that offers health insurance coverage shall collect uniform quality data that include a minimum uniform data set.... The Secretary [of Health and Human Services] shall specify (and may from time to time update) the data required to be included in the minimum uniform data set...and the standard format for such data. Such data shall include at least: (1) aggregate utilization data; (2) data on the demographic characteristics of participants, beneficiaries, and enrollees; (3) data on disease-specific and age-specific mortality rates and (to the extent feasible) morbidity rates of such individuals; (4) data on satisfaction of such individuals, including data on voluntary disenrollment and grievances; and (5) data on quality indicators and health outcomes, including, to the extent feasible and appropriate, data on pediatric cases and on a gender-specific basis."

The data collection provisions of H.R. 3605 were intended to support the patient's choice of physicians, but some observers believed they might actually have the opposite impact. The plans with the least choice for patients are HMOs and other organizations that permit only member physicians to provide services except under extreme circumstances. The plans with maximum flexibility for the patient are preferred provider plans, which allow patients to obtain medical services from any physician, but charge the patients more for physicians who are not a member of the plan. The costs of the data collection called for in Section 112 of H.R. 3605 would be substantially lower for HMOs than for preferred provider plans. This is because the HMOs have greater central control over patient medical records and over the process of routing patients to specialists. In contrast, large preferred provider plans may have thousands of doctors with no central repository of medical records and little consistency in recordkeeping. The process of sifting through different doctors' records to track the type and quality of treatment each patient received would be much more complicated for the preferred provider plans. If the law passed, they would be required to spend more on their internal recordkeeping and therefore would have to raise their rates. This would tilt the economic advantage further in the direction of the HMOs that provide less choice.

QUESTIONS

1. Explain why each of the six types of information system is or is not relevant to the data collection and data usage in this situation.
2. Assume typical questions about medical care include things such as how frequently diabetics are checked for high blood sugar, and what types of drug treatments are used for different types of cardiac patients. Propose a process that might be used for gathering and analyzing the data in an HMO. Explain how this might be done in a preferred provider plan.

Sources:

U.S. House of Representatives, *H. R. 3605, Patients' Bill of Rights Act of 1998, Section 112*, March 31, 1998, June 20, 1998 (http://thomas.loc.gov/cgi-bin/query/z?c105:h.r.3605:).

Weinstein, Michael. "In Health Care, Be Careful What You Wish For," *New York Times*, May 31, 1998, Sec. 4, p. 1.

CASE

Glaxo Wellcome: Accessing Unstructured Data Across a Multinational Enterprise

London-based Glaxo Wellcome is one of the world's largest pharmaceutical companies, with research and manufacturing efforts distributed around the world. Like any research-based firm in the pharmaceutical industry, a major part of the company's value is the knowledge in the heads of its employees and in the detailed information in widely dispersed research, clinical trial, and manufacturing documents and databases. The computerized part of that knowledge resides in many different repositories, including text and relational databases, groupware, document management software, Web servers, newsgroups, and file systems. Leveraging these resources for maximum results was traditionally difficult because Glaxo Wellcome had no enterprise-wide search capabilities. In a world in which information itself was expanding rapidly, researchers and others in the firm often needed to know where information existed in order to find it.

Glaxo Wellcome decided to address this issue by creating a "knowledge network" as part of its global "learning organization" initiative. The knowledge network project deployed Search'97, a catalog and search system produced by Verity, Inc., a California-based company whose products aid in retrieving information from a variety of sources including the Internet, corporate intranets, online documents, and CD-ROMs. The company's March 1998 announcement revealed plans to deploy the software to 10,000 users initially, and eventually to 30,000 users. This information system's goal is to help users search for and retrieve critical information without knowing where or how it is stored. The process of retrieving information using the search engine could also help in discovering information whose relevance had not been anticipated. As another part of the initiative, Glaxo Wellcome intended to use push technology to automatically route information to individuals or work groups based on user profiles that are stored in the form of queries.

One of the advantages of using a single search engine across multiple databases was that a single query could search all the available information. Search '97 operates by capturing and cataloging key concepts and features of documents, performing searches using this information, and organizing results into categories that can be defined by users or discovered on the fly from content, context, and metadata This form of knowledge indexing and retrieval tries to combine high-speed performance with concept-based search. Behind the scenes, the search engine also takes advantage of thesauri, word stemming, and linguistic analysis and other methods of query expansion. The response to a search includes a relevancy ranking of each potential source that is identified.

QUESTIONS

1. In what ways does Glaxo Wellcome's planned knowledge management system have characteristics of the six types of information systems?
2. Explain the extent to which this knowledge management system is guaranteed to find the most pertinent and valid information for any query.
3. Assume your university or business organization tried to create a knowledge management system. What information would it contain and how do you think users might access it?

Sources:

"Glaxo Wellcome Selects Verity for Worldwide Knowledge Management," Mar. 17, 1998, June 4, 1998 (www.glaxowellcome.co.uk/verity.html).

Verity, Inc. "Universal Access to Information Across the Enterprise," June 23, 1998 (www.verity.com/products/prd.html).

Product, Customer, and Competitive Advantage

6

Study Questions

- How can information systems change the scope and nature of a work system's product?
- How is the customer involvement cycle related to the customer's view of product performance?
- How are information systems related to competitive advantage?
- Why is it difficult to achieve sustainable competitive advantage through information systems?
- What is electronic commerce, and what new technical capabilities does it require?
- What are some of the opportunities to use information systems across the customer involvement cycle?

Outline

Opening Case

OTIS ELEVATOR: CENTRALIZING REPAIR DISPATCHING

Otis Elevator uses Otisline to achieve the responsiveness and quality essential to compete in the elevator service business. Otisline is a centralized system for dispatching mechanics to elevators requiring service. (See Table 6.1.) It uses a centralized database containing complete service records for each elevator installed. Prior to Otisline, local Otis field offices dispatched mechanics during normal working hours, while answering services used a duty roster to dispatch them after hours and on weekends and holidays. These answering services often handled multiple elevator service companies and rarely displayed great interest or ingenuity in ensuring that elevator service calls were answered promptly. Record keeping related to service calls was haphazard.

Otisline improved service by handling all calls for service at a centralized service center that receives 9,000 calls per day. Highly trained, often multilingual operators use complete information about each elevator to make sure that the right mechanic gets to the scene promptly. The system maintains detailed records and reports exception situations such as elevators with high levels of maintenance.[1]

The use of information technology extends to the service technicians and to the elevators. Using handheld computers linked to a nationwide wireless network, Otis field service technicians across the country can communicate instantly with a central office in Connecticut for technical assistance and job dispatching. Communication can be initiated from a location as remote as the inside of an elevator shaft. Before this wireless network was available, field workers needing to contact the office were forced to secure the elevator, leave the work site, search for a phone, call, and sometimes wait on hold while the elevator was out of order.

Additional enhancements include remote elevator monitoring, direct communication with trapped passengers, and monthly reports on each elevator for subsequent analysis of performance patterns. Customers purchase the remote monitoring function for an additional monthly charge. It uses a microprocessor to report elevator malfunctions to the dispatching office via modem.[2] In some cases this information can be used to fix problems before they cause elevator failure.

Beyond supporting the dispatching function, Otisline serves as a central conduit for exchanging crucial information among field service mechanics, salespeople, design and manufacturing engineers, and managers. For example, salespeople use Otisline to access an integrated database used for providing immediate quotes to customers.

Debate Topic

Although elevator maintenance may seem an extreme case, today's customers for most products expect high levels of post-sales service that must be supported by extensive information systems.

Otis Elevator is in the elevator business, not the information system business, yet its information systems are an important part of the products and services it offers customers. By centralizing dispatching and attaining better control of the maintenance process, Otis Elevator gives customers better service than would otherwise be available. Aside from supporting better maintenance, Otisline provides information to salespeople and is the basis of additional revenue from remote monitoring.

Otisline is cited often as an example of the competitive use of information systems because it benefits Otis Elevator's customers as well as internal operations. As you will see throughout this chapter, this case illustrates ideas that can help business professionals think about the customer and product of virtually any system, regardless of whether the customer is internal or external. This chapter starts with fundamental ideas about the way the customer views the product, the customer's entire cycle of involvement with the product, and the customer's criteria for evaluating the product. These ideas are then applied to a discussion of the competitive use of information systems, with special emphasis on electronic commerce (e-commerce) and electronically enhanced products.

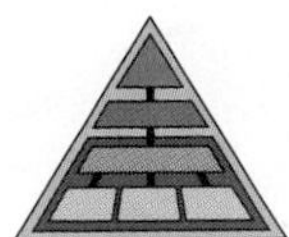

TABLE 6.1 Otis Elevator's Repair Service

CUSTOMER
- Building owners and people who use elevators

PRODUCT
- Elevator maintained in good operating condition
- Timely elevator repair
- History of service for each elevator

BUSINESS PROCESS

Major steps:	Rationale:
• Receive call about a problem • Dispatch mechanics • Perform repair steps • Track progress until the elevator is fixed • Update records	• Direct all calls for service to a centralized dispatching office. Use handheld terminals to maintain contact. Maintain records for anticipating and solving future problems.

PARTICIPANTS	INFORMATION	TECHNOLOGY
• Trained operators who answer calls for service • Local mechanics	• Notification of problem • Current status of all calls for service • Maintenance history of each elevator • Qualification and availability of mechanics	• Computer at headquarters • Handheld terminals • Commercial wireless network

THE CUSTOMER'S VIEW OF THE PRODUCT

The first step in thinking about the product from a customer's viewpoint is to describe it. This should start with the big picture rather than the details. We will summarize product architecture in terms of two sets of characteristics that are especially applicable for improving products of IT-enabled systems. The first of these is the *product's content* as a combination of information, physical things, and service. The second set of characteristics refers to the way the product is controllable during each instance of use and adaptable over longer time spans.

Combining Information, Physical, and Service Content

The product of a work system usually contains a mix of information, physical, and service components (see Figure 6.1). (Putting information first reflects our emphasis on IT-enabled systems.) An **information product,** in its purest form, consists of information and nothing else, such as a list of names downloaded using the Internet. Similarly, a pure **physical product,** such as a pound of sugar, has no significant information or service components. A pure **service product** is a set of actions that provide value to a customer who receives neither information nor physical things.

Most work system products involve a combination of information, physical, and service components, even if one or two of the three dominate the product's value. For example, a new car is certainly more than a physical product purchased as several thousand pounds of steel and plastic with numerous aesthetic and practical features. It also has a service component, either explicitly in the form of warranties, or implicitly in the form of the reputation of the dealer and manufacturer. In the last decade, its information content has also risen dramatically. The information content of older cars was limited to paper manuals and dashboard gauges. Newer cars have information-based features ranging from antilock brakes and collision avoidance devices to electronic maps. (See Figure 6.2.)

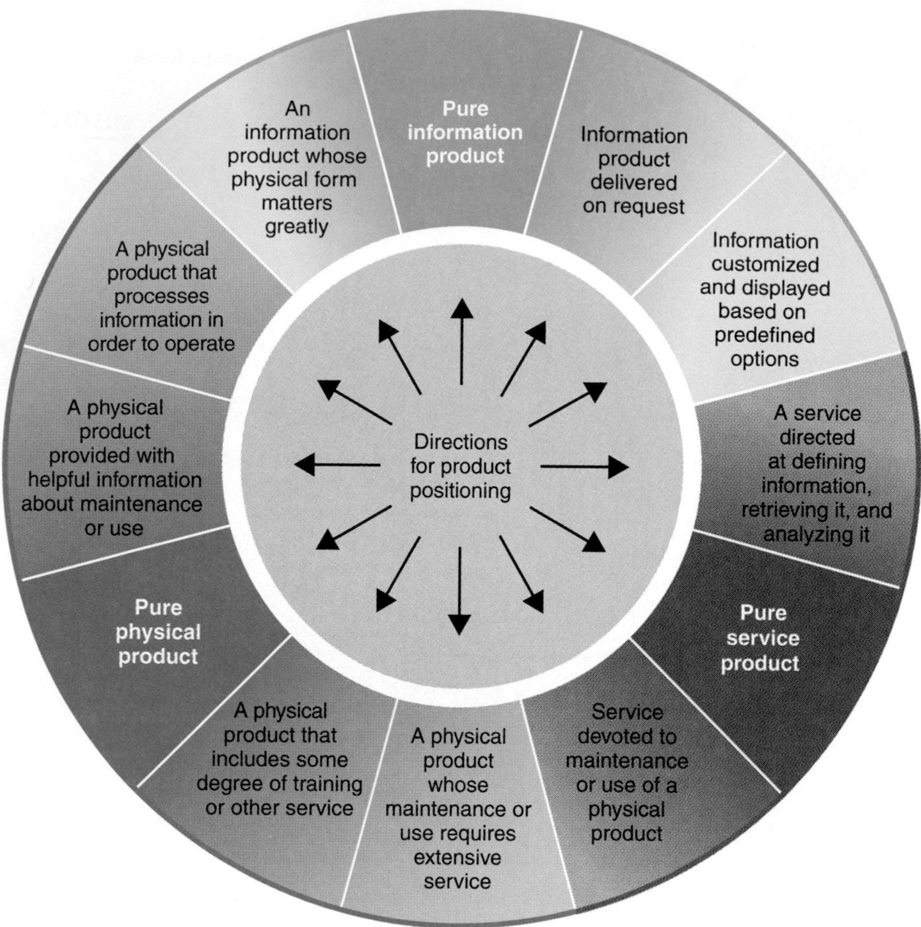

Figure 6.1
Viewing products as a combination of information, physical, and service components

Although some products are purely information, physical things, or service, the annotations along the sides of the triangle show some of the ways pairs of these components can be combined.

As an example of an information product, consider what has happened to encyclopedias over the last decade. Previously they were hardbound reference books occupying three or four shelf-feet of space. Today over half of the encyclopedias sold are in the form of CD-ROMs weighing ounces. By 1998, all 50 million words in a 32-volume Encyclopedia Britannica that costs $1,500 were available in a $100 product consisting of two CD-ROMs. Aside from requiring less physical space, the electronic encyclopedias provide some of the advantages of an interactive information product, such as the ability to show video segments, perform simulations, and link directly to material on other topics.[3]

The intermediate points connecting the three components in Figure 6.1 show some of the ways information, physical aspects, and service can be combined in a product. The automobile has changed from an almost pure physical product to a physical product that processes information in order to operate. Moving in the opposite direction, over half the encyclopedias sold have become purer information products as their physical form has become less important.

The relative balance of information and service is especially important for many IT-intensive products. Consider, for example, the product of a commercial marketing information service that provides weekly item-level sales data from a sample of supermarkets across the country. One way to position this product is as an information product containing an enormous database, a fixed set of preprogrammed reports, and a set of tools for ad hoc queries. Alternatively, it could be positioned as a combination of information and service by including an analysis service in addition to the massive database. This service would involve data analysis and marketing experts who would help corporate clients find the surprises and the trends in the data they receive. Whether the analyst role exists at all,

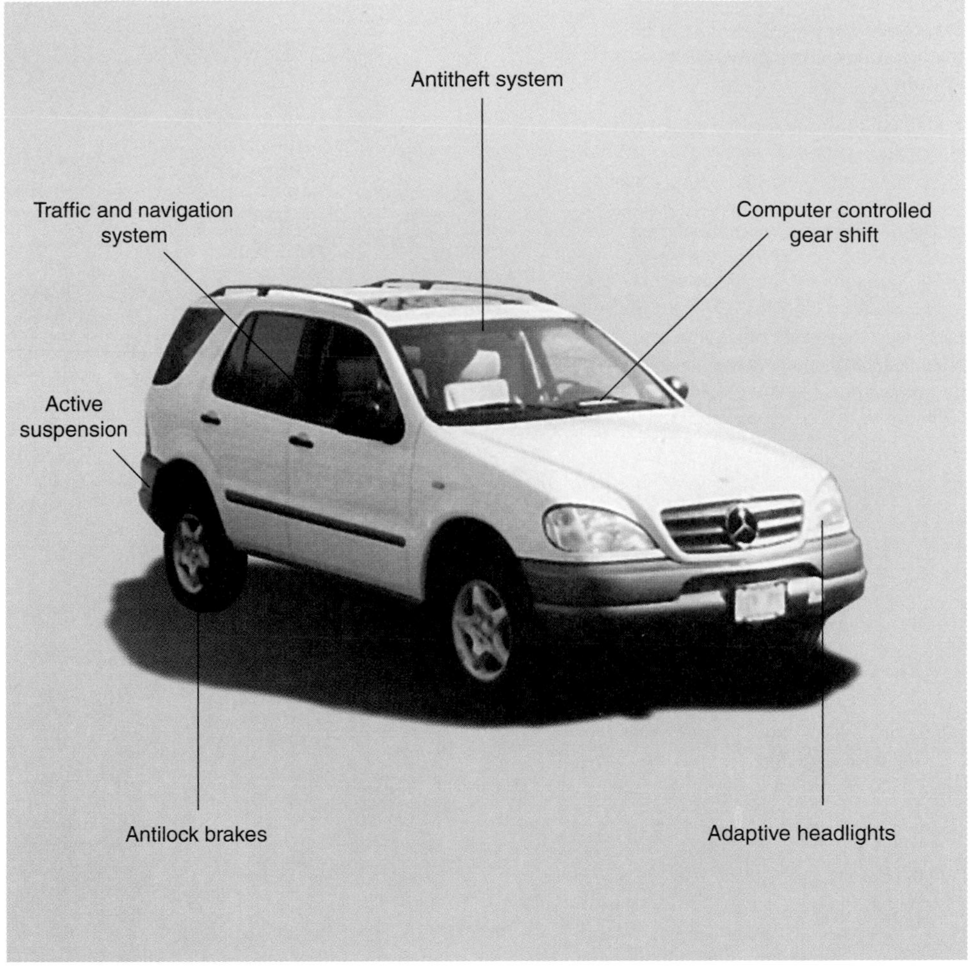

Figure 6.2
Information systems built into automobiles

Information systems play an increasingly important role in automobiles as many basic driving functions are controlled or supported using computers.

and whether it is placed in the producer organization or the customer organization is a key determinant of both customer satisfaction and system cost. Advances in hardware and software have made the range of choices much wider because it is now more feasible for the customers to manipulate the data themselves.

Directions for Product Improvement

To improve a product, it is sometimes useful to separate it into information, physical, and service components. Figure 6.3 illustrates how this method can be used to identify potential improvements. Consider the Resumix case introduced in Chapter 2. The starting point is an examination of a traditional HR department's résumé processing activities prior to installing Resumix. The HR department places ads, receives résumés, and forwards them to the managers doing the recruiting. The customers are the managers, and the product they receive is a prescreened stack of résumés. The value of the product is related to the résumé information it contains and the HR department's efforts to include only qualified candidates; however, its physical form is a stack of paper résumés. Its physical form limits the ways the information can be used.

Notice in Figure 6.3 that arrows A, B, and C indicate directions that lead to product improvement based on scanning the information into a computerized form and storing it in a structured database. The inconvenience of searching through paper résumés is now eliminated, and the information component becomes more powerful because the résumés can be ranked automatically based on criteria provided by the hiring managers. The product also expands in the direction of service because the scanned information

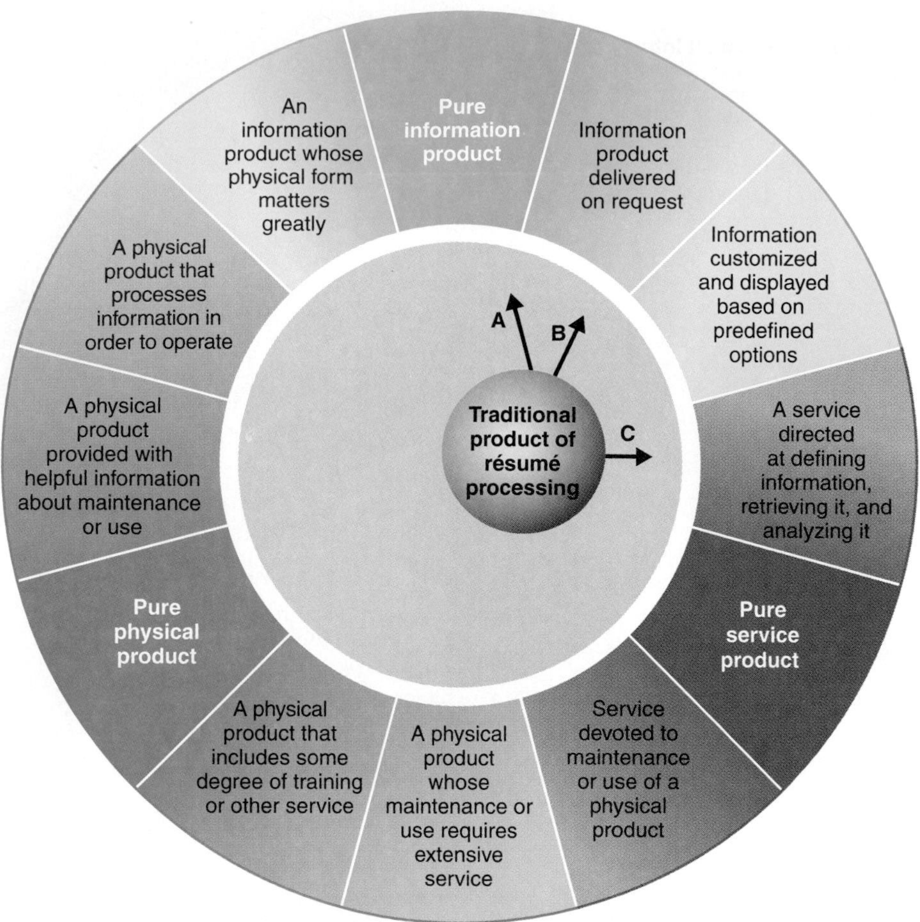

Figure 6.3
Directions for improvement in a traditional résumé processing system

Traditional résumé processing is an information processing service designed around the awkward physical form in which the information is received. Directions for improvement include (a) extracting the information to eliminate the inconvenience of working with paper (the physical form), (b) processing the information more effectively, and (c) providing additional services such as helping employees find openings within the company.

provides the basis for new services, such as allowing employees to find job listings that match their own qualifications.

The general purpose of the arrows in this type of diagram is to indicate a set of different directions, any or all of which might be pursued simultaneously to expand the product's scope and value. An information product might be improved by changing physically from paper to electronic form or by supplementing one electronic form such as CD-ROM with another electronic form such as a Web site. A physical product such as an automobile, copy machine, or elevator might be improved by incorporating information processing into its operation or by expanding the service that is part of the product. A service product such as medical care might be improved by using information more effectively in its delivery, such as by having real time access to complete medical records. It also might be improved by replacing some of its physical vestiges with information, for instance, by transmitting x-rays or electrocardiograms over a telephone instead of requiring the doctor and patient to always be at the same place.

Repositioning a product in the diagram or expanding its scope does not necessarily mean that a customer will receive more information, more physical things, or more service. To the contrary, a customer may be happier with less rather than more in any of the three areas. Consider, for example, the customer using the library or Internet in an attempt to research a particular question. More is not necessarily better if this customer wants to get to the answer quickly and doesn't want to be overwhelmed with information. Likewise, users of physical products often want less instead of more when they prefer products that are smaller, lighter, and less obtrusive. Similarly, owners of copy machines and elevators do not want more service; rather, they want the original product constituted so that it will require a minimum of maintenance-related service.

Controllability and Adaptability

Regardless of how a work system's product combines information, physical, and service components, the customer may want to control the product's function or appearance at any point in time, or may want to adapt its features and functions over time as needs change. Understanding this is important for analyzing work systems because the specific types of control and adaptability the customer wants can sometimes be accomplished in different ways. One way is to build additional features into the product itself. Another way is to change the work system that produces the product in order to create a richer set of product options that can be built in during production. Products such as boats and cars illustrate that controllability and adaptability existed in many forms long before computers, but successive advances in IT have led to a variety of powerful approaches based on the direct use of codified information.

IT enables controllability through three approaches: the "smart" product, the interactive product, and the programmable product. A **smart product** is preprogrammed to obtain information from its environment and act appropriately, such as the way automatic flood lights turn on for three minutes after detecting motion, and the way computerized vending machines in Japan keep track of their own inventory levels and replenishment needs. Smart products with more complex functions range from heat-seeking missiles to databases programmed to identify news and emerging trends. An **interactive product** provides immediate responses to interactive commands. The widespread use of the World Wide Web shows that simple forms of the interactive approach are quite acceptable to a broad range of people. While the same can be said for mortgage calculators and simple database queries, use of complex models and complex interactive queries by nontechnical users is very rare. A **programmable product** accepts instructions from the user and executes them later. Thermostats and timers for VCRs and coffee makers are examples of the programmable approach in which the user enters instructions that are later executed automatically when specific conditions related to temperature or time are met. The fact that so few consumers actually use the programmable features of a VCR demonstrates that building programmability into products for nontechnical users may be ineffective until the programming tools are simpler and more intuitive.

The key issue when providing adaptability is to support the product features and functions the customer really wants rather than just those that have already been defined or those that are easy to produce. This can be done via IT by making the product interactive or by making it programmable. It can also be done by building customization into the process that produces the product, so that each unit is produced based on specifications unique to a particular customer order. These specifications must be obtained from the customer and converted into a form that dictates the specific production process for each case. The desired degree of customization in a production process has major ramifications for how the business process operates, how efficient it can be, and how well the product matches customer desires. Chapter 1 explained that *mass customization* describes the ideal situation, namely, producing the product as though it were a commodity but using IT-based tools to customize it so that it fits customer needs exactly.

Controllability and adaptability are crucial characteristics to consider when thinking about information as the product of an information system. The extreme inflexibility of early MISs was largely due to the programming methods and hardware technology available at the time. The ability to incorporate current tools, such as database management systems, into the technical underpinnings has made today's MISs much more flexible. In addition to accelerating the design and programming processes, data retrieval and formatting functions in the newer tools have become part of the product itself. Current MISs may still generate the same set of computerized printouts every week, but they also bring many possibilities for direct control by permitting users to specify what information should be reported and in what format. This is an increasingly important part of the information system product because business issues are in constant flux and because once customers learn how to use an information system, they often see new adaptations that may generate unanticipated benefits.

Reality Check

THE CUSTOMER'S VIEW OF THE PRODUCT

This section described products as a mix of information, service, and physical components.

1. Identify several products in which all three components are important.
2. Explain how these products might be changed by providing more or less of these three components or by making them more controllable or adaptable.

THE CUSTOMER'S CYCLE OF INVOLVEMENT WITH A PRODUCT

Anyone who has ever waited on line to pay for gasoline or to check in at an airport knows that customer satisfaction involves much more than just the quality of a product the customer receives. As Konosuke Matsushita, founder of Matsushita Electric, stated over 50 years ago, well before the computer revolution: "We are responsible for delivering satisfaction to the customer not only by designing good products, but also by providing those products through carefully laid out distribution systems in which we should follow through to eliminate any inconvenience to our customers, such as difficulty in repair work."[4]

Matsushita's broad view of the overall product offering is that the basis of customer satisfaction is the complete **customer involvement cycle,** the customer's entire involvement with the product starting with defining the requirements and acquiring the product. Figure 6.4 shows a five-step version of the customer involvement cycle along with some of the opportunities for improvement within each phase. The steps include requirements, acquisition, usage, maintenance, and retirement.

Requirements: establishing what the customer wants, matching these requirements to the available alternatives, and, in some cases, customizing the product to fit the requirements.

Acquisition: determining the customer's acquisition cost, determining product availability, and performing purchase or acquisition transactions.

Usage: the customer's usage of the product, typically viewed in relation to the customer's processes.

Maintenance: the customer's efforts to maintain durable products over extended periods of time.

Retirement: whatever must be done to get rid of the product or its remnants once it is no longer useful to the customer.

Each of the five steps in the customer involvement cycle can be viewed as a separate subsystem that produces a product for the customer. Each of those products can be presented in terms of different combinations of information, physical, and service features. For example, the discussion of Otisline at the beginning of the chapter showed how information could be used more effectively as part of elevator service. That discussion emphasized the usage and maintenance steps in the customer involvement cycle and implied that information generated by Otisline might be useful in the requirements step for new customers. The discussion said nothing about the acquisition or retirement steps, each of which might provide other opportunities to improve customer satisfaction. The last part of this chapter will look across a variety of industries as it explains the entire customer involvement cycle in more depth.

The idea of the customer involvement cycle applies to both external and internal customers. It is used most frequently when thinking about external customers because a firm's success is directly related to how well it satisfies its external customers. Its use in thinking about internal customers is also warranted, however, because it reminds work

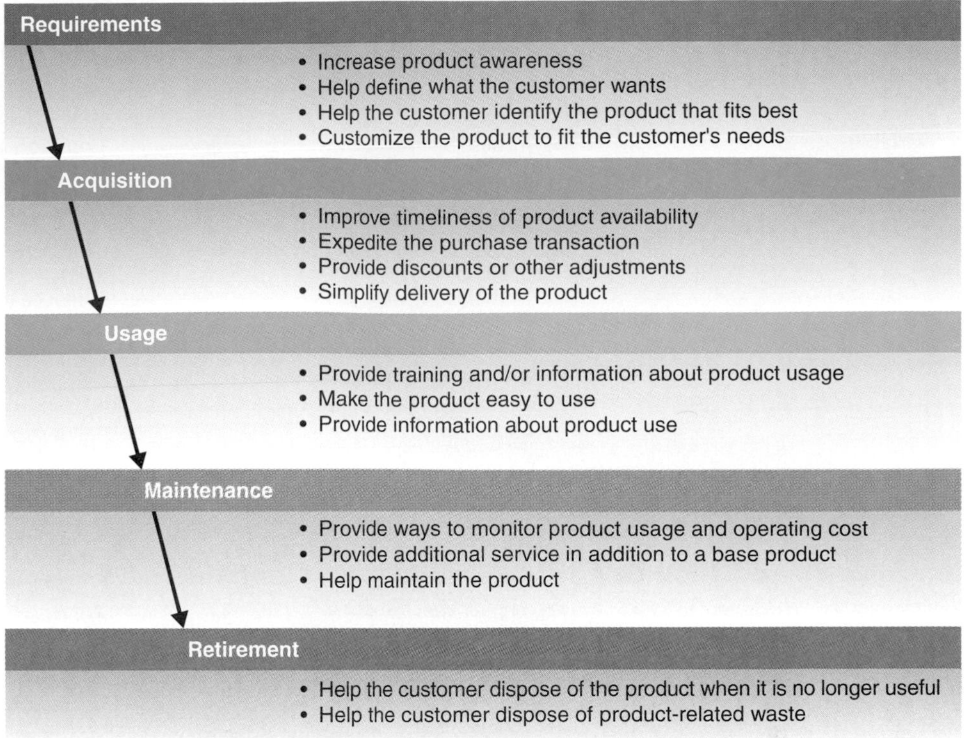
Requirements
• Increase product awareness
• Help define what the customer wants
• Help the customer identify the product that fits best
• Customize the product to fit the customer's needs
Acquisition
• Improve timeliness of product availability
• Expedite the purchase transaction
• Provide discounts or other adjustments
• Simplify delivery of the product
Usage
• Provide training and/or information about product usage
• Make the product easy to use
• Provide information about product use
Maintenance
• Provide ways to monitor product usage and operating cost
• Provide additional service in addition to a base product
• Help maintain the product
Retirement
• Help the customer dispose of the product when it is no longer useful
• Help the customer dispose of product-related waste

Figure 6.4
Opportunities to increase customer benefits across the customer involvement cycle

Each step in the customer involvement cycle provides a number of possible ways to improve customer satisfaction.

system participants that inwardly directed systems such as payroll, health benefits, and expense reimbursements also do have customers with a legitimate desire to feel satisfied in their complete experience with these systems.

Reality Check

THE CUSTOMER'S CYCLE OF INVOLVEMENT WITH A PRODUCT

This section described a five-step customer involvement cycle.

1. Describe the customer involvement cycle for the products you discussed in the previous reality check.
2. Explain ways in which changes in the customer involvement cycle might increase customer satisfaction for these products.

THE CUSTOMER'S CRITERIA FOR EVALUATING THE PRODUCT

Customers think about product performance in terms of a variety of performance variables. Table 6.2 identifies five product performance variables that can be used to evaluate the result of any step of a product's customer involvement cycle. The table also lists typical performance measures for each, plus common ways information systems are used to improve the product. Other possible criteria, such as image and aesthetics, are left out because information systems usually affect them only indirectly.

TABLE 6.2 Common Roles of Information Systems in Improving the Product of a Work System

Product performance variable	Typical measures	Common information system roles
Cost	• Purchase price • Cost of ownership • Amount of time and attention required	• Reduce internal cost of business process or increase productivity, making it easier to charge or allocate lower prices to customers • Improve product performance in ways that reduce the customer's internal costs
Quality	• Defect rate per time interval or per quantity of output • Rate of warranty returns • Perceived quality according to customer	• Insure the product is produced more consistently • Make it easier to customize the product for the customer • Build information systems into the product to make it more usable or maintainable
Responsiveness	• Time to respond to customer request • Helpfulness of response	• Improve the speed of response • Systematize communication with customers • Increase flexibility to make it easier to respond to what the customer wants
Reliability	• Average time to failure • Failure rate per time interval • Compliance to customer commitment dates	• Make the business process more consistent • Make the business process more secure • Build features into the product that make it more reliable on its own right
Conformance to standards and regulations	• Existence of nonconformance • Rate of complaints about nonconformance	• Clarify the standards and regulations so that it is easier to determine whether they are being adhered to • Systematize work to make the output more consistent

Notice that these variables often interact, sometimes by working together and sometimes by working in opposite directions. For example, cost and reliability issues overlap because poor reliability generates unwanted costs for the customer. Likewise, responsiveness, reliability, and conformance are sometimes viewed as partially overlapping aspects of quality. In other cases, performance variables such as responsiveness and reliability may oppose each other because the product variations needed to increase responsiveness might diminish reliability. Despite the overlaps and contradictions, it is useful to consider ways in which each of these variables helps clarify the customer's view of how good the product is and how it might be improved. At least a few of the five product performance variables could be irrelevant in any particular situation, but each performance variable should be considered, if for no other reason than to assure yourself that it is not important in a given situation. We will look at each of the performance variables in turn.

Cost

Cost is a prime determinant of customer satisfaction. When considering **cost,** we are not thinking about it in a strict accounting sense but as what the internal or external customer must give up in order to obtain, use, and maintain the product of a business process. This includes money plus time, effort, and attention that could be used for other purposes. This view of cost illustrates how the product of any work system involves cost to the internal or external customer even when no money is transferred.

There are many ways to use information systems to reduce costs felt by internal or external customers. These start with reducing the cost of acquiring or using the product, such as the way ATMs eliminate the time and effort of standing on line during bank hours or the way MCI provides special "friends and family" rates. Information systems can also be incorporated into the product to make it more efficient, such as the way computers control combustion in car engines. Information systems can also provide more usable billing data to promote efficiency, such as by analyzing telephone bills and telling customers what services and pricing options would minimize their future bills if the same usage patterns continue.

The cost felt by an internal or external customer can also be used as a tool for rationing the use of scarce resources. This is commonly done through a pricing scheme that motivates customers to use resources efficiently. An example of this type is the decision to bill internal users or departments for telephone and copier usage. The process of billing internal departments within the company absorbs time and effort, but this cost is often preferable to the cost of excessive usage due to treating telephones and copiers as free goods. Pricing can also be used to shift usage away from peak load periods, such as late morning and mid afternoon. Electric power utilities use peak load pricing strategies to spread out demand during peak periods and thereby reduce the need to purchase new power plants.

Quality

The concept of quality has been interpreted many different ways and spans many performance dimensions. Even though product quality is often linked to the consistency of the process that produced the product, we will view quality as a criterion by which the customer evaluates the product. Chapter 3 previously discussed consistency, productivity, cycle time, and other aspects of process performance.

For our purposes, **quality** refers to the customer's perception that the product has desired features and that these features are in line with the product's costs. For physical products, the perception of quality is related to function and aesthetics, such as the way information technology has been incorporated into automobiles in functions ranging from antilock braking to computerized directions using global positioning satellites. For information products, the perception of quality is related to accessibility and usefulness, such as the way graphical user interfaces made it easier for nonprogrammers to extract data from databases. For service products, the perception of quality is related whether the service seems complete and whether it is delivered attentively. One of the complaints about some HMOs is that doctors are so swamped they cannot provide high-quality service.

Responsiveness

With regard to customer satisfaction, **responsiveness** means taking timely action based on what the customer wants, such as when a sales clerk uses a company-wide inventory system to find an out-of-stock item at another store and has it shipped to the customer's home. As another example, many architectural firms now use computer aided design systems to provide simulated walk-throughs of proposed buildings; this sometimes enables them to make immediate modifications based on customer feedback. The highest levels of responsiveness often require creating or modifying a product or service based on a specific customer's needs, thereby increasing its value for that customer.

Responsiveness involves more than just speed. Even in today's fast-paced business world, convenience and personalized service are often more important than speed. As an example, AT&T Universal Card Services gave an employee a $6,000 award for suggesting that AT&T should give the customer a choice between a 10:00 A.M. delivery or a 3:00 P.M. delivery when a credit card is lost. Providing a choice instead of automatically sending new replacement credit cards using overnight delivery to arrive by 10:00 A.M. had the potential of increasing customer satisfaction while also reducing costs for AT&T because a 3:00 P.M. delivery would be cheaper.[5]

Computerizing a work system may increase responsiveness or may do the opposite, either by design or by accident. As managed care takes hold in medicine, for example, more medical decisions, such as how many sessions of psychotherapy to allow, are being constrained (and hence made less responsive) by partially computerized systems based on statistical data. As an example of responsiveness decreasing by accident, consider what happened when a Bay Area restaurant began using handheld terminals for taking orders. The terminals had many benefits, but they provided no way for waiters to record special customer requests, such as putting the sauce on the side. Service was faster and more reliable, but not as responsive to the customer.

Reliability

The **reliability** of a work system's product refers to the likelihood that it will not fail when the customer wants to use it. Although computerizing work systems often adds a layer of structure that increases reliability, there is no way to guarantee the computers are programmed correctly or that communication networks will always stay up. On April 13, 1998, a breakdown in AT&T's high speed data networks affected thousands of customers, such as Wal-Mart, about half of whose 2,400 stores experienced difficulties processing credit card purchases or updating inventories. AT&T had spent billions of dollars modernizing its networks and often boasted that they were "self-healing." In this case, however, the self-healing features that reroute data traffic when a cable is cut were useless because the major switches that perform the routing were down, apparently due to a software problem.[6] Eight years earlier, a previously unobserved bug in software used by AT&T's long distance telephone network prevented completion of 44% of the 148 million long distance calls on the network between 2:30 and 11:30 P.M. on January 15, 1990. That disruption left national sales offices and other large-scale telephone users unable to operate and led many corporations to consider using MCI and Sprint as backup suppliers of telephone service.[7]

One of the paradoxes of reliability is that measures taken to increase reliability are often the cause of failure. An ironic example is a power failure at an air traffic control center serving Chicago's O'Hare Airport. Thousands of airline passengers were delayed for hours because a contractor accidentally caused a short circuit while testing a system for preventing power failures. This was the second time in the same year that installation of an "uninterruptible power system" interrupted power at an air traffic center.[8]

Conformance to Standards and Regulations

Adherence to standards and regulations imposed by external bodies such as major customers, industry groups, or the government is a crucial issue for the product of many work systems. We will call performance in this area **conformance to standards and regulations.** Unlike cost and quality, conformance does not play a role in the return on investment, yet it is the driving force behind the way many work systems operate. The most obvious examples of conformance issues occur in work systems related to gathering and analyzing information related to paying taxes; nonconformance in these systems results in fines or even jail terms. In other cases, nonconformance with industry standards such as the shape of electric plugs, the width of a typical doorway, or the dimensions of a piece of paper is unacceptable because it would cause incompatibility with many other products used by the same customers.

Standards are precisely stated, widely publicized rules governing the size, shape, and operating characteristics of products or processes. The existence of an American standard for the size of copy paper (8½ by 11 inches) means that any paper supplier can provide paper fitting any copy machine or laser printer built for the American market. Different standards can coexist, as illustrated by the fact that Europe and Asia use different standard sizes for paper, and that people in America and continental Europe drive on the right side of the road while people in England and Japan drive on the left side. The chapters on information technology will explain why "competing standards" is a major competitive issue in the computer and telecommunications industries. The enormous growth and market power of Microsoft and Intel attest to the importance of controlling technical standards, in this case, the standards for personal computer operating systems and microprocessors.[9]

Where standards are either negotiated voluntarily or determined by the way things evolve in business or society, **regulations** are rules based on laws administered by federal, state, or local governments. International bodies such as the European Union also generate regulations. Regulations require businesses to operate in particular ways and to submit tax forms and tax payments consistent with rules. Depending on the size of the business, regulations may require additional information about hiring practices, energy utilization, waste disposal, and other topics. One of the most far reaching system-related regulations in current business is the conversion from national currencies to a new European currency called the euro. This conversion requires banks, corporations, and government agencies to overhaul their financial information systems. Invoices, tax calculations and bank statements will have to be changed from marks or francs to euros. By some estimates, the conversion could cost private industry $80 billion.[10]

Electronic data interchange (EDI) systems (mentioned in Chapter 1) exemplify the way conformance to standards applies across the customer involvement cycle. EDI is the electronic transmission of structured documents such as customer orders between companies. Before EDI, large companies like General Electric would spend around $55 to process each invoice because of paperwork and inconsistent data formats. In many cases, these companies told their suppliers that reducing paperwork costs was so important that the use of EDI was a requirement for doing business regardless of the particular features of the product being purchased. This forced changes in the smaller companies' internal information systems to permit linkage into the standardized EDI systems the large companies were establishing. In effect, EDI became an essential part of the product the large companies were buying.

Thus far we have surveyed the basic ideas for describing product architecture, the customer involvement cycle, and criteria for evaluating a product. These ideas are basically the same regardless of whether the product is directed at internal or external customers. With this background, we will now turn to the competitive uses of information systems in producing, extending, or servicing products for external customers. The last part of the chapter will discuss electronic commerce and electronically enhanced products, but first we need to look at the nature of competition.

Reality Check

EVALUATING PRODUCT PERFORMANCE

This section has discussed a number of product performance variables.

1. Identify two work systems, one with internal customers and one with external customers. Identify the product performance variables that seem most important and least important in each situation. Explain how you might measure those variables.
2. Assume someone actually measured each variable. Estimate what the person would find currently and what the person might find if the product were improved as much as seems conceivable.

USING INFORMATION SYSTEMS FOR COMPETITIVE ADVANTAGE

Organizations compete based on their products' value chains, the series of processes that create the value external customers pay for. **Competitive advantage** occurs when a product's value chain generates superior product features, quality, service, availability, lower cost, or other things customers care about. Competitive advantage comes from many sources. Some companies have a natural competitive advantage (for example, a steel mill that has lower transportation costs because it is near a good source of iron ore and coal). Others must create competitive advantage through superior product design, marketing, customer service, or distribution channels.

Whether and how a firm can use information systems competitively depends on the firm's strategy. Table 6.3 compares the basic strategies of two competitors in each of four industries. These examples show that organizations compete on a wide range of performance variables and information, service, and physical features. Although competitive

TABLE 6.3 Competitive Approaches in Different Industries

Industrial competition is based on a mix of cost and value.

Automobile A	Automobile B
• Solid car at reasonable price • Good for families • Good service • Long warranty	• Flashy foreign car • Excellent power and handling • Image associated with youth and wealth • Reasonably good repair record • Reputation for having the newest features
Hospital A	**Hospital B**
• Best service and best doctors • Excellent food • High ratio of nurses to patients • Pleasant rooms • Long-term success in difficult heart operations	• Lowest cost for the patient • High-volume general care • Few complex cases • Cooperative with local ambulance companies
Cereal A	**Cereal B**
• Product image aimed at children • Prizes in cereal boxes • Product features aimed at children	• Product image aimed at parents • Emphasis on nutritional values without sacrificing good taste • Good product features for the entire family
University A	**University B**
• Large university • All major specialties • Large faculty including famous researchers • Major intercollegiate sports programs • Substantial work-study opportunities	• Small private university • Substantial attention to individual students • Good athletic programs for students • Strong ties to alumni

situations vary widely, most companies adopt some combination of three idealized strategies described by Porter.[11] A firm using a **cost leadership strategy** competes on lower costs. A firm using this strategy can reduce its own costs, its supplier's costs, or its customer's costs, or it can raise its competitor's costs. A firm using a **product differentiation strategy** provides more value than competitors or eliminates the competitor's differentiation. A firm using a **focus strategy** sells its product or service into a restricted market niche with limited competition. While viewing strategy in terms of these idealized models is sometimes useful, a growing consensus in the 1990s is that most companies have to focus on both cost and differentiation in order to succeed in today's business climate.

Strategic Information Systems

Competitive use of information systems is one of many current approaches for creating competitive advantage or counteracting competitors' strategies. This differs from the use of early information systems, which typically had little to do with competitive advantage. These early systems focused primarily on support functions such as accounting, record keeping, and providing information for management. These tasks supported the primary activities on a product's value chain but affected a product's competitive stance only indirectly. Even if these systems reduced the organization's costs, the customer rarely perceived their impact directly.

More recently, organizations have integrated information systems into their products' value chains. Today these systems are so infused throughout entire organizations that many have become essential for a business to operate. Even if these systems provide no competitive differentiation whatsoever, they are often considered **mission-critical information systems** because their failure prevents or delays basic business activities such as selling to customers, processing orders, and manufacturing. The importance of mission-critical systems was reflected in a 62% plunge in the stock of Oxford Health Plans after an unanticipated quarterly loss in 1997. Oxford attributed the loss to problems with upgrades in basic systems for billing and reimbursement. Many bills had been sent out late over the course of eight months, and some customers balked when Oxford tried to collect back payments. Oxford had fallen hundreds of millions of dollars behind in payments to hospitals and doctors and had been forced to advance money to them without verifying they were obeying Oxford's cost-saving rules.[12] Had Oxford implemented the information system upgrades successfully, it wouldn't have fallen so far behind in its billing, it would have been able to make all its payments, and it would have avoided a devastating quarter. The mission-critical nature of many information systems is one of the reasons banks have spent enormous amounts to fix their Y2K problems. For example, Bank of America, the fifth largest U.S. bank, had 1,000 people examining 200 million lines of code in 1998 and expected to spend $250 million on the project. Most large banks seemed to be on track in dealing with the problem, but many smaller banks that lacked financial and technical resources were in deep trouble. Federal inspectors warned over 200 small to mid-sized banks that their Y2K progress to date was inadequate and that they might be forced to shut down unless they could show their mission critical systems would operate correctly.[13,14]

In contrast to the many mission-critical information systems most organizations rely on, a comparatively small group of systems called **strategic information systems** are designed to play a major role in an organization's competitive strategy. These systems typically increase the customer's perceived value by providing information and services with products, customizing products, eliminating delays, improving reliability, making products easier to use, bypassing intermediaries, or reducing transaction times. Otisline is one of many examples of this type of system.

The discussion of electronic commerce later in this chapter will present many other examples that are too recent to have a long track record, regardless of how successful they seem initially. To introduce the long-term dynamics of strategic information systems, we will discuss classic examples from Merrill Lynch and McKesson.

Merrill Lynch's Cash Management Account was introduced in 1977 to combine three previously distinct investment services: credit using a margin account; cash withdrawal using a check or Visa card; and automatic investment of cash in a money market. The Cash Management Account was aimed at customers who were tired of the confusion and inefficiency of having too many different accounts in too many different places. Combining these services required a state-of-the-art transaction processing system. Building the information system and developing the other business activities required for this type of financial product was so complex that Merrill Lynch enjoyed a monopoly for four years. It had gained over 450,000 new customers by the time its competitors could respond with a me-too product of a type that is now commonplace and is also easier to create because the underlying technology has improved.

McKesson, a distributor of pharmaceuticals, used what was initially an innovative system to help its customers simultaneously achieve two seemingly contradictory goals, reducing inventory costs and avoiding stock-outs. Pharmacies traditionally ordered from distributors using inefficient and error-prone methods. A pharmacy employee checked the pharmacy's inventory, recorded amounts needed, and mailed orders to distributors, who responded days later. Delays in all the steps and errors in transcribing information several times forced pharmacies to tie up money in large inventories. To minimize these problems, McKesson's system allows pharmacies to record their orders using a handheld, calculator-like terminal. Bar code labels on shelves make it unnecessary to even write product names. Orders recorded on the terminal are transmitted over phone lines to McKesson's computer system and entered automatically. McKesson attained a competitive edge by reducing its internal costs, reducing customers' internal costs, and providing better customer service. The benefits for McKesson included a reduction in order entry clerks from 700 to 15. From 1975 to 1987, McKesson's sales increased 424%, whereas its operating expenses increased only 86%.[15,16]

The Merrill Lynch and McKesson systems were both attempts to attain competitive advantage through product differentiation. Both were so successful that they created new expectations and changed the basis of competition in their respective industries. With the bar raised, competitors either had to create a different type of differentiation or had to build similar systems to eliminate the differentiation these strategic systems originally created. The me-too systems were built not for competitive advantage but because particular features or capabilities had become a de facto requirement to participate in the market. The ultimate result of many strategic information systems is that the capabilities in the system become a **competitive necessity** and are no longer a source of competitive advantage because all the major competitors do something similar.

In other words, even if a strategic information system is initially successful, there is no guarantee it will provide **sustainable competitive advantage.** If one firm can build a system, there is usually no reason why another firm or group of firms cannot copy the idea. The main challenge to sustainability is how long any single system or capability will provide advantage before its is copied, equaled, or even surpassed by competitors. The most sustainable sources of competitive advantage are the firm's culture, its personnel, its major business processes, and its special resources such as patents or land that cannot be copied. The fact that competitive advantage through information systems may be temporary does not invalidate this approach, however. During the four years Merrill Lynch's competitors struggled to catch up, Merrill Lynch expanded its customer base and could look to new opportunities while its competitors were matching its existing capabilities. The same issues about competitive necessity and sustainable competitive advantage are being played out in the late 1990s as companies try to exploit electronic commerce using the World Wide Web and private networks.

Competing by Increasing Value and Decreasing Cost

This chapter started with ideas about products and customers and has also addressed competitive strategies, competitive advantage, and strategic information systems. The next step is to identify common rationales for using information systems competitively. First we will consider how the value chain can be extended to include both suppliers and customers in the search for opportunities. We will then look at other areas of opportunity that involve improving the product, competing in terms of speed, and reducing the customer's cost.

Viewing Suppliers and Customers as Part of the Value Chain

Figure 6.5 shows how to extend the value chain concept to identify different ways information systems can affect the cost incurred and value received directly by the customer.[17,18] It shows a product's value chain extending from the firm's suppliers to the firm itself and to the firm's customers. Steps inside the firm and its suppliers include developing, producing, selling, delivering, and servicing the product's components or the product itself. Steps involving the customer directly include the steps in the customer involvement cycle. These include determining requirements, acquiring the product, using it, maintaining it, and retiring it (see Figure 6.4).

Each step in Figure 6.5 is an opportunity to increase value or decrease costs or prices, regardless of whether the improvements occur within the firm's internal operation or for a supplier or customer's direct benefit. For example, the types of supply chain management mentioned in Chapter 1 can help a firm manufacture its product with less waste and using less inventory. The basic approach is to create standardized electronic links and long-term agreements with suppliers. This helps the firm price its products competitively. Within the firm, information systems can improve sales processes by providing better information for salespeople and customers. These systems can also improve service processes by maintaining customer records and hastening response. In the customer's part of the value chain, information systems can help fit the product to the customer's requirements and can make the product easier to use and maintain.

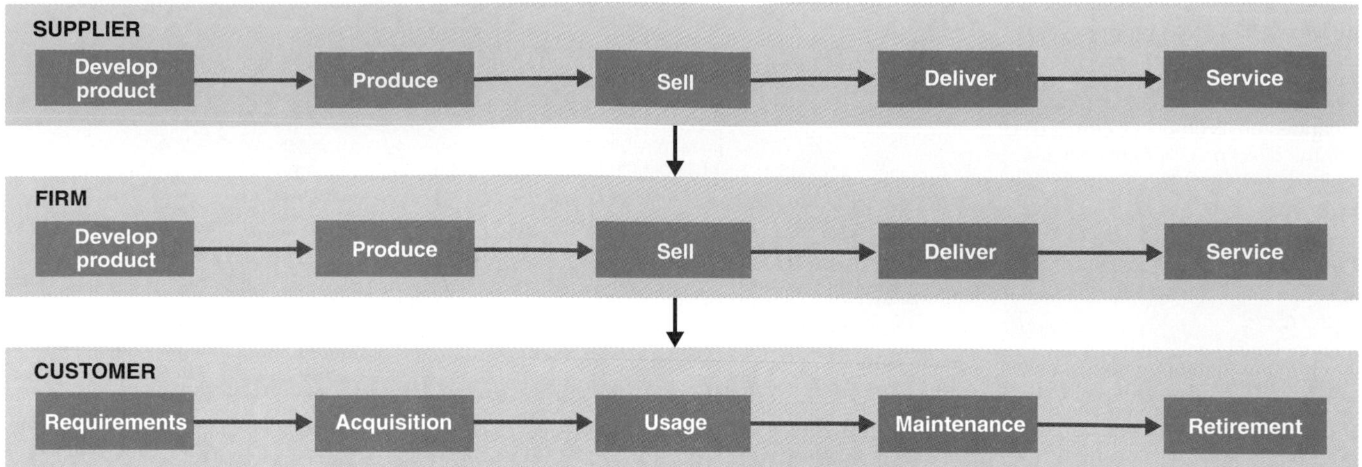

Figure 6.5
Extended value chain for a manufactured product

This extended value chain starts with business processes at suppliers, and includes business processes within the firm and business processes performed by the customer using the product. Each step in the extended value chain is an opportunity to reduce the cost or to add value for customers.

Making Product Features Competitive

Figure 6.3 used a product positioning approach for identifying potential improvements in the product of an internal work system that processed résumés. The basic idea was to characterize a product as a combination of information, service, and physical things, and then to identify ways to expand the product's scope or improve it in other ways. This same product positioning approach can be used to think about potential improvements in products directed at external customers.

Figure 6.6 uses this approach to characterize the opportunities available to Otis Elevator. Because an elevator is a physical thing that requires service, the original positioning in the triangular map identifies the product as primarily a physical product. In addition to making better elevators, Otis decided to expand the product in the direction of more information and better service. The information improvements include complete long-term tracking of each elevator's maintenance, along with the ability to use that information to expedite repairs and to do preventive maintenance. The service improvements are based on centralized dispatching, which ensures that repair technicians are notified quickly and that each incident is followed until the elevator is again in service.

Notice how product improvements can occur at any point along the extended value chain in Figure 6.5. In effect, the new dispatching system supports the Otis product line by helping repair technicians who are suppliers. The Otisline system provides internal savings for Otis Elevator but also improves the customer's usage and maintenance steps.

Competing on Time

The competitive strategies of some firms recognize that time has become a key corporate resource. **Competing on time** is a business strategy of providing more value by doing things faster, including bringing new products to market more quickly, responding more quickly to customer demand, and providing faster service. Many companies have slashed both time to design a product and time to manufacture it by more than 50%. They have done this by reorganizing workflows, removing unnecessary bureaucracy, and using information technology to eliminate redundant work and speed up necessary work. For example, CAD systems allow the use of computerized drawings and parts lists for the previous version of a product as the starting point for designing the next version. These systems also speed up the process of designing new components from scratch. Designs may be tested

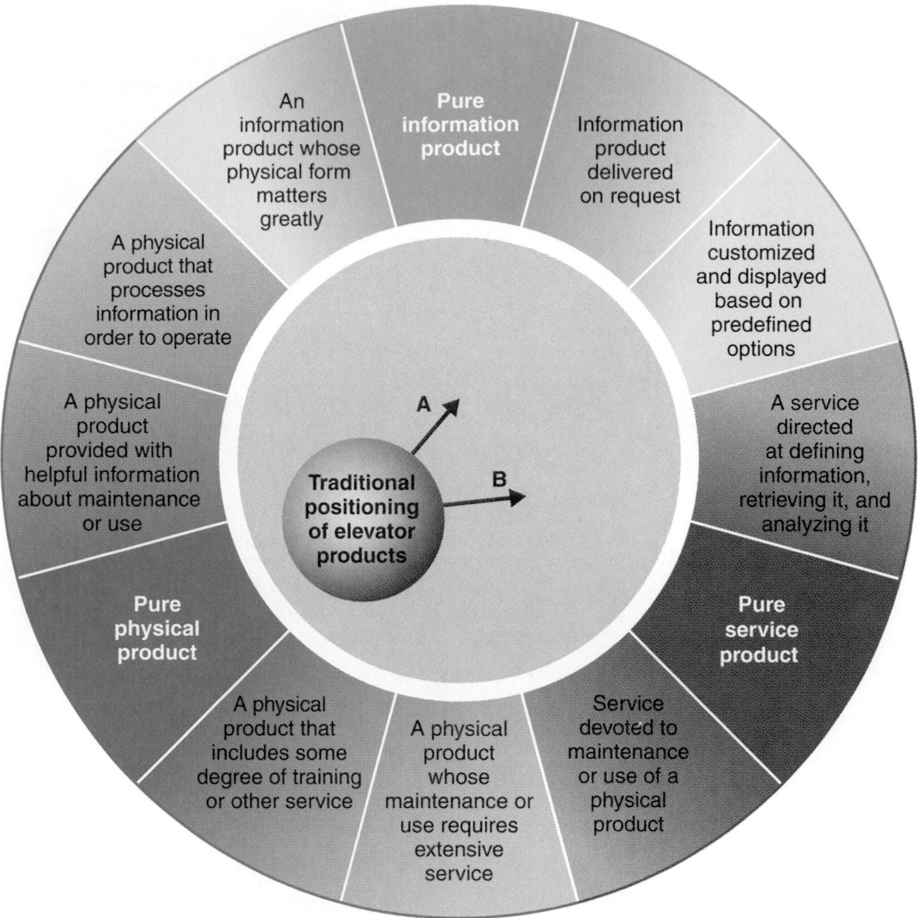

Figure 6.6
How Otis Elevator improved and expanded its product

Elevators are physical products. Otis expanded on its product by expanding it in the direction of information and service.

using simulation to avoid delay and expense of building unnecessary physical models or prototypes. On completion, some designs can be transmitted to the factory in a form that can immediately drive numerically controlled machine tools.

Thanks to information systems that track and coordinate sales, inventory, and orders, inventories have been slashed 50% or more in both manufacturing and distribution. The enabling technology includes bar coding to identify individual items and prevent data errors; data communications to consolidate the information from multiple locations; and rapid computing to convert the raw data into new orders, scheduled receipts, projected shortfalls, and other information needed to support customer demand with minimal inventory levels. Retailing and distribution are also areas where high degrees of integration have been achieved by integrating marketing, production, and distribution. The system is sometimes called **quick response**. At its core are bar code scanners that identify individual items and provide complete visibility of when each item is moved or sold. The benefits include not only inventory control but also increased profitability by avoiding out-of-stock situations that once cut sales by 25% to 40%.[19]

Competing on Cost

The way the WCA framework distinguishes between the product and the process is reflected in Figure 6.7, which illustrates how product-related costs borne by the internal or external customer differ from costs related to producing the product. This distinction is reflected in the performance variables shown in Table 2.5 in Chapter 2. The term *cost* is used as a performance variable perceived by the customer across the entire customer involvement cycle, whereas *productivity* is the cost-related term for measuring internal business operations.

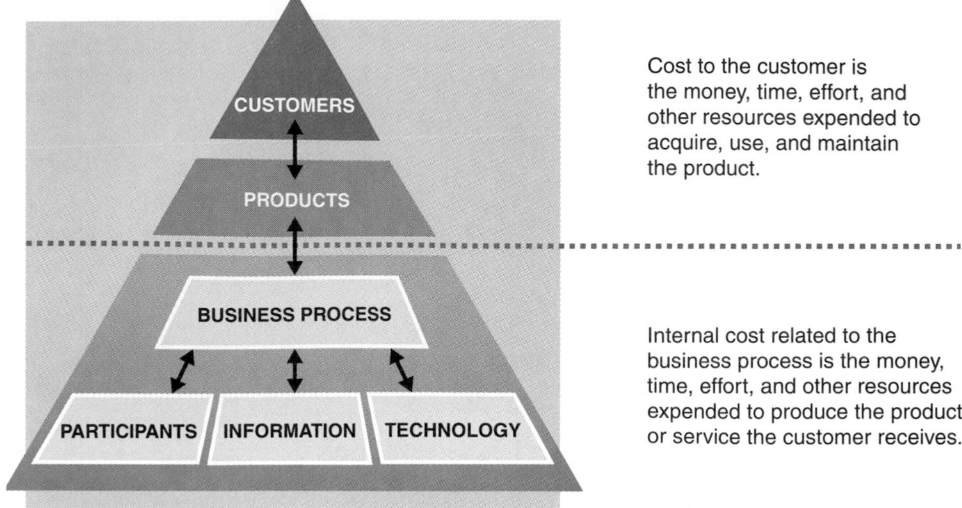
CUSTOMERS
PRODUCTS
BUSINESS PROCESS
PARTICIPANTS
INFORMATION
TECHNOLOGY
Cost to the customer is the money, time, effort, and other resources expended to acquire, use, and maintain the product.
Internal cost related to the business process is the money, time, effort, and other resources expended to produce the product or service the customer receives.

Figure 6.7
Internal costs versus costs borne by the customer

The analysis of a system should look at two types of costs: product-related costs borne by the internal or external customer and internal costs related to producing the product.

Many firms have used information systems to reduce the costs borne by their customers across the customer involvement cycle. Using information systems to improve internal efficiency is often a crucial part of a cost leadership strategy. The specific information system applications typically reduce manufacturing costs, eliminate excess inventory by building to order, automate customer service functions, or reduce the cost of product development.

An approach that is more visible to customers involves helping them reduce internal costs related to the product by providing cost control information related to its use. For firms such as telephone and insurance companies, this type of information may be readily available as a byproduct of the business relationship. Telephone companies have taken this approach by providing billing information in a useful form. Previously, businesses received paper telephone bills that were hundreds of pages long. This information was adequate for justifying the total bill but useless for analyzing how telephones could be used more efficiently. More recently, telephone companies have sent computerized bills to help their customers analyze telephone usage and reduce their costs. Insurance transaction data is also especially valuable in controlling costs. Instead of treating its claims data as a secret, Travelers Insurance analyzes the data for its customers. When the manufacturer Allied-Signal noticed a rise in some of its self-insured workman's compensation claims, data from Travelers pinpointed a large number of hand injuries by maintenance workers. Allied-Signal halved these injuries through better training and the use of gloves.[20]

The remainder of this chapter will extend these ideas about competing through product differentiation and cost reduction. Instead of covering these topics in general, it will focus on ways electronic commerce and electronic enhancement of products can be applied within each step of the customer involvement cycle.

Reality Check

USING INFORMATION SYSTEMS FOR COMPETITIVE ADVANTAGE

This section noted that many information systems are mission-critical but that some might be called strategic information systems because they are part of a firm's strategy.

1. Identify three mission-critical information systems in organizations you are familiar with and explain why you believe these systems are mission-critical.
2. Explain why you do or do not believe these can also be considered strategic information systems.

ELECTRONIC COMMERCE

Electronic commerce refers to the use of computerized systems in selling and distributing products. The Web and other electronic means are used to:

- inform a customer of a product's existence
- provide in-depth information about the product
- establish the customer's requirements
- perform the purchase transaction and, in some cases, deliver the product electronically if the product happens to be software or information

Electronic retailing, stock trading, banking, and publishing are typical examples of electronic commerce. We will discuss these areas along with some of the required capabilities, such as digital signatures and digital cash.

Electronic Retailing

Electronic retailing is selling products to external customers through a computer network rather than through traditional retail stores or person-to-person sales processes. The example of Amazon.com that opened Chapter 1 was an example of electronic commerce. Changes in the process of making airline reservations show how much is at stake in the way people purchase things. Figure 6.8 shows three of many possible processes for purchasing a seat on a flight. Using the first method, the customer works through a travel agent who uses a published airline guide but needs to call individual airlines to determine seat availability and to make reservations. The second method shows the travel agent using a computerized database of flight availability information. The third method depicts the customer using the Web to make the reservation directly, bypassing both the travel agent and airline personnel. In the first and second methods, the travel agent plays the role of broker by using information and expertise not readily available to the consumer; in the third method, however, the information system allows the customer to bypass the agent, and the travel agent loses a commission.

The availability of flight information on the Web is a significant threat to travel agents and other intermediaries who make a living by accessing and filtering information for customers. An increasing number of travelers see little advantage in working through a travel agency if its services involve little more than providing the same information and purchase options that online travel services provide. As with other electronic commerce examples, a traveler's choice between a traditional travel agency and an electronic one depends on

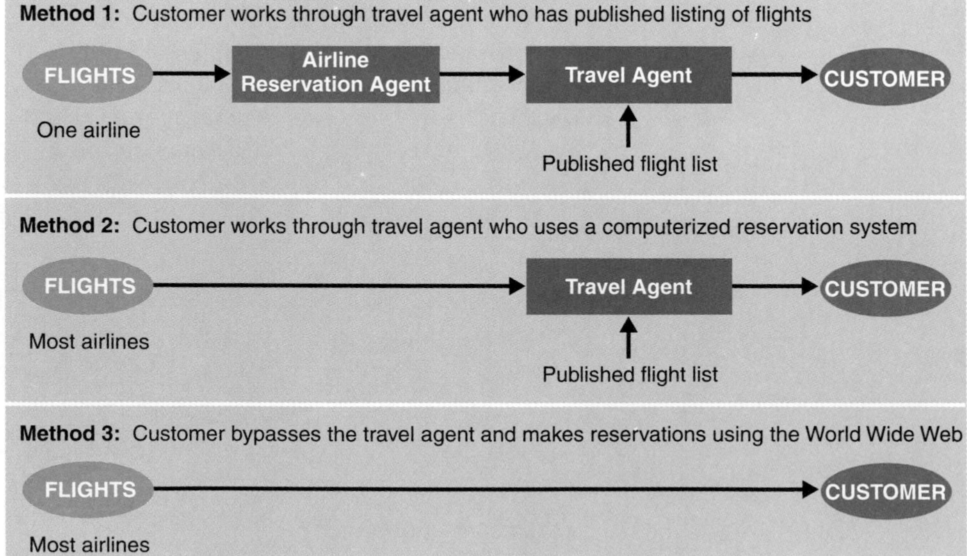

Figure 6.8
Three ways to make reservations

The first method is largely obsolete, although some airlines are still not listed on major computerized reservation systems. The second is the most common method today, but the third is becoming more popular through Web sites of travel agencies and airlines.

whether World Wide Web access is readily available, whether it would be quicker to use the human travel agent, and whether the price or seat availability might be better with either choice. Some travel agencies are still thriving, however, because their business approach is to provide special services that are more convenient and more valuable than what one can find on the Web.

Electronic Stock Trading

Electronic commerce creates threats and opportunities for brokers and intermediaries of all kinds—not only travel agents, but insurance brokers, loan brokers, stockbrokers, and brokers of food and mechanical parts as well. The threat to these intermediaries is that their customers will bypass them by obtaining information and meeting their purchasing needs through new, online channels. The opportunity for intermediaries is to use electronic commerce to create one of those new channels, thereby providing better service than a customer could otherwise obtain.

Opportunities that electronic commerce presents to intermediaries are exemplified by the evolution toward online trading led by companies such as Charles Schwab & Co., a discount financial stock brokerage. Schwab was built based on the idea of eliminating the investment advisory role of stockbrokers and providing only transaction processing services. In the early stages of this strategy, the company introduced personal computer software through which investors could obtain current price quotes and research reports from independent firms such as Standard & Poor's and could execute trades at a 10% discount from their regular low price. The popularization of the Internet took online brokerage activities to a new level of competition. Just as Schwab attacked traditional brokers by eliminating the investment advisory role, E*Trade and several other online brokerages competed with Schwab by offering even lower prices for trades entered using the Web, where Schwab also had its E-Schwab Web site.

By 1997 Web-based information and transaction capabilities spanned most of the customer involvement cycle for buying and selling stocks and bonds. Private investors could obtain readily available data and analysis software to identify stocks they wanted to buy and sell. Some of it could be accessed for free from the home pages of companies providing search engines and other services not specifically related to finance. Investors could make the purchases through Web transactions, touch tone phones, or human agents. Their stock and bond holdings and transactions could be tracked. They could obtain customer service information about the status of buy and sell orders. How the traditional brokerages would respond and whether they could maintain their much higher cost structure remained to be seen.

Electronic Banking

The banking industry relied on computers for decades before electronic banking created new ways to provide service. A first step in electronic banking for consumers was the advent of automatic teller machines (ATMs) popularized by Citibank in the late 1970s. Thanks to ATMs, Citibank tripled its depositors from 1978 to 1987, increasing its local consumer market share from 4.5% to 13%.[21,22] As happened in the Merrill Lynch case, the competition responded. Other banks banded together to produce their own network, the New York Cash Exchange, or NYCE, which began operations in 1985, and which Citibank eventually joined. More recently, several national ATM networks permit customers to withdraw money from ATMs in all major cities in the United States and some cities abroad.

The next step in electronic banking for consumers is to provide additional banking services and transactions through personal computers linked to the Web or to private networks. In addition to providing history and bank balance information, electronic banking permits people to pay bills without writing checks. The electronic banking customer starts by identifying checks that are written to the same payee repeatedly, such as checks for rent, water, electricity, and car payments. The electronic banking system makes it possible to enter the amount of the check and then have the bank transfer the money into the payee's account without ever handling a physical check. For fixed payments such as rent, the amount can be entered once and then transferred automatically each month. For the customer, these electronic banking functions eliminate the annoyance of balancing a checkbook and some of the uncertainty about whether or not the check arrived. For the bank, the computer-to-computer transfers performed in electronic banking are more automatic and less expensive than processing paper checks for handling payment transactions.

Like many aspects of electronic commerce, electronic banking is more complicated than it might appear. For example, assume that the payee is a national firm with many offices and a number of different bank accounts for different purposes. To pay the bill, you need to specify which account at which bank should receive the funds. That bank may be out of state, and the payee's accounts receivable system may not be set up to receive payments directed to its bank; it may require that payments go to its accounts receivable department. To minimize the chance that a payment transaction will be lost or delayed, a bank offering the electronic banking service must verify in advance that each payee is set up to receive funds in this manner. This is especially important if the electronic banking service combines multiple transfers to a given bank into a single transfer accompanied by a list of all payments that are included. Notice also that subsequent changes in the payee's banking relationships might result in confusion or lost payments. Electronic banking has advantages for people who write a lot of checks, but for others it is simpler to slip physical checks into preaddressed reply envelopes.

Electronic Publishing

Publishing has taken on a new meaning in the world of electronic documents. Traditional publishing involved designing and producing a fixed document, such as a magazine or book, and distributing paper copies of it. Electronic publishing still involves producing the document and distributing it, but the shift to electronic documents brings a wide range of new possibilities. During the production process the document itself can be customized to the needs or tastes of specific readers. A multimedia document can augment text and graphics with audio, video, and models the user can execute.

User controls that can be designed into the document include scroll bars, outlining, active internal links, links to other electronic documents, and even links to pages on the Web. The document can then be distributed in paper form or using a variety of electronic media including diskettes, CD-ROMs, and access through the Web. The document can be sold as a fixed, resellable object like a CD, or it can be sold more like software, based on a license that may be time-limited and may provide upgrades.

The Web provides one of the most intriguing areas for innovation in electronic publishing. Many print periodicals such as newspapers and magazines have created Web sites that provide excerpts from current editions and, in many cases, provide access to past editions and even search capabilities for finding information about specific topics. Some provide free access, but others, such as the *Wall Street Journal,* charge for access to archived articles. In similar fashion, a great deal of product-related information is available for free or on a subscription basis. One of the most significant trends in Web publishing is the juxtaposition of published content and advertising. Just as happens with television programs, advertisers view the electronic publication as a way to contact potential customers whether or not the authors had something very different in mind. (See Figure 6.9.)

The Technical Side of Electronic Commerce

Electronic commerce brings fascinating possibilities, but its success depends on resolving a number of tricky practical and technical questions. For example, how does the merchant know that the person buying something from a Web site is not an impostor? The reverse question applies for the customer, because it is also possible for a criminal to create a fraudulent Web site that sells nonexistent products. The technical side of electronic commerce occurs in the background. It includes validating transactions, protecting messages in transit, and transferring funds. (Chapter 13 on System Security and Control will explain

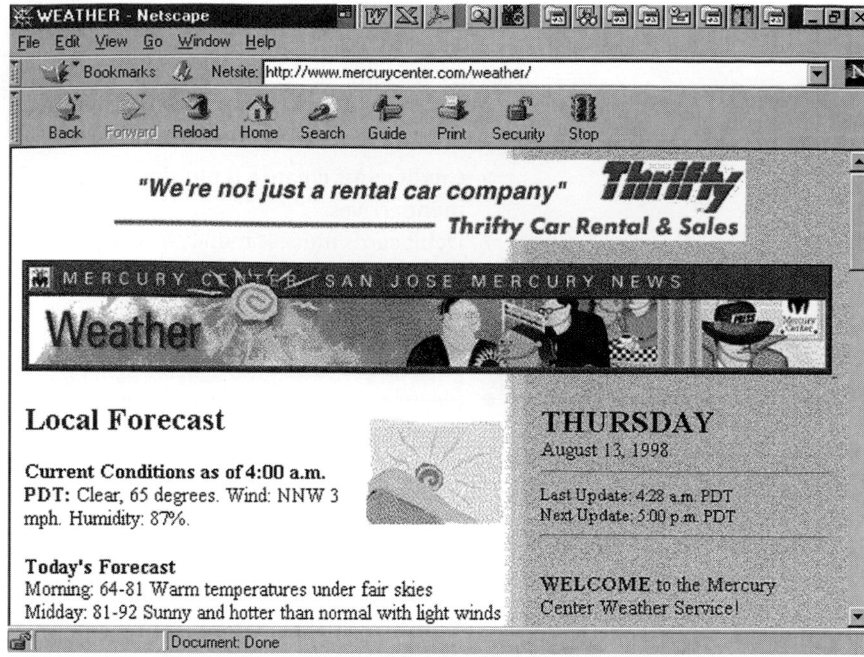

Figure 6.9
Advertising on the Web

Thrifty Car Rental has placed an ad in the San Jose Mercury's online edition, just as it might place an ad in the newspaper's daily paper edition or in the commercial breaks in a television show.

encryption methods that make intercepted information meaningless to a computer criminal.) Here we will look at validating transactions and transferring funds.

Validating Transactions

The feasibility of consumers performing transactions using personal computers and networks depends on the development and implementation of effective schemes for identifying buyers and sellers and validating transactions. Fraudulent purchase transactions involving forged checks, stolen credit cards, and other types of fraud are already a multibillion-dollar problem. Existing user name and password schemes are effective enough for restricting unauthorized access to private information in research reports and archival databases on the Web, but they aren't powerful enough to protect against fraudulent transactions that could create financial havoc.

An important step toward finding a practical way to validate transactions is the development of the **digital signature,** which serves the purpose of a written signature by verifying the origin and content of a message. A digital signature is a number produced through complex calculations involving the message itself and a private encryption key unique to the sender. The recipient can use a public key, another number associated with the sender, to decode the digital signature and thereby verify that the sender actually sent the message. (Chapter 13 explains private and public keys).

During a transaction, each party may want to verify the identity of the other party. This authentication can be done using a "trusted third party" called a **certification authority.** This is a company whose business consists of issuing digital certificates that provide an independent confirmation of an attribute claimed by a person offering a digital signature. A **digital certificate** is a computer-based record that identifies the certification authority, identifies the attribute of the sender that is being verified, contains the sender's public key, and is digitally signed by the certification authority. Certificate authorities, such as the company VeriSign, will probably offer different types of certificates, such as identifying certificates, authorizing certificates, transactional certificates, and time stamps.[23] Digital certificates enhance the security of electronic transactions by verifying the identity of two computers used in conducting electronic commerce. For example, Visa provides digital certificates to card-issuing financial institutions, and those institutions provide a digital certificate to the cardholder. At the time of the transaction, each party's software validates both merchant and cardholder before any information is exchanged.

Transferring Funds

Chapter 1 discussed debit cards, credit cards, smart cards, and electronic cash as alternatives to cash and checks for making payments. All of these options can be used to transfer funds. Specifically,

- Credit cards create a temporary loan due within a month after the credit card statement arrives.
- Debit cards transfer money from a buyer's bank account into a seller's bank account.
- Smart cards store a monetary value that can be increased by using a vending machine to transfer an amount such as $20 to the card, or can be decreased by using that card to pay for copies in a library or for telephone calls at a properly equipped pay phone.
- Electronic cash is like a smart card except that the cash balance is stored inside a computer rather than on a card.

The potential role of each of these approaches in the future of electronic commerce depends on a combination of economics and technology. The cost of credit and debit card transactions has dropped dramatically as computers and networks have become more efficient. For example, a typical credit authorization from an electronic terminal cost $0.35 in 1981 but costs less than $0.03 now.[24] This is far less than the cost of processing a check. Each card-based option can potentially store data other than just an amount of money. For example, each could store a person's signature, fingerprint, picture, or retina scan. Each could also store other personal information that might be useful in verifying that only an authorized person was performing the transaction.

The idea of electronic cash transfers the concept of a stored value card to a Web-based environment. A person wishing to use digital cash transfers money to a bank, which transfers the same amount to a **digital purse** that plays the role of the smart card in the computer. A user wishing to pay a small amount for accessing information or playing a game on the Web simply transfers digital cash from the digital purse to the online merchant. Unlike a credit or debit card payment, the payment transaction is completed when the electronic transfer occurs. No record of who paid for what is necessary because the information regarding the purchase is delivered immediately and because the amounts are small, perhaps even fractions of a penny.

Digital signatures, digital certificates, and digital cash are all part of a new wave of identification and payment options that are being developed. These options extend an earlier wave of options based on checks and various kinds of physical cards. The challenges of moving in this direction combine technical, commercial, and societal issues. The technical issues involve tradeoffs between security, cost, and convenience, with the most secure approach being to simply avoid Web-based commerce. The commercial issues emphasize the merchant and customer's willingness and ability to adopt the new methods and to integrate them with existing business processes. The societal issues range from how the government will handle regulation and taxation to whether electronic commerce will become a way to exclude a sizeable part of the population from economic life.

Reality Check

ELECTRONIC COMMERCE

This section identified a number of important areas of electronic commerce.

1. Identify three examples of electronic commerce in which you have participated.
2. In each example, explain the advantages and disadvantages of using this approach.

OPPORTUNITIES ACROSS THE CUSTOMER INVOLVEMENT CYCLE

The remainder of this chapter discusses additional opportunities to use information systems across the customer involvement cycle. The sections on determining requirements and acquiring the product contain a number of topics that tend to be more strongly tied to electronic commerce than to the topics related to using, maintaining, and retiring the product.

Determining Requirements

The process of determining requirements varies from product to product, depending on how the product is sold and whether it can be customized. The impact of information systems on requirements starts with traditional sales and marketing issues such as increasing a customer's product awareness, supporting the sales process, and matching products to the customer's requirements. For certain products, the requirements phase also permits the customer to specify how the product should be customized.

Increasing Product Awareness

Newspaper advertising, broadcast advertising, and paper catalogs are traditional ways to make customers aware that a product exists and might be worth purchasing. Traditionally, all three approaches have had a low yield rate because most of the people who see the message are not interested. Information systems that establish and use marketing databases have created many new ways to reduce this problem by exploiting **addressability,** the ability to direct specific messages to specific individuals or groups. By providing information such as purchase patterns, affiliations, and age, these databases make it possible to focus marketing resources on the individuals with a higher probability of making a purchase.

Addressability is the basis of **direct marketing,** the process of selling through mail or other forms of communication addressed to specific individuals. External sources of mailing lists include organizations that sell their membership lists, magazines that sell their subscription lists, and public record information such as births and home sales. Extensive transaction databases provide even more targeted mailing lists by permitting companies such as American Express to send mailers to specific groups of customers, such as those who made purchases from golf pro-shops, who charged symphony tickets, or who traveled more than once to Europe. Before these databases existed, direct marketing response rates of as little as 2% were considered acceptable. In contrast, Canon Computers used a 1.3 million customer database to achieve an extraordinary 50% response rate to a direct-mail solicitation asking printer owners if they would like information on a new color scanner for desktop publishing.[25] Similar effectiveness can sometimes be achieved with advertising on the Web because usage of many Web sites directly reflects personal interests and concerns. Instead of selecting individuals in advance and using addressability, Web advertisers can direct their message to whichever individuals happen to use a Web page related to a special interest such as auto loans, tropical fish, or Star Trek.

Combining customization techniques with addressability creates possibilities of directing different messages to different customers. For example *American Baby* adapts the mix of editorial and advertising pages to the age of the baby in each subscriber's household. It does this through a process called selective binding, in which different pages are included in a magazine depending on subscriber characteristics stored in a subscriber database. *Farm Journal* recognizes 5,000 different subclassifications of farm type and geographic region and produces a different edition for each.[26] Even small companies can use direct marketing techniques based on addressability. Some small clothes retailers maintain a customer list and record the color and size of each item sold to each customer. This enables them to send out pre-Christmas mailings to their customers' spouses mentioning Christmas gifts that might go well with "the tan slacks Pat purchased last month."

A form of direct marketing called **telemarketing** is the process of selling products and services by telephone. Although it requires nothing more than a telephone and a list of telephone numbers, important aspects of telemarketing can be automated. Having the telephone numbers on a computer makes it possible to dial phone numbers automatically, and even redial automatically if the line is busy. Once the telephone connection is established, the computer can display a script outlining the main points to be covered in the call. The script can even move into different branches depending on responses entered into the computer by the telemarketing agent. If any follow-up action is required, the system can record that data in the database for later use. If a product or service is sold, the sales transaction can be processed immediately. Any data gathered during the phone call can remain in the database to improve the targeting of future telemarketing efforts toward this account. For example a stockbroker might learn that a potential client will have funds to invest at a future time and is interested in long-term bonds.

Techniques used for direct marketing and telemarketing have raised controversy about privacy and confidentiality. An example is the public uproar that ended a joint venture between Lotus Development Corporation and Equifax. They had intended to sell Marketplace, a $695 CD-ROM product containing name, address, estimated income, and buying habit data for 120 million households in the United States. This product would have been a valuable source for direct marketing and telemarketing efforts of small businesses with a personal computer. Although large companies could already obtain the same data through Equifax, publishing the data on a CD-ROM made it much more accessible to anyone. Over 30,000 people cited violation of their privacy and demanded to be removed from the database.[27] Similar privacy concerns are felt strongly in Europe as well. In Finland and Sweden, laws require direct marketers to indicate the source of the addressee's name and address.[28]

Supporting the Sales Force

People often have the image of sales work as a matter of charming customers based on the salesperson's charisma and guile. Sometimes this may be part of the equation, but it is more useful to view selling as a business process involving many separate tasks, each of which must be performed well. For example, salespeople at AutoZone, an auto parts distributor with 822 stores, are expected to ask customers if they need help within 30 seconds after they enter the store. Regardless of whether the customer wants windshield wipers or hubcaps, the salesperson can provide helpful service by entering the make and year of the customer's car into an information system that responds immediately with the appropriate options.[29]

Table 6.4 shows some of the ways information systems can support various steps in the sales process for industrial products such as a copiers, tractors, or computers. The left-hand column shows the steps in the process, which begins with designing the sales program and identifying prospects. Some of the tasks included are unstructured, but most of them have enough structure to be supported using information systems, as shown in the right-hand column.

Matching to Customer Requirements

Information systems have been used in many ways to find products that match a customer's requirements. If the customer can specify a clear requirement, an information system can search for satisfactory options and may be able to rank them in terms of the customer's relative preferences related to cost, convenience, and other factors. This is what happens when an airline reservation system helps a traveler find a particular flight. Similar systems are used by real estate agents to identify homes or apartments that meet a client's needs and ability to pay.

In other situations the customer does not have a clear-cut requirement, but is willing to try out different options to decide which is preferable. Software is sometimes sold this way by letting the customer try it out within a Web site or letting the customer download it and use it for a limited length of time. The fashion and cosmetics industries have been innovative in their use of information systems for matching products to customer needs. For example, cosmetics companies such as Elizabeth Arden and Shiseido have used computers to augment their sales techniques. One system allows a cosmetologist to use a computer to try out a number of different make-up combinations electronically. Another determines the best product for an individual's skin type. These systems have generated dramatic sales increases at cosmetics counters.[30] Similarly, an electronic dressing room called a Magic Mirror has boosted clothing sales by projecting a woman's face, hands, and feet onto a clothed image that replicates her size and shape. This system makes it possible to "try on" a large number of outfits in a few minutes. After identifying

TABLE 6.4 **Supporting the Sales Process for an Industrial Product**

There are many ways to use information systems to support the sales process for industrial products. The sales process for consumer products is different, but many of the uses of information systems are similar.

Steps in the sales process	Ways to use information systems
Design the sales program and supporting materials	• Provide information and tools for analyzing strengths and weaknesses of past and current sales processes • Customize sales materials for specific groups of customers
Identify, prioritize, and contact prospects (potential customers)	• Create lists of prospects from commercially available mailing lists or from internal customer lists • Obtain information about individual prospects prior to sales calls
Meet with prospects to qualify their interest, explain the product, and counter objections	• Use communication technology to set up meetings • Use computers to demonstrate product options or simulate product operation • Use databases to provide information for justifying the purchase or countering objections
Negotiate pricing and delivery options	• Perform pricing calculations while exploring the customer's options • Link to corporate databases to find current product availability and delivery options
Take the order	• Perform the recordkeeping related to taking the order and conveying it to the delivery department
Follow up to maintain the customer relationship	• Maintain customer database • Perform customer surveys • Store and analyze warranty and repair data

the best choices, the shopper actually tries the clothes on. Sales increased 700% in an early use of this system.[31]

Customizing the Product

Another way to satisfy each customer's unique requirements is to customize the product so that it actually fits the customer's needs. There are two stages to ensuring a good fit. The first is to match product options with customer requirements to find the specific options that fit best. The second stage, customization, is the creation or modification of a product based on a specific customer's needs, thereby increasing the product's value for that customer. A tailor's adjustment of the length of a pair of pants is a form of customization. The result is not as customized as it would be if the tailor simply made the pants for the customer, but it is more customized than if the customer bought the pants and skipped the alterations.

Information products are especially amenable to customization because information is so fluid. Electronic publications can be personalized in two ways: by selecting the information to be transmitted to the individual or by transmitting all the information and then permitting the individual to select and view only the subset purchased. Figure 6.10 shows an example of greeting card customization. This starts with selecting among standard components but also allows the customer to introduce a totally personal message. The customized cards initially cost around $3.50, almost twice the cost of most greeting cards. Like any other competitive action however, customization is not guaranteed to succeed. By 1997 Hallmark had removed all of its 2,700 Touchscreen Greetings machines, and its competitor American Greetings had removed most of its 10,000 Createacard kiosks.[32] An intriguing idea had flopped due to a combination of the price, the time requirement, and the customer's interests and abilities.

Figure 6.10
Direct customer participation in customizing an information product

Hallmark Cards installed 2,700 computerized kiosks that customers could use to create customized greeting cards via touch-screen inputs. This method of creating customized cards failed commercially, in part because the customized cards were almost twice as expensive as most other greeting cards.

Financial instruments, such as futures contracts and options, are also information products and can be combined in many ways to match a firm's financial needs. Virtually any cash flow stream from a combination of securities can be swapped for another cash flow stream as long as a willing counterpart can be found.[33] For example, a firm that sells soybeans around the world can purchase a combination of commodity and currency options that meet its particular needs for protection against changes in soybean prices and currency exchange rates.

Customization is becoming an important competitive issue for many physical products as well. With the ability to link CAD systems to computer aided manufacturing (CAM) systems that control machines using CAD specifications, it is becoming more practical to tailor anything from clothes to machines based on the customer's requirements or wishes. This approach has been used extensively by the prefabricated housing industry in Japan. These businesses are set up to use mass customization by standardizing production even though the product is customized. Customers for prefabricated homes meet with salespeople to design their homes on a computer screen using representations of thousands of standardized parts. The completed designs are transmitted to a factory that produces the building's structural components on an assembly line. It takes one day for a crane and seven workers to put up the walls and roof of a two-story house. Finishing the job takes another 30 to 60 days.[34] The introductory case in Chapter 5 mentions another example, the Levi Strauss system of producing customized jeans.

Acquiring the Product

After determining the requirements, the next step is acquiring the product. Information systems can have competitively significant contributions at this point by improving product availability, by facilitating purchase activities, and by adjusting prices.

Improving Product Availability

Often people are willing to pay more for a product if they won't have to wait to get it or know they can get it soon. This is one of the reasons people buy clothes at full retail price instead of waiting for sales at the end of the season. Computerized inventory systems provide an effective way for some businesses to maximize merchandise availability without excessive inventory levels. Many large retail chains have developed extensive systems tracking the quantity on hand for every item in each store. These systems can assure availability in several ways. First, they ensure inventory is replenished quickly after items are sold. In addition, they make it possible to treat inventory at other stores as backup. For example, sales associates at the New York–based retailer Saks Fifth Avenue can use their regular point-of-sale terminals to order direct home delivery for an item located at another Saks store.[35]

One chain of stores that uses a computerized inventory system to the utmost is 7-Eleven of Japan. Its 5,000 convenience stores have limited shelf space but stock over 3,000 items. A network of point-of-sale terminals captures every sale and supports paperless inventory ordering for each store. The company plots the sales of individual products at each store by hour of the day and day of the week. This is essential for compact stores that can receive three deliveries a day within eight hours of ordering. Average daily sales per 7-Eleven store are 30% more than at Family Mart, its most direct rival. 7-Eleven analyzes the sales statistics to help the stores decide what products to sell and what products to eliminate.[36]

The Walgreen drugstore chain uses telecommunications to ensure the availability of prescription refills for its customers, even when they are from out of town. Each prescription Walgreen fills is stored in a corporate database accessible from any Walgreen store. This means that the same customer can get a refill at over 1,700 stores across the country. Walgreen's advertising tells its customers that the products it sells are one reason to do business with Walgreen and its communication technology is another.

Facilitating Purchase Activities

If the process of purchasing a product is complex or burdensome, information systems can improve the customer involvement cycle by facilitating purchase activities. This is certainly desirable in the health care industry, where the recordkeeping requirements of third party payers such as insurance companies force health care providers and customers to provide the same information repeatedly. One information system that addressed this issue was extension of the McKesson ordering system for pharmacies. As described earlier, the ordering system provided an online link from these drug stores to McKesson, thereby improving the efficiency and accuracy in the reordering process. Seeing that insurance companies paid for the pharmaceuticals many drug store customers purchased, McKesson built a system that collected funds from the insurance companies, thereby freeing the drug stores from involvement in this process. This system established linkages to insurance companies in addition to pharmacies and opened new strategic possibilities for McKesson.[37]

Other major manufacturers and distributors have tried to address the entire process by which businesses purchase products. Levi Strauss developed LeviLink, an extensive transaction processing add-on to their usual product offerings. Figure 6.11 illustrates this system, which was designed to help retail clothing stores, Levi's customers, at every stage in the retailing cycle. LeviLink uses bar code labels affixed on goods at the factory as the basis for material and sales tracking. This system reduced the time between the order and receipt of shipment from 40 days to as few as three. By 1990, electronic purchase orders through LeviLink represented 35% of domestic sales. Sales increased 20% to 30% in accounts using LeviLink because fewer customers left without finding the size or style they wanted. This sales increase was accomplished with lower inventory levels because ordering is tightly linked to sales and because the orders arrive quickly.[38] The system was subsequently reengineered to try to replenish all standard stock within three days (versus up to two weeks) and to change existing stock to a new fabric or finish in 30 days (versus up to six months). While information system improvements were essential, other changes were also required, such as changing the organization of distribution centers and the location of sewing and finishing facilities.[39]

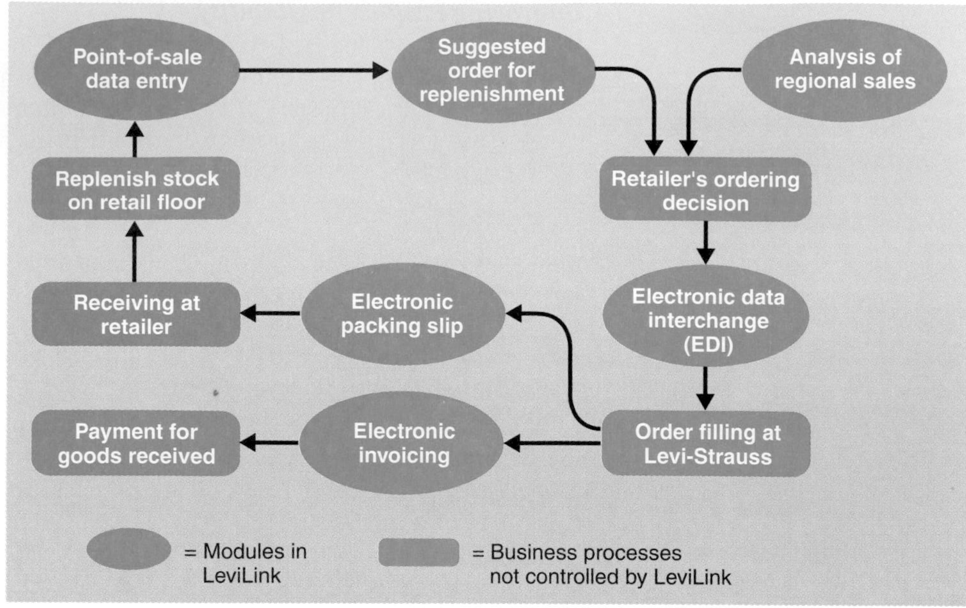

Figure 6.11
LevilLink services in the retailing cycle

This diagram identifies a subset of the services provided by LeviLink as part of a retailer's cycle of selling and replenishing inventory.

Some distributors and manufacturers have moved even further toward facilitating purchasing activities by literally taking over the management of inventory for their customers. Working with its hospital supply customers, Baxter International negotiates risk-sharing arrangements based on setting a cost target and sharing the savings or additional costs if expenses overshoot targets. Hospitals participating in the ValueLink inventory management program cede ownership and management of inventory to Baxter, which may even deliver supplies to hospital floors. At some hospitals, Baxter employees are on site 24 hours.[40] Although permitting a supplier to manage a firm's inventory is contrary to traditional business practices, some firms believe there is relatively little advantage in managing their own inventories if a large supplier can produce better results due to its information systems and knowledge of its own products. At minimum, most businesses would rather devote their scarce human resources to their core business activities rather than keeping supply inventories balanced.

Adjusting the Price

A very different competitive use of information systems involves making maximum use of information for pricing decisions. Sri Lankan villagers used the first approach when telephones were first installed in their villages. They used the phones to learn the current market prices in the capital city of Colombo before selling their produce to wholesalers who brought it to the market. This information helped the farmers increase their income by 50%.[41] A more technically sophisticated way to improve pricing decisions involves the use of transaction databases to understand the relationship between price and sales. During a Christmas season, Kmart realized its porcelain dolls were not selling as expected. Sales skyrocketed when the manager of toy merchandising cut the price from $29.88 to $24.99, but plummeted again when the price was reset near the original price. This process helped Kmart find a good selling price slightly above $25, and the dolls sold out for the season. With 2,400 stores, monitoring price response this way was possible only because Kmart had an integrated information system that could consolidate sales by product on a timely basis.[42]

Information systems can also be used for **market segmentation,** which is the process of dividing the market into different customer groups each of which is willing to pay different amounts for different types or levels of service. For example, MCI Communications developed a billing system that makes possible its Friends & Family service, which gives residential customers 20% discounts on calls to a dozen preselected locations. The information systems supporting this service helped MCI win market share and increase profits by maintaining its basic prices and giving a reduced price to a specific set of customers, many of whom switched to MCI only because of the special discount. Within several years, 10 million customers signed up, taking at least 4% of the consumer long distance market away from AT&T.[43]

Airline yield management systems are the heavyweight champions of market segmentation. Unlike products that retain their value from day to day, a seat on a specific flight has value until flight time and no value thereafter. **Yield management** systems try to maximize revenue by selling the same product (a seat on a flight) to different customers at different prices. Because vacation travelers can usually plan their trips longer in advance than business travelers, there is a natural segmentation in the market. Exploiting this segmentation, these systems charge higher prices for tickets purchased at the last minute and try to fill the planes by giving lower prices to vacationers who can reserve weeks in advance but wouldn't fly at higher prices. The economic challenge for these systems is to avoid two types of errors: selling too many cheap seats that last-minute travelers would have purchased at high prices and having too few cheap seats, resulting in empty seats on flights. These systems also have other challenges, however, such as maintaining customer satisfaction when people sitting next to each other on a flight have paid vastly different amounts for what they see as the same thing.

Market segmentation and yield management approach pricing from the supplier's viewpoint, but it is also interesting to look at ways the World Wide Web has created opportunities from the customer's viewpoint. For example, Caterpillar used an online auction to fill a $2.4 million order for hydraulic fittings for tractors. Instead of asking a few suppliers to submit bids by fax, Caterpillar invited 23 suppliers to an online auction and watched as they tried to outbid each other to fill parts of the order. Overall, Caterpillar saved around 6% compared to typical prices it would have paid. Private individuals trying to get the lowest prices on consumer items such as CDs have not been able to do something similar because it is not in the interest of online retailers. Efforts to find the lowest price for specific CDs using programmed "shopping agents" that search multiple Web sites have been stymied because major online retailers programmed their sites to reject inquiries by the agents.[44]

Using the Product

Making products more useful and easier to use is another way to apply information systems for competitive advantage. This can be done in three ways: incorporating electronic enhancements into products, providing better service, and providing the customer with accessible information or knowledge about the product.

Electronically Enhanced Products

Advances in semiconductor technology have made it possible to build computerized systems into manufactured products that traditionally existed without those systems. A simple example is a coffee maker. Although it is still possible to make coffee manually by dripping boiling water through ground coffee, some current coffee makers contain many programmable features. For example, they can be programmed to start at specific times and to grind coffee beans in specific ways. In this case, the computerized system offers convenience, but is not essential for the product's primary function. In contrast, some current jet fighters simply can't be flown by an unaided human being. The pilot determines the direction and speed of these jets, while a real time information system in the background performs adjustments that make sure that the jet remains stable enough to be controllable.

Automobiles are an everyday product in which information systems are playing an increasingly important role. Figure 6.2 showed that current or anticipated automotive electronic systems can improve driving performance and safety and may even reduce driving times. Systems that improve driving performance include computer controlled gear shifts and fuel injection systems that attain high fuel economy, active suspensions that sense and automatically adjust to bumps and potholes, and traction control systems that prevent brakes from locking. Safety systems include adaptive headlights that turn on and dim automatically, collision avoidance systems that warn of impending crashes, heads-up displays that make instrument readings appear in front of the hood, and antitheft systems that prevent the car from being hot-wired.

Current automotive navigation systems can track the location of a car and display it on a map. Future navigation gear may receive real time information from large-scale information systems that monitor traffic flows and congestion. By combining this information with map information, a navigation system could potentially suggest the route to any location that takes the least time. Such systems would maximize the use and safety of existing highways in congested areas. Like adding any new product feature, making cars "intelligent" has its risks, however. Chrysler's Neon auto had three recalls in its first year, one of which was to fix the computer.[45]

Information systems are also being built into so-called **intelligent buildings** which contain features that reduce the need for building maintenance and security personnel. Computer-controlled systems check the temperature of each floor, the location of every elevator, and the status of all doors (locked or unlocked). They turn the lights on when people enter offices and off 12 minutes after they leave. They maintain security by recording the electronic ID card used whenever someone enters a secured area. In the home market, control systems are being sold that allow homeowners to change light settings or set burglar alarms by phone. Electric utilities such as Detroit Edison have encouraged consumers to use home control systems to automatically turn on loaded dishwashers in the middle of the night when electricity usage and prices are low.[46]

Providing Better Service

Leading companies in many industries attempt to differentiate themselves by providing an extra measure of service for their customers. Consider the way national car rental firms such as Avis use information systems to provide high-quality service. From a busy traveler's viewpoint, every minute spent in the process of renting or returning a car is a waste of valuable time. In the early days of car rentals, the rental and return processes involved waiting in line and filling out paper forms. Today, Hertz and some of its competitors have minimized the waiting and paperwork in these business processes. Figure 6.12 shows the handheld terminal a service representative uses to record a car's mileage reading and gas-tank level. The handheld terminal uses a radio link to a computer network to transmit the check-in information and receive the billing information in return. For customers who presented a credit card when they rented the car, it can then print out a final receipt without requiring the customer to set foot in an office again. This process enhances Hertz's productivity while also ensuring the quality and responsiveness customers want.

Figure 6.12
Handheld terminal used to speed the process of returning rental cars

The system Hertz uses for checking in returned cars has competitive significance because user convenience is one of the ways Hertz differentiates itself from its competition.

Just as information products can be delivered on paper or in various electronic forms, service products can also be delivered in a variety of ways. A useful way to describe service delivery options is to think of a particular service as either a series of isolated encounters or part of an ongoing relationship.[47] Service through **supplier–customer encounters** occurs through interactions between customers and providers who are strangers. Service through a **supplier–customer relationship** occurs when a customer has repetitive contact with a particular provider and when the customer and provider get to know each other personally. Obtaining cash from a bank can be framed as an encounter with an ATM machine or faceless teller, or as part of an ongoing relationship with the staff of a local bank. Similarly, delivery of medical care can be framed as a series of encounters between the patient and whichever health care provider happens to be available, or as part of an extended relationship with particular providers. Information systems can improve either type of service delivery. For example, information systems can improve an encounter style of medical service by supplying complete and up-to-date patient information to any provider. Providing the information is not a replacement for a relationship with a medical care provider, but it decreases the chances that a total stranger will overlook something important that has already known and has been recorded. Similarly, information systems can contribute to a relationship style of medical care delivery by making record keeping and billing more efficient, and thereby permitting more attention to the relationship.

Providing Product Information or Knowledge

Another way to enhance a product is to provide better information or knowledge about the product itself. For example, because people frequently misplace owner manuals for household items, finding another way to provide such information would have many advantages. Even when manuals are available, many owner and user manuals are difficult to use because they are presented in broad context and they can't adjust to the user's knowledge or to the situation the user faces. Many manufacturers address these shortcomings by providing telephone hotlines staffed by human operators. More recently, firms have begun experimenting with using Internet "chat rooms," in which customers can exchange typed messages with trained customer service representatives. One consulting study estimated that servicing customers this way could cost as little as 20% of the cost of a typical phone transaction.[48]

A somewhat different approach is to provide information and knowledge add-ons in the form of information systems. For manufactured products, the information may provide a complete life history of the item, including the quality, ownership, and processing performed during manufacturing. The knowledge may focus on how to use the product effectively under different circumstances or how to solve common operational problems.

Information and knowledge products show some of the possible ways information systems can help customers use products effectively. Many commercially available templates, models, and expert systems make knowledge available to users in an active form. Interactive templates ask a series of questions or enforce a data collection format based on an expert's understanding of what is important in a particular type of situation. Models combine expert's ideas about the important factors in a situation to evaluate a decision mathematically or calculate an optimal solution. Expert systems support a decision process that imitates what an expert might do.

An example that demonstrates what is possible is the Mudman system developed by N. L. Baroid, a supplier of drilling muds used in oil wells. These muds are pumped into oil wells to lubricate the drilling process and carry away rock shavings. The engineers at the well collect and analyze up to 20 types of data, such as viscosity and silt content. Mistakes can cause serious problems with the well. To help differentiate its commodity product, N. L. Baroid built an expert system that helps with the analysis and recommends adjustments in the mud. At one site, Mudman diagnosed a contamination problem that people had misdiagnosed for a decade.[49]

Maintaining and Retiring the Product

Product maintenance is an important determinant of whether a customer's experience with a product is favorable. Products prone to excessive down time or catastrophic failure simply don't provide the value the customer expects. Information systems can be used to support maintenance and repair processes in a variety of ways, including providing maintenance information, linking to machines from remote sites, and even performing product upgrades automatically.

Supporting Maintenance and Repair Processes

Good information systems are an essential part of an effective field service operation. The Otis Elevator case at the beginning of the chapter described a system that supported field service through communication, storage, and data analysis. The communication role of the system was to ensure that technicians were contacted immediately whenever an elevator problem occurred. The informational role was to store a complete history of service calls to all elevators. This information could be used to identify long-term service problems and to monitor the emergency response process.

Product maintenance systems also serve many other functions. Some provide direct linkages to computerized parts inventories. These systems help field technicians find the parts they need and help them estimate when repairs will be completed; other systems provide direct guidance for repair people. Figure 6.13 shows a picture of a mechanic using one of these systems developed for Ford to analyze electrical problems. The system surveys computer chips built into the car. If the mechanic doesn't find the problem, the customer can borrow a five-pound recorder and turn it on when the problem reappears.

Using Remote Monitoring

Use of information technology to observe a building, business operation, or person from a distance is called **remote monitoring.** An everyday example of remote monitoring is the service burglar alarm companies provide using sensors that detect events such as a door opening, a motion, and a sudden impact such as breaking glass. On detecting any of these events, the automatic system notifies operators in a central location, who then try to decide whether it is a false alarm by phoning the premises or studying the signals from the sensors.

Many manufacturers of electronic equipment such as telephone switching systems and computers provide remote monitoring services as an add-on following an equipment purchase. Typically, these remote monitoring systems poll each machine nightly to try to identify electronic components that have failed or are going bad. Doing this frequently minimizes emergency calls when the customer's operations are disrupted by a hardware failure. This also makes it less likely that the customer will even notice equipment failures. In addition, these systems make it possible to perform some repairs by entering machine instructions over the phone, thereby reducing the cost of service calls.

Retiring Obsolete Products and Upgrading to New Versions

The continual sequence of upgrades required with software and many other information products demonstrates how information systems can be used in the final part of the customer involvement cycle, namely, retiring products whose useful life is over, removing them, and upgrading to current versions. The programs that perform these upgrades have stringent requirements because they could cause great inconvenience if they disable the old version and fail to perform the complete upgrade. At some point, information systems may even play a role in retiring physical products. For example, an owner registry for a product such as wall-to-wall carpet might be used to recycle the product in an effective way. Whether this type of use will develop remains to be seen.

BEING REALISTIC ABOUT WHAT INFORMATION SYSTEMS CAN DO

An honest perspective on the competitive uses of information systems must include something about the limits on what can be done. This is especially important because of the common tendency to exaggerate the importance and impact of IT. We have already noted

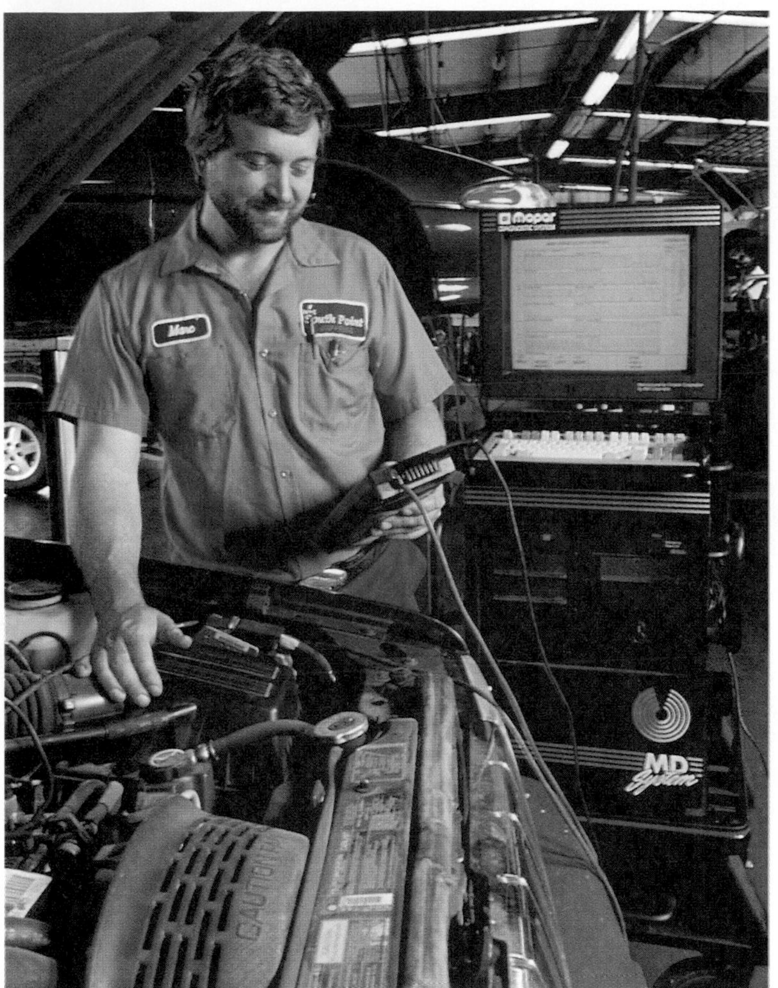

Figure 6.13
Ford's Service Bay Diagnostic System

Ford Motor Company's Service Bay Diagnostic System is designed to help mechanics with two of the most frustrating service department occurrences—intermittent problems and hard-to-find problems.

that competitive advantage through information systems is often temporary. We should say a bit more.

One of Many Aspects of Business

Because information systems are one of many components of operating a business, attributing success to this one component is often an exaggeration. "When the Dallas Cowboys were consistently winning football championships [in the 1980s], their success was attributed to the fact that computers were used to evaluate and select team members." But when Dallas did poorly, "not much was said about the computers, perhaps because people realized that computers have nothing to do with winning football games, and never did."[50] The author of this quote disagrees to some extent with the Dallas coaches. If they thought computerized systems have nothing to do with football games, they never would have used computers. On the other hand, attributing football success to computers does seem an exaggeration because other factors such as having top players and coaches are more directly related to success.

The general point behind this example is that information systems are one of many components of business. This is illustrated in Figure 6.14, which represents a business as an engine that contains a number of connected elements: strategy, leadership, culture, people, physical resources, systems, and information. Although it might seem obvious that these elements should be aligned, top managers often reflect on how difficult it is and how many years it takes to attain the degree of alignment that maintains competitive product performance in terms of cost, quality, responsiveness, reliability, and conformance with regulations and standards.

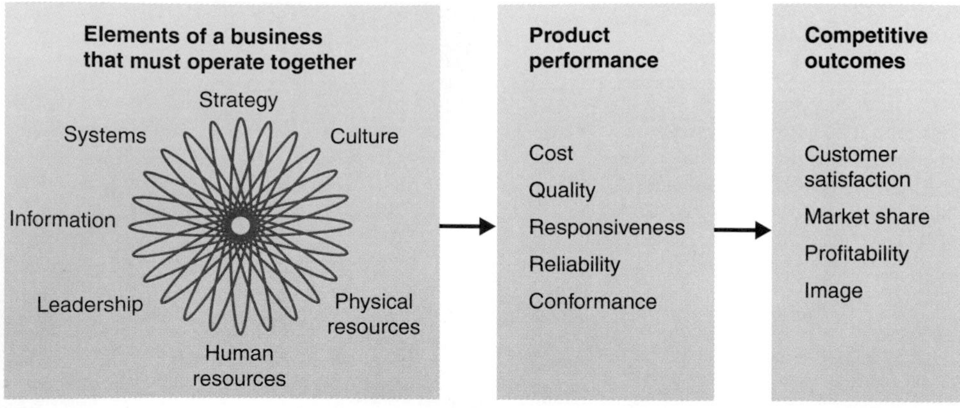

Figure 6.14
How elements of a business combine to determine competitive outcomes

Information, systems, and many other elements combine to generate the controllable product performance results that are the basis of competition.

This book emphasizes the part of Figure 6.14 involving information and systems, but it always recognizes that information systems are one of many components of business success. The figure also highlights issues about context, one of the five perspectives in the WCA method. Information systems operate within the context of the other components of business. Information systems that are inconsistent with a firm's strategy, culture, or staff capabilities may do more harm than good. For example, an information system that permits different divisions to track inventory using incompatible brand codes and incompatible computers may become an obstacle if the firm's strategy requires close coordination between divisions.

Not a Silver Bullet

Although examples of the competitive use of information systems abound, there is no guarantee that an attempt to use information systems competitively will succeed. Some strategic systems absorb huge amounts of effort and then fail before they are put into operation. This happened when the London Stock Exchange (LSE) tried to build Taurus, a paperless system for settling stock purchases and sales more rapidly than their existing system's two- to four-week cycle for recording transactions and transferring funds. This was crucial for the LSE because its two main competitors, the Paris and Frankfurt exchanges, could settle trades within four days. The project was canceled after ten years of work, $106 million spent by the LSE, and over $600 million spent by other financial institutions rebuilding their systems to make them compatible with Taurus. A project review revealed that the original system design was too complex because it tried to reconcile too many different interests. Completing it would have taken three more years and would have doubled its costs. Canceling Taurus left the future of the LSE in doubt, with some of its board members wondering whether London, Europe's leading financial center, really needed a stock exchange.[51, 52]

CHAPTER CONCLUSION

Summary

How can information systems change the scope and nature of a work system's product?

A work system's product is a combination of information, physical things, and service the customer receives. Products can also be described in terms of their controllability when being used and adaptability over time. Information systems can be applied to improve a product in any of these areas.

How is the customer involvement cycle related to the customer's view of product performance?

A product's customer involvement cycle is a customer's entire involvement with the product starting with defining the requirements and acquiring the product and including using the product, maintaining it, and retiring it. Each step in the cycle provides opportunities to increase customer satisfaction in terms of performance variables such as cost, quality, responsiveness, reliability, and conformance to standards and regulations.

How are information systems related to competitive advantage?

Competitive advantage occurs when a product's value chain generates superior product performance. Most firms have information systems that are mission-critical because their failure would prevent or delay basic business activities such as selling to customers, processing orders, and manufacturing. In contrast, strategic information systems are designed to play a major role in an organization's competitive strategy. These systems typically increase the customer's perceived value by providing information and services with products, customizing products, eliminating delays, improving reliability, making products easier to use, bypassing intermediaries, or reducing transaction times.

Why is it difficult to achieve sustainable competitive advantage through information systems?

Even if a strategic information system is initially successful, competitors are usually able to copy the idea. This is why information systems that temporarily provide competitive advantage often become a competitive necessity for all major players. The most sustainable sources of competitive advantage are the firm's culture, its personnel, its major business processes, and its special resources such as patents or land that cannot be copied.

What is electronic commerce, and what new technical capabilities does it require?

Electronic commerce refers to the use of computerized systems in selling and distributing products. Major areas of electronic commerce include: informing a customer of a product's existence, providing in-depth information about the product, establishing the customer's requirements, performing the purchase transaction, and in some cases, delivering the product electronically if the product happens to be software or information. The technical side of electronic commerce occurs in the background and includes validating transactions, protecting messages in transit, and transferring funds. New technical capabilities in this area include digital signatures, digital certificates, and electronic cash.

What are some of the opportunities to use information systems across the customer involvement cycle?

Applications in determining requirements include increasing product awareness, supporting the sales force in a variety of ways, matching available products to what the customer wants, and customizing the product. Applications in acquiring the product include improving product availability, facilitating purchase activities, and adjusting prices. Applications in using the product include electronically enhancing the product itself, providing better service, and providing product information or knowledge. Applications in maintaining the product include supporting maintenance and repair processes and using remote monitoring. Applications in retiring the product are primarily related to upgrading to new versions of software products.

Key Terms

information product
physical product
service product
smart product
interactive product
programmable product
customer involvement cycle
cost
quality
responsiveness
reliability
conformance to standards and regulations
standards
regulations
competitive advantage
cost leadership strategy
product differentiation strategy
focus strategy
mission-critical information system
strategic information system

competitive necessity
sustainable competitive advantage
competing on time
quick response
electronic commerce
electronic retailing
digital signature
certification authority
digital certificate
digital purse
addressability
direct marketing
telemarketing
market segmentation
yield management
intelligent building
supplier–customer encounter
supplier–customer relationship
remote monitoring

Review Questions

1. Why is it useful to think of products as a combination of information, physical things, and service?
2. What is the customer involvement cycle?
3. What performance variables other than cost are customers often concerned with?
4. What are Porter's three basic competitive strategies?
5. Differentiate between a mission-critical information system and a strategic information system.
6. Explain the relationship between competitive advantage and competitive necessity.
7. What is the meaning of "competing on time?"
8. What is the difference between credit cards, debit cards, smart cards, and electronic cash?
9. What is a digital signature?
10. Why is addressability important in direct marketing?
11. How are information systems used in acquiring a product?
12. How can information systems be used to help exploit market segmentation?
13. What is an electronically enhanced product?
14. Why is it useful to think of service delivery as a set of isolated encounters or as part of an ongoing relationship?
15. What are some examples of information systems built into automobiles?
16. How can information systems bring information or knowledge as part of a product?
17. What is remote monitoring?

Discussion Topics

1. Marui Department Store in Tokyo has over seven years of purchase history for 8 million customers. By integrating data from its customer and credit files it can target offers to individual customers, such as a designer watch offered to males who are 30 to 40, own a house, have purchased (or wife has purchased) a diamond or fur coat in the last two years, and currently have enough credit available.[53] Explain why this situation does or does not raise ethical issues.
2. One response to the privacy concerns raised by database marketing is the proposal that individuals should own all data about themselves and should be able to sell that data to others. This leads to the idea of a consensual database, in which a consumer might receive coupons, samples, or even money in exchange for yielding the rights to a personal transaction history. Identify some of the practical and ethical issues related to consensual databases and explain whether you believe that this form of marketing database could become widespread.
3. A university is considering automating parts of its course advising and enrollment process. One possibility is to automatically analyze a student's record and make a list of courses or groups of courses needed to graduate on time. Another possibility is to perform the registration process through a computer to avoid long registration lines. Explain why you do or do not believe these capabilities could have competitive significance for the university. Identify any other capabilities related to information systems that might have competitive significance.
4. Use the customer's parts of the value chain to identify a number of ways an automobile manufacturer's information systems could provide extra value for its customers.

Ernst & Young: Providing Consulting Through the Web

In May 1998, Ernst & Young announced that its online consulting service called Ernie had been nominated for a Computerworld Smithsonian Award. Each year, this award program honors visionary uses of information technology that produce positive social, economic, and educational change. Ernie was started in 1996 as an Internet-based consulting service for medium-sized companies that can benefit from the knowledge of consultants but cannot afford the high prices experienced consultants charge for extended engagements. Companies that use this service pay $6,000 per year for access to information on the Ernie Web site plus the ability to direct questions to E&Y consultants via e-mail.

The process of asking questions produces results by using information technology instead of much more expensive face-to-face meetings. After logging on using a company's password, the person needing help can access an extensive collection of Frequently Asked Questions (FAQs) in many areas. If the FAQs don't provide the answer, the user can direct the question to human experts by filling in a computerized form. In addition to the user's question itself, the form requests the general topic area (such as organizational change), general background information about the user's firm, and the selection of one of eight categories the Web site offers (accounting, corporate finance, human resources, information technology, personal finance, process improvement, tax, and other). The forms are routed to appropriate Ernst & Young consultants using its corporate intranet and a one-to-two page response comes back via e-mail within two days. Users can ask as many follow-up questions as they want.

The information directly accessible on the Ernie Web site can be used without the direct involvement of consultants. In addition to FAQs, in mid-1998 it included five "Ernie SuperTools." Ernie Diagnostix for supply chains provided a way to compare a firm's supply chain with those of top performing companies in an E&Y database. Ernie Software Selection Advisor provided an eight-step approach for selecting the right enterprise-wide software package. A technology selection tool provided a way of computing technology needs and taking advantage of E&Y's buying power. Ernie Business Analysis provided a way to commission an in-depth report to analyze competitors, markets, and industry trends. A link to the Gartner Group's self-paced courses provided a way for end-users, managers, and programmers to learn recent software applications. A 1998 extension called Ernie MediaWatch also linked Ernie to seven prominent trade magazines, including *HRfocus*, *Management Review*, *Real Estate Forum*, and *Management Accounting*. Linking to these magazines provides additional expertise and perspective that otherwise might not be as readily accessible.

Responding to predictions that Ernie would cannibalize E&Y's traditional consulting business, the firm's director of Internet service delivery said the firm had not viewed this as an important issue. "Bringing a team of consultants onsite remains the best way to implement large computer systems or to bring large-scale change to an organization....The pace of change is so fast today that there is a need for immediate support to help navigate the waters of change. That need hasn't always been there. Organizations used to have time to adapt to change. Now they don't. They need help today, and traditional consulting can't offer that kind of help. So Ernie is serving an entirely new market—the market for decision support."

QUESTIONS

1. What are the advantages and disadvantages of the direct service business model on which Ernie is built?
2. Review the rationale in the last paragraph and give examples to show how other businesses might or might not be able to use a business model similar to the one used by Ernie.

Sources:

Business Innovation Journal. "Selling Knowledge on the 'Net,'" Issue 1, June 16, 1998 (www.businessinnovation.ey.com/journal/issue1/features/body.html).

Ernst & Young, LLP. "Ernie: Your Online Business Consultant," June 16, 1998 (www.ernie.ey.com).

Rosenbluth International: Using IT for Worldwide Travel Services

People often think of a travel agency as a few people in a small office who provide vacation brochures and make airline, hotel, and rental car reservations. Rosenbluth International, the world's second largest travel service provider, has a far grander vision. In mid-1998 its press releases typically included a summary such as, "Rosenbluth International, headquartered in Philadelphia, Pa., USA, provides comprehensive corporate, leisure and meeting services worldwide. With annual sales in excess of $3.5 billion and 4,500 associates, Rosenbluth International has a global presence in 44 countries. Founded in 1892 and recognized as a leader in integrated information management technology, Rosenbluth International continues to develop innovative proprietary systems and software products which enable it to provide highly personalized service to its clients."

Its corporate Web site identifies a number of areas in which it uses information technology extensively. Custom-Res, its proprietary reservation system, incorporates client-specific data by automatically displaying negotiated fares, travel policy, preferred suppliers, and lowest fares during the reservation process, thereby encouraging accuracy and consistency with every transaction. E-Res, its electronic reservation system, is an agentless reservation tool enabling business travelers to book their own travel on their personal computers anywhere, anytime, while also encouraging compliance to corporate travel policies by linking to the global reservation system. Res-Monitor reviews each reservation daily and searches pricing databases for additional savings. Decision support capabilities for corporate travel management include a model for comparing alternative corporate travel arrangements offered by different travel providers, a tool for consolidating a client's global travel information from multiple travel service providers, and a reporting system for manipulating and analyzing corporate travel data. An expense management module helps reduce travel and entertainment (T&E) processing costs by combining bookings and billing data and tying together the client's travel, corporate card, finance, and T&E reporting for the corporation. This heightens corporate policy awareness, improves cash management, allows for greater expense control, and provides an accurate picture of current T&E expenditures and future trends. Some of these tools are licensed to Rosenbluth International by SABRE Decision Technologies, a division of The SABRE Group, Inc., which is a spin-off from American Airlines.

A press release when Perot Systems selected Rosenbluth as its single global travel management partner quoted Perot's global travel manager as saying, "This is a big step for Perot Systems in our efforts to reduce travel costs and to provide better services to our associates. By consolidating to one agency, we will be able to better track our air, hotel and rental car spending so that we can negotiate better deals, provide better management information to the cost center manager, implement new technology easier and, most importantly, provide an improved quality of service to our associates. Rosenbluth International was selected as our global travel supplier because they proposed the most creative and economical solutions. Additionally, there is great synergy between our corporate cultures and a commitment from their president and CEO, Hal Rosenbluth, to meet and exceed our expectations." Hal Rosenbluth had convinced his father to start using computers 20 years earlier and clearly believed in the power of technology. but he also saw the central role of people in providing service. This was one of the main points in a book he published called *The Customer Comes Second and Other Secrets of Exceptional Service.*

QUESTIONS

1. Explain the aspects of this situation that are about electronic commerce and the aspects that are not.
2. The co-owners of a small, local travel agency disagree about the strategy they should pursue. Terry believes they should take advantage of electronic commerce via the Internet. Lynn believes larger companies such as Rosenbluth would have an insurmountable lead in this area. Summarize your views of how they might use the Internet and what would determine their success in this strategy.

Sources:

Rosenbluth International. "Perot Systems Corporation Awards Rosenbluth International Its Global Travel Program," Philadelphia, PA, May 8, 1998. June 1, 1998 (http://www.rosenbluth.com/corporate/comm/pr_050898.html).

Rosenbluth International. "Travel Technology," June 1, 1998 (http://www.rosenbluth.com/corporate/comm/travtech.html).

7

Human and Ethical Issues

Study Questions

- What kinds of dilemmas do the impacts of information systems on people pose?
- What is the difference between machine-centered design and human-centered design?
- What are the characteristics of healthy work, and how do information systems affect these characteristics?
- How is computer-mediated work different from other types of work?
- What are the different ways to explain resistance to change?
- What are ethical theories, and how are they related to information systems?
- What are the major ethical issues related to information systems?

Outline

Opening Case

U.S. CONGRESS: CREATING NATIONAL DIRECTORY OF NEW HIRES

The U.S. Congress passed the Personal Responsibility and Work Opportunity Reconciliation Act of 1996 as part of an effort to change many aspects of the welfare system. One of its many provisions called for the creation of a National Directory of New Hires containing the name, address, social security number, and wages for each of the 60 million people hired into a full- or part-time job in the United States by all but the smallest employers. (See Table 7.1.) Several states already had state directories that had been quite useful. In Missouri, for example, child support collections had increased 17% in 1996 after the state required reporting of new hires even though its state directory did not cover people who had moved to different states. Welfare officials predicted that matching the federal and state directories would produce billions of dollars in child support payments. Under the new law, the directory would be available to state welfare and child support agencies. The Internal Revenue Service (IRS), Social Security Administration (SSA), and Justice Department would also have access for some purposes.[1]

Some privacy advocates voiced alarm about the new database, noting that most new hires have no child support obligations whatsoever. Including information about them in this database would be a threat to their privacy because so many agencies would have access to this information and because data in this type of database has not been totally secure in the past. This type of risk had been publicized in 1992, when an 18-month federal investigation found a ring of "information brokers" who allegedly bribed SSA workers to steal personal information. The going rate to obtain a ten-year earnings history within three to five days was apparently $175, of which $25 went for the bribe to the SSA worker. Buyers of the information apparently included private investigators, prospective employers, lawyers, and insurance companies.[2] In 1994 more than 420 IRS employees received some form of discipline for illegally browsing through tax returns of friends, relatives, and neighbors. Since that time the IRS has increased its training on privacy issues and has installed automatic systems to monitor data access by its employees. In 1997 the IRS Commissioner asked Congress for legislation that would add criminal penalties to the law that prohibits IRS employees from snooping into taxpayer records. This request followed shortly after a Federal appeals court reversed the 1995 conviction of an IRS employee who was also a Ku Klux Klan member. That employee had been convicted of using his computer terminal to look through tax records of other white supremacists he suspected of being informers for the FBI. The conviction was overturned because the prosecution failed to prove that the former employee had done anything with the information he collected.[3]

Debate Topic

Whether or not the database of new hires will help in enforcing child support obligations, creating this database and making it accessible unnecessarily infringes on the privacy of new hires who have no child support obligations.

The introduction of new technologies often has both positive and negative impacts far beyond the immediate problem they were supposed to solve. Technological change is not neutral because it can be used for good or bad ends, because the positive and negative impacts are often intertwined, and because many of the impacts are not anticipated.[4] The database of new hires illustrates these generalizations. It was proposed as a means of tracking down deadbeat parents, but it contains data about all new hires, perhaps jeopardizing the privacy of millions of people who aren't parents.

As information systems become more pervasive in today's businesses, managers need to think about the way systems depend on people and the way they affect people. Dependence on people starts with the system development process and extends to reliance on the knowledge and skills needed to use an information system effectively. Impacts on people occur in many areas. In some cases, systems affect them because they are participants; in others, because they are customers; in yet others, because they are being monitored. This chapter explores these issues and emphasizes the management dilemmas posed by today's

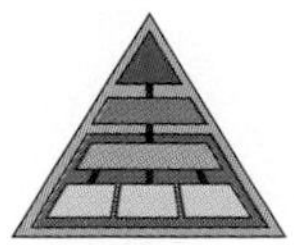

TABLE 7.1 Making New Hire Data Available for Enforcing Child Support Obligations

CUSTOMER
- Spouses to whom child support is owed
- State welfare agencies trying to enforce child support obligations

PRODUCT
- Identification of new address and new job of nonpaying ex-spouses
- Greater ability to enforce payment of child support

BUSINESS PROCESS

Major steps related to gathering data:
- Employers submit new hire identification quarterly
- Federal government consolidates this data into a single database

Major steps related to using data:
- Identify ex-spouses who have not met child support obligations
- Search for them in the database
- Take action, such as withholding part of their pay

Rationale:
- Ex-spouses with child support obligations sometimes move to avoid paying
- New hire data should be made available to enforce child support obligations

PARTICIPANTS	INFORMATION	TECHNOLOGY
• Employers • Federal government • State welfare agencies	• Name, social security number, address, wages, and employer for each new hire	• Computer system for storing the data • Network for accessing the data

technical capabilities. A theme throughout is that the social and psychological impacts on people are not caused by technology itself, but rather by the way technology is used.

TECHNOLOGY AND PEOPLE

IT-enabled systems are much more than IT applied to a business process. This is why the pictorial version of the WCA framework (Figure 2.6 in Chapter 2) contains a link between participants and the business process. Using a two-headed arrow for this link also says that the business process affects the participants and that their abilities, interests, and skills determine whether the business process is practical.

Human-Centered Design Versus Machine-Centered Design

For a work system to operate well, the division of labor between people and machines should take into account the particular strengths and weaknesses of both people and machines. Table 7.2 summarizes these strengths and weaknesses. It shows that people are especially good at tasks involving understanding, imagination, and the ability to see a situation as a whole. Machines are especially good at repetitive tasks involving endurance, consistency, speed, and execution of unambiguous instructions.

The challenge in the division of labor between people and machines is to give each the tasks they are best suited for and to design business processes that exploit their respective strengths and weaknesses. This is easier said than done. This chapter includes a number of examples of problems that occurred when work systems treated people somewhat like machines.

TABLE 7.2 **Human Versus Machine Strengths and Weaknesses**

Characteristic	People	Machines
Endurance	• Become tired and bored • Need variety • Need to stop to rest and eat	• Never become tired or bored • Don't need variety • Need to stop for servicing
Consistency	• Often somewhat inconsistent even when doing highly structured tasks	• Operate totally consistent with their programmed instructions
Speed	• Comparatively slow in storing, retrieving, and manipulating data	• Enormously fast in storing, retrieving, and manipulating data
Memory	• Often forget things • Time required for remembering is unpredictable • Able to retrieve information based on associations not programmed in advance	• Storage and retrieval times are predictable • In most cases can retrieve data based only on associations programmed in advance
Ability to perform programmed tasks	• Can perform highly structured work, but may find it boring and unsatisfying	• Can only perform totally structured tasks (which may be parts of larger tasks that are not totally structured)
Understanding	• Capable of understanding the meaning of work • Want to understand the meaning of work	• Incapable of understanding the meaning of work • Only capable of following unambiguous instructions
Imagination	• Can invent new ideas and associations • Can draw conclusions from data without using formulas	• Basically unable to invent ideas • In a few limited areas, can draw conclusions by combining specific facts in preprogrammed ways
Ability to see the whole	• Can recognize things as wholes in addition to recognizing details	• Recognize details and combine them into recognizable wholes only through appropriate programming

The contrast between human-centered design and machine-centered design is useful in thinking about the design of technologies and work systems. In **human-centered design,** the technology or business process is designed to make participants' work as effective and satisfying as possible. In **machine-centered design,** the technology or process is designed to simplify what the machine must do, and people are expected to adjust to the machine's weaknesses and limitations. Machine-centered design has been the tradition in many computerized systems, although there has been much progress in the last decade. An assumption within this tradition is that technology users will read and understand manuals, regardless of how arbitrary and illogical a system may seem. Another assumption is that people will follow procedures, regardless of how confusing or contradictory they are.

When accidents occur, this type of thinking leads to the conclusion that the user is the problem, rather than the technology or the system. Perrow's study of major accidents in power plants, aircraft, and other complex systems found that 60% to 80% of the accidents were blamed on **operator error,** mistaken or incorrect action by system participants who operate equipment or use information within systems.[5] For example, the commission investigating the partial meltdown at the Three Mile Island nuclear plant concluded that operator error caused the problem. Given the nature of human limitations, poor system design creating a high likelihood of operator error might have been blamed equally.

As an everyday example of machine-centered versus human-centered design, consider the way typical telephone calls are completed.[6] One person dials a number, a telephone rings in another location, and someone picks up the phone. This method is comparatively simple for the machine because it rings the same way regardless of whether the caller is a spouse, an acquaintance, a colleague from work, or someone trying to sell magazine subscriptions. From the user's viewpoint, there might be better ways to announce calls, such as by including with the ring a five second message identifying the caller and purpose of the call. Perhaps simpler, the system might ring differently for emergencies, family matters, calls by acquaintances, or uninvited sales calls. Although each alternative system has both advantages and disadvantages, the point is that the simplest system for the machine might not be best for the participants, customers, and stakeholders.

User Friendliness

Although often no more than a slogan, genuine user friendliness is an important outcome of human-centered design. Anything a person uses, ranging from everyday objects such as utensils and vacuum cleaners to technically advanced products such as computers and copiers, should be user friendly. User friendliness involves more than just cosmetic issues. Something is **user friendly** if most users can use it easily with minimal startup time and training, and if it contains features most users find useful. User friendly information systems are more productive because users waste less time and effort struggling with system features that get in the way of doing work.

Unfortunately, computers and computerized systems have often been more user hostile than user friendly. A technology is **user hostile** when it is difficult to use or makes users feel inept. Early computers were truly user hostile, because they were noninteractive and could be programmed only in languages appropriate for professional programmers. Advances in computer languages, interactive computing, and graphical interfaces were driven in part by the desire for user friendly computing.

Features and characteristics of computer systems can be designed to make them more user friendly or less user friendly. Genuinely user friendly computer systems help the user focus on the business problem rather than on the computerized tool being used to help solve the problem. In contrast, user hostile systems force the user to use codes and procedures that seem arbitrary and absorb effort that should go into doing useful work. Aspects of user friendliness are related to the nature of what the user must learn and remember, the nature of applications, the nature of application programs, and the nature of the user interface.

Nature of What the User Must Learn and Remember

A user friendly computer system interacts with the user in readily understood terms, never forcing the user to learn or pay attention to seemingly arbitrary or irrelevant details. Consequently, the user must understand basic principles but does not have to remember the precise spelling or grammar for commands. Multiple applications have similar organization and appearance and are therefore easier to learn. If the computer system operates this way, the user manual is basically a reference. The users can figure out how the computer system works mostly by playing with and modifying examples.

Nature of the Applications

A user friendly computer system provides easy ways to access and reuse previous work by the user or by others who built templates as starting points for users. Computer system flexibility fits task flexibility, permitting the user to do the task in whatever way the user finds easiest. The computer system is designed to minimize errors by users and to make it easy to fix any user errors that occur.

Nature of the Interface

In a user friendly computer system, input methods are tailored to the task at hand. Different methods are combined to make the work efficient. The menus are well structured, easy to understand, and consistent with menus in other applications. Ideally, the computer system adjusts to what the user knows. Novices see and use only basic features. Experts are not forced to interact the same way as novices. The user can name files or other objects with whatever names make sense instead of being constrained by computer restrictions such as the now outdated eight character limit for file names.

Technology as a Metaphor and Influence

the word **anthropomorphize** combines the ancient Greek roots for man (anthro) and form (morpho), and means to ascribe human attributes to an animal or object. One often hears statements such as: the computer *knows* the client's age, the computer *chooses* the best move in a chess game, or the computer *understands* the difference between discount prices and regular prices. Although basically a way to say the computer has stored certain data or performs certain preprogrammed processing, taken literally, terms such as *knows* and *understands* are extreme exaggerations of what computers can currently do. (See more on this in Chapter 9.)

"The computer *knows*" may seem a trivial concern, but what about "the computer *made a mistake*"? People who say that seem to experience computers as autonomous entities that can act on their own behalf and are therefore blamable. When things go wrong, these individuals might blame the computer instead of their company's policies or their fellow workers.[7]

Although there may not be a fancy word for it, the reverse of anthropomorphizing is using computer functions and attributes to describe people. Some psychiatrists have observed patients who work with computers all day and end up describing themselves and their relationships using computer terminology. These patients sometimes prefer computers to human company. Computers provide immediate, unambiguous responses and provide a tiny world a user can control. The world of people, with its slow responses, ambiguous messages, and disagreements is messier, more difficult to control, and in some ways less safe for these patients.

Extensive use of certain computerized systems may even affect the way people perceive the world. Noting that over 30 million American homes had Nintendo, a book about Nintendo[8] cited surveys showing that the Nintendo character Super Mario was more recognized by American children than Mickey Mouse. Childhood entertainment had once been imbued with Mickey's message: "We play fair and we work hard and we're in harmony." Mario's message imparts different values: "Kill or be killed. Time is running out. You are on your own."

The chapter has opened by identifying some of the relationships between technology and people. It is clear so far that computerized systems have meaning and impact far beyond basic functions such as storing and retrieving information. The next section goes into more depth by looking at positive and negative impacts on people at work.

Reality Check

TECHNOLOGY AND PEOPLE

This section discussed the relationship between technology and people in terms of human-centered versus machine-centered design, user friendliness, and technology as a metaphor and influence.

1. Considering several technologies you use or have seen used, identify several features you see as especially human-centered or user friendly, and compare these to features that are machine-centered or user hostile.
2. Considering computers, cars, or other machines, give examples of anthropomorphizing that you have encountered and explain why you do or do not believe this is a problem.

POSITIVE AND NEGATIVE IMPACTS ON PEOPLE AT WORK

The impacts of information systems on individuals vary widely. For some, new technology has brought professional and personal gains. For others, it has meant obsolescence and frustration. For some, work has become easier or more enjoyable. For others, it has become more difficult and sometimes intolerable. We will explore personal impacts by identifying characteristics of a healthy job and then looking at related impacts of information systems.

Table 7.3 summarizes the characteristics of a healthy job. People in healthy jobs use their skills in meaningful work, enjoy autonomy and social relations with others, have personal rights including some control over the demands of the job, and can have enough time and energy to participate in family and community life.[9] Based on these characteristics, the least healthy types of work are those with continual pressure to perform but little personal control. Examples include assembly-line workers, clerks who process business transactions, and telephone operators. These are jobs with rigid hours and procedures, threats of layoff, little learning of new skills, and difficulty in taking a break or time off for personal needs. Stereotypical high-stress jobs such as manager, electrical engineer, and architect are healthier because professionals have more control over their work.

Health and Safety

Researchers have found relationships between psychological well-being at work and physical health. People with active jobs involving initiative, discretion, and advancement have the lowest heart attack rates, even though these jobs often involve stress. People in high-strain jobs at the bottom of the job ladder have the highest rate of heart attacks. Even when such risk factors as age, race, education, and smoking are considered, those in the bottom 10% of the job ladder are in the top 10% for illness. These workers have four to five times greater risk of heart attack than those at the top 10% of the ladder, whose jobs give them a high sense of control.[10] The same type of pattern applies in the middle of the socioeconomic distribution. A study that followed 7,400 men and women with civil service jobs in London found that those in low-grade positions with little control over their responsibilities were at a 50% higher risk of developing heart disease than those in higher-level jobs. The author of the study concluded, "Our research suggests that illness in the workplace is to some extent a management issue.... The way work is organized appears to make an important link between socioeconomic status and heart attack."[11]

Information systems can have an impact on health because they are part of the job environment. The impact is positive if the system contributes to a person's feelings of initiative, discretion, advancement, and control. It is negative if the system reduces these feelings by diminishing skills, meaningfulness of work, autonomy, and social relations. We will see examples in both directions.

TABLE 7.3 Characteristics of a Healthy Job

Job characteristic	Meaning to you as an employee
Skills	You can use and increase your skills.
Meaningfulness	You understand and respect the importance of your work and understand how it fits into the organization's work.
Autonomy	You can control your work. You are not made to feel childish by the methods of supervision.
Social relations	Your job includes collaboration and communication with others.
Psychological demands	Your job includes a mix of routine demands and new but reasonable demands. You have some control over what demands to accept.
Personal rights	You feel that you have appropriate personal rights at work and have reasonable ways to settle grievances.
Integration with life outside work	The job does not interfere excessively with your ability to participate in family and community life.

Even though they may have generally healthier jobs, some professionals and managers believe their stress level has increased due to **information overload.** They believe information technology has contributed to this overload, and that routine use of v-mail, e-mail, fax, and personal computers has not been liberating at all. To the contrary, they feel unremitting work pressure because the technology brings work faster, and people expect immediate responses. The Nobel prize winner Herbert Simon described this phenomenon eloquently: "What information consumes is rather obvious: it consumes the attention of its recipients. Hence, a wealth of information creates a poverty of attention and a need to allocate that attention efficiently among the overabundance of information sources that might consume it."[12]

Using Video Display Terminals at Work

An additional aspect of information systems that has come into question is the effect of personal computers on intensive users. These individuals often suffer higher stress levels and related physical problems than other workers in the same businesses. This stress has been attributed to a combination of lack of control, feelings of being monitored, lack of social contact, and physical discomforts such as eyestrain and physical tension. A study comparing clericals who worked on video display terminals (VDTs), clericals who did not work on VDTs, and professionals who worked on VDTs revealed that clericals working on VDTs had the highest stress. They had to follow rigid work procedures and had little control over what they did. They felt they were being controlled by a machine. In contrast, the professionals who used VDTs experienced the least stress. They were newspaper reporters who found satisfaction in their work and had flexibility in meeting deadlines.[13]

Impacts specifically related to the physical relationship between people and their work environment are studied in the field of **ergonomics.** Many VDT operators suffer eyestrain, backache, and muscle tension (see Figure 7.1.) Some also suffer **repetitive strain injury** (RSI) such as carpal tunnel syndrome, which causes severe pain due to nerve irritation in the wrist. Figure 7.2 shows one of the modified keyboards that attempts to reduce these risks. The voice recognition systems mentioned in Chapter 8 may address this problem for at least some of the people who could dictate more and type less.

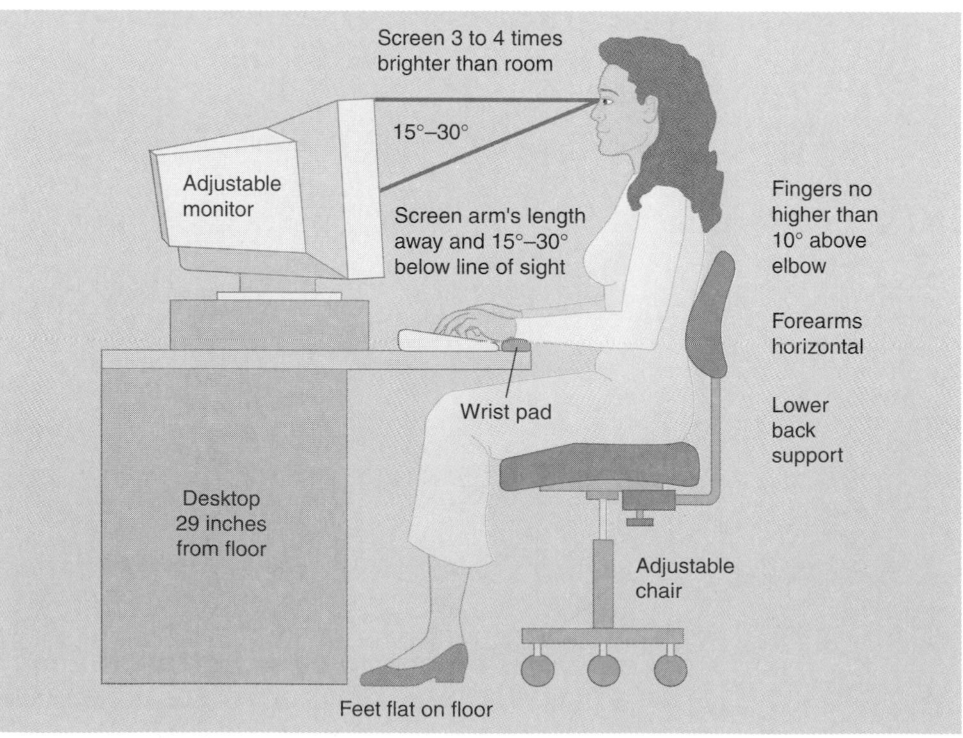

Figure 7.1
Guidelines for VDT users

This figure shows a person sitting at a VDT, practicing habits that help minimize eyestrain, reduce radiation exposure, avoid carpal tunnel syndrome, and reduce back pain.

Figure 7.2
Adapting the keyboard to the person

This is one of several ergonomically designed keyboards that try to reduce repetitive use injuries by permitting the typist's hands to remain in a more natural position.

A number of studies have raised concerns about the effects of electromagnetic emissions from VDTs. In one with a sample size too small for statistical significance, pregnant women who spent 20 or more hours per week working at VDTs were twice as likely as non-VDT users to suffer a miscarriage during the first trimester of pregnancy. Reviewing these findings and many others, a World Health Organization report concluded that "psychosocial factors are at least as important as the physical ergonomics of workstations and the work environment in influencing health and well-being of workers."[14] A more recent study of the effect of stress on female lawyers supported the general thrust of the WHO findings. This study found that female lawyers who worked more than 45 hours per week were five times as likely to experience great stress at work and three times as likely to suffer miscarriages as female lawyers who worked fewer than 35 hours per week.[15]

Autonomy and Power

Autonomy in a job is the degree of discretion individuals or groups have in planning, regulating, and controlling their own work. **Power** is the ability to get other people to do things. Information systems can cause increases or decreases in either area.

Information systems may increase autonomy whenever the individual can control the use of the tools. For example, a data analysis system might permit totally independent analysis work by a manager who previously had to ask for assistance to analyze data. Likewise, professionals such as engineers and lawyers can use information systems to do work themselves that previously would have required more collaboration and negotiation with others. (See Figure 7.3.)

In contrast, many information systems are designed to reduce autonomy. The need for limited autonomy is widely accepted in transaction processing and recordkeeping. Systems in these areas are designed to assure that everyone involved in a repetitive process, such as taking orders or producing paychecks, uses the same rules for processing the same data in the same format. If individuals could process transactions however they wanted to, tracking systems and accounting systems would quickly degenerate into chaos.

In other situations, a competition-driven push toward consistency and cost-cutting is leading toward increased electronic surveillance, especially where computerized systems are used continually as part of work. Even a decade ago, a survey found that over 6 million American workers were being monitored electronically.[16] For jobs using telephones intensively, this means someone may be listening in. For jobs involving sales transactions or anything else that can be tracked, every completion of a unit of work may be recorded and

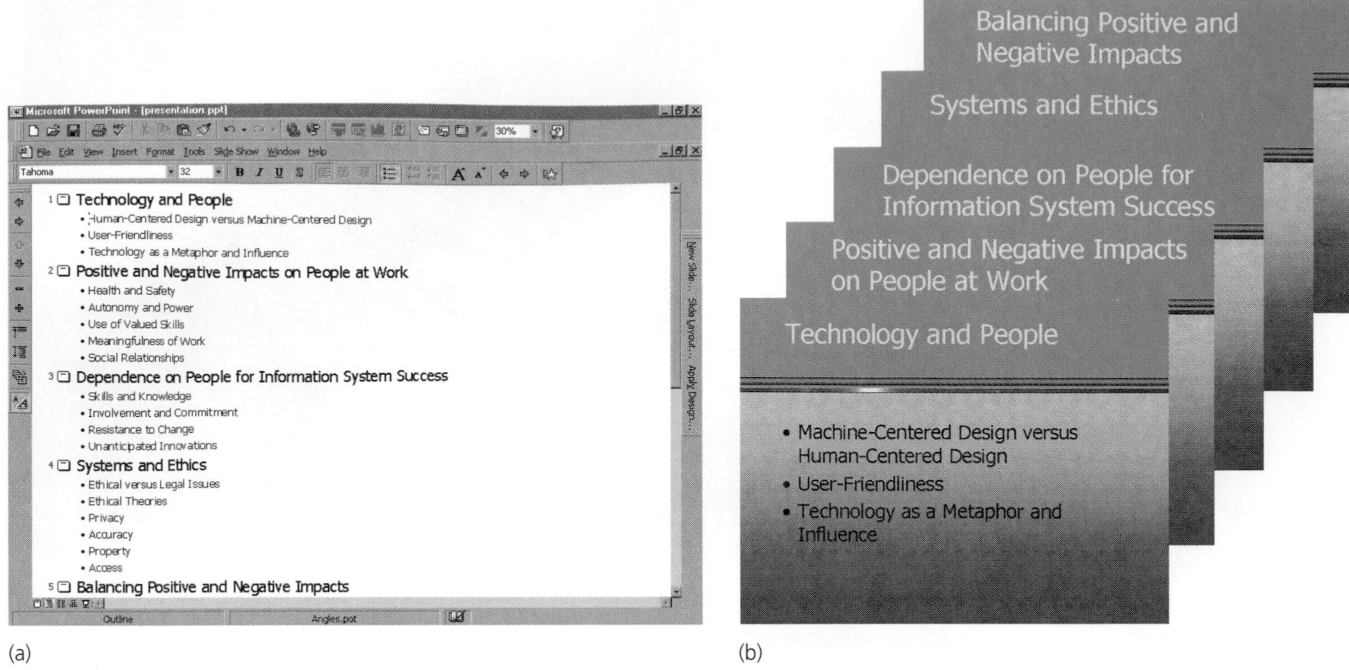

Figure 7.3
Increasing autonomy through tools

A presentation software package automatically converts this chapter's outline into the format and appearance of a professional-looking presentation. Using convenient tools like this makes business professionals more independent.

available for analysis by someone at a remote location. For data entry jobs, every keystroke may be monitored and statistics taken for speed and accuracy of work, and even time spent on breaks.

As a case in point, a company called WinVista developed software that monitors a personal computer and records every file that is opened, every Web site that is visited, and every e-mail message that is sent. The original version of this software was developed by two brothers who wanted to help their mother avoid more trouble with carpal tunnel syndrome by reminding her to take a break every 5,000 keystrokes. Although this software can be used to identify people who spend too much time playing games, it can also be used to improve work practices. For example, Metropolitan Life tested the software on insurance agents who use up to 50 different programs. The goal was to see how the best agents use programs and then to pass that wisdom on to other agents.[17]

Information systems that monitor workers closely and that decrease autonomy are often experienced as threats. Consequently, systems that increase employee monitoring may lead to resistance and may result in turnover of personnel, especially if autonomy is traditional in the work setting. In the trucking industry, for example, many formerly independent drivers are now among the most closely monitored U.S. workers. A decade ago truckers were able to set their own schedules as long as they occasionally called a dispatcher from a pay telephone. Today, 57% of trucking firms have computers on board each rig, and many trucks have antennas used to monitor the truck's exact location. The trucks' engines are programmed for efficient gear shifting, optimum idling times, and top speed. Truck drivers are happy to use cellular phones instead of lining up at pay phones, but some object to the monitoring and the limits on how they drive. Some have taken evasive action such as blocking their truck's satellite dishes or parking under a wide overpass to escape surveillance from the sky.[18]

Capabilities to monitor minute details of work may create the temptation to misuse the available information, but the way the information is used determines whether system participants feel as though "big brother" is watching. For example, recording conversations by telemarketers can help resolve disputes with customers even if it is never used for day-to-day monitoring of individuals. Similarly, random samples of calls can be used for training rather than for punishment. Given the natural tendency to wonder whether such systems are being misused, it is especially important for managers to explain whether they will be used for monitoring work, and if so, how they will be used.

Just as information systems can affect autonomy, they can also affect power by redistributing information, changing responsibilities, and shifting the balance of power in an organization. Across the entire organizational spectrum, information systems have increased the power of people who operate largely on facts and technical competence, and have reduced the ability of people to give orders based on the power of their position. The availability of information across business functions has also made it easier to resolve conflicts based on facts rather than on opinions and power.

Information systems have had an important impact in reducing the power of many middle managers. Higher-level executives can often use their MIS or EIS directly to get some of the information they once received from middle managers. In addition, they can use communication systems such as e-mail and v-mail to bypass middle mangers and go directly to the individuals who know the most about a particular situation or issue. Middle managers therefore may see information systems squeezing them from below and above.

Use of Valued Skills

Information systems may have either positive or negative effects on people's skills. As a simple example, consider what happens when you rely on a pocket calculator to do arithmetic. Although you usually get the right answer more quickly, your ability to do arithmetic without the calculator deteriorates through disuse. The calculator has the positive effect of helping you calculate more quickly and the negative effect of allowing your skills to decline.

New information systems have enhanced the skills in a wide range of jobs. MIS and EIS have provided information to managers that helps them learn how to manage based on analyzing facts rather than just on intuition. DSS and execution systems such as CAD have helped professionals analyze data, define alternatives, and solve problems in new ways.

Introducing information systems has also had the opposite effect in some cases, especially when the system automated the judgment and discretion in the work. Such systems redefined jobs by replacing the individual's autonomy and authority with computer-enforced consistency and control. Now a less skilled person could do the same task, and previous skills had less value. Reducing the value of skills previously needed to do specific types of work is called **de-skilling.**

Tasks most susceptible to de-skilling call for repetition, endurance, and speed, rather than flexibility, creativity, and judgment. Such tasks are highly structured and can be described in terms of procedures. In general they could involve processing data or could involve physical actions such as spray painting a new car. In some specific cases, de-skilling has occurred with the partial automation of decision processes once thought of as requiring years of experience. For example, managers of an insurance company once believed it took five years to become a reasonably good group health insurance underwriter. (An underwriter determines rates for insurance premiums.) The mystery in training new underwriters disappeared when a new system automated standard underwriting calculations. Although the system's purpose was to provide better customer service and reduce the stress of year end peak loads, it also de-skilled the job. New underwriters could be productive on simple cases within months, and the knowledge of the more experienced underwriters was less valued.[19]

Automating significant job components also tends to reduce people's skills by encouraging mental disengagement and "peripheralization," a feeling that one is at the periphery of the action. Consider the way automatic flight control systems built into new airliners (see Figure 7.4) allow pilots to almost become spectators. Many aviation experts wonder whether pilots of highly automated planes will be able to react quickly enough in emergencies. The quandary of how much control to put into automatic systems came up

Figure 7.4
Cockpit of a Boeing 777 airliner

Flying a modern jet requires a great deal of skill and experience, even though some aspects of a pilot's job have been automated.

when an airliner with highly automatic systems crashed after an unsafe maneuver at an air show, killing three people and injuring 50. Although the automatic system was suspect, it is also possible that pilot error caused the crash and that the automatic system prevented a worse crash by keeping the wings level after the plane hit a group of trees.[20] Regardless of how much training pilots receive in realistic flight simulators on the ground, there is also the question of whether this practice is enough. For example, the survivors of a 1989 DC-10 crash in Sioux City, Iowa, owe their lives to an experienced crew that managed to guide the plane to an airport despite an engine explosion that destroyed all of the plane's steering equipment.

Information systems may require that workers learn new skills. For professionals, the skills may involve new analytical methods or new ways to obtain information. For nonprofessional workers, the necessary skill may simply be literacy. Many companies are installing flexible manufacturing systems to permit the same manufacturing line to produce different products. When these systems were installed, many companies found that their workers were not literate enough to read the instructions for product changes or new machine set-ups. In some cases, the employees were foreigners who couldn't read English. In others, the employees were good workers who had not learned to read in school. In response to this problem, many companies now provide literacy training for employees.[21]

Meaningfulness of Work

Information systems can affect the meaningfulness of work in several ways. First, the information system can be set up to either expand or limit the scope, variety, and significance in the user's job. In addition, the mere fact that work takes place through the medium of a computer may affect the way people experience their work.

Variety and Scope of Work

The range of different types of things people do at work is called **task variety.** Most people desire variety in their work environments and get bored if the work becomes too routine and repetitive. **Task scope** is the size of the task relative to the overall purpose of the organization. Installing a single door lock on an automobile assembly line is a task with minimal scope. Assembling the entire door is a task of larger scope. Information systems can either increase or decrease the variety and scope of work.

Information systems reduce variety if they force the worker to focus on a small aspect of work. Consider what happened with the implementation of a computer-based dental claims system at an insurance company. With the previous paper-oriented system, the benefits analyst pulled information about each account from a set of paper files, checked contract limitations, completed the necessary paperwork, and returned the account information to the files. Analysts were often hired based on their prior knowledge of dental procedures, and they frequently discussed cases with their supervisors and other analysts. With the new computerized system, much of the information was on the computer, which also ran programs that assured claims were processed in a standard way. The analysts spent more time entering claim data into computers and less time using their knowledge and judgment. Claims analysts who previously knew a lot about each account started saying things like: "I don't know half the things I used to. I feel that I have lost it—the computer knows more. I am pushing buttons. I'm not on top of things as I used to be."[22] Within a year the system had increased productivity 30% to 40%, but at the cost of job satisfaction for the analysts.

Nature of Computer-Mediated Work

The fact that work is done through a computer may affect its meaningfulness to participants. Work done using computers, rather than through direct physical contact with the object of the task, is often called **computer-mediated work.**[23] Box 7.1 identifies different types of computer-mediated work and emphasizes the relationship between how work is done and how people experience their work.

There are many situations in which working through a computer affects the way workers experience their work. The **abstractness of work** is a related issue because computer-mediated work doesn't involve direct physical contact with the object of the task.[24] This work is designed to focus on symbols on a computer screen rather than a more tangible reality. Consider the example of a bank auditor. With a new system, he had less need to travel to the branches, talk with people, and examine financial paperwork. Although some tasks were quicker, he felt it was more difficult to define what information he needed. With nothing in front of him except numbers, he had a limited basis for figuring out what the numbers meant. The job had become abstract and for better or worse didn't feel like the kind of auditing he had done before.[25]

BOX 7.1 ***Different types of computer-mediated work***

The fact that work is done through a computer affects the way people experience their work and exercise their skills. The meaning of working through a computer is somewhat different in different types of computer-mediated work.

Computer-mediated production work: The worker enters instructions into a terminal attached to a robot or numerically controlled machine. Instead of the person holding tools and doing the work, the machine does the work based on instructions the person enters. The person becomes more like a programmer and less like a machinist.

Computer-mediated office work or record keeping: The worker uses a terminal to record and retrieve data instead of writing on paper. The work takes place through a keyboard and display screen. Because so much of the work goes through the computer, there is less reason to get up, walk over to a file cabinet, or even open a drawer. The computer becomes the only important physical object.

Computer-mediated intellectual work: The worker uses a computer as a tool for creating ideas, performing analysis, or doing other intellectual work. Computers allow analysis and manipulation of information in new and different ways. However, computerized systems may constrain both the form of the work and the ability to change to a different method after a major investment in one way of doing things.

Computer-mediated control or supervision: The worker receives instructions through a computer or is monitored based on the rate or accuracy of inputs into a computer. The nature of interactions with supervisors changes. The instructions come from the computer, and it is less necessary to interact with other people to find out what to do. The feedback is based more on data the computer recorded and less on the supervisor's direct observation.

Social Relationships

Social interaction at work is an important part of many people's lives that work systems can affect. In some cases computerized systems may create new possibilities for interaction by automating repetitive paperwork and calculations, thereby giving people more time to work on the issues that require interaction with others. Furthermore, communication systems such as e-mail and v-mail support additional contact between people separated geographically or organizationally.

Impacts of computerized systems on social relationships may also be negative, however. Jobs that require sitting at VDTs all day doing repetitive work tend to reduce social interaction. Even though the people in Figure 7.5 are in an open office setting, their work processes make the workstations their primary information source and work tool, and minimize interaction with their peers. People working in this type of environment may feel the lack of social contact and become alienated. Trends toward downsizing and telecommuting amplify isolation and alienation because they reduce the number of people working in organizations and permit these people to work from their homes.

The chapter started by discussing human interface issues such as human-centered design and user friendliness, and then described five areas in which information systems can have positive or negative impacts on people at work. The next section comes from the reverse viewpoint and looks at the impact of people on work system success.

Reality Check

POSITIVE AND NEGATIVE IMPACTS ON PEOPLE AT WORK

Positive and negative impacts on people occur in areas such as health and safety, autonomy and power, use of valued skills, meaningfulness of work, and social relationships.

1. Explain whether you or others you know have ever felt positive or negative impacts of information systems in any of these areas.
2. For the examples you identify, describe the extent to which you think the impact was the type of issue managers should be concerned with.

Figure 7.5
Impacts on the social side of work

The physical layout and the nature of this work forces employees to sit at their terminals while having little interaction with their peers.

DEPENDENCE ON PEOPLE FOR INFORMATION SYSTEM SUCCESS

The most brilliant state-of-the-art information system is a waste of time and effort unless people in the organization accept it and use it. Many information systems never work successfully in the organization even though the software operates correctly on the computer. This section looks at several areas in which system success depends on people.

Skills and Knowledge

Anyone who has learned how to use a computer recognizes that information systems operate successfully only if participants have the necessary skills and knowledge. These start with literacy and include knowledge about how to use computers for specific tasks and how to interpret information in the system. In what is often called an Information Age, it is troubling that industry surveys repeatedly conclude that a large percentage of workers lack important basic skills. In a 1997 survey of 4,500 manufacturers, 60% said their workers lacked basic math skills, 55% noted deficiencies in writing and comprehension skills, and 48% said their workers lacked "the ability to read and translate drawings, diagrams, and flow charts."[26]

Some companies have addressed skill and knowledge deficits by designing systems requiring minimal skills from employees. To attain consistent results with a labor force of 500,000 teenagers, McDonald's reduces work to procedures requiring little or no judgment. The system for producing golden brown french fries in consistent portions monitors the boiling grease and beeps to tell the worker to remove the fries. The worker then uses a special fry scoop designed to produce 400 to 420 servings per 100-pound bag of potatoes and make the fries fall into the package attractively. A former employee said he quit because he felt like a robot. Timers controlled every step of his work on the hamburger grill to produce consistent burgers in 90 seconds. He said, "You don't need a face, you don't need a brain. You need to have two hands and two legs and move them as fast as you can. That's the whole system. I wouldn't go back there again for anything."[27]

The McDonald's system represents an extreme, but it helps in seeing the range of system design choices. Many transaction processing systems are highly structured but still call on employees to exercise judgment. MIS, EIS, and DSS all call for knowledge in interpreting the data. Specialized information systems for professional work such as designing buildings or analyzing financial statements require a higher level of knowledge because the business process is much less structured.

System design is clearly important to work system participants, ranging from the teenagers working at McDonald's to professionals and managers doing highly skilled work. Because participants care about the ways work systems affect them, their acceptance of a system or resistance to it is a key determinant of its success. This acceptance or resistance is often tied to involvement and commitment while the system is being designed and implemented.

Involvement and Commitment

Using information system modifications to improve a work system requires changing that work system and overcoming the inertia of current ways of doing things. **Social inertia** is the tendency of organizations to continue doing things in the same way and, therefore, to resist change. Unless a business problem is both evident and painful, overcoming inertia often takes a lot of work. For some projects, more time and effort is spent in overcoming inertia than in the computer-related parts of information system development.

The main force against social inertia is involvement and commitment by participants and their managers. Low levels of involvement and commitment make it more likely that the information system will never reach its full potential or will fail altogether. If commitment is low, even an information system that has been implemented somewhat successfully may be used for a while and then gradually abandoned, soon making it seem that the project never happened.

Table 7.4 shows some of the possible levels of **user involvement** in an information system development project, ranging from noninvolvement to active ongoing participation

TABLE 7.4 Alternative Levels of User Involvement in System Development

These levels of involvement go from the lowest to the highest level.[28]

Level of involvement	Description of involvement at this level
Noninvolvement	Users are unwilling to participate, unable to contribute, or are not invited to participate.
Involvement by advice	User advice is solicited through interviews or questionnaires, but others make decisions about which features are included in the system.
Involvement by sign-off	Users approve the results produced by the project team, but are not actively involved in analyzing or designing the system.
Involvement by design team membership	Users participate actively in design activities, such as interviews of other users and creation of functional specifications and external specifications.
Involvement by project team membership, management, and project ownership	Users participate throughout the entire project, including initiation, development, implementation, and operation; a user representative manages the project; the user organization owns the project.

in the project team. Noninvolvement occurs if the users are unable to participate or if the system is to be imposed on them and they are not invited to participate. Noninvolvement may sound like a recipe for disaster, but it sometimes works, such as when a software package developed elsewhere is the most practical basis for a new information system and when the implementation of that package is well explained. Involvement through advice or sign-off uses a small amount of users' time to provide input that influences priorities and features and therefore reduces political problems.

Unfortunately, limited involvement often leads to overlooking system shortcomings and organizational issues that fuller participation would catch. The highest levels of involvement require ongoing participation by users in the project team. In some cases a user representative manages the project to make sure that it genuinely solves the problem. Higher levels of involvement make it more possible to address issues such as mutually inconsistent requests from different users, different needs that cannot all be supported due to resource constraints, and requested features or capabilities that the analysts believe are too difficult or expensive to provide.

The importance of involvement and commitment are clear from attempts to implement the same information system in four unrelated life insurance firms, Sun Alliance Insurance Group in the United Kingdom, National Mutual in Australia, and Prudential and Lutheran Brotherhood in the United States. All sold a full line of life insurance products and had a geographically diverse field sales force with a central home office. All attempted to implement an information system developed by Applied Expert Systems to perform comprehensive financial planning in areas such as cash management, risk management, income protection, general insurance, education funding, and retirement planning. The system used an extensive questionnaire to obtain data and produced a professional-looking personal financial profile and agent's report. Designed to create a better client relationship based on a thorough understanding of client needs, it seemed promising because early pilot projects in four organizations showed that profiling might increase the total premium per sales call between 10% and 30%. There were disadvantages, however, starting with the need for an extra sales call to obtain the client data. The profiles often suggested buying disability insurance, because people are more likely to become disabled than to die in the short term. Life insurance salespeople often disliked suggesting disability insurance, however, because the premiums are high and because the underwriting process for disability insurance causes delays. The move to profiling also changed the way information was controlled. Both new and experienced agents traditionally controlled their own client files, but with profiling, all the detailed client data was fed to the home office.

Figure 7.6 shows the number of profiles done per month in the four organizations. The pilot project peaked and then died out at National Mutual and Lutheran Brotherhood. In contrast, the use of profiling increased steadily at Sun Alliance and Prudential. Both firms that abandoned profiling implemented it through an approach that began with lead users and progressively widened availability to other participants. In these cases the system was presented to the salesforce much like a new insurance product that they could sell if they so desired. The initiative was championed by someone from headquarters who tried to persuade the sales force that the technology could help them. In the two firms where profiling succeeded, it became a central concept in training new agents and in the way the organization intended to operate. The implementation was done on a focused, office-by-office basis, with a senior manager taking an intimate role in training and implementation. In these cases, the involvement and commitment of both managers and agents contributed strongly to the system's growing use.[29]

The differing results at these four companies show that a system's success is determined partially by its features and partially by the development and implementation process itself. The likelihood of success drops if this process cannot overcome the inertia of current business processes or if the implementation itself causes resistance.

Resistance to Change

Even with a lot of effort to make the change process successful, many systems encounter significant resistance from potential users and others. **Resistance to change** is any action or inaction that obstructs a change process. Resistance may come in many forms, ranging from public debate about the merits of the system to outright sabotage. Public debate can be expressed through direct statements about system shortcomings or the reasons that the system is unnecessary or undesirable. Sabotage can occur through submission of incorrect data or other forms of conscious misuse.

Figure 7.6
Importance of involvement and commitment during implementation

These are the levels of utilization for similar expert systems installed at unrelated insurance companies. After several years, the system was used widely by two companies even though its use was discontinued at two others.

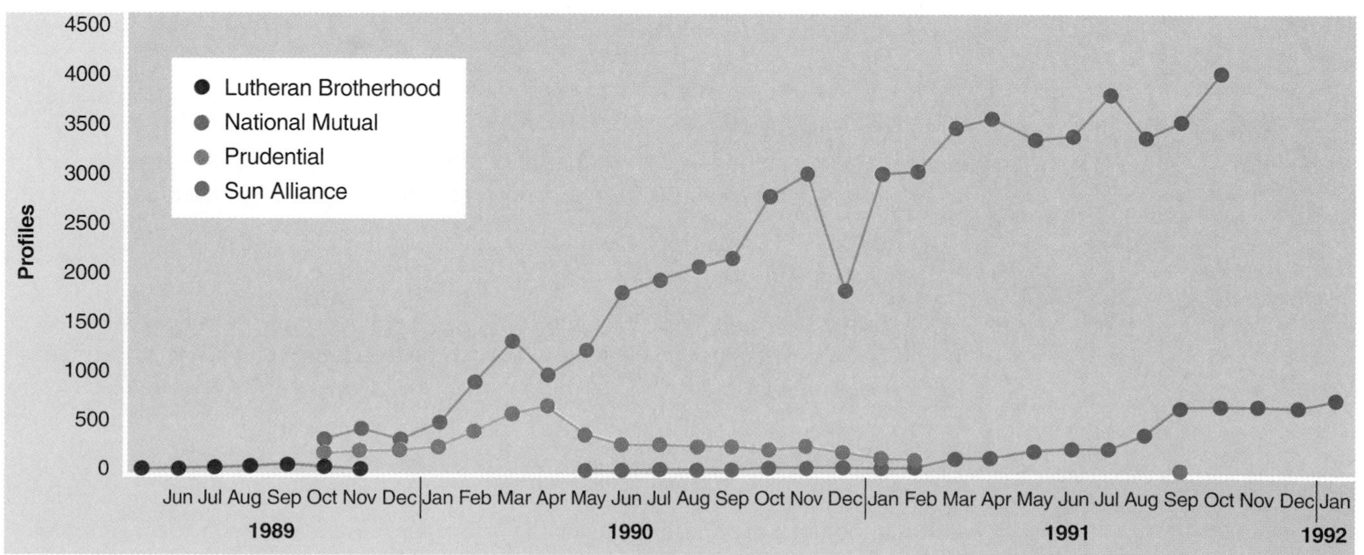

Between the extremes of public debate and sabotage are many less overt forms of resistance, including benign neglect, resource diversion, inappropriate staffing, and problem expansion.[30] A person resisting the system through *benign neglect* would say nothing against the system but would take no positive action to improve its chances of success. A person resisting through *resource diversion* would say nothing against the system but would divert to other projects the resources it needs. Resistance through *inappropriate staffing* involves assigning people to the project who lack the background and authority to do a good job. A final form of resistance is *problem expansion.* This is done by trying to delay and confuse the project effort by claiming that other departments need to be involved in the analysis because the system addresses problems related to their work.

Resistance is a complex phenomenon because it often comes from a combination of motives. It can be a highly rational response motivated by a desire to help the organization. For example, a manager might believe a new system is useless and might try to get others to agree. In contrast, resistance can have selfish or vindictive motives. For example, a manager might feel that the system will undermine personal ambitions or improve the prospects of personal rivals.

It is useful to think about resistance by looking for multiple causes. One approach is to say that resistance can be caused by people, or by the system, or by interactions between the characteristics of the people and the characteristics of the system.[31] Table 7.5 shows five typical person-related explanations of resistance. Next to each of these is a corresponding system-related explanation and an interaction-related explanation. The table illustrates how different individuals might cite different reasons for resistance to a particular information system. Highly committed members of the project team might view resistance as caused by the action or inaction of people. Users who didn't want the system might view resistance as caused by the system's characteristics. An unbiased observer might be more likely to cite all three types of reasons shown in the table.

Awareness of the different causes of resistance is helpful in anticipating implementation problems that may arise in a project. Table 7.5 implies that anyone who holds only one view of the causes of resistance may be missing important ways to improve the situation. Regardless of personal beliefs about which causes are foremost in any situation, considering the range of causes may lead to better implementation strategies.

Unanticipated Innovations

A final aspect of the impact of people on information systems is the unending stream of unanticipated uses. Some may be beneficial, others may just be unexpected, and yet other may create new problems. Because this chapter is full of examples of surprising uses and impacts, we will not discuss the topic further at this point.

Reality Check

DEPENDENCE ON PEOPLE FOR INFORMATION SYSTEM SUCCESS

People-related determinants of system success include skills and knowledge, involvement and commitment, resistance to change, and unanticipated innovations.

1. Identify situations you know about in which involvement and commitment had important impacts on the success or failure of a project or activity.
2. Think of an example of resistance to change in which you were the person resisting the change. Explain how you resisted the change and how you justified your position.

SYSTEMS AND ETHICS

Ethics is a branch of philosophy involving principles of right and wrong behavior related to other people. Ethics is a key concern for everyone involved with information and systems because of the many ways one's actions in this area can affect other people.

TABLE 7.5 Common Explanations of Resistance to Information Systems

Caused by people	Caused by the system	Caused by interactions
Perhaps the resisting users are not smart enough to understand the system's advantages.	Perhaps the system is too difficult to learn in a reasonable amount of time or too difficult to use effectively.	Perhaps the system is wrong for these particular users.
Perhaps users are involved in a political fight unrelated to the system.	Perhaps the system is causing a political problem for some of the users.	Perhaps the system will change the political distribution of power in the organization.
Perhaps users are lazy and want to continue doing things the outmoded way they have always worked.	Perhaps the system doesn't solve enough of the problem to make the change worthwhile.	Perhaps the system will help some users but harm others by increasing their work-loads or devaluing their skills.
Perhaps users' complaints about missing or poorly designed features are an excuse for not plunging in.	Perhaps the system is poorly designed.	Perhaps the system needs to be enhanced to make it more effective for these users.
Perhaps users are overly perfectionistic in their expectations.	Perhaps the system doesn't solve the problem well.	Perhaps the system doesn't meet expectations and needs to be improved.

Ethical Versus Legal Issues

Table 7.6 summarizes important distinctions between ethical issues and legal issues. Laws are a society's official statements defining proper behavior and governmental actions in response to improper behavior. Laws typically grow out of the society's ethical sense of right and wrong in dealing with people but never cover all ethical issues. Laws typically cover only ethical issues that can be described clearly, have impact on society, and are governed by commonly accepted ethical principles.

Ethical dilemmas are difficult choices related to ethical issues that may or may not be covered by laws. Here are examples of ethical dilemmas that occur every day in business and society:

- The supervisor of five telephone attendants has received numerous complaints lately and is considering secretly listening in on the attendants' phone conversations to monitor their service. Is this right or wrong?
- A software engineer working for a city government prints a file while debugging a computer program and notices that a large number of unpaid parking tickets have been canceled for several individuals, one of whom is an elected official. Is it right or wrong to publicize this?
- A manager under severe competitive pressure is thinking about installing a new computerized system that will eliminate the jobs of five people who will probably be unable to get equally good jobs anywhere else. Is this right or wrong?
- A programmer in a software firm is dissatisfied with the way a new information system has been tested and is considering telling his manager's boss that the system should not be distributed to customers, even though it has no obvious bugs. Is this right or wrong?

These situations all pose ethical dilemmas related to the impact of one person's actions on others, whether or not laws could be used to decide what to do. None of these dilemmas involves either conscious lawbreaking or malicious acts such as trying to hurt someone, steal something, or damage something mischievously. If malicious acts were involved, the perpetrator would be less likely to think about ethical dilemmas and more likely to think about the chances of being caught and the nature of punishment. In each case above, the person faced with the dilemma is trying to figure out what principles and values to apply in deciding what to do.

TABLE 7.6 **Distinctions between Ethical Issues and Legal Issues**

	Ethics	Laws and regulations
What is the basis?	Customs and beliefs about how people should treat each other	A combination of: • society's consensus about ethics • practical issues about what can be enforced • historical precedents from existing laws
Who is the judge?	Individuals	Judges appointed or elected through a governmental process
What is the price of nonconformance?	Criticism or ostracism	Legal penalties such as fines or jail sentences
Does the principle have geographical boundaries?	May differ from society to society or region to region	May differ from society to society or region to region

Ethical Theories

Over thousands of years, philosophers have proposed a range of **ethical theories,** principles that can be used as the basis for deciding what to do in ethical dilemmas. Some of these theories are based on the potential consequences of the action, whereas others are based on the way people should be treated. Here are simplified statements of three common ethical theories:

- *Maximize the overall good.* This theory says that people should choose to act in ways that maximize the overall good of society. As the examples in the preceding section illustrate, it is often difficult to decide what will maximize the overall good. Consider the manager who is trying to decide whether to install a system that will displace five people. That action may be part of the only practical strategy for the company's survival. On the other hand, there may be alternative approaches such as changing people's jobs but maintaining their salaries and working conditions.
- *Maximize personal good.* This theory says people should make choices that maximize their own personal outcomes. In business situations, this theory can be translated into a theory of employer rights whereby an employer has the right to treat any employee at the job site in any way the employer wants, limited only by the law. In the telephone attendant example, the supervisor might use this theory to justify listening in on the phone conversations, even though other methods of supervision might work equally well.
- *Treat others well.* This theory resembles the biblical rule of acting toward others as you would have them act toward you. It differs from the other two theories because it focuses on the actions one might take rather than the consequences of those actions. For example, someone following this theory might feel it is never appropriate to lie, whereas someone trying to maximize the overall good might feel that lying could be justified depending on the likely consequences. In business situations, the ethical theory of treating others well is translated into theories of employee rights based on personal respect, healthy working conditions, fair wages, and employment continuity.

Regardless of how the ethical principles are stated, ethical dilemmas such as those described above are difficult to resolve. Over time, societies and organizations gradually develop negotiated guidelines for what constitutes ethical behavior in that environment and what happens when these guidelines are broken. With technology changing so rapidly in today's world, people frequently face ethical choices with minimal precedent. This is one of the reasons major professional societies involved in information systems have issued codes of ethics for their members.

Now that several typical ethical dilemmas have been listed and several ethical theories have been introduced, it is important to identify some of the major ethical issues that face people working in information systems. These ethical issues are organized under the headings of privacy, accuracy, property, and access (summarized by the acronym PAPA[32]).

Privacy

Information systems can have impacts on two types of privacy, physical privacy and information privacy. **Physical privacy** is the ability of an individual to avoid unwanted intrusions into personal time, space, and property. **Information privacy** is the ability of an individual to determine when, how, and to what extent personal information is communicated to others.

Physical Privacy

Information technologies provide numerous opportunities to intrude on others. Computer-generated phone calls interrupt dinner to invite you to buy things you don't want or to give to a charity you may not support. Your fax machine runs out of paper due to a long, unsolicited fax. You receive junk mail you don't want. You receive electronic junk mail you don't want. (Sending such electronic junk mail is called **spamming** and is a controversial topic on the Internet.) Computer-generated "personalized" letters have no person at the other end. High-decibel speaker systems operate at such high volume that "one loud rock concert can leave patients with permanent tinnitus (ringing in the ears), and legions of frequent concertgoers now suffer high-frequency hearing loss," according to the director of audiology at the University of California at San Francisco.[33]

A variety of state and federal laws and regulations protect physical privacy. For example, the Telephone Consumers Protection Act of 1991 prohibits "any telephone call to any residential telephone line using an artificial or prerecorded voice to deliver a message without the prior express consent of the called party, unless the call is initiated for emergency purposes." This law was disputed in courts by owners of small businesses such as the A-Aa-1-Lucky Leprechaun chimney sweeping company in Keizer, Oregon. It had purchased a $1,800 system that dials telephone numbers, delivers a recorded sales pitch, and lets potential customers leave messages. Such calls are an intrusion for many households, but the business owners maintained this type of system is the key to their survival. In 1993 a court granted a preliminary injunction preventing the Federal Communications Commission from enforcing the 1991 ban. The judge wrote that the law might not make much of a dent in the volume of unsolicited telemarketing calls, and it could wipe out Lucky Leprechaun.[34]

The optional caller ID feature in current telephone systems raises many questions about physical and information privacy. Phones with **caller ID** display the caller's telephone number on a special unit attached to a telephone. This feature is useful for telemarketing and customer service because the caller's telephone number can trigger the retrieval of account information such as the latest bill and outstanding balance. Use of caller ID may also reduce nuisance calls because the person receiving the call will know the source. Caller ID is controversial because it raises questions about who should be favored, the caller or the person called. The person called would like to eliminate some telephone calls or respond more appropriately to others. But a caller with an unlisted telephone doesn't want that number exposed unnecessarily, and a person who anonymously calls a business to get price information doesn't want to automatically become part of that business's mailing list. In 1992 a Pennsylvania court ruled that caller ID was a form of illegal wiretapping.[35] At the same time, many other states permitted it subject to various limitations and caller options.

Pacific Bell offers a $6.50 per month caller ID option that displays both the caller's phone number and the name in which the phone is registered, regardless of whether the caller's phone number is unlisted (a $0.30 per month option). It also offers a free option of complete or selective "caller ID blocking," which prevents the number and name from being displayed on a caller ID unit. Pacific Bell advises people not to use complete caller ID blocking because these calls will not be accepted by phones with caller ID equipment that contains a feature called "block the blocker." (What would Alexander Graham Bell think about the way his invention developed?) In addition to caller ID, Pacific Bell offers a $3.50 per month "call screening" service that permits a subscriber to identify up to ten phone lines whose incoming calls would automatically be blocked with a message saying that the subscriber will not accept calls from that number. This service provides a way to add an unknown number to the list by dialing a code after receiving a call from that number.

A 1998 *Wall Street Journal* article described a different, less complex approach to the phone intrusion issue. According to a market research survey, around two-thirds of homes have answering machines and around half of these are used to screen calls. Contrary to previous social norms, increasing numbers of people simply don't answer their telephone at all until they know who is calling.[36]

Information Privacy

Most Americans feel that they should not be monitored without consent, that they should not have to divulge personal information, and that personal information they provide should be treated confidentially. Whereas most Americans think of privacy as a right, no specific provision in the United States Constitution guarantees the right to privacy. A century ago, innovations related to "instantaneous photographs" and newspapers led to the first influential article raising issues about privacy.[37] The issue then was right to be free from unwarranted publicity regarding private affairs. Just over 100 years later, concerns about privacy became front-page news when Britain's Princess Diana died after her car crashed while being chased by photographers.

Even with greater awareness of privacy today, concepts about privacy are by no means universal. For example, the idea of privacy was so much less prominent in Japan's traditionally group-oriented culture that a word equivalent to privacy didn't exist in the Japanese language.[38] On the other extreme, Article 18 of Spain's 1978 Constitution codifies a concept of privacy exceeding what one expects from American newspapers and television, especially in regard to public figures. It establishes a right to privacy, saying: "Rights to honor, personal and family privacy, and one's own image are guaranteed....The law shall limit the use of known information for the sake of guaranteeing honor and personal and family privacy of citizens and the full exercise of their rights."[39]

Widespread use of computers and computerized databases makes privacy a much broader issue than in the past. Each of us leaves a trail of computerized data every time we use a credit card, write a check, use medical insurance, or subscribe to a magazine. Data from various sources can be combined to create a very detailed picture of how you live, whom you associate with, what your interests are, and how you handle money.

Credit information firms such as Experian (formerly TRW), Equifax, and Trans Union have credit histories on 190 million Americans. A summary fact sheet about any one of these individuals can be obtained in several seconds by merchants and landlords all over the United States. Many other publicly accessible databases contain information about financial transactions, media preferences, driving records, political affiliations, insurance claims, and much more. For example, for $5 New York state sells a driver's personal data including height and weight, driving record, license revocations, vehicle ownership, and accidents and police reports.[40] These databases are used for many different purposes and are very valuable to people who need to make business decisions such as granting loans, renting apartments, and hiring employees.

There is considerable question about how much and which information about an individual should be available through a computerized information service. It is hard to know what personal information exists in these databases, whether it is correct, or who is actually using that information. It is also not clear what information is held in government databases and whether that information is more or less threatening than information in private databases. Finally, regardless of the true purpose of an information system, there is no way to guarantee the information in the system will be protected from someone intending to use it for an illegal or simply inappropriate purpose. The Web page for one firm in the personal information business advertises the availability of many types of personal information. Prices quoted in a separate letter to private investigators included $80 for long-distance phone records and $400 for ten years of medical treatment history. Some personal data can be pieced together through publicly available sources such as driver data. Investigators obtain other data illegally by misrepresenting themselves. For example, an investigator might call a credit card company with a tale about a wife who left ten days ago with a credit card. The investigator would claim he did not want to report the card stolen, but did want to know whether his wife was generating huge bills. An investigator who had served time in prison for perpetrating this type of fraud said this method of obtaining recent transactions usually worked for him.[41]

To demonstrate how easy it is to obtain private information about individuals, Jeffrey Rothfeder obtained fiscal histories, phone numbers, and consumer preferences of Dan Rather, Arsenio Hall, Dan Quayle, and others. Before publishing this information in his book *Privacy for Sale,* he wrote a letter to Rather, who hit the roof, saying Rothfeder's actions were akin to breaking into his home, stealing his diary, and publishing it. Publication of the book was delayed two months, and Rothfeder said that Rather's angry response reinforced the book's point that privacy really matters.[42]

Many other examples show how trails of computerized data have jeopardized common expectations of privacy. For example, as revenge against a magazine columnist who had written an article critical of computer hackers, a computer hacker broke into a national credit database and posted the columnist's credit card number on a national bulletin board. During the confirmation hearing of Supreme Court nominee Robert Bork, a list of the videotapes that he or his household had rented from a video store was printed in a Washington newspaper. When he rented those videotapes as a private citizen, he probably did not believe that the record of the rentals would become public information. Congress reacted swiftly with the Video Privacy Protection Act of 1988, but this involved only one of many types of transaction data that could be used to breach personal privacy.

Code of Fair Information Practices

Many aspects of physical privacy and information privacy have generated a discussion and debate. The following are five principles proposed within the U.S. Government in 1973 as the beginnings of a Code of Fair Information Practices related primarily to databases.

1. There must be no personal record-keeping systems whose very existence is secret.
2. There must be a way for an individual to find out what information about him or her is on record and how it is being used.
3. There must be a way for an individual to correct or amend a record of identifiable information about him or her.
4. There must be a way for an individual to prevent information about him or her that was obtained for one purpose from being used or made available for other purposes without his or her consent.
5. Any organization creating, maintaining, using, or disseminating records of identifiable personal data must assure the reliability of the data for their intended use and must take reasonable precaution to prevent misuse of the data.

These principles are equally applicable to personal information record-keeping systems in the government and in the private sector. With the collection of data by computerized systems whenever anyone uses a credit card, gets on an airplane, or even rents a video, implementing and enforcing this code would be an enormous undertaking. In many ways governments are no more sensitive to privacy issues than other organizations. For example, 34 states sell driver's license information including name, address, height, weight, age, vision, social security number, and type of car. Buyers include private investigators, who pay a few dollars for an individual lookup, and direct marketers, who receive complete databases to build targeted mailing lists based on personal characteristics.[43] Most people who apply for driver's licenses wouldn't imagine their personal information is made available this way. Nor would most people who submit a change of address card to the U.S. Post Office dream that this information is sold to organizations that use lists of recent movers for targeted marketing.

The availability of the World Wide Web to children has generated a facet of this problem that the Fair Information Practices committee probably didn't anticipate. "As millions of kids go online, marketers are in hot pursuit. Eager to reach an enthusiastic audience more open to pitches than an adult buried in junk mail, companies often entertain tykes online with games and contests. To play, these sites require children to fill out questionnaires about themselves and their families and friends, valuable data to be sorted and stored in marketing databases." For example, the Mars, Inc., site asked kids to search out fake M&M candy by supplying names and e-mail addresses of their friends. A spokesman for Mars said the search was "just part of the fun" and that the company doesn't keep the names or e-mail addresses.[44] Regardless of how the information is used, it is legitimate to ask whether children benefit from being trained to divulge private information in this way.

Reality Check

PRIVACY

This section discussed various aspects of privacy and the way computerized information systems may compromise your privacy. Explain what you think is acceptable in the following questions related to privacy.

1. To what extent should your medical records be available to your boss?
2. To what extent should your financial records such as credit card and car payments be available to anyone who pays for them?
3. To what extent should your conversations at work be monitored by your employer?
4. To what extent should you be able to avoid unwanted intrusions such as phone solicitations during dinner and electronic junk mail?
5. To what extent should there be limits on the types of information others can collect about you without telling you they are doing so?

Accuracy

Chapter 4 introduced the issue of information accuracy and indicated that it involved much more than questions about data errors. Figure 4.16 showed why managers should expect some degree of bias in analysis, proposals, and suggestions. Although some bias exists in any explanation from a personal viewpoint, bias becomes an ethical issue when relevant information is knowingly suppressed or misrepresented. This is a recurring ethical issue throughout business, government, and society. Here are several health-related examples reported in the news within one month.

suppression of information: Executives of Philip Morris admitted before a congressional committee that publication of a company study of the addictiveness of cigarettes had been suppressed.[45]

misrepresentation of information: The Agriculture Department gave the milk industry a dispensation allowing them to use the "low fat" label for milk with 2% fat even though all other products with the same percentage of fat do not qualify.[46]

acceptance of misleading information because it fits the rules: A watchdog agency demonstrated that the "smoking machines" used by the government to identify cigarettes as "low in tar and nicotine" actually "puff" the cigarettes in a way that absorbs much less tar and nicotine than an average smoker would absorb. This discrepancy, which exaggerates the benefits of smoking low-tar cigarettes, was known for years, but no one did anything about it.[47]

One case involves suppression of information while the other two involve varying degrees of misrepresentation. At the heart of all three are a set of ethical issues about accuracy, regardless of whether computerized systems are involved.

Storage of personal data in computerized systems brings an additional dimension to the accuracy issue because of harm that may occur when data in these databases is incorrect. Every year, people come forward with horror stories about not being able to rent an apartment because of a past dispute with an unfair landlord or because a data entry error became a virtually indelible mark against them in a database. A clerical error at the U.S. Treasury Department demonstrates the types of problems that can result from incorrect data. The error deleted the social security number of Edna Rissmiller, a 79-year-old widow. Soon thereafter her pharmacy refused to honor her insurance card and the government recollected a $672 pension check from her bank account. Her son William found it difficult to reestablish that she was alive. Her bank told him that as far as they were concerned, she was dead until he could prove otherwise.[48]

An increasingly important part of the data inaccuracy problem is **credit identity theft,** in which a criminal obtains a victim's social security number and other credit information and then uses the victim's name to commit fraud. Aside from commercial losses suffered by the credit issuers, which may cost several billion dollars per year, this type of theft creates an incorrect credit history for the person whose information is stolen. In one example, a Houston engineer discovered that someone at a Honda dealership in Florida had obtained his Equifax credit report. The identity thief used the engineer's social security number and other information on the Equifax report to obtain 24 fraudulent credit cards. The engineer and his wife tried to set the record straight for more than a year by writing to credit issuers, but their warnings seemed to be ignored. Their credit rating slipped and their bank of 11 years refused to give them a loan for their son's tuition. Eventually they filed a lawsuit against three credit bureaus and the banks that had ignored their pleas. They were offered a settlement to drop the suit and not go after the auto dealership.[49] In a similar story, a woman in Los Angeles sued Trans Union, which had produced an inaccurate credit report when she tried to buy a home. Someone had opened charge accounts in her name at 15 retailers across the country and had not paid the bills. Her lawyers showed that Trans Union had done very little when she tried to get the record corrected. In response, the company claimed it was the retailers' fault for accepting inaccurate credit information in the first place, and that she hadn't done enough to clean up her credit history. The jury found Trans Union had violated the Fair Credit Reporting Act and awarded her $200,000.[50]

Reality Check

ACCURACY

Many computerized databases contain inaccurate information about individuals that may cause them inconvenience and harm.

1. Explain why you do or do not think there should be a legal requirement for accuracy in public databases containing information about individuals. If the requirement existed, what do you think it should be?

2. If you were in charge of a database of financial and medical information about individuals, what do you think you might do to assess the accuracy of the data?

Property

Imagine that you were in a video rental store and saw someone steal a blank videotape. Imagine that the same person rented a videotape of a film and copied it. Both situations involve theft, but the nature of the theft seems different to many people. In the first case, the person stole a physical object. In the second case, the person stole the information recorded on the physical object. Although the information is more valuable than the physical object, many people act as though copying the information is not theft.

As children, we come to understand the concept of property and ownership by recognizing our own bodies, our own clothes, and our own toys. This concept of ownership involves physical things. If someone takes a child's toy, the child no longer has it. If the child has one toy and would like another like it, there is no instantaneous way to duplicate it. The world of computerized information products does not follow these commonsense features of the physical world. Someone can copy a movie, a piece of music, a computer program, or a database without changing it. The original owner still has the original even if a million copies were made, and a million unauthorized copies may be made, as the entertainment and software industries certainly know. By some estimates up to 97% of the software used in Thailand has been copied illegally, compared to as much as 40% in the United States. Estimates of pirated software in Europe range from 80% in Spain to 25% in the United Kingdom.[51]

Outright piracy is a clear case, but the widespread existence of electronic information on different electronic media has many difficult legal and ethical questions related to property rights for information. Databases, music, and video can all be stored, transmitted, and reformatted in a variety of ways. Techniques such as desktop publishing are making it increasingly easy to produce information by modifying other information, thereby leaving issues about rights to intellectual property even blurrier. Legal issues concerning property rights to information arise in many areas, such as the departure of employees to join the competition, the copying and modification of creative work, and the unauthorized "framing" of pictures and other information on the Web. Consider some examples:

departure of employees to join competitor firms: A key employee's departure to join a competitor firm often raises questions about whether intellectual property was taken. When a PepsiCo general manager for California accepted a job with Gatorade, PepsiCo sued, claiming that he was privy to its softdrink marketing plan. The general manager had to wait six months before joining Gatorade and was forbidden to disclose the plan. Similarly, when two employees of the roofing contractor Morlife left to form a new firm in the roof repair business, the court prohibited them from using a collection of business cards that represented much of Morlife's customer base, saying that the customer list was a trade secret.[52]

copying and modification of creative work: Digital sampling is a technology that can be used to record any sound and reproduce it at any pitch, in any combination, and in any tempo. An attorney was hired by the American Federation of Musicians Local 802 to look into the use of a sampled conga drum sound for the "Miami Vice" sound track. David Earl Jones, the drummer whose original sounds had allegedly been transformed into the sound track, had not been paid for this use of some of his best work and wanted compensation.

unauthorized "framing" of material on the Web: One Web site can contain a link to a second Web site, but it shouldn't be able to "frame" information from the second Web site so that it appears to belong to the first site. An important detail of framing is that it is possible to frame just part of a Web page. This makes it possible to display another site's information while cutting off its banner advertising and replacing it with other advertising. The contentiousness of the framing issue was clear when a small company called TotalNews, Inc., built a Web site that links to 1,100 other news sites, mostly through framing. An attorney for the *Washington Post* complained, "It's a completely parasitic Web site." An attorney for TotalNews countered, "They're just paranoid."[53] The *Times of London* went further by notifying a different site called News Index that it violated the paper's copyright by listing *Times* stories in its index and maintaining hypertext links back to stories at the *Times* site. The News Index disputed the charge, saying that the site's indexing, summaries, and links fall within "fair use."[54]

Intellectual property is different from other forms of property and has therefore become a specialty in the legal profession. In general, property is usually defined as an exclusive right to own and dispose of a thing. When the thing is an automobile, the ideas of ownership and disposal are reasonably clear. When it comes to information or knowledge, neither ownership nor disposal is as straightforward as with other forms of property. The preceding examples illustrate this question: Who owns the appearance of a product or the knowledge in the mind of the engineer or the musical sounds produced by the drummer? How would anyone know if the information in these cases were stolen? If a car is stolen and then found, it is usually possible to verify that it is the same car. What about the knowledge or the sounds, especially if they are used in a slightly different context and therefore modified or extended in some way?

Ownership rights for intellectual property have traditionally been protected in the United States by copyright, patent, and trade secret laws. Copyright laws protect the literary expression of an idea, not the idea itself, for the life of the author plus 50 years. Patent laws protect for 17 years inventions or discoveries having distinguishing features that are innovative, useful, and not obvious. Both copyrights and patents require public disclosure of the intellectual property that is being protected. Trade secrets are protected by contracts designed to ensure confidentiality. All of these tools have serious practical shortcomings at a time when new intellectual property products can be developed in months rather than years.

Altogether about 14,000 software patents have been awarded, and several patented information systems were mentioned earlier in this book. These include Merrill Lynch's cash management account (U.S. Patent #4,346,442 dated Aug. 24, 1982) and Mrs. Fields Cookies' staff scheduling system (U.S. Patent #5,111,391, dated May 5, 1992). The latter was titled "system and method for making staff schedules as a function of available resources as well as employee skill level, availability, and priority."[55] Scheduling employees is a common problem in most businesses and is used commonly as an example in operations research textbooks. Even if Mrs. Fields uses a truly unique technique, there are important practical questions about how anyone trying to develop a method for scheduling employees would know about this patent and how Mrs. Fields would enforce it. Although the U.S. Patent and Trademark Office had made it more difficult to patent software-related inventions, a July 29, 1994, ruling by the U.S. Court of Appeals for the Federal Circuit seemed to open the floodgates for new patents. That ruling declared that a general-purpose computer run by software can be patented because the program essentially creates a new machine.

Reality Check

PROPERTY

The special characteristics of information raise a number of issues about property. Explain what you think is acceptable in the following questions related to information as property:

1. To what extent should an engineer be allowed to take any of his or her original work for a company on leaving for another job?
2. To what extent should an executive who moves to another company be prevented from discussing the affairs of the company she left? Is there any practical way of doing this?
3. Under what circumstances should you be allowed to store or copy a magazine article, a book, a computer program, a taped rendition of a song, a football game broadcast on television, a videotaped movie?

Access

A citizen in an information society needs at least three things: intellectual skills to deal with information, access to information technology, and access to information. Although access to information and information technology have exploded in recent decades, the explosion has not been uniform. Some people have much greater access and others have much less, with impacts ranging from power in organizations to employment opportunities and job satisfaction.

Intellectual Skills

Consider the workers in a factory under great competitive pressure to automate using numerically controlled machines. Skilled machinists who may not have much formal education may be doing high-quality work based on 20 years of experience working with the previous generation of tools. To run the new machines, these workers would have to do a form of programming, and they may lack the necessary literacy and abstract reasoning ability.

Access to Information Technology

Access is also important for handicapped workers (see Figure 7.7). Both general purpose and specially adapted technology have helped people with vision, hearing, mobility, or dexterity impairments do a wide range of jobs that might have been difficult or unattainable for them. For example, voice recognition tools make it possible for people who cannot handle a mouse or keyboard to work effectively with computers. While certainly far from perfect,

Figure 7.7
Extending technology to increase access

These photos represent the many ways information technology can be used to aid people who have problems with muscular control, vision, or hearing. (a) Commercially available voice recognition capabilities that reached a new plateau of power in 1998 permit a user to enter data via dictation and to speak commands such as "print" and "copy" instead of typing them or pointing with a mouse. This allows a person with physical limitations to use a computer productively without touching it. (b) The Kurzweil reading machine uses synthesized speech to read texts to people with visual impairments. After working with a Kurzweil music synthesizer, the rock star Stevie Wonder encouraged Ray Kurzweil to build a reading machine. Years later, Stevie Wonder stayed up all night listening when he received the first release of the product. (c) This photo shows Stephen Hawking, one of the world's greatest physicists, whose use of a special data entry device and a voice synthesizer helps him participate in scientific research despite suffering from an advanced case of ALS, "Lou Gehrig's disease," which causes muscular degeneration.

(a)

(b)

(c)

voice recognition can also help people with hearing problems by capturing spoken words and converting them into text.

Cost-effective technologies that compensate for visual limitations include screen magnification, Braille printers, optical character recognition, speech recognition, and high-speed voice synthesizers. Although these new technologies have increased access for the visually handicapped, the graphical interfaces used in current software is a step backward for blind people. The problem is that the use of icons and mouse clicks relies on vision much more heavily than the use of text-based screen displays, which can be read aloud using a voice synthesizer. The release of GUI-based Windows 95 became a serious vocational threat to blind and visually impaired computer users. Microsoft responded by providing the "Active Accessibility" feature in Windows 95, which lets an automatic screen reader ask the operating system for descriptive information on the screen. Given the visual complexity of GUIs, there is still a long way to go in making current interfaces accessible.[56]

Access to Information

Ethical issues related to information access cut in many directions. Because people need information to participate in economic life, the extensive use of computerized information sources such as the Web raise questions about whether technical progress will divide the haves and have-nots in society even further. Coming from a totally different direction, the existence of pornography on the Web raises questions about whether and how information access should be restricted or controlled. A final question concerns the kind of access individuals should have to information about themselves. The three main credit bureaus will sell an individual his or her own credit report. Why shouldn't people have guaranteed, immediate, free access to information about themselves that resides in commercial databases, such as credit history databases and medical databases? The nature of the ethical issues we have discussed is that there are no easy answers, while at the same time it is very important to recognize the questions.

Reality Check

ACCESS

This section explained that access to information and information technology is an ethical issue in an information age. Explain the degree to which you agree with the following.

1. Businesses should not build internal systems that might exclude potential participants due to deficits in mobility, vision, or hearing.
2. Universities should not use educational materials that might exclude potential participants due to deficits in mobility, vision, or hearing or due to lack of access to technology such as personal computers and networks.

BALANCING POSITIVE AND NEGATIVE IMPACTS

Many readers probably came to this book thinking that technology was the main topic when one thinks about information systems. The WCA framework introduced in Chapter 2 emphasized that people play key roles as participants and customers. This chapter goes further by showing that information systems have impacts on people and raise human issues and ethical dilemmas.

As in many business situations, decisions about information systems often involve conflicts between positive impacts in some areas and negative impacts in others. Table 7.7 shows how many of the systems mentioned in this chapter had impacts of both types. You and your business colleagues may well decide that a system is appropriate, even if it will have negative impacts on some people. This issue should be understood and dealt with rather than ignored.

TABLE 7.7 Positive and Negative Impacts of Innovations Mentioned in This Chapter

Innovation	Positive impacts	Negative impacts
National database of new hires	Helps track down parents who fail to pay child support	Jeopardizes privacy of millions of workers who have no child support obligations
Software that monitors use of corporate networks	Identifies people who spend too much time playing games; identifies best users of particular software	Promotes feeling that Big Brother is always watching
Computerized systems for monitoring truck usage	Increased efficiency through better use of equipment and time	Reduced feeling of autonomy; feeling of being spied on and distrusted
Computerized systems for insurance underwriting	Better service to customers; shorter training time; better work conditions	De-skilling of experienced underwriters
Use of auto pilots in airplanes	Greater safety and consistency in many situations	Mental disengagement of pilots; de-skilling
Data processing automation of insurance claims	Greater productivity in claim processing	Decreased social interaction at work; feelings of alienation
Auditing through a computer system	Less need to travel to branches because the computer provides information	Increasing abstractness of work; difficulty relating numbers to reality
Highly structured work in fast food restaurants	Making it likely that somewhat unskilled workers will produce consistent results	Feeling that the work requires participants to act like machines
Development of national credit-rating services	Better information for decisions related to granting credit, renting apartments, and hiring employees	Possibility of incorrect decisions based on incorrect information in the database; possibility that information will be retrieved and used illegally
Use of profiling in insurance sales	Creates a better understanding of client needs; informs client about need for disability insurance	Makes the sales process lengthier and more complex
Proliferation of electronic information on various media	Ability to disseminate and use that information more effectively	New opportunities to steal that information and use it illegally

The examples in this chapter concerning negative impacts on people inside or outside an organization should also remind you to be skeptical in evaluating claims about the success and benefits of a system. A new system that ostensibly improves quality or responsiveness perceived by business process customers may nonetheless have negative impacts on job satisfaction, loyalty, and length of service of people within the organization. It may also raise ethical concerns related to privacy, accuracy, property, or access. Decisions about information systems clearly involve many factors other than technology.

CHAPTER CONCLUSION

Summary

What kinds of dilemmas do the impacts of information systems on people pose? Information systems can have positive or negative effects on people inside and outside of the organization. Positive impacts involve empowering people to do their work well by making work more enjoyable and by helping people grow professionally. Negative impacts involve eliminating jobs, de-skilling jobs, making jobs less satisfying, creating greater job stress, or reducing personal privacy.

What is the difference between machine-centered design and human-centered design?
In machine-centered design, the technology or process is designed to simplify what the machine must do, and people are expected to adjust to the machine's weaknesses and limitations. In human-centered design, the technology or business process is designed to make participants' work as effective and satisfying as possible.

What are the characteristics of healthy work, and how do information systems affect these characteristics?
People in healthy jobs use their skills in meaningful work, enjoy autonomy and social relations with others, have personal rights including some control over the demands of the job, and have enough time and energy to participate in family and community life. Especially unhealthy jobs are those with continual pressure to perform but little personal control. Information systems can provide tools and information that make jobs healthy, or they can contribute to work patterns and control methods that make work unhealthy.

How is computer-mediated work different from other types of work?
Computer-mediated work is work done through computers. This kind of work is more abstract than most other types of work because it does not involve direct physical contact with the object of the task. At least part of a worker's reality is of symbols on a computer screen rather than the more tangible physical world.

What are the different ways to explain resistance to change?
Resistance to change is any action or inaction that obstructs a change process. Resistance comes from a combination of motives. It can be a highly rational response motivated by a desire to help the organization, or it can have selfish or vindictive motives. Resistance to change can be explained as determined by people, determined by the system, or determined by interactions between the people and the system.

What are ethical theories, and how are they related to information systems?
Ethics is a branch of philosophy dealing with principles of right and wrong behavior related to other people. Ethics is related to information and systems because of the many ways one's actions in this area can affect others. Ethical theories are principles that can be used as the basis for deciding what to do in ethical dilemmas. Stated simply, three ethical theories related to information systems are: maximize the overall good, maximize personal good, and treat others well.

What are the major ethical issues related to information systems?
The major ethical issues related to information systems can be broken down under the topics of privacy, accuracy, property, and access. Privacy falls into two categories, physical privacy and information privacy. Issues related to accuracy involve incorrect conclusions drawn from incorrect data. Issues related to property start with the ease of copying data on electronic media and include the inability of existing laws to protect intellectual property. Issues related to access include access to information and access to technology.

Key Terms

machine-centered design
human-centered design
operator error
user friendly
user hostile
anthropomorphize
information overload
ergonomics
repetitive strain injury (RSI)
autonomy
power
de-skilling
task variety
task scope
computer-mediated work
abstractness of work
social inertia
user involvement
resistance to change
ethics
ethical dilemmas
ethical theories
physical privacy
information privacy
spamming
caller ID
credit identity theft

Review Questions

1. What is the difference between machine-centered design and human-centered design?
2. Compare the strengths and weaknesses of people versus machines.
3. What characteristics make computerized systems user friendly or user hostile?
4. What are the characteristics of a healthy job, and how are information systems related to these characteristics?
5. What characteristics of work determine whether people who use VDTs find their work stressful?
6. How can information systems affect a person's autonomy?
7. What is de-skilling? Explain whether information systems necessarily lead to de-skilling of their users.
8. What are some of the impacts of information systems on the meaningfulness of work?
9. Explain why user involvement in system development is related to implementation success.
10. What are the different forms of resistance to systems?
11. What is the difference between ethical issues and legal issues?
12. Compare three common ethical theories.
13. What is the difference between physical privacy and information privacy?
14. What are some of the issues related to the storage of personal information in databases?
15. Why would it be difficult to enforce a national code of fair information practices?
16. Why is the accuracy of information in publicly available databases an important problem?
17. How is intellectual property different from other types of property in terms of the ethical issues it raises?
18. In what ways is access an ethical issue?

Discussion Topics

1. Recognizing that two-thirds of all trucking accidents are caused by fatigue, alcohol, and drugs, the Federal Highway Administration funded Evaluation Systems, Inc., to develop a computerized driver-monitor system. At a set time, the driver pulls off the road and takes a simulated driving test that gives the driver orders such as turn left or turn on the lights. The results are transmitted via satellite to a central computer that compares them to the driver's baseline results. If the driver fails, a retest is given. If the driver fails again, the computer orders a rest and can prevent the truck from restarting until the driver passes the test.[57] Identify any human and ethical issues in this situation. Explain whether you do or do not believe this system should be used.
2. When Dr. Donald Miller closed his Taylors, South Carolina, family practice in 1991, he auctioned off the patient records for his 10,000 patients to the highest bidder, an auto junk dealer who paid $4,000. The dealer sold photocopies to some former patients for $25 each and eventually resold the records for $6,000 to a new doctor who moved into town.[58] Explain why ethical, economic, and practical considerations should or shouldn't have called for different actions.
3. A Georgia furniture store targeted residents of upscale neighborhoods in Atlanta suburbs with offers of free credit and a 25% discount on initial purchases but did not offer the same rates to residents of less prosperous adjoining suburbs.[59] Explain why this use of database marketing does or does not raise ethical issues. Would your answer be different if you knew that the targeted neighborhoods were primarily white and the nontargeted neighborhoods were primarily black?
4. Legal scholars Arthur Miller and Alan Westin have suggested that information privacy problems could be solved by giving individuals property rights in all personal information about themselves.[60] They, and not the credit bureaus, private firms, and government organizations, would own all information related to themselves. Identify legal, ethical, and practical issues that this approach raises.
5. The chapter emphasized the abstractness of computer-mediated work. Have you ever noticed this either in work or in play, such as when using a video game? If so, has it made your activity either more or less enjoyable, and in what ways?

CASE

Visionics: Applying Facial Recognition Software in Driver Registration

On April 15, 1998, Polaroid Corporation signed an agreement with Visionics Corporation to integrate Visionics' FaceIt facial recognition software into Polaroid's secure identification products for Departments of Motor Vehicles (DMVs). Integrating facial recognition software into the processing of driver's license applications should help combat identity fraud by making it extremely difficult for anyone to obtain multiple driver's licenses under assumed names.

Polaroid's press release stated that "computerized facial recognition works from a standard DMV photograph and does not require the collection of any additional information, making it convenient and non-invasive for the applicant. FaceIt extracts a "face print" from the photograph, similar to a fingerprint, which is unique to the individual. This print is resistant to changes in lighting, skin tone, eyeglasses, facial expression and hairstyle. When a new license application is submitted, the face print extracted from the digital photograph will be used to search the DMV database of millions of faces for potential duplication. The speed of the FaceIt search engine makes it possible to process thousands of images in less time than it would take a DMV agent to scroll through and verify an individual's address or the spelling of their name in a computerized driver license record."

According to the FaceIt Web site, the product utilizes a mathematical technique called local feature analysis that "represents faces in terms of statistically derived features from specific regions of the face. These features are used as building blocks that make it possible to quickly map an individual's identity to a complex mathematical formula." Using this type of transformation for a new photo and for every picture in a photo database makes it possible to quickly display the closest matches in order of similarity. The program can even recognize faces at angles of up to 35 degrees.

A number of other current or potential applications of facial recognition are mentioned on the FaceIt Web site. One of these is access control for PCs. A computer equipped with a video camera can lock a PC after a period of inactivity and start it again only after the user looks at the camera and is recognized by the software. The mathematical representation of the user's face can even be used as part of the key for encrypting information stored by the computer. Face recognition could be used in a similar way to control access to ATMs, thereby reducing the chances that stolen cards can be used or even eliminating the need for the cards. In time and attendance applications, facial recognition can make it unnecessary for employees to punch in and punch out. In a video surveillance application, a version of FaceIt can search live video of a crowd to find faces of individuals on a watch list. This might be used in an airport to identify known terrorists or in a department store to identify previously convicted shoplifters within minutes of their arrival. It might also be used to identify missing children.

QUESTIONS

1. The chapter emphasized that technology often has positive and negative effects. Identify some of the negative effects of this technology or explain why its effects are all positive.
2. Explain why you do or do not believe it may be necessary to create laws related to the proper use of this technology and the information it generates.

Sources:

Polaroid Corporation. "Polaroid and Visionics Team Up to Provide Facial Recognition Solutions for Departments of Motor Vehicles." Press release, Boston, April 15, 1998, May 12, 1998 (www.faceit.com/pr/polaroid.htm).

Visionics Corporation. "FaceIt: Computers Can Now Recognize Faces," May 12, 1998 (www.faceit.com).

The White House: Electronic Privacy Initiative

On May 14, 1998, Vice President Albert Gore announced a new Clinton Administration privacy action plan designed to give people more control over their own personal information. "We need an electronic bill of rights for this electronic age," the Vice President said. "Americans should have the right to choose whether their personal information is disclosed; they should have the right to know how, when, and how much of that information is being used; and they should have the right to see it themselves, to know if it's accurate."

In the area of medical privacy, Gore called on Congress to pass strict medical records legislation to restrict how and when an individual's medical records can be used, give each individual the chance to correct those records, and give patients the right to be informed about them.

In the area of commercial access to personal data, Gore announced a new "opt-out" Web site sponsored by the Federal Trade Commission and located at www.consumer.gov. This Web site will enable individuals to do three things: (1) prohibit companies from pre-screening their credit records without their permission, (2) prevent their drivers license data from being sold to data miners, and (3) remove their name and address from direct-mailing and telemarketing lists.

Gore also called on the federal government to review its own record-keeping to prevent personal information from being released. He also announced that the Administration will convene a "privacy summit" that will bring privacy and consumer advocates together with industry officials to explore privacy on the Internet as well as children's privacy.

The www.consumer.gov web site already existed at the time of the proposal. In addition to providing a wide range of information related to health issues, product safety, personal finance, and other topics, it provided a way to contact the Direct Marketing Association (DMA) to opt-out of direct mail marketing and telemarketing from many national companies. The DMA page provided a form that any consumer could fill out in order to register for its "mail preference service," a list provided to direct marketers and telemarketers for the sole purpose of removing a consumer's name and address from their mailing lists for five years. Filling out this form would reduce the number of solicitations an individual receives from national marketers of credit cards, sweepstakes, magazine subscriptions, and catalogs. It would not affect junk mail from local businesses and from organizations that do not use the DMA service.

QUESTIONS

1. Assume the U.S. government decided to adopt the proposed policies. Suggest systems that might be used to enforce the policies in each area.
2. Identify both positive and negative consequences of the policies and the systems you suggested in the first question.

Source:

Office of the Vice President. "Vice President Gore Announces New Comprehensive Privacy Action Plan for the 21st Century, press release, May 14, 1998, May 15 1998 (www.epic.org/privacy/laws/gore_release_5_14_98.html).

8

Computer Hardware

Study Questions

- What are the basic components of a computer system?
- What are the different types of computers?
- What are the organizational approaches to computing?
- How is client-server computing different from centralized computing?
- How is it possible for computers to process data of any type?
- What are the different approaches for increasing data manipulation speeds?
- What are the different forms of data input?
- What are the different forms of data storage?
- What are the different forms of data output?

Outline

Opening Case

MASSACHUSETTS GENERAL HOSPITAL: PILOT PROJECT ON VOICE RECOGNITION FOR RADIOLOGY REPORTS

Voice recognition has traditionally been one of the great challenges of computer science. Unlike inputs from a keyboard, spoken inputs are ambiguous because different people have different accents and speech patterns, because the words often arrive along with background noise interspersed with the speaker's "ahhs" and "umms," and because many words are homonyms, such as *to*, *too*, and *two*, or *read* and *red*. The first widespread commercial applications of voice recognition involved simple tasks, such as differentiating between the responses *one*, *two*, or *three* in a telephone-based customer service system. The first applications with a large vocabulary focused on work with a predictable vocabulary, such as dictating medical reports in particular medical specialties. These applications were speaker dependent; acceptable accuracy required the speaker to "enroll" his or her voice by speaking a specific set of words into a microphone. The speaker could not slur words together or speak rapidly. Instead, the speaker had to use "discrete speech" by pronouncing each word carefully and separately. Applications of this type developed by Dragon Systems and Kurzweil Artificial Intelligence had better than 95% accuracy. By 1997, Dragon, Kurzweil (acquired by Lernout & Hauspie), and IBM were all selling dictation programs that supported a general vocabulary.

Radiologists at Massachusetts General Hospital and Sloan Kettering Cancer Center participated in pilot studies of IBM's MedSpeak, a real time, continuous speech system for dictating radiology reports. (See Table 8.1.) The process for "reading" x-rays, CAT scans, and MRIs and producing the related medical reports is extremely time sensitive because radiologists are often paid by the report. In the traditional process, the radiologist looks at the films and dictates the report into a microphone at a typical rate of around 100 words per minute. Later, trained medical transcriptionists type the reports, sometimes making educated guesses at the meaning of unclear utterances, and sometimes making obvious corrections. The radiologist must check and sign the report, but in many cases may not see it until the next day, and may have seen 100 additional cases in the interim. With MedSpeak, the radiologist dictates the report into a microphone, and the words appear on the screen virtually as they are spoken. The radiologist can review the report, correct it, and sign it immediately without forgetting the details. Radiologists can also trigger repetitive sections of a report using a single phrase. In the pilot study the average time to dictate a report was 81 seconds with the traditional method and 109 seconds with MedSpeak after using it for five or more hours. Following the dictation, more corrections by the radiologist were required with MedSpeak because the medical transcriptionists could correct some errors themselves.

MedSpeak uses a 25,000-word, domain-specific vocabulary, plus probabilities that the words will appear in a particular order. Its recognizer function uses these probabilities to produce the most likely guess when ambiguities occur. Because the program is designed for native speakers, radiologists with heavy accents need to enroll their voices by using speaker-adaptive functions in MedSpeak. Although MedSpeak delivered continuous, accurate, speaker independent, real time decoding, many radiologists were reluctant to embrace the new system. Some of the reasons involved issues about speech processing, such as variability in accuracy and difficulty remembering commands to the program. Other reasons included general satisfaction with the existing process, aversion to computers, and reluctance to change the radiologist's role.[1] In a 120-word demonstration for a reporter, MedSpeak correctly captured terms such as mediastinal contour and pneumothorax and only made one mistake, writing "of which" rather than "for which." When someone else recited "Mary had a little lamb, her fleece was white," the program recorded: "Very heavily laminectomies with widest."[2]

Debate Topic

Even though current MedSpeak users can type their corrections using keyboards, the advances leading to MedSpeak demonstrate that keyboards will become a relic, much like the punched cards that were once used for data storage.

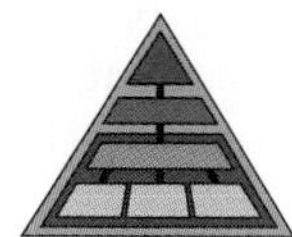

TABLE 8.1 Using Voice Recognition in Radiology

CUSTOMER
- Other doctors
- Patients
- Insurance companies

PRODUCT
- Medical records generated without lengthy delays and unnecessary reviews
- Greater standardization of medical records

BUSINESS PROCESS

Major steps before using MedSpeak:
- "Enroll" the user's voice if necessary

Major steps when using MedSpeak:
- Dictate the medical report
- Review the report and correct errors

Rationale:
- Use voice recognition to create text records immediately, and eliminate unnecessary typing and delays.

PARTICIPANTS	INFORMATION	TECHNOLOGY
• Doctors	• X-ray, CAT scan, or MRI image being viewed • Medical report interpreting the image	• Noise-cancelling microphone • Computer for interpreting the voice data • Keyboard for entering corrections

"Any sufficiently advanced technology is indistinguishable from magic."[3] This opening case is an example of why this famous quote from Arthur Clark applies to IT. Early computers seemed somewhat magical even though they required totally unambiguous inputs using punched cards or tapes. Current computer systems are starting to be able to decipher speech and handwriting. Voice recognition methods also illustrate that the distinction between hardware and software is becoming blurrier all the time. Doctors using MedSpeak see it as a machine (hardware), yet the greatest challenge in building the system was in writing the programs (software) for recognizing speech.

Computer systems are changing in many other directions simultaneously. At one time, the computer was a centralized piece of equipment that could operate only if run by highly skilled technicians. Today, millions of people use personal computers (PCs) routinely. Furthermore, with computer functions becoming distributed across networks, computer users in many firms may not know or even care about the physical location of the computer. New ways of thinking about computers are required as the traditional definitions of different types of computers become less meaningful.

Although business professionals do not have to be technology experts, they should have enough familiarity with basic concepts and terminology to participate effectively in discussions of technology investments that support work system operations. The overview of IT in this and the next two chapters includes computers and computer systems, programming, software and artificial intelligence, and telecommunications and networks. (Chapter 4 on Information and Databases covered DBMS.) These chapters do not explain the internal workings of technology in enough detail to make the feeling of magic disappear, but they do prresent ideas for thinking about functions performed by IT.

This chapter begins by identifying performance concepts that business professionals can apply when thinking about any type of technology. Its overview of computers and computer systems starts with a discussion of the different types of computers and computer systems. It looks inside the black box to describe how information is coded for a computer and how semiconductor devices form the internal basis of computers. The remainder of the chapter discusses computer system components for capturing, storing and retrieving, and displaying data. Throughout, the chapter refers to user and management concerns wherever these concerns are intertwined with the computer system topics.

PERFORMANCE OF INFORMATION TECHNOLOGY

Although all of the WCA perspectives are mentioned in this chapter, the coverage of IT in this and the next two chapters emphasizes architectural issues, such as different types of devices and how they operate together. We start with the performance perspective, because the continual announcements about ever greater computer and telecommunications capabilities often lead to questions about how to evaluate the significance of new technology investments.

Performance Variables for IT

Table 2.5 in Chapter 2 implied that technology performance could be summarized in terms of just four performance variables: functional capabilities and limitations, ease of use, compatibility, and maintainability. Table 8.2 shows that each of these four performance variables for IT is tied to a set of more specific performance variables. Notice that some of the terms used for IT performance are also used at other times for process or product performance. Also notice that Table 2.5 treated security as a performance variable for the process rather than the technology even though it is sometimes directly related to a technology issue.

Functional Capabilities

Functional capabilities of a particular type of information technology identify the types of processing it is supposed to perform and the degree of capability it has. Functional capabilities are often measured as capacity or speed, using terms such as number of instructions executed per second, amount of data that can be stored, and rate of data transfer. Another aspect of technology performance is reliability, the likelihood that the technology will continue operating without errors or unplanned interruptions. A final aspect of functional capabilities is operating conditions, which include issues such as how much something weighs, how much space it takes, and how much electricity it uses. While these questions may not seem to be technological issues, they often determine whether a particular technology, such as the laptop computer, is effective in a particular situation.

Because the productivity of a business process depends partially on the cost of the technology and other resources it uses, it is always important to think of performance in terms of **price-performance,** the relationship between the price of technology and the performance it provides. (The more general term is cost-effectiveness, the relationship between what something costs and how much it accomplishes.) For example, competition among personal computer manufacturers throughout the 1990s generated major improvements in both performance and price-performance. Computers became faster and more powerful (performance) at the same time that the price for any given level of processing power plummeted (price-performance). Similar improvements have occurred in all areas of computing for four decades.

Ease of Use

Although **ease of use** is often associated with the user interface, Chapter 7 explained why it is actually a broader idea including ease of learning how to use the technology, ease of setting it up, ease of becoming proficient, and ease of using it directly. Everyday experience with audio equipment such as a Walkman shows that features that contribute to ease of use include size, portability, user interface, and compatibility with technology standards such as the dimensions of the tape cassette. These same aspects of ease of use apply for business technology such as telephones and computers.

TABLE 8.2 Performance Variables for IT

Group of performance variables	Typical issue raised when using this term to describe a particular technology
Functional capabilities and limitations	*What types of processing is the technology supposed to perform and what capabilities does it have?*
• Capacity	How much information can it store or process?
• Speed	How fast can it process data or instructions?
• Price-performance	How many dollars does it cost per amount of information stored or for a given calculation speed?
• Reliability	How long will it likely continue operating without errors or unplanned interruptions?
• Operating conditions	How much space does it take up? How much does it weigh? What temperature does it require? How much electricity does it use?
Ease of use	*How easy is it to use this technology?*
• Quality of user interface	How intuitive and easy to learn is the method for instructing the technology to perform its task?
• Ease of becoming proficient	How much effort is required to become proficient in using the technology?
• Portability	How easy is it for the user to move the technology in the course of doing work?
Compatibility	*How easy is it to get this technology to work with other complementary technologies?*
• Conformance to standards	To what extent does the technology conform to accepted industry standards?
• Interoperability	To what extent does the technology use the same internal coding and external interfaces as other technology it must operate with or substitute for?
Maintainability	*How easy is it to keep the technology operating over time?*
• Modularity	Is it divided into modules that can be snapped together when building systems? Can these modules be replaced by equivalent modules if necessary?
• Scalability	Is it possible to significantly increase or decrease capacity without major disruptions?
• Flexibility	Is it possible to change important aspects of system operation without major disruptions?

Compatibility

Compatibility is important because most information technology is genuinely useful only in combination with other information technology. **Compatibility** is the extent to which the characteristics and features of a particular technology fit with those of other aspects of the situation. You understand the importance of compatibility and conformance to standards if you have ever wanted to plug an American hair dryer into a typical wall socket in Europe or Asia. The plug's shape is not compatible with the outlet's shape, and the hair dryer won't operate unless you have a special adapter. IT compatibility issues range from "technical" details, such as internal machine languages and data coding methods, to mundane issues such as the size of paper in copy machines and the shape of plugs.

Compatibility issues arise at several different levels. At one level, maintenance of two devices or programs is simpler if both of them operate according to the same standards even if they do not have to work together. At another level, the question is whether the two devices or programs can be used together, even if they use different brands of hardware or are written using different computer languages. This type of compatibility is called **interoperability.** An essential feature of Internet technology is the way it applies standards to permit convenient usage through a wide variety of otherwise incompatible computers and networks.

Maintainability

Maintainability is the ease with which users or technical specialists can keep the technology running and upgrade it to suit the changing needs of the situation. It is easier to maintain technology if the components are designed for modularity, separation into a set of components that can be developed, tested, and understood independently and then plugged into other related components to create a system or device. Dividing systems into modules makes them easier to build and understand because solving many small problems is usually easier than solving one big problem. The modules work together based on the way the outputs of one become the inputs of others. Scalability, the ability to significantly increase or decrease capacity without major disruptions, is another important aspect of maintainability because upgrading capacity beyond certain limits often requires a complete change in the technology. For example it is possible to hitch a trailer behind most cars, but if the trailer is too big, the car can't drive safely and it is necessary to switch to a truck.

Bits and Bytes: Technical Terms for Describing and Measuring Technology Operation

An unavoidable part of the basic vocabulary for discussing computers and peripherals is the units of measure used to describe amounts of data and rates of processing. These terms involve things such as the amount of information (number of bits and bytes), time (milliseconds and microseconds), speed of processing (MIPS, FLOPS, bits per second), and frequencies. Familiarity with these technical terms is useful because people use them to talk about computer and telecommunications devices just as they talk about cars using number of passengers, gas tank capacity, number of cylinders, miles per hour, and miles per gallon.

Measuring Amounts of Data

A key characteristic of any computer is how much data it must store and process. Amounts of data are described using the terms *bit, byte, kilobyte, megabyte, gigabyte,* and *terabyte*. A **bit** is a binary digit, namely, a 0 or 1. This chapter will show how any number, letter, or even picture or sound can be represented as a set of bits. A **byte** is 8 bits, whose 256 different possible combinations are sufficient to represent 256 different characters, including all ten digits (0, 1, 2, 3, ...), all 26 uppercase and 26 lowercase letters (a, b, c, ...), and all the common special characters (:,;,@,#,$, ...). The storage of computers is described in kilobytes, megabytes, gigabytes, and terabytes.

kilobyte (KB)	approximately 10^3 (one thousand) bytes
megabyte (MB)	approximately 10^6 (one million) bytes
gigabyte (GB)	approximately 10^9 (one billion) bytes
terabyte (TB)	approximately 10^{12} (one trillion) bytes

The term *kilobyte* is slightly inaccurate because it usually refers to 2^{10} bytes, which is actually 1,024 bytes. Similarly, megabyte is really 2^{20} bytes or 1,048,576 bytes, and the same pattern applies for gigabyte and terabyte. The random access memory (RAM) in the first PCs was stated in kilobytes, such as 16 KB or 64 KB. Now it is measured in megabytes, such as 16 MB or 32 MB. Typical computer diskettes can store 1.4 MB. Typical capacities for hard disks in early personal computers were 10 MB and 40 MB. Hard disk capacities in today's inexpensive personal computers exceed 1 GB.

Measuring Time

Because computers operate at speeds that are difficult to imagine, the typical time units for discussing their operation are fractions of seconds.

millisecond	10^{-3} (one thousandth of a) second
microsecond	10^{-6} (one millionth of a) second
nanosecond	10^{-9} (one billionth of a) second
picosecond	10^{-12} (one trillionth of a) second

Hard disks for PCs can access data in 12 milliseconds. Computers can execute machine language instructions in fractions of a microsecond. The switching speed of a semiconductor circuit is around 200 picoseconds, although switching speeds of 2 picoseconds have been produced in research labs.

Measuring the Rate of Data Transfer

Data transmission is measured in **bits per second (bps),** or thousands or millions of bits per second (kbps or mbps). The speed of data transfer over telephone lines and fiber optics depends partly on the medium and partly on the speed of the devices that encode and decode the message. Typical modems on PCs operate at 28.8 or 56 kpbs, although cable modems can operate at 1.5 mbps. Data travel over fiber optic cable at 100 mbps or more. The engineering term *baud* is sometimes used instead of bits per second. Baud refers to the rate of signal changes per second. If a device can send only off-on signals, its bits per second rate equals its baud rate. Higher speed devices that transmit individual signals with gradations finer than just 0 versus 1 can send messages whose bits per second rate is higher than their baud rate.

Measuring Internal Clock Speed and Transmission Frequency

Hertz is a measure of frequency. The internal clocks in most personal computers operate from 100 to 300 MHz. Data transmissions are broadcast at different frequencies. For example, AM radio is broadcast in the range around 1 MHz, FM radio is around 100 MHz, and satellite transmissions are around 10 GHz. Although clock speed is strongly related to computer speed, many other factors such as the computer's internal machine language affect a computer's data processing speed.

Hertz (Hz)	1 cycle per second
kilohertz (KHz)	10^3 cycles per second
megahertz (MHz)	10^6 cycles per second
gigahertz (GHz)	10^9 cycles per second

Measuring the Speed of Executing Instructions

The terms *MIPS, FLOPS, megaflops,* and *gigaflops* are used to describe the speed of executing instructions. **MIPS** is an abbreviation for one *m*illion *i*nstructions *p*er *s*econd. It is typically used in a context such as, "This microprocessor can operate at 50 MIPS." The term **FLOPS** stands for *fl*oating point *o*perations *p*er *s*econd. Floating point operations are the addition, subtraction, multiplication, and division of decimal numbers. FLOPS are a better measure than MIPS for talking about the computing power of computers used to do complex scientific calculations. Millions, billions, and trillions of FLOPS are called megaflops, gigaflops, and teraflops, respectively.

Although they are indicators of a computer's speed, MIPS and FLOPS tell only part of the story because the effective speed of a computer system also depends on other factors, such as internal data transfer speed and disk speed. Different types of computers also accomplish different amounts of work while operating at the same speed because they use different internal computer languages and process data in different sized chunks.

Technology Performance from a Business Viewpoint

Business professionals not directly involved with the IT industry often find the onslaught of product announcements and technical jargon overwhelming. What are they to make of all these announcements and all the new technical terminology? For example, how should they decide whether they really want client-server computing, object-oriented programming, or ISDN telephone systems?

From a business professional's viewpoint, it is important to separate two issues: (1) What does the organization want to accomplish? (2) What combination of currently available hardware and software provides the necessary capabilities, and at what cost? A given technological advance may support business capabilities that would otherwise be impractical or impossible. Alternatively, an advance may simply reduce costs compared to other methods for performing similar functions. Another possibility is that the more advanced technology will have no effect whatsoever because another part of the system is the limiting factor in overall performance. For example, assume that an inadequate rate of printed output has raised the question of whether to buy a faster computer. This may help if the current computer's speed limits the speed of printing, but if the limiting factor is actually the printer's speed, a faster computer probably won't help. Even when marveling at the incredible technical progress that has occurred, it is always worthwhile to remember that technology is just one part of a larger work system that also includes business processes, information, and human participants.

Reality Check

PERFORMANCE VARIABLES FOR INFORMATION TECHNOLOGY

The text cites a number of performance variables related to functional capabilities, ease of use, compatibility, and maintainability.

1. Explain how each of these performance variables does or does not apply to information technology you are familiar with, such as a personal computer or a home audio system.
2. Identify which of these performance variables seemed important the last time you or someone you know made a purchase related to using this technology.

OVERVIEW OF COMPUTER SYSTEMS

A **computer** is a device that can execute previously stored instructions. Because the instructions for performing a particular task are called a **program,** computers are programmable devices. A **computer system** consists of computers and computer-controlled devices that process data by executing programs. The physical devices in a computer system are its **hardware.** The programs are its **software.** Everything computer systems do can be boiled down to six functions: capturing, transmitting, storing, retrieving, manipulating, and displaying data. In Chapter 1, Table 1.2 defined each of these functions and showed some of the devices or technologies used to perform each of them. Later in this chapter we will look in more detail at devices for capturing, storing, retrieving, and displaying information. Chapter 10 on Networks and Telecommunications will discuss data transmission.

Basic Model of a Computer System

In the late 1940s, John von Neumann and his colleagues published a description of the internal architecture of an idealized electronic computer. Most computers from that time until today are based on extensions of this architecture, which involves a unit that performs calculations, a unit that controls the sequence of operations, a memory that holds data and programs, and input and output units. The earliest computers used vacuum tubes to store information. The engine that would eventually drive today's computers was unknown to von Neumann and his colleagues. Its basic component, a zero-one semiconductor switch called a transistor, was first invented at Bell Labs in 1948. Further breakthroughs such as the ability to embed an entire circuit on a chip and the first microprocessors did not arrive until 1958 and 1971, respectively.

In today's computers, one or more microprocessor chips made of silicon decode and execute programs, thereby serving as the computer's **central processing unit (CPU).** Microprocessors are linked to another type of silicon chip, **random access memory (RAM),** which stores instructions and data the microprocessor is currently using. The term random access implies that the microprocessor can directly address and access any data location in the RAM. A related term encountered frequently in discussions of computers is **read only memory (ROM).** Programs stored in this permanent memory cannot be changed because they control internal computer activities such as the way the computer boots up when it is turned on.

Input devices used for entering instructions and data into computers start with a keyboard and mouse. Other input devices include scanners, voice input devices, electronic cameras, touch screens, and electronic tablets. An **output device** displays data to people. The output devices for computers start with a monitor and a printer, and can also include speakers for sound output. **Storage devices** hold programs and data for future processing. Typical storage devices for computers include hard disks, floppy disk (diskette) drives, and other devices such as zip drives that are used for backups and transferring data between non-networked computers. Because input, output, and storage devices are usually considered to be options separate from the computer itself, they are often called **peripherals.**

Types of Computers

The original concept of computation, storage, input, and output has developed into many types of computers. This section focuses on computers whose users see them as computers rather than as components of other machines. A computer that is an internal component of another machine is called an **embedded computer.** Machines ranging from airplanes to television sets and automatic coffee makers contain embedded computers. Embedded computers used for controlling chemical and mechanical processes in industry are essential components of information systems for factory automation.

Nonembedded computers are classified based on a combination of power, speed, and ability to control or link to other computers or terminals. A reasonable first cut at computer categories includes personal computer, workstation, midrange computer, mainframe, and supercomputer. Although these categories have merged somewhat and have become less meaningful, they are still part of everyday terminology and they help in visualizing new options related to networked computer systems.

A **personal computer (PC)** is a single-user computer that sits on a desktop or can be carried around by the user. **Laptop** and **notebook computers** are portable PCs that fit into a briefcase but contain enough computing power and disk storage to support a business professional's personal requirements for word processing, spreadsheets, and storage of documents. Pen computers, which lack a keyboard and use an electronic pen for writing input on the screen, have been adopted in specific types of applications where keyboards are inconvenient and handwritten input is adequate. (See Figure 8.1.) A **workstation** is a powerful single-user computer used for computing-intensive work such as complex data analysis, graphic design, and engineering. Workstations often come with large screens needed to work with complex images. Although the first PCs could only run simple word processors, spreadsheets, and specialized applications, technical advances in hardware and software permit current PCs to perform tasks previously reserved for workstations.

Current PCs are divided into desktop and laptop units and are typically advertised in terms of their processing power, storage, and input and output devices. Processing power is summarized by the type of microprocessor and the amount of RAM and hard disk memory. The headline on a typical ad might mention a desktop computer with a 233 MHz Pentium microprocessor, 32 MB of RAM, and a 2.6 GB hard drive. Input and output features include the type of display and size of the screen, the speed of the modem, the speed of the CD-ROM drive, and the type of sound card. Features such as the size of cache memory (extremely fast temporary storage for instructions and data) and the speed of internal "bus" that transfers data to and from the microprocessor are also mentioned frequently because these technical features affect the computer's internal speed in processing instructions and moving data.

Midrange computers and mainframes typically perform all the processing for a large number of users working at terminals. **Midrange computers** (previously called minicomputers) are centralized computers typically shared by a department for processing transactions, accessing corporate databases, and generating reports. **Mainframe** computers are even more powerful; they are typically linked to hundreds or even thousands of terminals for processing high volumes of online transactions and generating reports from large databases. Mainframe systems contain extensive data storage capabilities. The tape library might contain thousands of tapes, and the computer center could include dozens of freestanding hard disk units containing enormous databases. Printed outputs could be produced on high-speed printers

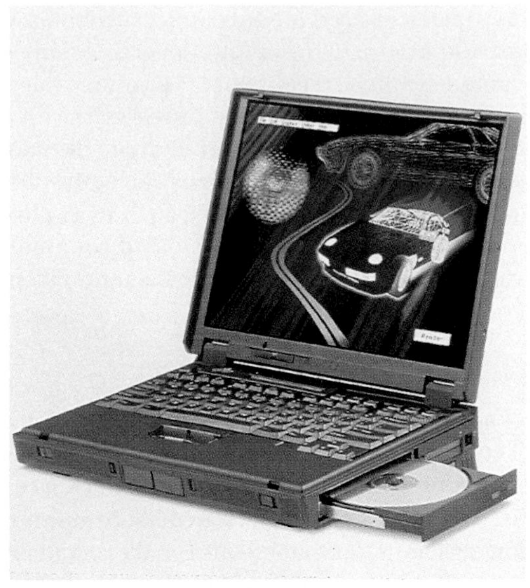
(a)

(b)

Figure 8.1
Portable computers

(a) This laptop computer contains more processing power than a top-end desktop computer had only several years earlier. (b) This pen computer is used for data input where a keyboard would not work.

at centralized locations or on low-speed printers at end-user locations. Mainframes are usually housed in environmentally controlled and physically secure computer rooms. (Figure 8.2 compares a mainframe computer with a desktop computer.) **Supercomputers** were initially thought of as computers designed for exceptionally high volume, high-speed calculation, rather than transaction processing. Such computers have been used for complex analysis problems such as simulations of the weather or the flow of air around a wing. More recent applications have occurred in banking, manufacturing, and data mining.

Twenty years ago the CPUs of mainframe computers operated at a much higher MIPS rate than minicomputers, which were much faster than the early PCs. By the 1990s, these computer categories started to break down because CPUs of both mainframes and advanced PCs started using similar microprocessors. This breakdown is hastened by the fact that the cost per MIPS for PCs is far lower than for mainframes. Improvements in raw computing power do not mean that PCs can replace centralized computers, however. Using PCs for applications that formerly ran on mainframes requires that they be linked together in a network. Midrange computers and mainframes are designed to accept inputs from many simultaneous users. PCs cannot support this type of application, regardless of whether they can perform an individual user's numerical calculations at the speed of a larger computer. Mainframe computers also tend to be more reliable than PCs for networked applications.

The trend toward computer networks has spawned a newer category of computers that overlaps with all the others. **Servers** are specialized computers linked to other computers on a network in order to perform specific types of tasks requested through those computers. Low-end servers are basically powerful PCs configured to perform specific tasks, such as finding data in a database, controlling printing, or controlling electronic mail. High-end servers perform similar functions for larger networks or larger databases and often compete with midrange computers or even mainframes. For example, in 1998 a top-end server from Compaq, originally a personal computer company, had 4 gigabytes of RAM and 708 gigabytes of disk storage, linked to 9100 personal computers, and cost half a million dollars.[4]

Many observers believe that mainframe computers will gradually evolve into database servers that control and update large databases. You will understand more about the role of servers after the following discussion of computer system architectures and client-server computing.

Computer System Architectures

Computer systems should be deployed in a way that mirrors business processes. If people work individually and rarely share their work products, computer systems should provide effective tools for individual work. If people work as a group, computer systems should

(a)

(b)

Figure 8.2
Comparison of a mainframe computer and a desktop computer

The IBM mainframe computer requires a large, environmentally controlled computer room. The desktop computer can be used in any typical office environment.

make it easier to share work. If the organization relies on a central database for orders, reservations, or inventory, computer systems should provide access to the database.

Figure 8.3 shows four alternative computer system architectures. The first is **centralized computing,** in which all the processing for multiple users is done by a large central computer. In **personal computing,** users have their own machines and rarely share data or resources. In **distributed computing,** users may have their own computers and the organization uses a network to share data and resources. In **network computing,** some of the computing is done on each user's computer, but the processing is controlled centrally. Each approach raises its own management issues concerning the effective and efficient use of data and equipment. Although the four approaches are introduced separately here, they may be combined in many ways in practice. (See Figure 8.3.)

Centralized Computing

This approach involves a single mainframe or midrange computer that processes data for multiple users. The first computerized systems for business transaction processing operated in batch mode and used punched cards for data input and storage. Later, online transaction processing permitted multiple users at terminals to perform transactions simultaneously. In this original form of online transaction processing, every input went directly from the terminals to the central computer, and it controlled all outputs to the users. The terminals in these systems were eventually called **dumb terminals** because they could not actually process information and served only as an input/output mechanism linking users with the central computer.

Approach to computing	Basic idea of the approach	Advantages	Disadvantages
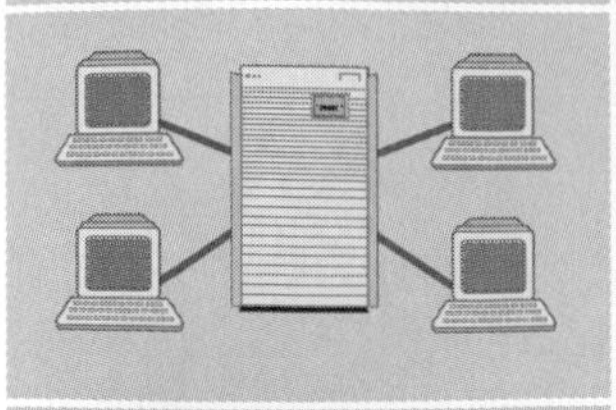	In **centralized computing**, terminals are attached to a central computer that performs all the computations and controls all the peripherals, such as printers.	• Greater security because all processing is controlled at a central location	• Central computer must perform computing and must do work to control the remote terminals • Total reliance on the central computer; if it goes down, so does the entire system
	In **personal computing**, individual microcomputers are used for individual work but are not linked in a network.	• Greater flexibility for individual users doing inherently individual work • Less impact from what others are doing using a computer	• Difficulty sharing the work individuals do • Duplication of underutilized hardware and software
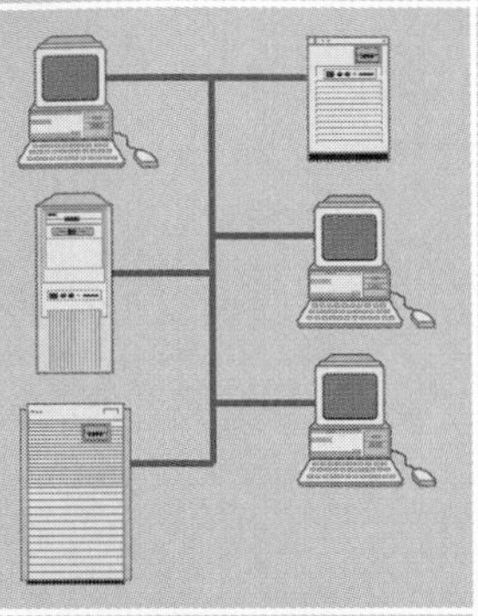	In **distributed computing**, multiple workstations are linked to share data and computing resources. The data and resources may be at the local site or may be elsewhere.	• Greater ability to share work, information, and resources • Ability to continue doing some useful work even if part of the network is down	• Complex to administer • Security more difficult because computing and data are so spread out
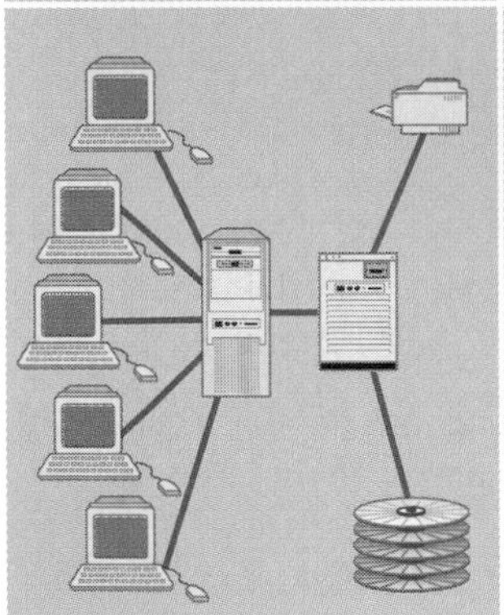	In **network computing**, multiple network computers are linked to a central server that controls their operation and that provides links to other servers.	• Greater ability to share work, information, and resources • Easier to administer than distributed computing	• Reliance on a central server • Limited processing ability at user's computer

Figure 8.3
Four approaches to computing in organizations

With the first computer systems, centralized computing was the only option. Personal computing arose as an alternative providing more flexibility to individual users. Distributed computing uses a network to share data and resources. Network computing tries to combine the benefits of centralized computing with the flexibility and responsiveness of distributed computing.

Using centralized computing to service multiple users has many shortcomings. First, the computer has to perform two types of work: It has to do the computing for the users, and it has to manage the status and progress of work being done for each online user. The operating system software that keeps track of the jobs uses a lot of the CPU's processing power. As a result, a substantial percentage of the available computing resources go toward controlling the job stream rather than accomplishing the work the users want. A second shortcoming is total reliance on the central computer. No work can be done using the dumb terminal if the computer or the telecommunications line goes down. A third shortcoming is the tight schedules and controls the central computer needs to balance the computer's workload to avoid peak-load problems when people across the organization want to use it simultaneously. These procedures support the processing scheduled in advance but limit users' flexibility in doing their own work.

Despite these problems of centralized computing, centralized functions are needed for many business operations. For example, order entry functions in many businesses such as airlines, distributors, and large manufacturers require online access to central databases by geographically dispersed users. Centralized computing has evolved in many ways to perform these functions while reducing the problems of totally centralized processing by moving some of the processing to other computers on the network. In addition, various forms of redundancy have been built in to improve overall system reliability.

Personal Computing

Computer system deployment changed dramatically in the late 1970s when personal computers first provided powerful computing to individuals and small businesses at an affordable price. In the 1980s, worldwide shipments of personal computers exceeded the shipments of the large-scale systems that had previously dominated the market. The basic idea of personal computing is that a computer should be available as a tool for individual work at any time. This approach is particularly effective for inherently individual work such as word processing, spreadsheets, presentations, personal calendars, and simple graphic design work. It also succeeds for small companies whose limited record keeping fits on a PC.

Major advances have occurred in areas where the first PCs were especially weak, such as awkward user interfaces, limited software capabilities, and data and software storage only on diskettes. When a **graphical user interface (GUI)** was incorporated into many programs, it allowed the use of a mouse or other pointing device to express commands by selecting icons or entries on pull-down menus. This advance provided a more user friendly interface by eliminating the need to memorize command languages, file names, and other details that previously made personal computing difficult for nonprogrammers. Another development, storage of data and programs on hard disks, made it easier to start programs, access data, and work with several programs at the same time. As the power of microprocessors increased, software such as spreadsheets and word processors could provide many more capabilities and operate much faster. PCs can support several activities at once; for example, they permit a user to print out a large document while doing other work on the computer. Portable laptop computers provided additional convenience because they run on rechargeable batteries and can be used even if an electric plug is unavailable for several hours. Overall, personal computing made computer usage practical and affordable on a much wider scale.

Distributed Computing

Despite all these advances, personal computing is a limited approach because people in organizations work together. Even departments that enthusiastically embraced PCs soon felt the need for individuals to share information and computing resources. The information included databases, phone messages, memos, and work in progress such as drafts of documents. The resources included printers, fax machines, and external databases.

In distributed computing, individuals do their own work on PCs or workstations and use a telecommunications network to link to other devices. Distributed computing improves coordination, helps in sharing data, messages, and work products, and permits sharing of resources such as printers. Data, messages, and work products are shared in two ways. First, an individual may send a message or file to other computers on the network. Second, an individual may access data residing on a hard disk attached to a different computer on the network. For example, an insurance adjuster using a portable computer can upload the day's data to a central database. Later, an insurance pricing analyst might access the claims database through another part of the network. The sharing of printers is accomplished by designating a computer on the network as a print server and sending print jobs to that computer.

Unfortunately the advantages of distributed computing come with a price, the need for controls and administration that make it more complex than personal computing. The need for greater controls is apparent from the fact that a given user on a network may want to share some files while restricting access to others. For example, a supervisor may wish to share work-related files with subordinates but keep employee salary review files private. This makes it necessary to state explicitly who can access what files. It is also critical to enforce standards to facilitate access to data controlled by someone else. The result is a more restricted environment than personal computing, but one in which people can work together more effectively. The degree to which computing should be distributed depends on tradeoffs between data transmission costs, user convenience, maintainability, and security.

Network Computing

One response to the complexity of distributed computing is to step back and ask whether networks of powerful PCs are unnecessarily expensive to maintain. Table 8.3 summarizes the Gartner Group's estimate that the total cost of ownership for a networked Windows 95 PC in a large organization is $9,785. A major part of this hardware and support cost comes from users changing configurations, installing nonstandard applications, and plugging in cards, thereby making every machine unique and greatly complicating troubleshooting and maintenance. Users sometimes cause expensive crises by downloading programs infected with viruses.[5]

A recent approach that addresses these problems is network computing, which uses advances in programming and telecommunications technology to combine the traditional benefits of centralization with the flexibility and responsiveness of distributed computing. This approach is based on networks of stripped down personal computers called **network computers (NCs).** The NCs do not contain hard disks, and therefore cannot store programs or data. The programs and data are all stored on centralized servers that download to the NCs whatever programs and data they may need at a particular time. Because NCs are designed to be controlled through a network, they typically cannot run the Windows 95 desktop operating system and are designed to run programs written in Java (a computer language described in Chapter 9). Aside from using cheaper computers,

TABLE 8.3 **Cost of Ownership for Personal Computers, Network Computers, and Net PCs[6]**

	Personal computer	Network computer	Net PC
Desktop			
• Equipment outlay	1850	980	1733
• Technical support and administration	2011	1310	1392
• End-user operations	3464	1799	2073
Desktop annual cost	7325	4089	5198
Network			
• Network equipment outlay	682	689	664
• Network tech support and administration	1190	841	973
• Network end user	588	392	434
Network annual cost	2460	1922	2071
Total costs	**9785**	**6011**	**7267**

centralizing the data and the programs eliminates much activity related to updating software versions and assuring data security and consistency. Key disadvantages of network computing are its reliance on centralized control and the relative immaturity of software designed to support this approach. A second alternative mentioned in Table 8.3 is the net PC, which can run Windows software but is more secure than a standard PC because it lacks a diskette drive.

The initial debate about PCs versus NCs and net PCs was surprisingly vehement. In some ways the NC seemed a manager's dream: a closed box with no slots for inserting messy diskettes or CD-ROMs, a way to eliminate some of the costly individualism of the PC environment, and a way to prevent workers from installing their favorite software. "What's a floppy disk?" asked Scott McNealy, CEO of Sun Microsystems. "It's a way to steal company secrets." Bill Gates, CEO of Microsoft, responded to NC promoters by saying they were trying to "portray PC's as an evil." He said the campaign against PCs espouses "grinch management," a short-sighted effort to take tools away from workers and control their behavior.[7] Regardless of whether network computers or net PCs replace PCs in corporate networks, it is very likely that both software and administrative procedures will evolve in a way that will reduce some of the excessive costs of administering and supporting PCs.

Client-Server and Beyond

The previous section introduced four ways to deploy computers in organizations. Because there is both speculation and controversy about the relative advantages of different forms of distributed computing and network computing, we will look at this in more detail. We start with the client-server concept, which was originally developed to support the early versions of the Internet, and which remains the basis of this important tool.

In **client-server architecture,** different devices on the network are treated as clients or servers. The client devices send requests for service, such as printing or retrieval of data, to specific server devices that perform the requested processing. For example, the client devices might consist of ten workstations within a department, and server devices might be a laser printer and a specialized computer, called a **file server,** dedicated to retrieving data from a database. In many networks, the file server is a powerful computer containing special data retrieval and network management capabilities. Some networks use other types of specialized servers such as print servers that execute requests for printing, mail servers that handle electronic mail, and communication servers that link the network to other external networks.

In effect, client-server computing is a way to modularize the work performed by computers. Figure 8.4 shows the difference between client-server and centralized mainframe computing in terms of the division of labor in handling the user interface, application program logic, and database access. Instead of having a mainframe computer control everything from the displays on user terminals through the application logic and the updating of the database, client-server divides these functions between specialized client and server components. There are actually many different forms of client-server computing, depending on factors such as the volume of transactions, whether the application is mission-critical, and whether the application is localized or enterprise-wide. The two-tier client-server approach shown in the figure is typically used in simpler situations. The three-tier approach is preferred for mission-critical, enterprise-wide systems that require stringent controls.

The advantages of client-server computing include user convenience, technical scalability, and greater ability to accommodate and maintain hardware and software from different vendors. User convenience starts with having a powerful PC that can serve personal computing needs but can also link into a network. Attaching a PC to a network instead of using a dumb terminal also means that the graphical user interface and the validation of data no longer have to be controlled by an overworked central computer. Scalability is improved because it is easier and less disruptive to add or enhance individual client or server devices instead of modifying a centralized system.

A client-server approach may accommodate hardware and software from different vendors with reasonable ease because the interfaces between each vendor's products and

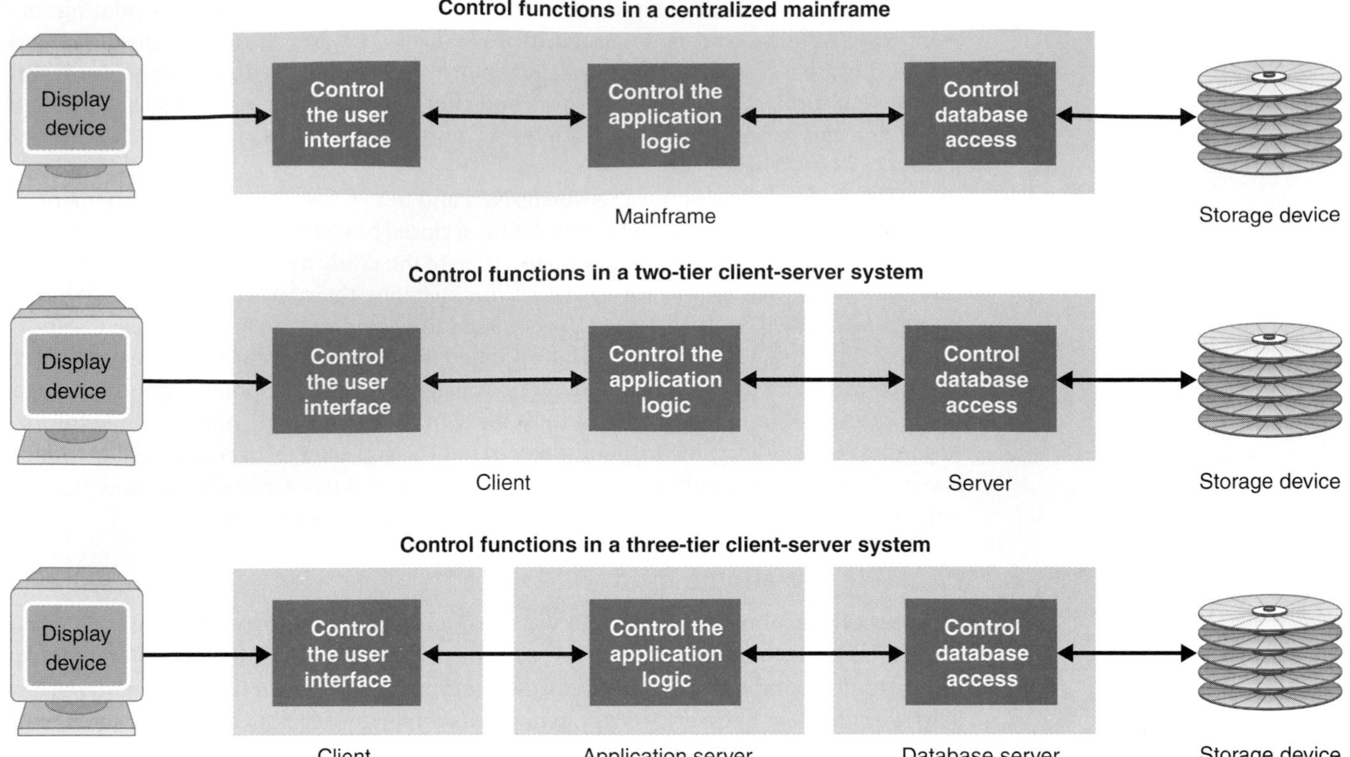

Figure 8.4
Client-server versus centralized mainframe computing

With the centralized mainframe approach, the central computer controls the user interface, the application logic, and database access. Permitting the same program to control aspects of all three elements makes it much more difficult to change the software over time. With a two-tier client-server, the application programs and user interface are controlled by the client workstation, while database access is controlled by the server. With a three-tier approach, application logic is controlled by an application server that links to both the client and a database server.

the other parts of the network are becoming more like off-the-shelf products. For example, a client device might request particular customer data from a network without "knowing" the type of database management system the server uses to store the data. The query simply goes to the right server, which contains off-the-shelf software that can interpret the query for the type of database it is using.

Network computing can be viewed as a variant of client-server that puts more of the processing in the server. The client computer in this approach is called a **thin client** because it does not store programs or data. Figure 8.5 shows how network computing applies client-server principles without storing programs or data on the client. The user logs on and wants to modify a word processing document. The server downloads the document along with part of the word processor. The user uses this module to modify the document but reaches a point where additional word processing capabilities are needed. The client machine detects the need for an additional module, automatically conveys that request to the server, and receives the required module. The user completes the document and stores it on a hard disk attached to the server. The user turns off the computer and the program modules that were used are erased from the client. These same modules will be downloaded again the next time they are needed. Surveys in 1997 and 1998 yielded inconclusive predictions about the near term adoption of this approach. Some planned projects would use network computers to replace dumb terminals while others would use them to replace PCs. Yet other planned projects stayed with PCs. Whether network computing would be widely adopted in the near term was a controversial issue.[8]

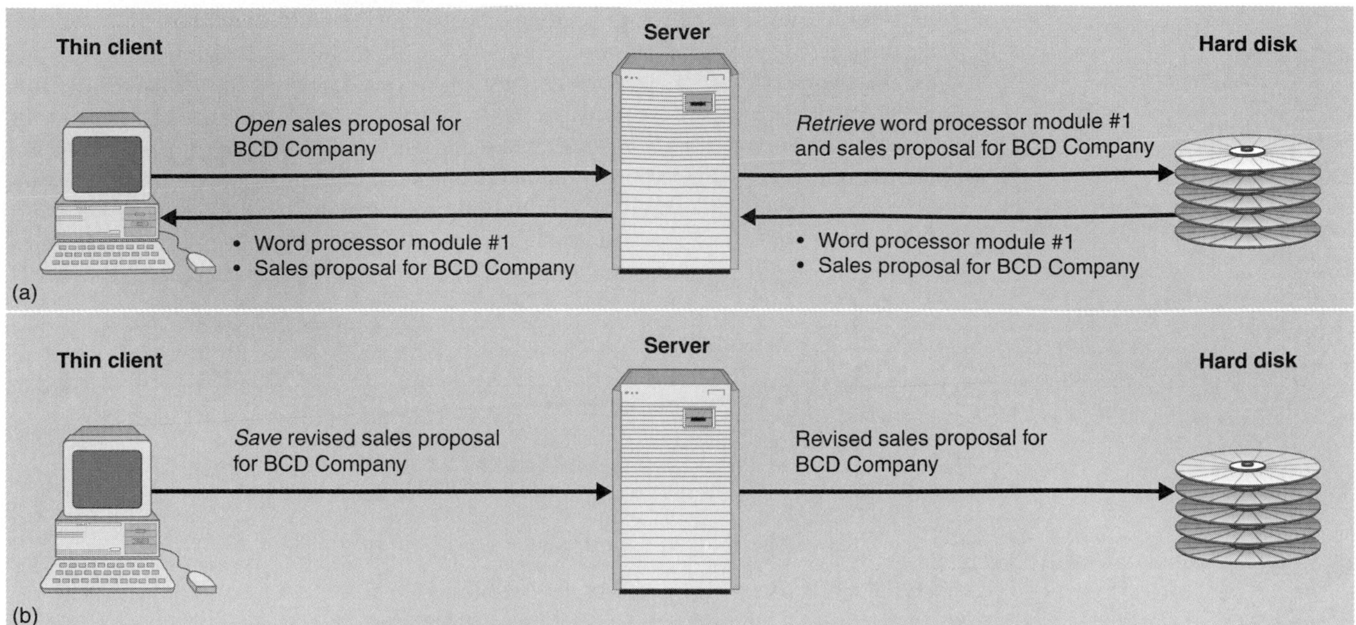

Figure 8.5
Network computing

In network computing, both programs and data must be downloaded from a server to the "thin client." (a) The downloading of an existing sales proposal and a word processor module to the client. (b) The revised document is saved through the server.

Middleware

The common requirement for using different types of hardware and software on the same network generated a need for new programming methods. These methods divide programming tools between client tools, such as methods for creating graphical user interfaces and validating data inputs, and server tools, such as database management systems. Between the client tools and server tools is another category of tool called middleware. **Middleware** controls communication between clients and servers and performs whatever translation is necessary to make a client's request understandable to a server device. There are several types of middleware. Distributed database middleware provides a common, high-level programming interface, such as structured query language (SQL), that packages information so that it can be used by multiple applications. In contrast, message-oriented middleware facilitates interaction with other applications and operating systems by sending data or requests in the form of messages.

Despite its advantages, client-server computing also has disadvantages. Many early adopters of client-server computing have found that it increases data and system administration efforts. In addition, since the interfaces and middleware translations between modular components take a certain amount of computing time, networks can be slow. The separation between clients and servers also requires using rapidly changing programming methods that are unfamiliar to many programmers.

Peer-to-peer architecture is an important alternative to client-server for small computer networks. In **peer-to-peer,** each workstation can communicate directly with every other workstation on the network without going through a specialized server. Peer-to-peer is appropriate when the network users mostly do their own work but occasionally need to exchange data. In these cases, it may be more efficient to keep data and copies of the software at each workstation to avoid the delays of downloading data and software each time a user gets started. Peer-to-peer has potential problems, however, in security and consistency. For example, with data at someone else's workstation, the data may be difficult to retrieve when that person is out of the office and the workstation is shut off.

Although the various forms of client-server, network computing, and peer-to-peer differ from traditional mainframe computing in the way they divide computing and data transmission tasks, they still require human infrastructure to perform many of the same centralized chores required in mainframe computing. Someone must set up the network and maintain it. Someone must make sure that the data files are defined properly, that the network provides adequate performance, and that it is secure from misuse. If the network delivers the software to the workstations, someone must make sure that the software is updated appropriately and that users know when it is updated. The combination of new administrative burdens and unfamiliar and sometimes immature programming technology have led many industry observers to question exaggerated claims about the benefits of these newer technologies, regardless of the fact that they put a high-MIPS microprocessor close to the user.

Reality Check

COMPUTER SYSTEM ARCHITECTURES

This section identifies four computer system architectures: centralized computing, personal computing, distributed computing, and network computing.

1. Identify times (if any) when you have used a computer system of each type.
2. Referring back to the performance variables in Table 8.2, explain how the architectures felt different from a user's viewpoint. If you have used only one, explain how you think the others might feel different to a user.

LOOKING INSIDE THE BLACK BOX

With this background on types of computers and organizational approaches to computing, we can now take a deeper look at what actually happens inside a computer system. We will introduce a series of computer-oriented topics, each of which will help you appreciate something about the way computers are used in business. Understanding the coding of data will help you understand why a single picture may be worth 10,000 words but may use 100 times as much storage in a computer system. Similarly, it will help you see why videoconferencing requires far greater data transmission capabilities than e-mail. The discussion of the semiconductors inside the computer helps you understand why it has been possible to shrink computer sizes and make them portable.

Coding Data for Processing by a Computer

To understand how computers operate, it is essential to understand the way any type of data including numbers, text, pictures, and sounds can be coded for processing by machines. This is not just a technical detail because it helps in understanding the capabilities and limits of current computers.

Binary Representation of Numbers

Before a computer can process data, the data must be converted into a form the computer can process. This section will show how any type of data (numbers, text, images, and sounds) can be represented as a organized set of bits (0's and 1's). Representing data as a series of bits is especially efficient because digital computers are built from components that switch between off-on (0-1) states.

Consistent with their off-on internal components, computers perform calculations using the base 2, or binary, number system. Figure 8.6 shows binary addition and multiplication tables to illustrate the advantage of using binary representation for the internal operations within a computer. The addition and multiplication tables involve only 4 entries instead of 100 entries that would be required for base 10 tables. This implies that the internal circuitry inside the computer is much simpler because binary representation is used. Because people work with base 10 numbers, computers automatically convert these numbers into binary form before they perform calculations. They then change the results back into base 10 for use by people. Figure 8.7 explains how to convert a number from our everyday base 10 number system into binary.

Figure 8.6
Addition and multiplication tables for binary numbers

Addition and multiplication tables for binary numbers have only four entries, each of which is either a zero or a one. Implementing these tables within a computer's circuitry is much simpler than implementing base 10 tables that would have to include 100 situations.

Addition table

+	0	1
0	0	1
1	1	10

Multiplication table

*	0	1
0	0	0
1	0	1

Binary Representation of Text

The memory inside most computers is organized in groups of eight bits. Eight bits, or one byte, is enough to uniquely identify 256 different characters (digits, uppercase and lowercase letters, punctuation marks, and special characters such as $ and @). The 256 possible configurations of a single byte can represent all characters used in English and most other languages that have alphabets. However, 256 different characters are not sufficient for coding the thousands of different Chinese characters, or kanji. This is one reason why computers were adopted slowly in the Far East.

The industry requirement for standard ways of coding data comes from the frequent need to move data between different brands of computers even if their internal operation is inconsistent. **ASCII** is one of several standard codes for representing letters, digits, and special characters on computer systems. ASCII stands for American Standard Code for Information Interchange. Table 8.4 shows how ASCII-8 represents letters and digits as sequences of 0's and 1's. Unicode is a superset of the ASCII character set that uses two bytes for each character rather than one and is therefore able to handle 65,536 combinations rather than just 256. It is important in the global market because it encompasses the alphabets of most of the world's languages.

Figure 8.7
Expressing numbers in base 2

This figure shows how to convert from base 10 numbers to binary numbers and vice versa.

The location of each digit in a base 10 number determines that digit's value.
For example, the base 10 number 3,597 can be expressed in powers of 10 as follows:

$$3597 = 3 * 1{,}000 + 5 * 100 + 9 * 10 + 7 * 1 = 3 * 10^3 + 5 * 10^2 + 9 * 10^1 + 7 * 10^0$$

Base 10 uses the 10 digits 0 through 9. In contrast, base 2 uses only two digits, 0 and 1. The location of digits in base 2 has the same effect as the location of digits in base 10, except that each position represents powers of 2 rather than 10. For example, the base 2 number 10111 (which is equivalent to the base 10 number 23) represents the following combination of powers of 2:

$$10111 = 1 * 2^4 + 0 * 2^3 + 1 * 2^2 + 1 * 2^1 + 1 * 2^0 = 1 * 16 + 0 * 8 + 1 * 4 + 1 * 2 + 1 * 1 = 16 \text{ (in base 10)} + 0 + 4 + 2 + 1$$

$$= 23 \text{ (in base 10)}$$

It is possible to express any base 10 number as an equivalent base 2 number by breaking it up into successive powers of 2. The base 10 example (3,597) is equivalent to the base 2 number 111000001101.

TABLE 8.4 ASCII-8 Code for Data

Digit	ASCII representation	Letter	ASCII representation
0	0101 0000		
1	0101 0001	A	1010 0001
2	0101 0010	B	1010 0010
3	0101 0011	C	1010 0011
4	0101 0100	D	1010 0100
5	0101 0101	E	1010 0101
6	0101 0110	F	1010 0110
7	0101 0111	G	1010 0111
8	0101 1000	H	1010 1000
9	0101 1001	I	1010 1001

Numerical Representation of Sounds and Pictures

Images and sounds can also be represented as a series of numbers and therefore as a series of 0's and 1's. The process of generating these numbers is called **digitizing,** and the result is called a digital representation of the image or sound. Figure 8.8 shows how an image can be digitized by dividing it into tiny squares and assigning a number to each square representing the shade in the square. Imagine that a 1-by-1 inch image is covered with a 200-by-200 grid that isolates tiny picture elements, or **pixels.** Each pixel is coded on a scale ranging from absolutely white to absolutely dark. With the 200-by-200 grid, the 1-inch-square image would be represented by 40,000 numbers, which could then be stored in a computer or transmitted. Representations of this type are actually approximations. The denser the grid, the more precise the representation, as was demonstrated by Figure 4.16 in Chapter 4. Four times as many numbers would be required to represent a color image, because color images can be represented as a combination of four colors such as red, blue, yellow, and black. The second part of Figure 8.8 shows that sounds can also be digitized by dividing their waveforms into tiny increments and coding each of these numerically.

The fact that any type of data can be represented as a series of bits means that a computer system can manipulate and transmit any type of data. Just as it can add numbers, it can change the shade of part of an image or can store and transmit audio data. Until the 1980s, computer systems rarely processed images and sounds because insufficient price-performance made it too expensive to handle the amount of data required for useful applications. Although most business data processing still involves numbers and text, image and audio applications have become commonplace. Image applications include creating engineering drawings, storing correspondence from customers, and displaying graphical information for decision makers. Audio applications include voice mail, controlling computers by voice commands, and even entering numerical or textual data by voice.

Data Compression

Digitizing images and video generates an enormous number of numbers. Consider a black and white 8-by-10 photograph digitized at the resolution of 200 dots per inch. Because each square inch contains 40,000 dots and the photograph contains 80 square inches, the digitized image would contain 3,200,000 numbers, more than enough numbers to represent every letter in every word in this book. A picture may be worth a thousand words, but it may require the same computer resources for storage and transmission as a million words.

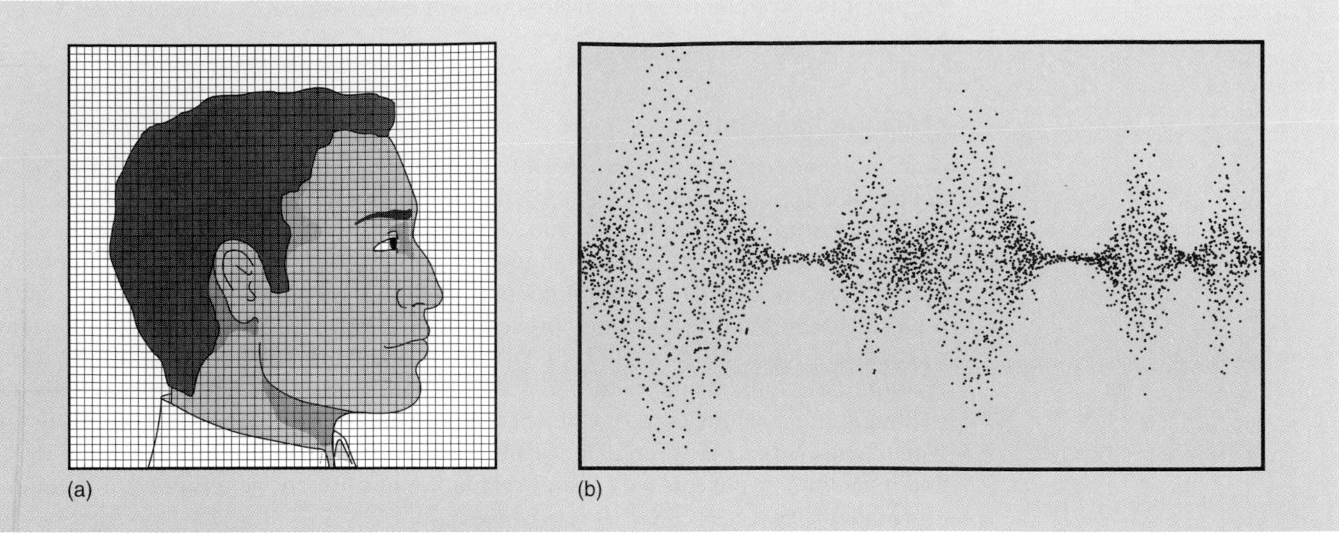

Figure 8.8
Digitizing images and sounds

(a) Black and white images can be digitized by subdividing them using a fine grid and then assigning a number to each point on the grid. The number for each point represents its value on a scale from absolutely white to absolutely black. The fineness of the grid (in lines per inch) determines the precision of the digitized image. (b) Sounds can be digitized by dividing their waveforms into tiny increments and coding each increment. The picture shows how voice waveforms can be represented.

Data compression is one of the ways to increase the storage and transmission capability of computer and communication hardware without upgrading the hardware. Data compression is the coding of data to remove types of redundancies that can be detected easily. The basic idea is to use computational techniques to compress data whenever it is stored or transmitted, and to decompress it whenever it is used. There are two groups of compression methods. **Lossless compression** is used for typical business data and text. It can shrink programs and word processing documents to roughly half their normal size, making it possible to squeeze more data into the same floppy disk or hard disk. Given that it applies to business data and text, the corresponding decompression process must recreate an exact duplicate of the original data. In contrast, **lossy compression** that actually loses some data can be used for audio, video, and some image applications in which minor degradations in data quality are much less important than drastic reductions in file size. Lossy compression of 90% or more for video signals helps make video conferencing possible. The sources of the reduction include taking fewer frames per second, transmitting only the parts of the picture that change from frame to frame, and identifying and coding special patterns within individual frames, such as areas of unchanging color.

Data Encryption

A special type of coding is sometimes used to prevent unauthorized or illegal use of data that can be stolen or intercepted while being stored or transmitted. **Encryption** is the process of coding data to make it meaningless to any unauthorized user. The encrypted data is meaningful only to someone who can use a special decoding process for converting the data back to the original form. Encrypting data is essential for performing financial transactions on the Internet and for transferring money electronically between financial institutions. It is also important to pay television operators who don't want their signals used for free. Some people encrypt data on their own PCs to prevent unwarranted access.

An example of a simple encryption scheme is to replace each letter in a word by the letter five positions after it in the alphabet. With this scheme, the word *encryption* would appear as *jshwduynts*. Because a scheme like this would be easy to figure out, real encryption schemes are much more complicated and typically involve complex manipulations of bit patterns. Several encryption techniques will be explained in Chapter 13 on System Security and Control.

Machine Language

Computers are devices that can execute previously stored instructions. Although the details of computer circuitry are immensely complicated, the basic idea of executing previously stored instructions is quite simple. Instructions a computer can execute directly are expressed in **machine language,** the computer's internal programming language. Different brands of computers may use different machine languages because their CPUs contain different microprocessors. For example, a server produced by Sun might use a Sparc chip, while IBM-style PCs from both IBM and Dell might use a Pentium microprocessor. The difference in machine languages implies that software written in the machine language of a particular type of chip will not run on a different type of chip. Box 9.1 in Chapter 9 will show a hypothetical example of a highly simplified machine language as part of an explanation of different generations of programming languages.

The details of a machine language have many important ramifications for a computer's internal efficiency. For example, the number of internal locations that can be referenced directly has a major impact on the effective speed of the processor that executes machine language instructions. The Intel Pentium uses **32-bit addressing,** meaning that it can address over 16 million (2^{32}) locations directly. Previous 8-bit or 16-bit processors could address only 64 (2^{8}) or 4096 (2^{16}) locations directly. Because machine language programs are often much larger than this, computers with 8- or 16-bit addressing had to do extra work to keep track of data in memory locations that they could not address directly. In addition to making it even harder to program these computers, limited address spaces slowed these computers down compared to what they might otherwise do. In 1993 Digital Equipment Corporation released a 64-bit microprocessor called the Alpha Chip, and Intel's IA-64 microprocessor scheduled for 1999 is also a 64-bit chip. This expanded memory addressing is important for processing multiterabyte data warehouses.

Approaches for Increasing Computer Performance

Increasing computer performance is a driving force for many applications. We will look at this topic in more depth by focusing on four approaches: making processors faster and more powerful, improving the instruction set, making specialized processors, and programming computers so that the processors operate in parallel. A fifth approach, distributing computing functions across a network, has already been introduced. That approach is based on dividing the computer system into specialized modules that perform particular tasks such as finding data in the database, interacting with users, or controlling printing.

Faster and More Powerful Processors

Developments in miniaturization and speed of computing devices have changed computers from room-sized machines to machines the size of a notepad. The first computers represented data using off-on switches that were wired together. Today's computers would not be possible without the **integrated circuit** that was first developed in 1958. The concept of the integrated circuit was that an entire electronic circuit could be embedded into a single piece of silicon called a **chip.** The **microprocessor** was another key development because it integrated control logic and memory on a single chip. (See Figure 8.9.) Extensions of this 1971 invention led to the development of personal computers and are the heart of current computers. Table 8.5 looks at the successive generations of microprocessor chips produced by Intel to date, showing advances in memory and speed, plus what those advances meant for PC users.

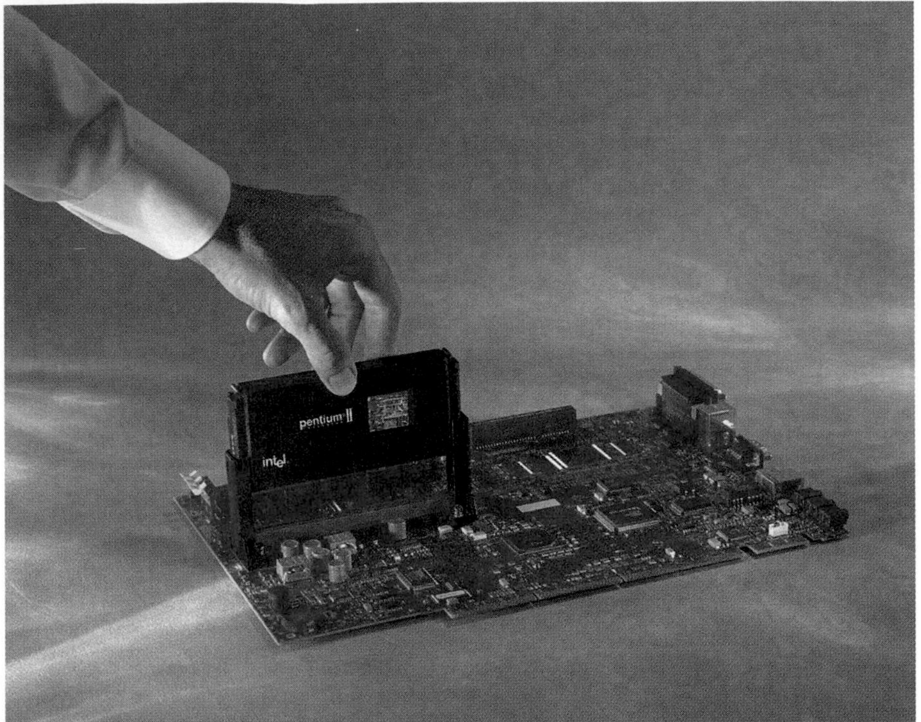

Figure 8.9
An Intel motherboard

The Intel Pentium II microprocessor is inside the rectangular plastic package being installed in the motherboard that controlls the operation of a computer.

In general, advances in computers have been related to advances in the miniaturization and integration of semiconductor chips. This miniaturization is accomplished through a complex manufacturing process that etches circuits on thin slices of silicon called wafers. Later, these wafers are cut into individual chips and put into small plastic packages. It is possible to increase the speed and reduce the power consumption of circuits by making the individual devices smaller, putting more devices on one chip, and packing them more tightly. Improvements in performance occur because the electrons travel a much shorter path and because off-on switching times decrease.

The existing 16-megabit memory chips contain over 16 million miniaturized transistors separated by etched lines around 0.5 microns wide. A **micron** is one millionth of a meter. By comparison, bacteria are about 8 microns wide, and a human hair is about 80. Chips of more than 64, 256 and 1024 megabits require line widths around 0.35, 0.25, and 0.18 microns, respectively. The Intel IA-64 architecture for microprocessors will require 0.18 micron technology. Beyond this point a switch to a new type of manufacturing equipment using ultraviolet light or x-rays instead of visible light may be necessary. When NEC produced a prototype version of a 4-gigabit memory chip, it used an electron beam technique not generally considered suitable for mass production.[9]

Faster and more powerful processors (plus similar improvements in hard disk storage) have led to vast increases in the power of the software that computers can execute. The first spreadsheet program, VisiCalc, was released in 1980 and occupied 29 kilobytes of memory on an Apple II computer. Current spreadsheet programs and their add-ons occupy many megabytes. Similar differences apply for word processors and other commonly used programs. The additional memory capacity makes it possible to include numerous capabilities that simply wouldn't fit in smaller memories. (The improvements in hard disk storage made it possible to store these large programs so they could be used.)

The combination of miniaturization and integration extends beyond the processors themselves and has contributed to major improvements in the cost-effectiveness of all computing equipment. Consider the way these developments powered the microcomputer

TABLE 8.5 Advances in Intel's Microprocessors

Successive generations of microprocessors from Intel, the industry leader, show the advances that occurred in the 1980s and 1990s.[10,11] Each new processor could run more complex software for PC users.

Processor #	Release date	Number of Transistors	Addressing	Initial MIPS	What this meant to a PC user
4004	1971	2,300	4-bit	0.06	This was the first microprocessor. It was developed for a desktop calculator.
8080	1974	3,500		0.06	This chip ran the first personal computer, the Altair, which was assembled by hobbyists.
8086/8088	1978	29,000	16-bit	0.3 MIPS	Chip for the first IBM PCs. Ran MS-DOS, the most common operating system for early PCs.
286	1982	134,000	16-bit	0.9 MIPS	Ran early versions of Microsoft Windows, but with poor performance.
386	1985	275,000	32-bit	5 MIPS	Ran early versions of Microsoft Windows, with adequate performance.
486	1989	1.3 million	32-bit	20 MIPS	Runs Microsoft Windows 95 with adequate performance.
Pentium	1993	3.2 million	32-bit	100 MIPS	Used for desktop computers and laptops.
Pentium Pro	1995	5.5 million	32-bit	300 MIPS	Better processing of multimedia data for engineering workstations; packaged with a speed-enhancing memory cache chip; primarily for servers and multiprocessor workstations.
Pentium II	1997	8 million	32-bit	500 MIPS	Designed to process video, audio and graphics data efficiently; primarily for high-end desktops and multiprocessor workstations.
Merced chip.[12] (code name) using IA-64 architecture	1999 (est.)	40 million (est.)	64-bit	1,000 MIPS (est)	Better support for high-end servers and work stations; useful for processing multiterabyte data warehouses due to 64-bit architecture.
Micro 2011 (prediction by Andrew Grove)[13]	2011(est.)	1 billion	Not mentioned	100,000 MIPS	Not known.

revolution of the 1980s. An IBM PC/AT built in 1984 using an Intel 286 microprocessor contained around 100 chips. One of the first chip sets built by the firm Chips and Technologies for clones of the PC/AT consisted of only 6 chips and cost $65. A much more powerful single-chip version cost $25 in 1990.[14] In 1998 National Semiconductor announced the first microprocessor chip that would consolidate on a single chip Pentium-class PC functions including graphics, audio, video, and communications. This chip was designed for high-performance PCs priced well below $1,000 and for widespread use in household appliances. Some analysts doubted, however, that such a chip could perform sophisticated computing functions as well as separate components operating together.[15]

Improved Instruction Set

Another approach to increasing speed is to change the types of instructions the individual processors perform. The **RISC** (reduced instruction set computer) microprocessor was developed to increase speed by using a simpler processor that operated faster. The concept of RISC was originally developed by IBM but was not commercialized at first for fear it would compete with IBM's existing technologies. Instead RISC was first exploited in the

1980s by other manufacturers. By 1989, RISC chips were helping increase computer speeds at an annual rate of 70%. In 1993 Digital Equipment Corporation used RISC technology in its 64-bit Alpha chip that could operate up to 300 MIPS and was later acquired by Intel. As the RISC advances were occurring, complex instruction set (CISC) microprocessors were also attaining performance improvements such as those shown in Table 8.5. Intel's 386, 486, and Pentium are all CISC microprocessors, whereas the PowerPC microprocessor developed by Motorola, IBM, and Apple used a RISC design. The design of Intel's IA-64 microprocessor due in 1999 seems to imply that Intel and its partner Hewlett-Packard believe that both "CISC and RISC are running out of gas."[16]

Specialized Processors

The chips recognized most widely by the general public are microprocessors that control PCs and dynamic RAMs that serve as memory. A second way to increase speed is to use specialized chips designed to perform a particular type of processing very efficiently. **ASICs** (application specific integrated circuits) are chips tailored to a particular application such as controlling a machine or a videogame. **DSPs** (digital signal processors) are specialized, single-purpose microprocessors devoted to processing voice or video signals. These chips are used in electronic musical equipment, voice mail systems, and video applications. A typical application is reducing audio distortion in cell phones. Doing this with regular microprocessors would be slower and wouldn't provide the level of performance needed. In a different area, several companies have developed special-purpose microprocessors optimized for running the Java programming language (discussed in Chapter 9) in conjunction with devices ranging from advanced cellular phones and pagers to Internet televisions and laptop computers. Rockwell's chip of this type uses one-thousandth the surface area of a Pentium II chip and 2% of the power of most microprocessors.[17]

Parallel Processing

As if progress due to miniaturization were not enough, many advances have also occurred by rethinking basic internal processing methods computers use. In **parallel processing,** a larger computation or query is divided into smaller computations or queries performed simultaneously. This idea is inconsistent with the traditional von Neumann architecture of general-purpose computers, which dictates that the computer fetches and performs one instruction at a time. Various forms of parallel processing have been used to build servers that contain multiple processors, thereby increasing the throughput of a single server instead of buying multiple servers. Parallel processing may be the only currently feasible approach for databases exceeding a terabyte in size. Intel's next generation chip, code named Merced, was designed using the IA-64 architecture that supports parallel processing more directly than previous microprocessors.

Parallel processing has been used in a number of ways, but it works only if programmers can figure out how to use the programming language, DBMS, and operating system to decompose the problems they are solving into subproblems that can be solved in parallel. Its first use was for complex scientific and engineering calculations that involved predicting weather patterns, studying fluid mechanics, and performing detailed simulations of physical systems. An important current use is in engineering workstations that generate photo-realistic images from detailed engineering specifications. Some of these systems simultaneously create an outline of the drawing, color it, shade it, and rotate it. Performing these tasks simultaneously allows speed and picture quality that would be impossible if everything were done in sequence. Business applications of parallel processing are typically based on querying and analyzing different parts of a huge database simultaneously. For example, Internet search engines can use parallel processing by converting a single query into several separate queries that can be performed simultaneously. A number of large companies have also started using parallel processing in data mining efforts aimed at finding and understanding otherwise obscure patterns in their own operational data.

Parallel processing may also have important applications in attempts to get computers to mimic intelligent behavior. Some artificial intelligence researchers see the human mind as a complex network of parallel processes. Although human consciousness focuses on one train of thought at a time, many other processes are going on in parallel in the background. These range from maintaining proper heart rate to filtering out background stimuli so that we don't get overloaded by all of the things happening around us.

Reality Check

INCREASING COMPUTER PERFORMANCE

The text discusses several approaches for increasing computer performance.

1. At a time when PCs can operate as fast as mainframes of the past, explain why you do or do not think computer performance is an important issue for users and managers.
2. Identify several situations in which inadequate computer system performance or improved computer system performance affected you directly.

The remainder of this chapter will discuss devices and media used for capturing, storing and retrieving, and displaying data. Chapter 10 will extend this picture by discussing data transmission.

DATA INPUT: CAPTURING DATA

Input devices used to enter data into computer systems range from keyboards and bar code readers to devices for voice and handwriting recognition. Before looking at specific devices, it is worthwhile to ask what characteristics an ideal input device should have. Like any other device, it should be inexpensive, reliable, accurate, and convenient to use. An ideal input device would also have characteristics unique to input devices. It should capture data automatically at its source and shouldn't require human intervention that might cause delays and might introduce errors. For example, it should be unnecessary for people to record data in one form (such as handwriting) and then transcribe into another form (by typing it). In addition, an ideal input device should do whatever is possible to ensure accuracy of the data. This section looks at several forms of data input involving keyboards and related devices, character recognition, and inputting images and sounds.

Keyboards and Pointing Devices

Although many Americans take keyboards for granted, even this familiar technology raises many issues, starting with the shape and layout of current keyboards. People who designed the first typewriters experimented with many different layouts before standardizing on what is called the "qwerty" keyboard because of the order of letters in the third row. Ironically, this layout of keys was developed to force people to type more slowly, thereby reducing the incidence of jammed keys in the mechanical typewriters of the time. Typewriters are no longer mechanical, but the qwerty keyboard has remained the standard.[18] Figure 7.2 showed another attempt to improve on the keyboard, in this case by adapting its shape to the shape of the hands.

Whether or not the qwerty keyboard is ideal for English, it simply doesn't fit many other languages, which have different alphabets or writing systems. Consider, for example, the problem faced by a consultant doing a training session in Belgium for Digital Equipment Corporation. The training center had three types of keyboards, Flemish, French, and U.S. English. Trainees switching between exercises sometimes had to use different computers that had different keyboards. Needless to say, the resulting confusion did not speed the training.

The whole idea of a keyboard containing a limited number of alphabetical symbols breaks down for Asian languages whose ancient writing system uses thousands of symbols called kanji, each representing an idea rather than an alphabetic character. Because it takes a long time to learn thousands of symbols, Japanese is written in two ways. Within the first few years at school, children learn approximately 100 kana, phonetic characters in two alphabets called hirigana and katakana. But since kana are rarely used by adults in business settings, computer usage requires a way to deal with kanji.[19] Figure 8.10 a shows a Japanese word processor that takes input in the form of kana and searches for the equivalent kanji. Difficulty dealing with kanji is a key reason why Japanese offices have not used computers as much as U.S. offices. Computers are becoming more widespread in Japanese offices as direct input of handwritten kanji becomes easier.

The basic idea of the keyboard has also been adapted to make it more effective for particular situations. Modified cash registers such as those used in McDonald's make it unnecessary for the cashier to remember the price of an item (see Figure 8.10b). Instead, the cashier presses a key that represents a particular type of hamburger or drink. The handheld terminal and touchtone phone made it possible to enter data from work locations without being anchored to a bulky VDT. Because the touchtone phone has no visual display, data input through a touchtone phone is a response to audio prompts from the computer system.

The last adaptation of the keyboard is to eliminate the keys altogether. The touch screen made it possible to enter data by pointing to a spot on a screen (see Figure 8.10c). Pointing on a touch screen is less precise than pointing with a mouse and is therefore limited to applications where pointing to areas of the screen suffices.

Figure 8.10
Data input examples

(a) Using a keyboard to enter Japanese Kanji characters is awkward. The first step is to type a word or sentence phonetically using either the English alphabet or a combination of two alphabetical forms of Japanese writing called Hiragana and Katakana. The computer uses a dictionary to find the equivalent Kanji. Since to different Kanji characters can sound the same (like "red" and "read"in English), the user must occasionally stop to select among such alternatives. (b) This specialized cash register permits the cashier to ring up a restaurant purchase without having to enter or even remember th price of each item. (c) This touch screen is used for buying airline tickets. This form of input is effective in applications involving user choices rather than extensive data entry.

(a)

(b)

(c)

The mouse and other pointing devices made it possible to point with more precision. The mouse was an important breakthrough for expressing commands to a computer. Before it was developed, users had to type commands such as "Print Cust_File." Users had to know the commands, syntax, and file names, and had to spell everything correctly, which made it difficult for users to control computers. With the mouse, touch screen, or screen designed for input using an electronic pen, a user can simply point to select the command and the file. Pointing is an excellent way to make computers easier to use, but it is not a way to enter large amounts of data. This is where the keyboard remains far more effective.

Optical Character Recognition

Several types of input technology are based on recognizing characters or special markings. **Magnetic ink character recognition (MICR)** was developed by banks as an early technology of this type. With MICR, account numbers are written on checks and deposit slips in a standard location and format using magnetic ink that can be recognized by special input devices. This technology expedites the clearing of checks and deposits.

Optical character recognition (OCR) applies a similar idea to capture machine-generated or hand-printed numbers or text. OCR involves two steps: capturing an image and then deciphering it. The deciphering step is a software function that consists of finding the individual characters, subdividing them into the equivalent of pixels, and identifying the input character by comparison with previously stored patterns.

Although OCR started with collecting data from forms filled in carefully by hand, bar coding to identify objects is the most important current application of the general idea. As you can see by looking at the bar code label on a grocery product, bar coding represents characters by using bars in a standard format. Bar code readers come in several forms. Some are stationary and scan the bar code as the object moves by. Others are more like pens that scan across a stationary object. Bar codes are often integrated into point-of-sale terminals used in department stores to record sales and track inventory. Bar coding makes it unnecessary for people to read the data and then copy it. Bar coding applications typically decrease the effort required to input data and increase accuracy substantially.

OCR for hand printing can be used with paper input forms or electronic tablets. For OCR to work with hand printing, either the person must be trained to write letters in a prespecified format or the computer must be trained to recognize an individual's printing. OCR is used with portable computers for applications such as checking inventory and writing parking tickets. However, existing OCR systems are not efficient for inputting large amounts of text and cannot decipher cursive handwriting accurately. OCR can also be used for inputting previously typed or typeset characters. For less than $500, a scanner and OCR program can input previously typed text at 500 words per minute with 98% accuracy (see Figure 8.11), which still means that someone will have to check the recovered text to identify the 10 words out of 500 that need corrections.

Capturing Pictures, Sounds, and Video

Earlier this chapter showed how every type of data can be digitized and can therefore be handled by a computer. Two approaches are used for inputting image and audio data into computer systems. One approach consists of simply recording or copying the data in a computer-readable form. This is what happens when a scanner captures an image and stores it in a computer system. Electronic cameras perform a similar function. (See Figure 8.12.) The other approach is to capture image or audio data and then, as part of the input process, do something to interpret what it means. This approach is used with voice recognition systems.

Voice recognition matches the sound patterns of spoken words with previously stored sound patterns. Work situations in which voice input is important include input while the speaker's hands are busy; input while mobility is required; and input while the user's eyes are occupied. Typical users are people looking through a microscope and not having to look away each time they make a note, or aircraft engine inspectors, who can use a wireless microphone and a limited vocabulary to issue orders, read serial numbers, or retrieve maintenance records. Voice recognition also has potential advantages for workers who lack reading or writing skills. At a Raytheon plant that produces circuit boards for

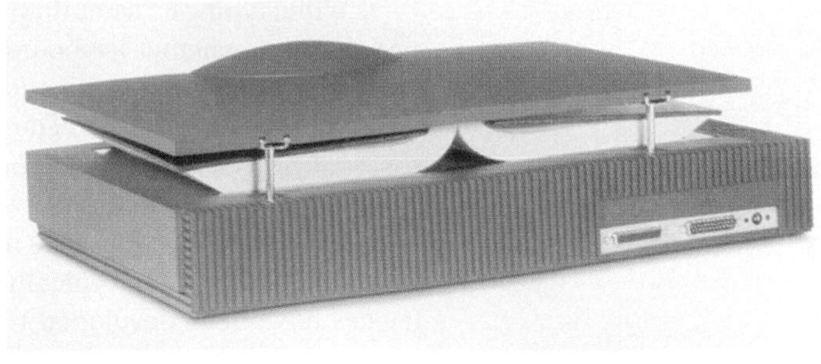

(a)

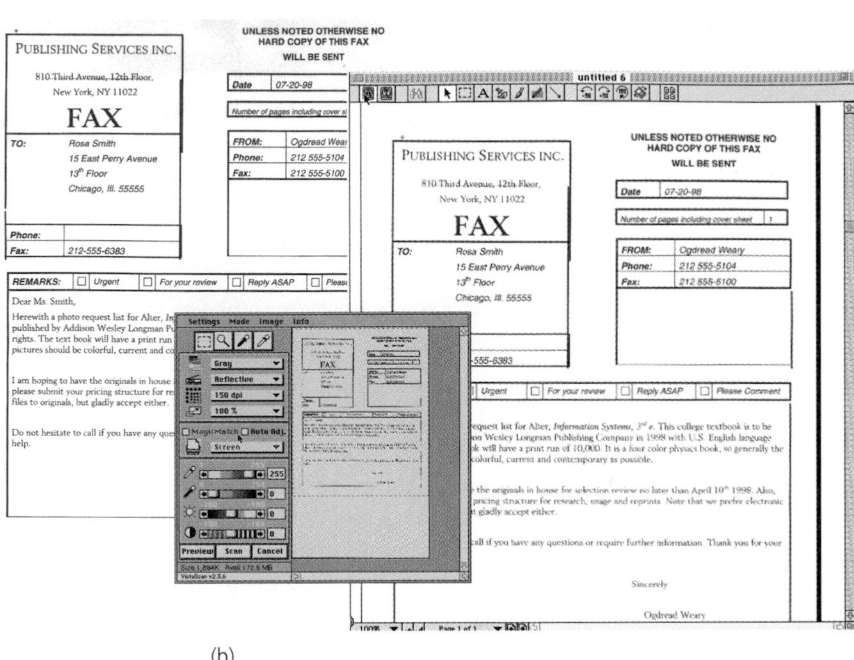

(b)

Figure 8.11
Optical character recognition

This flatbed scanner can be used to capture images and text in the form of a static picture. Converting the text back into a word processing document requires OCR software. The example shows a fax that has been scanned to capture text information in a form permitting further word processing.

Patriot missiles, inspectors gazing through microscopes dictate defect reports instead of writing them by hand. One special beneficiary was a Vietnamese refugee who had trouble reading and writing English, but had "trained" a voice recognition system to understand his pronunciation, as long as he said the words the same way each time.[20] Voice recognition is also becoming important in customer service applications. For example E*Trade, an online brokerage, provides its customers a voice recognition system that lets them manage their accounts and make trades 24 hours a day. The company's idea is to be able to market to anyone who is comfortable using a telephone.[21]

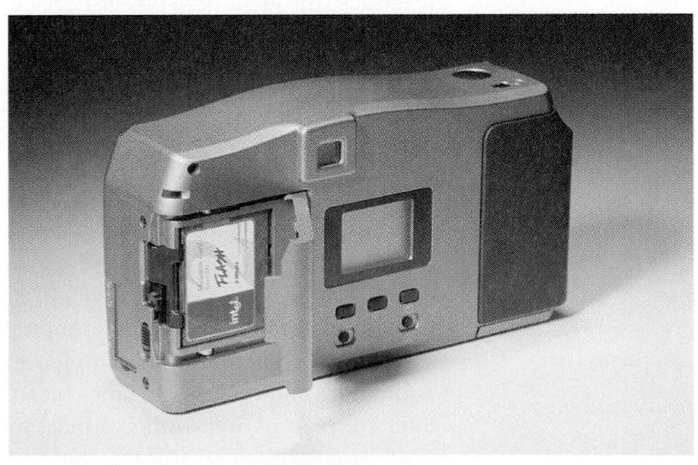

Figure 8.12
An electronic camera for input to a computer system

This electronic camera takes electronic pictures that can be downloaded to a computer. The camera can hold 20 images containing 640 x 400 pixels. This resolution is not as good as the resolution from a camera that uses film but is adequate for many purposes.

While typing is faster than handwriting for some people, there has been some speculation about whether keyboards will be bypassed in favor of direct voice input or handwritten input in many applications over the next several decades. Although no one knows what will happen, this type of development would have major impacts on managerial, professional, and clerical work. Bypassing keyboards may also be crucial for expanding computer use in China and Japan, whose use of kanji was mentioned earlier. Surprisingly, the complexity of these characters may help computers recognize them. Because the strokes in kanji characters are typically written in a particular order, handwriting-recognition devices have been developed that use the order of the strokes as information for deciphering the characters.

Reality Check

DATA INPUT

The text identifies a number of data input technologies.

1. Identify times (if any) when you have entered data into a computer system. Explain why the process seemed as efficient as possible, or alternatively, why it could probably have been improved.
2. Explain how you think you will input data or interact with computers in your career.

STORING AND RETRIEVING DATA

An ideal storage device should be able to store and retrieve any data immediately and in a minimum amount of space. Space used and storage and retrieval times are useful indicators for comparing storage technologies. This section looks at several forms of data storage: paper, micrographics, magnetic storage, optical storage, and flash disks.

Paper and Micrographics

Paper is a 2,000-year-old medium for storing data. Punched cards were the primary medium for storing data in the first computerized business systems (see Figure 8.13a). Although paper is easy for people to use when they are reading or annotating a document, it has many shortcomings. For one thing, it is so bulky that many large businesses have rooms full of paper records and documents. Finding specific data in a personal file cabinet can take seconds or minutes. Finding it in a firm's paper archives can take hours, days, or weeks, if it can be found at all. Another shortcoming is that paper is not conveniently computer readable even though OCR scanners can input text from paper documents.

Computer output microfilm is a solution to the bulkiness of paper that reduces pages of output to tiny images stored on film. A hand-sized card called a microfiche can store the equivalent of hundreds of pages of computer output. Although microfilm greatly reduces the amount of physical space required to store data, it is not conveniently computer readable, which makes it useful only for rarely accessed data. Finding a particular item of information using a microfilm or microfiche reader takes several minutes at best. Furthermore, microfilm cannot be changed once it is produced.

Magnetic Tapes and Disks

The shortcomings of paper media led to the development of media based on the magnetization or demagnetization of tiny locations on an iron oxide surface. The first of these was the **magnetic tape,** a plastic tape on which data could be stored using numerical codes. The ability to magnetize and demagnetize the same region of a magnetic tape without punching a hole means that the data on the tape can be modified by writing over it in a process similar to recording over an audiotape or videotape. Like entertainment audiotapes and videotapes, tapes for storing computer data are sequential devices whose data are read in their order of location on the tape. The fact that tapes must be read

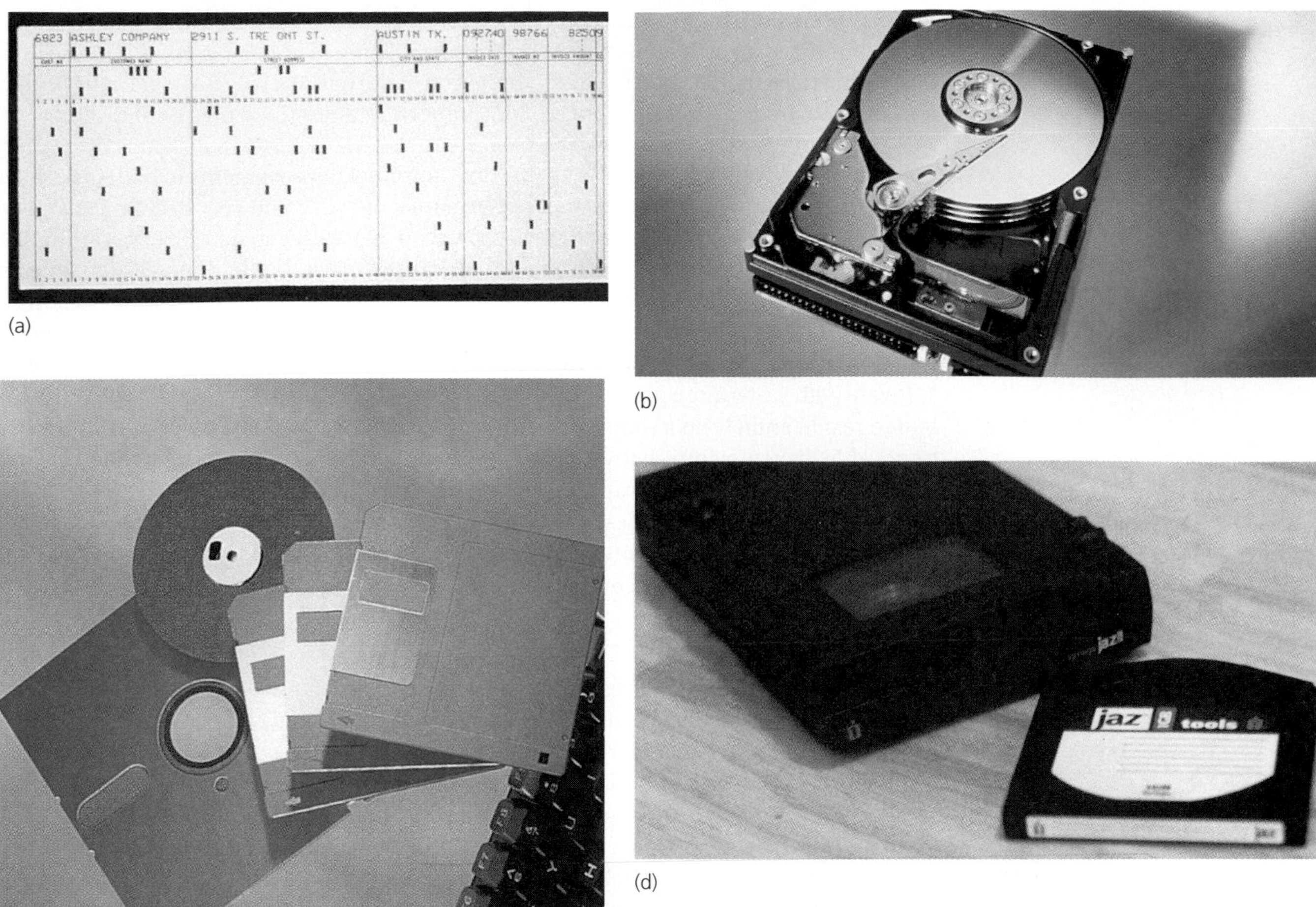

Figure 8.13
Data storage examples

(a) Early business data process was based on punched cards. The pattern of holes punched in each column represented the letter or number at the top of the column. A mechanical card reader sensed the holes. The typed line at the top of the card was for the convenience of the person looking at the card. (b) The first magnetic disks for PCs contained 10 to 40 megabytes of data. This hard disk is only 3.5 inches in diameter, but can hold a 2.1 gigabyte database and costs less then $500. (c) The circular object in the photo is the recording surface inside the plastic container that we often think of as the diskette. (d) This removable Jazz drive combines the high storage capacity of current hard disks with the portability of diskettes. The 3.5 inch disk holds one gigabyte of data.

sequentially greatly limits the types of processing they can be used for, but they are well suited for backup due to their speed and reliability.

Data can also be stored magnetically on a **hard disk,** which is a rotating device that stores data using magnetization and demagnetization methods like those for magnetic tapes. Like diskettes, hard disks store data in concentric circles called tracks. Unlike diskettes, many hard disks have multiple platters. While in use, a hard disk rotates continually. Whenever data are required, a program determines the location of the data on the disk and instructs a disk arm to look for the data at that point. The disk arm moves a read head into position over the correct track and performs the read. The data are read when the rotation brings the required location under the read head. Hard disks are also called DASDs, which stands for direct access storage devices. The special advantage of hard disks over tapes is their ability to access data immediately instead of having to read sequentially through all previous data on the device. A major disadvantage of hard disks is that they rely on continuous rotation at thousands of revolutions per minute with a read head just 15-millionths of an inch above the disk. Occasionally the read head crashes into the disk, destroying both the data and the disk. This is one of the reasons why it is especially important to make frequent backup copies of any important data stored on a hard disk.

Rotating disks come in a variety of sizes. Pocket-sized 3.5-inch diskettes commonly hold 1.4 megabytes of data (see Figure 8.13b). Continual improvements in hard disks have created the same type of exponential performance increase and cost decrease that chip improvements have created. The average capacity of hard disks sold in 1990 was around 60 megabytes. By 1998 this increased to around 3 gigabytes, a fifty-fold increase in 8 years. During this period the price of hard disk storage decreased by a similar ratio, making it possible to buy a gigabyte of disk storage for less than $100 (see Figure 8.13c). The combination of vastly increased RAM and hard disk capacities have made it practical to use PC software with vastly more powerful features and capabilities than the early PC software that had to reside entirely on a single diskette or within limited hard disk storage. Inexpensive removable disks providing between100 megabytes and 2 gigabytes of backup storage have created another important option for data storage and backup. For example a 100 megabyte zip disk that costs less than $10 holds the same amount of data as 70 diskettes. This technology permits business professionals to carry much of their frequently used data on a single portable disk even when they are not carrying a laptop.

Optical Disks

Optical disk technology involves the use of a laser beam to store or retrieve data as microscopic spots on a disk. The first optical disks came out in 1978 and competed with videotapes in the home entertainment market. Audio compact disks came out in 1982 and revolutionized the record business in the late 1980s. The **CD-ROM** was the first application of optical storage for business processing. CD-ROMs are 650 megabyte compact disks that can be read but not written on. They emerged in 1985 for publishing databases, directories, and encyclopedias. CD-ROMs make data readily transportable but were initially limited because the user could not change the data. The initial CD-ROM drives operated at 150 Kbps, but the more current drives operate many times faster. For example a 24X drive operates 24 times as fast as the initial standard.

Several additional optical disk options have been developed. Recordable CD-R disks along with a CD-R drive make it possible for anyone to master a CD-ROM just as they might make multiple copies of a diskette. Rewritable CD-RW disks use a somewhat different technology to produce CD-ROMs using media that can be rewritten up to 1,000 times. Unfortunately the different technology creates a different degree of reflectivity, which means that many CD-ROM and CD-R drives cannot read CD-RW disks. The **DVD** (digital versatile disk), which holds 4.7 gigabytes of data, enough for a two-hour movie, may eventually supplant CD-ROMs if and when the necessary standards are agreed upon.

Optical disks are used for two types of applications, based on whether the data can change. CD-ROMs are excellent for distributing large files of computer readable data ranging from software programs to technical manuals. They cost less than $1 to produce and therefore deliver data much more cheaply than diskettes. CD-R and CD-RW disks are used mostly for backup and long-term data storage of image data. Insurance companies and other paper-intensive businesses find optical storage especially attractive for this purpose. However, current erasable disk technology is too slow for high-volume online transaction processing.

Flash Memory

Although hard disks and optical disks can store an enormous amount of information, they are both mechanical devices with moving parts. They therefore have shortcomings involving the breakage of the moving parts and energy usage necessary to spin the disk and move the read/write mechanism. In contrast, the RAMs within the computer itself are semiconductor devices without moving parts. But they have the problem of losing information when the computer is turned off.

A **flash memory** is a semiconductor device that stores and modifies information while the computer is operating, but that also retains information when the computer is turned off. Currently flash memory chips are used in battery-powered products such as electronic cameras, cellular phones, and notebook computers. An early demonstration of the potential of flash memory came in 1993 with the Hewlett-Packard Omnibook 300, a 2.9-pound portable computer that could run on four AA batteries but was not very powerful by today's standards. The 10 megabyte flash memory chips (effectively doubled with data compression) were packaged in a card the size of a thick credit card inserted into one of four slots in the computer. Flash memory is still much more expensive per bit than RAM memory, but it illustrates yet another direction in which storage technology may develop.

Reality Check

DATA STORAGE AND RETRIEVAL

The text says that most managers and professionals can carry around most of the computerized information they need on a single 3.5-inch portable disk.

1. Explain why you do or do not believe you could store everything you have ever written and every test you have ever taken on a single portable disk.
2. Assume that someone develops a cheap electronic scanner that can capture an entire page in one second and can store it on a high-capacity hard disk. Explain how this would or would not affect you at school or work.

DATA OUTPUT: DISPLAYING DATA

Output devices display data for users. Aside from being inexpensive and reliable, an ideal output device would make it easy to convert data into the most useful information for the users. Early printers and terminals were limited because they were anchored to fixed locations and because they could not produce good graphical output. Recent advances incorporate graphics, images, voice, other sounds, and video. The capabilities that started becoming technologically feasible in the 1980s make it possible to go far beyond the forms of data output that are common even today.

We will look at output devices in the following categories: screen outputs, paper outputs, and audio outputs.

Screen Outputs

The most common device for interactive output on screens is the VDT monitor, such as those used with most PCs. Improvements in monitors over the years include higher resolution (more dots per inch), larger screen size, graphical outputs rather than just numbers and text, and color displays rather than just black and white. All of these improvements have made monitors easier to use and have permitted them to display better information to users. VDTs have shortcomings, however, such as being bulky and taking up a lot of space on a desk. Extensive use often leads to eyestrain. In addition, they give off electromagnetic radiation that may be a health hazard, at least for people whose desks are behind the monitors.

A great deal of work has been done to produce flat screens such as those used with laptop computers (see Figure 8.14a). By the late1990s the tiny black and white screens of early laptops had been replaced by 12-inch (diagonal) color screens that were much larger and much easier on the eyes. Flat screens for desktops are available but are substantially more expensive than VDT monitors with similar screen size. Flat screens are also used in factories where a wall-mounted screen is more convenient than a desktop device. Screen display technology is important not only for the future of computer displays but also for television screens.

Specialized displays of many other types have also been used. "Heads-up" displays originally developed for military applications have been used in some automobiles to project auto control panel information in front of the driver instead of forcing the driver to look down. In a more advanced version of this idea, Figure 8.14b shows a head-mounted display developed by Boeing to help workers performing complex wiring tasks in airplane manufacturing. This display uses semireflective lenses that permit the worker to see a wiring diagram transmitted from a computer superimposed on top of the circuit board being wired.

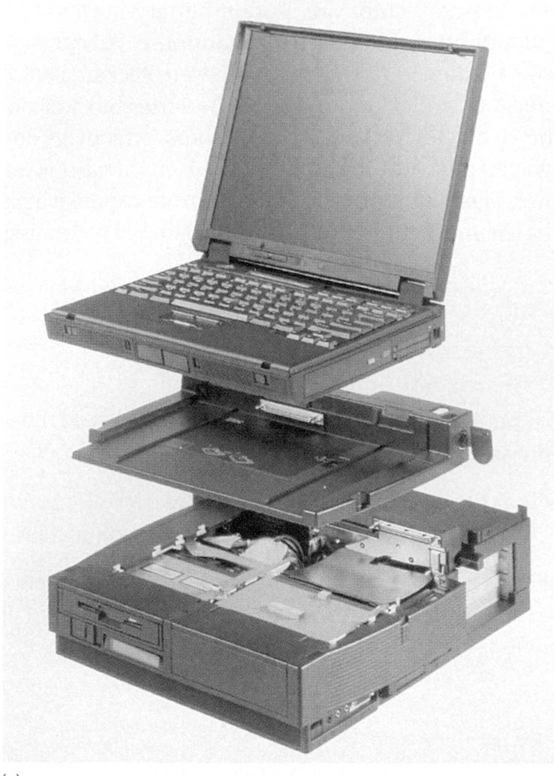

(a)

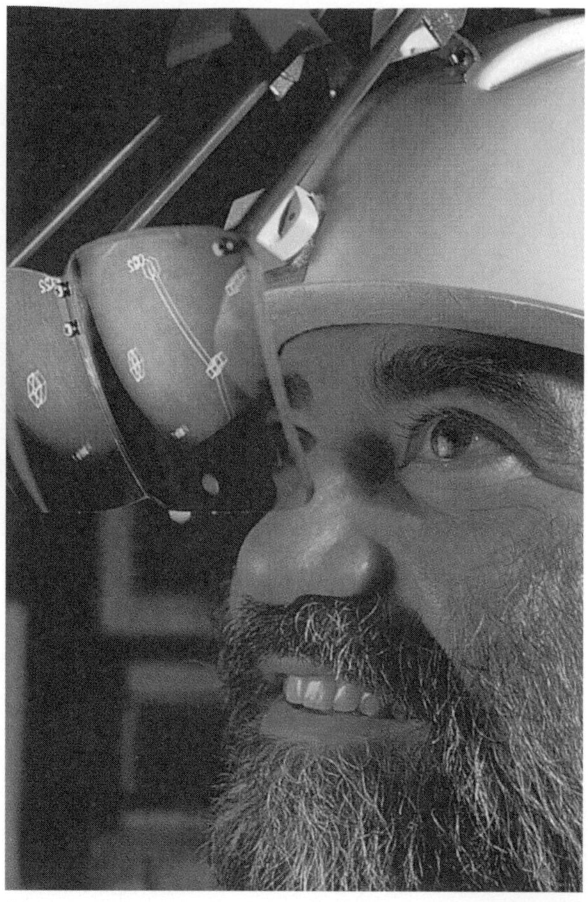

(b)

(c)

Figure 8.14
Data output examples

(a) This laptop computer's flat panel display allows portability while its docking mechanism supports usage within a network. (b) Boeing developed this head mounted display to help the production worker by projecting a wiring diagram into the visual field of the circuit board the worker is wiring. (You can see the projected diagram in the lenses.) The image changes when the worker turns or proceeds to a new task. (c) Unlike the small printers found in most offices,this plotter can print complex engineering drawings on large sheets of paper.

Paper Outputs

Many different types of printers are available for paper outputs from computer systems (see Figure 8.14c). The first computer systems used impact printers, which create marks on paper by hitting a print head against a ribbon. Nonimpact printers include inkjet printers and laser printers. Inkjet printers "spit" ink onto the paper. Laser printers create marks on paper by focusing laser beams on black particles of toner. It is now possible to buy a small laser printer for less than $400, whereas other types of personal printers may cost less than $200. Color also became a practical feature of printers in the early 1990s, with inexpensive color printers costing less than $500 but taking a comparatively long time to print text, and longer to print pictures.

Audio Outputs

Audio outputs are starting to appear more prominently in many business computer systems. In voice-mail systems and many systems for obtaining standardized data such as bank balances, prerecorded prompting messages help the user specify what information is needed. In applications such as voice annotation of spreadsheets and documents, users can hear a comment recorded earlier by someone else. In other computer audio applications, the voice sounds are synthesized. For example, Bell Canada uses voice synthesis to read locations of broken phone equipment to repair people and to tell them how to fix the equipment. Gradual refinements in speech synthesis have resulted in more natural-sounding synthesized speech, making future applications more likely.

This chapter has covered a variety of methods used for data input, storage, and output. Some, such as magnetic tapes, hard disks, and impact printers, have been used for decades. Others, such as voice recognition, are less common today but will have wider impact in the future. Although technological progress will continue, it is difficult to predict which technologies will be adopted widely enough to change the way people work.

CHAPTER CONCLUSION

Summary

What are the basic components of a computer system?
A computer system consists of computers and computer-controlled devices that process data by executing programs. The physical devices in a computer system are its hardware, and the programs are its software. Aside from the computer itself, a computer system also includes peripherals for input, output, and storage.

What are the different types of computers?
Embedded computers are internal components of other machines. Categories of nonembedded computers include personal computer, workstation, midrange computer, mainframe, and supercomputer. The newer category of server crosses many of the older classifications.

What are the organizational approaches to computing?
The organizational approaches to computing are centralized computing, personal computing, distributed computing, and network computing. In centralized computing, all the processing for multiple users is done by a large central computer. In personal computing, users have their own machines and rarely share data or resources. In distributed computing, users have their own computers and use a network to share data and resources. Network computing links stripped down network computers to central servers in order to combine the benefits of centralized computing with the flexibility and responsiveness of distributed computing.

How is client-server computing different from centralized computing?
In client-server computing, different devices on a network are treated as clients or servers. The client devices send requests for service, such as printing or retrieval of data, to specific server devices that perform the requested processing. It differs from centralized computing in terms of the division of labor in handling the user interface, application program logic, and database access. Instead of having a central computer control everything from the displays on user terminals through the application logic and the updating of the database, client-server divides these functions between specialized client and server components.

How is it possible for computers to process data of any type?
Digital computers are built from components that switch between off-on (0-1) states. Because eight bits, or one byte, is enough to uniquely identify 256 different characters, numerical data and text can be represented as a series of 0's and 1's. Pictures and sounds can be represented as 0's and 1's by breaking them into tiny elements and assigning a numerical value to each element.

What are the different approaches for increasing data manipulation speeds?
The approaches include miniaturization, improving the instruction set, using special-purpose processors, and using parallel processing. Miniaturization has been accomplished by changing the manufacturing processes to pack more individual devices into more highly integrated circuits. Improving the instruction set increases speed by combining individual instructions more effectively. Special-purpose processors are tailored to specific tasks. In parallel processing, a large computation is divided into smaller computations that are performed simultaneously.

What are the different forms of data input?
Keyboards are the dominant input device for business data processing but are used when a person has already captured (or just created) the data and is now entering the data into the computer as a separate step. Character recognition techniques such as optical character recognition and bar coding reduce the handling of data being entered into a computer system. Scanners capture images. Voice recognition systems bypass keyboard input, but are not as accurate.

What are the different forms of data storage?
The principal forms of data storage include paper, micrographics, magnetic storage, and optical storage. Micrographic devices reduce paper into miniature pictures on microfilm. Magnetic tapes and disks store data through the magnetization and demagnetization of tiny regions on an iron oxide surface. Magnetic tapes must be used sequentially, whereas disks can be used for direct access. Optical disks come in a variety of read-only, write-once, or rewritable forms. Flash memories use chips that retain data when the computer is turned off.

What are the different forms of data output?
The most common device for interactive output on screens is the VDT monitor, although flat screens have been used for portable computers and factory applications. Many types of printers and plotters are used for paper outputs. Audio outputs are used both for prerecorded messages and for synthesized interaction with computer system users.

Key Terms

functional capabilities
price-performance
ease of use
compatibility
interoperability
maintainability
modularity
scalability
bit
byte
bits per second (bps)
MIPS
FLOPS
computer
program
computer system
hardware
software
central processing unit (CPU)
random access memory (RAM)
read only memory (ROM)
input device
output device
storage device
peripherals
embedded computer
personal computer (PC)
laptop computer
notebook computer
workstation
midrange computer
mainframe
supercomputer
server
centralized computing
personal computing
distributed computing
network computing
dumb terminal
graphical user interface (GUI)
network computer (NC)
client-server architecture
file server
thin client
middleware
peer-to-peer
ASCII
digitizing
pixel
lossless compression
lossy compression
encryption
machine language
32-bit addressing
integrated circuit
chip
microprocessor
micron
RISC
ASIC
DSP
parallel processing
MICR
OCR
voice recognition
computer output microfilm
magnetic tape
hard disk
CD-ROM
DVD
flash memory

Review Questions

1. What is the von Neumann architecture and why is it important?
2. Identify the difference between an embedded computer and a nonembedded computer.
3. What is a server?
4. Describe the difference between centralized computing, personal computing, distributed computing, and network computing.

5. Why does distributed computing require more controls and administration than personal computing?
6. What is client-server architecture, and what does it accomplish?
7. Explain the role of middleware in client-server architecture.
8. How is peer-to-peer architecture different from client-server?
9. Why are base 2 numbers important in computing, and how is it possible to convert a base 10 number to base 2?
10. Define digitizing and explain what determines how closely a digitized picture resembles the original.
11. Why does high-resolution storage of a one-page picture involve more data than storing several hundred pages of text?
12. What are data compression and data encryption, and why are they important?
13. Describe the difference between 8-bit, 16-bit, 32-bit, and 64-bit addressing, and explain why this is important.
14. Explain the difference between RISC and CISC microprocessors and why this is important.
15. What is parallel processing, and why is it potentially useful for studying artificial intelligence?
16. Describe optical character recognition and how it operates.
17. How does voice recognition operate?
18. What are the advantages and disadvantages of optical disks?

Discussion Topics

1. This chapter mentioned information technology performance variables in four areas: functional capabilities and limitations, ease of use, compatibility, and maintainability. Assume you have a five-year-old PC and are considering buying a new one. Explain how each group of performance variables is or is not pertinent to your purchase decision.
2. Responding to Japan's 95% market share in flat panel displays, the U.S. government announced a nearly $1 billion "flat panel display initiative" providing incentives for American manufacturers to achieve full-scale manufacturing. According to the president of the U.S. Display Consortium, flat panel screens will be used in everything from autos to fighter planes, and on "every exit ramp on the Information Highway."[22] Explain why you agree or disagree that it is important for the United States (or any other leading industrial power) to have a significant share of this market.
3. Assume that computerized voice recognition is widespread. Identify some of the possible applications of this technology. How do you think it might affect you personally? How would it affect people you know?
4. Assume that a hand-printing pad and hand-drawing pad became standard components of both desktop and portable PCs. Would this have any effect on you? Identify some ways it might affect work practices in specific jobs.
5. It is now technically possible to carry around on a single portable disk all of the text data you have generated in your life. This includes your medical records, finances, homework assignments, papers, and so on. It also has enough room to store data you need for your current work, such as the syllabus for all your courses, scanned images for papers, and so on. Assuming this technology were available for free, what would you be able to do differently?
6. Estimate how many megabytes would be required to store this entire book. (Your answer will depend on your assumptions.) In making your estimate, consider the fact that the book contains both text and graphics. Based on your results for this book, estimate the number of bytes required to store all the books in a 600,000-volume college library. How many 650 megabyte CD-ROMs would this require?

Chicago Board of Trade: Giving Up on Stomp-Proof Handheld Terminals

For over a century, traders at the Chicago Board of Trade (CBOT) and Chicago Mercantile Exchange have used an open outcry bidding system to make trades, and paper cards to record those trades. Every day over 100,000 of these cards moved from the trading area, called the pits, to data entry clerks who entered the data into computers overnight. In the early 1990s the U.S. Congress demanded that the system be changed after an FBI sting operation led to indictments of dozens of traders for cheating customers by writing false entries on the paper cards and by "front-running," trading for their own accounts before performing clients' transactions. Congress didn't care about open outcry but demanded an audit trail requiring the use of computers.

The design of a computerized system that could be practical amidst the screaming and human gyrations in the pits was not obvious, however. Each trader needed a way to record trades, ideally a way that shared some of the advantages of paper, such as being light and very simple to use. Desktop computers and laptops just wouldn't do. Handheld terminals seemed promising but needed to bear up to the frenetic trading environment while being light enough and comfortable enough to hold for hours. Synerdyne, a small California design firm, bested over 100 competitors in a system design competition. They produced a handheld terminal whose specially designed contours maximized its "holdability." To retain the simplicity of old paper cards, the handheld terminals took handwritten input using a cordless, and therefore easily dropped, stylus made stomp-proof by encasing it in steel tubing. The terminal used radio waves to beam each trade directly to the exchange's computers. If the data from the buyer and seller don't match for some reason, the terminal gave a warning using a vibrating pad under the fingertip grip. At the end of the day, each trader could put the terminal in an electronic safe deposit box that checked the hardware and software and recharged the eight-hour battery. The plan to equip the exchanges with these devices was to cost $40 million but could reduce errors, cut back office costs, and make fraud much more difficult.

After spending over $20 million on this approach and several others, the CBOT abandoned the effort in 1998. The 14-ounce "Audit card" that was eventually produced was designed to be wireless, pocket-sized, connected to other traders, and able to recognize handwriting. Most floor traders opposed it as too slow and cumbersome. Problems included cost, weight, and inaccuracy of handwriting recognition. One director of the CBOT said: "If it's much bigger than the current trading card (which fits in a shirt pocket) teeth would get knocked out and glasses broken." Although other computerization initiatives focused on improving operational efficiency, close monitoring of the progress of trading was still lacking. Ironically, at roughly the same time the New York Stock Exchange announced plans to require mandatory electronic surveillance after several floor traders were charged with fraud.

QUESTIONS

1. What technology performance variables seemed especially important in this situation?
2. Explain why you do or do not believe the need for some version of the handheld terminal will disappear because the pits will be replaced by computer screens in brokers' private offices.

Sources:

Burns, Greg. "A Handheld Computer That's Combat-Hardened." *Business Week*, Apr. 18, 1994, pp. 94–95.

Lucchetti, Aaron. "New Gadget Loses Hope in Chicago," *Wall Street Journal*, Mar. 27, 1998, p. C1.

Media Lab: Trying to Produce a Book-Like Computer Display

Although it is possible to access enormous amounts of information using computers, the human factors of using paper media such as traditional books, magazines, and newspapers are attractive in many ways. For example, given a choice of reading articles in a paper magazine or reading exactly the same articles on a computer screen, most people would view this as no contest and would choose the paper magazine. A student lugging six heavy textbooks in a backpack might have second thoughts, however, and anyone looking at the amount of paper that is produced and discarded might wonder whether there is a way to enjoy the beneficial features of paper publications without the bulk, inflexibility, and waste.

One of many research projects at MIT's Media Lab is trying to address these issues. The Media Lab was founded in 1985 with the charter of inventing and creatively exploiting new media "for human well-being and individual satisfaction without regard to present-day constraints....The not-so-hidden agenda is to drive technological inventions and break engineering deadlocks with new perspectives and demanding applications." One part of the Media Lab is the MicroMedia Lab, which focuses on creating new electronic media. In mid-1998 its Web page identified a goal of "creating paper with microencapsulated cells that can freely rotate. Applying an electrical charge to these capsules changes their orientation and thus the same cells can display different images." In other words, the group was trying to develop a form of flexible paper that performs the type of function a computer screen performs.

The electronic paper would contain ultra-thin wires used to address tiny individual display cells electronically. The cells are around 40 microns in diameter, or around half the thickness of a piece of paper. If millions of these cells could be implanted on a flexible page and controlled electronically, it would be possible to make the paper into an electronic display. Use a binding to assemble multiple pages of this electronic paper and you have an electronic book with the potential of displaying the information in any traditional book. Imagine looking at a list of books or magazines, selecting the one you want, and then reading it using the electronic book. The student would only have one book to carry, and paper recycling would become less important. Furthermore, the electronic book would be able to handle forms of information such as models and animations that current computers can handle but current books cannot.

Through mid-1998 fundamental aspects of the electronic paper had been demonstrated, but a single page prototype did not yet exist. The chief researcher believed that most of the enabling technologies were feasible to produce. He estimated that a future electronic book might cost $2 to $4 per reusable page. Whether or not the electronic book would ever prove feasible, the research in the area showed it was possible to conceive of new ways to combine the easy usage and portability of a book with the information processing capabilities of computers.

QUESTIONS

1. Assume that further research created technology cheap enough for widespread adoption. What would have to happen in order for widespread adoption to succeed?
2. Assume this type of electronic book becomes available for less than $200 and assume that it is used widely. How would it affect the daily life of a student? Of a manager? Of a typical citizen?
3. What would be the implications for authors who receive royalties when books are sold? For the publishing industry which relies on copyrights to prevent unauthorized copying? For bookstores and libraries?

Sources:

Lehmann-Haupt, Christopher. "Creating a 'Last Book' to Hold All the Others," *New York Times*, Apr. 8, 1998, p. B1.

MIT MicroMedia Lab. "Electronic Paper," Online Posting, June 1, 1998 (http://physics.www.media.mit.edu/mm/elecpaper.html).

9

Software, Programming, and Artificial Intelligence

Study Questions

- What are the different types of software?
- How is programming like a translation process?
- What aspects of programming do not depend on the programming language?
- What are the four generations of programming languages?
- What are some of the other important developments in programming?
- What are operating systems, and why should managers and users care about them?
- What is the most basic limitation of programming?
- What is the relationship between artificial intelligence (AI), expert systems, and neural networks?
- What AI-related techniques other than expert systems and neural networks are beginning to attain prominence?

Outline

Opening Case

IBM: CREATING A CHESS PROGRAM THAT DEFEATED THE WORLD CHAMPION

Programming a computer to play high-level chess has been a challenge to the computer science community since the time of the earliest computers. Developed through many years of work by a talented and dedicated IBM team including a former U.S. chess champion, a chess computer called Deep Blue defeated Garry Kasparov, the world chess champion, in a 6-game chess match. (See Table 9.1.) Although chess is considered a hallmark of strategy and intellect, Deep Blue used a largely brute force approach. With its 512 microprocessors operating in parallel, it could evaluate 200 million board positions per second. It performed these evaluations by scanning the board for hundreds of factors such as pawn structure or the position of the king, and then combining these factors into a score for each move it considered. The program contained procedures for considering only plausible moves and countermoves. At the beginning of the game and in certain common endgame situations, it simply followed standard openings and other sequences of moves that are well known to experienced chess players. As the game developed, however, it often went through 10 or more levels of moves and countermoves before deciding what to do.

The machine's victory over the world chess champion led to speculation in many directions. Some believed that this was an important breakthrough for machine intelligence and indicated great promise to come. Others thought this merely demonstrated a great deal of concentrated effort on a situation that is limited by explicit rules of a type that do not exist in important real world problems. Some were very impressed with the unexpected move the machine made in the 35th move in the second game. After 2 minutes of calculation looking 11 moves ahead, it exchanged a pawn instead of moving a queen, thereby surprising most chess masters including Kasparov. Some members of the chess community also thought that one of the greatest players of all time simply played badly, perhaps because he felt disoriented playing against a computer instead of a human player. For example, one chess master noted that Kasparov lost the last game after making a "known" mistake on the 7th move of a common chess opening that is well known. Deep Blue didn't do extensive calculations at that point. It simply consulted its library of openings and instantly produced a winning move.[1] The game ended just 12 moves later. One columnist wrote that "Kasparov opened himself to an attack that no leading player ever lets himself fall into."[2] Kasparov himself said after the match that the arrangements would have to be different next time. Even before the match, he had complained that his past games were well documented but that the Deep Blue team had not made any of its games available for him to study while preparing for the match.

Debate Topic

Deep Blue's victory over the world chess champion illustrates that computers can demonstrate human-like intelligence or will do so soon.

Business professionals know that today's computers can do what seemed like science fiction just 40 years ago, such as recording every item sold by an international corporation, permitting nonprogrammers to create complex spreadsheets, creating realistic visual representations from engineering specifications, and retrieving data from servers around the world. The story of Deep Blue caught the world's imagination in 1997 because it also seemed like science fiction in many ways.

This chapter covers basic topics about software and programming that business professionals need to understand in order to work knowledgeably with information system developers and to appreciate what today's computers can and cannot do. Its major theme is the unending development of tools and techniques that make it easier to instruct computers to perform important business tasks.

To provide a better perspective on this series of triumphs of ingenuity and engineering skill, it is worthwhile to look at a problem that has not yet been solved, the problem of

TABLE 9.1 IBM's Chess Computer Plays World-Class Chess

CUSTOMER
- IBM's marketing and public relations efforts
- Computer science research community

PRODUCT
- A sequence of chess moves demonstrating world-class play

BUSINESS PROCESS

Major steps in preparing the program:
- Study strengths and weaknesses of previous chess programs
- Develop mathematical model for evaluating the board and searching for potential moves
- Codify chess knowledge such as standard openings and end games
- Build the chess computer
- Test the chess computer

Major steps in playing a game:
- Evaluate the current position
- Identify plausible moves
- Evaluate a sequence of likely countermoves and responses
- Select the best move

Rationale:
- Perform extremely deep search to find the best moves

PARTICIPANTS

Developing the program:
- Programmers
- Chess experts

Playing a game:
- None (the computer plays the game)

INFORMATION
- Previous chess games played by chess masters
- Board evaluation parameters
- Current status of the board during a game

TECHNOLOGY
- Programming language (not mentioned)
- Chess computer

programming a computer to understand and respond to questions about stories that four-year-old children can understand, such as:

> *Billy was invited to Sally's party. He asked his mother if she would like a kite. She said that Sally already had a kite and would return it.*

Here's the irony. People have programmed a computer to defeat the world chess champion, but no one knows how to program a computer to understand a simple story that children understand easily. The difficulty with the story is that many aspects of the situation are unstated or implied. We assume that Billy and Sally are young children (but not infants) and that Billy thinks Sally would like a kite as a birthday present. The word *she* in the second sentence refers to Sally because it is unlikely that Billy would be asking his mother if she (his mother) would like a kite, especially since the previous sentence referred to Sally's party. Even though the word *gift* did not appear in the story, we assume the kite is to be a gift because we know that children usually bring gifts to birthday parties. Apparently Billy's mother believes he understands that if Sally already had a kite she wouldn't want another. (If Sally already had a $100 bill, however, she probably would want another, especially as she got older.)

It was possible to program Deep Blue because the programming team had deep knowledge of chess and because the world of chess was completely described by explicit rules. We cannot yet program computers to understand everyday life because no one knows how to identify all the factors and describe how they interact. Between these two extremes are the real world problems that we can program using the tools and techniques that will now be explained. This chapter starts and ends with topics related to artificial intelligence in order to provide a deeper context for standard software topics such as the types of software, the process of programming, and the succession of ever more powerful programming languages.

TYPES OF SOFTWARE

The software in a computer system is the coded instructions, or programs, created by programmers or users to tell the computer system what to do. As summarized in Table 9.2, managers and users are affected directly or indirectly by four types of software: application software, end-user software, system development software, and system software. Although these four categories overlap in practice, the categories help in visualizing the different functions of software.

Application software processes data to structure or automate specific business processes. For example, application software in a sales department might include programs for forecasting sales, controlling purchase transactions, maintaining customer data, and sending bills to customers. This software may be built by a firm's programmers or may be purchased from an application software vendor. In either case, it is developed by analyzing specific work systems, deciding how they might be improved, and writing programs that improve work system operation by structuring or automating part of the desired process or providing better information.

Of all the types of software, application software has the greatest potential for competitive impact. This software is more tightly linked to business processes that the organization hopes will differentiate it from its competitors. Application software makes this business strategy possible. Effective use of the other types of software is still important, however, because it supports the organization's internal effectiveness and efficiency.

End-user software includes general-purpose tools such as spreadsheet programs, word processors, and DBMSs for personal computers. These general-purpose tools are designed for use by end users without programming assistance. They are used in two ways: (1) simply to get work done, such as writing a memo or performing a calculation and (2) to create personal systems for accomplishing particular business tasks repetitively.

TABLE 9.2 Four Types of Software

	Application software	End-user software	System development software	System software
What it accomplishes	Tells the computer how to perform tasks that structure or automate specific steps in business processes that apply only in specific settings	Tells the computer how to perform tasks that support general business processes that apply in many settings, such as writing memos or performing calculations	Helps analysts and programmers build information systems	Controls or supports the operation of the computer system so it can execute application software or end-user software
Example	Billing system, inventory system	Word processor, spreadsheet	Compiler, DBMS, CASE system	Operating system, utility program
Effect on end user	Automates or structures specific steps in business processes	Hands-on tools for the end user; may be used to develop small systems	No direct effect; helps technical staff produce better information systems	Controls computer system operations so that the end user can use it
Generality	Used for a specific type of business process in a specific business or group of similar businesses	Concerned with a general business process that could apply in many firms	Used to build a general class of systems, such as business applications	Concerned with how a computer operates, regardless of what business problem it is solving

End-user software is typically used to develop comparatively simple information systems that don't require a professional level of programming knowledge and expertise. It often permits end users to access and analyze data generated by large, complex systems developed by programmers. Users and managers are affected personally by end-user software because it is a fundamental tool for getting their work done efficiently. Firms that adopt this software especially well may enjoy some competitive advantage in internal efficiency.

Programmers and analysts use **system development software** in the process of building and enhancing information systems. Examples of system development software include compilers, database management systems, and computer aided software engineering (CASE) systems. Compilers translate programs written in languages such as COBOL or C++ into instructions that can be executed by computers. System development software affects managers and users in an important but indirect way because they can help programmers produce more benefits for an organization with the same level of effort. The ultimate impact is a combination of better information systems and lower costs.

System software, produced by programmers who are expert in a computer system's internal operation, controls the internal operation of a computer system. Examples of system software include operating systems and data communication software. An operating system controls the way programs are executed and the way computer system resources, such as disk space, are used. Examples for personal computers include Windows 98 and the Macintosh operating system. Data communication software controls the transmission of data among devices and computer systems. Other system software includes utilities for sorting and merging files and performing background functions related to maintaining computer systems.

Decisions about operating system software affect managers and users in several ways. Because programs are written to run under a particular operating system on a particular type of computer, the choice of an operating system affects the portability of programs and the ability to use purchased software. Operating systems also control the interface between users and computers. The popularity of graphical interfaces for personal computers demonstrates the importance of this aspect of operating systems.

So far, four types of software have been introduced, each of which plays a different role. Application software and end-user software have the most direct impact on the firm's business operations. Some forms of system software, such as operating systems, have a direct impact on ease of use, but other forms of system software along with system development software are oriented toward the technical staff.

Reality Check

TYPES OF SOFTWARE

This section identifies four types of software: application software, end-user software, system development software, and system software.

1. Think about the ways you have used computers. Give specific examples of each type of software that you have used, and explain why it was useful to you.
2. Software in every category is improving continually. For each example in the previous question, identify ways you think the software should be improved.

PROGRAMMING VIEWED AS A BUSINESS PROCESS

Programming is the process of creating instructions that a machine will execute later. This is done by organizing and communicating ideas in a form a machine can recognize. Setting a telephone to forward calls to another extension is a simplistic form of programming.

Setting up a spreadsheet to calculate budget alternatives is a more complex form. Building large transaction processing systems is a much more complex form. These instances all involve generating instructions that a machine will execute.

Because programming is a business process, programming performance can be evaluated using the terms in the WCA method discussed in Chapter 2. For example, the programs that are the product of the programming process can be evaluated in terms of cost to the customer (including learning time), quality, responsiveness, reliability, and conformance. The programming process itself can be evaluated in terms of rate of output, consistency, productivity, cycle time, flexibility, and security.

Infrastructure and context issues are important to consider for programming because it is part of the larger process of building and maintaining information systems (introduced in Chapter 1). Steps that precede programming include analyzing the problem, getting agreement on how the system should operate, and designing the computer system. Steps after programming include training users, implementing the information system in the organization, and maintaining it over time. The last three chapters of this book discuss these steps in depth. For now we are focusing on programming to help in understanding tools such as programming languages.

Programming as a Translation Process

Computers are programmed by writing computer programs. A **computer program** is a set of instructions in a programming language that specifies the data processing to be performed by a computer. Figure 9.1 shows that writing programs is part of a process of translating from what a user wants to accomplish into instructions that can be executed by a computer. Writing the programs expresses the user's ideas in a programming language. In most cases, these computer programs cannot be executed directly by the computer; instead, they must be translated into machine language. This additional step is performed automatically by other programs written by experts in the programming language.

The rules and limitations of the programming language affect both the programs expressing the user's ideas and the automatic translation process. The rules determine what kinds of statements and commands can be used in the programs, as well as the exact grammar for using them. Programs that perform the same processing but are written in different languages use different commands and different grammar. The automatic translation step uses the rules of the language as a guide in deciphering the programs. One reason programming languages contain so many seemingly arbitrary rules is to make this automatic translation practical.

Figure 9.1
Programming: a translation process

Programming is a process of translating a user's idea of what a computer should do into a set of instructions that a computer can execute.

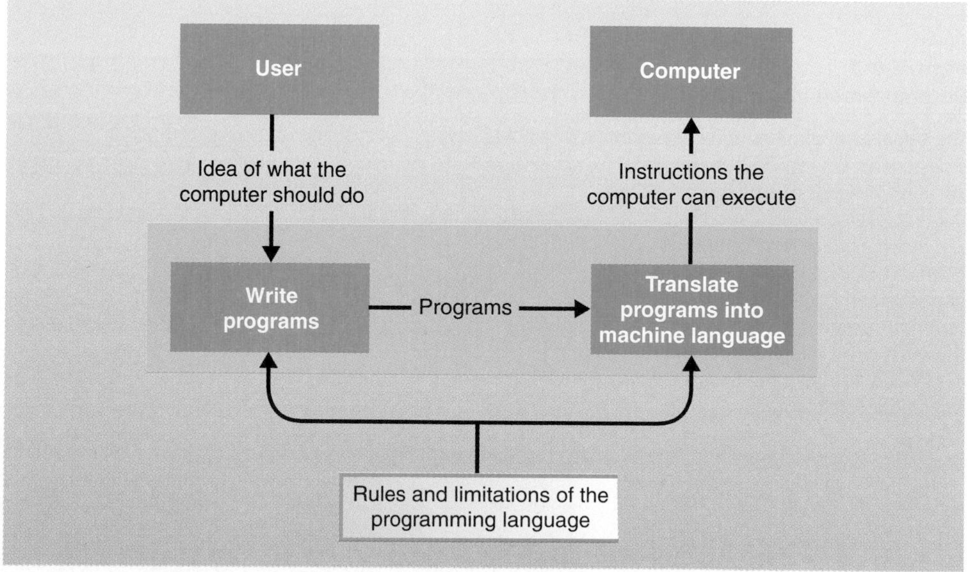

Organizing Ideas

Regardless of the programming language used, programming involves careful organization of ideas. The traditional technique programmers use for organizing ideas is **successive decomposition.** This "divide and conquer" strategy is consistent with the way process modeling with data flow diagrams divides business processes into successively smaller subprocesses. (See Chapter 3.) This strategy is an essential skill for programmers, who need to keep track of the various parts of complex problems. When successive decomposition is applied to programming, programs are divided into small, independent subprograms typically called **modules.** Modules are self-contained subsystems that produce predictable outputs from known inputs. Figure 9.2 illustrates how a program can be divided into a set of subprograms, which can be divided further. Decomposition into modules makes the logic of a program more apparent by separating the details of the modules from the overall logical flow.

Successive decomposition allows programmers to solve a problem with a module and then reuse that solution in new situations. This avoids reinventing program logic that has already been developed. For example, suppose that you want a computer to list every customer whose payments are delinquent. The same module that finds the next customer might also be used in a different program that sends a promotional mailing to specific categories of customers.

Even though most programming languages contain methods for successive decomposition, undisciplined programming still produces poorly organized programs. Such programs are difficult to test and to maintain. These problems led to the development of **structured programming,** a disciplined style of programming based on the successive decomposition. Structured programming has achieved wide acceptance because it results in programs that are much easier to create, understand, test, and maintain. Such programs have the following characteristics:

- The program code is divided into functional constituent parts called modules.
- The modules can be executed as independent programs.
- The modules are related to each other hierarchically.
- A main module at the top of the hierarchy controls program execution.
- Each module should have only one entry point and only one exit point.
- Each module should operate depending only on the input data and not on any information remembered from the last time it was used.
- The logical flow within any module should be specified using only three basic control structures shown in Figure 9.3: sequence, selection, and iteration. The use of GO TO

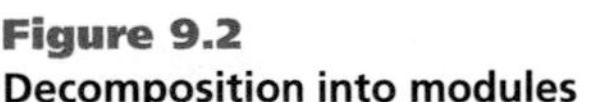

Figure 9.2
Decomposition into modules

The calculation of gross and net pay in a payroll system can be decomposed into several levels of subprograms. On the first level, the calculation is expressed as three smaller subprograms. Each of these is then divided into several modules, each of which could be specified in more detail to show the precise logic. (Note that the data flows between modules are not included in the diagram.)

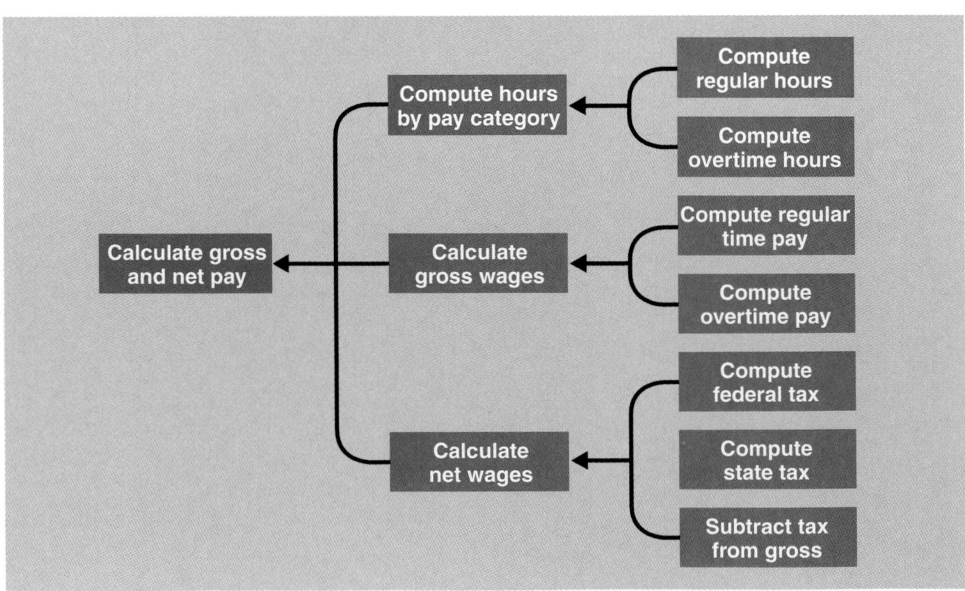

Figure 9.3
Three control structures used in structured programming

To make sure that computer programs are understandable and easy to maintain, structured programming calls for consistent use of only three control structures within programs.

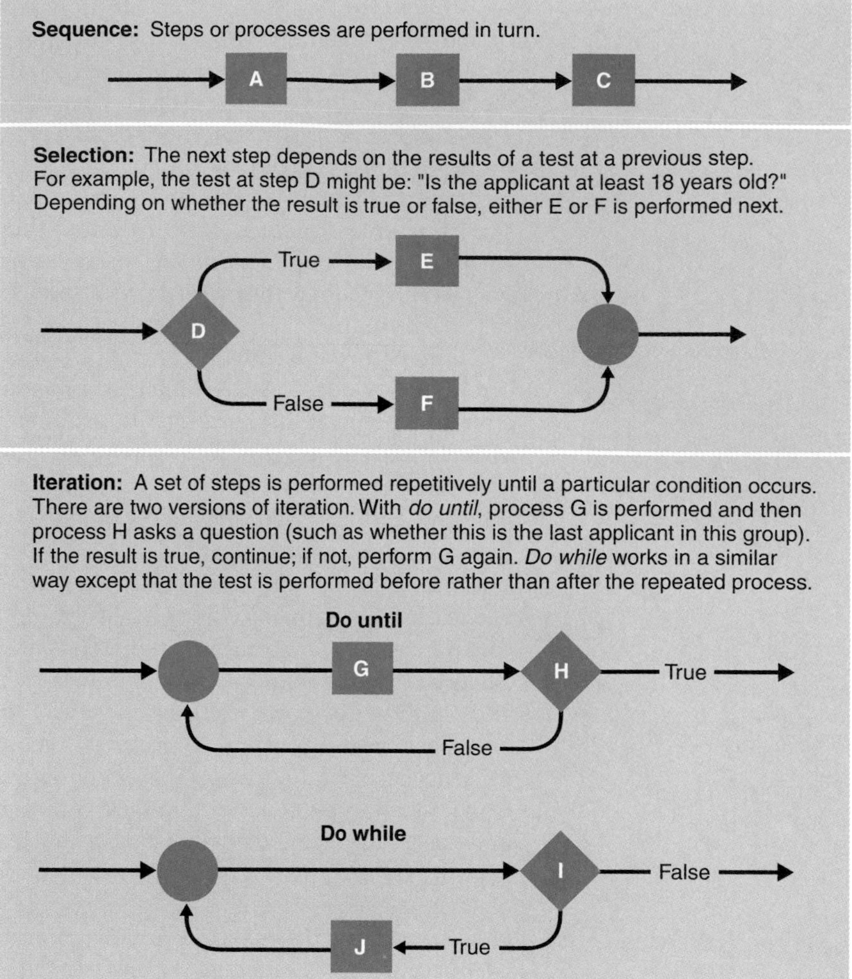
Sequence: Steps or processes are performed in turn.
A
B
C
Selection: The next step depends on the results of a test at a previous step. For example, the test at step D might be: "Is the applicant at least 18 years old?" Depending on whether the result is true or false, either E or F is performed next.
True
E
D
False
F
Iteration: A set of steps is performed repetitively until a particular condition occurs. There are two versions of iteration. With *do until*, process G is performed and then process H asks a question (such as whether this is the last applicant in this group). If the result is true, continue; if not, perform G again. *Do while* works in a similar way except that the test is performed before rather than after the repeated process.
Do until
G
H
True
False
Do while
I
False
J
True

statements that jump forward or backward in a program should be minimized or eliminated because a non-sequential flow tends to be confusing.

- Each module should be small enough to be understood easily.

Organization of ideas and structured programming are not just issues for professional programmers. Programs written by business professionals without programming training are often poorly structured. One reason spreadsheet models often contain errors is that spreadsheet software does little to encourage or enforce structured programming.

Testing Programs

Testing is the process of determining whether a program or system operates in the desired manner. A flaw in a program that causes it to produce incorrect or inappropriate results is called a bug. The process of finding and correcting bugs is called debugging. The two types of bugs are syntax errors and logic errors.

Syntax errors involve incorrect use of the programming language. The SQL translation of the user's query in Figure 4.6 in Chapter 4 demonstrates the meaning of syntax. The first line of the translation uses the term *select* because that command has a specific meaning in SQL. Conceivable English alternatives such as *find* or *look for* would be syntax errors because these terms are not recognized as commands in SQL and would be rejected. The syntax of programming languages has been a major stumbling block preventing nonprogrammers from developing information systems. Current user interfaces eliminate parts of this problem by permitting users to select from a list of commands instead of assuming that users will remember command names.

Logic errors, are bugs that cause a program to perform incorrect processing even though the program is syntactically correct. For example, it may calculate the tax on the entire purchase when it is supposed to exclude food items. Programs that operate correctly individually may also fail due to mutual inconsistencies when they are used together with other programs. Another possible logic error is that the program performs the intended processing but the initial intention when the program was designed was incorrect or too limited. In software firms, this problem has become a standing joke: Customer service people explain to customers that the way a particular program operates is a "feature," not a "bug." This means that the program operates the way it was supposed to operate, and the way the manual says it should operate, whether or not the user believes this makes sense.

Most programs initially contain bugs and inappropriate features regardless of how carefully they are first written. Business programs rarely work correctly the first time. The larger the program and the larger the number of interactions with other programs, the higher the likelihood of bugs. Furthermore, some bugs go undetected until after the program has been used in practice for weeks or months. Finding such bugs in important computer systems has given notoriety to a number of university students in the last few years. In 13 months spanning 1996 and 1997, university students hunting for bugs in available software found at least six. These included a way to booby-trap a Web page so that it would delete the files of anyone visiting it, a flaw in a Web browser's privacy protection for credit card transactions, a way to use Internet software to make unauthorized bank transfers, and a flaw in the encryption code that the U.S. government permits companies to export.[3]

Software bugs are an especially severe problem in situations where a single erroneous calculation could cause disaster. One of the most expensive isolated bugs to date caused a European Space Agency's Ariane 5 rocket to destroy itself when it went off course while transporting a pair of three-ton communication satellites into orbit in 1996. The bug existed in guidance system software that converted the sideways velocity of the rocket from a 64-bit format to a 16-bit format. The velocity number was too large to fit into 16 bits and caused an overflow error, which shut down the guidance system. A redundant backup version of the guidance system took over, but it failed in the same way milliseconds later because it was running the same software. The software should have checked before creating an overflow, but the programmers had not included this loop because the guidance code had been written for the Ariane 4, which was not as fast as an Ariane 5.[4] A similar overflow problem at the Bank of New York had been widely publicized in 1985 when it prevented the Bank from balancing its books at the end of a day in which it traded $23 billion in securities. The Bank had to pay $5 million interest to borrow that amount for one day because a 16-bit field overflowed the first time Bank performed more than 65,536 (2^{16}) transactions in a day.

Good practice in real world programming includes the development of a test plan for debugging the program and the system it is part of. The debugging of an individual program is sometimes called **unit testing,** which is usually done by testing a program under a wide range of conditions. For example, inputs that are transformed or that participate in program logic are set to typical values and to their high and low values in different tests. Tests using the high and low values often reveal bugs because the errors in the results they generate are often more obvious than errors in results calculated from typical values. In contrast to unit testing, **system testing** determines whether the entire computer system operates as intended. System testing is more complicated than unit testing because the number of possible combinations of conditions is much larger. Testing of programs and systems is a key area of computer science research because it is extremely difficult to prove that even a simple program is correct.

Surprisingly, it is often difficult to debug your own work because you are too familiar with the program's intent. Programmers testing their own work often test for what they think it is supposed to accomplish and decide that the program is correct, but they never test for situations or conditions they have overlooked. To avoid such omissions, many programming groups have someone else test a program after a round of unit testing by the programmer.

Reality Check

PROGRAMMING VIEWED AS A BUSINESS PROCESS

Basic ideas about programming include organizing ideas and testing programs.

1. What techniques do you use to test spreadsheets or other programs you write? Explain why you believe those techniques would or would not be adequate if the problem you were solving involved 20 times as many variables and relationships.
2. Explain how you feel about this statement: "I don't know whether my bank programmed its systems correctly, but I just have to trust those systems and assume that my checking account is being handled correctly."

The Changing Nature of Programming

The principle guiding progress in software is that people should be able to express themselves in a form that is easy and natural for them and that allows them to focus on their business problem and not on the details of representing the problem for the computer. Figure 9.4 identifies some of the major advances that were enabled by the hardware progress in Chapter 8; these advances have permitted greater focus on the business problem. The figure illustrates that these software advances have changed the balance of responsibilities between humans and computers. With the first machine languages, programmers performed 100% of the translation from the idea of what users wanted to accomplish into machine-executable code and kept track of minute, computer-related details about how programs operated. With each successive development, more of the translation is done automatically. The figure illustrates that we don't know whether programming methods will ever advance to the point where people can just say what they want and have it programmed automatically. The natural language that we use in everyday speech will remain ineffective for this purpose for the foreseeable future because it is so unstructured, and, as was illustrated by the story of Billy and Sally at the beginning of the chapter, so much is left unsaid.

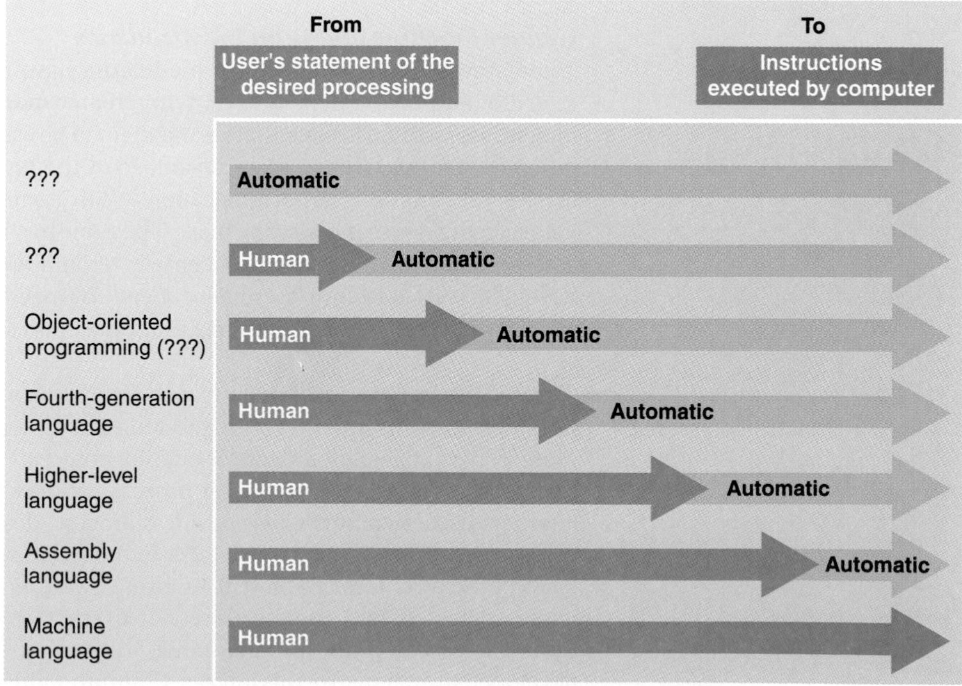

Figure 9.4
From user requirements to executable machine code

This figure summarizes the history of programming as a set of milestones in translating from what a user wants into instructions that can be executed by a computer. With each step, more of the translation is done automatically and less is done by a person. Where object-oriented programming belongs in this progression remains to be seen. The question marks at the top of the figure indicate future developments whose form and content are unknown.

Before discussing specific developments in programming it is useful to recognize some of the major trends supporting the automation summarized in Figure 9.4. In combination, these trends are changing the nature of programming by reducing the number of steps between specifying how the information system should help users and getting it to operate correctly on the computer.

Greater Nonproceduraltiy

People can increasingly express *what* should be accomplished instead of *how* it should be done by a computer. A program that specifies the procedures for how something should be done is described as **procedural.** One that specifies what should be accomplished, but not the procedures for doing it, is **nonprocedural.** For example, the query "Which sales territories were overforecast last month?" explains what the user wants, but not how the computer should answer the question. Greater nonproceduraltiy helps people specify the required processing in the terms in which they think about the problem. With greater nonproceduraltiy, programming is more directly linked to analysis, which is often done with diagrams such as data flow diagrams for process modeling (Chapter 3) and entity-relationship diagrams for data modeling (Chapter 4). As a result, less programming effort is needed to express the user's ideas in a programming language, and it is less necessary for people to make choices about computer-related details unrelated to the business problem.

Greater Modularity and Reusability

As discussed earlier, modularity is a form of division of labor in which systems are designed as a set of self-contained modules that work together, with the output of one module serving as the input of another. Modularity makes it easier to design and test systems because each function is isolated in one place. An important example of modularity is the separation between graphical interfaces that present information to users and database programs that find the data in databases. Early systems might have placed both functions in the same program, making it much harder to maintain. As software becomes more modular, it becomes less necessary for programmers to write programs from scratch. With the trend toward **reusability,** they are encouraged to reuse the work of others by cobbling together and modifying pre-existing modules. Typical reusable modules include programs that control windows on a screen, open and close files, find data in databases, or perform repetitive calculations. For reusability to be practical, programs must be created as carefully chosen modules and stored in a module library that makes reuse easy.

Greater Machine and Data Independence

Trends toward open systems and modularity have reinforced long-term trends toward machine and data independence. With greater **machine independence,** programs are increasingly written in ways that permit them to be executed on a variety of machines from different vendors. This is a key advantage of the Java programming language, which is used extensively for Internet applications. With greater **data independence,** programs are increasingly written in ways that make it possible to change the physical storage of the data without changing the program. Client-server applications with appropriate middleware have achieved a degree of data independence by making it possible to switch database software at the server without changing the application software at the client.

Tighter Links between Analysis and Programming

Although students often view programming as an end in itself, businesses see programming as part of a larger process of building and maintaining information systems (summarized in Figure 1.1). That larger process includes analyzing the problem, comparing alternatives, designing the new business process, designing the technical system, coding the system, testing it, implementing it in the organization, and maintaining it over time. Each of the advances in Figure 9.4 moves toward linking analysis and programming by eliminating steps between the expression of what people want (analysis) and the instructions for the computer (programming). A number of commercial products have been developed to systematize this linkage. **Computer aided software engineering (CASE)** systems differ in detail and scope, but they typically include process and data modeling, a comprehensive data dictionary, methods for designing the technical structure of programs and databases, and modules for creating user interfaces and reports.

As these four trends take hold even further, entire technical systems will become more self-explanatory because the programs will be less procedural, more modular, more machine and data independent, and more tightly linked to the analysis. This will make it easier for people other than the original programmers to understand what the entire system and the individual programs accomplish. Programmers should find it easier to modify programs when this becomes necessary. The four trends may seem very abstract at first blush, but they are basic ideas underlying much of the progress that has occurred in programming languages and techniques. One of the places where these trends are converging is in the increasing application of object-oriented programming.

The Trend Toward Object-Oriented Programming

Many software developers believe that major advances in programming are being created through applications of a programming philosophy called object-oriented programming (often abbreviated OOP). This general approach was invented in the 1960s with the simulation language Simula67 but did not become popular until the 1990s. Although OOP may seem to be an extension of the structured programming techniques mentioned earlier, there is more to it than that because it is a fundamentally different way of thinking about programming.

Object-oriented programming (OOP) treats data and programs in a way that may seem strange to someone who has programmed using the traditional languages that will be explained in the next section. Figure 9.5 illustrates the major OOP concepts. OOP starts by identifying *objects* and *classes*. Objects are the people or things about which data exist. Associated with an object are both data and actions that can be performed related to the object. For example, an object might be a document written using a word processor. Any particular document is a member of a *class* of objects called "document." Associated with that class of objects are *actions* that can be taken, such as opening it, closing it, saving it, or deleting it. These actions all have *methods* for performing the action. All members of a class of objects *inherit* the attributes of the classes that precede them in the object classification scheme. A document within the subclass "memo" therefore would inherit all attributes and actions related to documents as well as additional attributes and actions related specifically to memos.

In object-oriented programming all actions are controlled by *messages* passed between objects. For example, the object "user" could send a message to the object "Memo to A. Jones" telling it to open itself. If there are 10 different types of documents and one standard way to open a document, that method for opening documents would be attached to the object class "document" and inherited by all 10 types of document. To open a document of any type, it would only be necessary to send an "open" message along with any additional data required to perform this action. For example, the additional data might be the identification of the object sending the message because the method for opening documents might check whether the message came from an object permitted to open this document.

While it may seem strange to tell a document to open itself, treating things in terms of objects, classes, actions, inheritance, and messages encourages modularity and reusability. The most visible applications of object-oriented programming to date have been in graphical user interfaces, which can be described in terms of particular types of objects such as windows, menus, fields, and buttons. These same classes of objects apply regardless of whether the application is a billing system or a spreadsheet. It is therefore possible to program many methods only once and then reuse them for many different applications. Because the user interface and data handling make up a large part of many applications, OOP saves programming effort, simplifies overall system design, and creates more consistent-looking applications. Even though the many programming tools for OOP have not yet been developed fully, objects and object-orientation are becoming increasingly important across the information systems landscape. Object-orientation is also starting to transform the way programmers work and is increasingly common in applications. We will see in the next section that object-orientation is an important feature of newer programming languages such as C++ and Java.

Figure 9.5
Major concepts of object-oriented programming

The major concepts of object-oriented programming include classes, objects, inheritance, methods, message passing, and polymorphism. Building these ideas into the analysis and programming of an information system makes it easier to develop and maintain.

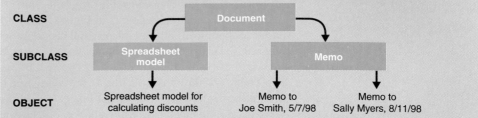

Classes and objects: Objects are the things about which data exists. Objects of the same type are grouped together into classes. Classes can include subclasses. In this example, speadsheets and memos are objects in the class *Documents*.

CLASS — Document

SUBCLASS — Spreadsheet model; Memo

OBJECT — Spreadsheet model for calculating discounts; Memo to Joe Smith, 5/7/98; Memo to Sally Myers, 8/11/98

Inheritance and methods: The objects within a class inherit the methods associated with the class. The methods are functions that can be performed on the objects in the class. In this example, associated with the class Documents are a series of methods such as opening, closing, saving, and printing. All of these are inherited by the objects in the subclasses.

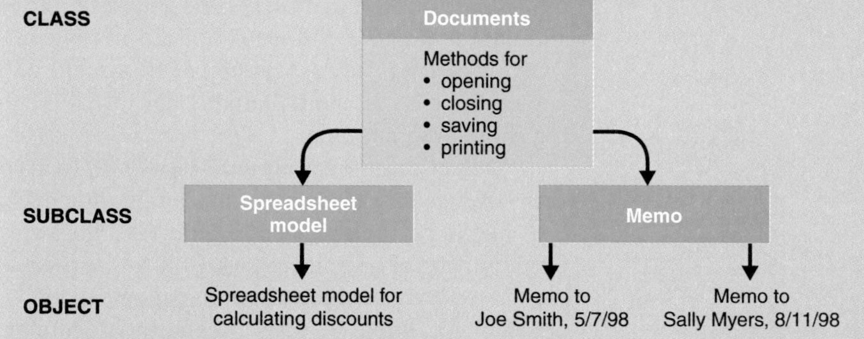

Message passing: The only way to communicate between objects is to send an explicit message.

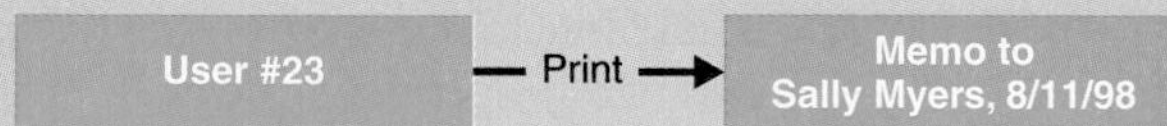

Polymorphism: The same message can be sent to objects in distinct yet similar classes to start an action that may be handled in a different way depending on the characteristics of the classes. While some aspects of printing are the same in this example, such as identifying a printer, other aspects are different, such as the need for a method for splitting the spreadsheet across columns and pages.

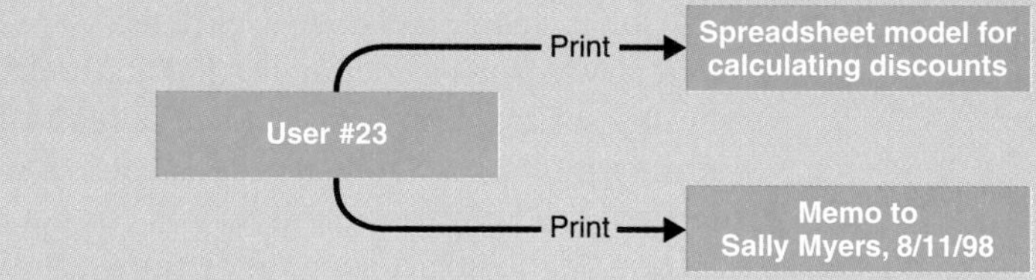

Reality Check

OBJECT-ORIENTED PROGRAMMING

Object-oriented programming is a fundamentally different way of thinking about the programming process.

1. Assume you were a programmer who had not used this technique but had many years of experience in traditional programming. Explain why you would probably be enthusiastic or unenthusiastic about OOP?
2. Assume you were an IT manager who recently heard about the advantages of OOP. How would you decide whether to pursue it in your organization?

FOUR GENERATIONS OF PROGRAMMING LANGUAGES

The progression from machine language to fourth generation languages and beyond is often called the **generations of programming languages.** We will summarize this progression to explain the directions in which progress is continuing to occur. Although business professionals do not work with machine language directly, starting from this point provides useful background for understanding the advances that are continuing today.

Machine Languages

The internal programming language for a particular chip is called its **machine language.** Although the first programmers had to write programs in machine language, today's application programmers no longer have to do so. Box 9.1 presents a hypothetical example that compares a highly simplified machine language with an assembly language. In this example, the instructions are performing the calculation

$$A = (B - C) * D + (E * F)$$

The machine language instructions in the box look nothing like the formula. Instructions in this hypothetical machine language consist of a numerical operation code and the location of the data item that is being added, subtracted, or multiplied. For example, the second instruction in the program is "37 - 202," which says "Add the contents of location 202 to the contents of the accumulator." Each instruction is in a physical location inside the computer; each data item is in a physical location that must be referenced explicitly by the program.

Writing programs in machine language is extremely difficult because it forces programmers to make many explicit choices they do not care about, such as the physical location of the data and machine language instructions. The code itself is also so inexpressive that it is difficult to understand what another person's machine language program is trying to do. Even the original programmer may find complex programs difficult to understand. Machine language programs are also difficult to modify or expand. Changes as seemingly simple as inserting several lines of code may require many corrections in location references. Major changes in data configurations or program flows are a programming nightmare. In addition, the lack of machine independence makes it necessary to rewrite a program for it to accomplish the same processing on a different type of machine. While machine language is essential for the internal operation of the machine, it is an inordinately difficult medium for business programmers to use.

Assembly Languages

Early programmers developed an ingenious solution to the shortcomings of machine language. The solution was to write programs using assembly language and then have the computer automatically translate those programs into machine language instructions. Box 9.1 illustrates that **assembly language** allows the programmer to write the program using the names of the variables (such as *A, B, C*) rather than the location of the data in the computer (201, 202, 203 in the machine language example). Working with the names of variables avoids the problems of physical references required in machine language programming and makes programs easier to write and maintain.

Programs called assemblers and loaders were developed to work together in translating the programmer's assembly language program into a machine language program. This translation includes a number of things. It converts all mnemonic operation codes (such as *add* and *sub* in Box 9.1) into the equivalent machine language codes (such as 37 and 46). More important to programmers, the translation identifies all variables in the program and assigns a machine location to each of them. When the program runs on the computer, a machine location is assigned for each translated instruction. Assemblers also perform other important functions such as identifying syntax errors and certain logical errors. For example, if a program statement says ADD *X*, but *X* does not yet have a value, the assembler identifies *X* as an "undefined variable."

BOX 9.1 *Comparison of machine language and assembly language*

A programmer wants the computer to calculate the value of the variable A using the formula

A = (B - C) * D + (E * F)

On the left is a set of instructions expressing this calculation in a hypothetical machine language. On the right is an equivalent set of instructions in a hypothetical assembly language. For example, the operation code "sub" in the third assembly language instruction is equivalent to the operation code 46 in the third machine language instruction. While programming in assembly language is easier than programming in machine language, it is still much harder than just stating the formula.

Machine language

To program in this machine language, one must specify the location of each instruction, the numerical operation code, and the location of the operand (the data item the instruction uses).

LI = location of instruction

OC = operation code

LO = location of operand

Assembly language

To program in this assembly language, one must specify the operation code and the name of the variable. Notice how the programmer had to make up a temporary variable that was not part of the business problem.

OC = operation code

VAR= variable name

Machine language instruction			*Meaning of instruction*	*Assembly language instruction*		*Meaning of instruction*
LI	*OC*	*LO*		*OC*	*VAR*	
101	19	—	Clear accumulator	cle	—	Clear accumulator
102	37	202	Add contents of location 202 to contents of accumulator	add	B	Add B to contents of accumulator
103	46	203	Subtract contents of location 203 from contents of accumulator	sub	C	Subtract C from contents of accumulator
104	52	204	Multiply contents of accumulator by contents of location 204	mpy	D	Multiply contents of accumulator by D
105	24	207	Store contents of accumulator in location 207	sto	T	Store contents of accumulator as a temporary variable T
106	19	—	Clear accumulator	cle	—	Clear accumulator
107	37	205	Add contents of location 205 to contents of accumulator	add	E	Add E to contents of accumulator
108	52	206	Multiply contents of accumulator by contents of location 206	mpy	F	Multiply contents of accumulator by F
109	37	207	Add contents of location 207 to contents of accumulator	add	T	Add T to contents of accumulator
110	24	201	Store contents of accumulator in location 201	sto	A	Store contents of accumulator in A

Despite the improvements embodied in assembly language, programming in assembly language retained many of the major drawbacks of programming in machine language. It remained a laborious, highly detailed, and error-prone activity. In addition, because assembly language is so directly related to the machine it runs on, transferring a program to a different machine language remained tedious and error-prone. The next step was to provide a better tool than assembly language.

Higher-Level Languages

The shortcomings of assembly language programming led to **higher-level languages** in the late 1950s. Also called third generation languages (3GLs), their purpose was to permit people to program at a higher level. In the assembly language example, the programmer is thinking about how to calculate *A* from the variables *B, C, D, E,* and *F.* Ideally, the programmer should be able to give the formula instead of having to break the calculation into 10 tiny steps. Higher-level languages permit concise statements of this type.

A program called a **compiler** translates higher-level language programs into machine language. For example, a compiler allows a programmer to simply write the equation in the example and translates the equation into machine language. In this type of translation process, the original program is called the **source code,** and the equivalent machine language program is called the **object code.** The object code is used each time the application is executed. When it is necessary to change the program, the changes are made in the source code, which is then translated into new object code. These procedures make it unnecessary to translate the source code each time an application is executed. In addition to allowing programmers to express arithmetic statements directly, compilers (along with system software) also provide automatic mechanisms for handling input, output, and data formatting. These mechanisms permit the programmer to use a command such as *PRINT* which is automatically translated into hundreds of machine language instructions that take care of all the details required for the computer to retrieve the data. These details are related to the internal operation of the computer and its interface with the printer and are of no interest to the application programmer, who simply wants certain data printed.

Interpreters perform a similar function in a different way. An **interpreter** for a higher-level language translates and executes each successive line of a program. The interpreted programs remain in source code, and object code is not generated for later use. Interpreted programs often run more slowly than compiled programs because the compiler can optimize the translation instead of being required to translate and execute each line. Compilers have major advantages when repetitive use and speed are important, but the use of interpreters makes it easier to debug programs and is fast enough in many situations. The Java language used for many Internet applications is an interpreted language.

The same higher-level language needs different compilers or interpreters for different types of computers because different microprocessors use different machine languages. This is an important issue related to the portability of programs between different types of computers. Ideally most application programs should be machine independent, and therefore able to operate on any computer with sufficient capacity. Although many higher-level languages were designed with machine independence in mind, compilers for the same language on different machines often have some inconsistencies. Consequently, programs written in a higher-level language on one type of computer may not run properly on another type of computer. Such programs must be retested on the second computer and may have to be modified before they can be used.

Many higher-level languages have been developed, but only a few have attained widespread use, including COBOL, FORTRAN, PL/I, BASIC, Pascal, ADA, C, C++, and Java. All of these were initially developed with a particular set of capabilities but have been modified and expanded through subsequent versions on different computers. Box 9.2 explains more about these languages.

Figure 9.6 compares three programming languages by showing how each can express the same simplistic program. COBOL is the traditional language for most business data processing. BASIC was originally developed as a simple language for teaching programming but has developed into Visual Basic, which is an important programming tool for programs run on personal computers. C++ is a newer language used frequently for developing new, industrial-strength software. To a nonprogrammer, the differences between these languages may appear superficial, but each important language has certain features that make it especially useful for a particular purpose. For example, the COBOL program contains a mandatory data division for defining the format of the data in the program. Capabilities related to data definition and the formatting of inputs and outputs are one of the major reasons COBOL is the most common programming language for business data processing.

BOX 9.2 *Higher-level programming languages*

FORTRAN (FORmula TRANslator) was introduced by IBM in 1957 as the first higher-level language. It was developed for scientific programming focusing predominantly on calculations and with relatively simple input and output requirements. Initially, it had few structured features.

COBOL (COmmon Business Oriented Language) was developed in 1959 by a committee whose goal was to produce a higher-level language for business data processing. These applications required extensive control of inputs and outputs but relatively simple calculations. Improved versions of COBOL came out in 1968, 1974, and 1985. In attempting to make COBOL programs self-explanatory, COBOL's designers permitted lengthy names of variables and subroutines and used sentence-like grammar. This design made programs extremely verbose but easier to maintain than FORTRAN programs. COBOL is the language used most commonly in existing business data processing systems, although it is used less frequently for newer systems. It is a good tool for organizing programming ideas through successive decomposition and contains some features supporting structured programming.

PL/I was introduced by IBM in 1964 as a single language that could be used for both business data processing and scientific calculations. It is extremely complicated because it incorporates and extends most of the capabilities of both FORTRAN and COBOL. PL/I did not replace COBOL because businesses were not convinced it was worth the expense to rewrite their existing COBOL programs.

BASIC (Beginner's All-purpose Symbolic Instruction Code) is an interpreted language developed at Dartmouth in 1965 as a simple language for teaching introductory programming. Students learning BASIC could write small programs within an hour instead of days or weeks. The early versions of BASIC were very limited. For example, the names of variables could only be one or two characters long in the early versions. Newer versions such as Visual Basic have added methods for creating graphical user interfaces and are used widely for designing programs that run on personal computers.

PASCAL was developed by Niklaus Wirth in 1971 as a tool for teaching and enforcing structured programming. It has become widely used as a teaching tool in computer science departments and is also used widely on microcomputers instead of BASIC. Its input–output capabilities are too limited for most business data processing.

ADA is a language developed by the Department of Defense in 1980 to try to standardize data processing for its weapons systems and to make programs more reusable to reduce programming costs. It is a structured language that encourages modular design and facilitates testing and reusing code.

C was introduced by Bell Laboratories in 1972 to combine some of the low-level machine control capabilities of assemblers with the data structures and control structures of higher-level languages. It is designed to be machine independent and is used to write programs that can be used on different types of computers. The UNIX operating system is written in C so that it, too, can be portable. C is used extensively for infrastructure programs and new software development.

C++ is a dialect of C that provides capabilities related to object-oriented programming. It is used by software firms to develop many of their new commercial applications. It is used extensively for new client–server applications.

Java was developed in 1995 as a general purpose, object-oriented, application-development language for producing programs that operate in a distributed environment involving many different platforms. Java programs execute within a "Java virtual machine" that can be controlled by a Web browser. Operating within this constrained environment means that Java programs are machine independent and therefore generate the same results on any CPU that is using a particular Web page. It also leads to a serious disadvantage, however, because programs written in Java run much more slowly than comparable programs that are optimized for a particular CPU. Programmers knowledgeable in C++ can become productive quickly in Java because it contains 90% of the constructs in C++ and leaves out some of its more complex features.

The language Java, which is partially derived from C++, requires a few additional comments because it has received so much publicity due to its emerging role in distributed computer systems. The original Java development in 1995 was an offshoot of an unsuccessful project at Sun Microsystems aimed at controlling the user interface for home appliances. The team created Java when it redirected itself toward creating a standard, machine independent language for distributed applications on the Internet. The approach for achieving machine independence was to require that small Java programs called **applets** run inside a constrained environment called a "Java virtual machine" that runs within a Web browser or other software. Java is machine independent because the virtual machine runs the same way on every computer. Java is secure because everything

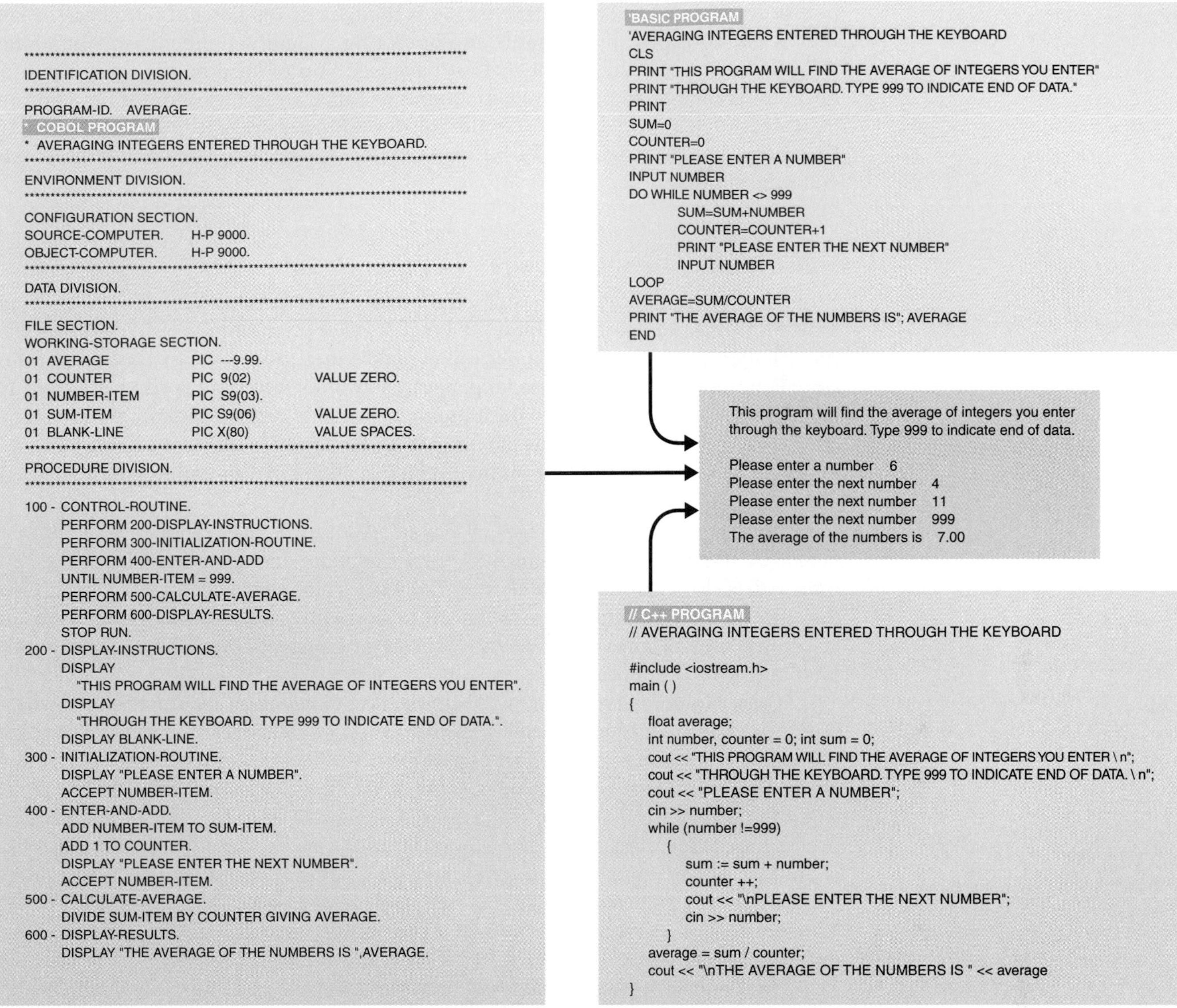

```
*****************************************************************************
IDENTIFICATION DIVISION.
*****************************************************************************
PROGRAM-ID.   AVERAGE.
* COBOL PROGRAM
* AVERAGING INTEGERS ENTERED THROUGH THE KEYBOARD.
*****************************************************************************
ENVIRONMENT DIVISION.
*****************************************************************************
CONFIGURATION SECTION.
SOURCE-COMPUTER.     H-P 9000.
OBJECT-COMPUTER.     H-P 9000.
*****************************************************************************
DATA DIVISION.
*****************************************************************************
FILE SECTION.
WORKING-STORAGE SECTION.
01  AVERAGE              PIC  ---9.99.
01  COUNTER              PIC  9(02)          VALUE ZERO.
01  NUMBER-ITEM          PIC  S9(03).
01  SUM-ITEM             PIC  S9(06)         VALUE ZERO.
01  BLANK-LINE           PIC  X(80)          VALUE SPACES.
*****************************************************************************
PROCEDURE DIVISION.
*****************************************************************************
100 - CONTROL-ROUTINE.
      PERFORM 200-DISPLAY-INSTRUCTIONS.
      PERFORM 300-INITIALIZATION-ROUTINE.
      PERFORM 400-ENTER-AND-ADD
      UNTIL NUMBER-ITEM = 999.
      PERFORM 500-CALCULATE-AVERAGE.
      PERFORM 600-DISPLAY-RESULTS.
      STOP RUN.
200 - DISPLAY-INSTRUCTIONS.
      DISPLAY
        "THIS PROGRAM WILL FIND THE AVERAGE OF INTEGERS YOU ENTER".
      DISPLAY
        "THROUGH THE KEYBOARD.  TYPE 999 TO INDICATE END OF DATA.".
      DISPLAY BLANK-LINE.
300 - INITIALIZATION-ROUTINE.
      DISPLAY "PLEASE ENTER A NUMBER".
      ACCEPT NUMBER-ITEM.
400 - ENTER-AND-ADD.
      ADD NUMBER-ITEM TO SUM-ITEM.
      ADD 1 TO COUNTER.
      DISPLAY "PLEASE ENTER THE NEXT NUMBER".
      ACCEPT NUMBER-ITEM.
500 - CALCULATE-AVERAGE.
      DIVIDE SUM-ITEM BY COUNTER GIVING AVERAGE.
600 - DISPLAY-RESULTS.
      DISPLAY "THE AVERAGE OF THE NUMBERS IS ",AVERAGE.
```

```
'BASIC PROGRAM
'AVERAGING INTEGERS ENTERED THROUGH THE KEYBOARD
CLS
PRINT "THIS PROGRAM WILL FIND THE AVERAGE OF INTEGERS YOU ENTER"
PRINT "THROUGH THE KEYBOARD. TYPE 999 TO INDICATE END OF DATA."
PRINT
SUM=0
COUNTER=0
PRINT "PLEASE ENTER A NUMBER"
INPUT NUMBER
DO WHILE NUMBER <> 999
        SUM=SUM+NUMBER
        COUNTER=COUNTER+1
        PRINT "PLEASE ENTER THE NEXT NUMBER"
        INPUT NUMBER
LOOP
AVERAGE=SUM/COUNTER
PRINT "THE AVERAGE OF THE NUMBERS IS"; AVERAGE
END
```

```
This program will find the average of integers you enter
through the keyboard. Type 999 to indicate end of data.

Please enter a number   6
Please enter the next number   4
Please enter the next number   11
Please enter the next number   999
The average of the numbers is   7.00
```

```
// C++ PROGRAM
// AVERAGING INTEGERS ENTERED THROUGH THE KEYBOARD

#include <iostream.h>
main ( )
{
   float average;
   int number, counter = 0; int sum = 0;
   cout << "THIS PROGRAM WILL FIND THE AVERAGE OF INTEGERS YOU ENTER \ n";
   cout << "THROUGH THE KEYBOARD. TYPE 999 TO INDICATE END OF DATA. \ n";
   cout << "PLEASE ENTER A NUMBER";
   cin >> number;
   while (number !=999)
      {
         sum := sum + number;
         counter ++;
         cout << "\nPLEASE ENTER THE NEXT NUMBER";
         cin >> number;
      }
   average = sum / counter;
   cout << "\nTHE AVERAGE OF THE NUMBERS IS " << average
}
```

Figure 9.6
Comparison of programs in COBOL, Basic, and C++

These three programs produce the same results (in slightly different format) and therefore illustrate some of the differences between three higher-level programming languages. This simple example actually uses poor programming techniques because 999 could be both a code and a number to be included in the averaging.

inside the virtual machine is referenced by name within the virtual machine rather than by memory address in the computer.

As a general-purpose language Java is applicable in many types of distributed computing other than Internet applications. For example, IBM's Lotus software division used Java to produce eSuite, a set of office applications designed for use on network computers. The attempt to make Java a computing standard encountered important commercial and political questions. Microsoft sent a letter to ISO, the International Organization for Standardization, saying that Sun wanted the benefit of an ISO standard but was unwilling to commit to an open process for developing the technology in the future.[5] In its advertisements IBM seemed to take the opposing view, saying, "since most business environments contain a wide variety of computing platforms, Java is just common sense. So is the idea of 100 percent pure Java—a Java that is not corrupted by offshoots and operating system dependencies."[6] Just a few months later, however, Hewlett-Packard accused Sun of keeping too tight a rein on developing new versions of Java and announced its own Java variant for noncomputer devices such as printers.[7] The continuing development and acceptance of Java is not only a question for programmers, but also a major strategic issue for competition in the computer industry.

Fourth Generation Languages

Other than programming languages for teaching, third generation languages are basically tools for professional programmers. The high level of programming skill needed to use these languages for business applications makes their direct use by business professionals impractical. Using these languages is arduous and time consuming even for professional programmers, and the amount of work for professional programmers has always exceeded programmer availability. These factors encouraged the development of new ways to make programmers more productive and to permit nonprogrammers to do programming work.

Fourth generation languages (4GLs) are a loosely defined group of programming languages that make programming less procedural than third generation languages. The term *4GL* is closely associated with query languages and report generators for retrieving data from databases, although 4GLs can also perform transactions using databases. Many 4GLs are subsets of larger products, such as DBMSs or integrated systems for designing and building business applications.

Query languages are special-purpose languages used to provide immediate, online answers to questions such as, "Which five customers in New Jersey had the highest purchases last month?" **Report generators** are special-purpose languages used to answer questions or to program reports that will be used repeatedly. The SQL in Figure 4.6 in Chapter 4 was an example of a query language. The query specification is nonprocedural. It identifies the desired output but doesn't say exactly how the computer should find the data or how the heading or body of the output should be formatted. Typical report specifications in a 4GL report generator once looked like a set of text statements but have moved to more of a graphical approach with the user specifying options using a mouse.

The benefits of 4GLs extend to both programmers and end users. Programmers need less time and effort to specify the required processing. Writing the same reporting program in COBOL might take 10 times as long because of all the details that must be incorporated into COBOL programs. End users benefit because 4GLs provide a way to obtain information without requiring the direct help of a programmer. The use of 4GLs for queries and report generation reduces the pressure on programmers to write reporting programs to support immediate information needs.

Although 4GLs have been adopted widely because of their advantages, they did not replace COBOL and other 3GLs for a variety of reasons. The existing investment in over 100 billion lines of COBOL code made rewriting all of these programs an enormous task with a questionable payoff, especially because it would involve a major training effort in addition to the program revisions. The capabilities of 4GLs were also too limited for a great deal of new development because they could not handle complex formats and logic and because they did not address many of the issues related to client-server computing.

The four generations of programming languages define an important stream of developments, which makes programming less procedural and permits the user to be more concerned with the desired processing or outputs rather than the specific method used for performing the processing. Although Japan's Fifth Generation research project and other projects have worked toward the next generation of programming languages,[8] no fifth generation of languages is used in business today.

Reality Check

PROGRAMMING LANGUAGES

The generations of programming languages illustrate progress in four directions: greater nonprocedurality, greater modularity and reusability, greater machine and data independence, and tighter links between analysis and programming.

1. Assuming you are a business professional whose job is not directly related to software development, explain why these trends might or might not matter to you.
2. As a spreadsheet user now and in the future, explain what these trends might mean to you.

OTHER MAJOR DEVELOPMENTS IN PROGRAMMING

While the four generations of programming languages represent an important stream of developments, they certainly don't encompass all that has happened. We will now look at other significant developments, including special-purpose languages, spreadsheets, and CASE systems. We discussed object-oriented programming earlier because of the change in programming philosophy that it signifies.

Special-Purpose Languages

General-purpose programming languages have an important shortcoming. They contain no ideas about the area of business or type of problem the programmer is working on. For example, even though COBOL may be used to program an inventory system or a financial system, it contains no specific ideas about inventory or finance. If you were a programmer analyzing the cash flow from a complex real estate investment, you would prefer to use a programming language that contained financial ideas, such as net present value and return on investment. You might save more time and make fewer errors if the language contained specific ideas about real estate investments.

Modeling languages, special-purpose languages for developing models, are used extensively in decision support systems. Unlike general-purpose languages, they contain specific capabilities that make it easy to build models. Many modeling languages contain financial functions. Some contain special ways of organizing data in two- or three-dimensional arrays for easy analysis. Others include methods for drawing a picture of a model and using that picture to check the consistency of the equations in the model. Figure 9.7 shows the way the modeling language Extend can be used to create a model for analyzing the operations of a car wash. Each of the building blocks was produced in advance and stored in module library. The programmer created this model by selecting and modifying the building blocks.

Spreadsheets

Like the 3GLs, the first modeling languages were effective only if used by programming professionals. Model building became much more practical for nonprogrammers with the advent of computerized spreadsheets. Excel and other spreadsheet programs are a special type of modeling language that can only be used to describe problems that fit into a spreadsheet format. Spreadsheet programs are used widely because many types of business calculations can be structured as spreadsheets and because the familiar spreadsheet format makes it unnecessary to struggle with a new way of thinking about problems. Spreadsheet software also provides an easy way for users to work with a model. Instead of forcing the users to name every variable, the spreadsheet permits users to recognize what each variable means based on the cell it occupies in the grid. Focusing on the cells and their specific locations also provides a virtually automatic way of formatting the outputs for printing, making it unnecessary to master a separate report generator.

Although these factors contribute to the popularity of spreadsheets, they sometimes result in spreadsheets that are inflexible and difficult to maintain. It is difficult to look at

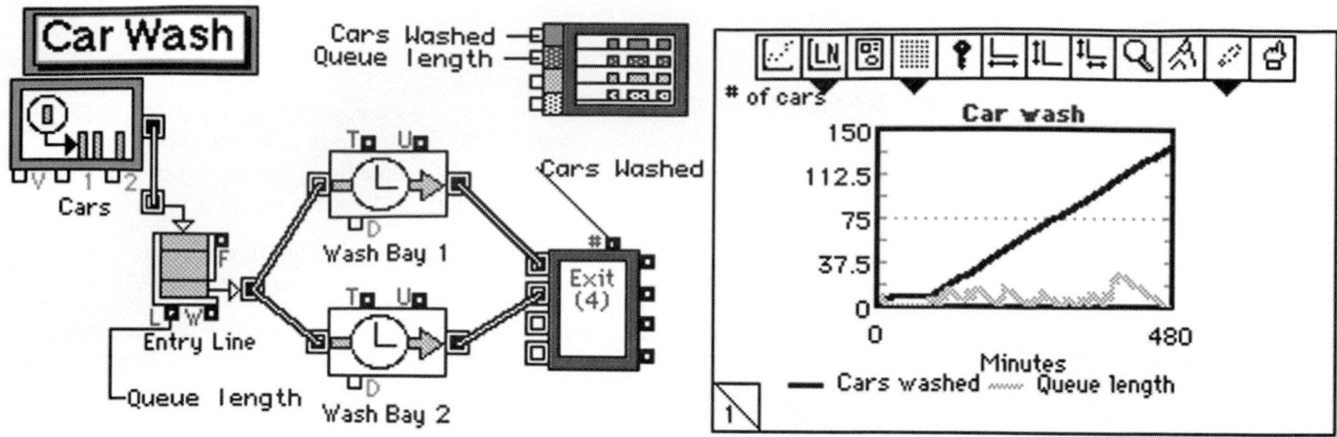

Figure 9.7
Graphical representation of a simulation

This is the graphical representation of a simulation developed using the Extend simulation system. The simulation was created by linking existing modules provided by the software vendor and specifying values of characteristics within those modules, such as speeds or capacities. Running this type of simulation many times generates statistics about average waiting times and other factors pertinent to improving the process.

spreadsheet outputs in different ways because the location of the cells is static. Users attempting to reorganize rows and columns run the risk of introducing errors. Figure 9.8 shows how the pivot table function in Excel made spreadsheets more flexible while maintaining the benefits of the spreadsheet approach.

Programming errors are a pervasive issue with spreadsheet models for several reasons. First, many of the people who build spreadsheet models are not trained in debugging techniques and therefore do not know how to check a model for accuracy. In addition, spreadsheet software permits a very casual style of model building that does little to encourage the characteristics of structured programming. A study by Coopers and Lybrand found that over 90% of spreadsheets with more than 150 rows contained at least one significant mistake.[9] A highly visible problem in debugging a spreadsheet model occurred when Fidelity's huge Magellan fund forecast a $4.32 per share capital gains distribution in November 1994 but distributed nothing. A clerical worker had put the wrong sign in front of a $1.2 billion ledger entry, creating an incorrect $2.3 billion gain in place of the real $0.1 billion loss. This probably affected the financial decisions of some Fidelity customers who may have sold to avoid the distribution.[10]

Computer Aided Software Engineering Systems

Computer aided software engineering (CASE) is the use of computerized tools to improve the efficiency, accuracy, and completeness of the process of analyzing, designing, developing, and maintaining an information system. CASE is based on the idea of improving quality and productivity by approaching system analysis and development in a highly structured and disciplined way. CASE products sold by different vendors overlap in many ways but also contain certain unique features.

Users of CASE products avoid reinventing methods that have been developed carefully and integrated into a consistent package. Ideally, CASE products increase coordination and reduce confusion by enforcing standard methods used by the entire organization. They establish effective methods for storing and using the data generated during systems analysis, design, and development. They also automatically check for inconsistencies and errors such as inconsistent data names or formats. They also make maintenance more efficient because the programs are constructed based on the same structures and standards.

CASE is sometimes divided into upper-CASE versus lower-CASE. **Upper-CASE** refers to tools used by business and IT professionals to describe business processes and the data needed by those processes. Upper-CASE techniques mentioned earlier in this text include data

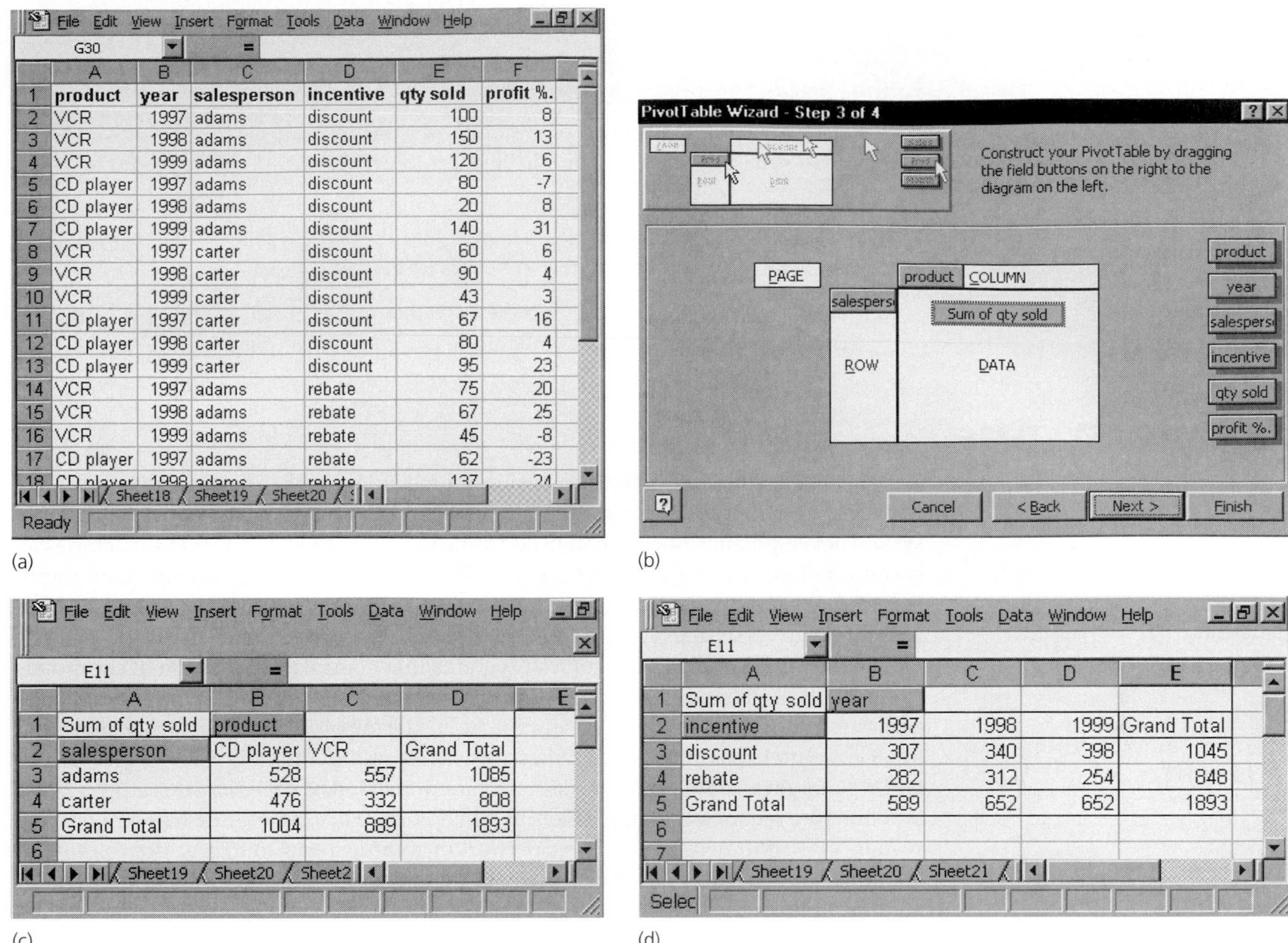

(a)

	A	B	C	D	E	F
1	product	year	salesperson	incentive	qty sold	profit %.
2	VCR	1997	adams	discount	100	8
3	VCR	1998	adams	discount	150	13
4	VCR	1999	adams	discount	120	6
5	CD player	1997	adams	discount	80	-7
6	CD player	1998	adams	discount	20	8
7	CD player	1999	adams	discount	140	31
8	VCR	1997	carter	discount	60	6
9	VCR	1998	carter	discount	90	4
10	VCR	1999	carter	discount	43	3
11	CD player	1997	carter	discount	67	16
12	CD player	1998	carter	discount	80	4
13	CD player	1999	carter	discount	95	23
14	VCR	1997	adams	rebate	75	20
15	VCR	1998	adams	rebate	67	25
16	VCR	1999	adams	rebate	45	-8
17	CD player	1997	adams	rebate	62	-23
18	CD player	1998	adams	rebate	137	24

(b)

(c)

	A	B	C	D
1	Sum of qty sold	product		
2	salesperson	CD player	VCR	Grand Total
3	adams	528	557	1085
4	carter	476	332	808
5	Grand Total	1004	889	1893

(d)

	A	B	C	D	E
1	Sum of qty sold	year			
2	incentive	1997	1998	1999	Grand Total
3	discount	307	340	398	1045
4	rebate	282	312	254	848
5	Grand Total	589	652	652	1893

Figure 9.8
Using a pivot table to make spreadsheets more flexible

The original table contains data about the quantity sold and profit percentage for different salespeople, different products, different years, and different sales incentives. The pivot table feature in Excel makes it possible to look at different slices of this data, such as sales by salesperson and product or sales by sales incentive and year. To convert from one view to another, the user switches the order and placement of the icons representing the various dimensions.

dictionaries, data flow diagrams for process modeling (Chapter 3), and entity-relationship diagrams for data modeling (Chapter 4). **Lower-CASE** is a set of tools used by programmers to facilitate the programming process. Screen generators simplify programming of data input screens by making it easy to place headings, instructions, comments, and the actual data entry fields anywhere on the screen with minimal effort compared to what is required in traditional programming. DBMSs for PCs all contain this type of capability, which was barely available for professional mainframe programmers just a decade ago. Report generators, which are often 4GLs, make it easy to program simple listings and reports based on the fact that reports typically contain headings, subheadings, totals, and subtotals of prespecified size and format in particular locations on the page. Some CASE products contain code generators that automatically generate computer programs from specifications that are not in a programming language. Code generators require a complete structured specification of exactly how the system should operate. Code generators convert those specifications into programs written in COBOL or other languages. CASE systems may contain many other tools and techniques that make system development more efficient, including the maintenance of subroutine libraries, the generation of data for testing, debugging techniques, and techniques for controlling changes in programs.

Reality Check

DEVELOPMENTS IN PROGRAMMING

This section mentioned a number of examples illustrating progress in programming. Despite that progress, many people still have trouble instructing VCRs to record television programs.

1. Based on the trends and examples, speculate about the way spreadsheet users may create spreadsheet models five years from now.
2. Based on the trends and the examples, speculate about the user interfaces for VCRs, microwave ovens, and other home equipment five years from now.

OPERATING SYSTEMS

Thus far, the chapter has focused on business applications and end-user software, both of which are designed to support the user's business processes. It has also covered the role of system development software in translating the ideas into object code that a machine can execute. Before finishing the chapter with efforts to program intelligence into computers, we will look at operating systems, a type of system software (rather than application software) that affects business professionals by controlling the computers they use.

Operating systems are complex programs that control the operation of computers and networks by controlling (1) execution of other programs running on the computer, (2) communication with peripheral devices including terminals, and (3) use of disk space and other computer system resources. When centralized computing was the norm, it was easier to generalize about operating system functions. Today, different operating system functions are required by different computing options. For example, the type of operating system that controls a client-server network has to deal with different issues than an operating system that controls a PC. To make things more complicated, operating systems are often intertwined with other layers of software including DBMSs, communication software, and middleware.

Operating systems differ in size and complexity. The first operating systems for personal computers, such as MS-DOS and CPM, were written by just a few programmers. As operating systems took on new functions, the amount of development work multiplied. Microsoft's Windows NT, an operating system for networked computers, cost over $150 million to develop with a team of 200 programmers, contained 4.3 million lines of code when it was first released in 1993, and has been developed much further since that time.[11] The discussion of operating system functions will start with the simplest case, personal computers.

Operating Systems for Personal Computers

The purpose of the operating system for a PC is to make it possible for you to do work by using application programs such as spreadsheets, word processors, or drawing programs. It does this by performing a variety of functions related to controlling the user interface, controlling access to data, controlling jobs in progress, and allocating resources. Regardless of whether the PC operating system is Windows 3.1, Windows 95, Windows 98, or one of the versions of the Mac OS, here are some of the operating system functions that affect a PC user:

- *controlling the user interface:* When you turn on a personal computer, the operating system displays startup information along with menus, icons, or other indications of the choices you can exercise. As you use the computer, the appearance of what you see on the screen is controlled by the operating system or by the interaction between the operating system and whatever application program is being used.
- *controlling tasks in progress:* When you select an application or document to open, the operating system recognizes your inputs and takes the action you request. If

you print something, the operating system controls the interface with the printer and reports problems, such as when the printer is out of paper. By supporting **multitasking,** operating systems permit the user to operate two or more programs concurrently on the same computer. For example, they permit a user to switch back and forth between a spreadsheet and a word processor without turning off one application in order to use the other.

- *controlling access to data:* When you access previously stored data through an application program, the operating system uses internal directories and other internal information to find and retrieve the data. Some operating systems can update one document automatically based on data changes in another document, for example, automatically updating a word processed report when changes are made in a spreadsheet, part of which is included in the report. The operating system can also ask for a password before permitting use of a restricted file.
- *allocating resources:* The operating system allocates memory while the computer is running. When you want to save a document or spreadsheet, the operating system decides where to store the data in the storage device. It makes sure that each file stored does not overlay files stored previously. If it is necessary to break the data into several blocks in different places on the storage device, the operating system keeps track of the different blocks. When you delete files, the operating system frees up the space so that it can be used again.

Operating Systems for Multi-User Computer Systems

Operating systems for mainframe computers and servers with multiple processors perform the same functions in much more complex situations. Instead of taking care of a single user, they run many jobs simultaneously for different users, taking into account the priority of different jobs. Some of the jobs involve online interaction with users. Other jobs are run in a background mode with the user detached. These operating systems make sure that the users, their data, and their various jobs do not interfere with each other. They also maintain computer system security.

Operating systems for multi-user computer systems monitor the current status of the system and decide when to start jobs. This is necessary because computer systems have a finite computing capacity, a specific number of peripherals of each type, and a finite capacity for communicating with the peripherals. The operating system considers resource availability when it allocates resources to jobs. For example, before starting a job that requires a tape drive, it allocates a specific tape drive to that job, and it delays the job if all tape drives are currently allocated to other jobs. Likewise, before permitting an online user to log on, it decides whether the capacity is available for that user. When multiple processors are involved, the operating system must also make sure that work being done by one processor does not interfere with work being done by another.

In networked computer systems, the **network operating system** establishes the links between the nodes, monitors network operation, and controls recovery processes when nodes go down or the entire network goes down. The network operating system must work in conjunction with the operating systems for the individual workstations on the network. This adds to the complexity of establishing and maintaining computer networks because the two operating systems (for the workstation and for the network) and the application software must all be compatible. It may also affect computer system performance by creating noticeable delays compared to doing individual work on a personal computer.

A number of different multi-user operating systems are used today. Older operating systems still used for mainframe and minicomputer applications from the 1970s and 1980s include IBM's MVS and Digital's VMS, both of which were upgraded substantially in 1995. Starting in the mid-1980s there was a shift away from these mainframe operating systems and toward a widely used multi-user operating system called UNIX, which was developed at AT&T's Bell Labs before the time of PCs. It was eventually given to universities for free because AT&T was not allowed to sell software at that time. Based on this history, it is not surprising that the Internet uses UNIX, which was written in the programming language C and was designed as a portable operating system. Although UNIX is used widely in networks of up to 1,000 users, early hopes that it would become a universal operating system working uniformly on all computers have not been realized. Currently used dialects of UNIX include IBM's AIX, HP/UX, Sun's Solaris, Digital's UNIX, SCO's UNIX, and several others. In 1993 Microsoft sold the first release of the Windows NT operating system, which contains both server and client components. By 1997 it could support corporate networks with up to 200 users. It overlaps with Novell's NetWare in the network operating system market and competes with the various forms of UNIX for new multi-user applications. Many observers believe that the client side of Windows NT will eventually replace Microsoft's client/desktop operating systems Windows 95 and Windows 98.

Why Operating Systems Are Important

Operating systems are a crucial component of any computer system because they can lock in some applications and lock out others. Current application programs and end-user software are written to run under a particular operating system. A program written to run under one operating system may not run under another operating system. Anyone who has attempted to switch between a *wintel* PC (that uses Windows on an Intel microprocessor) and an Apple Macintosh PC understands that switching to a different operating system often entails the expense of abandoning or modifying much existing software. Until the mid-1990s, even Microsoft Word documents or Excel spreadsheets produced on one platform could not be used on the other. Some degree of interoperability is now available because the file formats have been synchronized and because it is often possible to copy a document from one type of PC to a network and then from the network to the other type of PC. However, this still doesn't solve the problem of what to do about backward compatibility when successive releases of application software use inconsistent formats.

Department of Justice (DOJ) actions against Microsoft in late 1997 and 1998 showed that operating systems even raise anti-trust issues. In 1995 Microsoft had signed a consent decree with the DOJ prohibiting it from tying the sale of one product to another. Microsoft changed its licensing contracts as a result. The DOJ filed suit against Microsoft on Oct. 20, 1997, saying that it had breached the consent decree by requiring PC makers to ship Internet Explorer, Microsoft's Internet browser, as a condition of licensing the industry-standard Windows 95 operating system. The government suit said that Windows 95 and Internet Explorer are separate products and that Microsoft was using its near monopoly to restrict competition in the Internet browser market. In Microsoft's view the company had the absolute right of defining what went into its own products, and therefore had the right to declare the operating system and the browser an integrated product.[12] Whether and how this dispute would eventually affect the balance of power between Microsoft and other industry players such as Netscape, IBM, and Sun remains to be seen.

Reality Check

OPERATING SYSTEMS

This section discusses some of the functions of operating systems for personal computers, such as controlling the user interface, controlling access to data, allocating resources, and controlling jobs in progress.

1. Which operating systems have you used on a personal computer? What appeared to be the relationship between the operating system and the applications you ran, such as spreadsheets or word processing?
2. What aspects of the operating system could probably be improved? For example, was it extremely easy to learn, and did it do everything for you that you imagine an operating system could do?

STEPS TOWARD PROGRAMMING INTELLIGENCE INTO MACHINES

Programming advances to date have been impressive, to say the least, but there is still a long way to go. Figure 9.1 illustrated that programming is about translating from a vision of what is to be accomplished into instructions a machine can execute. Figure 9.4 showed that this translation is increasingly automatic, but that programming languages must still be used. We now round out the coverage of software and programming by looking at the limits of what it is possible to program computers to do.

Efforts to make computers more "intelligent" are often grouped under the general heading of artificial intelligence (AI), which first achieved prominence at a small conference of AI pioneers at Dartmouth in 1956. **Artificial intelligence** is the field of research related to the demonstration of intelligence by machines. This includes, but is not limited to, the ability to think, see, learn, understand, and use common sense.

Although AI research has led to important practical applications, the general topic of machine intelligence has spawned a great deal of hype, confusion, and speculation. As illustrated in Figure 9.9, people sometimes exaggerate computer intelligence and think of computers as gigantic brains. People often say a computer "knows" something, when they really mean that the computer program has access to that information. People often give undeserved credit or blame to computers, almost implying that the computer was responsible for something that happened in business or government. People often generalize about computer intelligence from isolated examples. People often use the terms "smart" or intelligent" to describe computer systems even though they don't come close to showing many types of intelligence that the least intelligent human employee shows every day.

The most basic limitation of programming is related to computer intelligence. This limitation is that no one knows how to program **common sense,** which is a shared understanding of how things work in everyday life. Even when programmers include every rule, exception, and special case that they can think of, something may still be missing. The

Figure 9.9
Images and headlines about machine intelligence

The two pictures illustrate the two questions underlying this section: What does artificial intelligence mean, and what are its current limits? (a) People sometimes think of computers as giant brains. Election day 1952 was one of the first situations in which computer intelligence was widely reported. Hours before the newscasters were willing to predict the outcome, a computer projected that Eisenhower would win. This was publicized as a demonstration of computer intelligence even though the projection was based on statistical formulas that are covered in undergraduate statistics courses today and can be used on any personal computer. (b) People may subconsciously believe part of the dream of human-like robots. This dream may inspire an image of computers that fuels some of the confusion about what computers can do today.

(a)

(b)

resulting programs may respond incorrectly or even disastrously when they encounter unanticipated or poorly understood situations or interactions of factors. In contrast, people usually exercise common sense about what they do and do not understand. When an unanticipated situation arises, they can recognize it as such and respond accordingly.

Figure 9.10 shows that programming greater intelligence into computers involves moving in two directions, increasing the scope of the information processed and increasing the degree of understanding of the information. Although the Deep Blue example at the beginning of the chapter has been trumpeted as a demonstration of computer intelligence, the figure would categorize this accomplishment as "following unambiguous instructions" related to "several predefined types of information about one type of situation." Deep Blue might seem intelligent if it were evaluated on its ability to create chess moves better than most human chess players. It would not seem intelligent if it were judged on how well it could converse about its strategy. The success with Deep Blue is impressive, but it is not as far along the scales in Figure 9.10 as the problem of trying to interpret the little three-sentence story about Billy and Sally at the beginning of the chapter. Interpreting that story would involve using "many types of information about many types of situations" in order to "understand a situation and use common sense."

The remainder of the chapter will briefly discuss six areas in which AI research that once seemed "far out" yet eventually led to important practical applications in business. (Important applications in other areas such as machine vision and robotics are not mentioned.) Table 9.3 identifies the six areas and notes the AI issue and approach to intelligence that eventually led to useful results even though computer intelligence has not yet been achieved. Each of these areas is related in some way to the general issue of interpreting or using ambiguous or incomplete information.

Natural Language Processing

Computerized natural language processing is applied in a variety of applications that are accurate enough to be useful even though none are perfect and the outputs produced by most require careful checking by people. Word processors contain spell checkers, grammar checkers, and auto-correct features that identify and correct likely spelling errors. Voice recognition programs provide over 95% accuracy even for continuous speech. Database query programs use situation-specific data dictionaries to convert natural language queries

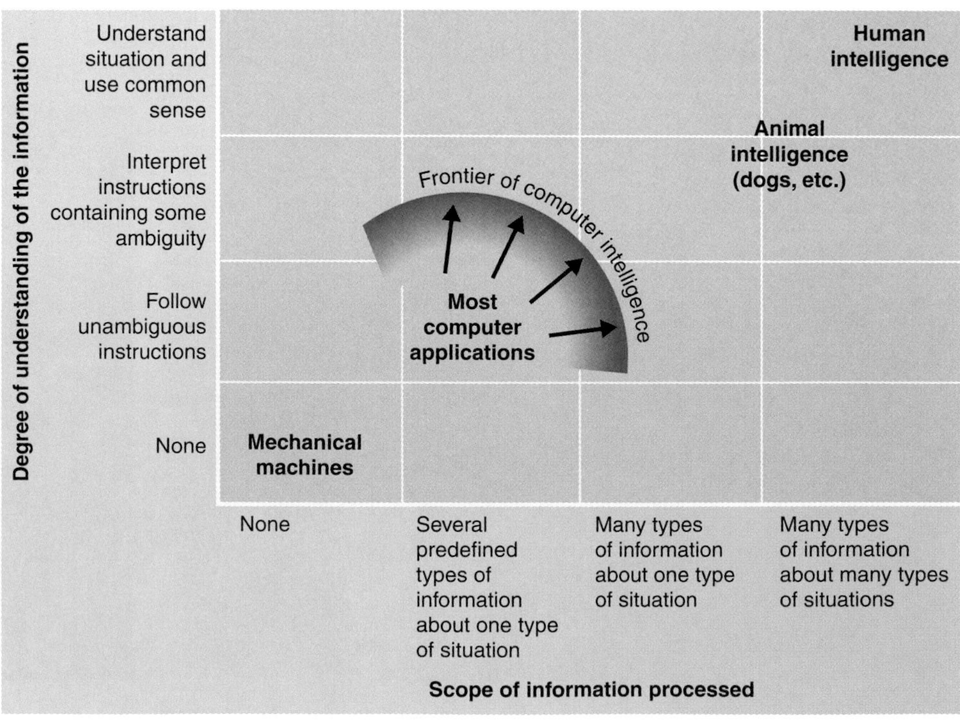

Figure 9.10
Visualizing what computers can be programmed to do

Computers are being incorporated into what were previously totally mechanical devices such as coffee makers and automobile brakes. Techniques for interpreting information such as voice and handwriting are being extended. More applications are being developed that handle many types of data. Despite these developments, computerized systems do not yet demonstrate common sense or understanding.

TABLE 9.3 Comparison of Practical Applications of AI Research

Type of AI application	AI issue	Approach to intelligence
Natural language processing	Understanding language	Use dictionaries, grammatical analysis, statistical techniques, and situation-specific knowledge if available.
Expert system	Understanding and reasoning about specific situations	Try to capture and apply an expert's understanding of a type of problem through a set of rules about reasoning.
Neural network	Learning how to make a specific type of decision	Use statistical methods to learn how to make good decisions by weighting various aspects of a problem situation.
Fuzzy logic	Reasoning method that avoids false distinctions	Perform reasoning by weighting multiple rules that can be posed using overlapping categories.
Case-based	Reasoning based on similarity of cases	Compare past cases to find the ones with greatest bearing on a current situation.
Intelligent agents	Exploring across a network to find desired information	Generate automated processes that operate autonomously.

into SQL queries. Automatic translation programs convert technical manuals and other noncolloquial documents into other languages. Information extraction services scan news articles to select the articles that might be useful to people interested in specific areas. All of these applications were influenced in some way by early AI and linguistics research on understanding natural language.

Based on this progress, it is reasonable to wonder whether **natural language,** the spoken or written language used by people to communicate with each other, will eventually replace formal programming languages. Each successive generation of programming languages allowed programmers to focus less on how the machine performs its work and more on expressing the desired result. It therefore might seem that natural language would complete the progression in Figure 9.4 because the translation from the user's ideas to machine language would be 100% automatic.

Natural language seems unlikely as a programming language for building application systems in the near future, however, even if the entire vocabulary could be defined with a dictionary. Statements in everyday natural language are often ambiguous and poorly structured. Even if the sentences are clear, in combination they are often inconsistent or illogical. Furthermore, people often misunderstand each other even though they share understandings about how the world operates. These problems of ambiguity, interpretation, and inconsistency would overwhelm any current attempts to program application systems using natural language because computers do not currently understand how the world operates. At minimum it would be impossible to test the resulting business application to ensure it operates correctly. Natural language is an interesting starting point for thinking about other applications of AI techniques because all of these applications were originally designed to deal with the use of computers to interpret or use ambiguous or incomplete information.

Expert Systems

The first expert systems were developed in the 1970s as part of AI research about developing ways for computers to "understand" situations in order to translate between languages and respond to queries from people. That research did not achieve its direct objectives but spawned techniques that were applied to many business problems within a decade. An **expert system** is an information system that supports or automates decision making in an area where recognized experts do better than nonexperts. Expert systems do this by storing and using expert knowledge about a limited topic, such as authorizing credit or analyzing machine vibrations. These systems produce conclusions based on data they receive. They are used either as interactive advisors or as independent systems for converting data into recommendations or other conclusions. An information system that performs calculations the same way that anyone would do them is not an expert system. For example, a computer program that converts Fahrenheit temperatures to Centigrade temperatures is not considered an expert system.

Expert systems are often called **knowledge-based systems** because they represent knowledge in an explicit form so that it can be used in a problem solving process. Many expert systems represent knowledge in the form of **if-then rules** stated in the form: *If* certain conditions are true, *then* certain conclusions should be drawn. An example of an if-then rule that might appear in an expert system for loan analysis is:

If: The applicant is current on all debts, and the applicant has been profitable for two years, and the applicant has strong market position,

Then: The applicant is an excellent credit risk.

A rule such as this would be used as part of the analysis of whether to grant a loan. The expert system might use several approaches for determining whether each of the three conditions is true. It might find the answer in a database or use data from the database plus other rules to conclude that the applicant is current on all debts. It might ask the user a direct question such as, "Is the applicant current on all debts?" It might also ask the user different questions and use other rules to conclude that the applicant is current on all debts. Regardless of how it found the data required by this if-then rule, the rule would be part of the knowledge that it uses systematically to support a decision process.

Like a human expert working on a problem, an expert system uses knowledge to draw interim conclusions based on whatever incomplete information is currently available about the situation. When it cannot reach a conclusion, it uses the knowledge to figure out what questions to ask or what information to retrieve in order to make more progress. In many situations, the expert system has enough information to draw partial conclusions but may not have enough information to resolve the situation completely. This is typical of what happens with human experts such as oil prospectors, advertising consultants, and doctors. Unlike human experts, however, expert systems do not truly understand the data and knowledge they are manipulating. This is why it is risky to trust expert systems to make decisions independently.

Applicability

Expert systems have been used in a wide range of applications spanning complex analytical tasks such as interpreting seismic data and procedure-oriented tasks such as making sure that the right paperwork goes out with an order or contract. Despite the breadth of possibilities, the characteristics that determine whether it is practical to build an expert system in a situation are the existence and availability of knowledge and the nature of the task. Expert systems are worth building only if experts perform the task better than nonexperts. They can be built successfully only where recognized experts exist. These experts must be willing to work with knowledge engineers to create the knowledge base and must be able to articulate the rules. Lack of a committed expert reduces the chances of success because the development of an expert system is time consuming and requires many iterations to elicit and codify the expert's knowledge. The practicalities of using expert systems also require reasonable agreement about the knowledge itself. Without such agreement, expert systems encounter difficulties when people try to use them.

Expert systems are applicable for tasks performed based on reasoning and knowledge rather than intuition or reflex. Playing basketball or driving a racecar therefore would not be good problems for using an expert system. Expert systems work best for tasks performed by a person in a time span ranging from a few minutes to a few hours. It may not be worthwhile to build expert systems for tasks taking less time; tasks that take longer are probably too complicated for this approach to succeed today. Expert systems also have a better chance for success when used for tasks that are routinely taught to novices. Such tasks are concrete enough to codify based on rules that use specific information. An example is the Cooper & Lybrand's ExperTAX system, which helps less experienced auditors work with small- to medium-sized client firms in gathering data for a tax planning analysis to uncover many decisions that will affect the client's tax liability for the year. Later, a tax expert prepares a written report that makes recommendations about the issues uncovered by the auditor's work with the client. ExperTAX thereby aids in identifying issues that need clarification but leaves the final recommendations to human experts.

Because they lack common sense and because they don't really understand the rules they use, expert systems don't recognize when they have reached the limits of what they "know." Unlike people, they also don't know how to break rules when it is necessary to do so. With these limitations, expert systems should be used only for the parts of tasks that can be described in terms of information and rules and that require no common sense. Except in problems that are totally understood, appropriate uses of expert systems divide responsibilities between the expert system and a person. The person is responsible for making the decision and exercising common sense. The expert system structures the analysis, makes sure that important factors haven't been ignored, and provides information that helps the person make a good decision.

Components

The five major components of an expert system are illustrated in Figure 9.11. The **knowledge base** is a set of general facts and if-then rules supplied by an expert. The *database* of facts related to the specific situation being analyzed may start as a blank slate each time the system is used or may begin with data that were gathered previously. For example, American Express's Authorizer's Assistant uses its database to retrieve all recent credit card charges by a customer as the starting point for its analysis of whether to approve a purchase. While analyzing a situation, many expert systems obtain additional facts by asking questions to the user or by querying other databases. For example, expert systems assisting in medical diagnosis may ask the doctor about particular conditions that would confirm or rule out possible diagnoses.

The **inference engine** uses rules in the knowledge base plus whatever facts are currently in the database to decide what question to ask next, either to the user or to other

Figure 9.11
Basic components of an expert system

An idealized expert system can be described in terms of five components.

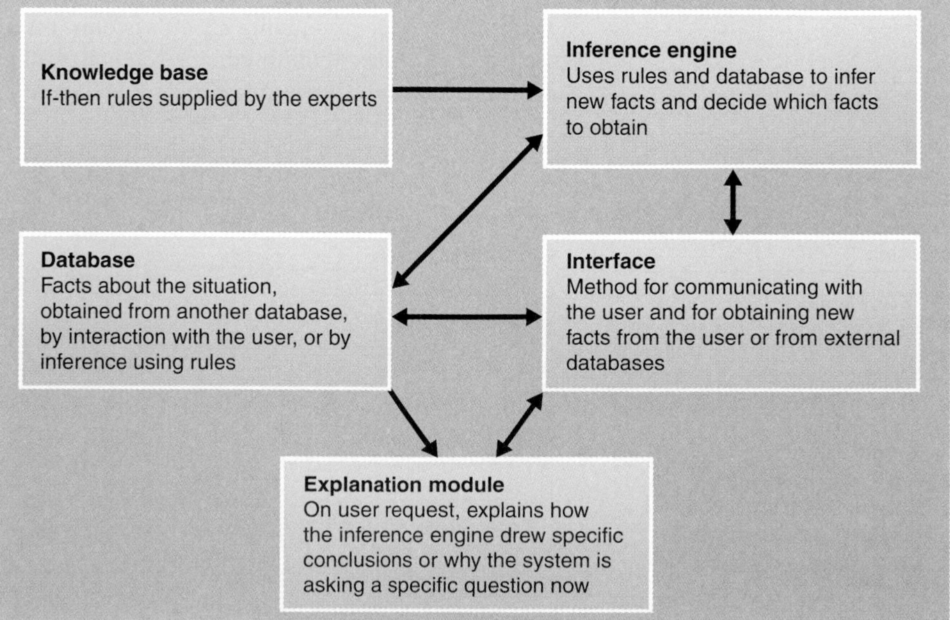

databases. Which questions are asked next depends on the current goal of the inference engine. For example, if the inference engine has identified five different facts that all must be true in order to confirm the current working hypothesis, it may ask five related questions in turn. If one of the responses is negative, the inference engine may then abandon the current line of reasoning in favor of a more promising one.

The *interface* is the way the expert system interacts with the user. The interface may operate as a set of text questions and answers, or it may be highly graphical if more effort is put in to make the interface easier to use. The **explanation module** is available to the user as a way to find out how a particular fact was inferred or why a particular question is being asked. The explanation either confirms the sequence of inferences that produced a conclusion or explains how a question may eventually lead to a conclusion.

Contrary to the idealized illustration in Figure 9.11, many systems that are often considered expert systems don't contain all of these components. For example, some expert systems don't contain an interactive interface for carrying on a dialogue with the user. Other expert systems don't have an explanation module but are still considered expert systems because they use knowledge to derive a conclusion.

How Expert Systems Perform Reasoning

As illustrated in Figure 9.12, the two main types of reasoning in expert systems are called forward chaining and backward chaining. Although they proceed in opposite directions, an expert system might use them in combination. An expert system using **forward chaining** starts with data and tries to draw conclusions from the data. Forward chaining is often used when there is no clear goal and the system is just attempting to determine all of the conclusions implied by the data. An expert system using **backward chaining** starts with a tentative conclusion and then looks for facts in the database supporting that conclusion. As part of backward chaining, the expert system may identify facts that would confirm or deny the conclusion and then look up these facts in a database or ask the user questions related to these facts. Backward chaining is used when an expert system has a specific goal, such as ruling out hepatitis as a possible diagnosis or deciding whether a business applying for a loan has a strong balance sheet.

A doctor's typical analysis process is a combination of forward and backward chaining. The doctor starts with a brief medical history and draws some tentative conclusions, such as the hypothesis that the patient might have a particular disease. The doctor then uses backward chaining to confirm or deny this hypothesis. The doctor obtains the necessary information by asking questions, performing physical examinations, or obtaining laboratory results.

Controlling the order in which rules are used and questions are asked to the user is a key design issue in building expert systems. Imagine a medical expert system that has thousands of rules about medicine but starts off with no facts about a patient. Asking questions in an arbitrary order would be inefficient and mind-numbing. Doctors avoid this

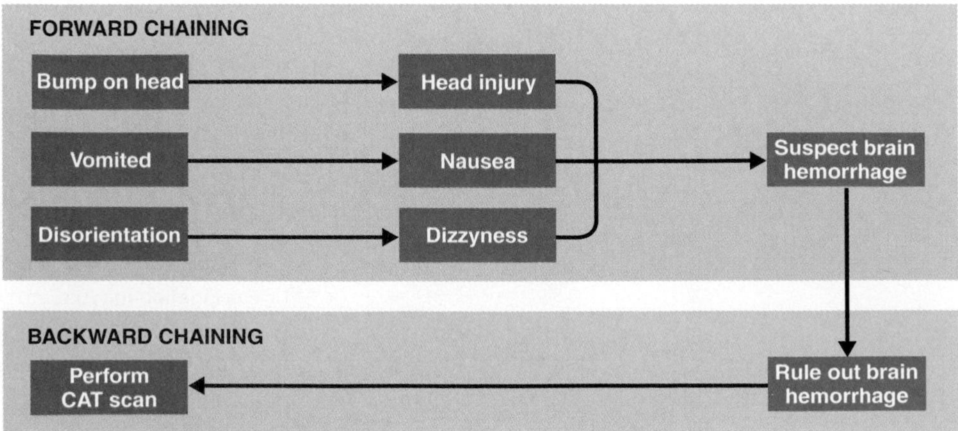

Figure 9.12
Forward chaining versus backward chaining

An emergency room physician examines a 3-year-old injured in an automobile accident. The child has a bump on his head, has vomited, and seems disoriented. Although the physician would immediately decide to perform tests to rule out a brain hermorrhage, an expert system confronted with this information might go through intermediate forward chaining steps.

problem by asking only those questions that are likely to affect diagnosis and treatment in the situation at hand. They ask those questions in an economical way by starting with broad screening questions. For example, determining that a patient has never had a heart problem can rule out an entire line of questions.

Why "Expert System" Is a Misnomer

The term *expert system* sets the expectation that a computer system will operate as well as a human expert. Although expert systems can mimic human experts, human experts have many characteristics that cannot be duplicated in expert systems today. Human experts learn by experience, restructure their knowledge, break the rules when necessary, determine the relevance of new facts, and recognize the limits of their knowledge. As human experts start encountering situations they are not familiar with, they understand they are approaching the limits of their expertise and become more cautious.[13] Although their performance usually degrades as they move into unfamiliar territory, human experts can perceive situations where the existing rules do not apply well and can decide what rules to break in order to solve a problem. They can apply common sense by noting that data is probably erroneous or that a particular rule or procedure was designed for one situation and doesn't really apply in another.

Expert systems have no way of showing this type of common sense and operate totally within the realm of the rules in their knowledge base and the facts they can obtain from a database or user. The only facts recognized by existing expert systems are the facts related to the "if" portions of the if-then rules in their knowledge base. Expert systems tend to either quit or make bad mistakes when they encounter situations not included in their knowledge base. It is possible to add new facts and new rules to an expert system, but each upgrade is like a program enhancement. A person must debug the revised system to ensure that the addition doesn't interfere with the rest of the system's logic.

Reality Check

WHAT CAN WE TRUST EXPERT SYSTEMS TO DO?

Use this section's coverage of expert systems to consider the following:

1. You are a passenger on an airplane and have just learned that it will be landed automatically by an expert system. How would you feel about that? Why?
2. You are a pilot and have just learned that the airline plans to buy airplanes containing an expert system that controls takeoffs and landings. How would you feel about that? Why?

Neural Networks

A **neural network** is an information system that recognizes objects or patterns based on examples that have been used to train it. Each training example is described in terms of a set of characteristics and a result, such as whether or not a loan was repaid. In its "learning phase" the neural network uses statistical methods to optimize a set of internal weights that relate each input to each of the possible results. Neural networks often operate well even if some of the information for a given case is missing because they perform identification and discrimination tasks by giving numerical weights to many different characteristics. They are used for tasks people perform even though there are no predefined formulas or procedures for performing these tasks. If a task can be performed well using known procedures, there is no reason to build a neural network.

To visualize the type of problem neural networks solve, consider the task of recognizing individuals based on physical appearance. People can do this readily, but it is hard to say how they do it. For example, people can usually recognize acquaintances even if part of their typical appearance is obscured because they are facing in different directions or are wearing sunglasses, hats, or heavy coats. Recognizing an individual involves much more than matching a few measurable characteristics such as height, shape, and coloring. Somehow our minds combine many different characteristics to recognize familiar individuals almost instantaneously even with incomplete information.

Neural networks operate based on a totally different approach from expert systems. Expert systems rely on an expert's ability to capture knowledge in the form of a knowledge representation such as rules. In contrast, neural networks are built assuming that no such explicit knowledge exists. Instead, they use mathematical techniques to "learn" how to recognize a particular type of pattern by combining the features from a set of training examples.

Neural networks were originally conceived as a way to study learning and intelligence. The idea of an evidence-weighing machine called a *perceptron* was invented by Frank Rosenblatt in 1959, but perceptrons went out of favor as a research area in the late 1960s, only to return in practical applications several decades later. The term neural network comes from seeing these systems as models of how the human brain operates. A human brain consists of up to 100 billion cells called neurons, each of which is linked to 1,000 or more neurons. The artificial neural networks described here usually contain only tens or hundreds of neurons and are tiny in comparison with what we might imagine as the neural networks in the brain.

Operation of Neural Networks

Neural networks take many different forms. One common form contains three or more layers of nodes called neurons. These layers include:

- a layer of input nodes representing each of the inputs to the recognition task
- a layer of output nodes representing the particular objects or patterns being recognized
- one or more intermediate layers representing intermediate associations between the input nodes and the output nodes. Nodes in these "hidden layers" have no meaning in advance, but the weightings of their inward and outward links serve as a medium for absorbing the patterns in the training examples.

Figure 9.13 represents a simplified neural network for deciding whether to approve or deny mortgage loans based on years at the current address, years at the current job, the ratio of salary to the loan amount, health, and credit rating. For each characteristic the input layer contains a separate neuron that is linked to each of seven neurons in the hidden layer. Each of those neurons is linked to the two neurons in the output layer. In all, this neural network contains 15 nodes and 56 links. The numerical weighting of each link is represented in the picture by the thickness of the line. The stronger the relationship between two nodes, the stronger the weighting.

The neural network learns by adjusting these weightings based on examples. As a starting point, each of the weightings is assigned randomly. This means that some of the initial weightings may make sense while others are totally wrong. Next the network receives a training example which includes the six input characteristics and whether the loan should have been approved or denied (based on the payment history for the actual loan). A mathematical procedure adjusts all of the weights to minimize the error the network would have made. Then the network receives the next example and performs the adjustment again. In real cases, a network might have 1,000 examples, and the entire sequence might be repeated 50 times to make sure the weightings converge to the best representation of the data. In some ways this process resembles the process by which a child learns to speak by making sounds and gradually adjusting them into clearly pronounced words.

After the training, the neural network would be ready to assist in mortgage loan decisions. Whether it serves as an advisor or actually makes the decision depends on the desired business process. Because it uses a weighting scheme involving many inputs, the neural network might give reasonably good results even for slightly novel examples, such as a combination of characteristics that had not been used in the training. The weighting

Figure 9.13
Using neural networks

The process of using neural networks starts by defining the network's structure. This is done by identifying the nodes in the input and output layer, creating the links to and from hidden layers, and deciding on the mathematical technique that will be used for learning. The next steps are creating a starting point for its training, training it, and then using it.

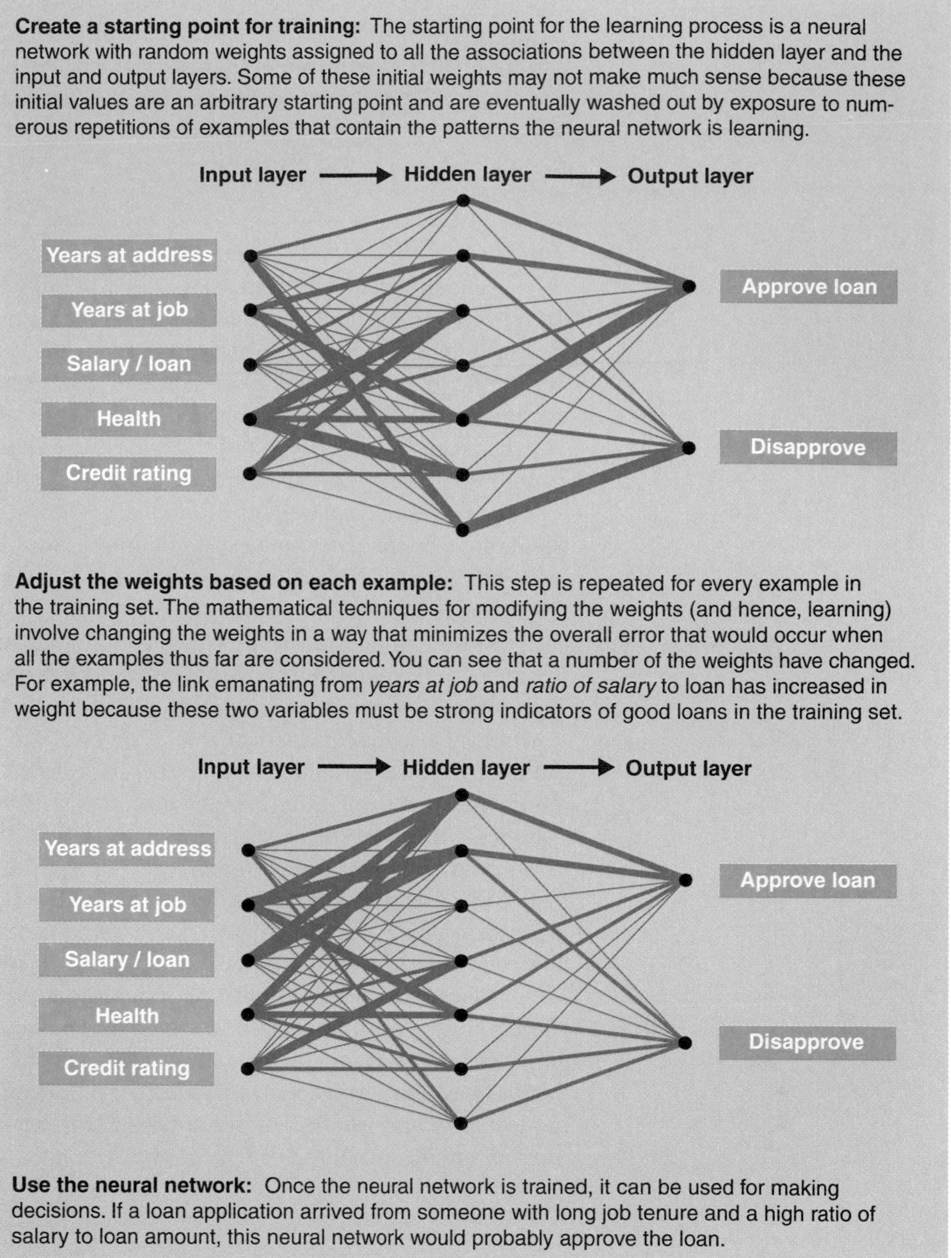
Create a starting point for training: The starting point for the learning process is a neural network with random weights assigned to all the associations between the hidden layer and the input and output layers. Some of these initial weights may not make much sense because these initial values are an arbitrary starting point and are eventually washed out by exposure to numerous repetitions of examples that contain the patterns the neural network is learning.
Input layer → Hidden layer → Output layer
Years at address
Years at job
Salary / loan
Health
Credit rating
Approve loan
Disapprove
Adjust the weights based on each example: This step is repeated for every example in the training set. The mathematical techniques for modifying the weights (and hence, learning) involve changing the weights in a way that minimizes the overall error that would occur when all the examples thus far are considered. You can see that a number of the weights have changed. For example, the link emanating from *years at job* and *ratio of salary* to loan has increased in weight because these two variables must be strong indicators of good loans in the training set.
Input layer → Hidden layer → Output layer
Years at address
Years at job
Salary / loan
Health
Credit rating
Approve loan
Disapprove
Use the neural network: Once the neural network is trained, it can be used for making decisions. If a loan application arrived from someone with long job tenure and a high ratio of salary to loan amount, this neural network would probably approve the loan.

process is also less sensitive to missing or inaccurate data than other types of classification schemes.

Applications of Neural Networks

Neural networks have been applied in many business and research settings, such as predicting business failures, rating bonds, predicting stock prices, trading commodities, preventing fraud, generating forecasts, and generating near-optimal schedules and routings in manufacturing and transportation.[14] They are especially applicable in situations where a large database of examples is available and where even experts cannot give rules for combining inputs to recognize patterns. An experimental neural network for analyzing electrocardiograms and other data in emergency rooms outperformed emergency room doctors. On 331 patients suffering from chest pain, the neural network recognized 35 of 36 heart attacks (97%) while the emergency room doctors identified 28 (78%).[15] Spiegel, Inc., used a neural network to determine which customers should receive their catalogs.

Mitsubishi Electric used a neural network in refrigerators to decide when to defrost, precool, and perform other functions. By dividing each day into 2-hour blocks and recording the frequency of door opening, this application has reduced temperature variations in food by 2.2°C. Neural networks have also been used to detect plastic explosives in airplane luggage. Plastic explosives cannot be detected by x-rays, but they can be detected by a gamma-ray frequency distribution generated when the baggage is exposed to a beam of neutrons.

Limitations of Neural Networks

At first blush a computerized system that learns automatically might seem like magic: turn it on and watch it learn. Like expert systems, neural networks are not magic. Even though neural networks do not try to capture rules from experts, the people who set them up should be experts who understand the important factors in the problem area and the techniques for defining, training, and validating these systems. With the help of experts on neural network technology, they must decide what factors to use as input nodes and output nodes, how to arrange the hidden layers, and what mathematical learning technique to use for adjusting the weights within the network. They must also gather a large set of representative training examples. The neural network's ultimate performance depends on how well it is designed and on how well the training examples capture the patterns it is trying to learn.

Another limitation is the need for a training database. If this database is too small or if it is not representative, the neural network may learn incorrect weightings. For example, a prototype of a loan approval system often approved loans for applicants with low income and rejected loans for applicants with high income. The training data had contained a number of loans for which certain low-income individuals were good credit risks. The neural network's weighting scheme eventually treated low income as a favorable characteristic.[16] In another case, a neural network was trained to distinguish between tanks, rocks, and other battlefield objects. However, all the pictures of the tanks had been taken with one camera and were slightly darker than the pictures of the other objects, which had been taken by another camera. The neural network had actually learned to distinguish between the cameras, not between tanks and other objects.[17]

Neural networks approach AI from a totally different viewpoint from expert systems. Expert systems require that knowledge exists and can be recorded in a form such as rules or frames. Neural networks do not start with explicit knowledge about a problem domain, but instead learn to recognize patterns by adjusting the weights of associations between nodes. How and whether either approach (or other approaches) will eventually mimic human intelligence remains to be seen.

Reality Check

VULNERABILITY TO TRAINING ERRORS IN NEURAL NETWORKS

Neural networks are vulnerable to training errors, but people are also vulnerable because they establish stereotypes based on just a few examples.

1. Identify some of the stereotypes you have heard people talk about that are probably based on just a few examples that may be unrepresentative.
2. Explain whether you think it is healthy or unhealthy to form stereotypes this way. For example, is it unhealthy to conclude that ice is dangerous after slipping once, or that people from Chicago are helpful after being helped once?

Fuzzy Logic

Fuzzy logic was invented to minimize a problem that occurs in expert systems and in many types of precise, formal reasoning. One of the expert system rules cited earlier included the phrase "if the applicant has been profitable for two years," and therefore recognized only whether it is true or false that the applicant has been profitable for two years. The trivial difference between a $1 profit and a $1 loss would affect the decision just as much as the difference between a $100 million profit and a $1 loss.

Fuzzy logic is a form of reasoning that makes it possible to combine imprecise conditions stated in a form similar to the types of descriptive categories people use. The term was coined in 1964 by Lofti Zadeh, a professor at Berkeley. The basic idea is to perform reasoning by combining rules stated in terms of conditions that may overlap. In the finance example, the conditions might include very profitable, somewhat profitable, slightly profitable, slightly unprofitable, and so on. Instead of forcing a precise cut-off between "somewhat profitable" and "slightly profitable," the reasoning system could treat these categories as somewhat overlapping, thereby reasoning in a manner similar to the way a person would reason. Better decisions might result from recognizing a range of conditions for the relevant factors and doing the analysis using logic based on shades of inclusion rather than just either-or categories.

Figure 9.14 shows that fuzzy logic would not require temperature conditions such as cool and cold to be mutually exclusive. Instead cool and cold could overlap because a temperature might have some degree of membership in coldness and some degree of membership in coolness. A rule about coolness could apply at the same time other rules about coldness or other characteristics apply. The fuzzy controller could come to a decision by combining all of the rules based on the relative degree of coldness, coolness, and other characteristics. This type of logic avoids artificial cutoffs that may lead to poor decisions when using either-or rules.

A famous fuzzy logic application is the controller of the subway in Sendai, Japan. This controller was built by observing the factors a human brakeman used to control the train using a manual brake. A key breakthrough in developing the system was the realization that the human brakeman knew the route and therefore began to apply the brake before the subway came to a downhill section. Eventually, the controller could control the trains so precisely that people standing on the train do not need to hold straps when the train starts or stops.

Figure 9.14
Fuzzy variables, fuzzy rules, and how they are combined

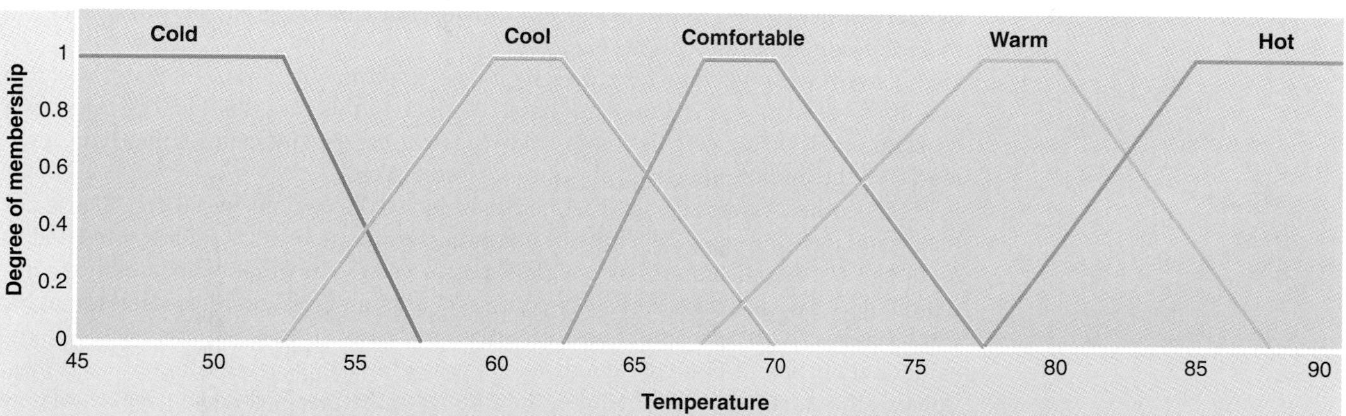

Instead of saying that 72° is either comfortable or warm, the fuzzy membership function shown here says that 72° gives a comfortableness rating of about 0.7 and a warmness rating of about 0.5.

If an air conditioner were based on crisp rules, it would have to decide whether the current temperature was comfortable or warm. Only one case could apply. But a fuzzy controller could use the following two rules simultaneously:

(1) If it is comfortable, then continue the current cooling level.

(2) If it is warm, then increase the cooling a little.

At a temperature of 72° both rules would fire, but their effect would be weighted by the degree of comfortableness (in the first rule) and the degree of warmness (from the second rule). Many other rules might fire at the same time. The fuzzy controller could weight all of these results to decide whether to increase, decrease, or leave the cooling constant.

Fuzzy logic has also been used effectively in many Japanese home appliances such as washing machines and vacuum cleaners and consumer electronics items such as video cameras. Matsushita's fuzzy washing machines use sensors and fuzzy rules to automatically adjust the wash cycle to the kind and amount of dirt (muddy or oily) in the wash water and the size of the load.[18] The applications in video cameras include automatic focusing, automatic exposure, automatic white balancing, and image stabilization. The autofocus technique reduces the amount of time needed to hunt for the right focus by using 13 rules, such as "If the sharpness is high and its differential is low, then the focus motor speed is low." The image stabilization detects unwanted movements caused by bumping and bouncing of platforms and jitters caused by shaking hands, and then corrects the shaken image as much as possible.[19] Using fuzzy logic in household appliances in Japan became such a fad that appliances are labeled as fuzzy or not, and people argue about whether a particular appliance truly deserves the label. Even with its commercial success in Japan, some observers believe that the use of fuzzy logic was much less important than simply building in sensors that monitor whatever process is being performed.

Case-Based Reasoning

Assume you are working at a manufacturer's customer service help desk, answering calls about many different models of many different products. Although there are shelves of manuals, finding the right information in those manuals takes a long time. Worse yet, the manuals explain how the product is supposed to work but often say little about the things that go wrong and how the customer could solve these problems. When Compaq Computer installed a case-based reasoning system to support the people at its help desk, the system paid for itself within a year.[20]

Case-based reasoning (CBR) is a decision support method based on the idea of finding past cases most similar to the current situation in which a decision must be made. CBR systems therefore maintain a history of past cases related to the topics under consideration. When a new situation arises, or a new call comes to the help desk, the decision maker identifies the characteristics of the situation and receives a list of related situations that have been analyzed in the past. Often the past solutions provide important clues or directly answer the current question. When the issue is resolved, the decision maker can add the case just solved as an additional instance in the database. In this way, a case-based reasoning system starting empty or with just one case can gradually be expanded to make it a valuable resource. (See Figure 9.15.)

Case-based reasoning resembles neural networks in one important way. Instead of operating based on rules, it operates based on data. In this case the data consist of past cases and their characteristics. Instead of trying to find the relationships in the data, however, CBR merely attempts to display the most similar case.

Like other systems using AI-related techniques, the systems based on CBR are not magic and have the same dependence on human infrastructure as systems unrelated to AI. Before a CBR application is set up, someone must study the situation to identify the initial categories of cases and the way the cases will be compared and retrieved. Although a CBR system can go into operation with only a few cases in its database, such systems achieve their potential as the database of cases grows to several hundred examples. Building the database of cases requires the administrative role of collecting reports of new cases, verifying these cases differ from cases currently in the database, and coding and indexing the new cases for inclusion and retrieval. Using CBR without this type of administrative effort undermines the system because the database fills up with redundant and confusing entries.

Intelligent Agents

Our nervous systems have the amazing ability to control many simultaneous processes at different levels of conscious awareness. Consider the different processes being controlled simultaneously by your nervous system as you drive a car to a familiar destination while chewing gum and having a strenuous political argument with a passenger. The argument might be at the highest level of consciousness, followed by awareness of the

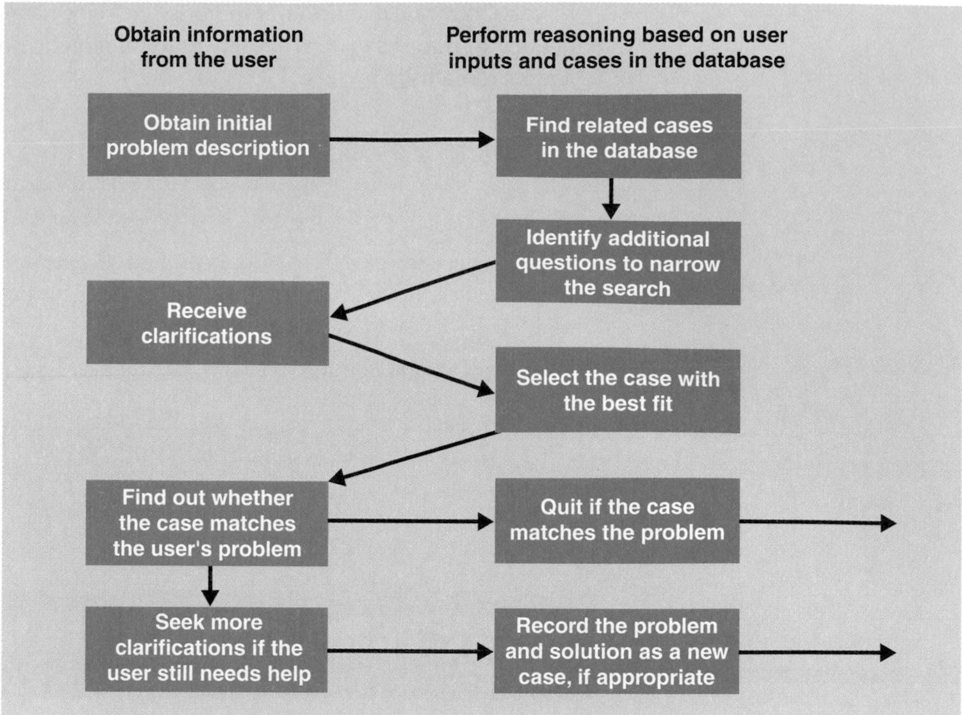

Figure 9.15
Logic of case-based reasoning

Case-based reasoning operates by finding a case in a database that is most closely related to the user's problem. When a new problem is solved, the information about that case is added to the database.

familiar driving route, and by the sensation of gum in your mouth. A simultaneous process of watching out for traffic hazards is going on in the back of your mind. In addition, body regulation processes such as maintaining your heartbeat and focusing your eyes are also continuing at a totally unconscious level. Suddenly a ball bounces into the street. Immediately the traffic hazard process takes over and you temporarily forget about the political argument. Seconds later your heart is racing from the jolt of adrenaline as you slam on the brakes.

Truly intelligent machines would require a capability to operate many simultaneous foreground and background processes and bring background processes into the foreground immediately when necessary. Although this type of machine does not yet exist, initial research on this problem led to the concept of an **intelligent agent,** an autonomous, goal-directed computerized process that can be launched into a computer system or network to perform background work while other foreground processes are continuing. An intelligent agent is a background process that sleeps until it wakes up on a schedule or until a trigger sets it into motion.

Possible intelligent agents include an e-mail agent, a data-mining agent, and a news agent. Each of these would operate in the background, performing information-related tasks that save time or increase the usefulness of information. The e-mail agent would scan incoming e-mail to identify the comparatively few incoming messages that call for the recipient to be interrupted instead of just going on a list to be read at the recipient's convenience. The data-mining agent would sort and filter data in a database to identify trends, surprises, and other new information a user might want. The news agent would scan articles on a computerized news service to cobble together a personalized daily news bulletin containing only articles of interest to a particular individual. Ideally this type of agent would be able to learn about the individual's changing interests instead of being told what to do by programming or check-off lists

Although past AI research[21] explored many ideas related to intelligent agents, the initial applications of intelligent agents look more like mainstream programming than AI. For example, an intelligent agent might be launched into a network to interrogate various travel providers to find the vacation that most closely suits someone's desires. A general capability that could perform this and similar tasks would involve many programming issues about data definition, standards, and telecommunications but very little about intelligence in the AI sense. Whether more intelligence will be programmed into intelligent agents remains to be seen.

Reality Check

FUZZY LOGIC, CASE-BASED REASONING, INTELLIGENT AGENTS

Fuzzy logic, case-based reasoning, and intelligent agents were discussed as three additional techniques with important current or potential application.

1. Identify examples of situations you have encountered or might encounter in which each of these techniques might be used currently or in the future.
2. For each example explain why the interpretation of ambiguous or incomplete information is or is not important.

CHAPTER CONCLUSION

Summary

What are the different types of software?
Application software processes data to structure and facilitate specific work practices. End-user software includes general-purpose tools (such as spreadsheet programs and word processors) designed for use by end users without programming assistance. System development software is used by programmers and analysts in the process of building and enhancing information systems. System software controls the internal operation of a computer system. Application software has the greatest potential for competitive impact because it is part of the specialized work systems that may differentiate an organization from its competitors.

How is programming like a translation process?
Programming is the process of creating instructions that a machine will execute later. Programming requires that a person organize and communicate ideas in a format that a machine can use. The use of programming languages automates part of the translation process. A programmer writes a program that expresses what the person wants. An assembler or compiler automatically translates that program into machine language instructions the machine can execute.

What aspects of programming do not depend on the programming language used?
Regardless of the programming language used, programmers have to organize their ideas and test them. The most common technique for organizing ideas is successive decomposition, the process of breaking up a problem into smaller and smaller subproblems. Testing is required for all programs to find and correct bugs.

What are the four generations of programming languages?
The generations are machine language, assembly language, higher-level language, and fourth generation language (4GL). Each succeeding generation is less procedural and permits programmers to use concepts more related to the business situation.

What are some of the other important developments in programming?
Object-oriented programming treats data and programs as if they are tightly intertwined, and uses concepts such as object, class, method, and inheritance to make programs more reusable. Other important developments include special-purpose languages for narrow types of problems, spreadsheets, and CASE systems. Special-purpose programming languages contain ideas about specific areas of business or types of analysis, such as financial calculations or queuing models. Spreadsheets are a special type of modeling language that permits millions of people to write

programs even though they are not professional programmers. CASE systems establish methods for storing and using the data generated during systems analysis, design, and development.

What are operating systems, and why should managers and users care about them?
Operating systems are complex programs that control the operation of computers and networks by controlling (1) execution of other programs running on the computer, (2) communication with peripheral devices including terminals, and (3) use of disk space and other computer system resources. Operating systems matter to managers because they regulate the efficiency of the computer system and because the choice of an operating system can lock in some applications and lock out others.

What is the most basic limitation of programming?
This limitation is that no one knows how to program common sense, which is a shared understanding of how things work in everyday life. Even when programmers include every rule, exception, and special case that they can think of, something may still be missing. The resulting programs may respond incorrectly or even disastrously when they encounter unanticipated or poorly understood situations or interactions of factors.

What is the relationship between artificial intelligence (AI), expert systems, and neural networks?
Artificial intelligence is the field of research related to the demonstration of intelligence by machines. This includes, but is not limited to, the ability to think, see, learn, understand, and use common sense. Expert systems are information systems that support or automate decision making in an area where recognized experts do better than nonexperts. Expert systems do this by storing and using expert knowledge about a limited topic. Expert systems are an offshoot of AI research about understanding language and understanding the world. Neural networks are information systems that perform discrimination tasks based on what they learn statistically from examples. They are also offshoots of AI research.

What AI-related techniques other than expert systems and neural networks are beginning to attain prominence?
Fuzzy logic, case-based reasoning, and intelligent agents are three techniques that are beginning to attain prominence. Fuzzy logic uses rules but assumes that the conditions and conclusions of rules are stated in an approximate way without forcing people to pretend their perceptions and beliefs are unrealistically precise. Case-based reasoning tries to provide guidance to decision makers by searching a database of past cases and displaying previous cases most similar to the current case. Intelligent agents permit creation of automatic background processes that find information or create danger warnings while other foreground processes are operating independently.

Key Terms

application software
end-user software
system development software
system software
programming
computer program
successive decomposition
modules
structured programming
testing
bug
debugging
syntax error
logic error
unit testing
system testing
procedural
nonprocedural
reusability
machine independence
data independence
computer aided software engineering (CASE)
object-oriented programming (OOP)
generations of programming languages
machine language
assembly language
higher-level language
compiler
source code
object code
interpreter
applet
fourth generation language (4GL)
query language
report generator
modeling language
upper-CASE
lower-CASE
operating system
multitasking

network operating system
artificial intelligence
common sense
natural language
expert system
knowledge-based system
if-then rules
knowledge base
inference engine
explanation module
forward chaining
backward chaining
neural network
fuzzy logic
case-based reasoning
intelligent agent

Review Questions

1. What are the four types of software, and which has the greatest potential for competitive impact?
2. Explain the significance of viewing programming as a business process.
3. In what sense is programming a translation process?
4. Why is successive decomposition important in programming?
5. Why is it necessary to test software?
6. Compare the two types of errors that can be found by debugging a program.
7. What is the difference between procedural and nonprocedural programming languages?
8. Define machine independence, and explain why it is important.
9. Why is it important to have tighter links between analysis and programming?
10. Identify the basic ideas of object-oriented programming.
11. Explain the difference between machine language, assembly language, higher-level languages, and fourth generation languages.
12. What prevents companies from abandoning COBOL in favor of 4GLs?
13. What are CASE systems?
14 Which operating system functions affect personal computer users?
15 Why would it be especially difficult to program in natural language?
16. Define expert systems, and explain how they improve the use of knowledge.
17. When are expert systems useful, and why can't they exercise common sense?
18. Identify the components of an idealized expert system.
19. Explain how a neural network operates.
20. What are the advantages of reasoning using fuzzy logic?
21. Define case-based reasoning, and explain how a CBR system typically operates.
22. Define intelligent agent, and explain why it should or should not be grouped with the other techniques related to artificial intelligence.
23. Why can't current computerized systems understand stories for 4-year-olds?

Discussion Topics

1. Someone has proposed that the job of programmer will be obsolete in 20 years, when users will be able to converse with computers in natural language. Explain why you agree or disagree.
2. Give examples of programming you perform in everyday life. Is anything notably easy or hard about this programming? How might programming in these areas become more complex?
3. Why is it comparatively easy to get an answer to a question such as, "List all customers whose current account balance is greater than $1,000," but much more difficult to answer a question such as, "List all of the customers we need to call to 'remind' them to pay their bills."
4. Read the following , answer the question, and then explain how your answer is related to the ideas in the chapter: Imagine that it is the year 2015. You have just come home after a hard day at work, and you are very hungry. As it does everyday, the home robot you purchased last year at a clearance sale says, "Good evening. I hope you have had a good day. Is there anything I can do for you?" On this particular evening, you would really like to have spaghetti and meatballs for dinner. How do you think you would communicate your request to the robot? How would the robot interpret and execute your request?

5. CHIPS, the Clearing House for Interbank Payments, transfers more than $1 trillion among 120 participating banks. System developers faced a unique problem when a system upgrade was needed. They could test the programs in a simulated mode, and could do trial installations on Saturdays, but could not test this entire, mission-critical system before putting it into operation because the banks did not have dual hardware and software. Fortunately nothing went wrong when they installed the changes on Aug. 17, 1992, because there was no fallback.[22] Use ideas in this chapter to explain the practical and ethical issues raised by this example.
6. Describe the process of attaining knowledge in anything you have ever studied outside of school, such as how to play baseball, play an instrument, or dance. Explain why it would or would not be possible for an expert system or neural network to learn how to do these things.
7. The manager of a $100 million company pension fund at Deere & Co. used a neural network to outperform common stock market indicators. At one point the neural network suggested the fund should invest 40% of its assets in bank stocks. The manager's boss overruled the neural network, but in retrospect the boss was wrong.[23] Explain why this experience should or should not convince the people not to overrule the neural network.
8. What would have to be done to build an expert system for coaching a basketball team? Why do you believe it is or is not possible to build such a system?
9. Did this chapter contain any examples that you consider to be machine intelligence? If so, what are the examples, and why do you believe these are examples of machine intelligence? If not, identify examples in the chapter that are closest to machine intelligence, and explain how the examples would be different if they were to truly demonstrate machine intelligence.

CASE

U.S. Navy: A Y2K-like Problem with Global Positioning Satellites

The U.S. global positioning satellite system was developed for the Department of Defense in the 1970s. It consists of 24 satellites whose continuous transmission of time and position information makes it possible to pinpoint any location on the surface of the earth to within about 100 meters for civilian use and to a closer tolerance for military use. Nonmilitary uses of GPS data include tracking the location of cars, boats, trucks, and even hikers in the wilderness. A basic GPS receiver now costs $250 or less. Over 2.5 million GPS units are installed in cars in Japan, where street and building numbering is haphazard. The high cost of in-car navigation equipment (over $1,000) has limited its use in the United States.

Unfortunately, a quirk in the way global positioning satellites are programmed will likely provide a preview of Y2K problems. The signals transmitted by the satellites include the date, and this is coded starting with the number of weeks since January 6, 1980. This number of weeks is stored in a 12-bit counter, meaning that the number of weeks since the first week goes to 1022, then 1023, and then rolls back to zero. The rollback occurs because 1024 is 2 to the 12th power and is too big for a 12-bit counter because it is expressed as a string of 13 bits, a 1 followed by twelve 0's. Any device relying on a GPS signal must correctly adjust for this rollover in the way it handles the signal. Otherwise it may give erroneous positions starting with the 1024th week, which begins at midnight of the evening of Aug. 21, 1999 and morning of Aug. 22, 1999. Had this counter been programmed as a 16-bit field, it could have continued for over 300 years without a rollover problem.

The official source of information about global positioning satellites is the U.S. Naval Observatory in Washington, DC. Its Web page explains when the rollover will occur and then says, "Once the rollover has occurred, it is the responsibility of the *user* (i.e., user equipment or software) to account for the previous 1024 weeks. Depending upon the manufacturer of your GPS receiver, you may or may not be affected by the GPS Week Number Rollover on 22 August 1999. Some receivers may display inaccurate date information, some may also calculate incorrect navigation solutions....Contact the manufacturer of your GPS receiver to determine if you will be affected by the GPS week number rollover." The Web page goes on to provide references for a number of GPS receiver manufacturers who may be able to provide information about whether their particular receivers will have a problem. It also refers the reader to another website, which warns, "On 22 August 1999, unless repaired, many GPS receivers will claim that it is 6 January 1980, 23 August will become 7 January, and so on. Accuracy of navigation may also be severely affected. Although it appears that GPS broadcasts do contain sufficient data to ensure that navigation need not be affected by rollover in 1999, it is not proven that the firmware in all receivers will handle the rollovers in stride; some receivers may claim wrong locations in addition to incorrect dates." It goes on to say that the problem is documented in ICD-GPS-200, par 3.3.4 (b) and that a July 1993 update of this document added a note saying that users must account for the rollover, but presenting no way to accomplish this.

QUESTIONS

1. Explain why the GPS week rollover problem is similar to the Y2K problem and why someone would design a week-counter using a 12-bit field.
2. Explain why you believe the Web-based warnings mentioned above are or are not adequate.

Sources:

Hafner, Katie. "Scooby Doo, Where Are You?" *New York Times*, May 14, 1998, p. D1.

Time Service Department, U.S. Naval Observatory. "GPS Week Number Rollover Approaches," Online Posting, May 15, 1998 (http://tycho.usno.navy.mil/gps_week.html).

Yourdon, Edward, and Jennifer Yourdon, *Time Bomb 2000*, Upper Saddle River, NJ: Prentice Hall PTR, 1998.

CASE

Cycorp: Building a Knowledge Base to Support Commonsense Reasoning

Developing techniques for capturing commonsense knowledge and building it into computerized systems is one of the greatest challenges of computer science. Capturing and codifying commonsense is difficult because the rules of thumb used in everyday life to understand language and to interpret the world are almost never published explicitly in books or dictionaries. Here are some examples:

- You have to be awake to eat.
- You can usually see people's noses, but not their hearts.
- You cannot remember events that have not happened yet.
- Once people die they stay dead.
- If you cut a lump of peanut butter in half, each half is also a lump of peanut butter; but if you cut a table in half, neither half is a table.
- A glass filled with milk will be rightside-up, not upside-down.

The CYC project began in 1984 at the Microelectronics and Computer Technology Corporation (MCC) in Austin, Texas, with the goal of codifying this type of knowledge. Cycorp, Inc., a 1995 spin-off of MCC, was founded to continue the development of CYC technology. In 1998, Cycorp had around 30 employees and a number of corporate sponsors who hoped to apply CYC technology in a variety of ways.

The CYC Web page describes CYC as a very large, multicontextual knowledge base and inference engine designed to "break the 'software brittleness bottleneck' once and for all by constructing a foundation of basic common sense knowledge. It is intended to provide a 'deep' layer of understanding that can be used by other programs to make them more flexible." Applications of CYC that are available or in development are in areas such as natural language processing, extracting information from databases, searching for examples in captioned databases (such as news photos or film clips), creating application-specific thesauruses, and retrieving information from the Web.

CYC technology includes a knowledge base, a representation language, an inference engine, interface tools, and modules designed for specific applications. The knowledge base is a formalized representation of commonsense knowledge including facts, rules of thumb, and methods for reasoning about the objects and events of everyday life. It consists of a vocabulary of terms and a "sea of assertions" about those terms. The assertions are related to causality, time, space, events, substances, intention, contradiction, belief, emotions, planning, and other aspects of human existence. New assertions are added continually. The knowledge base currently contains hundreds of thousands of assertions and is divided into hundreds of "microtheories," each of which is a set of assertions sharing a common set of assumptions. Various microtheories are focused on a particular domain of knowledge, a particular level of detail, a particular interval in time, and so on. Use of microtheories makes it possible to reconcile and resolve assertions from separate contexts that are both applicable to a situation but that may yield contradictory inferences. For example, in the context of total darkness you cannot see anything, and this seems to contradict the assertion that you can usually see people's noses. The CYC inference engine performs logical deductions using a variety of logical techniques. The vast size of the knowledge base requires that special inference techniques be developed, such as using microtheories to optimize the inference process by restricting search domains. Special purpose inference modules were developed for a few specific classes of inference. One such module handles reasoning concerning set membership or disjointedness. Others handle equality reasoning, temporal reasoning, and mathematical reasoning.

QUESTIONS

1. How is CYC related (or not related) to basic programming concepts such as computer program, successive decomposition, structured programming, debugging, syntax error, logic error, and reusability?
2. Explain how CYC might be used for data mining or for finding photos in an image database.

Sources:

Cycorp, Inc. "The CYC Technology," June 2, 1998 (http://www.cyc.com/tech.html).

Lenat, Douglas B. "CYC: A Large-scale Investment in Knowledge Infrastructure," *Communications of the ACM*, Nov. 1995, pp. 33–38.

10

Networks and Telecommunications

Study Questions

- What aspects of the convergence of computing and communications are important for understanding telecommunications?
- What are the steps in the basic telecommunications model?
- What are the advantages and disadvantages of the different forms of wire and wireless transmission?
- What is ISDN, and why is it important?
- What are the main differences between LANs, WANs, and VANs?
- Why are telecommunications standards important?
- How is telecommunications policy related to issues faced by managers?

Outline

Opening Case

FEDEX: MAXIMIZING THE VALUE OF INFORMATION

FedEx grew to a multibillion dollar company by providing reliable overnight delivery of high-priority, time-sensitive packages and documents. (See Table 10.1.) Its 590 airplanes, 40,000 trucks, and 137,000 people deliver over 2.9 million packages a day. After the parcels are picked up at the customer's site or dropped off at a FedEx location, they are rushed to the local airport and flown to a FedEx hub where they are sorted by destination, loaded on planes, and shipped to the destination airport. Packages designated for overnight delivery are delivered to their destination within 24 hours. To maintain a high degree of reliability in its shipping process, FedEx tracks each package through each step on its path from the shipper to the recipient. When the driver picks up the package, it is immediately logged using Supertracker, a portable, handheld computer containing a bar code reader for capturing the bar code identification on the package and a keyboard for entering additional information such as the destination's ZIP code. On returning to the truck, the driver inserts the Supertracker into a small computer that transmits the data by radio waves to the local dispatch center, which has a link to the COSMOS database. Within five minutes of initial pickup, the FedEx database contains the package's identification, location, destination, and route. The location data is updated automatically (using the package's bar code) as the package moves through each step on its way to the destination. Although package pickup and delivery involve a series of steps in different places, the combination of telecommunications and computing permits FedEx to know the location of every package at any time and to make sure that procedures are followed throughout. Any deviation would become obvious quickly.

The information in the system is used in many ways. Information about pickups and deliveries is the basis of customer billing. Detailed tracking information supports customer service by permitting customer service agents to tell customers where their packages are. Customers can dial into the FedEx Web site to obtain the same information. As a method for managing their own internal operations, FedEx developed a service quality index based on 12 types of events that disappoint customers, including late delivery, damaged or lost packages, and complaints. Even a delivery at 10:31 for a package promised for 10:30 is considered a problem. So that they will learn from past problems and mistakes, people throughout the company receive daily feedback reports identifying problems that occurred yesterday.[1]

As other major package delivery and shipping companies built similar systems, FedEx decided to expand from a package delivery company to a fully integrated corporate partner that picks up, transports, warehouses, and delivers all of a company's finished goods from the factory to the customer's receiving dock—with status data available every step of the way. For example, when orders are sent from Omaha Steaks' central computer to its warehouses, a FedEx tracking label is generated automatically. Omaha Steaks delivers the warehouse-fulfilled orders by truck to a FedEx hub, and FedEx delivers the steaks to the customer. As the result of a five-year project, FedEx performs most of the warehousing and distribution for National Semiconductor, which manufactures most of its products in Asia and ships them to a FedEx distribution warehouse in Singapore. National Semiconductor's mainframe sends a daily batch of orders over a dedicated line directly to a FedEx inventory-management computer in Memphis. FedEx sends the orders to its warehouse in Singapore, where they are packaged and shipped. This system reduced the average customer delivery cycle from four weeks to seven days, and reduced distribution costs from 2.9% of sales to 1.2%.[2]

Debate Topic

Manufacturing and marketing firms that rely on quick, reliable delivery of consumer products and spare parts should plan to transfer most of these delivery functions to logistics firms such as FedEx and UPS that have built processes and information systems that support quick, reliable delivery.

Initially, FedEx's service was about delivering packages. Gradually, an international information system supported by a telecommunications network became an important part of

TABLE 10.1 FedEx Applies Information Technology in Package Delivery

CUSTOMER

- Individuals and companies who want packages shipped
- Billing department

PRODUCT

- Quick, reliable shipment of packages from shipper to destination
- Excellent customer service such as the ability to report where any package is at any time

BUSINESS PROCESS

Major steps:	Rationale:
• Identify the package when it is picked up • Determine package routing • Move the package through checkpoints, recording its location at each step • Provide information to customer service reps • Provide information for billing	• Know exactly where each package is at all times. Convert this internal operational data into an aspect of customer service.

PARTICIPANTS	INFORMATION	TECHNOLOGY
• Pickup and delivery drivers • Workers in the sorting centers • Customer service reps	• Identification of the package • Routing of the package • Location of the package • Customer information	• Handheld terminal • Radio link to central computer system • Bar code readers in sorting centers • Central computer system

the package delivery service because this system kept track of each package at all times. Later, the telecommunications network became an essential part of FedEx's expansion into a corporate logistics business that required a highly distributed but tightly controlled information system.

The previous two chapters discussed computer systems, computer peripherals, and software. They mentioned distributed processing but said little about the role of telecommunications in distributed processing. This chapter will look at a variety of ways telecommunications is used and also at some of the technical details business professionals need to be aware of simply to read a current business magazine such as *Business Week* or *Forbes.*

APPLYING TELECOMMUNICATIONS IN BUSINESS

Telecommunications is the transmission of data between devices in different locations. Typical initial experiences with telecommunications include watching television, listening to the radio, and using the telephone. In these cases, the data transmitted are sounds and images. Telecommunications applications in business include transmission of data of every type. The term **data communications** often refers to telecommunications involving computerized data, but not voice.

In essence, the purpose of telecommunications is to reduce or eliminate time delays and other impacts of geographical separation. Telecommunications reduces the effect of geographical separation when people talk on a telephone and eliminates time delays when a customer links into a supplier's computer to order products. It provides both benefits when a system consolidates results from a company's branch offices.

Vital Role of Telecommunications

Only 20 years ago, business people often thought of telecommunications as telephone calls and paid little attention to it. Today, telecommunications is a requirement for business effectiveness and success. In many businesses, national or international networks are a competitive necessity for tracking inventories, taking customer orders, verifying product availability, and granting credit. Telecommunications systems have improved the effectiveness of sales and customer service work by creating immediate access to data. Also, telecommunications systems have changed the nature of internal communication within geographically dispersed organizations.

Telecommunications can also be a strategic business issue even if the organization resides in a single building. Consider the importance of the voice and data networks within a hospital. This infrastructure makes it possible to communicate doctors' orders, lab results, and other vital information needed to coordinate patient care. Despite this, hospital administrators traditionally focus on a myriad of other issues and often plan inadequately for the infrastructure needed to improve services for patients and doctors.

Telecommunications can address many different issues in a business. In some cases, the issue is operational efficiency; in others, telecommunications innovations lead to increased business effectiveness and competitive advantage. Although this chapter and many other chapters in this book mention telecommunications applications that have competitive significance, the effective use of telecommunications does not guarantee competitive advantage. In fact, many telecommunications applications such as EDI are more like requirements for doing business in some industries.

One way to visualize the importance of telecommunications in business is to look at the value chain and identify common telecommunications applications that have competitive significance. Table 10.2 lists applications in both primary and background activities along the value chain. Telecommunications reduces delays and eliminates unnecessary work in all these applications.

Convergence of Computing and Communications

Before discussing different types of networks and telecommunications technologies, it is useful to look more deeply at the convergence of computing and communications, a trend introduced in Chapter 1. We will discuss four aspects of this trend:

Reliance of Telecommunications on Computers

The earliest telephone systems included human operators who established telephone connections by plugging wires into a switchboard. Later, this work was automated using electromechanical switches that changed position to establish a circuit. Today, the long distance connections are made electronically by computers, even though some of the local connections are still made using electromechanical gear. Computers also monitor the traffic on the network and balance the loads on different parts of the network by determining which path across the network each telephone call will take. Several widely publicized failures of long distance telephone systems during the 1990s were caused by bugs in computer programs that controlled these networks.

Role of Telecommunications in Computing

During the first decades of computer use, people thought of computing as something that occurs when using a computer. More recently, the convergence of computing and communications has made distributed processing more practical, with the data virtually anywhere and the computing occurring anywhere. In the FedEx example, handheld computers performed some of the processing but then hooked into a computer in the truck, which transmitted data to a central database where other processing occurred. In this type of distributed system, users often do not care about the location of the computers and data as long as they can do their work conveniently. The organization cares, however, because the location of computing and data affects costs, security, control of the data, and many other important issues. Figure 10.1 illustrates how distributed computing is increasing the overlap between what people think of as computing and what they think of as telecommunications.

TABLE 10.2 Examples of telecommunications applications

Value chain activity	Typical telecommunications applications
Product development	• Share data with other departments and with customers to make sure the product meets market needs and is manufacturable. • Work together with others who have simultaneous access to the same computerized data and drawings.
Production	• Transmit orders to suppliers' computer systems for immediate action. • Receive orders from customers for immediate action. • Transmit customer specifications to automated machines in the factory. • Collect quality data across the manufacturing process to analyze quality.
Sales	• Provide prices and production data to customers. • Obtain data from headquarters while traveling or visiting customers. • Transmit orders to the factory. • Permit customers to enter orders directly. • Transmit credit card purchase data for quick credit approval.
Delivery	• Receive delivery orders. • Track merchandise in the delivery process. • Confirm receipt of order.
Customer service	• Receive requests for service from customers. • Transmit data to customers to help them use the product or fix problems. • Dispatch repair crews.
Management	• Receive consolidated data from across the organization. • Maintain personal communication with people throughout the organization.
Finance	• Transfer funds to suppliers. • Receive funds from customers. • Complete transactions related to financing of the organization.

New Options in Wire and Wireless Transmission

Figure 10.2 shows how progress in wire and wireless transmission is creating a wide range of telecommunications options. In metropolitan areas, wireless transmission of radio and television broadcasts is being superseded by cable broadcasting, which can provide more choices and higher quality reception. At the same time, direct satellite broadcasting is creating a new wireless option. Similarly, the first telephone networks transmitted conversations only through copper wire. The inconvenience of transferring data through wire has led to the emergence of portable telephones and data transmission through satellites. At the same time, however, fiber optic cable has greatly increased the amount of data that can be transmitted by wire transmission.

New Combinations of Data and Computing

In Chaper 1, Figure 1.8 showed some of the new combinations of data and computing that have emerged by combining certain elements of telephone, telegraph, broadcasting, and data processing. For example, electronic mail takes some of the function of a telegraph but

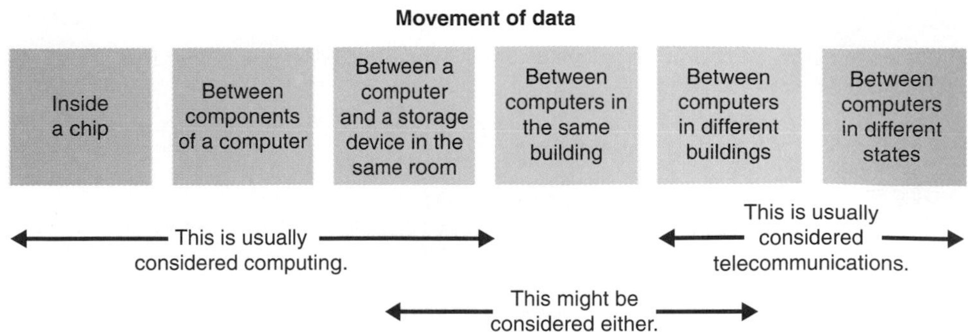

Figure 10.1
The unclear boundary between computing and telecommunications

This figure shows that there is no precise boundary between computing and telecommunications.

uses a computer to generate and receive the message. Voice mail uses a computer to control recording and retrieval of the voice message that might have been missed. Video conferencing applies the idea of video from television broadcasting to expand what would have been a telephone conversation. Many new combinations of data and computing can be expected in the future.

Making Sense of the Terminology and Details

Like computer systems, telecommunications systems present us with a large number of technical terms and choices. Although many business professionals may think they don't care about such things, these technical choices do determine what types of telecommunications applications are possible, and at what cost. You need an introduction to telecommunications technology because business professionals with no understanding of the types of networks or technical options have difficulty contributing to discussions of how a telecommunications infrastructure can be used effectively and economically to support an organization's mission.

Recognizing both the need to understand telecommunications basics and the need to avoid a deluge of terminology, this chapter proceeds by introducing a simple model of the steps in telecommunications and identifying some of the options for different parts of the model. The model is based on familiar telephone systems but raises many of the choices that also apply for data communication networks.

The reason for the various choices and types of equipment is the same as the reason for different types of computer system equipment. Recall how Table 8.2 identified technology performance variables under the general headings of functional capabilities, ease of use, compatibility, and maintainability. All of the issues identified in that table apply to telecommunications just as they apply to computers, peripherals, and software. Table 10.3 shows examples of telecommunications choices related to these performance variables plus security, which is a special concern for telecommunications.

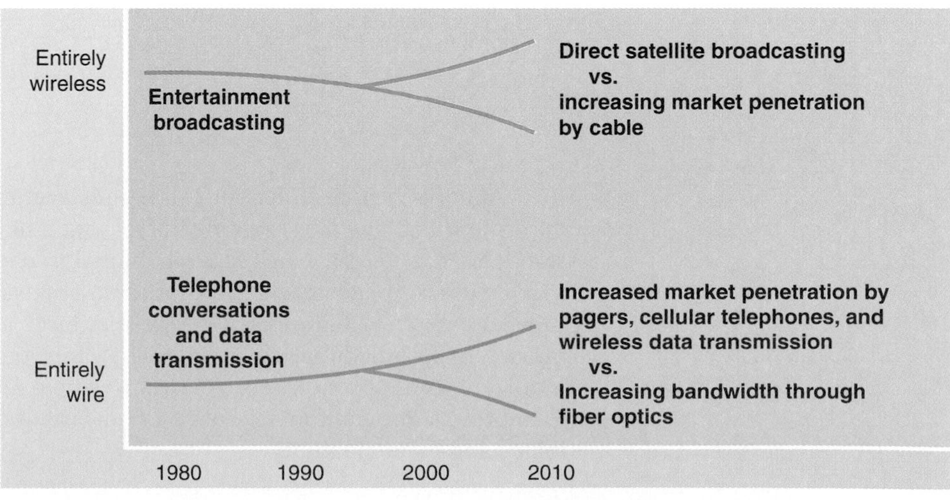

Figure 10.2
New options for wire and wireless transmission

Local wireless entertainment broadcasting is being superseded by transmission through cable at the same time cable is seeing new competition from satellite television. Similarly, telephone conversations are increasingly transmitted using wireless methods at the same time that fiber optics vastly increases data transmission bandwidth. (The diagram shows the direction of change rather than absolute amounts.)

TABLE 10.3 Performance Variables and Related Telecommunications Choices

Performance variables	Examples of telecommunications choices related to each performance variable
Functional capabilities and limitations	
Capacity	• Each transmission medium operates in a particular capacity range in terms of data transmission speeds and distances covered. • Multiplexers increase the effective capacity of a line by combining multiple transmissions and separating them out when they are received.
Speed	• The promise of the Information Superhighway is limited by practical constraints on data transfer rates and capacity. • Transmitting voice communications through a satellite introduces a noticeable delay in response.
Price-performance	• Fiber optic cable has far more data carrying capacity than twisted pair or coaxial cable, but is more expensive. • Cellular phones are more convenient than fixed-location phones, but are much more expensive.
Reliability	• Networks sometimes fail altogether, calling for alternative routes and other forms of backup. • Data degrades as it moves through a physical medium, motivating the use of digital transmission and calling for the use of repeaters to boost the signal. • Data networks can use encryption to prevent unauthorized access.
Operating conditions	• Clouds, rain, and buildings interfere with some wireless transmissions. • Weight and portability of cellular phones affect their use. • Telephone switches require uninterrupted electric supply.
Ease of use	
Quality of user interface	• Digital transmission provides clearer transmission than analog transmission.
Ease of becoming proficient	• Proficiency with basic telephone capabilities systems is almost immediate, but many users never learn the more advanced features, such as transferring phone calls.
Portability	• Portable phones are convenient for many purposes.
Security	
Ease of interception	• Analog cellular calls are comparatively easy to intercept.
Cost of security	• Encryption requires additional calculation capabilities built into telecommunications devices.
Compatibility	
Conformance to standards	• Telecommunications operates based on many *de facto* and *de jure* standards.
Interoperability	• Multiple inconsistent standards exist in computer networking, such as OSI, SNA, and TCP/IP.
Maintainability	
Modularity	• Data networks are modularized so messages can follow the routing that is least busy at any time.
Scalability	• PBXs can handle particular numbers of lines and then need to be upgraded.
Flexibility	• There is often a need to upgrade or downsize networks.

Many telecommunications decisions are difficult because these goals pull in opposite directions. For example, increasing a network's compatibility with external standards may increase its maintainability but decrease its functional capabilities by making it slower. Increasing a network's ease of use by simplifying aspects of its operation may make it incompatible with standards and may have positive or negative impacts on its functional capabilities. As we introduce the technical aspects of telecommunications networks, it is important to remember that the purpose of each option is to improve some combination of functional capabilities, ease of use, security, compatibility, and maintainability.

Reality Check

CONVERGENCE OF COMPUTING AND TELECOMMUNICATIONS

The text mentions four aspects of the convergence of computing and telecommunications: the reliance of telecommunications on computers, the role of telecommunications in computing, new options in wire and wireless transmission, and new combinations of data and computing.

1. Think about ways you have used computers and telecommunications in your everyday life. What aspects of this convergence have you felt personally?
2. Some people think that televisions will be more like computers in the future. What could this mean and how is it related to the convergence of computing and telecommunications?

FUNCTIONS AND COMPONENTS OF TELECOMMUNICATIONS NETWORKS

A **telecommunications network** is a set of devices linked to perform telecommunications. Each device in a network is called a **node.** The nodes of a network can include many types of devices, such as telephones, terminals, secondary storage devices, and computers. The nodes can be a few feet apart or thousands of miles apart. The data transmitted from one node to another are often divided into small chunks called *messages*. The overall amount of data transmission on a network is often called the *traffic* on the network.

Connectivity, the critical objective of telecommunications, is the ability to transmit data between devices at different locations. Although connectivity refers to machine linkages, it allows people in different parts of an organization to communicate with each other and share and coordinate their work. Connectivity therefore supports business processes but has a technical side that managers must appreciate.

Basic Telecommunications Model

Figure 10.3 shows the basic functions of a telecommunications network along with the network components that perform those functions. This explanatory model is based on familiar telephone networks. We start by looking at each step briefly.

The first step in telecommunications is generating the data to be moved to another device. For example, a telephone caller generates data by speaking, just as an ATM user generates data by keying it into the ATM terminal. A salesperson may generate data by using a push button telephone as a terminal. A computer may generate data for an overnight transfer of transactions to headquarters by copying the day's computerized transaction log.

However the data is generated, it must be converted from the original form into a form for transmission. This process is called **encoding.** In a telephone conversation, the telephone mouthpiece encodes sounds into electrical impulses. In transmitting a picture by fax, the original image is encoded when it is digitized by a scanner. In a system for transferring funds electronically from one bank to another, the encoding uses encryption to make the signal meaningless to anyone intercepting it for unauthorized use.

Next comes the process of directing a signal from its source to its destination. This process is called **switching** and is comparable to the process of switching a train from one railroad track to another. Telephone systems require switching decisions because the data may follow alternative paths from its source to its destination. Switching is automatic in most current telephone systems. A computer assigns each outgoing telephone call to one of the firm's outgoing lines. An instant later, a computer or mechanical device in a telephone company switching station chooses among alternative physical paths to establish the circuit between the parties on the call.

A path along which data are transmitted is called a **channel.** Both wire and wireless channels are used frequently. Telephone systems once used only copper wire channels.

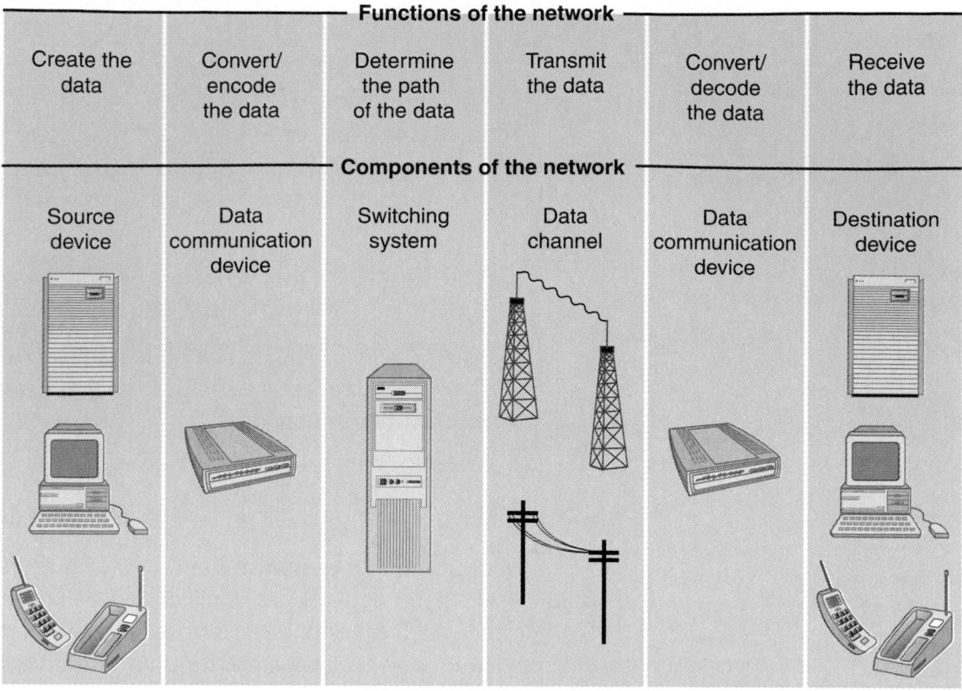

Figure 10.3
Functions and components of a telecommunications network

Network components can be understood in terms of the various functions a network performs. Notice that some of the functions can be performed at several different times by different equipment in different places during the same transmission.

Fiber optic cable made of ultrapure glass is now an alternative for networks with high data volume. Air or space is the channel for wireless transmission, which eliminates some of the restrictions of wires. Telephone systems use wireless channels for many types of transmissions. A cordless telephone in a house covers a few feet of air, whereas transmission through a communications satellite uses a channel covering 22,300 miles of space in each direction. Many applications use several different channels. For example, a single telephone call may be transmitted through several wire and wireless channels.

On arrival at the destination, the data must be converted from the coded form back to the original. This conversion is called **decoding.** In a telephone conversation, the telephone handset decodes the data back into audible sounds. In electronic funds transfer, the decoding process reverses the encryption step that preceded data transmission.

Finally, the decoded data are received and restored to the original form. This form may be a reproduction of the original sounds for a telephone conversation, a reproduction of the original document for fax transmission, or identical data for transmission of computer data.

To apply the telecommunications model to a specific situation, consider a telephone call from a person in a car on a freeway in Los Angeles to a person in an office in Paris. Figure 10.4 shows the steps of creating, encoding, switching, transmitting, decoding, and receiving data. Notice how several switching and transmission steps are included in this process.

Figure 10.3 showed the functions directly involved in moving data, but it left out a crucial background function. **Network management** is the process of monitoring the network's operations and reallocating work among different parts of the network so that it can handle its workload. Every large network requires major efforts in network management. Figure 10.5 shows the network management center used by AT&T for its long distance lines.

The steps in the telecommunications model rely on technology for generating signals at precise frequencies and moving and receiving those signals with minimal data loss. Although users and managers needn't be involved in complicated technical details, they do need to recognize common telecommunications choices related to the basic functions. Next, each of the functions and components are covered in more detail, focusing on the types of things users and managers should know. The discussion is divided into four sections: generating and receiving data, encoding and decoding data, switching, and transmitting data.

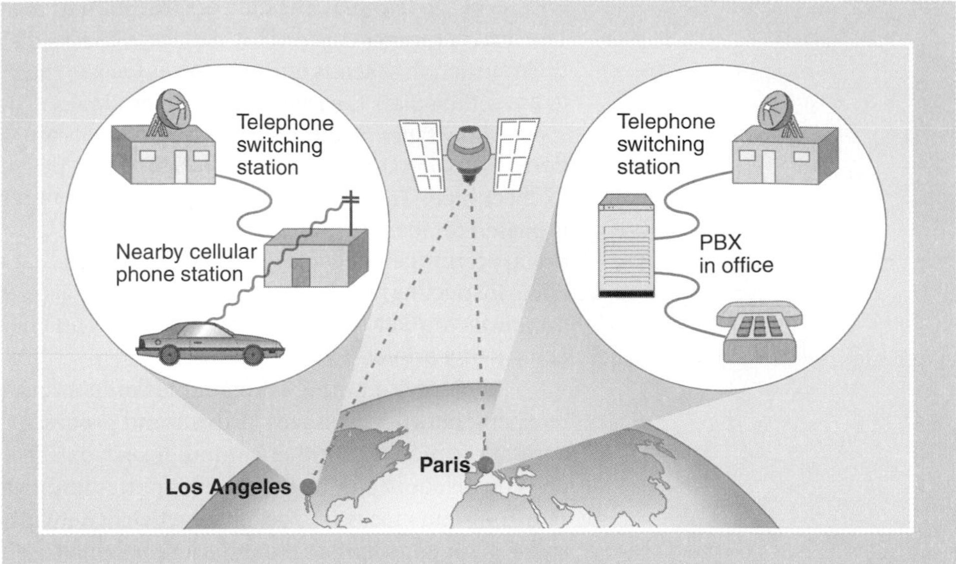

Figure 10.4
Los Angeles to Paris by telephone

This diagram shows one of many possible routings for a telephone call between Los Angeles and Paris.

Generating and Receiving Data

Telecommunications systems can use many types of telephones, terminals, secondary storage devices, computers, and other devices for generating and receiving data. In some systems, the data are generated by a handheld terminal and transmitted to a computer elsewhere. In a paging system, the data are generated by a person using a pager and received by a person using a beeper. In a large building's automatic air conditioning system, a computer receives readings from sensors and then generates commands that are sent to the cooling equipment. We will talk about telephones later and will look now at roles of computers in generating and receiving data in telecommunications systems.

The variety of terminals in telecommunications systems is expanding continually. The progression from dumb terminals to intelligent terminals was explained in the discussion of distributed computing in Chapter 8. Regardless of whether some of the processing

Figure 10.5
AT&T's long distance control center

AT&T's Network Operations Center balances resource utilization on AT&T's long distance network, which includes 114 interconnected switching centers in the United States.

is done at the terminal, the data are transmitted to a computer called the host computer. The **host computer** controls the database, checks the inputs for validity, and either accepts the transaction or sends error messages back to the terminal. A touch tone telephone used to enter data plays the role of a dumb terminal.

Many types of special-purpose terminals are used in telecommunications applications. The special-purpose terminals for ATMs permit only numerical inputs. Those used to check credit cards before granting credit also contain a slot through which the credit card is passed for identification. Handheld terminals play a key role in applications where stationary terminals are too awkward. For example, car rental company employees use them while inspecting returned cars to enter the mileage and gasoline level. The terminals may broadcast the data to the office for generating an invoice or may print a receipt themselves using a tiny printer.

An entire computer is sometimes used as communication gear for originating and receiving network messages. A **front-end processor** is a computer that handles network communication for another computer such as a mainframe that processes the data. The division of labor between the two computers improves the efficiency of the overall system. The front-end processor is set up for efficient network communications, whereas the mainframe is set up to update the transaction database efficiently.

Thus, the equipment that generates or receives a message on a network can range from a telephone or a tiny special-purpose terminal to a computer. After creating the data, the next step is to encode or decode the data.

Encoding and Decoding Data

Data transmission requires that data be encoded as electrical or optical signals, transmitted, and later decoded. The basic choices in encoding and decoding data are related to two factors:

1. *Whether the original data are naturally analog or digital.* Sounds, images, and video are naturally analog because they are continuous and depend on their shape for their meaning. Numbers, text, and other characters used in written language are naturally digital because they are discontinuous, separable codes with a specific meaning.
2. *Whether the data are transmitted in analog or digital form.* Transmitting data using **analog signals** means that the signal varies continuously in a wave pattern mimicking the shape of the original data. Transmitting data using **digital signals** means that the signal is represented as a series of 0's and 1's.

Analog Data, Analog Signal

Figure 10.6 summarizes the physical method for analog encoding and decoding. The starting point is a **carrier signal** recognized by both the sending and receiving equipment. As shown in the figure, the carrier signal literally carries the encoded data and is itself a wave that swings back and forth in steady cycles. A typical telephone handset encodes sounds using the type of process shown in the figure. The handset at the receiving end decodes the signal by subtracting out the carrier signal.

Digital Data, Analog Signal

To transmit computer-generated digital data over a standard analog telephone line, a **modem** (*mo*dulator/*dem*odulator) is used at each end of the transmission. The sending modem superimposes the pattern of 0's or 1's on the carrier signal. The receiving modem subtracts out the carrier signal to reconstruct the original pattern of 0's and 1's. Different modems send signals at different speeds, which are measured in bits per second (bps) or baud. (Chapter 8 explained why the term *baud* is sometimes used instead of bits per second because some devices can transmit individual signals with gradations finer than just 0 versus 1). Early modems operated as slowly as 300 bps, although modems for PCs commonly operate at 28.8 or 56 Kbps. Limited modem speed is often

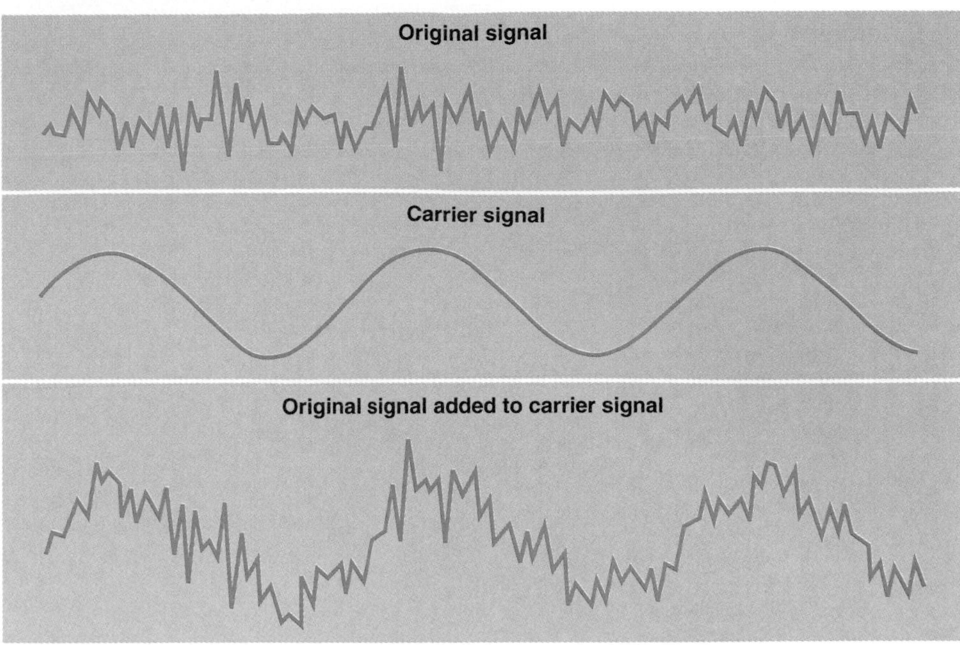

Figure 10.6
Superimposing a signal on a carrier wave

To encode sounds for analog transmission, their wave pattern is added to a carrier signal. The receiver decodes the message by subtracting out the carrier signal.

frustrating when using the World Wide Web from home computers. By 1998, 1.5 Mbps **cable modems** that permitted Internet access through cable television connections were available to about 10% of U.S. homes, but only a small fraction of these had bought them.

Digital Data, Digital Signal

With digital signals, the data are not superimposed on a carrier wave. Instead they are just sent down the channel as a series of electrical or optical on/off pulses. In digital transmission, modems are replaced by other electronic devices that transmit the data in a precise pattern and recognize the data at the other end. Responding to the threat of cable modems, major regional telephone companies in the United States formed a consortium with Compaq, Intel, and Microsoft in 1998 to apply asymmetric digital subscriber line (ADSL) technology in 1.5 Mbps digital modems for use on regular phone lines. U.S. West's initial version of this type of service cost around $200 plus a subscriber fee of over $40 per month.[3] The media research firm Jupiter Communications predicted that cable modems would provide high-speed access to 6.7 million homes by 2002, while ADSL would be limited to about half as many homes because the cable companies would probably push cable modems more actively than telephone companies would push ADSL.[4]

Analog Data, Digital Signal

Using a digital signal to transmit analog data such as an image or sound requires that the data be digitized. As was discussed in Chapter 8, the digitized image or sound is only an approximation of the original. The quality of the image or sound received depends on the precision of the digitizing process.

Significance of Analog Versus Digital Transmission

Table 10.4 shows that the four possibilities are not just a technical detail. The choice of type of data and type of transmission signal affects the quality of the data received, the cost of the transmission system, and the receiver's ability to manipulate the data as part of the decoding process.

The first telecommunications applications encoded analog data such as voice and video using analog encoding methods. Analog encoding of discontinuous, coded data such as numbers and text was necessary to transmit computer-generated data using

TABLE 10.4 **Transmitting Analog or Digital Data Encoded in Analog or Digital Form**

Original type of data \ Type of encoding	Transmission using an analog signal	Transmission using a digital signal
Original data in analog form, such as sounds, images, and video	*Method:* superimpose the "shape" of the data on a carrier signal; receive the signal and subtract out the carrier wave to reconstruct the original signal	*Method:* digitize the sounds or images to approximate them using a stream of 0's and 1's; receive the stream of 0's and 1's and reconstruct the approximation
	Examples: transmit voice using traditional telephone lines or radio broadcasting; use a fax to digitize a picture and then transmit it over a typical analog telephone line; transmit video in traditional television broadcasting	*Examples:* transmit voice using a digital telephone line, transmit voice via satellite, transmit television using cable
	Advantages: basic idea of the early telecommunications applications	*Advantages:* can manipulate the data more effectively and can have mixed forms of data as new transmission services emerge
	Shortcomings: signal degrades as it moves through the channel; can boost its power, but cannot restore its shape	*Shortcomings:* greater processing requirements at the nodes and greater data transmission capacity required of the network
Original data in digital form, such as numbers and text	*Method:* superimpose a stream of 0's and 1's on a carrier signal; receive the signal and subtract out the carrier wave to reconstruct the original signal	*Method:* transmit a stream of 0's and 1's by sending them through the channel as a series of pulses
	Examples: use a modem to transmit data from one computer to another via analog telephone line	*Examples:* transmit computerized data in a local area network
	Advantages: permits using typical telephone lines to transmit computerized data	*Advantages:* low error rate
	Shortcomings: not as efficient as simply sending the 0's and 1's down the channel; limited by base frequency of the analog signal	*Shortcomings:* cannot use standard analog telephone technology for these applications

typical analog telephone lines. Digital encoding was the natural way to transmit computer-generated data, but required digital transmission media. Continuous data can be transmitted using digital transmission media after being digitized.

The differences between analog and digital representations of data affect the quality of the transmission. The quality of analog data depends on preserving the precise shape of the waveform as it moves through a wire or through space. If the signal degrades gradually during transmission, there is no way to regenerate it. It is possible to boost the signal using a device called a repeater, but it is not possible to correct any distortions in its shape. With digital data, reconstructing the signal using a device called a regenerator requires only the ability to differentiate between the 0's and the 1's and make them sharper. Digital coding also provides many ways to use special bits for error checking and correction.

One of the most important differences between analog and digital data is that digital data can be manipulated readily. This issue underlies the struggle during the 1990s about standards for **high definition television (HDTV),** a new standard for broadcasting and receiving television signals. If the standard were totally analog, as some competitors suggested, the result would be clearer pictures than the previous standard allowed. If the standard were digital, the result would be both clearer pictures and greater ability to manipulate the data. It would be possible to give the user new types of choices that would make a television more of a controllable, interactive medium. For example, at some point it might be possible to let the viewer of a televised baseball game decide what seat to see it from. This would be possible because the data transmitted for the game would include the game itself and metadata telling the television set how to interpret the various components of the signal.

Directing Data from Source to Destination

After the signal is encoded, it must move from the source to the destination. For special applications with high data volumes, it may be cost-effective to lease a **dedicated line,** a telephone line used exclusively by one firm for transmitting voice or computerized data between two locations.

In contrast, public telephone networks are used for typical telephone communication and for lower volume computerized data. These networks often have alternative paths from a source to a destination and contain switching systems that decide what path each message will take. Figure 10.4 showed the switching steps that might occur to connect a telephone call from a car in Los Angeles to an office in Paris. Ideally, it should seem to the caller that there are only two steps: dialing the call and speaking to the person in Paris a few seconds later. The switching process therefore should be transparent to the user, even though there might be a number of data transmission steps with separate switching decisions between them.

A **switch** is a special-purpose computer that directs incoming messages along a path and therefore performs switching in a network. Some types of switches control transmission across national telephone networks, whereas others control the distribution of telephone calls within a building. The first type of switch routes long distance telephone calls through long distance lines that cross the country. When a particular line gets very busy or is out of operation, these switches automatically assign telephone calls to other lines. Likewise, local telephone switching stations use switches to create the temporary circuits for telephone calls. These switches are still electromechanical rather than computerized in many local stations. A different type of switch called a private branch exchange (PBX) distributes calls within a customer site. Functions of PBXs are covered later in the discussion of telephone networks.

Different switching methods are used in different situations. The **circuit switching** used for telephone calls sets up a temporary circuit between the source and destination; when the telephone call is terminated, the temporary circuit is also terminated. Without circuit switching, it would be necessary to maintain permanent circuits linking all pairs of telephones. Switching for a local telephone call usually occurs in a local telephone switching facility. Switching for a long distance call can involve several steps, depending on how many different physical links are established in the temporary circuit.

Although a switching process has always been required for any telephone call, switching technology has become much faster and more highly automated over the years (see Figure 1.11 in Chapter 1). In the first telephone systems, all telephone calls required a manual switching step at a local telephone office. At that time, some forecasters believed that the maximum number of possible telephone calls would be limited by the number of telephone operators who could be hired. Today, most central telephone offices in the United States use digital switching equipment, although the loop from the central office to the home or office is usually analog.

When data are transmitted infrequently from a large number of nodes, **packet switching** is typically used. In this process, a temporary circuit is not established. Instead, the message is divided into a series of segments or packets, each of which contains addressing and control instructions in addition to several hundred bytes of data in the message. These routing instructions are executed automatically as the message moves through the network. The message is reassembled when all of the packets reach the destination. Data transfer on the Internet is based on packet switching.

Packet switching has the advantage of allowing multiple users to share the same transmission facilities because packets from different users can be interspersed on the same line.

This is consistent with what can also be done for nonpacketized analog or digital data by **multiplexers,** devices that collect signals from multiple terminals and interweave these signals so that they can be transmitted more economically on a single high-speed channel. A mirror image of the interweaving process is used to separate the messages during decoding.

The basic idea of packet switching also brings disadvantages. The process of creating packets, directing them through a series of routers during transmission through a complex network, and then reassembling them at the destination involves delays for computing done at different points in the network. These delays are inconsequential for most data communication, but make it difficult to maintain telephone conversations using packet switching. Reliability is also a problem because packets sometimes are lost. In addition it is more difficult to guarantee a given level of service with packet switching.

Initial attempts to provide **Internet telephony,** the use of the Internet to carry on voice conversations while bypassing telephone company billing systems, required special equipment at the sending and receiving sites and produced results whose quality was inadequate for typical commercial uses. Both large telephone companies and small start-ups are working on better forms of Internet telephony. One approach is to link through the Internet, thereby avoiding even local access charges, but to perform most of the point-to-point transmission on a private data network. Another approach is to bypass the Internet altogether and simply use a private packet switched network as a telephone network. Internet telephony potentially includes much more than just voice conversations. By integrating telephony with data transfer, travel agents could use voice and video to discuss travel plans and merchants could show merchandise and take orders.

Moving the Data Through Transmission Media

The two methods for moving data from a source to a destination are wire and wireless transmission. In wire transmission, a signal moves through a "wire" such as a telephone wire, coaxial cable, or fiber optic cable; in contrast, wireless transmission moves the signal through air or space. Different types of wireless transmission use different wave frequencies and require different types of receivers. Common categories of wireless transmission include radio and television broadcasting, microwave, radar, and satellite transmissions.

Wire and wireless transmission have changed places in many applications such as television broadcasting. In addition to the fact that it can provide more channels, cable television is becoming more popular in some areas because it can deliver a stronger and more reliable signal than broadcast television. In contrast, telephones started with wire transmission and are becoming wireless. Wireless telephones are popular because they can perform the functions of fixed telephones without the inconvenience of being anchored to one location.

Although data transmission involves many technical issues, business professionals should recognize several important characteristics of data transmission systems. For analog transmission, **bandwidth** was originally defined as the difference between the highest and lowest frequency that can be transmitted. This term is also used in relation to digital transmission, but it is usually thought of as the capacity of the channel stated in megabits or gigabits per second. In practice, networks with higher bandwidths can transmit more data. For example, voice transmission requires a bandwidth of around 4 KHz, whereas television requires a bandwidth of around 6 MHz, over 1,000 times as great. This is why television cannot be transmitted on a voice-grade telephone line. Cable television is practical because fiber optic cable has enough bandwidth to transmit television signals for many different channels at the same time. To demonstrate the range of capacities and requirements in current telecommunications, Table 10.5 lists data rates related to topics discussed later in this chapter. Table 10.6 shows the historical improvement in data rates. The starting point is a century earlier than the starting point for computers, but the recent rate of improvement is as fast or faster than that of computers.

Bandwidth limitations are a major obstacle reducing the practicality of what has been called the **information superhighway,** the idea that everyone in the United States should have virtually unlimited access to information in electronic form. A simple example illustrates the problem: Assume you want to download a 600-page novel using a 56 Kbps modem. If the novel contained no pictures but had 300 words per page and an average of 6 characters per word (including spaces), the transmission time would be 2.5 minutes. If

TABLE 10.5 Data Rates Related to Different Telecommunications Technologies

Data rate	Telecommunications channel or device
6 to 30 Kbps	Wireless network services for mobile workers
28.8 or 56 Kbps	Data transfer through a typical modem for a PC
64 Kbps	Uncompressed, digitized voice
112 Kbps	Basic rate ISDN for twisted pair wire using 2 data channels
1.5 Mbps	T-1 phone line, commonly used for transferring business data between company sites; also, primary rate ISDN for twisted pair wire using 23 data channels
1.5 Mbps	Cable modems and ADSL modems
10 Mbps	Ethernet standard for local area networks using coaxial cable
100 Mbps	Fast ethernet; also, FDDI (Fiber Distributed Data Interface) standard for local area networks using fiber optic cable
155 Mbps	Data switch using asynchronous transfer mode (ATM) technology
1 Gbps	Gigabit ethernet
2.3 to 9.2 Mbps	Transmission to a large satellite terminal
12 to 274 Mbps	Microwave transmission at frequencies between 2 GHz and 18 GHz[5]
2 Gbps	Typical data rate for a single strand of fiber optic cable
3 terabits per second	Data rates achieved in a lab by Bell Labs using fiber optic equipment in 1997[6]

the information superhighway were to provide video on demand, its bandwidth would have to be staggering. Chapter 8 explained why a single high-resolution picture might contain as many bits and therefore might take as much transmission time as the text of the entire novel. Video involves 10 to 30 images per second and a single copy of the movie *Jurassic Park* contains about 100 billion bytes of data. Even when compressed 25 to 1 by removing redundant background information that doesn't change from frame to frame, this is still 4 billion bytes.[7] Assuming you wanted to download the movie onto a 4-gigabyte hard disk, the data transmission time at 56 Kbps would be 555,555 seconds, or about 6.4 days. While no one intends to download movies using 56 Kbps modems, the example shows that the promise of the information superhighway must be tempered by the limits of what is practical with current technology.

TABLE 10.6 Historical Improvements in Data Rates[8]

Year	Data rate	Technology
1844	5 bps	Telegraph
1876	2 Kbps	Telephone
1915	30 Kbps	Transcontinental copper telephone cables
1940	7.6 Mbps	Coaxial telephone cable carrying 480 voice calls
1956	1.3 Mbps	Transatlantic telephone cable carrying 36 voice calls
1962	0.8 Mbps	Telstar, the first communications satellite, carrying 12 voice calls
1983	45 Mbps	First fiber trunk line between New York and Washington, DC
1996	2.5 Gbps	Phone companies install new, much faster fiber optic equipment for long distance lines
1997	100 Gbps	Ciena promises to deliver 100 Gbps fiber optic equipment in 1998
1997	3000 Gbps	Data rates achieved in a lab by Bell Labs using fiber optic equipment

Even if faster modems were available, there is still the question of how high speed signals would be transmitted into homes and small businesses. This issue is frequently called **the last-mile problem** because installing a high speed data line for every home and business would be enormously expensive even if the local telephone infrastructure provided a high bandwidth phone line in the street.

Data loss is another important characteristic of data transmission systems. **Data loss** occurs during transmission when the physical properties of the data channel or the presence of other signals weakens or distorts the signal. Causes of data loss include *noise* (due to movement of electrons in the transmission medium), *crosstalk* (interference between signals in an adjacent channel), *echo* (reflections of signals), and *attenuation* (due to distance). Telecommunications channels use devices called repeaters to amplify the signal before too much of it is lost. Because both wire and wireless systems may transmit many different signals at the same time, preventing mutual interference between signals is essential. For example, interference between signals is an important reason why a geographical area can have only a limited number of television and radio stations. Using too many frequencies within the limited range of frequencies set aside for radio and television broadcasting would cause distortion.

Next, we will look at available choices in wire and wireless transmission.

Wire Transmission

Wire transmission requires that wires and cables be manufactured, installed, and protected from damage. Wires and cables take up space, can be messy to install, and get in the way. However, wire can transmit vast amounts of data with high quality and little interference from other signals. Three types of wire media are illustrated in Figure 10.7.

Copper telephone wire is often called **twisted pair** because it consists of a pair of copper wires that are twisted to help minimize distortion of the signal by other telephone lines bundled into the same sheath of cable. Copper wire is used for voice transmission and for low volume data transmission. These wires are the slowest medium for data transmission but can be used over long distances. Using typical switching and transmission methods, the data rate for copper telephone wire is up to 64 Kbps. The main advantage of copper wire is that so much wire is already in place in businesses and in telephone networks. But it also has disadvantages. It transmits data slowly and is heavier and bulkier than fiber optic cable. Also, it is vulnerable to unauthorized intrusion because messages traveling through telephone wire generate electrical emissions that can be sensed.

Coaxial cable consists of a copper data transmission wire surrounded by insulation, electrically grounded shielding, and a protective outer insulator. It is used in local area networks and for other data transmission covering less than 10 miles. Its advantages include data transmission speed of 10 Mbps or more, little distortion from external signals, and easy modification of networks without disrupting service. However, it carries signals only a short distance and is limited for secure applications because it is comparatively easy to tap into.

Fiber optic cable contains an ultrapure glass core, a layer of "cladding," and a plastic covering. Unlike copper wire, fiber optic cable carries data in the form of light. Its data

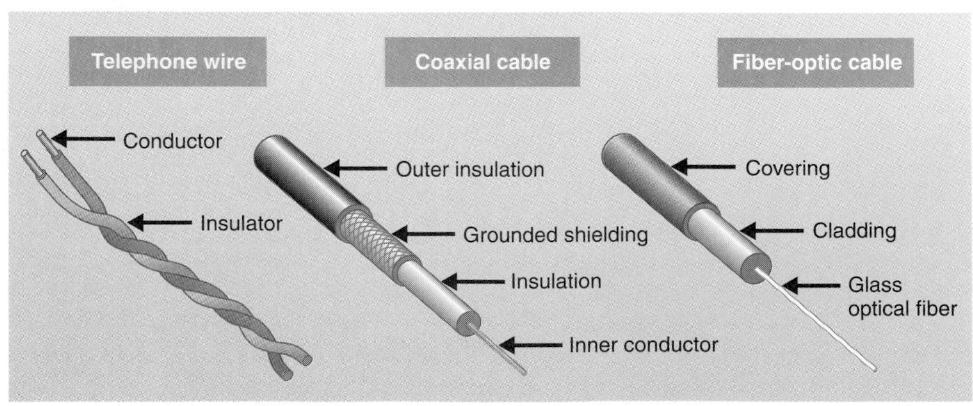

Figure 10.7
Three types of wire media

Twisted pair telephone wire, coaxial cable, and fiber optic cable have different physical configurations because the "wire" for transmitting the data in each case has different physical characteristics.

transfer rate of 100 million bits per second or more is much higher than the rates attainable with copper wire because the frequency of light is much higher than the frequencies used with copper wire. A single strand of optical fiber can carry 8,000 telephone conversations, and there are many strands of fiber in a single cable. Fiber optic cable carries most of the long distance traffic in the United States. Fiber optic cable has other advantages. It is 20 times lighter than copper wire, very difficult to tap into, and has comparatively little data loss because the glass fiber is ultrapure. Recent advances increased the capacity of fiber even further through wave division multiplexing, in which different colors of light can be used to transmit 100 separate channels simultaneously through a single strand of fiber. Fiber also has some disadvantages, however. The use of light frequencies in fiber optics transmission requires expensive, high-speed encoding and decoding. Fiber optic cable is also difficult to splice because the glass itself is only as thick as a hair. Consequently, although fiber optic transmission is cost-effective for high-volume applications, it is too expensive for many low-volume applications.

Wireless Transmission

Wireless transmission does not need a fixed physical connection because it sends signals through air or space. Figure 10.8 shows four common types of wireless transmission. The differences in scale and complexity among these four applications are enormous. Building and launching a communications satellite costs over $100 million, whereas a cordless telephone costs under $100.

Cordless and cellular phones both achieve portability by moving from wire to wireless channels. Cordless phones for a home transmit to a base unit within a small radius, such as 100 feet. Cellular phones transmit signals to a grid of cellular stations that are linked to the wire-based telephone network. Cellular phones originally operated only within metropolitan

Figure 10.8
Four examples of wireless transmission

Wireless transmission ranges from cordless telephones within buildings to satellite transmission covering thousands of miles.

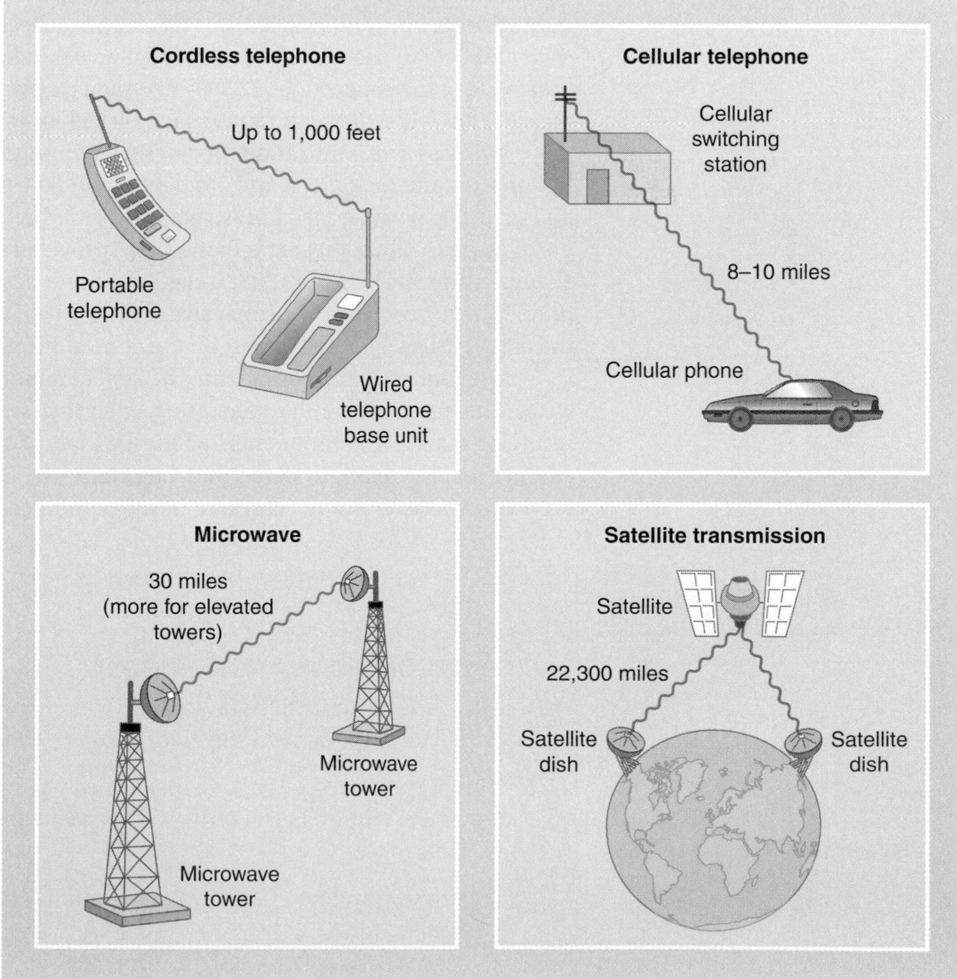

areas with nearby cellular stations, but many cellular networks have now expanded outside these areas. The convenience of cellular phones is offset by several shortcomings. First, at least in the United States, they are expensive and often cost $0.30 to $0.45 per minute. (In Israel and other countries with different regulatory goals, cellular prices are far lower.) In addition, the signals can be intercepted. Stories of intercepted calls abound, ranging from conversations of political and business leaders to embarrassing phone conversations by Great Britain's Prince Charles and Princess Diana while their marriage was breaking up.

Although not as visible in everyday life, microwave transmission was the earliest of the four types of wireless transmission in Figure 10.8 to attain common use. It has been used for several decades to transmit both voice and data. Because earth-based microwave transmission is restricted to line of sight, microwave towers must be placed no more than 30 miles apart unless they are located on mountains or tall buildings. The line of sight restriction limits the use of microwave transmission within city centers. Microwave transmission can also be disrupted by atmospheric conditions and is comparatively easy to intercept.

Telecommunications satellites move in geostationary orbits that remain 22,300 miles above the same part of the earth. At this altitude, the satellite can send signals to earth stations up to 11,000 miles apart. These satellites can carry 40,000 simultaneous telephone calls or 200 television channels. Satellite communication has many advantages. Because it doesn't use a wire channel and doesn't need earth-bound relay towers, it can be used in remote areas. Unlike undersea telephone cables, satellite earth stations can be placed near the people who use them and are therefore easier to maintain and repair. Unlike wire transmission, the cost of satellite communication is the same regardless of the distance between the sender and receiver on earth.

Common use of satellite communication became more practical in the late 1980s as the cost and size of transmission equipment decreased. **Very small aperture terminals (VSATs)** can even transmit and receive data from computer terminals. VSATs are used widely in both data communication and broadcasting. For example, oil drilling companies can use VSATs to transmit data from drilling platforms for analysis at headquarters. Large retailers such as Wal-Mart and K-Mart use VSATs to transmit daily sales data. Unfortunately, only a finite number of satellites can operate in the 22,300-mile-high geostationary orbits. The problem is not that the satellites will collide, but rather that their signals will interfere with each other.

Wireless communication provides telecommunications opportunities for emerging nations, remote rural areas, and other regions where it is impractical or inefficient to build and maintain a wire-based infrastructure. Even where a wire-based infrastructure is being installed gradually, cellular telephones have provided an important option. In Thailand, for example, the wait for installing a regular phone has been over a year, whereas cellular phones have been more readily available. Many believe Thailand's economic expansion in the early 1990s depended in part on the communication afforded by cellular phones.[9]

The functions and components of a telecommunications network have been covered so far. The functions include generating, encoding, switching, transmitting, decoding, and receiving data. The components include a variety of computers and terminals, communications gear, switching systems, and data channels. The next section looks at the different ways these functions and components are combined into different types of networks.

Reality Check

BASIC TELECOMMUNICATIONS MODEL

The basic telecommunications model includes creating data, encoding data, determining the data path, transmitting data, decoding data, and receiving data.

1. Thinking about every way you have used telecommunications, which of these steps have required your active involvement and which have basically been invisible to you?
2. Explain why and how you think this should (or should not) change in the next five years.

TYPES OF NETWORKS: A USER'S VIEWPOINT

The functions and components are building blocks of various types of networks used to improve business operations and compete more effectively. The discussion of types of networks starts with the most familiar, a telephone network. It then looks briefly at broadcasting networks because everyday tasks such as ordering products, performing financial transactions, and obtaining information may eventually apply the same cable and satellite systems used for delivering entertainment. Next, three types of networks that transmit data between computerized devices are discussed: local area networks (LANs), wide area networks (WANs), and value added networks (VANs). LANs and WANs are data transmission systems owned and controlled by the enterprise that uses them; VANs provide a commercial service to customers.

Telephone Networks

Americans take telephones for granted in everyday life because they are available to virtually anyone and almost always work. People in other parts of the world don't take telephones for granted because they may be unavailable, because the network isn't reliable, or because it may take years to install a telephone. For example, the lack of an up-to-date telephone system has been a significant stumbling block slowing the transformation of East Germany to West Germany's level of commerce.

Many aspects of telephone networks, including the encoding of speech, wire and wireless telephones, and alternative transmission media have been discussed so far. We will look in detail at two aspects of telephone networks: the PBXs that perform switching and ISDN, a digital telephone service whose capabilities exceed those of traditional analog telephone service. Business professionals need to recognize features of technical systems such as ISDN and PBXs because of their impact on both users in the organization and telecommunications costs.

PBXs

A **private branch exchange (PBX)** is a special-purpose computer that controls telephone switching at a company site. PBXs reside at the company site, although a service called Centrex performs similar functions from a telephone company office. In its simplest form, a PBX automates functions formerly performed by switchboard operators who plugged wires into a grid. All incoming calls go to the PBX, which connects them automatically or directs them to an attendant who uses a keyboard to redirect them as is appropriate. Outgoing calls also go through the PBX, which automatically assigns each call to an available outside telephone line. Using a PBX permits a company with 50 telephones to have only 5 or 10 outside lines, depending on how frequently employees use the telephone. If all of the outside lines are in use, someone trying to make a call has to wait until a line becomes free. Likewise, incoming callers will get a busy signal if all the incoming lines are occupied.

PBXs have moved far beyond merely connecting telephone calls and now provide a wide range of features directed at making communication more convenient and effective, such as call waiting, call forwarding, and voice mail. PBX features directed primarily at decreasing costs include reducing the number of outside telephone lines, providing internal extensions, and determining least cost routings. The method for reducing the number of outside lines was explained above. Providing internal extension numbers permits people to make calls within the same site using only extension numbers and without making a chargeable outside call. Least cost routing is the automatic determination of which carrier to use for each outgoing call.

With so many capabilities, PBXs are complex, and keeping them operating effectively takes work. For example, data tables assigning physical telephone outlets to individuals' phone extensions must be updated each time someone moves from one office to another. Deciding how to use PBXs requires a lot of planning and attention to how people can use telephones more effectively.

ISDN

ISDN (integrated service digital network) is a set of standards whose adoption provides additional telephone capabilities without scrapping existing copper telephone lines. By providing integrated service, ISDN offers consistent ways to handle voice and computer data in telephone networks. As a digital network, ISDN provides for digital transmission of both voice and computer data on the same copper telephone lines that were previously used for analog transmission. A firm switching to ISDN must install totally digital telephone gear, thereby replacing all analog on-premises telephone equipment, including even the telephone handsets.

ISDN provides a number of capabilities that reduce equipment costs and make equipment use more effective. It permits the regular telephone network to link personal computers and handle data transmission that would otherwise require expensive leased lines. The higher volume ISDN service, called the primary rate interface (PRI), uses multiple channels for linking computers, local area networks, and PBXs into the telephone network at up to 1.5 Mbps. This ISDN service permits telephone wire to serve as cabling for small network applications. ISDN's basic rate interface (BRI) provides two voice or data channels that operate at 64 Kbps.

ISDN permits connection of a voice telephone and a personal computer on the same call. Transmitting both voice and computerized data with one phone connection makes it possible for people to see and discuss the same spreadsheet or engineering drawing at the same time. This capability, called screen sharing, helps people work together on complex financial or technical topics even when they aren't in the same location. By increasing transmission speed, ISDN also cuts transmission time for fax or graphical images and therefore makes it more practical to transmit images, including x-rays, engineering drawings, and advertising designs.

ISDN has been used in trials since 1986 and is being installed for applications that require its additional capabilities today. Its national adoption requires that all telephone company switching stations use digital ISDN switches. Although it brings some important advances, ISDN's ultimate success is far from assured. Many forecasters believe it will be bypassed by other options that provide more capacity at lower prices.

Broadcast Networks

Like other parts of the telecommunications world, broadcast networks for radio and television are changing rapidly. Delivery of the signal via cable rather than through the air marked an important departure from the past. Fiber optic cable can deliver many channels with high-quality pictures because it can carry a vast amount of information. Instead of being restricted to whatever programs are acceptable to a wide audience, cable viewers should be more able to find programs they genuinely prefer. Beyond giving more choices of what to watch, future cable systems may make it much easier for viewers to control the time when they watch it. After all, why should people watch programs only at the times a broadcaster considers best for attracting the largest audience?

In addition to changing the entertainment industry, multiplying the amount of information available through a television may lead to future developments affecting many aspects of business and communication. For example, people may ask why two separate information cables should come into the house, one for telephone and one for television. Why shouldn't the same cable support two-way telephone communication, one-way television, and possible extensions of each? Time Warner's Full Service Network, an early experiment in this area, attempted to create a vast range of choices including video-on-demand, telecommunications, and interactive multimedia services, such as home shopping, education, and video games. It never went beyond 4,000 subscribers, perhaps because the public wasn't ready, and perhaps because the offering wasn't good enough. The Internet, on the other hand, has been used successfully for shopping, business information, and many other services. Providing the Internet to the home using cable's bandwidth could provide much richer forms of home shopping. This is one of the reasons why Microsoft spent over $400 million to buy WebTV. No one knows what will really happen in this area, but it is important to recognize that today's entertainment systems may evolve into essential business and communication tools of the future.

Next we turn to LANs, WANs, and VANs, networks devoted primarily to data generated by computerized systems.

Local Area Networks (LANs)

Local area networks (LANs) connect personal computers and other equipment within a local area, such as a floor of a building. LANs are used widely in small businesses and in departments of larger businesses. They help people share equipment, data, and software, and help them work together more effectively. They may also link to wide area networks (described later).

Applications of LANs

Chapter 8 introduced distributed computing, which provides users many benefits of both centralized computing and personal computing. LANs provide access to more computing power, data, and resources than would be practical if each user needed an individual copy of everything. They provide the benefits of personal computing, such as not being forced to do personal work through a central computer that can get bogged down when its capacity is shared by many users. They also provide a number of ways to make an organization more efficient and effective through sharing equipment, sharing personal files, sending messages, sharing databases, and effective software administration.

- *sharing equipment:* As shown in Figure 10.9, LANs can link multiple workstations to one laser printer, fax machine, or modem. This makes a single piece of equipment available to multiple users and avoids unnecessary equipment purchases.
- *sharing personal files:* LAN users can select personal files that they want coworkers to see, such as engineering drawings, department plans, contracts, or drafts of memos. Coworkers can look at these files without delays for printing paper copies.
- *sending messages:* LANs can be used to transmit and manage electronic mail.
- *sharing databases:* LANs can be used for accessing shared databases. The LAN in Figure 10.9 is set up for this purpose because it contains a file server for retrieving data requested by the workstations. The file server is linked to a disk that contains shared databases, such as the firm's customer list and telephone directory. When a workstation needs data in a shared database, it sends a request message to the file server, which performs the retrieval from the disk and sends the data to the requesting workstation. This arrangement avoids maintaining redundant copies of data. In addition to not wasting storage, having the databases in one place avoids problems with inconsistent data.
- *administering software:* Instead of storing separate copies of spreadsheet or word processing software at each workstation, the LAN can deliver a temporary copy to a workstation that needs the software. Handling software this way assures that everyone uses only the latest version of the software. Upgrading to a new software version involves only one replacement instead of finding and replacing each copy. This approach also reduces the number of copies of the software that must be

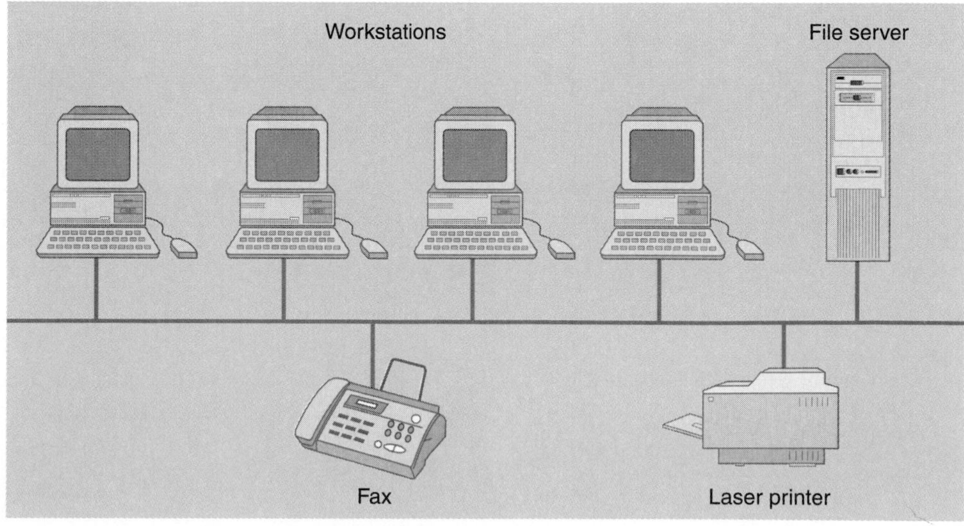

Figure 10.9
A typical local area network

This LAN permits the users at workstations to share a laser printer and a fax machine, and to receive e-mail and share files. It also allows them to share a database that is accessed through a file server.

purchased. For example, if no more than 10 out of 25 people on a LAN typically use a spreadsheet at the same time, the firm can purchase a license for 10 copies instead of 25, and can use the LAN to monitor the number of copies in use.

Like many other forms of wire telecommunications, LANs are becoming wireless for some applications. (See Figure 10.10.) While the advantages of not having to string the wires are obvious, there are some disadvantages, such as problems in maintaining signal quality and concerns about electromagnetic radiation in the workplace. An attempt to develop a wireless LAN to be used in commodity trading turned out to be controversial for other reasons. A proposed system would give traders handheld terminals for recording the trades and transmitting them to a central computer using radio waves. Much of the impetus was from regulators concerned that traders were using information illegally to trade for their own accounts just before executing large trades for other accounts. The handheld terminals for recording trades in real time generated little enthusiasm from most traders, however, due to concerns about the weight and discomfort of carrying the terminals around instead of pieces of paper they could put in their pockets.[10]

Technical Aspects of LANs

Although LANs link devices rather than telephone conversations, they need to perform many of the same functions as PBXs. They route messages from source to destination, ensure the destination nodes are ready to accept the messages, and monitor network utilization. Network operating systems and protocols control the flow of data between the devices on the network and handle requests for data. Control of a LAN includes preventing a node from sending a message until the network is ready to process it correctly and taking care of situations where a node is not ready to receive a message because it is busy.

LANs (and other networks) may be configured in different ways. A network topology is the pattern of connections between the devices on a network. There are many possible network topologies, each with its own advantages and disadvantages. Table 10.7 shows three representative network topologies: the star, ring, and bus.

LANs use a variety of methods for their internal communication, one of the most common of which is **token passing,** which is used in ring topologies. A token is a bit pattern that circulates between nodes. To transmit data, a node appends the data to the token. When the token arrives at the destination node, it adds a notation that the data have been received, and the token continues back to the sending node. The sending node removes the packet and the token continues circulating.

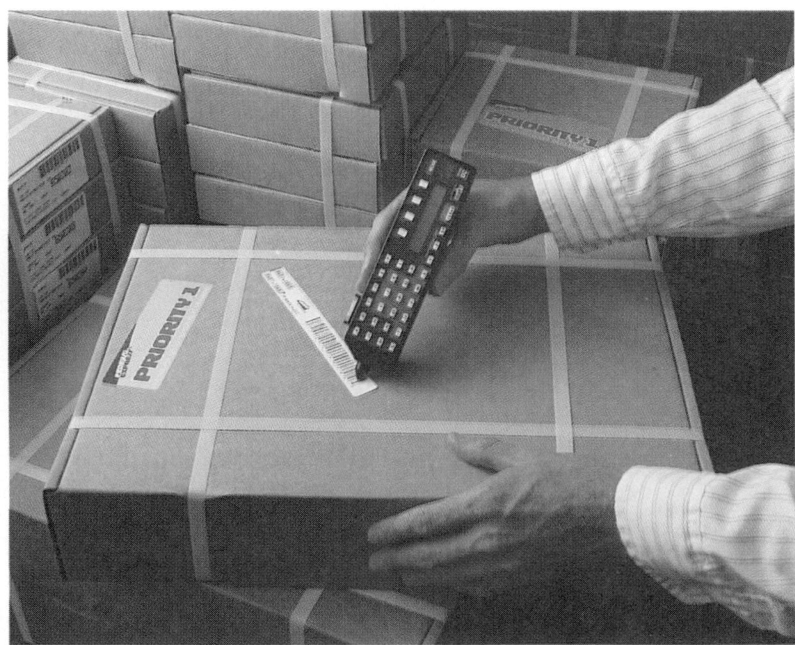

Figure 10.10
Handheld terminal used in a wireless LAN

This handheld terminal transmits data about packages to a computer within a LAN.

Most LANs use either twisted-pair telephone wire or coaxial cable. Fiber optic cable is used rarely for LANs because it is difficult to install and expensive. LANs use two types of data transmission: baseband and broadband. Most LANs are baseband networks. In **baseband** networks, the entire capacity of the cable is used to transmit a single digitally coded signal. Ethernet is a common baseband network that uses coaxial cable and operates at 10 Mbps or 100 Mbps. In **broadband** networks, the capacity of the cable is divided into separate frequencies to permit it to carry several signals at the same time.

It is often necessary to link several sections of one LAN, or to link a LAN to another network. For example, a LAN with 100 users might run more efficiently if it were divided into several distinct LANs that are linked. Links between LANs and between LANs and other networks are accomplished using routers, bridges, and gateways, all of which are a combination of hardware and software. A **router** links two parts of the same LAN or two compatible LANs by looking at each message and directing it to a node on the other network, if appropriate. Routers permit two LANs to operate like one from a user's viewpoint, thereby making it simpler for someone in a department to send data to someone in another department. A **bridge** links two networks by converting the addressing data from one into addressing data in the appropriate protocol for the other. A router may also select among alternative paths for each message, thereby balancing the traffic on the network. A **gateway** permits communication between computers on incompatible networks. It does this by translating the data format of an incoming message into the data format of the destination network.

TABLE 10.7 Representative network topologies

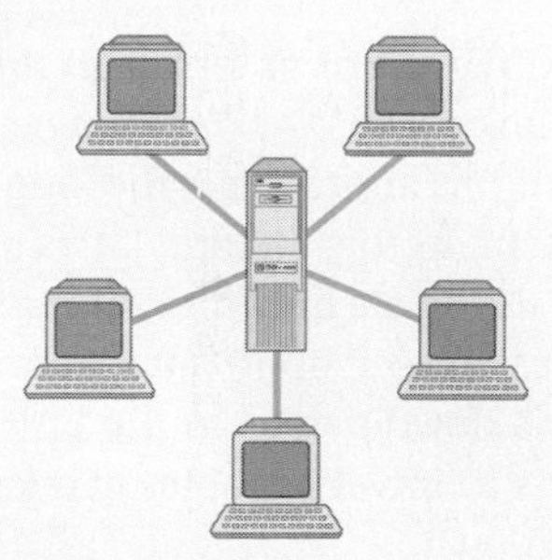

In a **star topology,** all messages go through a central node that serves as a switch, receiving messages and forwarding them to a destination node. Because every node is attached to the central node, a star network requires at most two links for a message to move from one node to another. A star network typically uses circuit switching and can integrate voice and data traffic. It provides good control because all messages go through the same node. It is also easy to expand without disrupting ongoing processing. However, a star network may have reliability problems because the entire network is down whenever the central node is down. The expansion of a star network is limited by the processing power of the central node. In addition, the cost of linking every node to the central node becomes excessive as the number of nodes grows and if the nodes are far from the hub.

In a **ring topology,** the nodes are linked directly without a central server, which means that messages between nodes must be retransmitted by all nodes between the source and destination. Unlike a star network, the network control and processing are distributed to each node on the network. If any node is disabled, messages must be routed around that node to keep the network operating. Adding or subtracting a node while the network is in operation requires special effort to keep the network running.

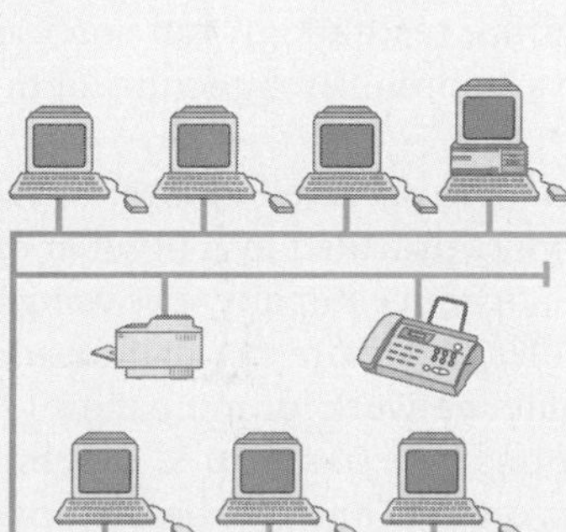

A **bus topology** attaches each node to a central channel called a *bus.* Each device on the network can access any other device directly by using its address on the bus. All messages are "heard" by every device on the network, but only the addressed device responds to a message. Bus topologies are easy to expand because the addition or loss of a node has no direct effect on any other node. As with a ring, control is distributed among the nodes. Network performance degrades as traffic increases, however, because each message requires the attention of each node. LANs commonly use bus or ring topologies. Ethernet is a common baseband network that uses a bus topology.

Wide Area Networks (WANs)

Wide area networks (WANs) are telecommunications networks that span a wide geographical area such as a state or country. WANs are used for many different purposes. Some are designed as a communications backbone for a large distributed organization. For example, North Carolina–based NationsBank has a WAN that connects 65,000 people around the United States.[11] Other WANs focus on a particular transaction processing application, such as taking orders, making reservations, or tracking packages. Many WANs are used to transfer and consolidate corporate data, such as daily transaction summaries from branches. HP uses a WAN to manage its 90,000 desktop PCs by permitting all HP users to download new desktop applications from centrally controlled servers, thereby ensuring that PC configurations and software releases are uniform throughout the organization.[12]

WANs are often implemented in the form of a **virtual private network (VPN),** a private network configured within a public network. Telephone companies have provided nonswitched leased lines for decades by dedicating portions of their high-capacity trunk lines to links between specific company sites. VPNs go a step further by supporting communication to any point within the private network but not supporting communication outside. This type of VPN service costs more than a pure leased line approach, but a telephone company manages the network. An example of a multifirm VPN is the Automotive Network Exchange, which lets thousands of companies in the auto supply chain swap CAD files, e-mail, and other information. This VPN may eventually link as many as 40,000 companies involved in manufacturing, financing, and insuring cars and trucks.[13] Today there is tremendous interest in building VPNs that use the Internet to provide a secure and encrypted connection between two points. These VPNs are run by Internet service providers (ISPs), who are responsible for maintaining bandwidth, network availability, and security.

As Figure 10.11 illustrates, WANs can link to workstations or terminals through LANs. The LANs perform local data processing, and they link to the WAN for data needed or provided beyond the local environment. An example of this approach is the long-term direction of Apollo, the United Airlines reservation system. In this system, LANs are gradually being installed at travel agencies to replace dumb terminals linked to midrange computers and mainframes. The LANs maintain local copies of reservation data. New reservations are uploaded through the WAN, and travel data is downloaded to the LANs. With this arrangement, agents who are booking reservations at travel agencies can keep working even if the WAN or one of the central computers is down.

An important problem related to both WANs and LANs is the difficulty of designing flexible networks that can evolve while retaining a great deal of flexibility. A technology that might play a role in this evolution is **asynchronous transfer mode (ATM),** which has the same acronym as automatic teller machine but means something entirely different. It is a form of high bandwidth switching that provides connectivity between a variety of networks including LANs and WANs, the majority of which still use other technologies. For example, most LANs use one of the forms of Ethernet. ATM is a connection-oriented service, in contrast to the packet switching method used by the Internet. One of its advantages is the ability to "reserve service" to guarantee the bandwidth for the connection. ATM is still an immature technology, but some observers believe it is the most likely technology to provide a common architecture for public, private, and on-premises networks in the future.

As with LANs, important developments have also occurred in wireless WANs. (See Figure 10.12.) For example, wireless network services provided by a number of vendors make it possible for mobile employees to obtain data from company sites using handheld terminals without using a telephone and regardless of where the data resides. About 7,000 Sears technicians use the ARDIS wireless data network for more than 130 million wireless messages annually.[14] In a typical use of this type of network, a technician can locate a required part in the company's inventory, order it, and tell the customer when it will be available. This reduces the separation between the office and the field and thereby

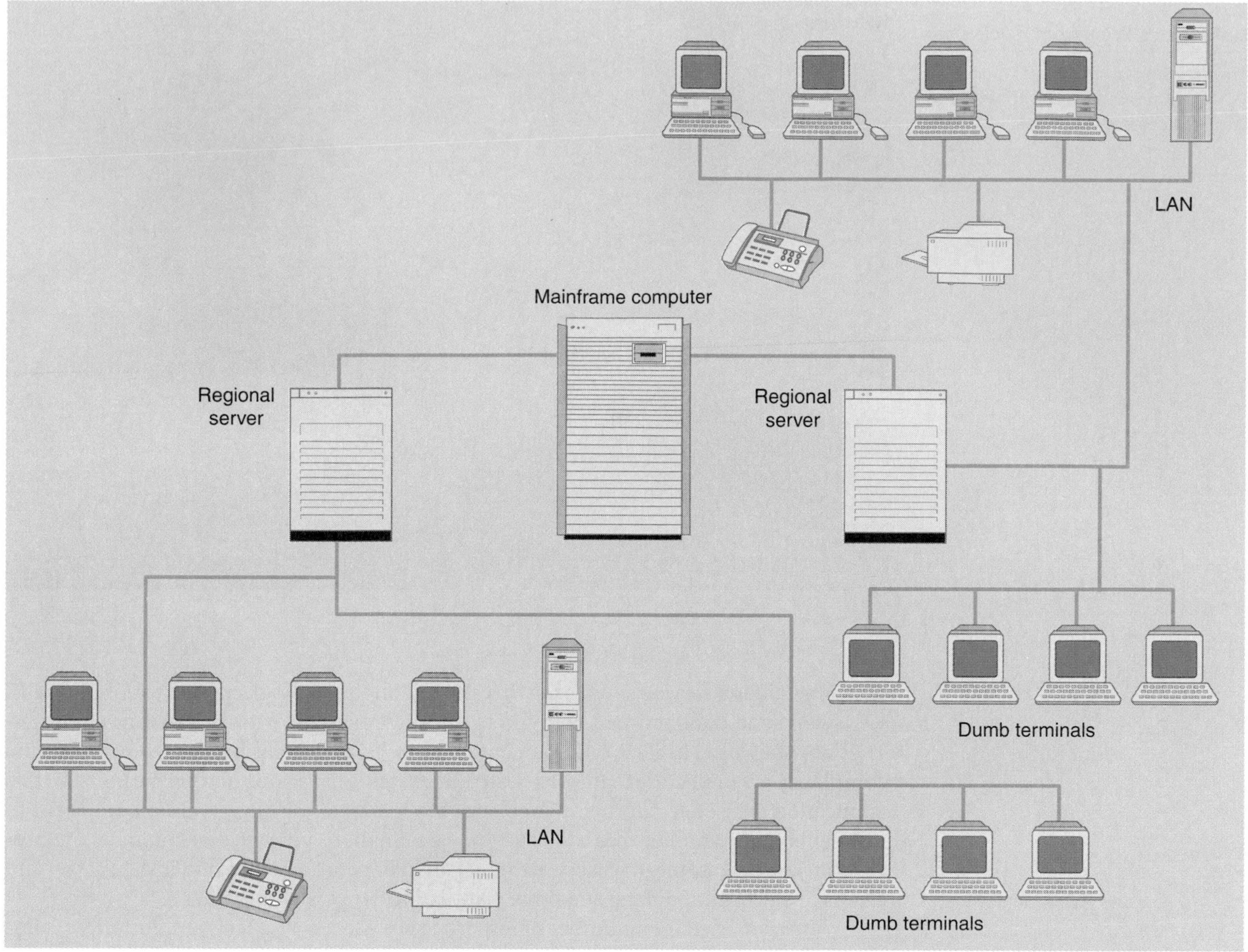

Figure 10.11
A WAN that includes several LANs

This WAN includes several LANs, each of which links to the rest of the network through regional servers.

improves the efficiency of field service and sales work. It also permits a local office to send new instructions to a service technician driving to a service call that is now unnecessary because the customer fixed the problem. Although the promise of wireless network services was not attained in the 1990s due to a combination of high cost and low data rates (between 6 and 30 Kbps), many believe these services will be adopted more widely in the near future.[15]

Due to their size, complexity, and response time requirements, WANs must be managed carefully by telecommunications experts. Work can grind to a halt or costs can expand if WANs are set up inefficiently or used inappropriately. The difficulty of keeping networks operating is one of several reasons for using VANs, which are described next.

Value Added Networks (VANs)

Value added networks (VANs) are public data networks that "add value" by transmitting data and by providing access to commercial databases and software. VANs are complex technical systems that have traditionally used packet switching so they can be accessible from many different types of workstations. The use of VANs is usually sold by subscription, with users paying for the amount of data they move. As a way to transmit computerized

Figure 10.12
Linking to a WAN from a police car

This officer is linking into a wireless WAN that provides access to several law enforcement databases.

data, they offer a service similar to what the telephone networks do for telephone calls. VANs can send data between computers in different cities or even different countries. They are often used in electronic data interchange (EDI) systems because they reduce the complexity of connecting to the disparate EDI systems of various trading partners. In this application they collect forms in an electronic mailbox, translate and forward them to recipients, and guarantee they will reach their destinations intact. Other common VAN services include electronic mail, access to stock market data and other public databases, and access to electronic banking and other transaction processing services.

VANs are used for a number of reasons. They are a cost-effective solution for companies that need data communication services but don't want to invest in setting up their own private networks. They are commonly used by companies that lack the technical expertise to maintain a network. Even small companies can enjoy the benefits of data communications by using VANs and leaving the technical details to the vendors. VANs permit companies to use part of a network instead of paying a large fixed cost for their own underutilized network. VANs also provide for easier expansion because they are set up to use their capacity efficiently and to bring in new capacity if necessary. Finally, VANs can provide convenient access to data that would not otherwise be available.

The widespread acceptance of the Internet is creating an alternative to VANs for many applications that do not involve huge amounts of data. For example, Cummins Engine plans to keep its EDI system for its major customers such as automobile companies because their data-intensive orders require several hours of data transmission time even with a high-speed line. At the same time, Cummins plans to let small customers and suppliers use the Internet for low-volume transactions. Similarly, Boise Cascade will continue using EDI with its major customers, even though it saved $1 million in one year by allowing 1,300 smaller trading partners to post electronic orders using the World Wide Web instead of submitting paper and fax forms that require expensive manual processing.[16]

LANs, WANs, and VANs differ in scope, performance requirements, and technology. For example, the reliability and data transmission requirements for a LAN used to link three personal computers to a single laser printer are minimal compared to the requirements for a large WAN providing rapid response to any of thousands of terminals in an airline reservation system. When a VAN is down, the services provided by that VAN are essentially out of business until it comes up again.

Reality Check

TYPES OF NETWORKS

This section discussed types of networks including telephone networks, broadcast networks, LANs, WANs, and VANs.

1. Explain how the functions or capabilities of networks have or have not affected you in your everyday life.
2. What human and ethical issues arise from advanced network capabilities?

TELECOMMUNICATIONS STANDARDS

Technological standards have been a crucial issue ever since the industrial revolution called for interchangeable parts. Abraham Lincoln illustrated this point in the fall of 1863 when he signed a bill standardizing railroad gauges at 4 feet 8½ inches between the rails, rather than the 5-foot measure that permitted bigger loads. This was bad engineering but made sense politically at the time because most of the 5-foot track that was going to have to be torn up was in the South.[17]

Standards are an equally crucial issue today because they make it practical to build networks containing hardware from different vendors (see Figure 10.13). Standards involve important tradeoffs. They may disallow certain features or capabilities that are valuable in a particular situation but are inconsistent with the standard. Standards may also contradict the features vendors have built into their own proprietary products. This strikes at fundamental competitive issues because vendors often rely on their own proprietary data architectures as strategies to lock out competitors. The enormous market value of Microsoft and Intel demonstrates the huge potential rewards for controlling standards.

Standards can be divided into de facto standards and de jure standards. **De facto standards** are standards established by the fact that a product dominates a particular market. Examples of de facto standards in personal computing include Windows 95 and the machine language of Pentium microprocessors. **De jure standards** are standards defined by industry groups or by the government. Many de facto standards become de jure standards when analyzed and ratified by industry standards associations.

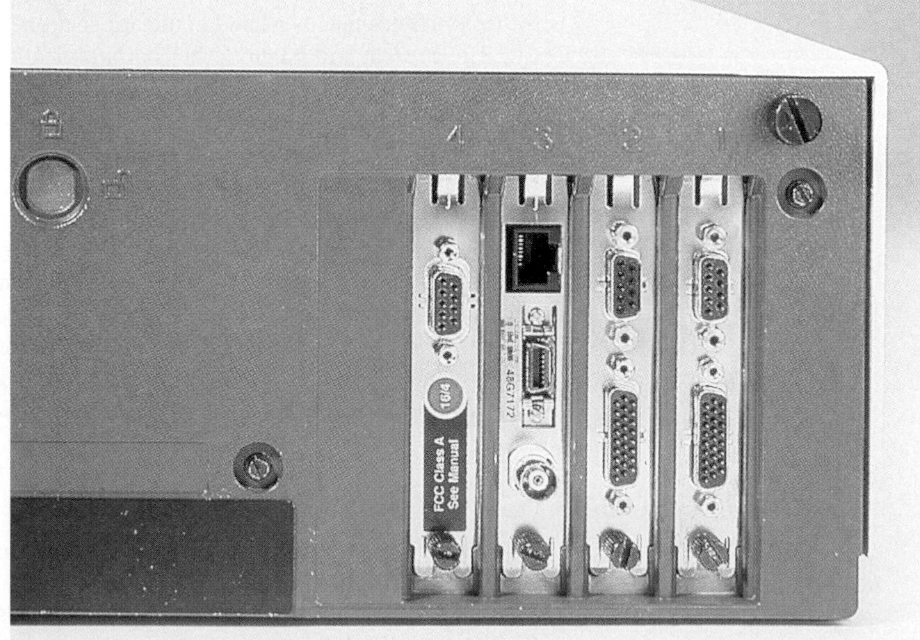

Figure 10.13
Standards that are visible in hardware

This rear view of a personal computer shows standard plug configurations for serial ports and a network interface card. Conformance to accepted standards permits the use of many different brands of peripherals.

The **OSI** (Open Systems Interface) **reference model,** a framework for defining standards, is useful for appreciating the complex nature of networking standards even though support for the model itself may be wavering. It was created to guide the development of standards for communications between networked systems, regardless of technology, vendor, or country of origin. These standards cover all aspects of network operations and management. Developed by an industry consortium called the International Standards Organization, the OSI reference model identifies issues that specific standards should address. At each level the standards themselves are expressed through **protocols,** which are precisely defined rules, codes, and procedures for linking devices or transmitting data between devices. The various protocols needed to implement the OSI reference model cover topics such as establishing, maintaining, and terminating connections, routing information packets, controlling errors, disassembly and reassembly of messages, multiplexing and demultiplexing of messages.

The OSI model divides a network's operation into seven layers, each having well-defined and limited responsibilities. Each layer receives data from an adjacent layer, performs specific processing tasks, and passes the data up or down to the next level of the hierarchy. At the bottom, level 1 is concerned with the physical attachment of devices and looks at issues such as what type of plug to use. Intermediate levels are concerned with the formatting of messages, methods of transmission, and error correction. At the top, level 7 is concerned with the logic of the application itself. Breaking network operation into these layers makes it easier to identify and solve problems, and it simplifies adding enhanced capabilities because they can be installed a layer at a time. Figure 10.14 explains the seven levels of the OSI reference model in more detail.

Although the Internet is based on a somewhat different five-layer model, the OSI layers are useful in identifying some of the important standards that have made it possible for millions of users to access Web sites around the world. At the physical layer, the standards that define fiber optic transmission were the key. At the data link layer, extensions of the original bps standards related to ethernet for LANs and frame relay technology for WANs were essential in making transmission of images effective. At the network layer, **TCP/IP** (Transmission Control Protocol/Internet Protocol) defines the way data packets are constructed and addresses are specified. TCP/IP was developed in the late 1960s and early 1970s to permit information sharing between different computers running incompatible operating systems. At the application level, the **HTTP** (Hypertext Transfer Protocol) became the key standard for coding and displaying pages on the World Wide Web. The skyrocketing acceptance of the World Wide Web led software developers in other areas of computing to begin using HTTP for file transfers and transmission of Java applets.[18] Other frequently encountered protocols and extensions related to the application layer are shown in Table 10.8.

The content and quality of telecommunications standards affect not only the commercial fortunes of individual vendors but also the long-term ability to achieve connectivity. In the digital cellular phone market, for example, different vendors are using incompatible technologies called time-division multiple access (TDMA), code-division multiple access (CDMA), and GSM. All can process calls digitally and can be used for data transmission, but they operate quite differently. TDMA multiplexes conversations for one to three users using the same frequency and then reassembles the original signals quickly enough to give the illusion of continuous sound. CDMA breaks conversations into segments that travel on different frequencies and are later reassembled. GSM is a variant on TDMA that dominates Europe's wireless market. TDMA is the older and more stable technology, but CDMA has the potential to transmit more conversations on a limited number of frequencies. These "technical details" will have direct bearing on which competitors can offer the best price/service tradeoff.

TELECOMMUNICATIONS POLICY

This chapter closes with a brief discussion of telecommunications policy. This is a topic whose impacts range from personal concerns such as what telephone service will be available at what price through regulatory issues such as who will be allowed to broadcast on which radio frequencies.

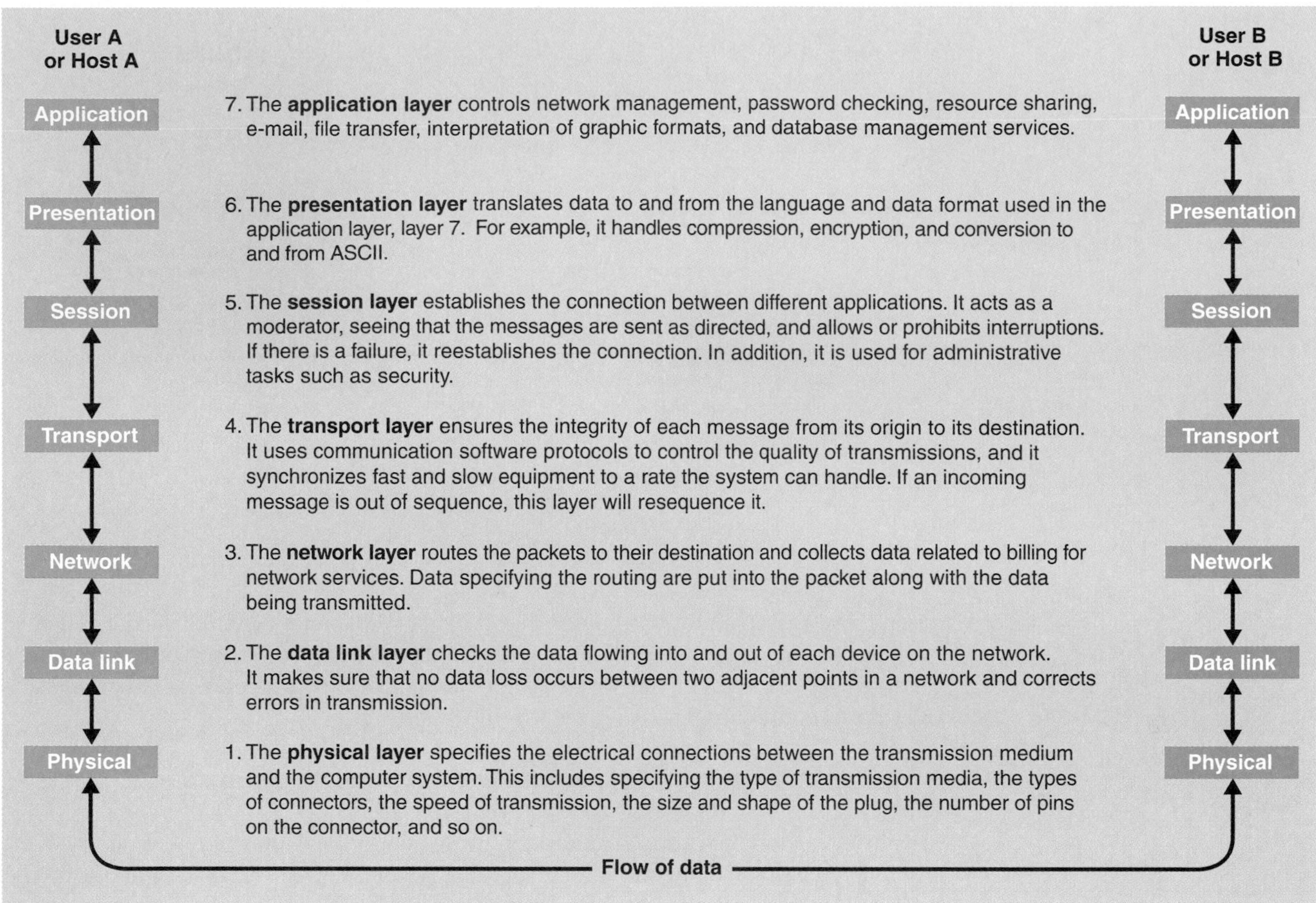

User A
or Host A
User B
or Host B
Application
Presentation
Session
Transport
Network
Data link
Physical
7. The **application layer** controls network management, password checking, resource sharing, e-mail, file transfer, interpretation of graphic formats, and database management services.
6. The **presentation layer** translates data to and from the language and data format used in the application layer, layer 7. For example, it handles compression, encryption, and conversion to and from ASCII.
5. The **session layer** establishes the connection between different applications. It acts as a moderator, seeing that the messages are sent as directed, and allows or prohibits interruptions. If there is a failure, it reestablishes the connection. In addition, it is used for administrative tasks such as security.
4. The **transport layer** ensures the integrity of each message from its origin to its destination. It uses communication software protocols to control the quality of transmissions, and it synchronizes fast and slow equipment to a rate the system can handle. If an incoming message is out of sequence, this layer will resequence it.
3. The **network layer** routes the packets to their destination and collects data related to billing for network services. Data specifying the routing are put into the packet along with the data being transmitted.
2. The **data link layer** checks the data flowing into and out of each device on the network. It makes sure that no data loss occurs between two adjacent points in a network and corrects errors in transmission.
1. The **physical layer** specifies the electrical connections between the transmission medium and the computer system. This includes specifying the type of transmission media, the types of connectors, the speed of transmission, the size and shape of the plug, the number of pins on the connector, and so on.
Flow of data

Figure 10.14
The OSI reference model

The OSI reference model divides network operation and management into seven layers. Layers 1 through 4 are responsible for moving data from one place to another, whereas 5 through 7 handle the exchange of data between application programs. Communicating between two programs running on two different computers requires going through each step in some way.

Figure 10.15 shows a framework for thinking about telecommunications policy in terms of issues and stakeholders. The issues include questions such as what products and services will be available at what prices, what level of access will be guaranteed to whom, what societal resources will be allocated to telecommunications in what ways, and how will telecommunications be regulated for efficiency and effectiveness. The stakeholders in most of these matters include telecommunications suppliers, customers, regulators or policy makers, and society in general. Telecommunications policy is a complex area because the issues cut so many ways. We will address it by summarizing recent history and discussing several areas of controversy.

Until 1984, AT&T was a telephone monopoly servicing most of the telephones and telephone networks in the United States. A consent decree between AT&T and the Justice Department in 1984 broke up AT&T's telephone service monopoly. This change left a long distance company (AT&T) and seven regional operating companies that handle local telephone calls. Often called the Baby Bells, the regional operating companies originally included Ameritech, Bell Atlantic, BellSouth, Nynex, Pacific Telesis, Southwestern Bell, and US West, although several have subsequently merged. The consent decree prevented the Baby Bells from selling equipment, carrying long distance calls, and manufacturing telephone equipment. Subsequent rulings permitted them to enter new lines of business including some information services, but these services couldn't manipulate the data they transmit. Their potential competitors in information services include cable television

TABLE 10.8 TCP/IP Protocols and Extensions Related to the Application Layer

Network and e-mail users frequently encounter the TCP/IP protocols and extensions, including the following:

- Telnet: a protocol that supports access to remote computers. It makes it seem as though the user's terminal is attached to the remote host.
- File Transfer Protocol (FTP): a protocol that permits transfer of files between computers on a network.
- Post Office Protocol (POP): a protocol for storing e-mail and downloading it when a user logs on.
- Simple Mail Transfer Protocol (SMTP): electronic mail protocol permitting e-mail between computers.
- Multipurpose Internet Mail Extensions (MIME): extensions to SMTP permitting transfer of messages containing additional data types.
- Hypertext Transport Protocol (HTTP): protocol for sharing hypertext information on the World Wide Web.

companies, newspapers, companies that provide VANs, long distance carriers such as MCI, Sprint, and the new AT&T, and most recently, companies that provide information services over the Internet. The broad span of companies and potential products and services raises many complex issues, such as the following:

Why should the government permit some companies, but not others, to sell products in a particular line of business?

Permitting the original telephone monopoly avoided duplication of telephone systems and made the original investment in telephone systems less risky. The limitations on the Baby Bells were designed to prevent them from using their local telephone monopolies to block access to long distance carriers and to freeze out local competition from smaller companies. This rationale was consistent with U.S. antitrust laws but left questions about

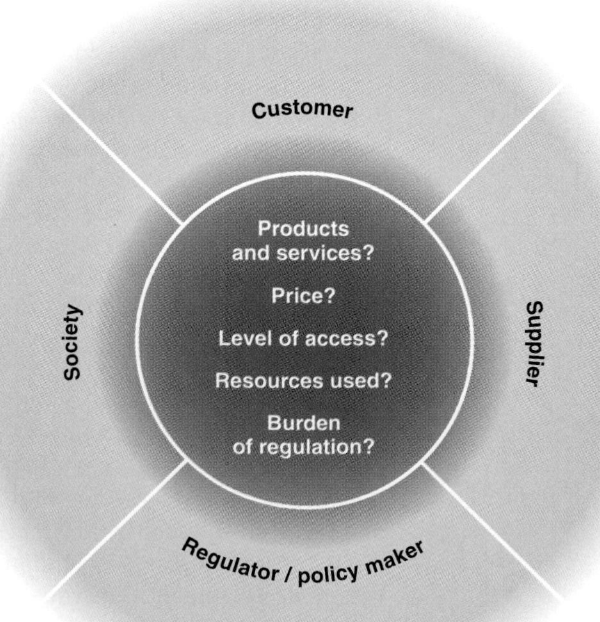

Figure 10.15
Telecommunications issues and stakeholders

Customers, suppliers, regulators and policy makers, and society as a whole are all stakeholders in telecommunications issues such as what products and services will be provided at what price, what level of access will be guaranteed, what societal resources will be used, and how much burden regulation will cause.

economic efficiency, customer satisfaction, taxation, and even national security. The Telecommunications Act of 1996 eliminated many of the restrictions in the 1984 consent decree by permitting the Baby Bells to enter the long distance telephone business after satisfying a 14-point checklist of conditions guaranteeing that their competitors will have fair access to residential customers. In 1998 a federal judge struck down some of these provisions by declaring that they unfairly prevented the Baby Bells from competing in the long distance business. The judge ruled that Congress had essentially pronounced the Bells guilty of antitrust violations without a trial, in violation of the Constitution.[19] The ruling was highly controversial, especially since the Baby Bells had actually lobbied in favor of the Telecommunications Act because they believed it would open new opportunities for them.

Another aspect of the story is that direct descendants of the old AT&T are only part of the telecommunications picture of the 1990s. For example, if cable television companies could run fiber optic cable into a house, why should or shouldn't they be able to provide telephone service? Similarly, why should or shouldn't a telephone company be able to provide cable television or other information? Who should be able to provide wireless communication services, and under what conditions?

The telecommunications world is both dynamic and highly uncertain because all the players have many options for new alliances, new services, and new types of competition, and because everything they try to do is judged by both regulators and the marketplace. The Internet has proved a major wild card in this area, especially with the promise of Internet telephony. This is a threat to the lucrative market for long distance and international calls because it creates a way to provide services that completely bypass existing billing systems that record each call. It is an opportunity because combining telephone calls with multimedia data on the Web creates many new ways for companies to communicate internally and with customers.

What should be the rationale for regulating telecommunications and setting prices?

When AT&T agreed to purchase McCaw Cellular Communications for $12.6 billion in 1993, it told the Federal Communications Commission (FCC) that its ultimate goal was the provision of affordable, nationwide, radio-based telephones, with features and quality comparable with the wireline network and with capacities to bypass the local land-line network. The FCC mandated that AT&T pay local telephone companies $14 billion to connect into their networks, funded by a 5.5 cent-a-minute charge on interstate calls.[20] Bypassing the local telephone companies would save AT&T a great deal of money, but the Baby Bells and local telephone companies had competitive responses of their own. In the same year as the AT&T's McCaw purchase, New York state regulators approved a plan designed by Rochester Telephone Corp. allowing Time Warner's cable unit to provide local telephone service by linking its cable lines with Rochester Telephone's local network. In exchange, Rochester Telephone was allowed to split into two companies, a regulated unit owning the network and providing access to its competitors, and a nonregulated unit to bundle and sell telecommunications services.[21]

Deals such as these lead some observers to complain that U.S. telecommunications policy is being determined by antitrust policy rather than by national telecommunications needs. In other countries where antitrust is not an issue, monopoly telephone companies are able to plan their products and services based on their view of what is needed for telecommunications. For example, Nippon Telegraph and Telephone, Japan's main telephone company, has a long-term goal of using only digital switches by the year 2000 and running fiber optic cable to all houses and offices by 2015.[22] In contrast, telecommunications planning in the United States depends on the plans of a number of separate companies. Meanwhile, the various nations in the European Community have negotiated about a coherent plan for Europe.

Who should be able to use specific public resources, such as radio frequencies?

This question shows how public issues and interests intersect with technology. All wireless transmission uses a particular frequency in the electromagnetic spectrum, regardless of whether the transmission is a television program, a cellular telephone call, or computerized data. (See Figure 10.16.) To prevent different uses of wireless transmission from interfering with each other, governments allocate specific frequency ranges to specific uses. Within those ranges, the governments allocate specific frequencies to individual users, including radio and television broadcasters and businesses that use certain frequencies for data communications. Because there are only a finite number of frequencies, the electromagnetic spectrum shown in the figure can be considered a scarce resource that has been allocated by governments. Such allocations are always controversial. There is no widely accepted right way to decide that a particular radio station or wireless service provider should own a particular frequency in a region. In the past these frequencies were granted outright. In the mid-1990s, the government auctioned around 200 megahertz that it still controlled. An important issue at that time was how or whether to protect the interests of small, innovative businesses that larger rivals could easily outbid. Several years later the question was whether or how to bail out several companies that had overpaid. On an international scale, many Third World nations have complained that the industrialized world has too much control over the frequencies used for satellite communication. They argue that these frequencies are a finite resource that is allocated unfairly today.

To what extent is universal access possible and to what extent should it be guaranteed?

In 1994 Vice President Gore told a telecommunications conference, "We cannot tolerate—nor in the long run can this nation afford—a society in which some children become fully educated and others do not; in which some adults have access to training and lifetime education and others do not. Nor can we permit geographic location to determine whether the information highway passes by your door."[23] He proposed five principles related to difficult tradeoffs between private sector and public sector concerns:

1. encouragement of private investment (primarily by removing regulatory impediments)
2. preservation of competition
3. open access to the network (through uniform standards)
4. universal service (to be assured primarily by the private sector)
5. flexible and responsive government[24]

Disagreements related to these principles cover a wide range of issues, including who will pay for universal access and whether most people want access to anything other than entertainment. Access to information and technology was one of the ethical issues discussed in Chapter 7. In a society sensitive to differences between haves and have-nots, access to new telephone, text, and video services is an important political and practical issue as well.

Business professionals don't confront issues such as these every day, but they need to be aware that their ability to use telecommunications will be shaped by a dynamic and unpredictable interplay of technology, business strategy, and government policy.

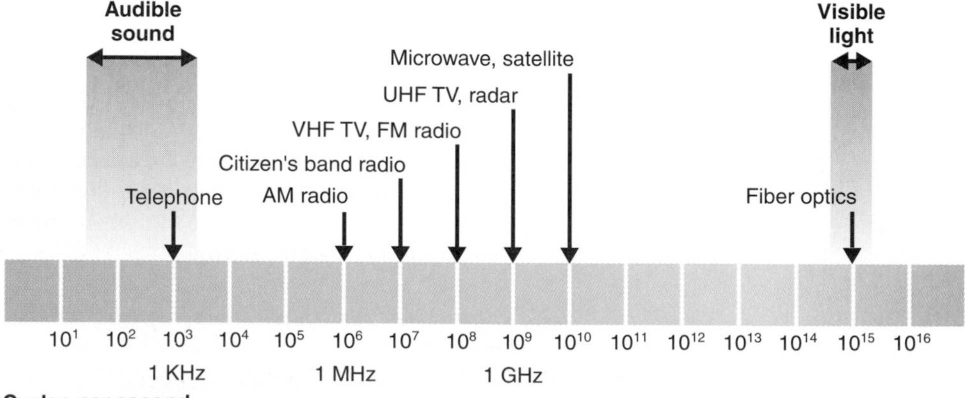

Figure 10.16
The electromagnetic spectrum

Various parts of the electromagnetic spectrum have been allocated for different uses.

Reality Check

TELECOMMUNICATIONS POLICY

The text mentions a number of impacts of telecommunications policy.

1. Explain why you do or do not believe telecommunications policy has affected you in your everyday life.
2. What human and ethical issues arise in discussions of telecommunications policy?

CHAPTER CONCLUSION

Summary

What aspects of the convergence of computing and communications are important for understanding telecommunications?

Communications capabilities have become essential to many computer systems, especially with the trend toward distributed computing. Roles of computers in telecommunications include making long distance connections, monitoring the traffic on the network, and balancing the loads on different parts of the network by determining which path across the network each telephone call or data packet will take.

What are the steps in the basic telecommunications model?

Telecommunications is the movement of data between devices in different locations. Telecommunications starts with generating the data. The encoding step converts data from an original form into a form for transmission. The switching step directs the signal from its source to its destination. Data can be transmitted using a variety of wire or wireless channels. On arriving at the destination, data are decoded into the original form.

What are the advantages and disadvantages of the different forms of wire and wireless transmission?

Wire transmission requires that the wires be installed and protected from damage. This is difficult in remote geographical areas and in locations where wires would take up too much space. Although a great deal of copper wire is already in place, it transmits data slowly, is heavy and bulky, and generates electrical emissions that can be intercepted. Coaxial cable is much faster but can be tapped into easily. Fiber optic cable can transmit vast quantities of data, is very light, and generates no electrical emissions, but it requires complex electronics and is difficult to splice. Wireless transmission is the only effective method for many applications, but it can be intercepted and can be disrupted by physical objects or atmospheric conditions.

What is ISDN and why is it important?

ISDN (integrated service digital network) is a set of standards whose adoption provides additional telephone capabilities without scrapping existing telephone lines. By providing integrated service, ISDN offers consistent ways to handle voice and computer data in telephone networks. As a digital network, ISDN provides for digital transmission of both voice and computer data on existing copper telephone lines. By increasing data transmission speeds, ISDN eliminates some needs for expensive leased lines. It cuts transmission time for graphical images and permits connection of a voice telephone and a personal computer on the same call.

What are the main differences between LANs, WANs, and VANs?

These three types of networks transmit data between computerized devices. Local area networks (LANs) connect computers and other equipment within a local area, such as a floor of a building; they help people share equipment, data, and software. Wide area networks (WANs) link geographically separated locations. Some WANs are used as a communications backbone for a large organization; others focus on a particular application, such as taking orders or making reservations. Value added networks (VANs) are public data networks that "add value" by transmitting data and by providing access to commercial databases and software.

Why are telecommunications standards important?
Telecommunications standards make it practical to build networks containing hardware from different vendors. However, they may disallow valuable capabilities that are inconsistent with the standard. Standards may also contradict the features vendors have built into proprietary products. This strikes at fundamental competitive issues because vendors often rely on their own proprietary data architectures as strategies to lock out competitors.

How is telecommunications policy related to issues faced by managers?
Telecommunications policy is one determinant of who owns telecommunications networks, what products come to market, and who can sell these products. The issues in this area range from economic efficiency and customer satisfaction to national security. The allocation of broadcasting frequencies, both nationally and internationally, is a question that has major impacts on business and security interests.

Key Terms

telecommunications
data communications
telecommunications network
node
connectivity
encoding
switching
channel
decoding
network management
host computer
front-end processor
analog signals
digital signals
carrier signal
modem
cable modem
high definition television (HDTV)
dedicated line
switch
circuit switching
packet switching
multiplexer
Internet telephony
bandwidth
information superhighway
the last-mile problem
data loss
twisted pair
coaxial cable
fiber optic cable
very small aperture terminal (VSAT)
private branch exchange (PBX)
ISDN (integrated service digital network)
local area network (LAN)
token passing
baseband
broadband
bridge
router
gateway
star topology
ring topology
bus topology
wide area network (WAN)
asynchronous transfer mode (ATM)
value added network (VAN)
de facto standards
de jure standards
OSI reference model
protocol
TCP/IP
HTTP

Review Questions

1. Identify some of the ways telecommunications affects value chain activities.
2. Identify and define the telecommunications functions in the basic telecommunications model.
3. Describe the difference between analog and digital signals.
4. What does a modem do?
5. What is the difference between circuit switching and packet switching?
6. Why is Internet telephony an important challenge to established telephone companies?
7. Why would it take a long time to transmit a movie over a telephone line?
8. Explain some of the performance differences between twisted pair, coaxial cable, and fiber optic cable.
9. What are the advantages and disadvantages of communication via satellite?
10. Identify some of the functions performed by PBXs.
11. What is ISDN, and why isn't it used everywhere?
12. What is a LAN, and what are some common uses of LANs?
13. Identify important differences between star, ring, and bus topologies.

14. Explain why it is possible for a WAN to contain a number of LANs.
15. What is a VAN, and what are the advantages and disadvantages of using VANs?
16. Explain the difference between de facto and de jure standards.
17. What is the OSI reference model, and what do its layers represent?
18. Discuss some of the issues in telecommunications policy.
19. Why is the electromagnetic spectrum a scarce resource?

Discussion Topics

1. A congressional panel began a broad investigation after learning that the online service America Online sold data on one million subscribers to direct marketers at the rate of $100 per 1,000 names. For additional fees direct marketers can get selections based on ZIP code, income, operating systems, and ages of users' children.[25] Given that an online service can track everything a user does online, explain your view of acceptable privacy guarantees in this part of "cyberspace."
2. According to 1994 data from the International Telecommunications Union, 71% of the world's phone lines were in countries with 15% of the world's population. In Latin America only 7% of the population had access to a phone line, and only 1% had access in most of Asia and Africa.[26] Explain whether disparities in telephone access have an unfair impact on global competition. What might the less developed countries do about this situation?
3. You have just seen two commercials. In one, an executive has received an important message by pager while driving. In the other, an executive relaxing under an umbrella on an isolated tropical beach is using a portable computer for a videoconference with people in the Paris home office. Use ideas about data transmission to compare the situations and to explain what would make the second situation feasible.
4. Assume that the U.S. Congress totally deregulated telecommunications. Based on ideas in this chapter, identify five major impacts this development might have.
5. Assume that you could have advanced PBX and ISDN capabilities for your home telephone. Would these capabilities make any difference in the way you use the telephone?
6. What kinds of telecommunications capabilities would be required for a large multinational food company to provide any employee with instant access to any data in the entire company? What types of data handling capabilities would this require? Aside from technical capabilities to transmit data, explain why you do or do not believe this is practical.

CASE

Network Solutions, Inc.: Maintaining Internet Domain Names

Did you every wonder who registers and maintains Internet domain names, such as www.ibm.com or www.purdue.edu? Furthermore, what would have happened if you had applied for ibm.com before IBM did? Would you have made a fortune by selling that name to IBM? Since 1993, an agreement with the U.S. National Science Foundation has delegated control of domain name registry system for .com, .org, and .net addresses in the United States to a Virginia-based company called Network Solutions, Inc. (NSI). The company's responsibilities include registering domain names and transmitting updated names and addresses to the servers that control the flow of information through the Internet. These servers receive a Web user's request for a Web page, transmit it to the appropriate server, and then transmit the response back to the user's computer.

The process of registering a new domain name is straightforward. Domain names are activated upon request, on a first-come, first-served basis. The registrant fills out an electronic form that includes the domain name, the name of the organization registering the name, various contacts, and the primary and secondary server host names and net addresses. Within seven days after domain name activation, an invoice is sent to the billing contact by both postal and electronic mail, and payment is due within 30 days. If payment is not received by the due date, the domain name is deactivated, deleted from the database, and made available for registration by someone else.

Originally there was no fee for registering domain names; new rules in 1995 called for a $100 initial registration fee and an annual renewal fee of $50; in 1998 the fees dropped to $70 and $35.

NSI has a defined dispute resolution process for situations in which a registered domain name infringes on another firm's registered trademark. A dispute of this type occurred when a 12-year-old nicknamed Pokey received the registration of www.pokey.org as a gift from his father. A toy company called Prema previously had a registered trademark for a character named Pokey and applied for a domain name, only to find it was already taken. The dispute resolution process started, and lawyers for both sides got involved. Ultimately Prema recognized that the domain name was not being used for commercial purposes and decided not to pursue the matter. No one knows whether the same thing would have happened if the name in question were IBM or Microsoft.

The dependence of the entire Internet on the proper handling of domain names became especially apparent on July 17, 1997, when an operator at NSI sent a corrupted master list of domain names and the corresponding Internet machine addresses to the nine main servers that control Internet traffic. NSI distributes the list daily at 2:30 A.M. to reflect updates during the previous day. In this case, the employee responsible for monitoring the process ignored a warning that a data consolidation program had failed and released the corrupted database to the network. This effectively wiped out the domain names of more than one million companies in the .com and .net domains. NSI detected and corrected the problem by 6:30 A.M. By that time, thousands or even millions of e-mail messages had been returned as undeliverable, while untold numbers of users had been unable to contact websites whose addresses were temporarily garbled. Sporadic problems extended through the day. This appeared to be the most extensive network breakdown that had ever occurred. The fact that a simple, isolated human error could wreak so much havoc caused many people to reflect on how crucial the Internet has become in the daily life of businesses and individuals around the world and how vulnerable it is to accidents or sabotage.

QUESTIONS

1. Identify the major processes described in the case. For each process, identify several important measures of performance.
2. Review the chapter's discussion of different types of networks and explain the areas in which NSI seems to play a crucial role in today's electronic commerce.
3. Some observers have argued that having a single central keeper of Internet addresses makes electronic commerce a riskier proposition than it might otherwise be. Explain why you agree or disagree.

Sources:

Machlis, Sharon. "Might Makes Right in Name Fight," *Computerworld*, Apr. 20, 1998, pp. 51–52.

Markoff, John. "Minor Error Throws Internet into Disarray," *New York Times*, July 18, 1997, June 2, 1998, (http://www.nytimes.com/library/cyber/week/071897network.html).

CASE

France Telecom: Moving from Minitel to the Internet

In 1974 the French telephone system had one of the lowest penetration rates in the industrialized world, less than 7 million phones for 47 million citizens, and French leaders voiced concerns that American domination of telecommunications and computers threatened France's technological and cultural independence. In 1975 French President Valéry Giscard d'Estaing asked two researchers to suggest a strategy to computerize French society. Their 1978 report led to a major project to modernize the French telephone infrastructure under the national telecommunications monopoly France Telecom. One part of that project was the 1983 launch of a videotex system to increase telephone usage and therefore help recoup the investment expenses. This system used dedicated, inexpensive 8-inch terminals called minitels to display text information transmitted over the phone lines. The initial plan included just two applications, an electronic telephone directory and classified ads. A decision to subsidize the service by providing the minitels for free was a key step in achieving rapid adoption, although the system attracted a great deal of controversy. Newspaper publishers argued that it would decrease their classified ad revenues;

some politicians argued that it could be abused by the state to control information; others argued it could be used to distribute pornography. Negative publicity related to a system crash in 1985 due to excessively heavy traffic posed a further challenge.

By the late 1980s, 95% of the population had access to telephones. By 1992, the year before the first graphical Web browser became available, 48.5% of the French working population had access to minitels, and the entire system was known by the name Minitel. Its 6 million subscribers used 110 million hours of connect time to access 20,000 information services. These services included information about entertainment events, train schedules, television and radio programs, jobs and classified ads, interactive games, banking services, grocery and home shopping, comparative pricing, and many other consumer services. Almost every bank, for example, developed its own minitel-based home banking system to allow their customers to check the status of their accounts, order checks, pay utility bills, and trade stocks. Average monthly usage of the terminals was 90 minutes, a decrease from 106 minutes in 1986. In 1992, use of the electronic phone directory represented 43% of the calls but only 21% of the connect time. An electronic mail system was introduced in 1991, as were newer types of minitels that had to be leased.

By 1998, 35 million French subscribers dialed in regularly and purchased billions of dollars in goods from 25,000 vendors. Minitel service was available for $10 per month plus a connection time fee that varied with the service being used. The small terminals were cheap and clunky but provided a safe way to make purchases via credit card or via smart cards that are popular in France. The national railroad SNCF used Minitel for selling tickets and for answering 25 million inquiries per year.

Despite its widespread usage, Minitel was showing its age. Unlike text-based Minitel, the Web supported multimedia information and access to a far wider range of information and services. The Internet industry scoffed at French companies that sell types of information on Minitel that are typically available for free on the Internet. In a 1997 speech, Prime Minister Lionel Jospin said Minitel could end up hindering the development of new and promising IT applications and could soon have dire repercussions on competitiveness and employment. Few French consumers saw why they should purchase PCs and pay for phone connections and Internet access when the Internet contained little French content. Consequently, only 3% of the French population used the Internet, versus 20% in the United States and 9% in the United Kingdom and Germany. Reluctant to give up its cash cow, France Telecom planned to build a new $500 next-generation terminal that could access Minitel and the Internet, but that would be simpler to use than a PC. A 1998 press release from France Telecom predicted 10 million French Internet users by the year 2000.

QUESTIONS

1. Compare the usage and history of the Minitel system and the usage and history of the Web.
2. Explain how this story illustrates ideas in this chapter related to telecommunications standards and policy.
3. Explain why you do or do not believe France should eliminate the Minitel system in favor of the Web or something like it.

Sources:

Cats-Baril, William L., and Tawfik Jelassi. "The French Videotex System Minitel: A Successful Implementation of a National Information Infrastructure," *MIS Quarterly*, Vol. 18, No. 1, Mar. 1994, pp. 1–20.

France Telecom. "1997 Results Confirm Growth—France Telecom Financial Results in Line with Forecasts," Press Release, Mar. 18, 1998, June 2, 1998 (http://www.francetelecom.com/nr/nr_prre/nt_prre 3-18-98 97results.htm).

Strassel, Kimberly L. "Gallic Passion for Minitel Thwarts L'Internet in France," *Wall Street Journal*, Mar. 27, 1998, p. B1.

11

Information Systems Planning

Study Questions

- What is an information system plan?
- Why do users and managers have to participate in information system planning and development?
- How is information system planning linked to business planning?
- What are some of the strategic issues in information system planning?
- What are the key issues in balancing centralized versus distributed processing and control?
- How is cost/benefit analysis used in making investment decisions about information systems?
- What are the basic elements of project management for information system projects?

Outline

Opening Case

OWENS CORNING: INTEGRATING ACROSS BUSINESS UNITS

Owens Corning manufactures building supplies such as fiberglass insulation and roofing materials and sells them to building contractors and to building supply distributors such as Home Depot. In 1991 the company faced challenges on all fronts. It was deeply in debt due to a financial restructuring five years earlier, and its revenues were shrinking slowly. Internally it had 200 incompatible systems dedicated to specific tasks such as invoicing for specific product lines. Externally, the company was out of step with the direction in which the market was moving. The company was organized around different product lines, meaning that retailers dealt with four service centers and four sets of bills. Builders and remodelers also saw few benefits in this product line orientation because they were less concerned with selecting the right brand of a particular material such as insulation and far more concerned with timely, convenient acquisition and delivery of all the materials for a project. Furthermore, although the company wanted to provide a complete "envelope" for a house, including shingles, waterproofing, siding, and other materials, there were significant gaps in the product line.

Owens Corning embarked on a long-term effort to reorient the entire company. (See Table 11.1.) It acquired 14 smaller manufacturers to fill in the products it lacked. It reorganized sales so that salespeople sold the entire company's whole line instead of just one product line. One of its most daunting tasks was a complete overhaul of its hodgepodge of outdated and incompatible information systems. A new head of IS was hired in 1994. After reviewing the state of existing information systems in the light of the company's strategy, he and his staff decided that an integrated information system was needed so that sales people could enter orders, reserve inventory, and produce consistent bills.

In what was virtually a "bet the company" strategy, Owens Corning embarked on a two-year rush project to replace its old order fulfillment, manufacturing, inventory, distribution, and financial accounting software with SAP's R/3 program, an integrated, but notoriously complex, enterprise software package. The head of IS insisted that half the staffing for this project would have to come from the business units, not the IS group, and that its success would be defined in business terms, such as a 50% reduction in inventory.

By mid-1995 the project team of 250 people was housed at Toledo headquarters to maximize internal coordination and minimize delays in answering questions. It was divided into five groups, each focused on a different set of processes. Each group included representatives from local business units and IS and business professionals from across the company. Councils with members from all five groups made sure that each process meshed with other processes. In some areas, such as production planning, SAP's capabilities were not as good as those in homegrown systems. However, because the company's strategy required greater integration, the project team and local business operations sometimes had to be satisfied with "good-enough reengineering" rather than insisting on the best way to perform each process. Project cost through 1997 was $110 million for a combination of analyzing how to use SAP, setting it up on the computers, and training people to use it. Estimated benefits were $15 million in 1997, $50 million in 1998, and $80 million in 2000.[1,2]

Debate Topic

Owens Corning took a huge gamble in devoting so much money to an unproven reengineering project. Although the project succeeded, a more incremental approach would have been more prudent.

The SAP project at Owens Corning is an example of how information systems can play a crucial role in a company's strategy. The lack of an integrated information system was clearly an obstacle to the company's strategy of manufacturing and selling a complete product line and providing customers a unified view of the company. The price of change was high, however, over $100 million, and in some cases, the inability to use homegrown processes whose fit to local conditions was better than any of the options available through

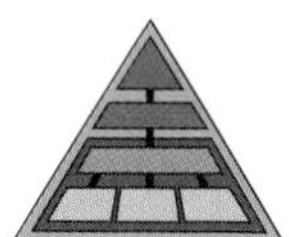

TABLE 11.1 Owens Corning Reorients Its Operations

CUSTOMER
- Building supply companies and contractors that purchase building materials from Owens Corning

PRODUCT
- Reengineered work systems that are more responsive to market needs

BUSINESS PROCESS

Major steps:
- Create a vision for how company operations should change
- Select SAP R/3 as the approach for improving information systems
- Create a large project team at headquarters
- Analyze how to use SAP
- Install SAP on computers
- Train people to use it
- Use SAP in practice

Rationale:
- Replace multiple, incompatible information systems with an integrated information system that makes it possible to serve customers more effectively.

PARTICIPANTS
- Project team consisting of half business professionals and half IS professionals
- Users who were trained and then used the new information system

INFORMATION
- Company strategy
- Project goals
- Details of business operations
- Selected options for using SAP

TECHNOLOGY
- SAP R/3 software package
- Computers and other hardware

SAP. Overall, this case involved a series of IS planning issues including aligning information systems with business strategies, deciding what projects to do, and deciding who should work on those projects.

This is the first of three chapters about building and maintaining information systems. Aspects of these topics such as the phases of building and maintaining systems were introduced early in Chapter 1 and will now be explained in more depth. This chapter covers information system planning at both the strategic and project levels. It introduces many of the issues in the IS planning issues that every firm should address in some way. Regardless of whether the firm has one employee or 100,000, it is still necessary to decide what will be done, who will do it, when they will do it, how it will be done, and what are the desired results. Chapter 12 covers alternative approaches for building and maintaining information systems. Chapter 13 covers information system security and control.

The WCA framework can be used throughout these chapters to visualize the work systems that are discussed and to think about alternative ways of doing the work. For example, there are a variety of IS planning methods, but there is often a question about whether the payoff is worth the time and effort expended. Likewise, there are many ways to create financial justifications of IS investments, but participants often wonder whether these justifications have much bearing on actual decisions. There are also various ways to build systems, each with its own advantages and disadvantages. Moreover, there are many methods for controlling and protecting systems, each with its own costs, benefits, and risks. Approaching Chapters 11, 12, and 13 with the WCA framework in the back of your mind will help you use the ideas when you participate in planning, building, or managing systems.

A final comment is necessary about the use of the abbreviations *IT* and *IS*. This is a book about information systems (IS) which use information technology (IT), but many journalists and business and technical professionals write or say things that imply information systems exist under the general umbrella of IT. To give a flavor for how people often talk about this area, this chapter usually refers to the IS department and IS plan, but then to IT professionals and IT resources.

THE PROCESS OF INFORMATION SYSTEM PLANNING

The work of planning, building, and managing information systems can be viewed in work system terms and can be described, evaluated, and improved just like any other work system. The same issues apply, such as identifying the customer and product of the business process and finding a balance between the business process, participants, information, technology, and the results expected by the customer.

What Is an Information System Plan?

Planning is the process of deciding what will be done, who will do it, when they will do it, how it will be done, and what are the desired results. Table 11.2 shows that information systems planning requires addressing these questions at several levels. At the strategic level, the questions are about the firm's overall priorities and goals for information systems and the technical and organizational approaches that will be used. At the project level, the questions boil down to two types of concerns: first, what specific capabilities are required in each system, and second, who will do what and when will they do it to produce the specific results needed in a specific project, such as building a new sales tracking system or retraining users of a customer service system that has been changed.

Information system planning should be an integral part of business planning. Business planning is the process of identifying the firm's goals, objectives, and priorities, and developing action plans for accomplishing those goals and objectives. **Information systems planning** is the part of business planning concerned with deploying the firm's information systems resources, including people, hardware, and software. Figure 11.1 illustrates the similarity between information system planning and planning in various

TABLE 11.2 **Planning Questions for Information Systems**

Issue	Strategic level	Project level
Who?	• What are the responsibilities of the IS department and the user departments? • Which vendors will perform major functions that are outsourced?	• Who will work on each project? • Who will decide how the business process should operate? • Who will manage and support the system after it is in operation?
What?	• What are the major things that the IS department must do so that the firm can accomplish its goals?	• What specific capabilities are required in the information system? • What will be the individual steps in each project?
When?	• What are the major completion dates that the firm can rely upon?	• When will the individual steps in each project be completed?
How?	• What technology will be used to do the work? • What technology must be available so that the work can be done well? • What capabilities must the firm have to compete in the future?	• How will system development techniques be used to produce the desired results? • How will the IS department and user departments work together on the project?
Desired results?	• How will business processes change in terms of detailed operation and controllable results?	• What will be the deliverable results from each step in each project?

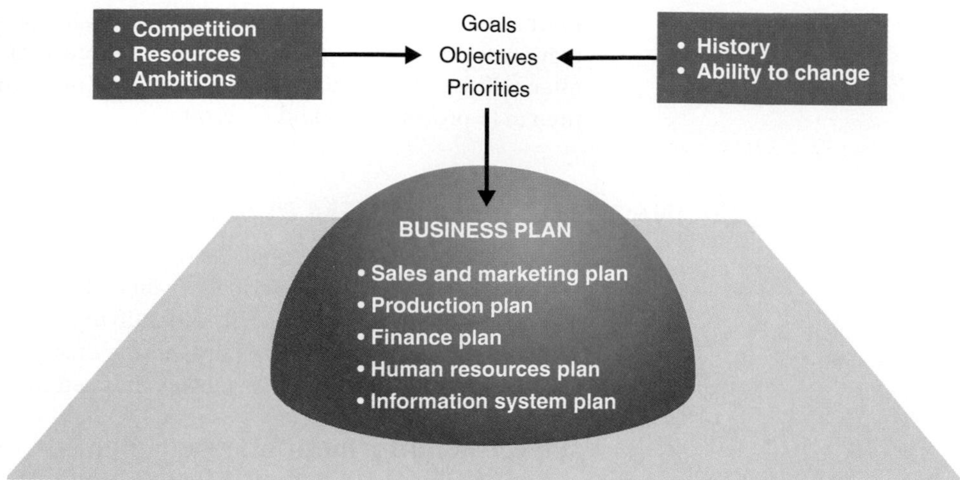

Figure 11.1
The information system plan as part of the business plan

The plan for each functional area (and for information systems) should be based on the firm's goals, objectives, and priorities. The individual plans in each of the areas are part of the business plan and should be consistent with it and support it.

functional areas. The goals, objectives, and priorities of the business should drive all the plans. Furthermore, although each plan is produced by specialists in a particular department, all the plans should support the same strategy and goals. From this viewpoint, the unique aspect of the IS plan is that it concentrates on IS projects.

Challenges in IS Planning

The specific steps and procedures for creating an IS plan vary from company to company, depending on factors such as the way the company manages its various planning and control cycles and the extent to which IT professionals are centralized or dispersed into the business units. Often missing from explanations of IS procedures, policies, and standards is the way the procedures and policies address the major challenges in IS planning.

Difficulty Foreseeing and Assessing Opportunities

It is sometimes said that IS strategies become apparent only after they have been accomplished. Consider the Sabre reservation system, which is often considered a major factor in American Airlines' competitive success. That system was not initially designed as a major competitive strategy. Rather, it evolved through four distinct stages over 30 years. It began in the early 1960s as a response to American Airlines' inability to use manual methods to monitor its inventory of available seats. Although a technical achievement for the time, it was a far cry from the powerful system later accused of presenting biased displays to travel agents so they would see and select American Airlines flights for their clients.[3] A similar story applies for the order entry and inventory control system American Hospital Supply (later acquired by Baxter International) built for its customers in hospital supply departments. From its start as a simple way to keep track of orders, it evolved into a major competitive tool by providing such complete service that customers found it expensive to switch to other suppliers. But competitors eventually offered similar systems, leading to frustrating situations in which a hospital might have to use different systems, including different terminals, for different vendors. Starting in 1988 Baxter moved to an EDI-based system called ValueLink, which permitted it to provide just-in-time delivery not just to hospital loading docks, but to nursing stations and supply closets. A proprietary order entry system for Baxter's own product line had changed into a service system allowing Baxter to manage a hospital's inventory of products from multiple suppliers.[4] (See Figure 11.2.)

The point of both examples is that it is usually difficult to foresee the way information system innovations will develop. As with many complex products, users typically identify new uses and possible improvements that the inventor never imagined. Consequently, IS plans should be reviewed periodically and systems should be designed to be flexible and extendable.

Figure 11.2
Evolving from an ordering system to a service partnership

The early predecessor of Baxter International's ValueLink system was a computerized order entry system. With ValueLink, Baxter shares risk in managing a hospital's inventory of supplies.

Difficulty Assuring Consistency with Organizational Plans and Objectives

A fundamental problem with IS planning is that individual departments within companies have their own priorities and business practices and often have difficulty working toward a mutually beneficial plan. This issue is especially significant if a large organization attempts to develop an information architecture and infrastructure that spans departmental boundaries. Even if mutual benefits seem likely, the process of developing the plans takes a lot of time and effort, and the rewards may be distributed unevenly.

Difficulty Building Systems

Large information systems are complex creations that often take years to build and involve many organizational, political, and technical tradeoffs. In many system development efforts, only a small cadre truly understands what the system is trying to do and how it will operate both organizationally and technically. It is not surprising that even major business organizations such as American Airlines, Bank of America, Chemical Bank, and the London Stock Exchange have suffered costly project failures. For every failure reported in the press, many smaller failures are never reported, and for every unreported failure there are many semifailures, systems that were developed and installed but never came close to accomplishing their goals. The difficulty of building systems is one of the reasons IS investments require management attention.

Difficulty Maintaining Information System Performance

Each of the six elements of the WCA framework points to things that can go wrong with information systems. Regardless of whether the system performs as it was designed, the customer may be dissatisfied for a variety of reasons. The products and services produced by the information system may not have the cost, quality, responsiveness, reliability, and conformance expected by its customers. The business processes within the system may lag in productivity, flexibility, or security. Participants can cause problems through anything from inattention to criminality. The information in the system can cause problems due to anything from occasional inaccuracy to fraud. Furthermore, the technology can impede or stop the business process by degrading or failing. Each of these problems can be anticipated to some extent and a preventive response can be planned, but at the cost of more effort, more attention, more expense, and less flexibility.

Difficulty Collaborating with System Builders

Business professionals and IT professionals sometimes talk past each other as if they come from different worlds. Nonspecialists talking to lawyers, doctors, or scientists often recognize the resulting frustrations. Specialists may have trouble translating their specialized knowledge and worldview into terms nonspecialists genuinely understand. Nonspecialists may feel they can't speak the lingo and can't even explain their concerns, no less engage in a genuine dialogue about alternatives. Even if they trust the specialists, they are left with a queasy feeling of operating too much on trust and too little on mutual understanding.

Attaining a genuine dialogue is important because the business professionals and the IT professionals each bring knowledge and understanding essential for system success. Many IT professionals have worked on different types of information systems and may be able to suggest approaches the business professionals would not have imagined. They know what is easy and difficult to do with computers. They know how to analyze, design, program, and debug computerized systems. They know what it takes to make an information system maintainable over time. Business professionals have the most direct experience of the business problem but may not have much experience articulating the problem systematically. Even if they can use spreadsheets and data analysis tools proficiently, they may not appreciate the problems of building maintainable systems for supporting business processes. Quite justifiably, they often want a quick solution to their business problem and lack patience for the delays required to build robust systems.

Principles for IS Planning

A series of management principles apply to IS planning and to the topics covered in the next two chapters as well.

Support the Firm's Business Strategy with Appropriate Technical Architecture, Standards, and Policies

Finding the right balance between what should be decided centrally and what should be decided locally is one of the major issues related to planning, building, and managing information systems. If people or departments plan, build, and manage their own systems their own way, opportunities for coordination and economies of scale are lost. In large companies, immense amounts of time and effort have been wasted trying to bridge technical gaps and inconsistencies between multiple systems that all do roughly the same thing, such as generate paychecks or keep track of purchases. If central authorities make too many decisions about systems, however, some of the best knowledge about differing local needs and conditions will be ignored. Individuals or departments with genuinely different needs will then have to do extra work to get around the shortcomings of whatever was decided centrally.

Although different firms have come to different conclusions about the balance between centralization and decentralization, most have concluded that some issues should be decided centrally. The key issues involve tools for building and maintaining systems, the general architecture for information, and technical standards such as what personal computers and operating systems to use. With today's rapid organizational change, consistent decisions in these areas make it much easier to keep information systems operating effectively even as the business reorganizes.

Evaluate Technology as a Component of a Larger System

Specific hardware and software products should always be evaluated in their own right and as a component of an overall system. Consider what a highway engineer said about the rebuilding of certain highway overpasses after the 1994 San Fernando Valley earthquake: "When we strengthen some of the older structures using the newest highway technology, what we are basically doing in many cases is moving the likely point of failure from one place to another." In a similar way, having the latest microprocessor may not change system performance at all if the system continues using old software whose internal design cannot take advantage of the new microprocessor's speed. Likewise, the latest hardware and software may have little impact if the training and support for participants is inadequate or if the right data is not available.

Recognize Life Cycle Costs, Not Just Acquisition Costs

The discussion of a customer's view of a product in Chapter 6 was based on a customer involvement cycle in which the customer perceives costs and benefits across the entire cycle of learning about a product, customizing it, using it, and maintaining it. In a similar way, the costs of any information system typically far exceed the cost of acquiring the hardware and software. For example, the discussion of network computers in Chapter 8 showed that a typical large company's costs related to personal computers is several times what the computer itself might cost. (See Table 8.3.) The difference consists of costs incurred to install the computer and use it effectively. These costs are related to wiring the computer to a network, buying software, training users, and providing support for users.

Design Information Systems to Be Maintainable

Anyone who has ever tried to remodel a house recognizes the value of designing information systems to be maintainable. The difficulty of doing the home improvements depends on what you find when you tear open the wall. The work is much easier if you have an accurate blueprint or wiring diagram telling you where to look and what to expect. Information system users whose main computer experience is with their own spreadsheets often have trouble understanding why it takes so long to build and implement information systems. Unlike spreadsheet models developed for temporary, personal use in analyzing a current situation, many information systems must last for years and must be maintainable long after the original system builders have moved to other jobs. This requires that the systems be constructed and documented carefully, and that the documentation be updated whenever the system is changed. In general, it is also easier to maintain systems if the parts are simpler and are designed as modular components meant to be plugged into other components that are consistent with accepted industry standards.

Recognize the Human Side of Technology Use

A point made repeatedly throughout this book is that people are part of the system. A technically spectacular system may still fail if its human participants are unwilling or unable to play their part effectively. Similarly, even technically primitive systems can often be very successful when supported and understood by active participants. The human side of technology use is one of the reasons the process of designing systems and implementing them in organizations requires involvement and commitment by system participants and their management. Processes for planning, building, and managing systems should be designed accordingly.

Support and Control the Technical System

Important as the human side of the system is, the technical side should also be supported and controlled. Information systems need care and maintenance in much the same way as cars or houses. If care and maintenance are ignored, systems gradually degrade and become more prone to failure from overloaded databases, incorrect data, faulty documentation, or human error. This leads to the question of who should do maintenance work. The trend toward decentralization and outsourcing leaves less of this work in the hands of centralized groups. These groups often have greater technical depth than individual functional departments and greater company allegiance than outsourcing vendors who have their own external business agendas. Consequently, the support and control of technical systems is just as much a planning issue as deciding what new information systems to build.

Planning Role of the IS and User Departments

A firm's information systems department is usually responsible for producing the IS plan in conjunction with the user departments, such as marketing and finance. As happens in other departments, managers in the IS department start the planning process by reviewing their progress on the existing plan. They look at special problems, such as systems approaching obsolescence. They confer with managers in the user departments to learn about user priorities and needs for system improvements, new systems, and user support. IS department managers also look at the needs of their own department such as training, hiring, and personnel development.

Many questions and issues arise as an initial IS plan is produced and reviewed. Users are often frustrated by how long it takes to build new systems and how much effort it takes to make what might seem like small changes to existing systems. The IS department often feels frustrated by its inability to keep up with many of the business's pressing problems.

It is especially important to allocate resources carefully because most firms don't come close to having the IT resources needed to develop all of the information systems that people in the company say they need. It is not unusual for a central IS department to have over a two-year backlog of committed projects, with many other requests simply turned down or never submitted formally because of the minimal chance that they would be acted upon. In the late 1990s, the need to devote resources to the Y2K problem created even more pressure on IS departments.

Chief Information Officer

Recognizing the importance of information systems in corporate success, some firms have designated the head of the IS department the **chief information officer (CIO),** just as the head of finance is the CFO and the chief executive of the company is the CEO. By leading the IS function, the CIO has special responsibility for making sure that the IS plan supports the firm's business plan and provides long-term direction for the firm's system-related efforts.

The role of CIO calls for a rare mix of business skills and technical knowledge. CIOs too focused on computer technology may have trouble being accepted as business professionals working for the overall good of the firm. CIOs too focused on general business issues may have trouble resolving the technical issues in creating a practical plan for adopting new technologies essential for future business practices. Throughout the 1990s, career turmoil among CIOs was so common that some claimed CIO stood for "career is over." Regardless of whether individuals succeeded in filling an ambitious role, the strategic nature of IS leadership is increasingly clear.

User Roles in IS Planning

Even though the IS department compiles the IS plan, members of user departments also have important planning responsibilities. Because information systems exist to help them do their work, they have to ensure that the right systems are developed and are used effectively and efficiently. Members of user departments participate in IS planning in various roles including sponsor, champion, and steering committee member.

- **Sponsors** are senior managers who recognize the importance of an information system and make sure resources are allocated for building and maintaining the system. In addition to funding, the crucial resource is people from the user department who would be doing their regular work if they were not working on the information system project. For example, an accounting manager might spend months as the user representative in a project building a new accounting information system.
- **Champions** are individuals who recognize the importance of an information system and exert effort to make sure that the system is recognized as important by others in the organization. Champions may not have direct control of resources for the system, even though they promote its success.

- **IS steering committees** meet to make sure the IS effort reflects business priorities These committees typically include knowledgeable representatives from user groups plus members of the IS department. Responsibilities of these committees range from identifying problems to reviewing system proposals and long-term IS plans.

Because IS planning efforts inevitably face questions about resources for maintaining existing systems versus resources for building new systems, we will look at this issue next.

Allocating Resources between New and Old Information Systems

An IS plan allocates resources such as budgets and programmer time between different possible uses of those resources. Major uses of those resources include maintaining existing systems, developing new systems, supporting users, and trying out new ideas and techniques.

Maintaining Existing Information Systems and Supporting Users

Keeping existing information systems operating efficiently and effectively as business conditions change often absorbs 60% to 80% of the planned work in an IS plan. This work can be split into three categories: user-support, system enhancements, and bug fixes.

User-support projects include helping users with applications developed by the IS department, with applications purchased from outside vendors, and with performing individual work on personal computers. The individual work typically involves personal use of tools such as spreadsheets, word processors, and presentation graphics. Because of the ongoing nature of user-support projects, many firms have staffed separate groups devoted to helping users develop and maintain their own applications, especially applications that extract data from corporate databases. Ideally these groups should reduce costs and increase effectiveness by standardizing on a few types of hardware and software, offering training programs for users, and helping users analyze and solve their own problems.

Enhancements are improvements in an existing system's function without changing its fundamental concepts or operation. Work system participants who care about what the information system does are often able to suggest many desired enhancements. The list of suggestions usually grows as users learn what the information system can and cannot do in its current form, and as they think up new ways to use it to greater advantage. Many IS departments could assign every programmer to enhancements and barely make a dent in the list of suggestions from their users.

Bug fixes are projects directed at correcting bugs in existing systems. Bugs are flaws in systems that cause them to produce incorrect or inappropriate results. All large information systems (and most small ones) contain bugs. The planning issue is to decide how much effort should go into fixing them. Because important bugs may be discovered during the period covered by the plan, IS plans should reserve time and effort for bug fixes even though the specific bugs to be fixed may not be known in advance.

Bugs are usually divided into priority-based categories. Bugs that prevent people from doing their work or prevent departments from operating effectively receive the highest priority and usually preempt other scheduled work. Bugs that cause minor problems for the user are typically fixed when convenient. Minor bugs with little impact on users' ability to do their work may never be fixed.

New Development, Infrastructure, and Other Projects

Resources not assigned to maintaining existing information systems and supporting users can be allocated to a variety of other projects, including new application development, IT infrastructure projects, and research projects.

Major new application projects provide new types of capabilities for users rather than small improvements in existing application systems. New application projects can be divided further into projects that require new technology, knowledge, and methods, versus systems for which existing knowledge and methods suffice. Projects that require new technology, knowledge, or methods are usually riskier than those applying currently used approaches. To reduce the likelihood of high visibility failures, only a limited number of high-risk projects should be undertaken at any time.

IT infrastructure projects install and maintain the hardware, software, and human support organizations that are used by application systems. The types of infrastructure projects users see most directly include installing and maintaining computers, telecommunications networks, and messaging systems. Also important but not as visible to users are infrastructure projects emphasizing system development tools.

Research projects evaluate new methods or technology to determine how they might be used. The research may involve finding out about the existence of new tools and trying them out. When a new technology seems applicable, the firm typically does a **pilot project,** a limited, experimental application to get experience with the new technology. Pilot projects are usually done with users who are particularly interested and wish to be innovators. Although these projects use a small percentage of a firm's IS resources, they are important because they help bring about innovation and change.

Just looking at the different types of projects helps you see that IS planning involves much more than just making a list of the new systems to be developed. Many IS professionals feel frustrated that so little of their effort can go into new development.

Project Roles of IS Professionals

IS projects vary greatly in size and complexity. In small system development projects, just a single person or several people may play all the necessary roles without defining them explicitly. For example, if a small business buys and uses an accounting package, a user or IS professional may purchase it from a software vendor, install it on a personal computer, train other users, and consult the vendor's customer support staff for questions. Various roles may be combined into a single person's job responsibilities in this way.

In large projects involving hundreds or even thousands of people, many distinct roles are assigned to individuals. Box 11.1 briefly defines common roles in typical major projects, such as developing online transaction processing systems used for day-to-day operation of large companies. Teams of analysts, programmers, and, possibly, programmer-analysts produce the application software. Technical writers produce the user documentation. Computer operators keep the computer systems running and make sure the reports are produced at the right times. The system manager makes sure that the computer system itself is maintained. The user support staff makes sure that the users are trained and are receiving benefits.

Many of the same roles apply even if the project involves acquiring and installing an application package sold by a software vendor. For example, systems analysts still need to determine the requirements, and the user support staff still has to train the users. Programming may also be required to tailor the purchased software to the firm's needs or to link the resulting data to the firm's other internal systems.

This introduction to IS planning started by saying that planning is the process of deciding what will be done, who will do it, when they will do it, how it will be done, and what are the desired results. Thus far we have seen some of the roles in IS planning and the types of projects the plan includes. With this background we can now look at the strategic issues and project-level issues that must be faced while developing the plan.

Reality Check

ISSUES IN PLANNING

A plan is a statement of what will be done and how and when it will be done. Strategic-level plans are different from project-level plans.

1. Identify any project you have worked on (preferably with other people). Whether or not a plan existed for that project, summarize some of the things that could have been included in the strategic-level plan and in the project-level plan.
2. Explain why you agree or disagree with this statement: IS plans should be fundamentally similar to any other type of business plan because a plan is just a statement of what will be done and how and when it will be done.

BOX 11.1 ***Roles of information system professionals in building and maintaining information systems***

Large system development projects involve many roles such as the following.

- *Project managers* manage the people doing the work to make sure that project goals are accomplished. Among other things, project managers develop schedules, monitor work for completeness and quality, and help in resolving conflicts and questions that arise. Project managers in IS departments typically started as programmers or systems analysts and showed they could take responsibility for larger parts of projects.
- *Application programmers* convert a general understanding or written description of a business problem into a set of programs that accomplish the required computer processing. Their jobs include designing the programs and database, coding and testing the programs, and producing the related program documentation.
- *Systems analysts* perform the analysis to decide how a new or updated system can help solve a business problem or exploit a business opportunity. They communicate part of the results to programmers who write the programs.
- *Programmer-analysts* play the role of both programmer and analyst in situations where it is more effective to combine these roles.
- *Technical writers* produce user documentation and training material.
- *Computer operators* make sure that a computer is running, that tapes and removable disks are loaded and unloaded, and that jobs such as backups and database reconfigurations are performed on time.
- *Database administrators* control the definition of all items in a shared database and monitor the performance of the database.
- *System managers* manage computer installations and make sure that the hardware is configured properly and that the operators do their jobs.
- *Systems programmers* write programs related to the operating system and internal operation of the computer system. This is a more specialized job than programmer, which generally refers to someone who produces programs related to business applications.
- *User support staffs* help the users use the system by providing training, answering questions, and collecting change requests.

STRATEGIC ALIGNMENT OF BUSINESS AND IT

Strategic alignment of the business effort and IT effort is the central issue in IS planning. Figure 11.3 combines ideas from two[5,6] of the many strategic alignment models. It differs from most of these models because it illustrates two distinct rationales that strategic alignment should balance simultaneously. The primary rationale (indicated by the darker arrows) is that the business needs, opportunities, and strategy should determine both how the firm and its processes are organized and how its information systems should operate. In turn, both the firm's processes and organization and its IT needs, opportunities, and strategy should dictate the form and operation of the IT infrastructure. Because IT infrastructure takes a long time to change, however, a series of restrictions pushes in the opposite direction. Today's IT infrastructure is a key determinant and limiting factor in how the business can actually operate today. It is also a determinant of needs for changing IT as well as being a limiting factor in how much can be accomplished at what pace. In turn, business organization and processes and IT needs are both limiting factors that constrain a business's realistic opportunities and strategic options.

This section surveys some of the strategic issues related to alignment between business and IT. It starts on the business side of Figure 11.3. First it looks at critical success factors, which are used to foster strategic alignment by identifying information needed for the business to succeed. It continues by discussing IT-related ideas often used as the rationale for changing business processes and organizations. These ideas include reengineering, downsizing, and the trend toward enterprise information systems and interorganizational systems. Moving to the IT side of the figure, the next topic is IS architecture and its relationship to centralization versus decentralization. The topic of strategic alignment is addressed directly through a method for articulating a business-driven IT infrastructure. Outsourcing is then discussed as a central issue in a firm's overall IT strategy. A final topic is international IT issues.

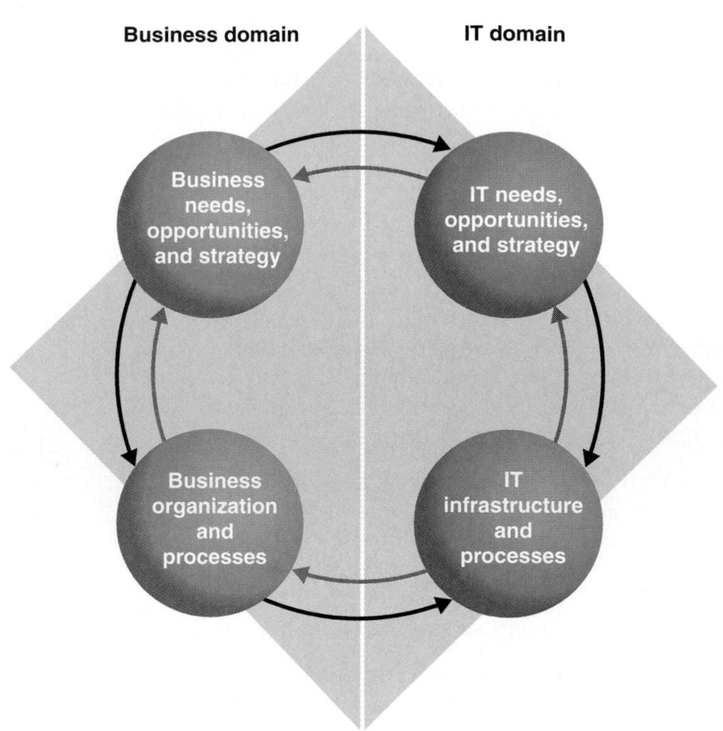

Figure 11.3
Strategic alignment of business and IT

The dark arrows represent business requirements as the starting point for strategic alignment between business and IT. The light arrows illustrate a completely opposite set of linkages that start with strengths and shortcomings in the IT domain.

Consistency with Business Priorities

Because information systems exist to support work systems that carry out a company's plans, it might seem obvious that a company's IS plan should be linked to its business plan. Obvious or not, this has not always happened. Only 36% of the CEOs interviewed in a 1989 survey[7] believed that the deployment of IS resources in their firm supported their company's business plan. With the extensive attention IT has received in the 1990s, many companies are now more careful that IS plans truly reflect business needs.

Critical success factors (CSFs) is an idea that leads to strategic alignment by highlighting the way better information might help the firm achieve its business goals. **Critical success factors** are the things that must go right for a business to succeed. The first step in using the CSF method is to identify the firm's primary mission and the objectives that define satisfactory overall performance. Next, executives identify the CSFs. Most businesses have relatively few of them, and these typically come from sources such as the structure of the industry, the firm's competitive strategy, its industry position or geographic location, environmental factors surrounding the firm, and temporary operating problems or opportunities.[8] Examples for one firm included improving customer relationships, improving supplier relationships, making the best use of inventory, and using capital and human resources efficiently and effectively. The third step is to identify the pertinent indicators or measures of performance for each CSF. For example, customer relations might be measured in terms of trends in customers lost, new customers, the ratio of customer inquiries to customer orders, or on-time delivery. The fourth step is to decide which measures are most important and then make sure that IS plans provide means for collecting and using this information.

The benefits of using the CSF method start with a shared understanding of what is critical to a company. This aids executive communication about important company issues and influences priorities for system development. Although the CSF method provides a useful framework in many situations, like any technique it should be applied with care and has some important weaknesses. It is more effective when used with senior managers rather than middle managers who focus more on their own areas and are less aware of the organization's overall CSFs. Furthermore, some managers who focus on day-to-day operations rather than planning may have difficulty dealing with the conceptual nature of CSFs.[9]

Finally, since CSFs focus on issues in specific areas of business, they may not be very helpful in making investment decisions about IT infrastructure shared between different areas.

Reengineering and Downsizing

Reengineering is a highly publicized idea that became an umbrella term for a variety of internal corporate initiatives in the early 1990s. Michael Hammer, the consultant who popularized the term, initially said that **business process reengineering (BPR)** is "the fundamental rethinking and radical redesign of business processes to achieve dramatic improvements in critical contemporary measures of performance, such as cost, quality, service, and speed."[10] Highly publicized examples such as Ford's accounts payables system (the opening case in Chapter 3) made reengineering a guiding principle for projects aimed at changing key business processes such as the way insurance companies handle claims and the way manufacturers design products.

A basic tenet of reengineering is that nothing about an organization or business process is sacred. The way things are done today may reflect nothing more than many years of trying to do things the same way even though the business environment and customers changed. Therefore, the business process of tomorrow may be completely different. Common outcomes of business process reengineering include combining several jobs into one, permitting workers to make more decisions themselves, defining different versions of processes for simple cases versus complex ones, minimizing situations when one person checks someone else's work, and reorganizing jobs to give individuals more understanding and more responsibility.[11] Many reengineering efforts also result in significant staff reductions.

The promise of business process reengineering captured the imagination of American managers in the early 1990s, and many impressive successes were announced. But it was also seen in many quarters as a slogan or umbrella term under which any important project might be explained and as a convenient excuse for layoffs. For example *Fortune* quoted a telephone company executive who said, "If you want to get something funded around here—anything, even a new chair for your office—call it reengineering on your request for expenditure."[12] The author Paul Strassmann was even more skeptical: "There's nothing new or original about business process reengineering. It's just a lot of old industrial methods, recycled and repackaged to seem like the latest in management science....Reengineering excels more in its packaging than in its substance. Its purpose is to make the purging of past staffing gluttony more palatable."[13]

Because of the radical restructuring it calls for, most firms attempting major BPR projects have found them difficult and risky. The President of SIM, the leading organization for IS executives, expressed part of the problem as follows: "One way to judge if you are reengineering: The first time you bring it up, if no one screams, 'Are you crazy?' then it is not a reengineering project." The same article cited a report coauthored by Michael Hammer speculating that the failure rate for reengineering projects is likely on the order of 70%.[14] A 1994 survey of 350 executives by the consulting firm Arthur D. Little concluded that more than 85% of the respondents were dissatisfied with the results, and 60% encountered unanticipated problems or unintended side effects related to turf battles, lack of management buy-in, and inadequate implementation skills. By the late 1990s even the original gurus of the area had rethought their message and concluded that the main point was an emphasis on improving processes rather than radical change for its own sake.

One of the reasons reengineering became controversial was its common association with **downsizing,** the effort to increase corporate efficiency by changing processes in order to reduce the number of people a firm employs. Some corporate initiatives that were presented as reengineering projects seemed to the participants much more like employee elimination projects. Downsizing was sometimes recast as *rightsizing*, but that didn't placate many of the employees who were laid off or who had to do their own previous work plus that of others who were laid off. The combined push for reengineering and downsizing raised many questions about loyalty and incentives. After all, why should someone be loyal to a company that is not loyal to its employees? An issue like this may seem far afield from how IT can help firms reengineer processes, but it is pertinent to planning decisions because the ultimate success of reengineering, downsizing, or any other major change depends on both the business and economic rationale and the ability of the organization to implement the changes successfully.

Enterprise-wide and Interorganizational Systems

The Owens Corning case at the beginning of the chapter is about an effort to integrate an organization's core information systems for order fulfillment, manufacturing, inventory, distribution, and financial accounting. Many large organizations have struggled with this type of integration issue because incompatibilities between information systems designed to solve local problems that existed years ago make it much more difficult to attain world-class performance today. The firms such as SAP, Baan, Peoplesoft, and Oracle that sell enterprise-wide software flourished in the late 1990s as ambitious expectations became the norm for short cycle times, fast response, unified action within the firm, and efficient data exchange with customers and suppliers. Enterprise resource planning (ERP) systems introduced in Chapter 5 provide one piece of the puzzle because they store data in an integrated database and because the data formats can be coordinated across a supply chain. These "technical details" make it possible to avoid the inefficiencies of trying to work with other people who are using incompatible business processes, data, and computers.

As illustrated by the fact that Owen Corning assigned 250 people to its ERP team, the effort of analyzing basic business processes and identifying the ERP options that fit best for both enterprise-wide and local reasons can be enormously expensive and time consuming. Just as there are many success stories, there are also horror stories of companies going far over budget on these projects. For example, a failed ERP implementation contributed to the bankruptcy of Foxmeyer Drug. The requirement for extensive involvement and coordination across so many functions implies that this type of investment requires strong agreement and commitment by top management. Accepting this requirement, CEO George Fisher participated in the executive council for Kodak's $500 million SAP implementation. Actually it was a reimplementation because the first attempt had failed. This council made sure the options chosen followed company priorities rather than divisional priorities. In another example, Dell Computer scuttled an SAP implementation that was designed to integrate many parts of the business. Dell decided to use only part of the software because using such highly integrated systems would make it difficult for Dell to respond to the rapid changes in the PC marketplace.[15]

Interorganizational information systems reflect the customer- and supplier-facing side of the integration issues addressed by ERP. These systems transmit information between different firms as part of ongoing business processes involving suppliers and their customers, such as designing custom products, entering orders, transmitting invoices, making payments, and servicing the product. Electronic data interchange (EDI) for entering orders, sending confirmations, transmitting bills, and transferring funds has been used in this type of system for many years. Many of these systems were developed by industry-specific trade groups for the mutual convenience of industry members, who naturally wanted to focus their efforts on whatever the industry was producing, be it automobiles or chemicals, instead of wasting resources on deciphering standard information coded inconsistently in paperwork from various suppliers or customers. A more recent development is the extranets described in Chapter 5, which use Internet technology in private networks that provide information to customers, such as detailed product descriptions, frequently asked questions about different products, maintenance information, warranties, and how to contact customer service and sales offices. Much of this information was formerly difficult for customers to access because paper versions of it at the customer site became scattered and outdated.

One of the most complex areas in which interorganizational information systems are applied is the integration between ERP packages and supply chain management. For example, Farmland Industries, a $9 billion agricultural cooperative in Missouri purchases everything from grain to livestock for more than 1,400 independent farm cooperatives, which in turn sell these supplies to local farmers. Farmland has implemented SAP's ERP product, but the local cooperatives still use their own point-of-sale, accounting, and inventory management systems. Maximizing the benefits to all concerned would involve greater integration across the entire supply chain.[16]

Interorganizational systems are also part of the trend toward **virtual organization** approaches, in which major aspects of core processes such as design, production, and delivery are outsourced to other organizations that specialize in these areas. Virtual organizations exist by agreement of their members and sometimes need immediate access to shared information in order to operate efficiently, such as when a delivery firm takes over the warehousing and distribution of spare parts for a computer manufacturer. Without good interorganizational information systems, the term *virtual organization* is no more than a slogan in such situations.

Thus far we have looked at aspects of strategic alignment that fit on the business side of Figure 11.3. Next we will look at the IT side by looking at IS architecture, centralization and decentralization in deploying IT, business-driven IT infrastructure, and outsourcing of IT-related activities.

Information System Architecture

The term *architecture,* which was explained in Chapter 2 as one of five perspectives for thinking about a specific system, is also used in IS planning. A firm's **information system architecture** is the basic blueprint showing how the firm's data processing systems, telecommunications networks, and data are integrated. A firm's information architecture is a highly summarized answer to the following questions:

- What data are collected?
- Where and how are the data collected?
- How are the data to be transmitted?
- Where are the data stored?
- What applications use the data, and how are these applications related as an overall system?

Just creating an organized list of IT assets sometimes shows major problems in IS architecture. For example, in 1993 General Motors had 27 e-mail systems, ten word processing programs, five spreadsheet programs, and seven business graphics packages. GM's director of desktop computing said, "We probably had one of every system that had ever been made." GM decided to standardize to eliminate this low-value variability. Three years later every PC user at GM worked on the same configuration: Windows 3.1, Microsoft Office, and Lotus Notes running on high-end Compaq PCs. No software outside the standard configuration was even allowed on the computers without special approval.[17]

Legacy systems are a part of IS architecture that sometimes make it more difficult to improve the work systems they support. **Legacy systems** are old, and often technically obsolete, information systems that still exist because they perform essential data processing such as accounting and customer billing in many firms. Many of these systems were initially built in the 1960s or 1970s and still use programming methods that are 20 years out of date even after numerous enhancements. The many changes to these systems are often poorly documented, and the people who made the changes have often left for other jobs. The difficulty of operating and upgrading these older information systems is one of the reasons companies such as Owens Corning have adopted SAP and other enterprise software packages. (See the opening case.) Unfortunately for IS staffs, obtaining funding to overhaul technically fragile legacy systems is often difficult because the benefits are indirect and largely related to greater flexibility and reliability in the future. Other large projects that could use the same funds often generate greater immediate business benefits. Legacy systems frequently remain in place until a business-driven rationale emerges, such as the need for enterprise-wide integration, the need to serve customers more effectively, or the risk of system failure due to Y2K problems.

The choice of a computing platform is another important part of IS architecture. The term **platform** is used to describe the basic type of computer, operating system, and network that an information system uses. The choice of a platform has long-term ramifications because most application software is programmed for a particular platform. This implies, for example, that software written to operate on servers that use the Windows NT operating system will have to be reprogrammed and retested before they can run on servers that use the UNIX operating system. Sharing information and applications while using different platforms is often a waste of resources and can become a nightmare if incompatibilities are serious. Consolidating from multiple platforms to a unified platform to make the infrastructure more efficient is rarely a prized project. The benefits are in the background and are often less visible to users than direct benefits from application enhancements. Consequently, the choice of a platform for large shared applications has long-term implications and should be considered carefully.

Although IS architecture may seem like a technical issue, it should reflect a strategic, managerial view of how an organization operates. IS architecture may be a constraint to a firm's business strategy because it determines the practical range of business and product strategies the firm can employ. Consider a bank whose new business strategy is based on combining checking accounts, savings accounts, credit cards, and loans into a simplified account relationship. This strategy can be used only if customer IDs for each of the separate products can be grouped into single combined accounts. In addition, the bank can provide 24-hour response to customer queries only if all the data is in an immediately accessible database rather than on paper files at branches. The wrong IS architecture would doom the business strategy.

Centralization Versus Decentralization

A primary issue in any IS architecture is the balance between centralization and decentralization. As with many other organizational endeavors, overcentralization results in overly rigid systems that cannot handle local variations. Similarly, excessive decentralization creates systems that may solve local problems but may not conform or interface well enough to solve problems that cross departments. Decisions involving centralization and decentralization often hinge on debates about efficiency (using the least resources to produce a given output) and effectiveness (producing the right output). Centralization is often more efficient because it eliminates redundant resources and effort. Assuming that decentralization is technically feasible, it is often more effective because it allows people to make the right decisions for their own local situations. Key factors in centralization and decentralization include location of the hardware, location of data, standards, and ownership and management control (see Table 11.3).

TABLE 11.3 **Centralization Versus Decentralization**

	Highly centralized	Intermediate	Highly decentralized
Hardware configuration	Central computer, remote terminals	Distributed network linking local data centers	Independent local data centers, personal computers
Data location	Centralized database	Central database plus local databases	Local databases
Hardware and software choices	Central decisions	Central guidelines, local choices	Local choices
Ownership and control	Central information systems group	Central services, system ownership by user departments	User departments
Organizational affiliation of IS staff	Central IS group	Highly technical IS roles affiliated with central group, less technical roles in user organization	Most IS roles affiliated with user organization (except infrastructure and planning)

Location of Hardware and Data

Computer hardware owned and managed within a corporation can exist at any or all of the following levels: corporate headquarters, regional processing centers, site processing centers (for individual factories or offices), department processors, work group processors, and individual work stations. The most centralized approach is to have all of the computers in a centralized computer center, with telecommunications links to terminals at other locations. The least centralized approach is to provide employees with their own personal computers and allow them to perform and control their own data processing. Figure 11.4 shows how most large firms use intermediate configurations that combine a centralized data processing facility with local data processing centers and networked personal computers for individuals or offices. Centralized locations process data that must be shared across the company or that can be processed most efficiently in a centralized way. Local data centers process data that should be shared within a division or geographical location but are not needed elsewhere in the company. The personal computers are used for individual data processing.

In distributing data, the most centralized approach is to have all the data at a centralized location; the least centralized is to allow individuals to maintain their own data. Intermediate configurations employ a centralized database for data that must be accessed across the organization, plus local or individual databases for data pertinent only to an office or individual. Centralized databases are used for corporate accounting, corporate inventories, and other data that must be controlled at the corporate level and accessed broadly. Firms frequently compromise between convenience and accessibility of local data and control and maintainability of centralized data. They do this through various forms of database replication or through downloads that make locally relevant data available to local users even if transactions update the central database. Many large companies have extensive telecommunications networks for moving data to and from centralized databases.

Standards, Ownership, and Guidelines for Action

Establishing corporate standards is essential for efficiency, even if the hardware and data are physically decentralized. Corporate standards determine which hardware and software can be purchased and what procedures to use in deploying the information systems. Standards for hardware and data make it easier for people to share their work. They are also

Figure 11.4
Intermediate degree of distributed processing

Most large firms use intermediate degrees of centralized data processing, with local data processing centers and personal computers for individuals or offices.

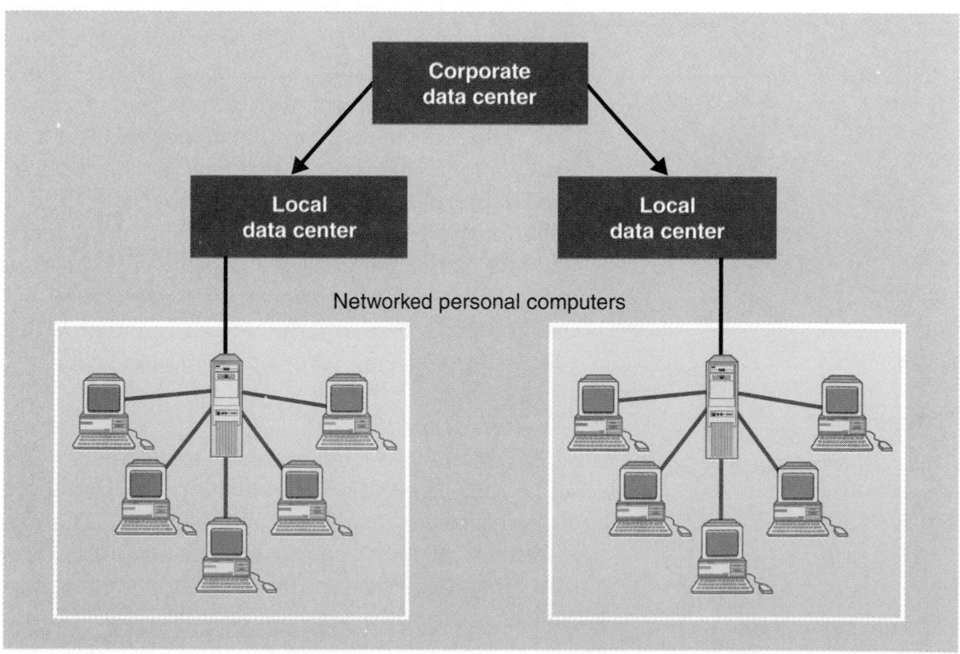

necessary for economies of scale in purchasing equipment, training personnel, and using data. Without standards, individuals and departments can make independent decisions about which hardware and software to buy, often resulting in incompatible systems. The existence of incompatible systems may not affect individuals doing their own individual work but is grossly inefficient when data or models must be shared by many users. Having standards doesn't guarantee that systems will be consistent but does increase the chances of realizing economies of scale.

Regardless of where hardware and data reside, the question of ownership is always an issue. For example, who should own a division's sales forecasting system: the marketing department or the IS department? With a centralized approach, a central IS department owns and controls all information systems and a request to change a system would go to that department. A decentralized approach would say whatever group uses the information system should own it. Permitting decentralized ownership of information systems leads to greater responsiveness to change requests but may result in systems that are not well controlled. For example, a company using a decentralized approach found that one of its important information systems had absolutely no documentation. The developer, a flamboyant individual who liked helping users but hated writing documentation, had left the company. Had the system been under central control, it probably would be documented but might not have had as many of the features users wanted.

Whether or not a central IS group owns the information systems, there are still important reasons to have general guidelines for building and administering these systems. At minimum such guidelines reduce the organizational inefficiency of learning how to install, interface, and manage unnecessary variations on the same basic technologies. But the guidelines can go further by talking about the way the organization's systems should be justified and built. For example, the guidelines might say that a formal cost/benefit analysis must be done for any system beyond a particular size, or that data should be captured when first created. To support interoperability even when different types of hardware or software are used, the guidelines can cover things such as eliminating redundant data definitions, defining uniform transmission standards, separating data definitions from the programs that use them, and establishing uniform programming environments.

Issues concerning location, ownership, and control of resources are by no means unique to information systems. Questions about centralization versus decentralization occur in all business functions whether or not computerized systems are involved. In sales, the question is often whether several product divisions will share the same sales force or distribution channels. In production, it is whether product divisions will share factories and research labs. In each case, the decision incorporates the company's history, economies of scale from centralization, advantages of focus from decentralization, and other personal, political, and economic issues.

Issues about centralization or decentralization are often even more complicated for information systems because the technology itself adds a layer of professional expertise, details, inertia, and confusion. Each approach has its advantages. Centralization may enhance the IS department's effectiveness and long-term potential. It also increases the ability to maintain standards for quality, consistency, and maintainability. Decentralization may avoid bureaucracy and lengthy system development backlogs. Decentralization also makes it possible to experiment locally and grow in smaller increments, and to continue processing work even when one computer is down.

Position of the IS Staff

The division of labor between user and IS departments is based on organizational history and practical tradeoffs. With a highly centralized approach, the programmers, analysts, and support personnel are in the IS department. This maintains professional affiliations with systems activities and may lead to greater professional depth in their discipline. But it may also separate them from the users and reduce responsiveness to user needs. In a decentralized approach, the programmers and analysts are in the user department, which tends to generate greater loyalty to the user department and greater understanding of the application. It also reduces their affiliation with other professionals in their field, however, and may ultimately reduce their technical depth. Table 11.4 lists some of the commonly cited differences between IS professionals and typical IS users. Like most generalizations about groups of people, there are many counterexamples to the differences listed in the table. No individual should be treated on the basis of a stereotype.

The balance between centralizing and decentralizing the IS staff may affect the success of information systems. With too much centralization, users often feel that they don't receive enough support and that the IS department doesn't appreciate their needs. With too much decentralization, servicing of small requests may be effective but there is less of the centralized focus and planning needed to achieve economies of scale and to develop strategic information systems.

Describing a Business-Driven IT Infrastructure

A firm's **IT infrastructure** is the shared technical and human resources used to build, operate, and maintain information systems included in the firm's IS architecture. Figure 11.5 summarizes the elements of the IT infrastructure that supports a firm's value chain. IT infrastructure is a long-term investment shared across various departments and applications. Operating a firm's IT infrastructure often consumes more than 50% of its IT budget.[18] Any feasible IS plan must include provisions for operating and upgrading this infrastructure to support changing business needs.

Because many aspects of IT infrastructure involve technical issues that seem far removed from business issues, it is often difficult for executives to participate effectively in discussions about the long-term strategy for IT infrastructure. A promising method proposed by Broadbent and Weill is called the **management by maxim** framework, which begins by considering "the company's strategic context, synergies among business units, and the extent to which a firm wants to exploit those synergies. The strategic statements or business maxims are derived from the strategic context and identify the firm's future direction. Starting from the business maxims, business and IT managers together identify IT maxims, which express the company's need to access and use information and the technology resources required."[19]

Table 11.5 illustrates this approach by looking at a hypothetical chain of hardware stores and identifying its business maxims in six aspects of business strategy along with related IT maxims in five aspects of IT strategy. If the business maxims were to change, the IT maxims would change accordingly. For example, if this chain saw no synergies through analyzing the transaction information from its various stores, it would not put as much effort into the overnight consolidation and data mining efforts. Similarly, if the stores themselves would benefit from closer cooperation, the IT maxims might say something about using IT to improve store-to-store communication.

TABLE 11.4 Commonly Cited Differences between IS Professionals and Typical Users

Type of difference	Tendency of IS staff	Tendency of user department
Professional orientation	Allegiance to profession	Allegiance to firm
Language	Language of computers	Language of business
Interests and recognition	Technical elegance	Practical solutions produced quickly
Project goals	Long-term maintenance	Practical solutions produced quickly
Work style and content	Analytical work related to computers	Work through people

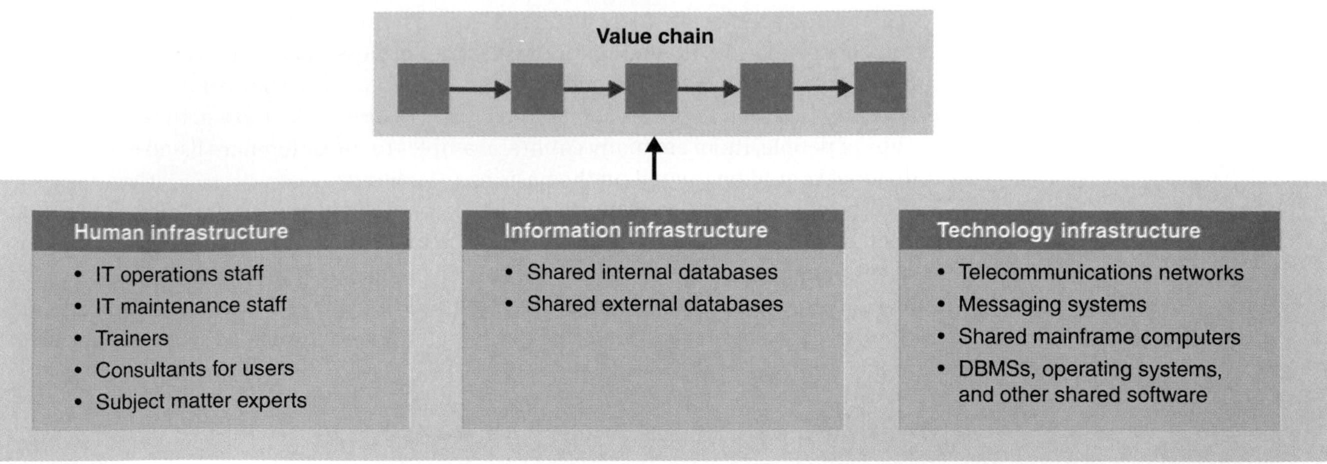

Figure 11.5
Typical elements of IT infrastructure

IT infrastructure that supports the value chain includes human infrastructure, shared databases, and technology infrastructure.

Firms that have performed this type of analysis, regardless of whether they called it management by maxim, have arrived at vastly different IT strategies based on their business needs. Amcor, a large Australian firm that makes packaging, corrugated boxes, cans, and plastic containers chose a highly decentralized IT strategy because its various business units had unique cultures and rarely shared customers. Its IT strategy was to focus on local accountability and minimize central mandates. In contrast, the auto and motorcycle manufacturer Honda saw itself as "a global network with 83 production facilities in 39 countries that supply Honda products" around the world. It enhanced its communications network to improve its parts system for all products.[20] In another case, the health care supplier Johnson & Johnson saw that it needed to create stronger partnerships with its large customers because the health care industry was changing. Its customers wanted to deal with a limited number of vendors, but J&J was organized as over 100 separate product divisions, each of which dealt with customers through its own marketing and sales arms. J&J's IT infrastructure in 1995 was not designed to support a unified external view of J&J due to inconsistent connectivity and data standards across the divisions. These inconsistencies made it more difficult to exchange data and generated a great deal of duplicated effort. J&J decided to move toward greater connectivity and data standardization through common financial, purchasing, order entry, accounts payable, payroll, and human resources systems.[21]

Outsourcing

Another key issue in attaining strategic alignment is the extent to which IT infrastructure, programming, training, support, and other IT-related activities will be outsourced. When used in general conversation, the term **outsourcing** denotes any product or service that is purchased from another firm. For example, all major auto companies outsource manufacturing of many components. Likewise, many firms outsource their cafeteria to food service companies. In general, companies outsource the products and services they do not want to or are unable to produce themselves. Competitive pressures of the 1990s have increased outsourcing across all industries by forcing companies to focus on the unique functions they do best, such as manufacturing at the lowest cost or providing excellent customer service in retailing.

Outsourcing of computer hardware, telecommunications services, and systems software such as operating systems and DBMSs is a long-standing practice in IS departments. These departments also purchase end-user software such as spreadsheets and word

TABLE 11.5 Business and IT Maxims for a Hypothetical Chain of Hardware Stores

Business maxims	IT maxims
Cost focus • Low cost retailer for consumers.	*Expectations for IT investments* • IT investments provide common infrastructure and systems to minimize these concerns for the local stores.
Value differentiation perceived by customer • Low prices supported by reasonably good service. • Reliable availability of medium to low priced hardware and building supplies. • Major distributor for particular suppliers and brands.	*Data access and use* • All sales data available to central purchasing nightly. • Local access to local customer and prospect list, plus corporate access for data mining and analysis.
Flexibility and agility • Stay focused in hardware market, expand slowly into related products for kitchens and gardens. • Detect and exploit trendy new products.	*Hardware and software resources* • Support consistent, automatic processing of repetitive transactions. • Standardize on minimum number of platforms to minimize cost of support.
Growth • Gradually expand across the United States and Canada. • Grow revenues using targeted discounts to bring back customers for repeat purchases.	*Communications capabilities and services* • Support nightly consolidation of daily sales transactions to help identify product and pricing trends. • Support EDI to minimize transaction costs.
Human resources • Staff stores with people who enjoy home remodeling projects. • Maintain pleasant work environment but assume high turnover in store personnel due to relatively low salaries.	*Architecture and standards approach* • Control IT architecture and standards centrally to minimize cost.
Management orientation • Maximize ability of local stores to satisfy needs of local markets. • Support stores with standardized systems and information, but permit local autonomy in decision making. • Share information about hot products and trends.	

processors because there is no reason to reinvent tools a software company specializing in these products can provide much more cheaply. Although these examples involve products and services bought from other firms, this is not the type of IT outsourcing that has become controversial.

The controversial side of IT outsourcing involves hiring outside organizations to perform functions often performed by IS departments. Business application software was one of the first areas for this type of outsourcing, with many firms purchasing commercial systems for common functions such as keeping track of inventory, purchase orders, and customer orders. Buying commercially available application software makes sense when there is nothing unique or competitively significant about the way the firm wants to perform the business function. Firms attempting to attain competitive advantage from a unique way of performing a business function typically cannot buy readily available commercial software to support the function because any other company could also buy it.

Maintaining computer centers and telecommunications networks is another common area for outsourcing. Companies deciding whether to do this look for reasons they can perform these functions more efficiently and effectively than firms whose main business is in this area. By performing these functions for many customers, outsourcing vendors may have more experience doing the work and greater ability to negotiate quantity discounts with hardware and software vendors. They may also be more able to pick up the slack if key staff members at a particular site leave.

Taken to an extreme, outsourcing of IT activities would mean having a very small IS department limited to developing IS plans and negotiating with outsourcing vendors.

This is risky due to the reliance on an outside firm to perform essential functions including building and maintaining application systems. Because the outsourcing vendor would have so much of the knowledge about the company's information systems, the company might end up lacking the staff and vision needed to produce competitively significant systems. If the outsourcing vendor developed business problems of its own, the company's basic data processing could be thrown into chaos. Even without a calamity, a ten-year outsourcing contract might spawn other problems by not anticipating evolving business requirements.

There is a common belief that IT operations should be outsourced wherever they do not provide strategic advantage, but several studies questioned this belief because it led to problems and disappointments in the majority of the cases observed. Outsourcing vendors were not necessarily more efficient than internal IS groups, which could often achieve similar results. Five- or ten-year contracts were signed in situations in which business conditions and availability of technology could not be predicted more than a few years in advance. Outsourcing vendors had their own separate profit motives and business issues. Companies considering outsourcing should have been more skeptical of slogans describing outsourcing vendors as "partners" and should have written outsourcing contracts with greater care. Regardless of whether an IT operation was strategic or a commodity, a company's overarching objective should have focused on maximizing flexibility and control so that it could pursue the best options as conditions changed. The overall conclusion was that managers should not make a one-time decision to outsource, but should structure outsourcing contracts in a way that permitted competition to provide the best IT services over time.[22,23]

International Issues

A final aspect of strategic alignment involves international issues that have become more important as business has become more international and as more information systems cross national boundaries. Some of these systems are internal management and control systems of multinational companies. Others are links between companies in one country and customers, suppliers, and agents elsewhere. The significance of these systems is growing because they provide a way to reduce the limitations of time and geography.

International issues start with a basic fact that things just work differently in different places, especially when different histories, cultures, and languages are involved. These differences appear at many different levels and make it necessary to retest basic assumptions about how things work. Shirts may button differently, paper may be a different size, doors may open differently, people may drive on the other side of the street, and, as shown in Figure 11.6, the power cord of a computer made in one country many not fit another country's wall sockets.

Technical incompatibilities in hardware, software, and data standards often make it difficult to transfer or share software between countries. An example is the international differences in the formats of numbers and dates. The date 6/8/99 means June 8, 1999, in the United States and August 6, 1999, in Europe. The same date would be written 99/6/8 in Japan. This simple discrepancy necessitated changes in hundreds of programs when the software company Consilium first installed its manufacturing system at Siemens in Germany. Companies in Italy face a different incompatibility problem with the European Union's conversion to the euro. Italy's national currency, the lira, is expressed in whole numbers only. Programs written for the lira may therefore use integer fields for monetary

Figure 11.6
American and French electrical plugs

American appliances need special adapters in order to use electrical outlets in France and other countries around the world.

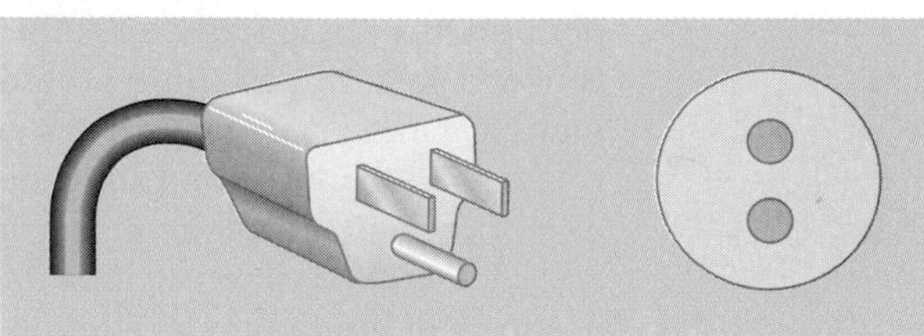

amounts instead of decimal fields. The move to the euro will require testing or revision of all those programs.[24]

Social and political issues cause many types of confusion and inefficiency in systems used in more than one country. These problems start with incomplete personal communication caused by speaking different languages. At a deeper level, differences in laws, work rules, accounting practices, and general expectations of workers may make information system practices from one country impractical in another. For example, labor agreements in different countries might differ on whether information can be recorded that indicates how well or how quickly a particular worker performed a particular work step. National culture is another issue. For example, red is generally a symbol of good luck in China, but writing text in red might be confusing in China because it is often reserved for notes ending a romantic relationship. Similarly, when DHL set up new account numbers in China, none could begin with four because the spoken word sounds a lot like the word for death.[25]

Telecommunications is an area where regulation, economics, and quality are especially intertwined. In the United States, telecommunications is highly competitive and there is a tradition of high quality, customer orientation, and rapid service. In many other countries telecommunications is controlled by government monopolies that are less customer-oriented and may take a year or more to install a telephone. A British bank had to write off $10 million in the mid-1980s when it tried to move some of its transaction processing to Paris using packet switching over a leased telephone line. According to the French government telephone monopoly, sending packets via a private network was illegal and the system had to be scrapped.[26] Reliability was an issue when Kentucky Fried Chicken wanted to operate its corporate distribution system in Mexico. They could not use the system because the phone lines available through Telmex could not provide enough reliability in transferring information on sales from individual stores to KFC headquarters.[27]

Economic issues in international information systems are obvious to any international traveler who has noticed how much more a phone call costs when it goes from Europe to the United States rather than in the reverse direction. A number of "callback services" have been formed just to exploit this imbalance. Callers from Europe can dial a U.S. number and hang up. This triggers a telephone switch that returns the call and provides a U.S. dial tone. The caller from Europe enters the desired telephone number and is connected. Because the bill at the end of the month is calculated at U.S. rates, it may be 50% to 70% lower than it would have been at European rates. Needless to say, many national telephone monopolies are not pleased with these callback systems. The Kenyan government took out newspaper ads warning callback users they could be prosecuted. Japanese telephone companies pressed regulators for a ban on this service.[28] In 1997 France and Germany, which impose value added taxes of 21% and 15% on all goods and services including telephone calls, announced plans to start imposing sales taxes on callback services. The U.S.–based callback services doubted the taxes could be collected because the service would be occurring in the U.S.[29]

A final international issue is the laws some countries have passed concerning the handling of data linked to individuals, especially in transborder data flows. For example, in 1989 France temporarily stopped Fiat from transferring its French personnel records to Italy because privacy laws there did not meet French regulations.[30] More recently, the European Union (the United Kingdom, France, Germany, Spain, Italy, among others) adopted a privacy policy for trade throughout Europe. Starting in late 1998, European citizens are guaranteed rights including the right of access to their data, the right to know where the data originated, the right to have inaccurate data rectified, and the right to withhold permission to use their data for direct marketing. Article 25 of the directive prohibits European countries from sending personal information to countries that do not maintain adequate privacy standards. Because the United States has few privacy guarantees of the types covered, direct marketers in the United States may not be able to access personal data about European citizens. If this were enforced, U.S. companies selling to European customers would be prohibited from using direct marketing practices that are legal in the United States. At minimum, the new European protections may force international firms to reconsider their data collection policies. A case illustrating the issues here involved Sweden's demand that American Airlines delete from its data collection systems all health and medical information about Swedish passengers unless they explicitly consented to retention of the data.[31] Any company wishing to transmit personnel records, credit card data, and customer data across national borders must take into account the laws of all nations that might be affected.

Reality Check

STRATEGIC ISSUES FOR IS PLANNING

This section discussed a series of strategic issues for IS planning.

1. Consider any major purchase you or your family have made in the last few years. For example, it could be a car, a computer, or a college education. Explain the extent to which that purchase did or didn't fit into a strategic plan.
2. Explain why strategic planning is or isn't relevant for the decision you identified.

SELECTING SYSTEMS TO INVEST IN

The decision to build an information system is an investment decision, as is the decision about which capabilities to include in the system. The strategic issues from the previous section provide guidelines for these investments, such as building systems that are consistent with the business plan, the architecture, and the company's approach to distributed processing and outsourcing.

Although these ideas provide some guidance and eliminate some options, there is no ideal formula for deciding which systems and capabilities to invest in. Many IS departments could double and still not have enough people to do all the work users would like. In practice, many IS departments allocate a percentage of their available time to different project categories, such as enhancements, major new systems, and user support. But within each category they still need to decide which systems to work on and what capabilities to provide. Cost/benefit analysis may help with these decisions.

Cost/Benefit Analysis

Cost/benefit analysis is the process of evaluating proposed systems by comparing estimated benefits and costs. Cost/benefit analysis should occur only after the proposed system has been analyzed and designed using a method like the WCA method, which clarifies key issues in areas such as system architecture and performance.

Cost/benefit analysis requires that estimated benefits and costs be expressed in dollars. If the benefits are substantially greater than the costs, the project may be worth pursuing. Cost/benefit analysis can be used in several ways. First, it is a planning tool to help in deciding whether the new system is a worthwhile investment compared to other uses of resources. In addition, it may be used as an auditing tool to determine whether a project actually met its goals.

Although the idea of comparing estimated costs and benefits sounds logical, it has limitations. It is most appropriate when the system's purpose is improving efficiency. If its purpose is providing management information, transforming the organization, or upgrading the IS infrastructure, predicting either the benefits or the costs is more difficult. Furthermore, because cost/benefit analyses are usually done to justify someone's request for resources, the numbers in a cost/benefit study may be biased and may ignore or understate foreseeable project risks. Key issues for cost/benefit analysis include the difference between tangible and intangible benefits, the tendency to underestimate costs, and the effect of the timing of costs and benefits.

Tangible and Intangible Benefits

Benefits are often classified as either tangible or intangible. **Tangible benefits** can be measured directly to evaluate system performance. Examples include reduction in the time per phone call, improvement in response time, reduction in the amount of disk storage used, and reduction in the error rate. Notice that tangible benefits may or may not be measured in monetary terms. However, using a cost/benefit framework requires translating performance improvements into monetary terms so that benefits and costs can be compared.

Intangible benefits affect performance but are difficult to measure because they refer to comparatively vague concepts. Examples of intangible benefits include better coordination, better supervision, better morale, better information for decision making, ability to evaluate more alternatives, ability to respond quickly to unexpected situations, and organizational learning. Although all of these goals are worthwhile, it is often difficult to measure how well they have been accomplished. Even if it is possible to measure intangible benefits, it is difficult to express them in monetary terms that can be compared with costs. All too often, project costs are tangible and benefits are intangible. While hard to quantify, intangible benefits are important and shouldn't be ignored. Many of the benefits of information systems are intangible.

Tendency to Understate Costs

A common flaw of cost/benefit studies is the understatement of costs. Careless cost analysis often includes the cost of hardware, software, and programming but omits other costs related to problem analysis, training, and ongoing operation of the system. Table 11.6 separates some of the more apparent costs of information systems from some of the costs that are easy to overlook. Notice how the time and effort of user management and staff is easy to overlook in each of the four phases of an information system (see Figure 1.1). This is

TABLE 11.6 **IS Costs That Are Easy to Overlook**

Cost/benefit analysis is often used to justify system projects. Effective use of this technique depends on estimating both the obvious costs and the costs that may be hidden.

Phase	Costs easily assigned to a project	Costs that are easy to overlook
Initiation	• Salary and overhead for IS staff • Cost of communication and travel related to the project • Consulting fees (if any)	• Salary and overhead of user staff and management involved in the analysis • Other work that is displaced in favor of work on the project
Development	• Salary and overhead for IS staff • Equipment purchase and installation costs • Purchase (if any) of system or application software	• Salary and overhead of user staff and management involved in the analysis • Site modifications such as wiring offices
Implementation	• Salary and overhead for IS staff and trainers • Cost of communication and travel related to the project	• Salary and overhead of user staff and management involved in the implementation • Disruption of work during implementation process • Salary of users during training and initial usage
Operation and maintenance	• Salary and overhead for IS staff • Software license fees (if any) • Depreciation of hardware	• Salary and overhead of user staff and management involved with system maintenance activities

because their salary and overhead is already accounted for in the work they normally do. For many systems, training, implementation, and troubleshooting absorb so much time and effort that their cost far exceeds the original cost of the hardware and software.

Timing of Costs and Benefits

The cost and benefit streams from an information system project occur at different times. The timing of costs and benefits in the customer service system in Figure 11.7 is typical in that many costs precede any benefits. The shape of the cost curve reflects different staffing levels at different points in the system building process. The figure shows that the benefits start in month 6 and increase to a high level when implementation is complete. If these estimated cost and benefit streams actually are accomplished, the cumulative net benefit of having the system will become positive during month 11. If development takes longer than planned or if the benefits accrue more slowly than originally anticipated, net benefit becomes positive later.

The cost of any information system includes the cost of buying the hardware, building or buying the software, and the cost of ownership. The **total cost of ownership (TCO)** includes the cost of implementing, operating, and maintaining it. For many information systems, the cost of only the implementation is much higher than the cost of the original development because training and conversion require work by all of the users. Total cost of ownership is therefore a key performance variable for any information system.

Risks

A surprisingly large percentage of information system projects either fail to attain their goals or attain them only after the expenditure of more time and effort than was initially anticipated. Common disappointments include:

- Desired benefits are not achieved.
- The project is completed late or over budget.
- The system's technical performance is inadequate.
- There is lack of user acceptance.
- Shifting priorities reduce the project's importance.

Because information system development is a risky endeavor, the risks should be considered in some way while deciding which projects to start. To anticipate the risks inherent in a proposed system, it is possible to compare the proposed system to a situation with minimum risk:

> The system is to be produced by a single implementor for a single user, who anticipates using the system for a very definite purpose that can be specified in advance with great precision. Including the person who will maintain it, all other parties affected by the system understand and accept in advance its impact on them. All parties have prior experience with this type of system, the system receives adequate support, and its technical design is feasible and cost effective.

The further a system development situation deviates from this ideal situation, the greater are the inherent risks. This does not mean that only low-risk systems should be developed. Companies developing only low-risk information systems are not learning much in this area and are probably attaining lower benefits than they might. The appropriate use of comparisons with this ideal situation is to identify areas of risk and then determine implementation strategies for managing those risks.

Financial Comparisons

IS steering committees often select among proposed IS projects by reviewing formal proposals and deciding how to allocate resources among them. The proposals usually include a formal justification stated in terms of the likely monetary costs and benefits. Expressing costs and benefits in dollars provides a useful way to compare and rank projects, even though dollar benefits are hard to estimate for projects involving major changes of business processes or IS infrastructure. Going through a formal justification process also eliminates

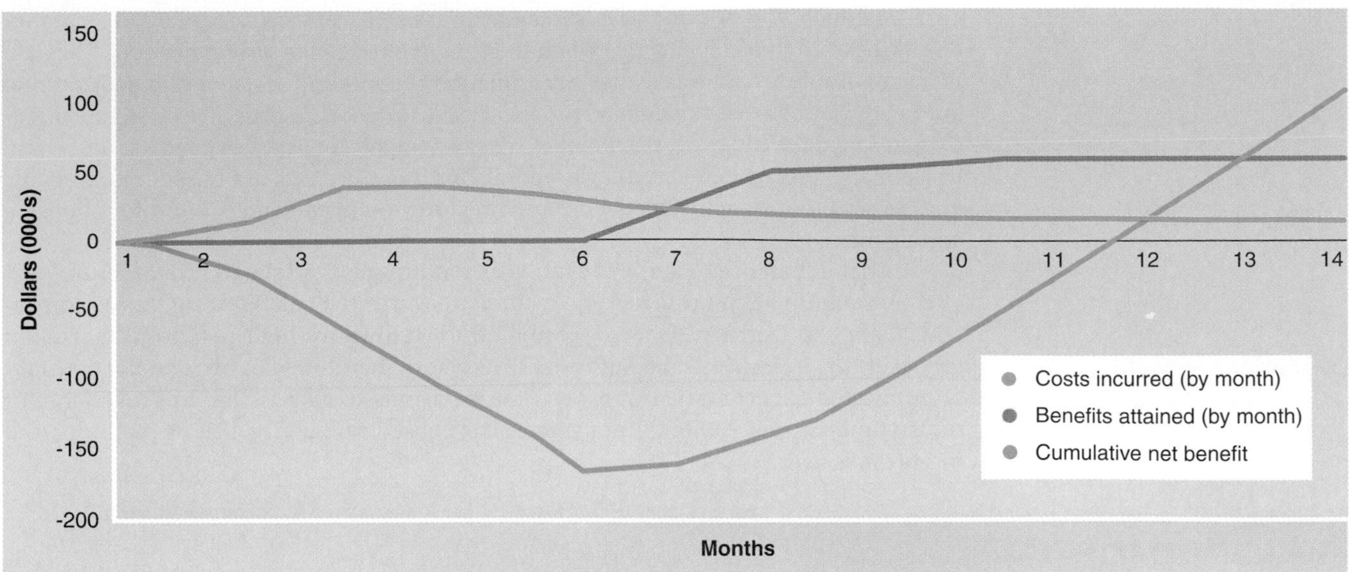

Figure 11.7
Estimated benefit and cost streams

In these estimated costs and benefits of a new system, costs are incurred before benefits are attained. The cumulative net benefit (total benefits minus total costs) is negative until month 11 even though the benefits start in month 6. Monthly costs decrease after the system goes into operation but continue for the life of the system. This estimate includes minimal maintenance. Costs will be higher if more maintenance is needed.

some projects because their sponsors cannot devise a plausible justification that satisfies cost/benefit criteria.

Common criteria used for comparing and ranking projects include net present value, internal rate of return, and payback. These three measures take into account the cost and benefit streams that go into a cost/benefit analysis. All three are thoroughly explained in introductory finance courses.

Net present value (NPV) is the estimated amount of money the project is worth to the firm, taking into account the cost and benefit streams and the time value of money. The ratio between the value of a dollar today and a dollar a year from now is reflected by the *discount rate* applied. NPV is calculated by taking the difference between benefits and costs in each period, discounting to the present, and adding up the resulting terms. Given two otherwise equally beneficial projects, one would prefer the project with the higher NPV. However, NPV favors larger projects (with higher benefits and costs). NPV of mediocre large projects can exceed that of very good small ones.

Internal rate of return (IRR) is a way to convert NPV into a form that makes projects more directly comparable. A project's internal rate of return is the interest rate one would have to receive on its cost stream to produce the same ultimate return as the project. IRR is computed by treating the discount rate in the NPV formula as a variable, setting NPV to 0, and solving for the discount rate. Many organizations use IRR as a *hurdle rate* by funding only projects whose IRR is at least 12% or 15%.

Payback period is the time until the project's net benefit becomes positive. Given two projects with equivalent long-term benefits, the one with a shorter payback period is preferred. A shorter payback period reduces the risk that the project will miss its targets. The division head of a large bank that often missed system deadlines decided to use payback as a primary criterion for selecting projects. Until system development performance improved, no systems with a payback of over 6 months would be approved. The division could not even consider very large projects involving significant change, but its development efforts were brought under control.

Although NPV, IRR, and payback can serve as useful controls on resource allocations, use of these criteria is ineffective when they are applied to the wrong projects. They are most applicable for projects with easily estimated benefits and costs, such as projects that automate part of a well-understood process. Because major changes often generate unanticipated benefits and costs, the financial return on highly innovative systems is often hard to estimate. Managers realize that proposals for these projects are based on unreliable guesses and that purely financial criteria may provide insufficient insight for choosing among them.

Strict adherence to guidelines such as requiring an estimated rate of return over 15% may eliminate innovative projects that are worth the risk. Viewing this as a problem, American Express allocated $5 million for innovative high-risk projects. One of the resulting projects was the Authorizer's Assistant mentioned in Chapter 9. This highly publicized expert system improved the decisions of agents who approve large or unusual purchases. Although not undertaken based on NPV or IRR, it paid for itself many times over.[32]

Reality Check

COST/BENEFIT ANALYSIS

This section discussed costs, benefits, and risks, and financial criteria that can be used to compare projects.

1. Consider any major purchase you or your family have made in the last few years, such as a car, a computer, or a college education. Identify the costs, benefits, and risks of several alternatives you considered or should have considered.
2. Explain why cost/benefit analysis would or wouldn't have been helpful in that decision.

PROJECT MANAGEMENT ISSUES

A project plan outlines initial answers to the *who, what, how,* and *when* questions summarized in Table 11.2. Answering these questions before starting a project helps organize the work and helps keep it on track. A project plan is especially important in IS projects because unanticipated technical and organizational problems often arise. At minimum, having a plan helps in identifying surprises and evaluating their impact. This section will look at two types of issues related to project plans, division of labor between the IS department and users and challenges of staying on schedule. The next chapter will look at alternative approaches for building information systems.

Division of Labor between the IS Department and Users

There are many ways to allocate IS personnel and responsibilities between the IS department and user departments. Mixed results with projects totally led by IS departments have encouraged giving user departments responsibility for the information systems they use. Even many technical roles for these systems have been moved into user departments.

As an example, Figure 11.8 shows how a food company divides work between the user departments and the IS department. The shaded and unshaded areas in the figure show that jobs closer to the application and user tend to be in the user department, whereas those closer to the machine and technology tend to be in the IS department. The location of jobs shown in Figure 11.8 is actually a change from the way this company operated previously, when programmer-analysts and systems analysts were in the IS department. These jobs were moved into the user departments to increase responsiveness to user needs.

However the work is divided, people in both the IS department and the user department should recognize staffing issues mentioned in the section on centralization versus decentralization. These issues make it all the more important to keep projects on schedule.

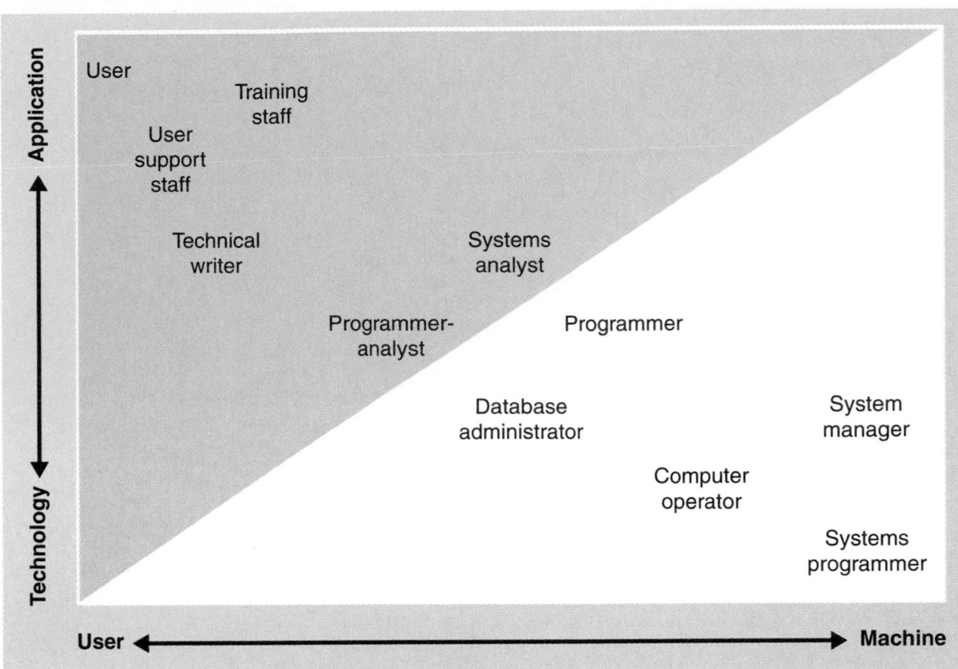

Figure 11.8
Possible boundary between user and IS departments

Many of the jobs in this figure could be in either the user department or the IS department. The shading indicates one possible way to divide the work. Jobs in the shaded area are assigned to the user department, and the others are assigned to the IS department.

Keeping the Project on Schedule

IS projects have an unfortunate tradition of exceeding budgets and missing schedules. Project participants and users can help avoid these problems by appreciating the need for project goals, deliverables, and schedules, and by recognizing some of the special challenges in these projects.

Goals, Deliverables, Schedules

Effective project management requires clear, measurable goals. A **project goal** is a result that should occur if the project is carried out successfully. For example, a project's goal might include staying within a $250,000 budget; project completion by June 30, 1999; average order confirmation time of 15 minutes; and average customer satisfaction rating of 4.7 six months after system installation. The first two goals involve the process of building the information system; the last two involve the organization's operation after system installation. Each goal is specific enough to measure. Without such goals, it is impossible to evaluate project completion or success.

In addition to their own unique goals, IS projects share commonsense goals in the back of any project manager's mind: creating the right system, creating it efficiently, making sure it works properly, and making sure it can be maintained and enhanced. Although these goals might seem obvious, too many system development efforts create the wrong system, create it inefficiently, fail to make sure it works properly, or create it in a form that is difficult to maintain. Systems miss the mark frequently enough that the picture in Figure 11.9 has become a cliché.

The essence of project management is controlling tasks that occur in a particular sequence and have an expected duration. Dividing a project into steps, or subprojects, clarifies what needs to be done and helps the people doing the project understand exactly what they have to do and how their work fits into the overall project. This approach also supports a project management process of monitoring progress and recognizing problems early enough to make mid-course corrections.

Each step in an IS project produces one or more deliverables. **Deliverables** are tangible work products, such as documents, plans, or computer programs. Specifying the deliverables expected with each step is a way to make sure the work is progressing. The steps simply aren't finished until deliverables are completed. In combination, the deliverables in IS projects provide a running history of what was done, when it was done, and why

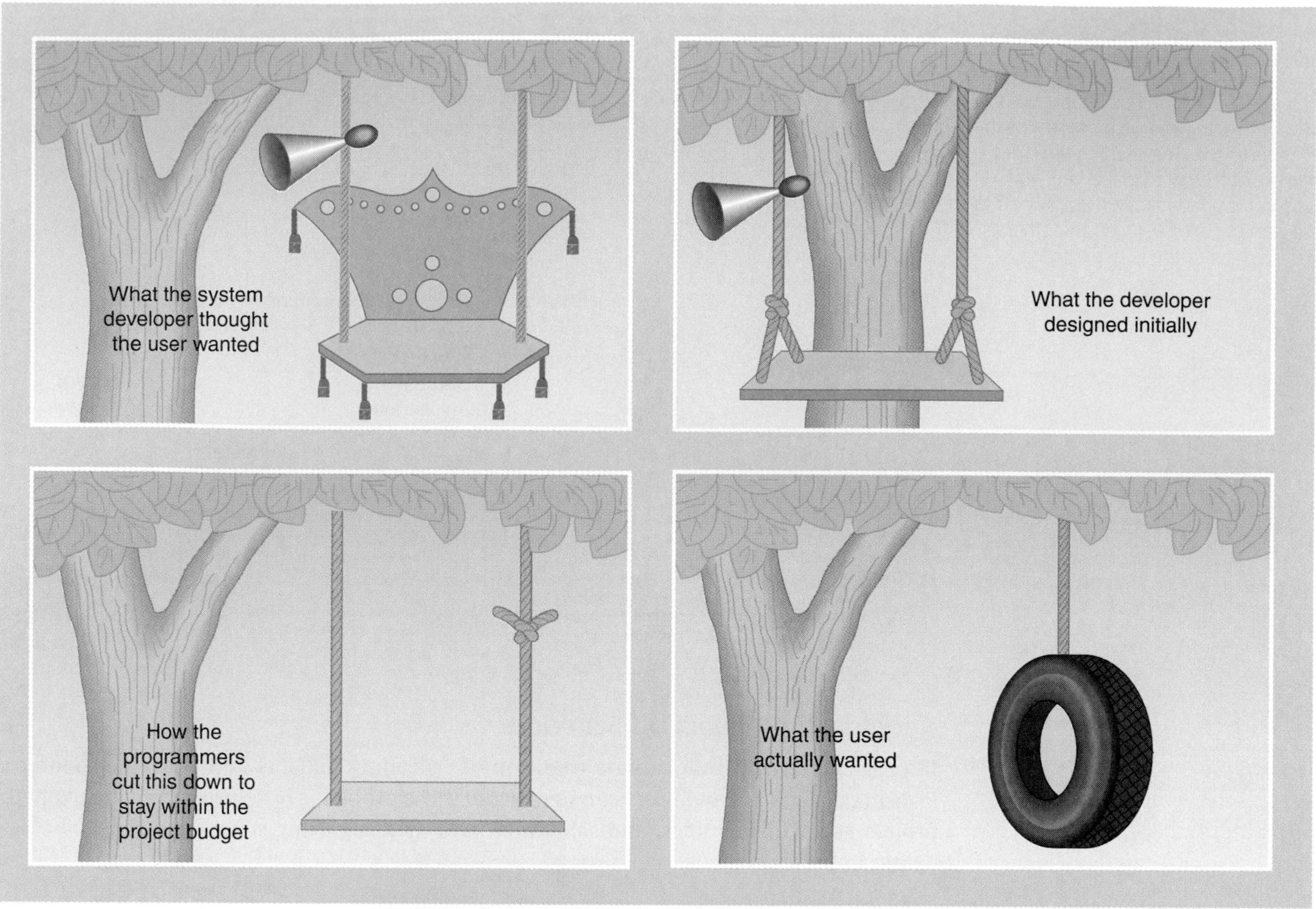

Figure 11.9
Why is it hard to develop the right system?

This figure illustrates a dilemma that has frustrated a generation of system developers.

it was done. The deliverables for each step in a project form the basis for work done in subsequent steps.

The deliverables are produced according to a schedule. A **project schedule** is a terse project description identifying the timing of major steps and who will do the work. Many project management tools have been developed to record and update schedules and track progress versus schedules. Most IS projects use **Gantt charts,** illustrated in Figure 11.10. Gantt charts represent a schedule visually by displaying tasks along with their planned and actual start and completion times and resource requirements. The tasks may or may not overlap in time and may or may not have mutual dependencies. Resource requirements may be stated in terms of person-months, dollars, or time allocations for specific individuals.

Gantt charts are excellent tools for communicating with project groups, identifying problems, and deciding what corrective action to take. A quick glance at a Gantt chart shows whether a project is ahead of or behind schedule. In team meetings, Gantt charts are effective in reviewing progress, identifying problems, and explaining why resources must be shifted. Gantt charts and similar management techniques depend on the quality of schedule data. If the tasks are stated vaguely, it is difficult to say when they are completed. If people are reluctant to report problems or if they say tasks requiring more polishing are "almost complete," the Gantt chart will display and amplify misleading data.

Managing IS projects involves balancing system scope and quality against schedule performance. Participants are often overoptimistic about how long the work will

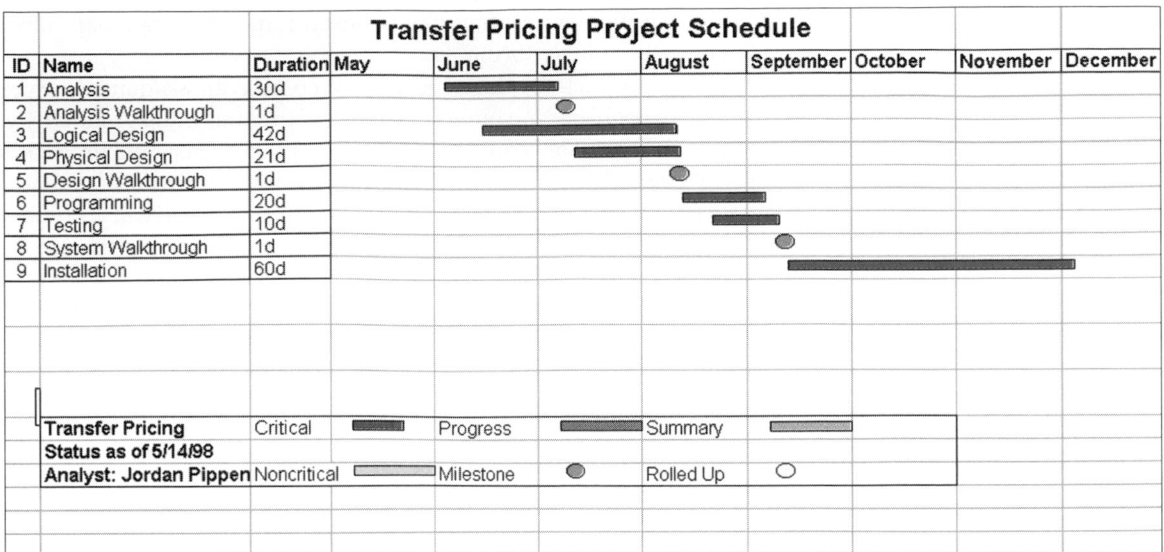

Figure 11.10
Gantt chart

This Gantt chart shows the planned sequence and timing of the different steps in an information system project. Among other things, it shows that physical design will start about halfway through logical design, that programming will start just before a design walkthrough, and that installation will take almost three months.

take, especially because projects often encounter unanticipated complexities. Possible responses to problems and slippages include maintaining the project's scope and schedule, changing the project's scope, changing the schedule, or adding more resources. Maintaining an unrealistic schedule causes morale problems and staff turnover. Reducing the scope may create a feasible project that doesn't solve the user's problem; extending the schedule may cause unacceptable delays. Making up for delays and other problems is often difficult because of the learning required if the staff is expanded. Losing a key individual from an IS project is an especially difficult problem due to the loss of knowledge.

Challenges in Information System Projects

Many of the challenges of project management mirror those of any other form of management: assigning the right people to the right jobs, getting people to do high-quality work, getting people to report their progress realistically, and resolving issues and disputes. Especially important in project-oriented work are estimating project scope and duration, minimizing rework on completed steps, and recovering from delays.

Estimating project scope and duration: It is difficult to estimate the scope and duration of projects for a number of reasons, including uncertain project scope, changes in scope, individual differences in productivity, and the way work is distributed in projects. Because the first phase of an IS project is basically a research project to appreciate the true nature of the problem and to identify a cost-effective solution, project scope is only partially known when the first project estimates are made. Even after this research is finished, important details involving both the business situation and the technical solution may remain poorly understood. Projects also change in scope because the business situation changes or because the users learn that their original understanding of the situation was off the mark. Both of these issues often cause **requirements creep,** continual increases in project scope that make project completion a moving target. A survey of 160

IS professionals found that 80% believed requirements creep "always or frequently" affected schedule performance.[33]

Vast productivity differences between individuals doing IS work cause additional estimating problems. An often cited study of programming productivity factors found that a mediocre team developing software often takes over four times as long as a superior team.[34] Even when the development team is known in advance, such wide productivity differences make it difficult to estimate what any individual will accomplish.

The combination of estimation difficulties, requirements creep, and individual differences often results in difficult practical and ethical dilemmas, starting with the common reluctance to pass on the bad news to the managers. People who are evaluated on the basis of meeting schedules are tempted to underplay problems that endanger schedules, even if this means that the result of the work will be less useful.

Minimizing rework on completed steps: Although some steps of an IS project may be performed simultaneously, many steps build on the outputs of previous steps. Ideally, it should not be necessary to return to previous steps to correct errors and omissions that become apparent later. In reality, each succeeding step tests the feasibility of conclusions from previous steps. Conclusions or outputs from previous steps may have to be changed because more is understood now or because the previous work contained errors. Consequently, there is often some rework even though a project is described as a sequence of successive steps.

Recovering from delays: The most natural unit for estimating the size of system development projects and tracking their progress is the *person-week* or *person-month*. A manager therefore might describe a new application as a 20 person-month project, meaning anything from 1 person for 20 months to 20 people for 1 month. If this 20 person-month project falls behind by the equivalent of 5 person-months, it might seem possible to bring in the equivalent of 5 additional person-months of work to get back on schedule. This tactic often fails for IS projects, even if it might work for other projects.

In the early 1970s, Fred Brooks summarized the difficulty of getting IS projects back on schedule by coining the term the **mythical man-month.**[35] (The more current term *person-month* is used here.) Brooks deemed the man-month (person-month) mythical because it implied people are interchangeable and can be added to a project at any time. In fact, people are interchangeable only in projects that require little knowledge, communication, or learning.

Participants in an IS project must understand its goals and strategy, the plan for doing the work, and the technology used; they must coordinate with other workers. A great deal of effort must go into training and communication. Bringing a new worker into a project requires a knowledgeable worker to spend less time doing productive work while bringing the new worker up to speed. Adding many new workers to an ongoing project can temporarily halt progress. The mythical person-month is therefore one of the reasons it is so important to keep projects on schedule. The amount of communication and coordination time absorbed by large project teams is also a reason to avoid allowing a project to get too large too soon.

Reality Check

PROJECT MANAGEMENT

This section discussed project management issues related to division of labor between users and technical specialists and keeping the project on schedule.

1. Consider a significant project you or your acquaintances have been involved in during the last few years. Identify any important issues related to the division of labor or related to keeping the project on schedule.
2. Explain any special issues that were unrelated to division of labor or keeping the project on schedule.

SYSTEMS ANALYSIS REVISITED

Chapter 2 defined systems analysis as a general process of defining a problem, gathering pertinent information, developing alternative solutions, and choosing among those solutions. By covering many different facets of information systems, this book's main purpose is to help you understand how to analyze these systems from a business professional's viewpoint. This is why tools such as the WCA framework, data flow diagrams, and entity-relationship diagrams were introduced in the first few chapters. This last section looks at the process of gathering information during systems analysis. The discussion is equally applicable to IS planning and to building and maintaining information systems (covered in the next chapter).

Information Sources for Analyzing Systems

Common sources of information for analyzing information systems include interviews, documentation of existing systems, inputs and outputs of existing systems, on-site observation, questionnaires, and examination of similar systems.

- *Interviews:* Interviewing users and their managers is probably the most obvious method for gathering information about a system. After all, who should understand the situation better than the participants?
- *Inputs, outputs, and documentation of existing systems:* An existing information system's input screens and output reports can give a good idea of what data are available and what data people use. System documentation often helps explain why the system exists, what business problems it solves, and how it solves them. However, documentation may be so detail-oriented that it doesn't explain the purpose of system features. Also, if the system has been modified many times, it is likely that the documentation will be outdated.
- *On-site observation:* One of the best ways to understand how a system operates is to go to the site and observe it for several days, or even weeks. If possible, an analyst should even try to perform some of the work the participants perform. Analysts who never observe the current system in action often misunderstand the problem they are trying to solve.
- *Questionnaires:* Questionnaires can be used to gather information from users, managers, and other stakeholders in the project. This method is especially useful when there are many geographically dispersed stakeholders, making it impractical to interview everyone. Although questionnaires sometimes bring in ideas that would otherwise be missed, people often fill them out in a perfunctory way because they are busy with other things and feel uninvolved in the project.
- *Benchmarking:* **Benchmarking** is the analysis of similar systems in other companies to provide both perspective and new ideas about the situation being analyzed. Many companies use this approach in their total quality management (TQM) efforts. In addition to new ideas, interviewing users of similar systems may produce insights about why particular system features are effective or ineffective.

Each of these methods provides a way to obtain information when analyzing a system. Using different methods is important because systems analysts often discover that things said in interviews are inconsistent with what they find when they observe systems in action. We will look at the interviewing process in more detail because interviews are used so commonly.

Performing Interviews

Although talking to users might seem like a simple task, a surprising number of problems may reduce interview effectiveness. Table 11.7 summarizes some of these, which include missing viewpoints, superficial information, and distorted information. Minimizing these problems involves careful preparation, execution, and follow-up, including an insistence on understanding the situation rather than just making a list of what the users apparently want.

Careful preparation for an interview includes gathering background information before the interview and going to the interview with a clear goal and a list of key questions. Conducting an interview without a clear goal, such as understanding a user's problems or understanding a user's information requirements, wastes time and leads to garbled

TABLE 11.7 Common Problems Encountered by Analysts Interviewing Users

Analysts encounter a number of problems while interviewing system users, but many problems can be prevented by paying attention to typical causes.

Problem	Typical cause	Preventive action
Missing viewpoints	Users unwilling or unable to participate	Make involvement of key users a condition for doing the project
	Stakeholders who are not invited to participate	Include all groups affected by the system
Superficial information	Lack of preparation by the analyst	Learn about the business setting; prepare before the interview
	User's assumption that only minor changes are possible	Don't just ask for the user's wish list; understand the reason for the user's problem rather than just the suggested solution
Distorted information	User responses based on user aims other than the system, such as political position in the organization	Obtain multiple viewpoints to confirm data and conclusions Be sure users know the purpose of the interview
	Analyst misunderstanding or biasing the user's response	Learn about the business setting Prepare before the interview

conclusions. Having a list of questions helps you focus the discussion and helps the respondent understand the interview's purpose. Although the discussion may move to unanticipated topics that are important, starting with a list of questions helps keep the interview on track and helps you recognize important observations. Prior knowledge of the organizational setting, business process, and other aspects of the situation helps you understand what the user means. It also avoids giving the user the impression of wasting time explaining things you should know. Being prepared keeps you focused on receiving information and helps you avoid putting words in the user's mouth.

Although interviews differ in content and feeling, there are common rules of thumb for interviewing:

- Make sure that the interviewee knows the reason for the interview. In too many cases the interviewee is unclear about the purpose and may withhold information or cooperation as a result.
- Ask **open-ended questions,** which invite the interviewee to provide more information than a yes or no. For example, ask "How do you use the customer file?" rather than a yes-no question such as "Is the customer file useful?"
- Validate responses by restating them and by comparing other people's responses. Different people often disagree about problems, causes, and priorities. The greater the disagreement, the more difficult it will be to design and implement a successful system.
- Pay attention to body language (both yours and the interviewee's). Uninterested or antagonistic interviewees often project a different feeling from those who genuinely want the project to succeed.
- Close the interview by reviewing some of the main points covered, thanking the respondent, and requesting permission to call back if you need clarification or additional information.

Follow-up after an interview is also important. Avoid the strong temptation to file your notes and go on to other work without analyzing what was said. In complex projects, it may even be worthwhile to rewrite your notes. If you neglect doing this, weeks later you may not understand much about what was said or why. Reviewing your notes also encourages you to follow up on unclear responses or on questions you hadn't raised during the interview.

It is much better to ask more questions than to develop an information system based on misunderstandings.

These guidelines for gathering information are useful in IS planning, in system development projects (discussed in the next chapter), and in many other areas of business. The guidelines help project participants stay focused and help them avoid unnecessary difficulties in projects that already have many challenges.

CHAPTER CONCLUSION

Summary

What is an information system plan?
A plan is a statement of what will be done, who will do it, when they will do it, how it will be done, and what are the desired results. At the strategic level, IS plans focus on priorities and goals for information systems and the technical and organizational approaches that will be used. At the project level, they focus on specific capabilities required in each system and on who will do what and when will they do it to produce specific results.

Why do users and managers have to participate in information system planning and development?
Even though the IS department compiles the IS plan, members of user departments have to ensure that the right systems are developed, are used efficiently and effectively, and have the desired impact.

How is information system planning linked to business planning?
IS planning is the part of business planning concerned with deploying the firm's IS resources. Like plans in all business functions, the IS plan should support the strategy and goals in the business plan and should be linked to the plans in the functional areas.

What are some of the strategic issues in information system planning?
The issues most directly related to business activities include attaining consistency with business priorities, supporting the redesign of business processes called for by reengineering and downsizing, and attaining the right level of internal and external integration by deploying enterprise-wide and interorganizational systems. Strategic issues more related to how IT is deployed include designing an appropriate IS architecture, finding the right balance between centralization and decentralization in the IT effort, defining a business-driven IT infrastructure, and outsourcing the right IT functions.

What are the key issues in balancing centralized versus decentralized processing and control?
The key issues focus on the extent to which information system location, ownership, and control should be dispersed to different parts of the organization. Excessive centralization often results in rigid systems that cannot handle local variations. Excessive decentralization often solves local problems but often doesn't solve problems that cross departments and misses opportunities for economies of scale.

How is cost/benefit analysis used in making investment decisions about information systems?
Cost/benefit analysis is the process of evaluating proposed systems by comparing their estimated benefits with their estimated costs, both expressed in dollars over a time horizon. Key issues for cost/benefit analysis include the difference between tangible and intangible benefits, the tendency to underestimate costs, and the effect of the timing of costs and benefits.

What are the basic elements of project management for information system projects?
Like any business project, IS projects have goals, deliverables and schedules, and roles and responsibilities. The essence of project management is controlling tasks that occur in a particular sequence and have an expected duration. Dividing a project into steps with specific deliverables clarifies what needs to be done and helps the people doing the project understand exactly what they have to do and how their work fits into the overall project.

Key Terms

information systems planning
chief information officer (CIO)
sponsor
champion
IS steering committee
user support
information center
enhancement
bug fix
pilot project
critical success factor (CSF)
business process reengineering (BPR)
downsizing
interorganizational information systems
virtual organization
information system architecture
legacy system
platform
IT infrastructure
management by maxim
outsourcing
cost/benefit analysis
tangible benefits
intangible benefits
total cost of ownership (TCO)
net present value (NPV)
internal rate of return (IRR)
payback
project goal
deliverables
project schedule
Gantt chart
requirements creep
mythical man-month
benchmarking
open-ended questions

Review Questions

1. Describe the difference between strategic-level and project-level plans for information systems.
2. What is IS planning and how should it be related to other planning in a business?
3. Identify important user roles in information systems planning.
4. How much of a typical IS group's work is typically involved with keeping existing systems operating, and what types of projects does this include?
5. Identify some of the roles of IS professionals in building and maintaining information systems.
6. What are critical success factors, and how are they used in IS planning?
7. Explain why business process reengineering is a controversial topic.
8. How are interorganizational information systems related to virtual organizations?
9. What is the significance of legacy systems and platforms in IS architecture?
10. How is the idea of management by maxim related to the strategic alignment of IT infrastructure?
11. In relation to centralization versus decentralization, what are the major issues involving standards and ownership?
12. Why is outsourcing controversial?
13. Describe some of the problems that often arise when information systems span two countries or are moved from one country to another.
14. Explain the difference between tangible and intangible information system costs.
15. Why is the timing of costs and benefits important in evaluating proposed information systems, and how does it affect financial measures such as NPV, IRR, and payback?
16. Describe the characteristics of information system projects with minimal risks.
17. Why are goals, deliverables, and schedules important in project management?
18. What limits the effectiveness of Gantt charts and other project management methods?
19. Explain the idea of the "mythical man-month."
20. Describe some guidelines for interviewing during information system projects.

Discussion Topics

1. Assume that you had been an IS manager at XYZ Corp. for the past 12 years and have just been informed that the outsourcing contract signed yesterday transferred all major IS operations to a leading outsourcing vendor. As part of the deal, you and your staff are to become employees of the vendor, which has different salary scales, different benefits, and a different culture. Ignoring any laws that might apply to this, what economic or ethical responsibilities did XYZ Corp. have toward you and your colleagues as it negotiated this contract?
2. A noted software expert has stated that "the introduction of new CASE tools may cause a short-term productivity problem that will impact the current project....Most organizations have found that productivity typically declines for the first 3 to 6 months after the introduction of CASE tools, and sometimes by as much as 25% during the first year."[36] Explain how this phenomenon is related to IS planning topics covered in this chapter.

3. To improve customer responsiveness in its consumer banking group in the early 1980s, Citibank decided to "decentralize its information process capabilities quickly to as low a level of responsibility and control as possible....Instead of increasing responsiveness, Citibank soon found itself drowning in a sea of systems, unable to collect, store, disseminate, or analyze vital information." Citibank quickly recentralized its information management processes.[37] Explain how Citibank's experience is related to issues covered in this chapter.
4. "When a company budgets $1 million to develop a new software system it is, in fact, committing to spend more than $4 million over the next five years. Each dollar spent on systems development generates, on average, 20 cents for operations and 40 cents for maintenance. Thus, the $1 million expenditure automatically generates a follow-on cost of $600,000 a year to support the initial investment."[38] Explain whether this quotation seems surprising to you and how it is related to topics covered in this chapter.
5. In talking about information system planning, this chapter mostly takes the viewpoint of a large firm. Which topics in the chapter seem equally applicable to a small firm or individual? Which topics seem less applicable?
6. You are nearing the end of a seven-month system development project. Last week, the leader of one of your teams estimated his group was 95% finished. This week, he says he may have been a bit optimistic and his team is probably only 85% finished. He asks you to assign two more programmers to his team to help him finish. What ideas from the chapter would you think about before responding?

CASE

Cemex: Incorporating IT into a Cement Company's Strategy

Founded in 1906, Cemex is one of Mexico's few truly multinational companies. It is the largest cement company in the Americas and one of the three largest cement companies in the world, with revenues of $3.7 billion and close to 51 million metric tons of production. Cemex and its subsidiaries engage in the production, distribution, marketing, and sale of cement, ready-mix concrete, and related materials. Its strategy includes focusing on cement and concrete products, diversifying globally to cushion against volatility in local markets, developing efficient production and distribution processes, using IT to increase flexibility, improve customer satisfaction, and reduce bureaucracy and excess staffing, and providing training and education for employees. Its state-of-the-art Tepeaca facility supplies one fifth of the Mexican market and may be the lowest-cost cement producer in the world, with operating costs of $25 per ton, roughly $10 lower than the industry average, and emissions far lower than legal requirements. In 1992 Cemex purchased Spain's two largest cement companies, reviewed their operations thoroughly, invested in facilities, and reduced the workforce dramatically, such as by consolidating 19 offices into one. With continued diversification in the 1990s, Cemex has operations in 22 countries. It is also Latin America's biggest corporate debtor, with over $4 billion in debt.

Although it was a laggard in IT usage through the 1980s, Cemex is now widely recognized as a company that uses IT extensively and views IT as an integral part of its long-term strategy. Lorenzo Zambrano, a Stanford MBA whose family owned a third of the stock, became its CEO at age 41 in 1985. In 1987 he hired an information system director and gave him the mandate of developing Cemex's then primitive IT capabilities. Within a year, dispersed operations were being linked via satellite. In one case, a cement plant in a town with only 20 telephones used a satellite dish to transmit voice and data, thus bypassing Mexico's chaotic phone system. By 1998, managers could use the satellite-based communications network to monitor operations and market conditions all over the world and to communicate using voice, video, Lotus Notes, and other technologies.

Application areas that demonstrate the importance of IT include management information and control of operations. Cemex managers can immediately link to any of the 18 plants in Mexico and immediately access the status of each cement kiln, recent production data, and even the deployment of trucks dispatched by different cement and concrete distribution centers. Financial statements are available two days after the end of the fiscal month, an endeavor that used to take a whole month and took 50 days for a facility in Venezuela acquired in 1995. Eliminating these lengthy delays in evaluating production, costs, and sales volume helps in running a lean, low-cost operation by making it possible for management to take action quickly instead of waiting almost two months to just receive the data in some cases.

Use of IT in controlling operations occurs at many points. Cemex's ready-mix delivery trucks are equipped with dashboard computers that allow tracking using global positioning satellite technology. A central dispatcher in a region constantly reroutes the trucks as customers cancel, delay, or speed up orders. This system generated a 30% decrease in the number of trucks and also increased customer satisfaction because it allows customers at chaotic construction sites to change their orders with just 15 minutes' notice instead of the six hours previously required. Information systems also track process and production information, such as the chemical composition of cement being produced, the reasons for kiln problems, and the delivery routes of trucks. To help workers use information effectively, Cemex provides monthly training and began a program to give workers the equivalent of high school or college degrees.

QUESTIONS

1. Based on the case, identify what seem to be some of Cemex's business and IT maxims.
2. What issues related to centralization and decentralization seem to apply in this case?
3. Review the discussion of international issues and explain which of those issues, if any, apply to this case.

Sources:

Dolan, Kerry A. "Cyber-cement," *Forbes*, June 15, 1998, pp. 60–61.

Dombey, Daniel. "Well Built Success," *Industry Week*, May 5, 1997. June 3, 1998 (www.cemex.com/articles/indeng.htm).

Rozenberg, Dino. "Cemex: A System for Worldwide Manufacturing," *Manufactura*, May 1998 edition, June 2, 1998 (www.cemex.com/articles/manueng.htm).

CASE

Unisource Worldwide: Scuttling an ERP Project

Unisource Worldwide is the largest marketer and distributor of paper goods and supply systems for packaging, food-services, and janitorial use in North America. It was formed as a spin-off from Alco Standard Corp. in December 1996. The company had been built largely through acquisitions, 41 of them in 1996, and had 14,000 employees in 143 operating divisions at 426 facilities. A nationwide implementation of SAP enterprise software had begun in 1994, starting with human resources, financial, and distribution modules. The company had planned to complete the implementation in two years and budgeted a total of $300 million over 10 years. But three years into the project the newly created firm Unisource decided that the SAP software was not a good fit. Unisource had hoped to replace multiple legacy systems and consolidate 11 service centers using the SAP R/3 product. Unfortunately, each service center had its own way of processing orders and doing procurement, meaning that the SAP rollout would be very expensive and time consuming. Most of the $168 million spent in the first three years of the project had gone toward outsourcing and consulting fees.

A letter to shareholders at the beginning of its 1997 Annual Report, stated: "In 1997 we began the initial implementation of our SAP-based North American Distribution System (NADS). NADS was installed in two small divisions served by our Fort Washington, Pennsylvania, customer service center. Implementation has been far more time consuming and costly than anticipated....It is extremely important that our information technology programs meet our future requirements in a cost-effective way. For that reason, this past October we commissioned an in-depth study designed to review NADS and our present IT programs and to evaluate our options for the future....In the meantime, we will focus the NADS implementation on the divisions serviced by Fort Washington. Savings from our refocused NADS implementation program will be redirected to converting our legacy systems to be Year 2000 ready." The discussion of the company's financial condition went on to say: "The potential alternatives related to the information technology program re-evaluation include, but are not limited to: (i) abandon NADS and the SAP software platform; (ii) retain NADS and SAP but significantly scale back implementation until benefits in relation to costs are validated; and (iii) consolidate current legacy systems to three to four integrated non-SAP systems."

A news release on Jan. 21, 1998, announced plans to streamline the company by moving from a regional to a functionally aligned organization structure, closing or consolidating underperforming and overlapping locations, and implementing more consistent business practices across the company. As many as 50 locations and 800 employees would be affected by these moves. The main targets of the restructuring would be the five regional offices, each of which has a full headquarters staff, and its computerized management information system. The CEO stated: "Our results during our first year as a public company did not meet our expectations. In fact, they have been a significant disappointment." A second news release on the same date announced "a new IT strategy" along with a $168 million writeoff of "capitalized development and related costs associated with the company's IT system." A study led by the company's chief financial officer had concluded that NADS would not cost-effectively meet the company's information technology needs. The CFO said that "SAP was designed primarily for manufacturing applications and is more complex than is required for marketing and distribution operations. Also, the extensive and continuing customization required for our business environment makes it prohibitively expensive to install future upgrades and enhancements to the system." The statement went on to say that Unisource would instead focus on enhancing and consolidating its existing legacy systems and would begin by consolidating those systems into one Y2K-compliant application that should be completed by the middle of the company's 1999 fiscal year.

QUESTIONS

1. How does this case differ from the Owens Corning case at the beginning of the chapter?
2. How is this case related to major ideas in this chapter?
3. Explain why you do or do not believe this chapter provided guidance that might have helped prevent this expensive failure.

Sources:

Stein, Tom. "SAP Installation Scuttled," *InformationWeek*, Jan. 26, 1998, p. 154.

Unisource Worldwide. "General discussion," 1997 Annual Report. Online Posting, June 2, 1998 (http://www.unisourcelink.com/_7lettershare.html).

Unisource Worldwide. "Unisource Announces Plan to Streamline Company," Press Release, Jan. 21, 1998, June 2, 1998 (http://www.unisourcelink.com/press28.htm).

Unisource Worldwide. "Unisource Reports First Quarter Earnings," Press Release, Jan. 21, 1998, June 2, 1998 (http://www.unisourcelink.com/press29.htm).

Building and Maintaining Information Systems

12

Study Questions

- What are the four phases of information system projects, and what are the key issues in each phase?
- What types of issues are addressed by the different system development processes?
- How does the traditional system life cycle solve the control problem of keeping a project on track?
- What are the advantages and disadvantages of prototypes?
- What are the advantages and disadvantages of application packages?
- What are the advantages and disadvantages of end-user development?
- How is it possible to combine system development approaches into a system's life cycle?

Outline

Opening Case

MICROSOFT CORPORATION: BUILDING SOFTWARE PRODUCTS

Microsoft has become one of the world's most valuable corporations by writing software used in over 100 million computers. Each software product is distributed in successive releases. In the planning stage for each release Microsoft identifies the new capabilities that customers request plus those that it wants to include for its own strategic reasons. (See Table 12.1.) It divides the planned release into three parts in order of priority. If it runs out of time on the release, it eliminates the lower priority items.

Microsoft's programming process tries to maintain overall discipline and project control while permitting small teams to do their own work independently. It does this by assigning specific portions of each release to small teams consisting of three to eight programmers and the same number of testers. Permitting each team to operate independently maintains the team's sense of responsibility and permits it to exercise creativity in the way it does its work. The teams attempt to meet goals for providing specific capabilities but do not start with the type of detailed specification that would be necessary if the software was designed to control mission-critical processes such as the operation of the space shuttle. Around 30% of each release is often the result of discoveries about unanticipated connections and relationships.

The method for maintaining overall control of the project is sometimes described as "synch and stabilize" because it tries to synchronize what people are doing as individuals and as members of parallel teams while it also tries to stabilize the product in increments as the project continues. At the heart of this approach is the "daily build," a daily test of whether the most recently debugged version of all the separate modules of the product still operate together and still produce correct results for examples that the previous release could handle correctly. One of the few rules developers must follow is that they have to transmit their latest tested version by a particular time in the day so that the project team can assemble and recompile the latest completed version of all components, and can therefore create a new "build" of the product that can be tested. Any code preventing the build from compiling must be fixed immediately. As the release date approaches, the list of known bugs is carefully monitored. Many releases are distributed with known bugs, but these can often be corrected with program patches that can be downloaded through the Internet.[1]

Debate Topic

Microsoft's business success is based in part on an unethical practice of distributing imperfect software.

Microsoft's "synch and stabilize" method is one of a number of possible methods for programming new releases of commercial software. Microsoft chose this method because it met Microsoft's goals and because it fit the talents and culture of its programmers. Other organizations attempting to produce commercial software might need to use very different methods. Furthermore, business organizations building and maintaining internal information systems would have to adopt a method that included implementation in the organization. Otherwise, whatever was programmed would have no impact and would be a waste of time and money regardless of whether the firm happened to use a "synch and stabilize" method for programming.

This chapter's purpose is to explain different ways to build and maintain information systems in organizations. Business professionals need to understand options related to software and system development processes because many IS projects encounter serious problems that ultimately affect business results. For example, a survey of 300 large companies by KPMG Peat Marwick, a big six accounting firm, discovered that 65% had at least one project that went grossly over budget, was extremely late, and ultimately produced results of little value. Peat Marwick called such a project a **runaway,** as in a "runaway train."[2] Chapter 1 mentioned other studies by consulting companies that revealed similar problems.

TABLE 12.1 **Microsoft Programs Software for a New Release**

CUSTOMER

- Customers who purchase Microsoft's software
- Microsoft itself, because it must create a basis for new releases and because the software reflects its strategy

PRODUCT

- New release of a software product

BUSINESS PROCESS

Major steps:

- Identify features customers want and features Microsoft wants for strategic reasons
- Decide which features to include in a release
- Divide the work among small teams and break each team's work into three phases
- Program and test features in each module
- Perform a daily build to make sure all parts of the product work together
- Decide which features to delay to subsequent releases
- Test the entire release
- Package and distribute the new release

Rationale:

- Produce releases that combine what the customers want and what Microsoft wants to produce
- Maintain creativity and responsibility by assigning subprojects to small teams
- Maintain control and compatibility by doing a daily build

PARTICIPANTS

- Programmers and testers

INFORMATION

- Features to be included in the release
- Programs
- Examples for testing
- Project plan

TECHNOLOGY

(Not mentioned in the case)

- Programming languages
- Debugging techniques
- Computers that run the programs

This chapter starts by reviewing the four phases of an information system originally introduced in Chapter 1. (See Figure 1.1.) These phases can be used as a least common denominator for discussing and comparing alternative methods for building and maintaining information systems. With this background, the chapter summarizes and compares four alternative models for performing the four phases. These alternative approaches include the traditional system life cycle, prototypes, application packages, and end-user development. Microsoft's synch and stabilize method is actually a response to some of the shortcomings of the traditional system life cycle. Because each approach has advantages and disadvantages, project managers need to decide on the combination of these approaches that makes the most sense in any particular situation.

As you read this chapter, remember that building an information system is a business process. Like other business processes it has an architecture that ultimately affects its internal performance and the product it produces for customers. Product performance can be evaluated in terms of cost to the customer, quality, responsiveness, reliability, and conformance. Internal process performance can be evaluated in terms of rate of output, consistency, productivity, cycle time, flexibility, and security.

In addition, please recognize that understanding this process requires attention to the difference between the information system that is being built and the work system that is being improved. The terms *system, work system,* and *information system* will be used carefully throughout the chapter. Because it is tedious to say "the information system and the work system it supports" repeatedly, the term *system* is used alone when the distinction between the information system and the work system is unnecessary for the point being made or when the term applies to both simultaneously, such as "the new system was ineffective."

PHASES OF ANY INFORMATION SYSTEM

The starting point for building or improving an information system is the recognition of a business problem or opportunity and the belief that a better information system might create benefits by improving the operation of a work system. Next comes the refinement of that idea into a specific statement of what the work system should accomplish, how the improved information system should help, and what parts of the information system will be automated. Analysts or designers decide how to create computer programs that accomplish the automated functions on specific hardware. The technical staff either writes the programs or buys them. The organization acquires whatever hardware is needed. The programs are tested to ensure the correct functions are performed in the correct manner. A team implements the information system in the organization through a process involving user training and conversion from the previous information system. The information system then goes into operation and is modified as necessary for further improvements in the work system. Eventually the work system or the information system may be absorbed into other systems or terminated.

Regardless of whether the software is produced by the IS department, the user department, or by an outside vendor, this general process can be summarized in terms of four phases: initiation, development, implementation, and operation and maintenance. Notice that authors from different disciplines use the terms *development* and *implementation* in different ways. In this book, the term development refers to the phase concerned with designing, programming, and testing a computer system. This is the second of four phases for any successful information system. Consistent with common usage, the verb *develop* is also used here in a general sense, as in "Acme developed a sales system." For programmers, the term *implementation* often refers to the process of designing and programming a computer system. Because this is a book for business professionals, the word *implementation* is used in the way they typically use it, namely, to refer to making the information system and the improved work system operational in the organization. Defined this way, implementation is the third phase of the system life cycle. Notice that the implementation phase was not discussed in the Microsoft case, which focused on the development phase for a new release of a commercial software product applied in totally different situations by different users. Each of the four phases will be discussed in turn.

Initiation

Initiation is the process of defining the need to change an existing work system, identifying the people who should be involved in deciding what to do, and describing in general terms how the work system should operate differently and how any information system that supports it should operate differently. This phase may occur in response to recognized problems, such as data that cannot be found and used effectively, or high error rates in data. In other cases, it is part of a planning process in which the organization is searching for ways to improve and innovate, even if current systems pose no overt problems. This phase concludes with a verbal or written agreement about the directions in which the work system and information system should change, plus a shared understanding that the proposed changes are technically and organizationally feasible.

A key outcome of this phase is an understanding of a proposed information system's purposes and goals. Errors in this phase may result in information systems that operate on the computer but don't support the organization's goals. Because it is possible to change a system after it goes into operation, design errors in the initiation phase may not be fatal to the project. However, they are especially expensive because the subsequent effort in developing both the information system and the work system are based on these errors. Figure 12.1 demonstrates the importance of identifying design errors early in a system development process by showing how the cost of design errors escalates the later they are discovered.

Some projects never go beyond the initiation phase. For example, the analysis in this phase may show that the likely costs outweigh the likely benefits, or that the system is technically or organizationally impractical. Other system efforts are abandoned because people cannot agree on system goals or because too few people in the organization care about the problem the system addresses. Although no one wants to invest time and effort in a project and then stop it, stopping a project at this phase is far better than pouring time and effort into something that will probably fail.

Development

Development is the process of building or acquiring and configuring hardware, software, and other resources needed to perform both the required IT-related functions and the required functions not related to IT. This phase starts by deciding exactly how the computerized and manual parts of the work system will operate. It then goes on to acquire the needed resources. If the hardware isn't already in place, development includes purchasing and installing the hardware. If the software isn't in place, it includes purchasing the software, producing it from scratch, or modifying existing software. Regardless of how the hardware and software are acquired, this phase includes creating documentation explaining how both the work system and the information system are supposed to operate. The development phase concludes with thorough testing of the entire information system to identify and correct misunderstandings and programming errors. Completion of development does not mean "the system works." Rather, it only means that the computerized parts of the work system operate on a computer. Whether or not the "system works" will be determined by how it is actually used in the organization.

A key goal of the development phase is assuring that work system and information system features really solve problems the users want solved. This is sometimes difficult because many users are unable to describe exactly how a better information system might help them. They also may not see that system modifications could help them in some ways but might become a hindrance in other ways. Another key goal is to perform the technical work in a way that makes it easier to modify the information system as new needs arise.

Implementation

Implementation is the process of making a new or improved work system operational in the organization. This phase starts when the software runs on the computer and has been tested. Activities in implementation include planning, user training, conversion to the new information system and work system, and follow-up to make sure the entire system

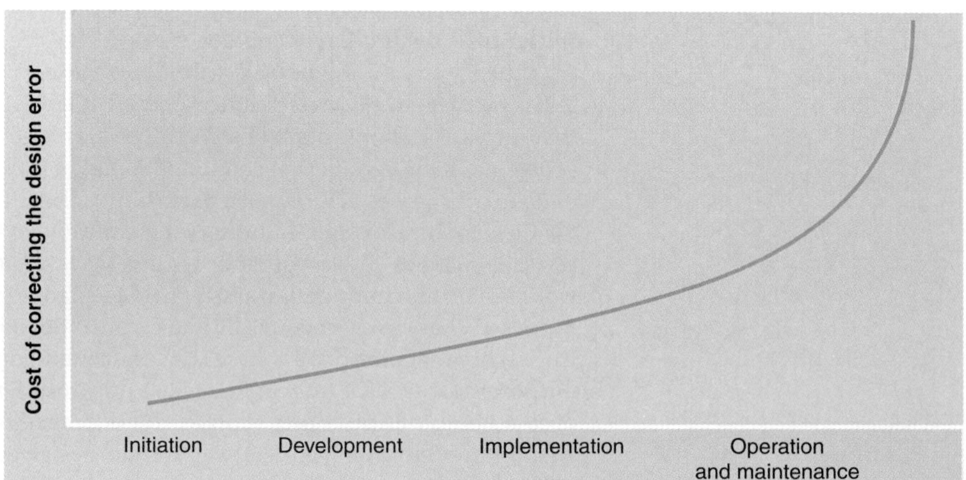

Figure 12.1
Costs in design errors detected at different times

The later a design error is detected, the more expensive it is to correct because so much rework and retesting is required.

is operating effectively. The implementation phase may involve a major change in the way organizations or individuals operate. Conversion from the old to the new must be planned and executed carefully to prevent errors or even chaos. For information systems that keep track of transactions such as invoices and customer orders, the conversion process requires some users to do double work during a pilot test, operating simultaneously with the old and new systems. Running two information systems in parallel helps identify unanticipated problems that might require information system or work system modifications before implementation is complete.

Political issues related to power and control within the organization often become visible during implementation. For example, implementing an integrated sales and production system might make computerized production scheduling data directly accessible to a sales department. Ideally, this data should help sales and production work together. However, it might also permit sales to exert new pressure on production, which formerly had sole access to the data. The new system's cooperative rationale might be replaced with a win-lose feeling. Such issues should be identified and discussed as early as possible.

Operation and Maintenance

Operation and maintenance is the ongoing operation of the work system and the information system, plus efforts directed at enhancing either system and correcting bugs. At minimum, this requires that someone be in charge of ensuring that the work system is operating well, that the information system is providing the anticipated benefits, and that the work system and information system are changed further if the business situation calls for it.

People tend to overlook the significance of this phase. To the IS staff, building new information systems often seems more challenging and creative than keeping old ones effective as needs change. Perceiving this phase as less creative, users may assume that upgrades should be easy. In fact, the operation and maintenance phase is often challenging. For example, consider the response time and uptime requirements of information systems companies rely on for taking customer orders or managing factories. Once an information system is in operation, users expect it to work. Downtime and bugs must be dealt with immediately, which requires the ability to diagnose and correct problems under time pressure.

Furthermore, the longer an information system has been in operation, the harder it is to change. Original developers who understood it best may have different jobs; documentation becomes outdated; infrequently used parts of the system fall into disrepair. Programmers become justifiably wary of changing the system because a change in one location is more likely to cause a bug elsewhere. In turn, work system participants are less likely to get the changes they want and start to complain about the IS department's unresponsiveness and the system's ineffectiveness. Ideally, the business process chosen for building an information system should minimize these problems.

The four phases of any information system have now been described. This model serves as a least common denominator for understanding and comparing different types of business processes used for building and maintaining systems. Figure 12.2 shows how the end product of one phase is the starting point of the next. It also shows some of the reasons for returning to a previous phase even though the four phases ideally occur in sequence.

Table 12.2 summarizes problems and issues that must be dealt with in order for each phase to succeed. Different business processes are used to perform the individual phases depending on the type of system, the problem it attempts to solve, and the situation in which it will operate. In some situations, the requirements are clear and easily agreed upon; in others, no one may be able to describe the requirements clearly until they have an information system to try out. In some cases, existing technology will be used; in others, new technology must be mastered and used for the first time in the organization. In yet other situations, buying application software from a vendor may be a better choice than building it from scratch. The next section explains and compares alternative processes used in these different situations.

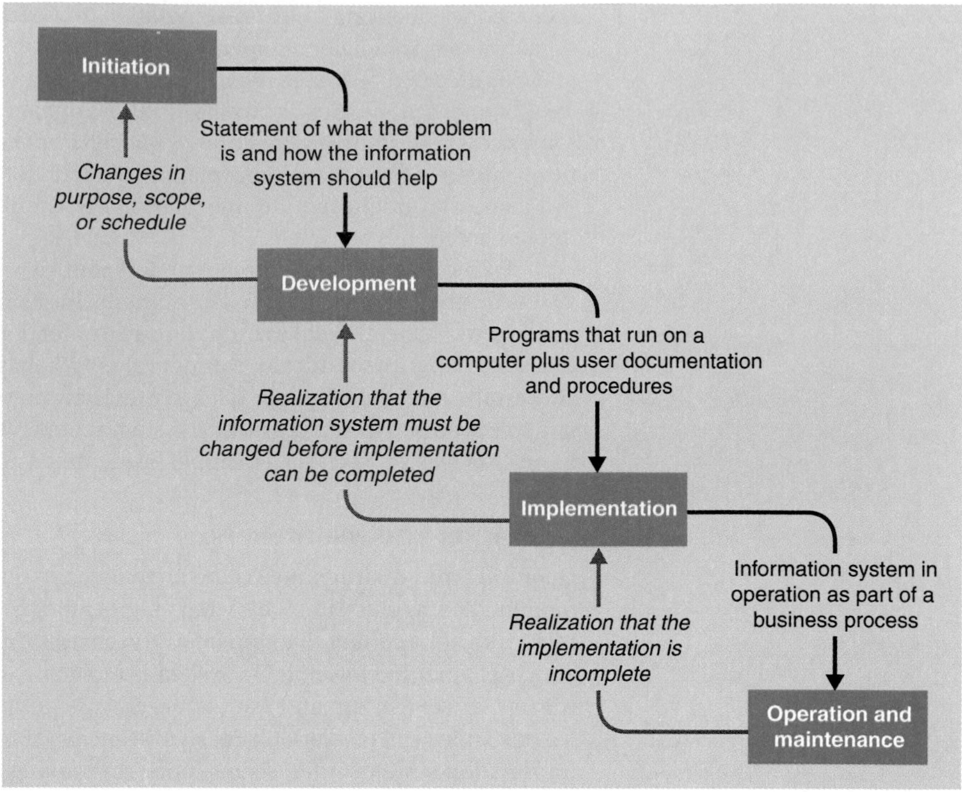

Figure 12.2
Links between the four phases of an information system

This diagram shows how the end product of the first three phases of an information system is the starting point of the next phase. It uses italics to show why it is sometimes necessary to return to a previous phase. The products of the steps shown here differ slightly from those in Figure 1.1 (Chapter 1) because that diagram referred to the phases of any work system, not just an information system.

Reality Check

PROJECT PHASES

This section explained the four phases of an information system project and explained why it is sometimes necessary to return to a phase that was previously considered complete.

1. Think of a project or team effort that you or your acquaintances have been involved in. Explain how well each of the four phases applied in that project.
2. Explain which of the issues in Table 12.2 are most related to important aspects of your project. (Because your project might not have involved an information system, you may have to restate the issues.)

OVERVIEW OF ALTERNATIVE APPROACHES FOR BUILDING INFORMATION SYSTEMS

This chapter summarizes and compares four alternative models for performing the four phases of building and maintaining an information system. These alternative approaches are summarized in Table 12.3 and explained in the sections that follow.

The **traditional system life cycle** uses a prescribed sequence of steps and deliverables to move reliably from user requirements to an information system in operation. These deliverables are related because each subsequent step builds on the conclusions of previous steps. The traditional system life cycle tries to solve a *control* problem by keeping the project on track. This type of process became popular in response to numerous system development efforts that went out of control and either failed to produce an information system at all or produced a system that did not solve the users' problem effectively. Accordingly, the traditional system life cycle establishes tight controls to guarantee that

TABLE 12.2 Common Issues and Problems in Each Phase of an Information System

Phase	Common issues and problems
Initiation	• Can we agree on the purposes and goals of the proposed system? • Are the requirements unnecessarily elaborate and expensive?
Development	• Can we assure that the system genuinely solves the user's problems? • Can we assure that users will participate effectively in the design process?
Implementation	• Can we convert effectively and painlessly from the old system to the new system? • Can we solve political issues related to changes in power relationships?
Operation and maintenance	• Can we keep system performance and uptime at acceptable levels? • Can we correct bugs and enhance the system to keep it focused on current business problems?

technical and organizational issues are addressed at each step. The controls are project deliverables ensuring that each step is completed in turn and documented carefully. Box 12.1 explains how the **capability maturity model (CMM)** tracks the extent to which an IT organization uses this type of life cycle in its development work. Notice that that model focuses on building software, rather than the larger problem of creating or modifying work systems in an organization.

A **prototype** information system is a working model of an information system built to learn about its true requirements. Firms build prototypes to solve a *knowledge* problem of not knowing exactly what the system should do to address an important issue. In this situation, the user needs some way to get a feeling for how the system should operate. Accordingly, a prototype is built quickly to help the user understand the problem and determine how an information system might help in solving it.

An **application package** consists of commercially available software that addresses a specific type of business application, such as sales tracking, general ledger, or inventory control. Firms acquire application packages to solve a *resource and timing* problem by using commercially available software that performs most of the functions desired. The IS department installs and operates this software instead of building customized software from scratch. This approach reduces the delays in developing custom software, reduces risks due to technical uncertainties and possible changes in the business problem, and reduces the resources needed to solve the problem.

TABLE 12.3 Differences between Four System Life Cycles

Life cycle approach	Issue addressed	Summary of method
Traditional system life cycle	Control	Go through a fixed sequence of steps with sign-offs after each step and careful documentation.
Prototype	Knowledge	Quickly develop a working model of the system; use the model to gain experience and decide how the final system should operate.
Application packages	Resources and timing	Purchase an existing information system from a vendor; customize the system if necessary.
End-user development	Responsiveness	Provide tools and support that make it practical for end users to develop their own information systems.

BOX 12.1 ***The capability maturity model***

The capability maturity model was developed by the Software Engineering Institute to track the extent to which an IT organization uses predictable, manageable processes for building information systems. By using recordkeeping and assessment tools based on this model, an IT organization can determine how its processes compare to a theoretical ideal and can see how quickly it is moving toward that ideal. As with many such detailed tracking methods, there is controversy about whether the extensive recordkeeping is worth the effort. For example, the model's training and recordkeeping requirements may slow down IT work for several years. Whether or not the model is adopted fully, it provides a useful way to think about why information system projects often miss their targets for functionality, schedule, or budget. The model rates the organization's practices on a five point scale.[3]

Level 1—initial	Processes are ad hoc and sometimes chaotic. Because few processes are defined, successful projects often depend on heroic individual effort.
Level 2—repeatable	Basic project management processes are used to track cost, schedule, and functionality. The discipline exists to repeat previous success with similar projects.
Level 3—defined	Both management and technical processes are documented and integrated into a standard software process for the organization. Projects use an approved, tailored version of the standard software processes.
Level 4 —managed	Detailed measures of the software process and product quality are collected and that information is used to understand both the product and the process in quantitative terms.
Level 5—optimizing	Continuous process improvement is facilitated by quantitative feedback from the process and by doing pilot studies of innovative ideas and technologies.

Approximately 62 percent of U.S. IT organizations operate at level 1 and around 25 percent are at level 2. This means that only around 15 percent have attained a degree of stability that gives credibility to schedules and project plans. Only 2 percent have attained level 4 or 5.[4] Based on these statistics, industry experts are skeptical about the credibility of schedules for Y2K projects whose failure could be catastrophic.[5]

End-user development is the development of information systems by work system participants (end users) rather than IS professionals. Firms apply end-user development to solve a *responsiveness* problem involving the inability of IS departments to keep up with individuals' changing information needs. The idea is to allow end users to produce their own information systems without requiring development by programmers. This is accomplished by giving end users spreadsheets, database packages, report generators, analytical packages, and other tools that can be used by nonprogrammers. End-user development is effective only for information systems that are small enough that an IT professional is not needed for design, programming, testing, and documentation.

We will now explain each of the four alternatives in more detail.

TRADITIONAL SYSTEM LIFE CYCLE

The goal of the traditional system life cycle is to keep the project under control and assure that the information system produced satisfies the requirements. The traditional system life cycle divides the project into a series of steps, each of which has distinct deliverables, such as documents or computer programs. These deliverables are related because each subsequent step builds on the conclusions of previous steps. Some deliverables are oriented toward the technical staff, whereas others are directed toward or produced by users and managers. The latter ensure that users and their management are included in the system development process.

Although there is general agreement about what needs to be done in the traditional system life cycle, different authors name individual steps and deliverables differently. Many versions of the traditional system life cycle emphasize the building of software and deemphasize what happens in the organization before and after software development.

Because this book is directed at business professionals, its version of the traditional system life cycle emphasizes implementation and operation in the organization in addition to software development.

Initiation

The initiation phase may begin in many different ways. A user may work with the IS staff to produce a written request to study a particular business problem. The IS staff may discover an opportunity to use information systems beneficially and then try to interest users. A top manager may notice a business problem and ask the head of IS to look into it. A computer crash or other operational problem may reveal a major problem that can be patched temporarily but requires a larger project to fix it completely. Regardless of how this phase begins, its goal is to analyze the scope and feasibility of a proposed system and to develop a project plan. This involves two steps, the feasibility study and project planning, which produce the functional specification and a project plan.

The **feasibility study** is a user-oriented overview of the proposed information system's purpose and feasibility. A system's feasibility is typically considered from economic, technical, and organizational viewpoints.

- *Economic feasibility* involves questions such as whether the firm can afford to build the information system, whether its benefits should substantially exceed its costs, and whether the project has higher priority than other projects that might use the same resources.
- *Technical feasibility* involves questions such as whether the technology needed for the information system exists and whether the firm has enough experience using that technology.
- *Organizational feasibility* involves questions such as whether the information system has enough support to be implemented successfully, whether it brings an excessive amount of change, and whether the organization is changing too rapidly to absorb it.

If the information system appears to be feasible, the initiation phase produces a functional specification and a project plan. The **functional specification** explains the importance of the business problem; summarizes changes in business processes; and estimates the project's benefits, costs, and risks. The **project plan** breaks the project into subprojects with start and completion times. It also identifies staffing, resource requirements, and dependencies between project steps.

The functional specification is approved by both user and IS personnel. It clarifies the purpose and scope of the proposed project by describing the business processes that will be affected and how they will be performed using the system. Functional specifications once consisted primarily of prose. With the advent of diagramming tools such as data flow diagrams and entity-relationship diagrams (Chapters 3 and 4), functional specifications have become much easier to read and understand. These visual representations help explain how the work systems will be improved and what general role the computerized parts of the system will play. Functional specifications typically do not explain exactly what data, reports, or data entry screens will be included. This more detailed description is produced in the development phase.

Development

The development phase creates computer programs (with accompanying user and programmer documentation) plus installed hardware that accomplish the data processing described in the functional specification. This is done through a process of successive refinement in which the functional requirements are translated into computer programs and hardware requirements. The purpose of the various steps and deliverables in the development phase is to ensure that the system accomplishes the goals explained in the functional specification. These steps are summarized in Figure 12.3.

The first step in the development phase is the **detailed requirements analysis,** which produces a user-oriented description of exactly what the information system will do. This step is usually performed by a team including user representatives and the IS department.

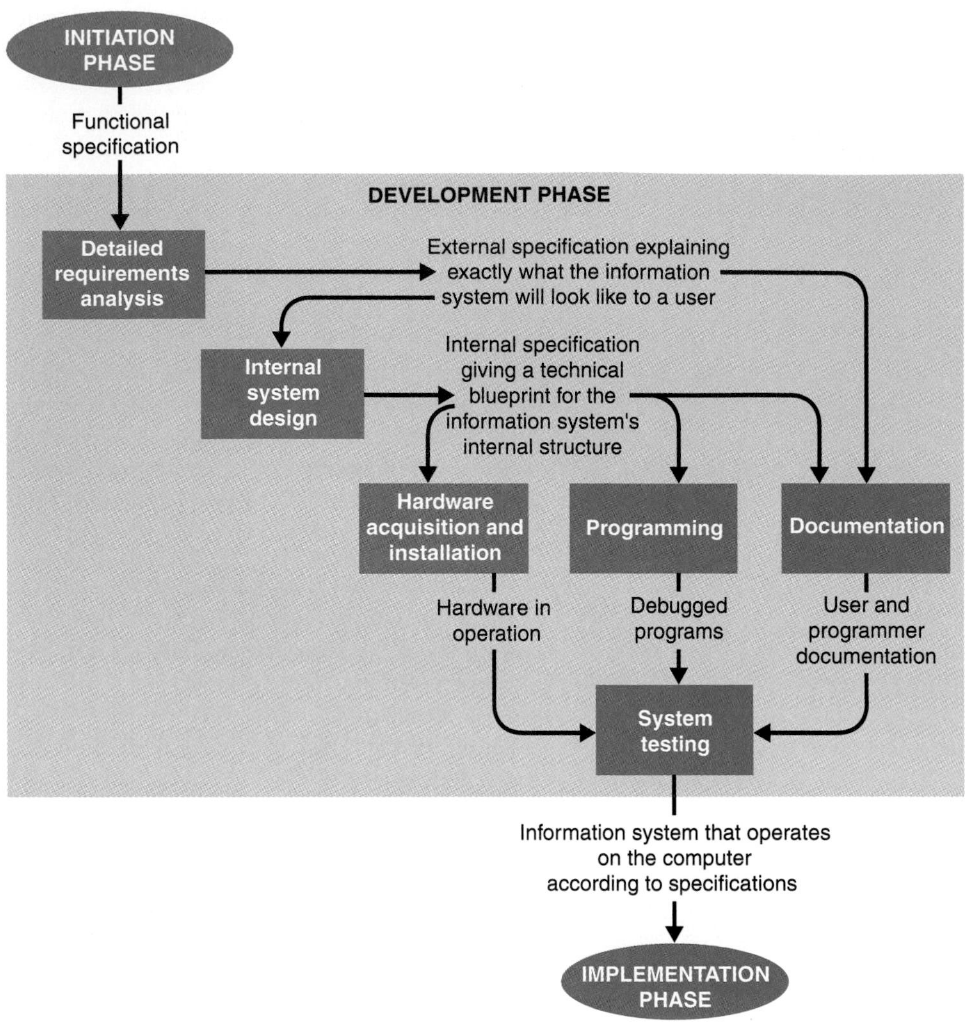

Figure 12.3
Steps in the development phase of the traditional system life cycle

The development phase of the traditional system life cycle starts with the detailed requirements analysis based on the functional specification from the initiation phase. The resulting external specification is used for the system's internal design, which outlines the structure of the programs and specifies hardware requirements. System testing occurs on completion of hardware installation, programming, and documentation. The development phase ends with an information system that operates on the computer according to the specifications.

It produces a document called the **external specification.** Building on the functional specification, the external specification shows the data input screens and major reports and explains the calculations that will be automated. It shows what information system users will see, rather than explaining exactly how the computer will perform the required processing. Users reviewing this document focus on whether they understand the data input screens, reports, and calculations, and whether these will support the desired business process. By approving the external specification, the users and IS staff signify their belief that the information system will accomplish what they want.

The next step is **internal system design,** in which the technical staff decides how the data processing will be configured on the computer. This step produces the **internal specification,** a technical blueprint for the information system. It documents the computer environment the system will operate in, the detailed structure and content of the database, and the inputs and outputs of all programs and subsystems. Users do not sign off on the internal specification because it addresses technical system design issues. Instead, the IS staff signs off that the internal specification accomplishes the functions called for in the external specification the users have approved.

Thus far the discussion has focused on software. Because the software will work only if there is hardware for it to run on, an essential step in the development phase is **hardware acquisition and installation.** For some information systems, this is not an issue because it is a foregone conclusion that existing hardware will be used. Other systems require a careful analysis to decide which hardware to acquire, how to acquire it most economically, where to put it, and how to install it by the time it is needed. Factors considered in hardware acquisition decisions include compatibility with existing hardware and software, price, customer service, and compatibility with long-term company plans. Computer hardware can be purchased or rented through a variety of financing arrangements, each with its own tax consequences. A firm's finance department usually makes the financing arrangements for significant hardware purchases. Especially if new computer hardware requires a new computer room, lead times for building the room, installing the electricity and air conditioning, and installing the computer may be important factors in the project plan.

In firms with large IS staffs, users rarely get involved with the acquisition, installation, and operation of computer hardware. Much as with telephone systems, users expect the hardware to be available when needed and complain furiously whenever it goes down. This is one reason computer hardware managers sometimes consider their jobs thankless.

Programming is the creation of the computer code that performs the calculations, collects the data, and generates the reports. It can usually proceed while the hardware is being acquired and installed. Programming includes the coding, testing, and documentation of each program identified in the internal specification. Coding is what most people think of as programming. The testing done during the programming step is often called **unit testing,** because it treats the programs in isolation. The documentation of each program starts with the explanation from the internal specification and includes comments about technical assumptions made in writing the program, plus any subtle, nonobvious processing done by the program.

A number of improvements in programming methods have made programming faster and more reliable. Structured programming (explained in Chapter 9) is often used to make the programs more consistent, easier to understand, and less error prone. Fourth generation languages (4GLs) also expedite programming for some systems. However, as should be clear from all of the steps leading up to coding and following coding, coding often accounts for less than 20% of the work in developing a system. This is one of the reasons 4GLs and other improved programming tools do not drastically shrink the system life cycle for large systems, even when they slash programming time.

Documentation is another activity that can proceed in parallel with programming and hardware acquisition. Both user and technical documentation is completed from the material that already exists. The functional specification and external specification are the basis for the user documentation, and the internal specification and program documentation are the basis for the programmer documentation. With the adoption of CASE tools described in Chapter 9, more of the documentation is basically a compilation of data and diagrams already stored on a computer. Additional user documentation is usually required, however, because different users need to know different things depending on their roles. People who perform data entry tasks need to understand the data entry procedures and what the data mean; people who use data from the system need to understand what the data mean and how to retrieve and analyze data, but do not need to know much about data entry details.

After the individual programs have been tested, the entire information system must be tested to ensure that the programs operate together to accomplish the desired functions. This is called the **system testing,** or integration testing. System tests frequently uncover inconsistencies among programs as well as inconsistencies in the original internal specification. These must be reconciled and the programs changed and retested. One of the reasons for Microsoft's "synch and stabilize" method is to eliminate the surprises and extensive rework that might occur if system testing showed that programs were incompatible. Although system testing may seem an obvious requirement, inadequate system testing has led to serious problems. For example, a new trust accounting system put into operation prematurely by Bank of America on March 1, 1987, lost data and fell months behind in generating statements for customers. By January 1988, 100 institutional customers with $4 billion in assets moved to other banks, several top executives resigned, and 2.5 million lines of code were scrapped.[6]

An important part of testing is the creation of a **testing plan,** a precise statement of exactly how the information system will be tested. This plan includes the data that will be used for testing. Creating a testing plan serves many purposes. It encourages careful thought about how the system will be tested. In addition, a thorough plan increases the likelihood that all foreseeable contingencies will be considered and that the testing will catch more of the bugs in the system.

It should be clear that the development phase for a large information system is a complex undertaking, quite different from sitting down at a personal computer and developing a small spreadsheet model. Explicitly separating out all the steps in the development phase helps to ensure that the information system accomplishes the desired functions and is debugged. Such an elaborate approach is needed because the system is a tool of an organization rather than an individual. An individual producing a spreadsheet is often trying to solve a current problem with no intention to use the spreadsheet next month, much less that someone else will need to decipher and modify it next year. In contrast, the traditional system life cycle assumes that the information system may survive for years, may be used by people who were not involved in its development, and may be changed repeatedly during that time by people other than the original developers. The steps in the traditional life cycle try to make the long-term existence of the information system as efficient and error-free as possible.

Implementation

Implementation is the process of putting a system into operation in an organization. Figure 12.4 shows that it starts with the end product of the development phase, namely, a set of computer programs that run correctly on the computer, plus accompanying documentation. This phase begins with **implementation planning,** the process of creating plans for training, conversion, and acceptance testing. The training plan explains how and when the user will be trained. The conversion plan explains how and when the organization will convert to new business processes. The acceptance testing plan describes the process and criteria for verifying that the information system works properly in supporting the improved work system.

Training is the process of ensuring that system participants know what they need to know about both the work system and the information system. The training format depends on user backgrounds and the purpose and features of both the work system and the information system. Users with no computer experience may require special training. Training for frequently used transaction processing systems differs from training for data analysis systems that are used occasionally. Information systems performing diverse functions require more extensive training than systems used repetitively for a few functions. Training manuals and presentations help in the implementation by explaining what will be different with the new work system and new information system. After the previous methods have receded into history, other types of training material are more appropriate.

Following the training comes the carefully planned process of **conversion** from the old business processes to new ones using the new information system. Conversion is often called *cutover* or *changeover*. It can be accomplished in several ways, depending on the nature of the work and the characteristics of the old and new systems. One possibility is to simply choose a date, shut off the old information system, and turn on the new one while hoping that the work system will operate as intended. This is risky, though, because it does not verify that the information system will operate properly and that the users understand how to use it.

Consider the following example: The State of California installed an optical disk system to streamline the process of doing title searches (establishing ownership and identifying indebtedness on a property) for borrowers who wished to purchase property. Previously, there was a 2- to 3-week delay between the borrower's loan request and the bank's receipt of a confirmation that the title was clear. The new system was to reduce this delay to 2 days. Both the vendor and several state officials recommended that the existing manual system remain in full operation during the conversion in case of problems. However, the Secretary of Finance rejected the request for an additional $2.4 million, and the manual system was simply shut down when the optical disk system came up. Unfortunately, software bugs plagued the new system, and the resulting logjam of 50,000

Figure 12.4
Steps in the implementation phase of the traditional system life cycle

The implementation phase starts with an information system that operates on the computer, but not in the organization. Implementation planning creates the plan for training the users, converting to the new business processes, and formal acceptance by the users.

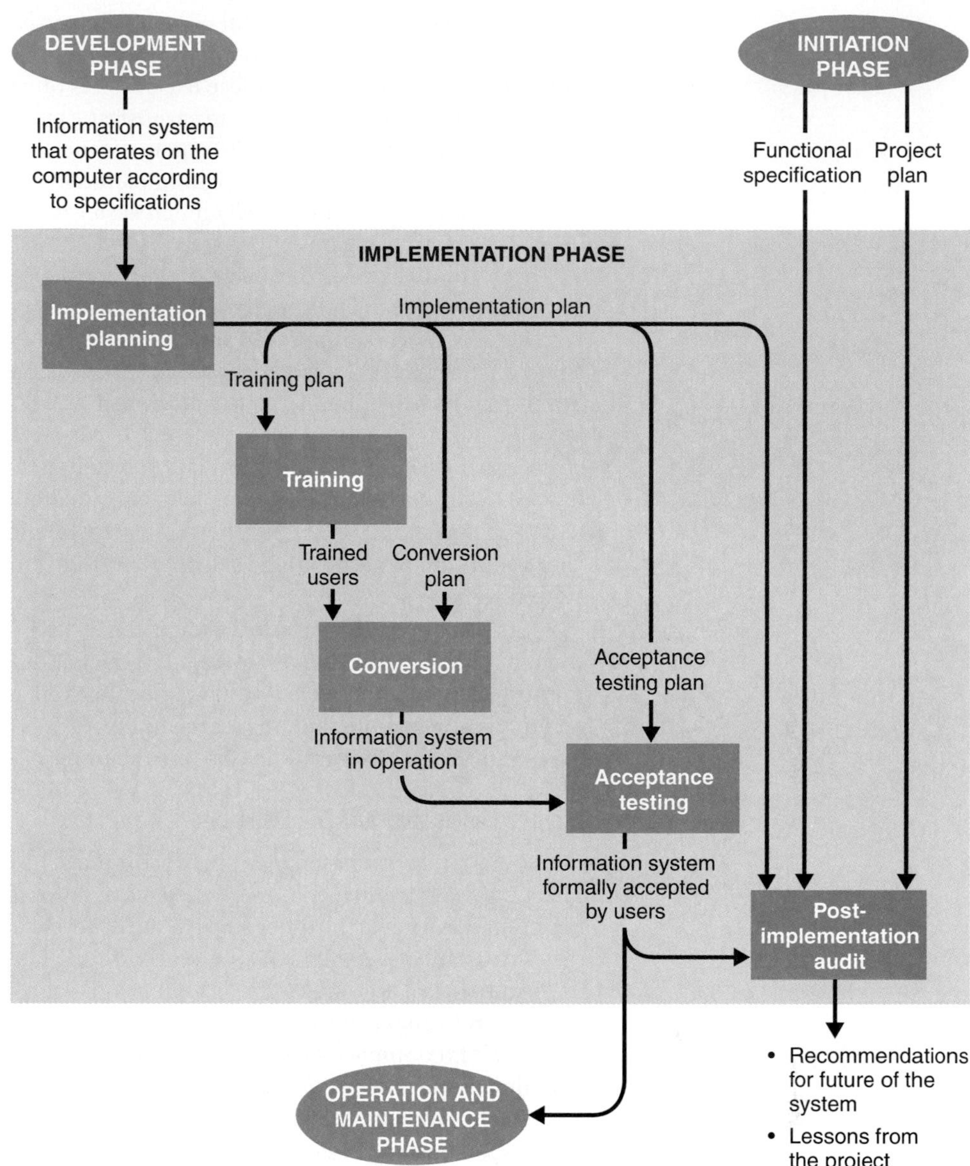

loan requests delayed title searches for up to 10 weeks. The new system was shut down for repair, and the old manual system reinstated. The Assistant Secretary of State said that some banks almost went out of business because of the slow turnaround.[7]

To minimize risk and wasted effort, most conversions occur in stages, which can be done in several ways. A **phased approach** uses the new information system and work system for a limited subset of the processing while continuing to use old methods for the rest of the processing. If something goes wrong, the part of the business using the new system can switch back to the old system. The simultaneous use of the old system and the new system is called **running in parallel.** Although this involves double recordkeeping for a while, it verifies that the new information system operates properly and helps the users understand how to use it effectively within the new work system.

Conversions from one computerized system to another are often far more difficult than users anticipate. Part of the problem is that computerized data in the old system must be converted into the formats used by the new system. Inconsistencies between the two systems frequently lead to confusion about whether the data in either system are correct. Furthermore, programs that convert the data from one system to another may have their own bugs, thereby adding to confusion and delays.

Conversion requires careful planning because even minor problems can be blown out of proportion by people who don't want the new system and use the problems as an opportunity to complain. For these reasons, it is often wise to do a **pilot implementation** with a small group of users who are enthusiastic about the system improvements. Ideally, their enthusiasm will motivate them to make the effort to learn about the changes and to forgive minor problems. After a pilot implementation demonstrates that the new information system works, it is usually much easier to motivate everyone else (including the skeptics) to start using it.

Acceptance testing is testing of the information system by the users as it goes into operation. Acceptance testing is important because the information system may not fit, regardless of what was approved and signed off in the external specification. The business situation may have changed; the external specification may reflect misunderstandings; the development process may have introduced errors; or the implementation may have revealed unforeseen problems. For all these reasons, it makes sense to include an explicit step of deciding whether the information system is accepted for ongoing use. If it doesn't fit user needs, for whatever reason, installing it without changes may lead to major problems and may harm the organization instead of helping. Acceptance testing also solidifies user commitment because it gets people in the user organization to state publicly that the system works.

The **post-implementation audit** is the last step in the implementation phase, even though it occurs after the new system has been in operation for a number of months. Its purpose is to determine whether the project has met its objectives for costs and benefits and to make recommendations for the future. This is also an opportunity to identify what the organization can learn from the way the project was carried out.

Operation and Maintenance

The operation and maintenance phase starts after the users have accepted the new system. This phase can be divided into two activities: (1) ongoing operation and support and (2) maintenance. Unlike the other steps in the life cycle, these steps continue throughout the system's useful life. The end of a system's life cycle is its absorption into another system or its termination.

Ongoing operation and support is the process of ensuring that the technical system components continue to operate correctly and that the users use it effectively. This process is similar to the process of making sure a car or building operates well. It works best when a person or group has direct responsibility for keeping the information system operating. This responsibility is often split, with the technical staff taking care of computer operations and a member of the user organization ensuring that users understand the system and use it effectively.

Day-to-day computer operations typically include scheduled events such as generating summary reports for management and backups of the database. The **operations manual** specifies when these jobs should be done. For transaction processing systems essential to the operation of the business, a member of the technical staff also monitors computer-generated statistics related to response times, program run times, disk space utilization, and similar factors to ensure the programs are running efficiently. When the database becomes too full, or when response times start to increase, the technical configuration of the information system must be changed. This is done by allocating more disk space, unloading (backing up onto tape or discarding) data that are not current, or changing job schedules.

Maintenance is the process of modifying the information system over time. As users gain experience with a system, they discover its shortcomings and usually suggest improvements. The shortcomings may involve problems unrelated to the information system or may involve ways that the information system might do more to support the work system, regardless of the original intentions. Some shortcomings are bugs. Important shortcomings must be corrected if users are to continue using an information system enthusiastically.

Handling enhancement requests and bug fix requests is both a technical challenge and a delicate political issue for IS departments. The technical challenge is ensuring that changes don't affect other parts of the system in unanticipated ways. The traditional life cycle helps here because documentation and internal design methods enforce modularization and make it easier to understand the scope and impact of changes. The political issue for most IS departments is their inability to support even half of the enhancement requests they receive. For new or inadequately planned information systems, some departments have more enhancement requests than they can even analyze. In this environment, it requires both technical and political skill to keep users satisfied. Users are often frustrated by how long it takes to make changes. What might seem to be a simple change to a person who "programs" spreadsheets is often vastly more complex in a large information system. Changes often require retesting of other parts of the system and sometimes spawn changes in several levels of documentation.

The steps in each of the four phases of the traditional system life cycle have now been introduced. Table 12.4 outlines the steps in each phase and makes two major points in addition to the details it presents. First it shows that users are highly involved in three of the four phases. In other words, building information systems is not just technical work done by the technical staff. It also shows that each step has specific deliverables that document progress to date and help keep the project under control.

The traditional system life cycle is a tightly controlled approach designed to reduce the likelihood of mistakes or omissions. Despite its compelling logic, it has both advantages and disadvantages. Adherence to fixed deliverables and signoffs improves control but guarantees a lengthy process. Having specific deliverables due at specific times makes it easier to monitor the work and take corrective actions early if the work starts to slip. But the schedule of deliverables sometimes takes on a life of its own and seems as important as the real project goals. When merely going through the motions of producing deliverables on schedule, participants may be tempted to turn in work that is incomplete and to approve documents they do not truly understand.

The traditional system life cycle is the standard against which other approaches are compared. Project managers who want to bypass some of its steps still need a way to deal with the issues they raise. The chapter looks next at three alternative approaches based on different assumptions and priorities: prototypes, application packages, and end-user development.

Reality Check

THE TRADITIONAL SYSTEM LIFE CYCLE

The traditional system life cycle is organized around a sequence of steps and deliverables.

1. Assume you were buying or renting a house or apartment that you plan to live in for five years. You want to make a plan for this process. What will the steps be, and what will be the deliverable for each step?
2. Explain the ways your process reflects some of the ideas in the traditional system life cycle. (Because this is a different problem, your process should differ from the traditional life cycle in many ways.)

PROTOTYPES

The traditional system life cycle enforces tight controls to ensure that the resulting information system performs according to requirements and is maintainable. The prototype approach emphasizes a different issue. Prototypes are used when the precise requirements are difficult to visualize and define because the business process must be changed substantially.

A **prototype** information system is a working model built to learn about how an improved work system could operate if it included an improved information system. The prototype's goal is to test possible information system features as a way of determining what the requirements should be. Instead of asking users to imagine how a proposed work

TABLE 12.4 Steps and Deliverables in the Traditional System Life Cycle

Phase/step	Degree of user participation	Key deliverable, plan, or document	Key participants
Initiation			
• Feasibility study	High	Functional specification	User representatives, management, and technical staff
• Project planning	Medium	Project plan	User representatives, management, and technical staff
Development			
• Detailed requirements analysis	High	External specification	User representatives, management, and technical staff
• Internal system design	None	Internal specification	Programmers and technical staff
• Hardware acquisition and installation	None	Hardware plan	Technical staff
		Hardware operational	
• Programming	None	Individual programs debugged	Programmers
• Documentation	Medium	User and programmer documentation	Technical staff and users
• System testing	Medium	Test plan	Programmers and users
		Completed system test	
Implementation			
• Implementation planning	High	Implementation plan	Training staff, users, and management
• Training	High	Training materials	Trainers and users
• Conversion	High	System in use	Users and project team
• Acceptance testing	High	System accepted	Users and project team
• Postimplementation audit	High	Audit report	Users and management
Operation and Maintenance			
• Ongoing operation and support	Low	Operations manual	Technical staff
	Low	Usage statistics	Technical staff and users
	High	Enhancement requests and bug fix requests	Technical staff and users
• Maintenance	Medium	Maintenance plan	Technical staff and users
• Absorption or termination	====== ======	====== ======	====== ======

system and the supporting information system might operate, the prototype approach allows them to work actively with a model of the information system. This helps them identify the features they need. It also helps identify impractical features that originally seemed to be beneficial.

A prototype system's purpose is similar to that of a prototype automobile. For example, assume that an automobile designer wants to test a new type of steering. A prototype would be designed specifically to test the steering. The steering system and suspension would be produced carefully, but the prototype might not have a paint job, back seat, or radio. These features would be put in later when the design is completed.

A prototype information system might contain a rough model of the data entry screens but might lack error checking because this would not be necessary to demonstrate the concept of the system. Because only a small sample database would suffice for a demonstration, no effort would go into making the prototype efficient. If the system contained a model, it might calculate approximate results just to show the types of outputs the final system would produce. Later versions would check the inputs, make the model more elaborate, and make its outputs look more complete.

Prototype information systems are sometimes classified as throwaway prototypes or evolutionary prototypes.[8] A **throwaway prototype** is designed to be discarded after it is utilized to test ideas and is especially useful for comparing alternative designs for parts of a system. These prototypes can be programmed for a personal computer even though the final system will use a vastly different approach. An **evolutionary prototype** is designed to be adapted for permanent use after the ideas are clarified and should be built using the programming tools that will be used for the final information system.

The phases of building and using a prototype are covered next. Table 12.5 summarizes important characteristics of each phase.

Phases

The phases of a prototype approach differ from those of a traditional system life cycle because the approaches have different assumptions. The traditional system life cycle assumes users understand the requirements, and that the main issue is to guarantee that requirements are followed in a disciplined way. Prototyping assumes users either cannot say exactly what the proposed information system should do or would have difficulty evaluating a written specification. Using a highly iterative approach, it proceeds by building a succession of "quick and dirty" versions of the system. The users look at each iteration and suggest improvements, continuing this way until they know what they want. At this point, they and the technical staff decide how to complete the project. Figure 12.5 shows the iterative process used in the prototype approach.

Initiation

The initiation phase begins with a request to build an information system in response to a business problem or opportunity. Because the problem isn't well understood, or because the users are unable to say exactly what they want, users and developers start by building a prototype instead of writing a functional specification. For this approach to succeed, the users must be willing and able to enter an iterative design process. Issues about completeness and consistency of the requirements are addressed as the users study successive versions.

TABLE 12.5 System Life Cycle Based on a Prototype

Phase	Characteristics
Initiation	Users and developers agree to develop a prototype because they need experience with a working model before designing a final system.
Development	Working iteratively with users, a prototype is developed and improved. Later, decide whether to complete the prototype or switch to a traditional life cycle.
Implementation	Accomplish parts of implementation along with development as users work with the prototype system. Dispel skepticism about whether the system will meet users' needs.
Operation and maintenance	May be similar to a traditional life cycle. May require less maintenance because the system fits users' needs more accurately. May require more maintenance because the system is not constructed as well.

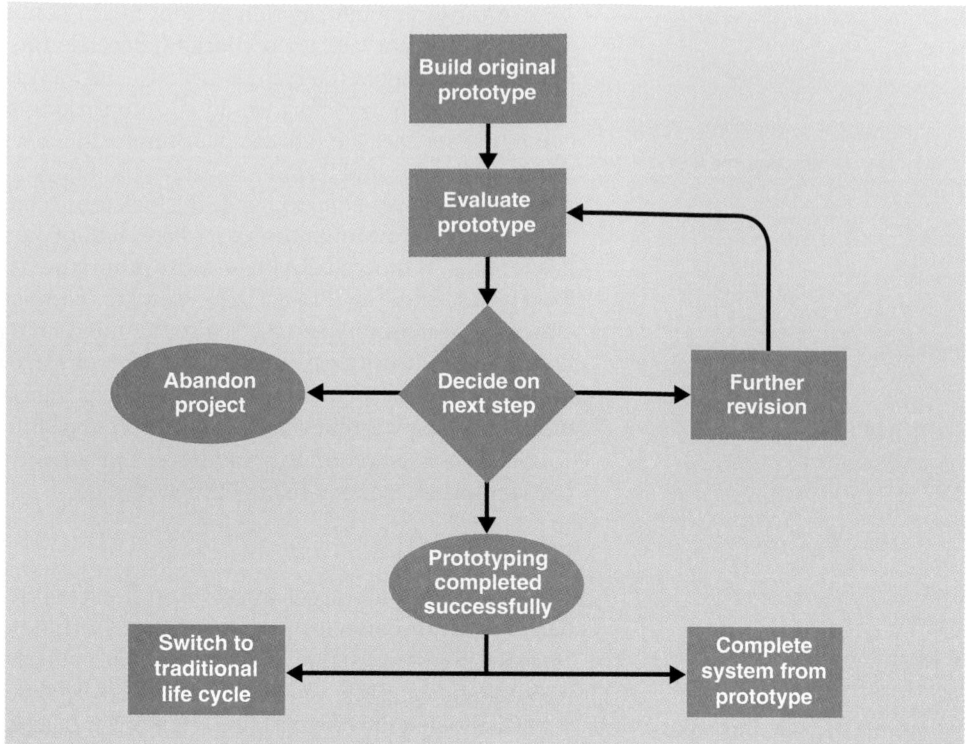

Figure 12.5
Using a prototype approach

Building an information system using a prototype is an iterative process. It involves evaluation and revision of a model system until the users and system builders understand the problem well enough to decide how to complete the project.

Development

The development process emphasizes speed and rapid feedback. It begins by developing an initial prototype that demonstrates some of the desired processing but is far from complete. Next come a series of iterations, each modifying the prototype based on user comments about the most recent version. The technical approach for this process differs from what would be used in a traditional life cycle. Instead of using a programming language that would support high-volume transaction processing, a prototype might be built using a 4GL or DBMS for personal computers.

Once the requirements are clear, the users and technical staff must decide how to proceed. They might conclude that the project should be abandoned. Although no one wants to start a project only to abandon it, the prototype reduces the time and resources absorbed by a project that won't succeed. If the project is to continue, one approach is to complete the prototype using the code that has been generated thus far. Another is to shift to a traditional system life cycle by writing a functional specification and external specification based on what has been learned and then doing the internal design based on the desired level of information system performance. Shifting to a traditional system life cycle is especially appropriate for an information system that will have a long life or will be critical to the business. If the system is primarily for management reporting, or if business problems are changing rapidly, extending the prototype might be a better choice.

Implementation

When using a prototype, part of the implementation is done in parallel with development. Users try out the prototype during successive iterations and become familiar with what it does and how it can help them. Systems developed this way may require less user training in the implementation phase. Active user participation in the development phase may offset skepticism about whether the results will be beneficial. For users who didn't participate in the prototyping, the training should be similar to the training they would have received in the traditional system life cycle. The conversion step should be similar to that of the traditional approach.

Operation and Maintenance

The operation and maintenance phase of an information system developed using a prototype should be similar to that of a system developed with the traditional life cycle. However, the characteristics of the development process contribute to both advantages and disadvantages that occur during the operation and maintenance phase.

Advantages and Disadvantages

The advantages of prototyping come from creating a more accurate idea of what the users really need. Starting from a better understanding has impacts on each remaining phase. During development, users have a tangible information system to work with instead of abstract specifications that may be difficult to visualize. This helps them provide useful feedback and may terminate an infeasible project before too much wasted effort. During implementation, the system may be more on target than it would have been otherwise. Early user involvement may also reduce skepticism and create a climate of acceptance about the new system. The impact during the operation and maintenance phase may be a reduced number of changes because of a better initial fit with user needs.

Building prototypes is much easier today than it was in the past because programming technology is much better. In particular, DBMSs, 4GLs, and CASE systems all contain screen generators (see Figure 12.6), report generators, and data dictionaries that make it easier to set up a model application quickly. Furthermore, because these same tools may be used for building the production version of the system, the transition from a prototype to a running system is much easier than it once was.

Using prototypes has disadvantages, however. The process of developing a prototype may require greater involvement and commitment by key users who are already busy with their regular work. Continual changes while analyzing succeeding versions of the prototype may be difficult for these users. The succession of rapid changes may also require an unusual level of skill and commitment by the IS professionals. This process can be frustrating because the users are often saying that the prototype is not right. It can also be stressful because rapid iterations imply frequent deadlines in producing the next version. On the other hand, system developers often find building prototypes exciting because they produce tangible results quickly and get considerable feedback about their accomplishments.

Figure 12.6
Creating a data input form

This Microsoft Access wizard permits a programmer to set up a data input form with minimal effort by automatically laying out a data input form after the programmer identifies the items that will appear on the form. It is an example of the programming advances that have made prototyping much easier.

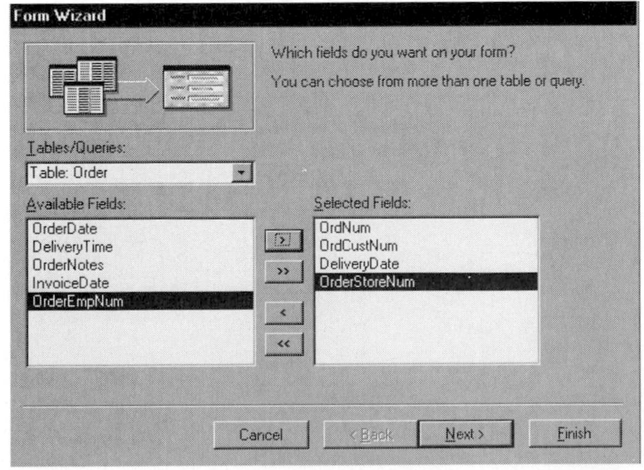

(a)

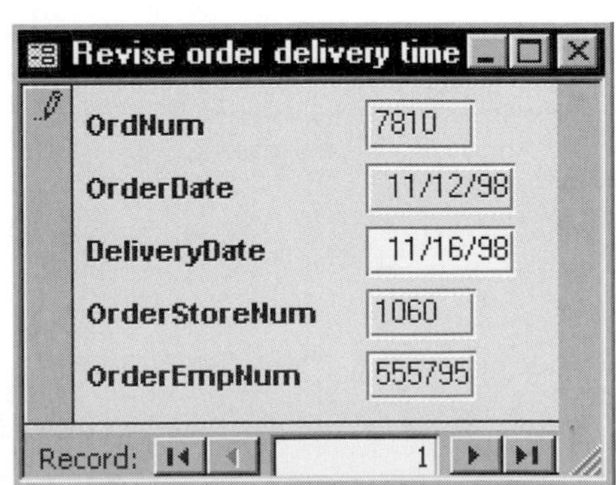

(b)

The shortcuts that make rapid prototyping iterations possible sometimes undermine the final system's technical foundations. This is a problem for prototypes put into use without being revamped technically. Internal design, programming, and documentation are not as sound as they would have been under the traditional life cycle. As a result, information system performance and reliability may suffer, and the system may require more maintenance than if the traditional life cycle had been used. The users of a prototype may also fail to appreciate its fragility and may not understand why the IS staff insists on revising a system that appears to work properly. Prototypes are built to demonstrate ideas. Even if the prototype eventually defines the final information system's general appearance, much more work must be done to assure reliability and adequate performance in real use. A prototype that looks good still is not successful in real use if it operates ten times too slowly, shuts down due to internal flaws, or has inadequate backup and recovery capabilities.

Prototypes are not the only alternative for bypassing parts of the traditional life cycle. Another is to purchase an application package previously developed by another firm.

APPLICATION PACKAGES

Although every company is unique in some ways, many information systems are similar across groups of companies. For example, the payroll systems in two small construction firms could be quite similar. Because there are thousands of such firms, this similarity leads to a business opportunity to develop and sell a payroll information system that many firms can use. Such systems typically start with custom work done for one or several firms. When the system works well for the original users, the software vendor markets it to other firms with similar requirements. The software vendor gradually adds more features to support a wider range of customers. Such systems often contain a number of modules and are therefore called application packages. The potential customers for most application packages have similar size and are in a particular market segment. For example, an appointment scheduling system sold to clinics with several doctors might not fit large clinics, which need different business processes for scheduling appointments. Figure 12.7 shows relationships between the modules of a type of information system that is commonly purchased as an application package.

Purchasing an application package reduces the time delay until a system can be operational. It also reduces the amount of system development work that is needed. However, as will be apparent by looking at the phases of acquiring and using an application

Figure 12.7
Example of a commercial application package

Manufacturing resource planning (MRP) systems such as this one are often application packages rather than internally built systems. The complexity of designing and integrating all the modules gives software vendors competitive advantage versus in-house IS groups in building and maintaining these systems.

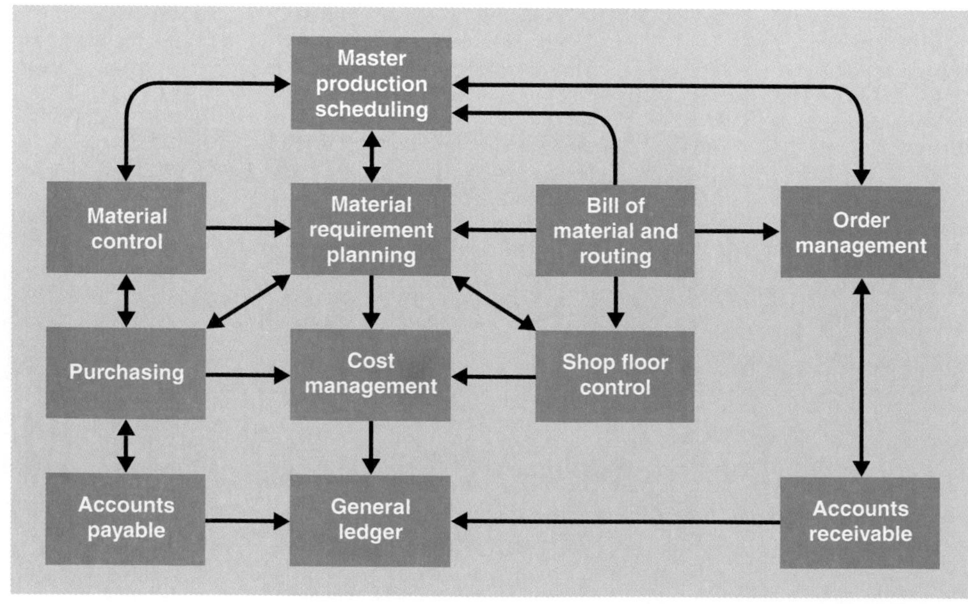

package, the life cycle for these systems still requires a great deal of effort and commitment. Table 12.6 shows some of the special characteristics of the phases of using an application package.

Phases

It might seem that buying an application system from a vendor would bypass most of the work of building and maintaining the information system. In fact, the company's staff must still work on all four phases to ensure that the right application package is selected and is set up and supported properly. For large applications such as factory management systems, several years of effort may pass before the new information system is fully operational and delivering benefits.

Initiation

The initiation phase may occur much as it would in the traditional life cycle, with a business problem or opportunity motivating a proposal to develop a new system. It may also start with a software vendor's sales call trying to convince the firm's management that the firm could use the vendor's product.

Regardless of how the project begins, it is often useful to produce a functional specification just as is done in the traditional life cycle. The functional specification represents the firm's perception of the problem and the required information system capabilities. It helps in deciding which vendors to consider and in selecting a software package. Failure to produce a functional specification can give vendors too much leeway in shaping the firm's view of its own problems.

Development

Although purchasing an application package changes the development phase, many development activities are still required. It is still necessary to decide exactly what features are needed, to test the software, and to tailor parts of the documentation for use within the firm. The process of clarifying user requirements and evaluating packages from different vendors involves the same issues as the first part of the development phase in the traditional life cycle. Instead of writing a formal external specification, the project team invites vendors to present their products and to provide live demonstrations. These demonstrations may be set up like prototype installations, with a small number of users using the application package on real data to understand how it works.

The firm may perform benchmark testing. **Benchmarking** an application package involves running a test application with the same volumes of input, output, data access, and data manipulation that the final application will have. Benchmarking sometimes

TABLE 12.6 **System Life Cycle for Acquiring an Application Package**

Phase	Characteristics
Initiation	May start with user's or manager's recognition of a business problem or with a sales call from a vendor.
Development	The vendor develops the software, although the purchaser still performs some typical development activities, such as determining detailed requirements. Development may include customization of the software and user documentation.
Implementation	Implementation starts by deciding exactly how the package will be used. It often relies on the vendor's staff because they have the greatest knowledge of the system.
Operation and maintenance	Operation occurs as it would with a traditional life cycle. Maintenance is different because the vendor maintains the software based on requests from customers and demands of the market.

reveals that an application package performs the right processing but cannot support the required volume of transactions. To compare products systematically, the project team may issue a **request for proposal (RFP),** which converts the ideas in the functional specification into a checklist of required capabilities and features. The vendors respond by explaining how their products meet the requirements.

Choosing among competing application packages is often difficult because each has advantages and disadvantages and few satisfy all user requirements. It may be unclear which features are or are not important. Business factors also matter, such as the vendor's financial strength and long-term viability. The selection process is based partially on information from vendors who emphasize their strengths and de-emphasize weaknesses. Good vendors avoid selling poorly matched software, however, because unhappy customers usually hurt a vendor's reputation. Poorly matched software also has implementation problems that often waste vendor time and resources.

In competitive situations with large, expensive application packages, vendors often try to be the first one in the door and try to "help" the buyer analyze the business problem. They do this to influence the problem statement so that the vendor's product appears to be a better fit than a competitor's product. For example, if vendor A's product runs on the UNIX operating system and vendor B's runs on Windows NT, vendor A may try to influence the company to view a UNIX platform as a requirement. Simultaneously, vendor B might try to include features that are difficult to obtain through UNIX.

When all is said and done, it is always possible to argue about the requirements. In fact, they are the result of a process of learning about alternative ideas and deciding which ones seem most important. Different people doing the same task might come up with different requirements.

Regardless of how the requirements are developed, it is necessary to select a vendor and product. Consider a retailer deciding what payroll software to purchase. To make the selection, it has identified a series of important characteristics under various headings, including application features, technical features, vendor comparison, and economic comparison. The retailer wants to decide by evaluating each alternative in terms of each characteristic and then combining these scores. More important characteristics have higher weighting in the final score. Box 12.2 illustrates this type of analysis. It weights each characteristic between 0 and 3 based on importance, evaluates each characteristic between 0 and 10 for each alternative, and calculates an overall score. Package B is preferred, but not by much.

In reality, the type of analysis in Box 12.2 is only an input to the decision and is often used as a sanity check to make sure that a significantly less preferable alternative is not chosen. One of many problems with over-reliance on a numerical comparison is that both the weightings and the ratings can be manipulated to some extent to give either of two close alternatives a slightly better score. Frequently, the real decision hinges on just several characteristics, such as whether the software runs on the right platform, whether the vendor is financially sound, and whether the vendor seems willing to change the software to suit the customer.

Implementation

The implementation phase begins by deciding exactly how the application package will be set up and used. This decision is necessary because most application packages contain a broad range of options to satisfy different customers' needs. A typical approach is to set up a trial installation of the information system and compare the choices for important options.

System documentation provided by the vendor must often be extended with a training manual tailored for a specific setting. For example, the vendor's manual may show how an order-entry system works for a paper distributor. A hardware distributor's users will learn about it most easily if the examples in the training manual are about hardware products.

The conversion from the existing system to the new system requires the same types of planning and training needed in a traditional life cycle. One key difference is related to

BOX 12.2 ***Selecting an application package***

The table below illustrates a common method for evaluating and comparing application packages. The results of this analysis are one of many types of information used in the selection. The table compares competing application packages A, B, and C based on four groups of characteristics. Each alternative has a score for each characteristic. For example, A has a score of 9 for completeness. Each characteristic also has a weight. For example, completeness has a weight of 2.5. The weighted score for each characteristic is the weight times the score. For example, the weighted score for completeness for A is 9 * 2.5 = 22.5. The total score for each alternative is the sum of its weighted scores. In this example, B is the preferred alternative with a total weighted score of 172.9.

		A	*B*	*C*	*A*	*B*	*C*
Characteristic	*Weight*	*Score*			*Weighted score*		
Application features							
completeness	2.5	9	7	8	22.5	17.5	20.0
quality of reports	1.0	9	5	9	9.0	5.0	9.0
ease of use	2.3	5	9	6	11.5	20.7	13.8
documentation	2.8	3	9	7	8.4	25.2	19.6
Technical features							
use of DBMS	2.8	8	7	3	22.4	19.6	8.4
transportability	0.8	2	5	6	1.6	4.0	4.8
expandability	1.2	4	5	5	4.8	6.0	6.0
Vendor comparison							
financial strength	2.0	9	7	5	18.0	14.0	10.0
management strength	1.3	6	9	8	7.8	11.7	10.4
commitment to product	2.6	4	7	9	10.4	18.2	23.4
Economic comparison							
purchase price	2.0	7	5	7	14.0	10.0	14.0
maintenance contract	1.5	7	7	8	10.5	10.5	12.0
consulting charges	0.6	5	6	8	3.0	3.6	4.8
conversion cost	2.3	5	3	5	11.5	6.9	11.5
Total weighted score					**155.4**	**172.9**	**167.7**

information system knowledge because the main experts on the purchased software are employees of the vendor rather than the firm that uses it. An expert on the software should be available during the implementation. The expert could be a vendor employee or a company employee who knows enough to troubleshoot problems that occur during implementation.

Operation and Maintenance

Operation and maintenance for application packages is similar to this phase in the other approaches. Someone must be responsible for ensuring the information system operates efficiently on the computer and is used effectively in the organization. There must be a process for collecting enhancement requests and acting on them, and there must be a process for installing new software releases, starting with an analysis of their possible impact on users.

Application packages are unique because the vendor has the greatest expertise about the package and owns the responsibility for enhancing it. Most vendors enhance their products based on customer feedback and their own long-term plans. They typically send out new releases every 6 to 12 months. A **release** is an upgraded version of the software that the customer must install. Ideally, the vendor and customer should cooperate closely. The vendor should be available for questions and should base future enhancements on product usage. The vendor should respond quickly when bugs are found, especially if the bugs prevent users from doing their work. Figure 12.8 shows how the vendor's responsibilities fit into the phases of the system life cycle.

Product enhancements are a delicate issue in vendor-customer relationships. As happens with in-house development, vendors of application packages used in multiple sites soon have long lists of enhancement requests. Some of these require major product changes. Vendors usually work with their customers to identify the genuinely important enhancements. They also explain that many desired enhancements cannot be done. Managing relationships with vendors requires business and negotiation skills. These relationships require the ability to exert pressure to get the vendor to do what you want, but without having direct management authority over vendor personnel.

To protect themselves and their customers, vendors usually provide application packages under license agreements allowing the customer to use the software but not change it. To minimize dissatisfaction about receiving information in the wrong format, vendors usually provide database formats and links to 4GLs. Features such as these help customers program their own reports, even if they are not permitted to change the transactions or database structure. Limiting customer changes prevents the customer from contaminating the database.

Advantages and Disadvantages

There are many reasons to purchase application packages. Benefits accrue sooner and the risks of cost and schedule overruns drop because the purchased software is available immediately, rather than months or years from now. Purchasing software helps a firm focus its resources on producing and selling whatever product or service it provides. Because the application package is the vendor's product, it will usually be documented and maintained better than in-house software. Vendors may also produce better features because they study the same problem in many companies. Finally, the firm's IS department may not have the knowledge, experience, or staffing necessary to produce the software.

With these advantages, purchasing an application package might usually seem a good choice. Unfortunately, the features in these products may not fit well. Firms using application packages often have to compromise on the business processes they want. As mentioned in reference to Owens Corning and Kodak examples in Chapter 11, this has been an especially difficult issue for firms attempting to implement enterprise resource planning (ERP) systems. A rarely used alternative is to purchase application software and then modify it to suit local requirements. A key shortcoming of this alternative is that application vendors usually won't maintain software modified by customers. Even without customized changes, users of major application packages typically pay 10% to 15% of the package's purchase price per year for maintenance, support, and new releases.

Figure 12.8
Vendor responsibilities for application packages

When an application package is used, the vendor's staff plays major roles at each phase of the system life cycle.

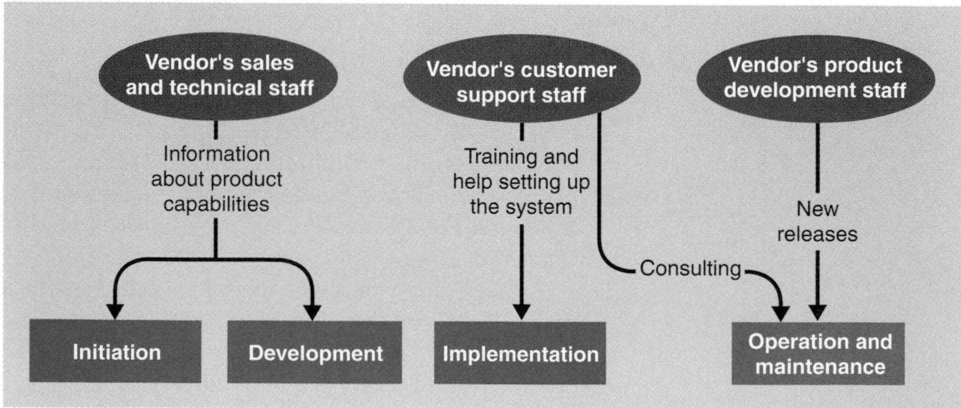

Control of the long-term direction of the software is also an issue because the vendor makes that decision. Because many customers provide inputs about desired enhancements, individual customers may have little control over software that controls their business processes. In addition, there is the risk that the vendor will go out of business, leaving no reliable way to maintain the software.

Application packages require the company's IS staff to analyze, install, and maintain software developed elsewhere instead of developing new information systems themselves. IS professionals recognize that these evaluation and maintenance roles require knowledge and professionalism and are critical to the organization. However, these roles sometimes receive less professional credit and fewer accolades in the organization. Some IS staff members and users resent having to conform to the restrictions of software developed elsewhere. NIH ("not invented here") is often cited as a reason purchased software encounters problems.

Finally, although application packages can support specific data processing needs, they rarely provide sustainable competitive advantage because any competitor can usually buy the same package. Some firms have a strategy of using application packages for functions that don't provide competitive advantage but are necessary for running the business, such as accounting, payroll, and human resources. Acquiring application packages in these areas frees up resources for other applications that help differentiate the firm in its market.

The alternatives described thus far all assume that professional programmers will develop an information system for users. The next process assumes that the users are able to develop their own information systems.

END-USER DEVELOPMENT

In the 1980s the term **end-user computing (EUC)** became popular as a description of computing that was truly the tool of the end user. EUC was originally viewed as the direct, hands-on use of computer systems by end users whose jobs go beyond entering data or processing transactions. The personal computer revolution of the 1980s made end-user computing possible through the use of personal productivity tools such as word processors, spreadsheets, online appointment calendars, electronic mail, and presentation graphics. Linkage of PCs into networks later permitted end-user computing to evolve and include many forms of everyday access to corporate data.

End-user development is a form of EUC in which users rather than programmers develop small data processing systems or models. Typical tools for end-user development include spreadsheets, DBMSs, 4GLs, and data analysis software. Figure 12.9 shows one of the capabilities that makes end-user development easier to perform.

End-user development became possible with the advent of spreadsheets and small DBMSs that could be used and controlled by people not trained as programmers. It is a partial solution to a severe overload problem in most IS departments, many of which have two-year backlogs of scheduled work. In this situation, users may feel it is pointless to request additional changes to existing systems, and the IS staff feels frustrated at not being able to provide good service. If the users could just change report formats or build small data processing systems, they would get more of what they want and the IS department's backlog would shrink. The technical staff would be more able to focus on major problems and opportunities, rather than continually changing old information systems. Table 12.7 outlines important aspects of this approach.

End-user development applies only where requirements for response time, reliability, and maintainability are not stringent; where the project is limited to a department and not on a critical path for other projects; and where proven technology is used. Unassisted end-user computing may be inappropriate even if high performance levels aren't needed. For example, the error rate in even simple spreadsheets is high because users often lack knowledge of testing methods and other programming disciplines that are needed to debug spreadsheets.

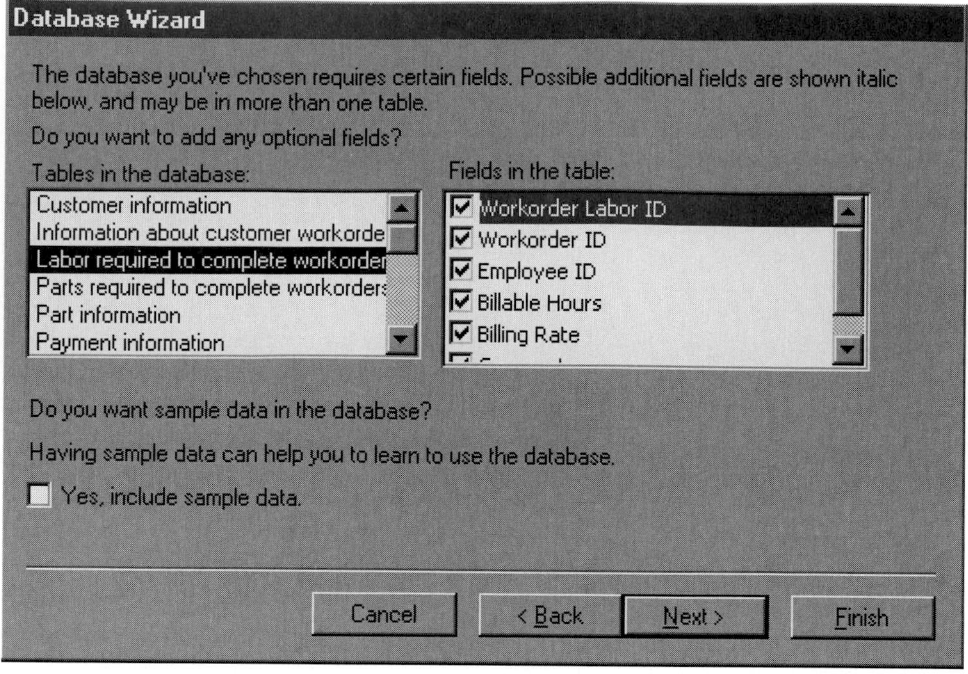

Figure 12.9
A tool for end-user development

This wizard in Microsoft Access provides a series of possible starting points that can be used in typical end-user development efforts.

Phases

The phases of end-user development are based on the fact that the end user does the work and is responsible for the results.

Initiation

The user identifies a problem or opportunity that can be addressed with end-user technology. For example, a sales manager might need an information system for keeping track of sales prospects. Support staff may help in defining the problem more clearly and in identifying how the available tools can help. A functional specification is bypassed because the problem scope is small and because an explanation for someone else's approval is unnecessary.

Development

End-users take responsibility for their own systems, deciding what they need and developing it using tools appropriate for them. Success often depends on the availability of IS staff who support the end-user developers with training and consulting. In most firms, end

TABLE 12.7 **System Life Cycle for End-User Development**

Phase	Characteristics
Initiation	Because the user will develop the information system, a formal functional specification is unnecessary.
Development	The user develops the system using tools that do not require a professional level of programming knowledge. Information systems that are critical to the company or have many users require more extensive testing, documentation, and usage procedures.
Implementation	Implementation is simplified because the developer is the user.
Operation and maintenance	End users are responsible. Long-term maintenance and technical quality become larger issues because the end users have other work to do and are not professional programmers.

users must use computers and software supported by a central IS department. Figure 12.10 shows the various roles that the IS department plays in end-user development.

Implementation

End-user development simplifies the implementation phase because the end user doesn't need training about the application. Training of other information system users is easier because an end user is an expert on both the system and how it fits into the department's business processes. Likewise, system acceptance may be less of an issue because end-user developers are so attuned to what is needed.

Operation and Maintenance

End users are totally responsible for the operation and maintenance of systems developed through end-user development. They decide when and how these systems will be used and create whatever documentation is needed. They perform backups and are responsible for system security. End users also determine what enhancements and corrections are needed and make those changes. When those systems are critical to the company, controls must be enforced to establish system security and to maintain the systems.

Supporting the Users

Successful end-user computing must deal with a number of issues involving hardware, software, training, data availability, data security, and systems analysis (see Table 12.8).

Because end users are not hardware experts and have other work to do, the IS department typically supplies and manages computers and workstations. The IS staff produces guidelines about what equipment will be supported. This consistency makes the computers cheaper to acquire and service. Instead of acquiring computers and network components one at a time, firms can get volume discounts. Rather than trying to keep different types of computers operating, the firm's hardware staff can concentrate on one or several types. Similar issues arise for software. Although individuals might have their own favorite spreadsheet or word processor, using many different products is inefficient. Firms often arrange **site licenses,** blanket contracts covering the use of a particular software product at a particular site by a particular number of users. (The number of simultaneous users can

Figure 12.10
Roles in end-user development

The IS staff plays many crucial roles in end-user development even though end users develop and maintain systems.

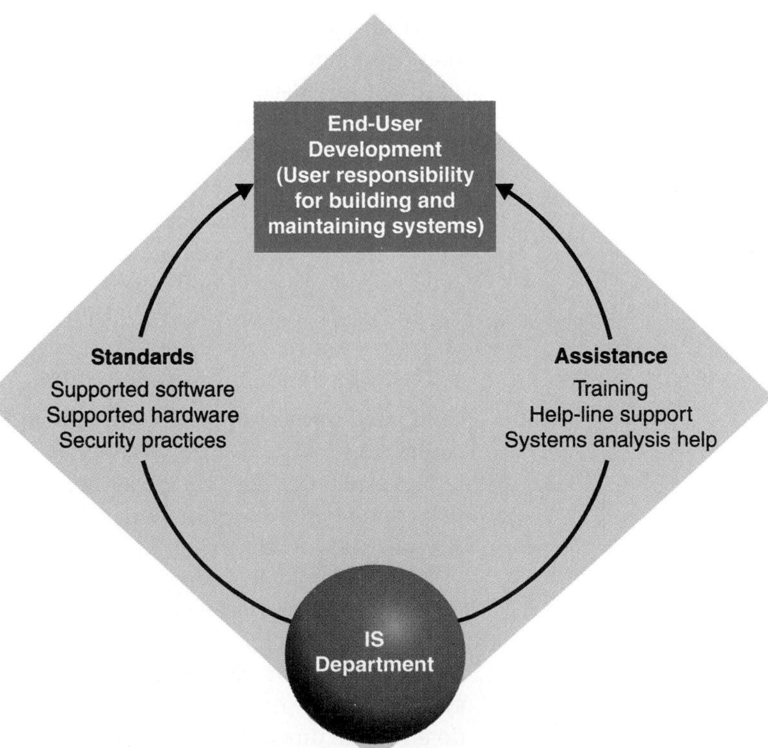

TABLE 12.8 **Common Approaches to Issues in End-User Computing**

End-user computing raises many issues that should be handled consistently to avoid wasted effort by users and the IS staff.

Issue	Common approach
Hardware selection and maintenance	The IS staff selects the types of hardware that can be pur chased and maintains the hardware.
Software selection	The IS staff selects the spreadsheet software and other end-user software that can be purchased and used.
Training	The IS staff provides training for end users on selected hardware and software.
Data availability	End users control their own data and share data using LANs. Corporate data are downloaded from central computers.
Data security	Limit access to only the data users need.
Systems analysis	Help end users with systems analysis and design where necessary. Provide help lines and other types of support.

be controlled through LANs that supply the software when needed.) Using only compatible software also makes it easier for users to work together. At minimum it eliminates obstacles to teamwork. Training is an area where restricting the hardware and software available to end users has important advantages. End-user training is often required for successful end-user computing. It is much easier to offer training and assistance for a small number of hardware and software choices.

Data availability is crucial when end-user applications need data residing on other computers. For example, consider a human resources manager who needs data to analyze a proposed benefit program. Some of the data may reside elsewhere on a network and therefore may need to be downloaded. Greater access to data raises questions about data security. End-user computing entails security risks because end users have individual control over what they do with data. Downloading data to a workstation with a floppy disk drive makes it easier to steal data. Consequently, the data available to end users must be limited to what they legitimately need. This limitation is far from foolproof, however, because many users need sensitive data, such as customer lists, pricing arrangements, and product design data.

End users often lack the system-related experience of IS professionals and need help in analyzing and designing systems and troubleshooting problems. Firms provide this help in various ways. Many deploy internal consultants to help end users by providing advice but not developing systems themselves. Many have set up help lines that can answer questions related to computers and systems. Many have established small groups that support end-user development by selecting and maintaining hardware and software, training end users, and providing consulting.

Advantages and Disadvantages

Compared to the complexity of the traditional life cycle, end-user development almost sounds too good to be true. It reduces the need for programmers and minimizes the problem of explaining requirements to people unfamiliar with the business. It eliminates the delays and political negotiations in resolving requirements and in implementing the system once it is developed.

Unfortunately, end-user development applies only to a limited set of situations. It works best where problems can be isolated from each other so that users can take full responsibility for both data and programs. Among other factors, the limitations of end-user development are related to the development tools used, the technical quality of the system, and the need for long-term maintenance. Because end users have other work to do and little time for learning to program, their tools are not the same as those designed for professional programmers. Many end users can use spreadsheets, small DBMSs, 4GLs, and statistical packages. Almost none can use programming languages or complex DBMSs requiring a professional level of involvement and understanding. Tools for trained programmers are needed to produce maintainable information systems involving shared databases and stringent response time or security requirements.

Technical quality is another issue for information systems built by end users. These systems are often less well designed and constructed than systems built by IS professionals. They are also more prone to bugs because end users are inexperienced in debugging. These issues may not be a problem in systems built for temporary, personal use by an individual, but matter greatly for systems with many users over a sustained period. Long-term maintenance is an especially important issue for complex applications involving many users. End-user developers may also find that long-term maintenance interferes with their primary job responsibilities. Like it or not, the support staff may be drawn into system maintenance roles when these situations occur.

Reality Check

END-USER DEVELOPMENT

This section explained end-user development and some of its advantages and disadvantages.

1. Think about your personal experience in developing spreadsheet models or doing other work related to computers. How comfortable would you feel if you had to develop a small system by yourself for keeping track of customers or calculating customer bills?
2. What kind of help do you think you would need?

DECIDING WHICH COMBINATION OF METHODS TO USE

The four life cycle models described so far are idealizations, each involving different processes and emphasizing different issues. Understanding these issues helps in deciding what methods to use for a project. After comparing the advantages and disadvantages of the four alternatives, this section will conclude with ways to combine features of different processes into an approach appropriate for a particular situation.

Comparing Advantages and Disadvantages

Table 12.9 compares the advantages and disadvantages of the four alternatives. Many of the principal disadvantages of each approach are the mirror image of its principal advantages.

The traditional system life cycle establishes control to avoid developing information systems that miss the mark or are difficult to maintain. But these same controls are sometimes burdensome and may take on a life of their own. When this happens, the project team starts going through the motions of producing deliverables but puts less effort into responding to the users' changing needs.

Prototypes focus on helping the user identify the requirements based on real understanding. Rapid iterations of prototypes support this but often produce software that is more difficult to maintain than software designed carefully before programming begins. When the prototype takes shape, the users often wonder why they cannot put it into operation immediately. In addition, the process of simultaneously developing ideas and coding requires programmers and users who are willing and able to work iteratively.

Application packages keep company resources focused on the company's business, rather than on building information systems to support the company's business. But the company does not have complete control over how the package works. Business processes may have to change to conform to the logic built into the package. Furthermore, desired enhancements may never appear because the vendor's other customers may not find these enhancements important.

TABLE 12.9 Advantages and Disadvantages of Four System Life Cycles

Life cycle	Advantages	Disadvantages
Traditional system life cycle	• Forces staff to be systematic by going through every step in an idealized process • Enforces quality by maintaining standards and reinforcing the expectation that the system will be produced to spec • Lower probability of missing important issues in the requirements analysis	• May produce excessive documentation; users feel buried in paperwork • Users are often unwilling or unable to study the specs that they approve • Takes too long to go from the original ideas to a working system • Users have trouble describing requirements for a proposed system
Prototype	• Helps clarify user requirements before the design is cast in concrete • Helps verify the feasibility of the design • Promotes genuine user participation in design • May produce part of the final information system	• May encourage inadequate problem analysis • User may not give up the prototype • May require "superprogrammers" • May generate confusion about whether or not the information system is complete and maintainable
Application package	• Software exists and can be tried out • Software has been used for similar problems elsewhere • Shortcuts delays for analysis, design, and programming • Has good documentation that will be maintained	• Controlled by another company that has its own priorities and business considerations • Package's limitations may prevent desired business processes • May be difficult to get needed enhancements if other companies using the package do not need those enhancements • Lack of intimate knowledge about how the software works and why it works that way
End-user development	• Bypasses the IS department and avoids delays • User controls the application and can change it as needed	• Creates fragile systems because an amateur does the programming • May eventually require consulting and maintenance assistance from the IS department

End-user development may be more responsive to end-user needs because it bypasses the IS department and avoids delays. However, it is only appropriate for systems that are limited in organizational scope, easy to debug, require little maintenance, and can be built using tools appropriate for end users.

Combining System Development Approaches

Although the four life cycle models might seem mutually exclusive, it is possible to combine their features into the approach for a given situation. Here are some ways to combine their features:

- Use a prototype as part of a traditional system life cycle. It may be difficult to produce a good functional specification or external specification without providing some hands-on experience. Therefore, include a prototyping phase in the original project plan, but insist that an internal specification be written as the basis for the internal design of the final information system.
- Use a small application package as a prototype. Shortcut the analysis process by purchasing an inexpensive application package and determining why it would or would not fit the situation. Identify required features it contains or lacks, as well as its unnecessary features. If it is well documented, use its documentation as a reference for clarifying business terminology and even helping the programmers understand an unfamiliar business situation.
- Adopt aspects of a traditional life cycle to purchasing an application package. Start with a functional specification. This makes it easier to evaluate alternative application

packages. Purchasers of a packaged system can use appropriate parts of the traditional life cycle to be sure the problem is understood, the information system well tested, and the implementation well organized.

- Add an end-user development component to the traditional life cycle. Use the traditional life cycle to create the core of the information system based on a solid internal design and carefully controlled data updates. Develop user reports or inquiries using a 4GL that can be taught to users. Let the users develop their own reports using the original report programs as starting points and as demonstrations of good programming style. This maintains control of data while providing some of the advantages of end-user development. For complicated reporting requirements, use a programmer.

Other variations on the four life cycle models have been used but won't be covered in detail here. In the **phased approach,** the information system is built through a sequence of iterations of development, implementation, and operation. The idea is to address a small and manageable part of the problem, observe how this information system works, and then identify another small project that would lead to improvements but not have the risk of a lengthy project.

Joint application development (JAD) is another important variation. Its distinguishing feature is a carefully prepared two- to four-day meeting bringing together user representatives and IS staff members. At this meeting they analyze the business problem and come to a shared understanding of what must be done. JAD tries to eliminate misunderstandings that often persist despite lengthy user interviews during the analysis needed for functional specifications and external specifications. Bringing people together this way increases user participation and gives the user community a greater feeling of ownership for the information system. Some believe JAD also saves a lot of time that would be spent in a lengthy analysis.

However, some research on JAD has found that JAD may not live up to its promise. In a genuine problem solving dialogue, both business professionals and the system builders freely express their opinions, understandings, and concerns about the situation. One exploratory study found that JAD workshop activities were focused on system developers' models and terminology, and that the business area personnel were expected to participate on those terms with little or no training.[9]

There are clearly many ways to build systems. The four life cycle models are just that, models that express a particular approach. System builders applying any of these approaches should be aware of their advantages and disadvantages and should develop a project plan that truly fits the situation, just as Microsoft did in the opening case.

CHAPTER CONCLUSION

Summary

What are the four phases of information system projects?
Any information system, regardless of how it is acquired, goes through four phases: initiation, development, implementation, and operation and maintenance. Initiation is the process of defining the need to change an existing work system, identifying the people who should be involved in deciding what to do, and describing in general terms how the work system should operate differently and how any information system that supports it should operate differently. Development is the process of building or acquiring and configuring hardware, software, and other resources needed to perform both the required IT-related functions and the required functions not related to IT. Implementation is the process of making a new or improved work system operational in the organization. Operation and maintenance is the ongoing operation of the work system and the information system, plus efforts directed at enhancing either system and correcting bugs.

What types of issues are addressed by the different system development processes?
The traditional system life cycle tries to solve a control problem by keeping the project on track. A prototype information system is a working model of the system built to learn about its true requirements. Firms acquire application packages to solve a resource and timing problem by using commercially available software that performs most of the functions desired. Firms use end-user development to solve a responsiveness problem involving the inability of information systems groups to keep up with changing information needs of individuals.

How does the traditional system life cycle solve the control problem of keeping a project on track?
The traditional system life cycle establishes a series of phases and steps with deliverables that must be completed before the step is completed. Key deliverables for the initiation phase include the functional specification and the project plan. For the development phase, they include the external and internal specifications, hardware plan, programs, testing plan, completion of system testing, and user and technical documentation. For implementation, they include the implementation plan, training materials, formal system acceptance, and post-implementation audit report. For operation and maintenance, they include the operations manual, maintenance plan, and completion of specific enhancements.

What are the advantages and disadvantages of prototypes?
The advantages of prototyping come from using a tangible working model instead of abstract specifications to clarify what the users need. During implementation, the system may be more on target than it would have been otherwise, and subsequent changes during operation may be reduced. However, developing a prototype may require exceptional developers and excessive involvement by key users. Users may not appreciate the incompleteness and technical fragility of a prototype.

What are the advantages and disadvantages of application packages?
Application packages reduce system development work, thereby reducing delays and helping a firm focus its resources on products or services it creates. They are often documented and maintained better than software built in-house and may provide better solutions. However, they often fit a firm's business processes only partially and the firm lacks long-term control of the package's direction.

What are the advantages and disadvantages of end-user development?
End-user development reduces the need for programmers, avoids the communication overhead of explaining the requirements to a technical staff, and eliminates the delays and political negotiations. However, it applies only to a limited set of situations and works best where problems can be isolated from each other so that users can take full responsibility for both data and programs. The resulting information systems are often less well designed and more prone to bugs than systems built by IT professionals.

How is it possible to combine system development approaches into a system's life cycle?
A prototype can be used as part of a traditional system life cycle. A small application package can be used as a prototype to shortcut the analysis process. A structured approach can be used when purchasing an application package. An end-user development component can be added to the traditional life cycle.

Key Terms

runaway
initiation
development
implementation
operation and maintenance
traditional system life cycle
capability maturity model (CMM)
prototype
application package
end-user development
feasibility study
functional specification
project plan
detailed requirements analysis
external specification
internal system design
internal specification
hardware acquisition and installation
programming
unit testing
documentation
system testing

testing plan
implementation planning
training
conversion
phased approach
running in parallel
pilot implementation
acceptance testing
post-implementation audit
ongoing operation and support
operations manual
maintenance
throwaway prototype
evolutionary prototype
benchmarking
request for proposal (RFP)
release
end-user computing (EUC)
site license
phased approach
joint application development (JAD)

Review Questions

1. Identify the four phases any system goes through, and some of the common issues and problems that occur in each phase.
2. Why is it sometimes appropriate for a system project never to go past the initiation phase?
3. What are the links between the four phases and some of the reasons for rework of a previous phase?
4. Describe the four alternative approaches for building systems and the main issues addressed by each.
5. What different types of feasibility are considered in a feasibility study?
6. Identify the main deliverables from the development phase, and explain why additional phases are necessary after development.
7. When in the traditional life cycle is user involvement greatest? Least?
8. What are the different approaches for converting from a previous system to a new system?
9. Explain reasons for using pilot implementations, acceptance testing, and post-implementation audits.
10. How is using a prototype different from using a traditional system life cycle?
11. What are the two types of prototypes?
12. Why is it still necessary for a firm to do a lot of systems analysis work when it purchases an application system?
13. What types of characteristics are considered when selecting among several application packages?
14. When working with an application package vendor that sells an established product, what may a firm expect to receive from the vendor during each of the four phases?
15. What are the advantages and disadvantages of using application packages?
16. Under what circumstances is end-user development appropriate?
17. Why do firms arrange site licenses with software vendors?
18. How is it possible to combine features of different life cycle models into the approach for building any particular system?

Discussion Topics

1. A code of ethics developed by three Swedish trade unions that organize computing personnel stated that computer professionals only take part in projects with the time and resources to do a good job, only develop systems in close collaboration with the user, and refrain from tasks aiming at control in ways that can be of harm to individuals.[10] Explain why you do or do not believe any computer professional would conform to these rules at all times.
2. Assume that your entire class had two months to write a single combined term paper. Within a broad guideline that the paper must be about some topic related to information systems, the class must decide on the topic and produce the paper. The class has asked you to decide how to do the project, what the steps will be, and who will do what work. What process would you propose for performing the project? What problems or difficulties are likely to occur in this project as you have outlined it? Compare your approach to the traditional system life cycle, explaining major similarities and differences.

3. Based on the description of Microsoft's "synch and stabilize" model at the beginning of the chapter, explain where you think Microsoft is operating on the capability maturity model in Box 12.1.
4. The information systems manager at Balboa Hardware decided to take a stand. "We have had too many system failures. As of today, don't even think about a new information system unless you use a traditional system life cycle." Use the ideas in the chapter to explain the implications of this statement.
5. Should the development process for the different types of systems identified in Chapter 5 be different? If so, explain what the differences should be. If not, explain why there should be no differences. The answer in either instance should use ideas related to the alternative processes in this chapter.
6. Explain any relationships between the critical success factors method described in Chapter 11 and the various system development processes described in this chapter. If the relationships are unimportant, explain why.

CASE

B-Tree Systems, Inc.: Verifying Embedded Systems

Heart pacemakers, anti-lock brakes, digital cameras, and fax machines all have something in common. Each of these devices contains programs built into "embedded systems" that control device operation. These embedded systems must be created and tested just as business information systems must be created and tested. An important difference, however, is that the embedded systems are typically mission-critical for the device. Bugs in these embedded systems can result in device failure, with consequences ranging from mild annoyance to tragedy, depending on the type of device. The challenge of thorough testing is frequently compounded by competitive pressures to bring products to market quickly while also providing an abundance of features that add complexity. For example, the embedded software in a current digital camera may contain 500,000 lines of code.

B-Tree Systems, Inc., is a Minnesota-based company that provides systems and support services for verifying software on embedded PC and microprocessor devices throughout the product development cycle. Its mission is to enable vendors to develop and deliver high-quality electronic products more efficiently. B-Tree Systems was founded in 1982 as a hardware and software consulting firm. It entered the testing business in 1988 when it helped a pacemaker manufacturer discover product flaws that had been overlooked. B-Tree Systems formalized its understanding of testing by creating a set of methods and tools for automatic system verification. The traditional process of testing devices by putting them through their paces manually is time consuming, repetitious, and unreliable due to human error. B-Tree's automated process makes it more possible to simulate and test all the conditions that the embedded system can be confronted with. This makes it possible to test many more conditions, to run multiple tests with greater consistency and reliability, to run the tests unattended, and to generate the test results automatically. These steps help streamline regulatory certification processes.

B-Tree's concurrent verification techniques support verification throughout the product development cycle instead of just testing when the product development is complete. This means that defects will be found earlier in the cycle and that product redesign late in the cycle will be less likely. A closed-loop testing environment is accomplished through automatically executed test scripts written using C-language commands. The product development cycle starts with requirements specification and design. The corresponding requirements verification captures the requirements in a structured design model and runs the model in real time to test for incorrect, incomplete, or omitted requirements. B-Tree's tools are used during this phase to develop the structured design model, test cases, and verification scripts. The test case tables are a set of test conditions with the corresponding inputs and expected output values of all system variables needed to verify the requirements. The second step in the product cycle is prototyping and development. The corresponding verification step tests new modules as they become available by compiling new "software builds." Catching problems while the recent changes are fresh in the developer's mind facilitates rapid correction. At the system integration phase, the verification process tests the functionality of hardware and software components when integrated into larger functional units. Finding the problem at this stage often takes more time than fixing it. B-Tree provides noninvasive analysis tools that provide a detailed view of internal dataflows without changing the system being tested or its performance. At the initial release stage, a final validation occurs. Test results from the requirements phase are now used as expected values when scripts from that phase are reused.

QUESTIONS

1. Explain the similarities and differences between the life cycles for typical business information systems and for products that contain embedded systems.
2. The Strategic Defense Initiative in the 1980s was a project aimed at creating a satellite-based anti-missile defense capability. It generated great controversy among computer scientists because of questions about how it could be tested. Explain how this case illuminates those questions.

Sources:

B-Tree Systems, Inc. "What Is Concurrent Verification?" June 3, 1998 (http://www.btree.com/AutomatedTest/verifi/index.html).

Mamis, Robert A. "When Chips Fail," *Forbes ASAP*, June 1, 1998, pp. 87–88.

CASE

FAA: Trying to Overhaul the Air Traffic Control System

The information system air traffic controllers use to control airplanes in the air and on the ground is a mission-critical system whose failure would endanger hundreds or thousands of lives. Its ideal design goals include minimizing delays, maximizing airport efficiency, and ensuring the safety of passengers and crews. Unfortunately, it uses obsolete computers and workstations and displays only part of the potentially available information that air traffic controllers might be able to use in normal situations and emergencies. Computer failures have occurred occasionally at control centers, leaving the air traffic controllers with little to work on but guesses and projections from last known locations. Although not usually associated with the computer failures, in 1997 there were 225 near misses by aircraft flying too close together, up 22% from 1996.

In 1981 the Federal Aviation Administration (FAA) proposed a project to overhaul the entire air traffic control system by building the Advanced Automation System (AAS) with an initial installation in Seattle in 1992. In 1984 IBM Federal Systems and Hughes were chosen as finalists for the contract. After three years and $500 million of FAA expenditures on prototypes, the FAA selected IBM's $3.6 billion fixed cost contract in 1988. The Government Accounting Office (GAO) warned that this was unrealistically low. The FAA pushed for an unprecedented 99.99999% reliability, no more than three seconds of downtime per year. Contrary to the wishes of the air traffic controllers, who wanted to retain paper strips they used to chart the progress of planes, the FAA wanted to accomplish the same type of function with a few keystrokes in a totally paperless environment. This was not achieved with the available technology. A report in 1992 found significant technical flaws in the work to date, including the inability to reach the required peak load of 210 coordinated consoles in a single facility. Six months later, IBM announced a 14-month delay. The FAA and IBM both proposed a number of changes and finally agreed to freeze technical requirements by April, 1993. Later that year, Loral purchased IBM Federal Systems.

In 1994 a new FAA administrator revamped the AAS team and later threw out major portions of the AAS design, deciding to emphasize Display System Replacement (DSR) in a new contract with Loral. A mock-up of the new display caused major controversy at the 1995 air traffic controllers' convention because it did not adequately handle the paper strips used to chart the progress of the planes. In 1994 the FAA administrator also launched a project to use global positioning satellites to make sure that aircraft would not fly on collision courses. An initial system design by one contractor was deemed unreliable in 1995, and a $475 million contract went to Hughes Electronics in 1996 to continue the work. The FAA administrator left the government in 1996. During 1996 and 1997 the scope of the technical requirements expanded to include as many as six new satellites and additional navigation aids on each airplane, including 180,000 small, general aviation planes. By 1998 the future of this project was in doubt. Meanwhile, work continued on the new terminals for air traffic controllers. On Mar. 5, 1998, the next FAA administrator testified that the FAA was closer to solving what air traffic controllers described as a hazardous flaw in the new hardware and software the agency planned to install nationwide starting in late 1998 or 1999. The controllers had complained that the design of the Standard Terminal Automation Replacement System (STARS) may hinder air traffic control because the system's windowing software frequently blocks icons that represent aircraft on the screen. In February, 1998, a human factors team had solved 87 of 98 remaining issues. The administrator said "I am optimistic that all the human factors issues will be resolved."

QUESTIONS

1. How are these problems related to the ideas about planning and building information systems in the two previous chapters?
2. Some observers cite the actual safety record of air traffic in arguing that the FAA's problems have not been a direct cause of airliner crashes and therefore are overstated. Explain why you agree or disagree.
3. What do you believe the FAA should do now?

Sources:

Bourlas, Stephen. "Anatomy of a Runaway: What Grounded AAS," *IEEE Software*, Jan. and Mar. 1996, reprinted in Robert L. Glass, *Software Runaways*, Upper Saddle River, NJ: Prentice Hall, 1998, pp. 56–64.

Cole, Jeff. "How Major Overhaul of Air-Traffic Control Lost Its Momentum," *Wall Street Journal*, Mar. 2, 1998, p. A1.

O'Hara, Colleen. "FAA Works With Controllers to Solve Unsafe STARS Design," *Federal Computer Week*, March 6, 1998. June 3, 1998 (www.fcw.com/pubs/fcw/1998/0302/web-stars-3-2-1998.html).

13 Information System Security and Control

Study Questions

- What are the main types of risks of accidents related to information systems?
- What are the different types of computer crime?
- What issues magnify the vulnerability of information systems to accidents and crime?
- What measures can be taken to minimize accidents and computer crime?
- What are the different ways to control access to data, computers, and networks?

Outline

Opening Case

LONDON AMBULANCE SERVICE: A MAJOR SYSTEM FAILURE

The London Ambulance Service (LAS) covers a population of 6.8 million people, carries over 5,000 patients every day, and receives up to 2,500 calls a day. (See Table 13.1.) Its goal is to respond to calls in an average of 14 minutes. A previous system for dispatching ambulances in response to medical emergencies had divided London into three separate zones and had communicated with ambulances through a combination of two-way radio, telephones, and computer displays in vehicles. Operators in the dispatching center received calls about emergencies and worked with local ambulance stations to identify the nearest available ambulance and then dispatch it to the site. A new system was developed to treat all of London as a single zone. It effectively did away with radio and telephone calls to stations and permitted the computer to dispatch ambulance crews automatically based on the location of the patient and of available ambulances. Unfortunately the new system had not been completely tested or debugged when it was put into operation on October 26, 1992. As the night progressed, calls were missed, several ambulances were dispatched to the same emergency, and operators in the dispatching center were swamped with computerized exception messages. Some emergency callers could not get through for up to 30 minutes. Between 10 and 20 people probably died because ambulances arrived up to three hours late. A spokesman for LAS called the situation "a complete nightmare."

A formal inquiry into this disaster concluded that neither the computerized parts of the system nor the human participants had been ready for full implementation. The software was neither complete nor fully tested. The computer system's performance under a full load had not been tested. The dispatching staff and ambulance crews had no confidence in the new information system and had not been fully trained. Physical changes in the dispatching room meant that the staff were working in unfamiliar positions without paper backup and were less able to collaborate on problems they had previously solved jointly. The automated dispatching approach required virtually perfect information, but the information it received was imperfect due to incomplete status reporting from the ambulance crews, poor coverage (black spots) in the radio system, a radio communications bottleneck, and technical inconsistencies between the mobile data terminals and the central computer. Imperfect data in the dispatching system caused inappropriate and duplicated allocations of ambulances to emergencies. A swarm of computerized exception messages plus an increased number of call backs when ambulances did not arrive slowed the work even more. As the ambulance crews became more frustrated, they became less likely to press their status buttons in the right sequence, making the information even less accurate. Problems with the system had been predicted by the owner of a company whose bid to build the system had been unsuccessful. In several memos to LAS management he had warned that the planned system would be "an expensive disaster" and that its rule-based, analytical approach could not be as effective as an experienced operator in the small minority of difficult cases.

The day after the system failure the dispatching staff reverted to a semimanual approach in which the computer stored data but the decisions were made while contacting an ambulance station near the incident. This approach worked well until November 4, when the computer system slowed down and then locked up and could not be rebooted. The dispatchers reverted to completely manual dispatching. The computer problem turned out to be a software bug that prevented the computer from releasing a small amount of memory each time a vehicle mobilization was generated. This bug had little impact initially, but it gradually tied up more memory until the computer could no longer operate.[1,2]

Debate Topic

It is likely that better technology (such as cellular phones and global positioning satellites) adopted widely in the years since the LAS disaster would have minimized or eliminated the problems that occurred.

Even though this book's first 12 chapters mentioned many problems that have occurred with computerized systems, those chapters emphasized the great progress that has been

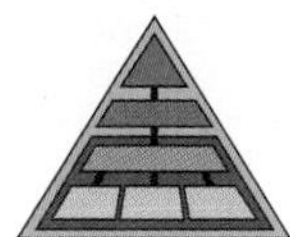

TABLE 13.1 London Ambulance Service: an Information System Disaster

CUSTOMER
- People requiring emergency medical care
- Ambulance drivers requiring information about where to pick up patients requiring emergency transportation to a hospital

PRODUCT
- Location of next pickup, selected to minimize delays and communicated immediately

BUSINESS PROCESS

Major steps:
- Track the location of all ambulances
- Receive telephone notification of an emergency situation requiring an ambulance
- Decide which ambulance should respond to the emergency
- Notify the ambulance driver
- Track the disposition of each call

Rationale:
- Treat all of London as a single zone
- Automate many of the dispatching decisions

PARTICIPANTS	INFORMATION	TECHNOLOGY
• Dispatching staff • Ambulance drivers	• Location of people having medical emergencies • Location of ambulances • Geography of London	• Telephone • Radio transmitters and receivers • Computer program making dispatching decisions

made not only in technology, but also in attaining personal and organizational benefits through information systems. To round out the picture, this chapter focuses on problems that may occur with these systems, and on approaches for minimizing these problems.

The London Ambulance Service case was chosen to start this chapter because it is one of relatively few cases (thankfully) that illustrate many different things that can go wrong even with systems that lives depend on. The software was not fully debugged. The information system and work system were not fully tested. The system was implemented before the participants accepted it. The method was based on an unrealistic assumption of perfect information. The information itself was inaccurate. The hardware failed.

This chapter starts by discussing project failures and quickly moves to different types of threats to information system security. It then explains a number of common measures for reducing those threats. The many examples throughout the chapter illustrate the threats are widespread and are not restricted to situations involving inept management. No system is foolproof, but careful use of established methods reduces the risks substantially and increases the likelihood of enjoying the benefits.

THREAT OF PROJECT FAILURE

The first threats to any computerized system occur while the system is being built. Table 13.2 lists common reasons for failures during each of the four major phases of a system life cycle. Although the previous chapter covered some of the problems that occur during information system projects, this brief section serves as a reminder that development and

TABLE 13.2 Common Reasons for Project Failure at Different Project Phases

Information system projects can be terminated at any of the four phases. Terminating a failing project sooner is better than letting it waste resources unnecessarily.

Phase	Common reasons for project failure
Initiation	• The reasons for building the system have too little support. • The system seems too expensive.
Development	• It is too difficult to define the requirements. • The system is not technically feasible. • The project is too difficult for technical staff assigned.
Implementation	• The system requires too great a change from existing work practices. • Potential users dislike the system or resist using it. • Too little effort is put into the implementation.
Operation and maintenance	• System controls are insufficient. • Too little effort goes into supporting effective use. • The system is not updated as business needs change.

implementation failures are serious threats. In development failures, the system never runs successfully on the computer. In implementation failures, the system runs on the computer but fails to attain the hoped for benefits when used by the organization.

Development Failures

A complex project abandoned during the development phase was the Confirm reservation system, a strategic system being built as a partnership between AMR (parent of American Airlines), Hilton and Marriott hotel firms, and Budget Rent-A-Car. In 1992 the project dissolved into accusations and lawsuits, with AMR writing off $109 million. AMR claimed that the three partners deviated from an agreed-on plan to build a common reservation system and pressed AMR to build three separate systems within Confirm. AMR said that its partners bombarded it with an unending flurry of change requests, failed to provide necessary information, and made poor staffing assignments. The project had also encountered technical design problems making it impossible to integrate its transaction processing component with its decision support component. AMR fired or reassigned 22 IS managers at about that time.[3]

The Confirm project had a number of things in common with other project failures mentioned previously, such as the Medicare claims system (Chapter 1), London Stock Exchange system (Chapter 6), and Bank of America trust system (Chapter 12). These projects had none of the characteristics of the idealized low-risk project described in Chapter 11. They were complex both technically and organizationally. They required inputs from many stakeholders in business situations in which new information and new priorities were emerging continually. Projects of this type often encounter a combination of unreasonable expectations, insufficient resources, technological risk, and inadequate project methodology and staff.

Implementation Failures

Many information system projects that survive the development phase limp through an ineffective implementation and never generate the planned benefits. For example, CompuSys (disguised name of a computer manufacturer) had developed a successful system for verifying existing sales orders to be sure they were complete and consistent before shipping the computer to the customer. CompuSys decided to extend this approach to generate error-free configurations before even quoting prices to the customer. An information system was built over several years with participation of sales reps and eventually produced more accurate configurations than average sales reps could produce. A survey showed that 75% of the reps had tried the information system, but only 25% were using it, and that dropped to 10% within three years. An expensive revamping resulted in a much more effective user interface but no change in usage patterns because sales reps had little motivation to use it. They were evaluated and paid based on sales revenues, not on correct configurations. Furthermore, they actually felt disincentives because this information system was not completely linked to a pricing information system and therefore made it more difficult to complete the paperwork for a sale. Building the new information system without considering the participants' incentives wasted a lot of time and money.[4]

Regardless of who is to blame, this example hints at many of the elements of disappointing implementations: inconsistent priorities, incomplete communication between the developers and the users, and inadequate follow-up to assure the information system is used effectively. Many types of systems have encountered related problems. For example, LANs are often sold based on the claim that they help people work together. But many LANs generate only modest benefits because they have little impact on the way people work together, even though they may be useful for sending electronic mail and sharing printers. Implementation problems such as these are sometimes cited as an important reason for what is sometimes called the "productivity paradox," in which companies with substantial investments in information technology often have no better competitive success than similar companies without those investments.

The remainder of this chapter will focus on system problems and failures that occur or become evident in the operation and maintenance phase.

THREAT OF ACCIDENTS AND MALFUNCTIONS

Many people assume that information systems will work as they are designed to work, that they will operate reliably, and that the information generated will be correct. When these assumptions are proven wrong, the consequences can be disastrous. This section looks at risks of accidents originating from seven causes: operator error, hardware malfunctions, software bugs, data errors, damage to physical facilities, inadequate system performance, and liability for system performance.

To help in visualizing the range of risks from accidents, Figure 13.1 assigns each type of risk to a single element of the framework. Do not assume that each type of accident is totally caused by the element it is associated with, however. For example, saying that a particular accident involved operator error might seem to imply participants are at fault. But the technology might have been difficult to use and the business process might have been designed based on unrealistic assumptions about human capabilities. Interactions between causes of accidents is a key point as we look at each type of accident in turn.

Operator Error

A prime cause of accidents is **operator error,** a combination of inattention, nonconformance to procedures, or other error by participants in a system. A disastrous example occurred in 1995 when an American Airlines jet crashed into a mountain while approaching Cali, Colombia. Because winds were calm, an air traffic controller had offered the pilot an unusual route while descending into Cali to help make up time lost due to a delay taking off from Miami. The pilot or co-pilot tried to "reprogram the onboard computer using a radio beacon at an intermediate point, Rozo, but erroneously entered only the letter 'R,' not the full name, as is required for that beacon. The letter 'R' identified 'Romeo,' another beacon on the same frequency but 132 miles northeast of Cali." The pilot was supposed to verify the data but did not, and the plane turned onto an incorrect course. About a minute later the crew recognized something was wrong and tried to turn back toward Cali. They continued their descent even though they did not find a navigational

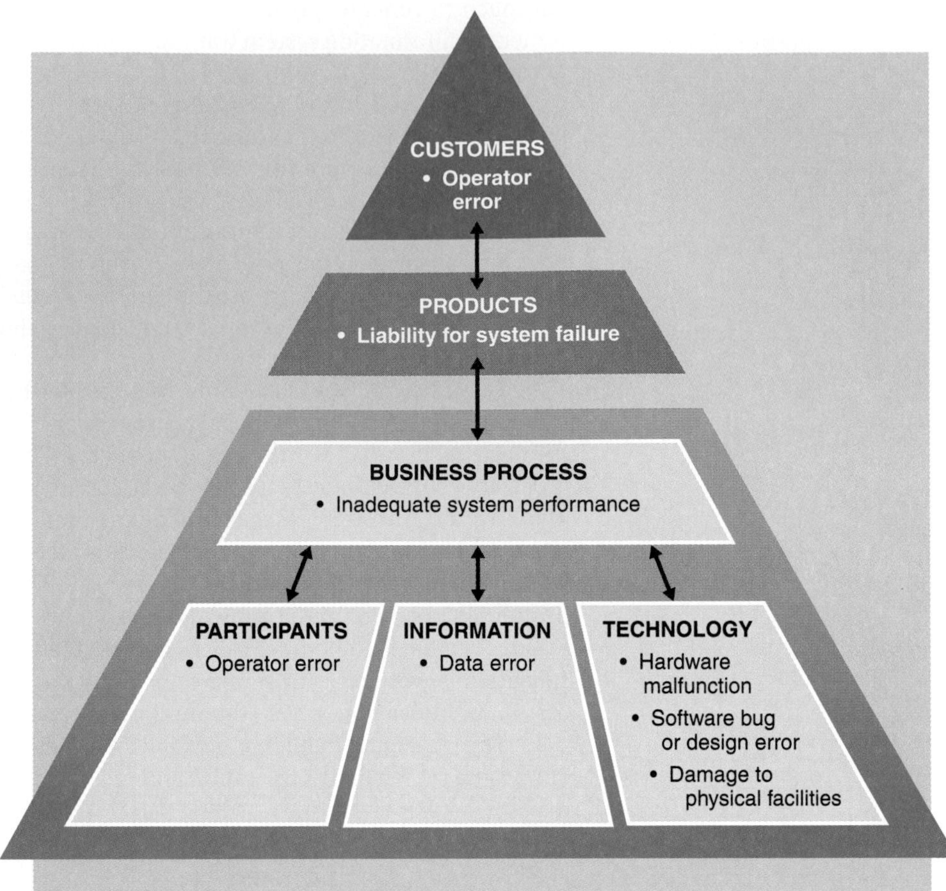

Figure 13.1
Seven types of risks related to accidents

Seven types of risks related to accidents can be associated with individual elements of the framework although the cause of the problem is often a combination of factors.

beacon that they should have passed. While not blaming the air traffic controller, an inquiry's report noted "he knew something was wrong because the pilots' requests 'made little sense,' but he was unable to tell the pilots his suspicions 'because of limitations in his command of English.'"[5]

A careful study of accidents in complex systems such as nuclear plants, dams, tankers, and airplanes found that 60% to 80% of major accidents were attributed to operator error, but that many factors other than operator carelessness contributed to the problems. These factors included flawed system design, poor training, and poor quality control.[6] One of that study's main examples was the partial meltdown at the Three Mile Island nuclear plant in Pennsylvania. A commission blamed the problem on operator error, but the operators were confronted with an enormously complex technical system, incomplete or contradictory information, and the necessity to make decisions quickly. The nature of the system increased the likelihood of operator error. The same thing happened in the flight to Cali.

Several factors magnify the risk of operator error. It is often difficult to anticipate how systems will really work in practice and how users will adapt to them. User adaptations and shortcuts may cause errors the designers never imagined. In addition, people tend to become complacent when a system seems to operate correctly. They begin to assume it will continue to operate correctly and put less energy and care into checking for errors. Who would anticipate that a pilot would enter the wrong code, or that the code R would stand for Romeo, 132 miles away, rather than Rozo, which was nearby? Similarly, who would have anticipated that an astronaut on the Mir space station would nearly cause a disaster by accidentally disconnecting a cable, thereby disabling the computer that kept the Mir's solar panels facing the sun?[7] Obviously, "the system" should have prevented these things from happening. The main point is that all systems are vulnerable to human error.

Reality Check

OPERATOR ERROR

This section mentioned that 60% to 80% of major accidents in one study were attributed to operator error, but that many factors other than carelessness contribute to operator error.

1. Identify times you or your acquaintances have been guilty of operator error in everyday life, for example by accidentally erasing an audio tape or by backing up when intending to go forward.
2. What factors caused the operator error in these cases? Was it ever caused by poor equipment design that somehow encouraged the operator error?

Hardware Malfunctions

Although significant hardware malfunctions are becoming more and more infrequent as computer technology improves, these problems do occur occasionally. A highly embarrassing hardware flaw was publicized in late 1994 when Intel acknowledged that the division function of its Pentium microprocessor occasionally calculated incorrect answers on divisions involving more than five significant digits. Consider the following calculation:

$$4{,}195{,}835 - (4{,}195{,}835 \div 3{,}145{,}727) * 3{,}145{,}727$$

Basic algebra says the answer should be zero since $a - (a \div b) * b = 0$, but the flawed Pentium's gave the answer 256. Intel had known about this problem for months before it became public but had downplayed it because most users don't do division calculations with five significant digits. Intel eventually took a $475 million write-off to account for replacing defective chips. The previous 386 and 486 chips also had math errors that were corrected.[8]

A far more frequent source of hardware malfunctions is incompatibilities between different components that are assembled in a single device or system. A *New York Times* reporter received an angry call from a colleague who had purchased an IBM Thinkpad 560 laptop based on his favorable comments about this product. The laptop crashed continually, often losing data. The IBM service facility replaced the motherboard under warranty, but the problem persisted. Eventually IBM found that the problem was an optional, non-IBM memory module that the dealer had added. This module worked fine with other IBM notebooks but was incompatible with certain power-saving peculiarities of the Toshiba chips used in this particular model.[9]

Another frequent and noticeable site for hardware failure is the electrical power and telecommunication networks that provide the infrastructure computerized systems depend on. For example, the entire NASDAQ stock exchange went down for 34 minutes in1994 because a squirrel shorted out a power line despite the local electric utility's previous attempts "to improve the squirrel-proofing of power lines in the heavily wooded area" near the computer center.[10]

Vulnerability to hardware malfunctions is often magnified by user disbelief that hardware can malfunction. As has occurred in airplane and nuclear plant accidents, it may be unclear whether the malfunction is in the hardware or in the warning system. Furthermore, as software functions are integrated into hardware, what is seen as hardware can have bugs just like software.

Software Bugs

A **software bug** is a flaw in a program that causes it to produce incorrect or inappropriate results. The Y2K problem introduced in Chapter 1 is an enormously expensive group of bugs related to the same problem, the fact that computers will perform many date-related calculations incorrectly around the year 2000 because of the tradition of coding the year with two digits rather than four to save space in the computer's memory or in storage media. IS staffs of large companies with aging legacy systems look forward to the year

2000 with trepidation because the transition from 1999 to 2000 may reveal previously undetected bugs that have lain dormant for decades in undocumented programs. A preview of the type of problem that will occur in some companies is the result of a software bug at an aluminum smelting plant in New Zealand. The plant's control systems stopped on midnight, Dec. 31, 1996, because the programmers had failed to plan for the 1996 leap year. The 366th day of the year caused the plant's control programs to halt, allowing huge furnaces to overheat.[11]

The U.S. Internal Revenue Service is spending around one billion dollars on the Y2K problem. To the extent to which it is not fixed on time, tax returns will go unprocessed, refunds will not be sent, and taxpayers may be told they owe 99 years' interest on disputed deductions. The project of reducing the likelihood of these problems requires the IRS staff to analyze 88,000 programs containing 60,000,000 lines of computer code that is up to 30 years old. The U.S. General Accounting Office has urged the IRS to set up a contingency plan that might even involve shifting some of the processing to computers outside the agency.[12]

Isolated software bugs have caused significant financial losses even in large, well-run organizations. Examples mentioned earlier include the telecommunications software bugs that crippled AT&T long distance networks for a day in 1990 and 1998 (Chapter 6) and the guidance system bug that destroyed an Ariane 5 rocket in 1996 (Chapter 9). Complex models are also susceptible to bugs. The Bank of Tokyo-Mitsubishi reported that its New York–based financial derivatives trading unit had lost $83 million because its computer model undervalued its position.[13]

Software bugs are a fundamental problem with computerized systems because there are no infallible methods for proving that a program operates correctly. The best-tested software may still have bugs after testing is complete. Even if it were possible to prove that a program operates correctly relative to its design specs, there is no guarantee that it will operate correctly under unanticipated circumstances. This was certainly illustrated by the example in Chapter 3 concerning the missile detection system that warned of an impending nuclear attack after spotting the moon rising over the Soviet Union.

Data Errors

Data errors are another source of risk. Information systems in everyday life frequently contain errors such as incorrect phone numbers or addresses. It is possible to check for some errors automatically, such as determining whether a number is within a specified range or whether a ZIP code is valid. Unfortunately, validity checks such as these cannot detect many errors. For example, a system that checks whether an employee's age is between 18 and 70 usually cannot determine that 12/10/54 was accidentally entered instead of 10/12/45. Many errors due to carelessness and inattention therefore cannot be detected automatically.

Seemingly small data errors sometimes have major impacts. In 1996, the 20231 ZIP code used exclusively by the U.S. Patent and Trademark Office was somehow canceled by the Washington, D.C., post office. Nobody noticed for several weeks until Mobil Corporation called to ask why time-sensitive applications it had sent to the patent office had been returned unopened, saying that the ZIP code had been discontinued. An estimated 50,000 letters to the patent office were returned before the problem was rectified.[14] An address-related problem also occurred at Network Solutions, Inc., the company that controls Internet addresses. Because a computer operator ignored alarms warning of problems with the computer that updates these addresses, corrupted address data were sent to ten other computers that direct messages to machine addresses across the network. Thousands or millions of attempts to send e-mail or access Web pages may have failed.[15]

Data errors have even impacted the stock market. A clerical error on March 25, 1993, caused a 12-point drop in the New York Stock Exchange's Dow Jones index in the last few minutes of trading. An institutional investor had sent Salomon Brothers a computerized order to sell $11,000,000 of stock spread over 400 companies. A clerk entered this order into Salomon Brothers' system incorrectly, typing 11,000,000 in the "shares" box rather than the "dollars" box on a data entry screen. The system automatically allocated the 11,000,000 shares among the companies and generated individual sell orders. The sell orders for under 99,999 shares of individual stocks on the New York Exchange were handled automatically by SuperDot, the Exchange's small-order system. Larger orders and orders for stocks on the NASDAQ exchange went to traders who looked at the size of the orders, concluded they were mistakes, and canceled them. The estimated cost of the error for Salomon Brothers was at least $1 million to repurchase shares sold and make up for lower prices received.[16]

Significant data errors are sometimes caused by malfunctions of automatic sensors. In a disastrous example in 1996, 70 people died in an Aeroperu plane crash because maintenance workers who were polishing the plane forgot to remove tape and paper covers used over pressure sensors that are about one inch in diameter. Just before the crash, the pilot radioed that his instruments had gone haywire. One automatic system indicated the plane was flying too slowly and would fall out of the sky while another sounded an alarm because the plane was flying too fast. When the plane hit the water, the captain's instruments were showing an altitude of 9,500 feet. People examining the wreck found masking tape over the sensors. To avoid a repetition, Boeing planned to manufacture brightly colored covers for the pressure sensors.[17]

Some data errors are related to the incentives that motivate people to enter incorrect data. One manufacturer developed a system that consolidated all records by customer number. Late in the project it discovered that salespeople created a new customer number for each sale, even to existing customers, because they received larger commissions for opening new accounts. The company scrapped the project after discovering the database contained more than 7,000 customer numbers for McDonnell Douglas, a single large customer.[18]

Damage to Physical Facilities

Physical facilities and equipment may be vulnerable to a wide range of environmental threats and external events. In the last few years, computer facilities have been damaged by fires, floods, hurricanes, and earthquakes. Computer and telecommunications equipment may be disabled by power failures and network breakdowns occurring far from the site. Damage to physical facilities doesn't require a natural catastrophe. In 1991, a telephone maintenance crew accidentally cut a fiber optic cable that provided 40% of New York City's long distance service. Because an AT&T operations center had not been notified that the work was being done, computers had not been programmed to give priority to data transmissions for air traffic control. Consequently, New York's three main airports lost their long-range radar for 102 minutes. Several days later, a U.S. Sprint cable broke, disrupting calls to and from Chicago.[19] In another example, airborne dust from a 1997 ceiling renovation made it hard to breathe at a New York air traffic control center, forcing it to rotate crews and operate on a limited basis for almost 10 hours. This set off cascading delays that affected air travel across the United States and caused cancellation of 150 flights.[20] In all three cases, individuals and businesses were affected by events miles from their facilities. Firms relying on information systems need to protect their own facilities and need to prepare for impacts of problems elsewhere.

Inadequate System Performance

Inadequate system performance occurs when a system cannot handle the task that is required of it. The London Ambulance Service example at the beginning of this chapter is certainly a case in point. Another highly visible example occurred during the stock market crash of October 19, 1987. The New York Stock Market's "real-time" information system of stock prices ran two hours late as more than 500 million shares of stock were traded, three times the average daily volume at that time. Investments during the 1990s brought the NYSE's capacity to over 1.4 billion shares per day, but some delays were still experienced at the brokerage firms on the busiest days.

Inadequate system performance also occurs in many mundane situations. For example, an overloaded computer may provide poor response time for interactive users or may generate the summary report on yesterday's production too late for this morning's production meeting. America Online (AOL) experienced this type of problem when it switched to a $19.95 flat rate for unlimited service but did not have enough modem and computer capacity to support all of its users. In early 1997 some of its users filed a class action lawsuit alleging that the company had misrepresented its service. Later in the same year a bug in its e-mail system caused a series of three- to five-hour shutdowns.[21] The need to maintain adequate performance is one reason to build information systems carefully and monitor their performance.

Liability for System Failure

Liability is legal responsibility for one's actions or products. Every type of accident mentioned thus far can result in a liability claim against a firm or individual. This is an especially serious potential problem in medical systems. Chapter 2 described how a bug in a computer program controlling an x-ray machine caused a patient's death by setting the machine to deliver 100 times the prescribed exposure to radiation. Potential liability is one of the reasons medical expert systems have largely remained confined to research tools rather than common tools for doctors. Whoever created or sold such a system might be held liable if it produced an incorrect diagnosis.

Liability is also an issue in business software. In 1994 Kane Carpet Co. of Secaucus, N.J., was in court trying to prove that after 22 consecutive profitable years and growth up to $90 million in sales, it had gone out of business due to flaws in an inventory system it purchased from McDonnell Douglas. Although the system seemed to work well at a flooring company in Houston, within a week of its installation in 1989 Kane experienced severe problems filling orders and quoting correct prices and credit terms.[22]

Liability related to information systems is complex because so many different things can go wrong. Given the potential for product liability lawsuits, software vendors are usually careful to avoid claiming their software is bugfree. Their license agreements usually state that any problems resulting from the use of the software are the user's fault. The Y2K problem raises many additional questions about liability because everyone in the industry knew about this problem years in advance. Legal experts have estimated that litigation about Y2K problems might involve amounts exceeding $1 trillion. As an indicator of things to come, a law firm filed a class action lawsuit in December 1997 on behalf of anyone that purchased SBT Pro Series software prior to March 1, 1997. The complaint alleged that the software manufacturer breached the warranty on the product based on the inability of older versions of the software to recognize dates starting with the year 2000. Software users could simply convert to version 3.0 of the software, but it contains functional upgrades that could take months to test and implement. The law firm's position was that SBT should provide a Y2K compliant version of release 2.0 or should provide release 3.0 for free.[23] Hoping to protect Silicon Valley hardware and software companies, a California legislator drafted a bill that would limit the damage awards to costs of repairing or replacing hardware and software and would restrict punitive damages. Some industry observers argued the bill was ill-conceived because it would allow some vendors to do sloppy work on a well understood problem.[24]

The seven types of risk mentioned thus far are all related to things that go wrong unintentionally. Before discussing security measures that reduce these risks, the next section will look at computer crime, which is anything but accidental.

Reality Check

RISKS RELATED TO ACCIDENTS

This section gave examples of seven different types of risks related to accidents.

1. Look at the categories and identify an example of each type of problem or something similar that you have personally encountered, regardless of whether a computer was involved.
2. Explain why you do or do not believe there is anything unique about the way these problems arise in relation to computerized systems.

THREAT OF COMPUTER CRIME

Computer crime is the use of computerized systems to perform illegal acts. It can be divided into two main areas: theft, and sabotage and vandalism. Computer pranks are included as illegal activities because they often have at least the potential for significant harm. Also, they may be difficult to differentiate from sabotage and other forms of destructive behavior.

Computer crime is growing more worrisome as computerized systems become more pervasive. The potential for significant damage to commercial interests and national defense through computer viruses and other forms of computerized sabotage has been demonstrated clearly. Weaknesses exploited often involve technical gaps between what a computer system is capable of enforcing and what it is expected to enforce. Other weaknesses involve gaps between computer policies, social policies, and human behavior.

There is no single profile for computer criminals. They range from application programmers and clerical personnel to managers and accountants. In general, perpetrators of computer crime can be divided into employees, outsiders, and hackers. *Employees* use their knowledge of how a business operates to identify opportunities for theft or sabotage and to obtain easy access to the resources they need for their criminal activity. *Outsiders* often have a somewhat more difficult task because they must learn how to penetrate a system without having easy access to information about how it works. **Hackers** are less concerned about personal gains or damage they might cause. Instead, they commit computer crime for the "fun" or intellectual challenge of breaking into a computer.

Despite its seriousness, computer crime is not treated in the same way in our society as other types of crime. Perhaps this is because the perpetrators seem less physically threatening to victims than other criminals. Perhaps it is because companies victimized by computer crime are hesitant to suffer adverse publicity. Regardless of the cause, to date many convicted computer criminals have received mild treatment. In some cases, they have even taken jobs as security consultants after receiving minor punishments.

As illustrated in Figure 13.2 the vulnerable points in computerized systems include people and procedures in addition to hardware, software, and data. A detailed look at many cases that are called computer crime reveals that the computer played a relatively small role compared to the role of bypassed procedures and forged transaction documents. Most of the following examples might have been stopped through better organizational procedures and safeguards.

Theft

Computer-related theft can be divided into five categories: theft of software and computer equipment, unauthorized use of access codes and financial passwords, theft by entering fraudulent transaction data, theft by modifying software, and theft by stealing or modifying data.

Theft of Software and Equipment

Theft of software and computer equipment has become a major problem for hardware and software manufacturers and for companies that use computer equipment. Part of the temptation is that software, chips, and computer equipment are both small and valuable. On Nov. 10, 1997, armed robbers stole an estimated 200,000 certificates of authenticity and 100,000 CD-ROMs from a Microsoft manufacturing facility in Scotland. The certificates could be worth as much as $16 million if affixed to counterfeit Microsoft operating system products.[25]

Theft of computers also causes problems because of the value of data on the computers. The theft of a desktop computer stolen from Visa International may have cost the company $6 million and caused headaches for thousands of credit card holders because the computer contained information on 314,000 credit card accounts. Several banks that issued the cards blocked the affected accounts and issued new cards, with Visa agreeing to cover the cost of around $20 per account.[26]

Unauthorized Use of Access Codes and Financial Passwords

Telephone credit card numbers, PBX access codes, ATM passwords, and regular credit card numbers have all become major targets of criminals. AT&T's manager of corporate security estimated that fraud costs the telephone industry, and hence its customers, $2 billion per year.[27] Many companies have been victimized by criminals stealing PBX access codes used to route telephone calls through the company's PBX to get reduced corporate rates and simplify accounting. Until the theft is detected and the access code switched off, it is used to make foreign long distance calls from pay phones and to arrange drug deals and other illegal activities.

Criminals steal telephone credit card numbers and PBX access codes in many ways. "Shoulder surfers" use binoculars, video cameras, or just good eyesight and number memory to spy on people entering telephone credit card numbers while making long distance calls in airports. Company insiders may also steal these codes. For example, an MCI Communications employee was arrested in 1994 for stealing 60,000 calling card numbers and selling them to an international crime ring. MCI officials estimated the entire loss was more than $50 million.[28]

Many schemes have been used to steal PIN (personal identification) numbers for ATMs. Criminals have scanned cordless and cellular telephone signals looking for people using bank-by-phone services. They have stolen data using wiretaps, thereby capturing data moving from one location to another. In 1998 a Russian citizen admitted to using passwords stolen from Citicorp customers to carry out illegal transfers from his apartment in St. Petersburg. He used the passwords to withdraw $400,000 of $12 million that was illegally transferred. Citibank stated it did not know how an accomplice stole the passwords.[29]

Theft by Entering Fraudulent Transaction Data

Entering fraudulent transaction data is the simplest and most common method of theft in computer-related crime. Box 13.1 lists major categories of transaction-related fraud. Such frauds are perpetrated by forging documents, bypassing procedures, or impersonating

Figure 13.2
Threats related to computer crime

Various types of threats related to computer crime can be associated with individual elements of the framework although computer crimes often involve a variety of factors.

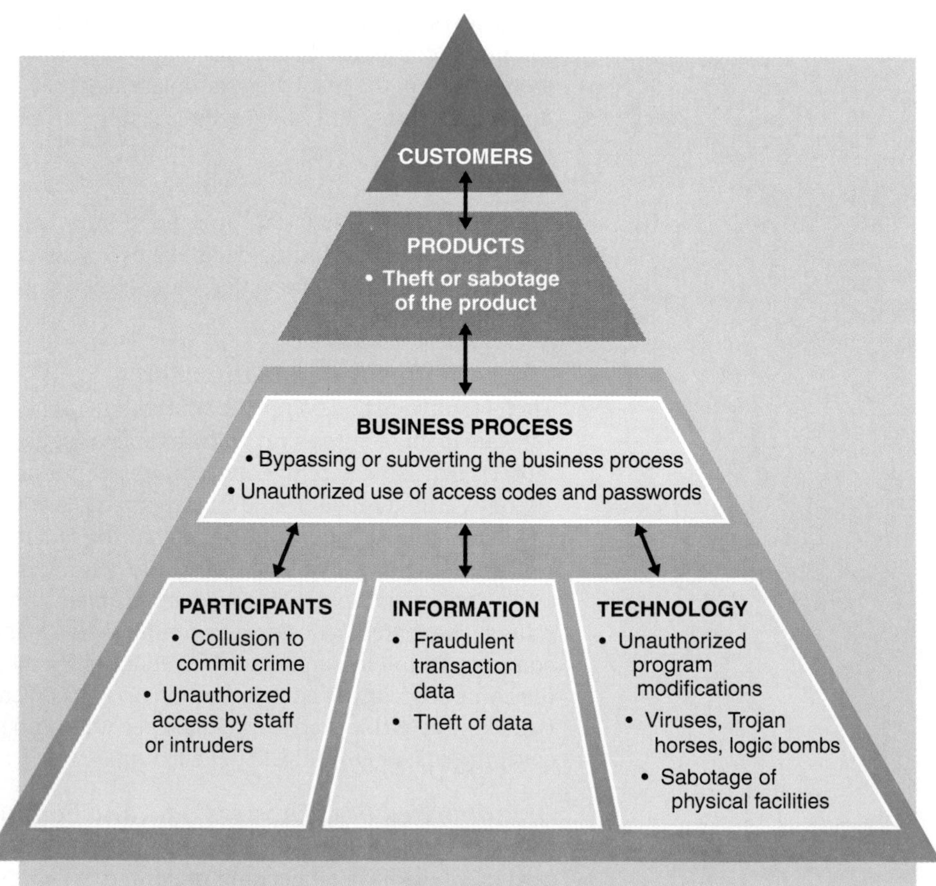

someone. The criminals who do this often know little about computers. In these cases, what is commonly called computer crime often relies less on knowledge of computers and much more on knowledge of how business systems operate. Many businesses have easy targets for this type of crime because their internal systems are managed carelessly.

Not surprisingly, transaction fraud is a major threat to online retailers. In 1995 Cyber Source, which runs an online retail store, had a week in which fraud exceeded legitimate sales. This type of fraud can put a merchant out of business because credit card companies hold merchants responsible for any fraudulent purchases made when the signature cannot be verified. By late 1997 Cyber Source had reduced the fraud rate to less than one percent of sales by using a computer model that looks at 150 factors to calculate the risk of fraud in the purchase.[30]

Theft by Stealing or Modifying Data

Stealing or modifying data is yet another form of computer crime. One way to steal data is by removing physical media such as paper documents, tapes, or diskettes. There are many stories of salespeople taking a customer list on leaving a job. The pervasive use of personal computers and diskettes makes this easy to do. Product and process specifications are

BOX 13.1 ***Examples of fraud committed using transaction processing systems***

Listed below are some of the many ways to commit fraud using transaction processing systems.[31] These types of fraud are usually perpetrated by insiders who generate fraudulent transaction data.

Forgery: The criminal produces fraudulent checks, ID cards, or even money. Desktop publishing technology such as scanners, drawing programs, and laser printers have made forgery easier than ever before. Figure 13.3 shows an example of this type of forgery. The American Bankers Association estimated that counterfeiters aided by laser printers and color copiers forged $2 billion worth of checks as far back as 1992.[32]

Impersonation fraud: The criminal impersonates someone else, accesses that person's account electronically, and steals money or information. One criminal recognized that bank computers handle deposits based on the magnetic account number at the bottom of deposit slips and not by the depositor's signature. This thief substituted specially coded deposit slips in the place of general deposit slips available in the bank lobby for customers who forget their own personalized slips. For the next three days, all deposits made with these fraudulent deposit slips were credited to the thief's account. The thief withdrew the money and vanished before the depositors' checks started to bounce.

Disbursements fraud: The criminal gets a company to pay for products or services it never received. This is often done by learning the procedures and paperwork through which purchases are made and the receipt of material is verified. Pinkerton Security and Investigation Services suffered this type of fraud when an accounting employee transferred money out of a company bank account into accounts set up for bogus companies at another bank. This employee needed a superior's approval before making a transfer but was once asked to cancel a former superior's approval code. Instead of canceling it, she started using it herself. Normally the reconciliation of different accounts would have caught the discrepancies, but she was also supposed to do these reconciliations. Eventually caught in an audit, she pleaded guilty to stealing over $1 million and was sentenced to prison.[33]

Inventory fraud: The criminal modifies inventory records or causes inventory to be shipped to a location where it can be stolen. In one case, employees of a railroad changed the boxcar inventory file to indicate that over 200 boxcars were scrapped or destroyed. These boxcars were then shipped to another railroad company's yard and repainted.

Payroll fraud: The criminal pads an organization's payroll with nonexistent employees or leaves former employees on the payroll after termination. In one example, an employee of a welfare department's data center stole $2.75 million by creating a fictitious work force. He used fake social security numbers and created input data that generated weekly checks through a payment system. He and several collaborators intercepted the checks and cashed them.

Pension fraud: The criminal embezzles funds from pension payments. Typically, the criminal keeps a deceased person on the file but sends that person's pension check to his own account. To test the existence of this problem, the State Retirement Board in Boston asked 14,500 pension recipients to submit proof they were still alive. They received responses from only 13,994.

Cashier fraud: Cashiers steal part of the cash payments received from customers. For example, a ticket clerk at the Arizona Veterans' Memorial Coliseum was caught issuing full-price basketball tickets, selling them, and then recording the transactions as half-price tickets by entering incorrect codes into the computer.

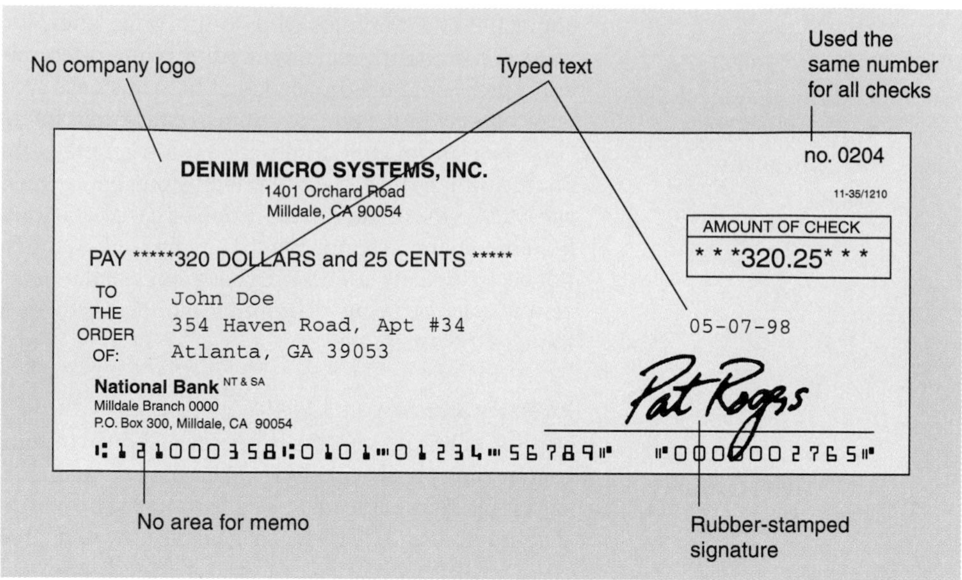

Figure 13.3
Check forgery

A number of flaws suggest that a check may be forged.

another valuable type of data that can be stolen this way. Unlike other forms of theft, it is often possible to steal computerized data without visibly affecting what is stolen.

New communication technologies such as cellular telephones, electronic mail, and voice mail have created new possibilities for theft. In a 1993 federal court case in Boston, Standard Duplicating Machines (SDM) accused its rival Duplo Manufacturing of "a prolonged and surreptitious campaign of business espionage" by stealing voice-mail messages to steal business. The evidence involved recorded product inquiries on SDM's voice-mail system that were answered the next day by Duplo's sales people. The lawsuit zeroed in on an employee hired by Duplo shortly after he was fired by SDM and was based on after-hours calls into SDM's toll-free 800 number from Duplo and from his home. Apparently SDM had not terminated telephone passwords for the terminated employee.[34]

Theft by Modifying Software

Some programmers have committed computer crime by modifying software so it performs differently when it encounters a particular account number or other triggering condition. One technique is to accumulate fractions of pennies on financial transactions and add them to a personal account. Presumably no one would notice and no one would be harmed. Because this technique involves shaving thin slices from transactions, it is sometimes called a *salami swindle.*

Individual criminals sometimes operate alone when they steal in this way, but software modification sometimes involves collusion with business executives. In what was called the largest criminal tax case in Connecticut history, top executives of Stew Leonard's, a sprawling dairy store that had received awards for entrepreneurship and customer service, pleaded guilty to conspiracy. They had stolen $17.5 million in cash receipts between 1981 and 1991 and used a computer program to modify the company's records to fool the auditors. The investigation began not through auditors' efforts, but when U.S. Customs agents stopped Leonard as he boarded a flight to a vacation home in the Caribbean with $80,000 in undeclared cash.[35]

Sabotage and Vandalism

Perpetrators of sabotage and vandalism try to invade or damage system hardware, software, or data. They may range from hackers to disgruntled employees to spies. Although some hackers may not intend to cause harm, sometimes they do so by making mistakes. This happened in a famous case in which a Cornell graduate student was convicted of a felony after trying to demonstrate a weakness in the Internet in 1988 using a program that created copies of itself and transmitted them across the network. Although the program was supposed to spread slowly, it spread rapidly due to a programming error and accidentally disrupted 6,000 computers and wasted nearly $100 million of time and effort.

The Internet has created many new possibilities for sabotage and vandalism. Kevin Mitnick, a hacker who had broken into many computers, was eventually caught after an Internet service provider (ISP) discovered he had stored 20,000 credit card numbers on its computer.[36] Public Access Networks Corp., another ISP that hosted almost a thousand corporate Web sites, was virtually shut down for several days when a hacker bombarded its site with requests to send information.[37]

Disgruntled employees who understand a computer system's operation and its weak points are especially dangerous perpetrators of computer crimes. Disgruntled employees have erased, modified, and even kidnapped data and programs. Although little is said about sabotage by spies, the fact that 14-year-olds have penetrated military networks surely implies there are possibilities for computer system sabotage by spies.

A number of programming techniques have been used for sabotage and vandalism:

- A **trap door** is a set of instructions that permits a user to bypass the computer system's standard security measures. Trap doors are frequently put into programs by programmers to make it easier for them to modify the software. The Internet program that disrupted 6,000 computers used a trap door left by programmers.
- A **Trojan horse** is a program that appears to be valid and useful but contains hidden instructions that can cause damage. For example, a Trojan horse could identify a particular account number and bypass it or could accumulate differences due to rounding and place them in a particular account.
- A **logic bomb** is a type of Trojan horse whose destructive actions are set to occur when a particular condition occurs, such as reaching a particular clock time or the initiation of a particular program. Logic bombs are sometimes used for computerized vandalism and revenge. In a 1998 federal court case, for example, prosecutors believed that a programmer who had been fired by Omega Engineering of Bridgeport, New Jersey, created a logic bomb that went off 20 days later, deleting all of the company's design and production software and disabling its backup and recovery facilities. Total damage was estimated at $10 million.[38]
- A **virus** is a special type of Trojan horse that can replicate itself and spread, much like a biological virus. A virus attached to a program is loaded into the computer's memory when the program is loaded. The virus is programmed to find and insert a copy of itself into programs or files that do not contain it. When those programs are executed, the copy of the virus starts up and attempts to replicate the virus again. Another type of virus is a macro virus, which infects documents and can be transmitted via e-mail. Viruses are introduced into company computer systems in many different ways. Macro viruses are a common and serious threat because they can be transmitted accidentally if attached unknowingly to legitimate documents and e-mail. This is one of the reasons it is important to use a virus scanner on incoming documents before opening them. Other sources of virus infections include unauthorized disks, downloads from bulletin boards, sales demo disks, and repair or service people. Even Microsoft itself distributed a demonstration CD-ROM to journalists but had to follow immediately with a warning to throw it away because it was infected with a virus.[39]

A 1997 survey by the National Computer Security Association found that virtually all medium and large organizations in North America (99.33%) had experienced at least one computer virus infection, and that the average infection rate was 406 of 1,000 machines. The rate of infection in February 1997 was over five times higher than a year earlier.[40] The cost of removing viruses and taking preventive measures has been estimated at several billion dollars a year. The chance of sabotage through viruses is also very real. Six years after the Chernobyl nuclear disaster contaminated an area the size of Delaware, a disgruntled employee inserted a virus into the computer system used to monitor a nuclear plant in Lithuania. Fortunately control room engineers saw indications that fuel rods were overheating. Whether or not this virus could have led to a meltdown, the mere fact that it could be introduced into the computer system shows the potential danger from lax security.[41] Earlier speculation that viruses might be used for warfare was proven valid in the Persian Gulf War. U.S. Intelligence agents in Amman, Jordan, replaced a computer chip in a French-made computer printer with a chip designed by the U.S. National Security Agency to disrupt a mainframe computer when the printer was used. Later this printer was attached to a mainframe used by Iraq's air defense system and caused data to vanish from computer screens.[42]

Theft, sabotage, and vandalism are intentional threats to information systems, whereas accidents (covered earlier) are unintentional threats. Many of the intentional and unintentional threats result from characteristics of systems, people, and the business environment. These causes of vulnerability are discussed next to lay the groundwork for the subsequent overview of measures to maintain system security.

FACTORS THAT INCREASE THE RISKS

Many examples of system-related accidents and crime have been presented to demonstrate the reality and breadth of the threat that must be countered by effective management and security measures. Although each example involved a unique situation, interrelated conditions such as carelessness, complacency, and inadequate organizational procedures increased the vulnerability to both accidents and crime. Table 13.3 shows particular conditions that increase vulnerability to each type of accident or crime. Behind the conditions in Table 13.3 is a combination of issues related to three themes: the nature of complex systems, human limitations, and pressures in the business environment. Because most system security measures are related to these themes, they will be discussed before system security measures are presented.

The Nature of Complex Systems

Many complex systems rely on many different human, physical, and technical factors that all have to operate correctly to avoid catastrophic system failures. Consider how a simple power outage at a New York City AT&T switching station at 10 A.M. on Sept. 19, 1991, was magnified by a combination of power equipment failure, alarm system failure, and management failure. When workers activated backup power at the station, a power surge and an overly sensitive safety device prevented diesel backup generators from providing power to the telephone equipment, which automatically started drawing power from emergency batteries. Workers disobeyed standard procedures by not checking that the diesel generators were working. Operating on battery power was an emergency situation, but over 100 people in the building that day did not notice the emergency alarms for various reasons: some alarm lights did not work; others were placed where they could not be seen; alarm bells had been inactivated due to false alarms; technicians were off-site at a training course. At 4:50 P.M. the batteries gave out, shutting down the hub's 2.1 million call per hour capacity. Because communication between the region's airports went through this hub, regional airport operations came to a standstill, grounding 85,000 air passengers.[43,44]

In addition to relying on everything to work correctly, computerized systems are often designed to hide things users don't want to be involved in, such as the details of data processing. Although usually effective, this approach makes it less likely that users will notice problems. In addition, users often try to bypass computerized systems by inventing new procedures that are convenient but that may contradict the system's original design concepts. The more flexible a system is, the more likely that it will be used in ways never imagined by its designers.

Information system decentralization and multivendor connectivity also affect security. As networked workstations become more common, the ability to access, copy, and change computerized data expands. Electronically stored data in offices are highly vulnerable because many offices are low-security or no-security environments where people can easily access and copy local data and data extracted from corporate databases. Storage media such as diskettes, and even the computers themselves, are easy to move. Data channels such as electronic message systems and bulletin boards may be poorly controlled. These areas of vulnerability all result from the worthwhile goal of making information and messages available and readily usable.

TABLE 13.3 Conditions That Increase Vulnerability

	Type of threat	Conditions that increase vulnerability
Threats from unintentional occurrences	Operator error	• Difficulty in anticipating how systems will really work in practice and how users and others will adapt to them • Complacency in assuming the system will operate as it is supposed to • Lack of energy and care in assuring systems work properly
	Hardware malfunction	• Disbelief that hardware can malfunction • Difficulty deciding whether the hardware or the warning system is malfunctioning
	Software bugs	• Inadequate design and testing • Unanticipated factors that affect system operation • Inability to prove software is correct
	Data errors	• Flaws in procedures • Inability of software to detect many types of errors • Carelessness and inattention
	Damage to physical facilities	• Inadequate backup • Inadequate physical security related to natural phenomena • Inadequate protection against failure of important external systems
	Inadequate system performance	• Inadequate design • Unanticipated peak loads or demand variations
	Liability	• Inadequate limitation on liability • Inadequate system quality
Threats from intentional actions	Theft	• Inadequate design of computer system or human processing • Existence of many easy targets for theft • Distributed systems
	Vandalism and sabotage	• Inadequate prevention of unauthorized access • Inadequate software change control • Inadequate organizational procedures

Human Limitations

To make things worse, many users of office systems are unsophisticated about system security and ignore it. Other human limitations increasing system vulnerability include complacency, carelessness, greed, and limited ability to understand complex systems.

Complacency and carelessness lead users and managers to assume systems work correctly. Pepsi-Cola's managers in the Philippines were certainly surprised when a "computer error" in their Numbers Fever promotion generated 800,000 winning numbers inside of bottle caps instead of 18. With a promised prize of one million pesos ($40,000) for each winner, Pepsi-Cola found itself in a public relations and legal nightmare. It certainly did not have $32 billion to pay the claimants and tried to appease them by spending $10 million to give 500 pesos ($20) to each claimant with a winning number.[45]

Complacency and carelessness also lead to lax enforcement of security systems. Controls designed to prevent disasters in computerized systems are often ignored by the people who are supposed to enforce them. A 1991 U.S. General Accounting Office (GAO) audit of U.S. stock markets turned up 68 security and control flaws. Three of the exchanges had no computer backup facilities; two had no alternative power supplies for trading floors; two had telecommunications equipment that could be used to modify data; combustible materials were found in a computer room.[46]

Greed and other human frailties increase vulnerability because they provide a motive for computer crime. People having personal problems related to drinking, drugs, gambling, or other difficulties may see computer crime as a way to solve their problems. People who want revenge on their employer or supervisor may also resort to computer crime.

Human limitations of system developers also have an impact. Even with the best CASE techniques, it is sometimes difficult to visualize exactly how a complicated information system will work. Many individuals understand parts of systems, but few understand all of a complex system. Inability to anticipate how the system will operate under all circumstances leads to accidents and increases the chances of computer crime.

Pressures in the Business Environment

The business environment increases vulnerability by adding pressures to complete systems rapidly with limited staffs. Information system vulnerability may not be considered adequately when development decisions are driven by needs to maximize return on investment. In the rush to meet deadlines with insufficient resources, features and testing that reduce vulnerability may be left out. Hallmarks of careful software development work may be curtailed, such as thorough documentation, careful design reviews, and complete testing. These things happen not only in information systems, but also in many other large projects. For example, after years of delays, the billion-dollar Hubble space telescope was launched into orbit with a warped mirror that had not received a standard final test on earth. A special mission of the space shuttle was needed to correct the flaw.

The competitive environment has even pushed companies to reduce their executive-level attention to security. Despite the argument that having a high-level security expert is more important to many organizations today than it ever was in the past, a number of high-profile businesses have shifted these responsibilities to their end-user departments. For example, First Boston Corporation eliminated its corporate executive position for data security and recovery based on its attempt to eliminate layers of management and give more local control to end users.[47]

METHODS FOR MINIMIZING RISKS

Many threats related to accidents and computer crime were covered to demonstrate why positive action to minimize these threats is essential. Figure 13.4 represents these actions as a series of business processes in a value chain for establishing and maintaining system security. The remainder of the chapter will use the following order to explain the basic sequence of steps for developing the system properly, establishing security, controlling operations, and anticipating problems:

- Build the system correctly in the first place.
- Train users about security issues.
- Once the system is in operation, maintain physical security.
- Given that it is physically secure, prevent unauthorized access to computers, networks, and data.
- Having controlled access, make sure transactions are performed correctly.
- Even with transaction controls in place, motivate efficient and effective operation and find ways to improve.
- Even if the system seems secure, audit it to identify problems.
- Even with continuing vigilance, prepare for disasters.

None of the methods mentioned in the remainder of the chapter are foolproof because many problems cannot be foreseen. However, consistent and thorough attention to the security and control value chain reduces the likelihood of accidents, computer crime, and ineffective usage.

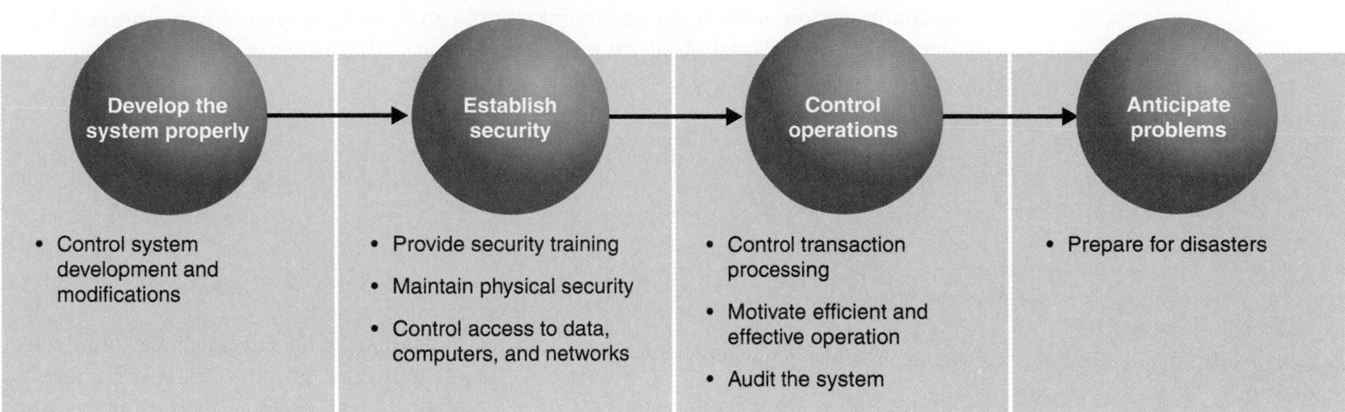

Figure 13.4
Value chain for system security and control

Information system security and control involve a number of separate business processes that combine to reduce the risk of accidents, crime, and ineffective use.

Controlling System Development and Modifications

Software quality control is the process of assuring that software is developed efficiently, debugged completely, and maintained carefully and efficiently. Software quality control usually implies careful adherence to a structured system life cycle, regardless of whether the software was built in-house or by a vendor.

Maintaining software quality also calls for careful testing of any vendor-supplied software before it is distributed in the organization. Although this may seem unnecessary because the software and computers should work properly, we have already seen many systems that did not work as intended. Problems and vulnerabilities of many systems are linked directly to bugs and design flaws that can be found through testing.

Another aspect of maintaining software quality is to prevent infection by viruses. Although there is no foolproof way to do this, effective measures include controlling access to the system, using only authorized, vendor-supplied software, and using vaccine programs to identify and eliminate known viruses. It is particularly dangerous to use programs from any sources that may not have been controlled carefully, such as public bulletin boards, public domain (free) software, pirated software, and diskettes that may be infected.

Software change control systems provide a procedural approach for maintaining software quality and preventing unwarranted changes in systems. Software change control applies the idea of segregation of duties to the development and maintenance of computer systems. Figure 13.5 illustrates the sequence that occurs whenever a program is changed:

1. The programmer documents the change to be made and then checks out the programs to be changed. When these programs are checked out, no one else can check them out or change them.
2. The programmer changes the programs and tests them.
3. The programmer transfers the modified programs to another person authorized to check them. That person reads the documentation of the desired change, studies the before and after versions of the programs, tests them, and signs off that they are correct.
4. The system administrator replaces the old versions of the programs with the new revisions. A journal is kept detailing when each change was made, what it entailed, who revised the program, and who checked it.

Many variations on this sequence have been used. For example, many IS organizations use structured walk-throughs in which the programmer explains the code to other programmers to be sure it is consistent and easy to understand. As with many other forms of quality review, this sequence is cumbersome and isn't foolproof. When enforced, however, it makes it more difficult for people to tamper with programs.

Providing Security Training

Complacency, carelessness, and lack of awareness all increase the likelihood of accidents and computer crime. Companies should train users to be aware of security concerns and to understand how these concerns are related to rules and procedures. Every employee who uses a computer or is at all involved with transaction processing should be familiar with the issues this chapter raises. They should also know some of the signs of suspicious activity and the company's procedures for reporting that activity.

Although the many examples presented here and the huge costs of telephone fraud and viruses show why this type of training and awareness is important, many companies do not follow through adequately. Large losses are not surprising when employees are unaware of the risks or know that company management doesn't care.

Maintaining Physical Security

Maintaining physical security is essential for protecting computing and communication facilities. Physical security measures should take into account threats including accidents, uncontrollable external events, and attack by intruders. Physical security starts with simple measures, such as forbidding eating, drinking, and smoking near computer equipment. Just dropping a cup of coffee can damage equipment and erase data.

Physical access controls guard against physical access to computer facilities and data. The general guideline is to keep unauthorized people out of computer rooms, communication centers, and data storage locations. Contrary to that guideline, one author recalls a security consulting assignment in which his elevator accidentally stopped at the floor of a large casino's computer center at 11:00 P.M. He and an associate walked up to a locked door marked "Computer Center—No Admittance." They rang the bell, were admitted by a computer operator without saying a word, and wandered through the computer

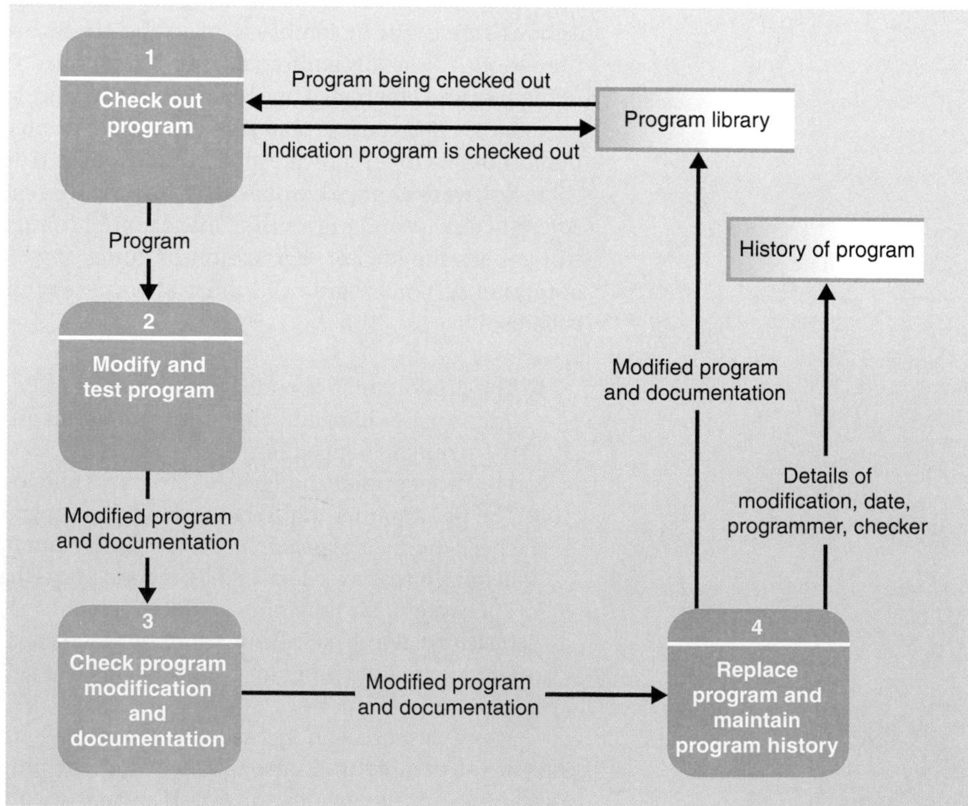

Figure 13.5
Software change control

Software change control creates a division of responsibility in which one person modifies and tests a program, and others check the changes and move the changes back into the program library.

center for ten minutes before leaving. If they had been disgruntled heavy losers rather than security consultants, they might have done substantial damage.[48]

Firms go to great lengths to protect critical data processing facilities, and rightfully so. Concerns about physical security for its reservation system led American Airlines to build an underground facility in Tulsa, Oklahoma. With its extreme reliance on that system, foot-thick concrete walls and a 42-inch ceiling seemed justified.

Controlling Access to Data, Computers, and Networks

After providing for physical security, the next set of measures involves controlling access to data, computers, and networks. Security measures should restrict access to confidential information and enforce mandatory ground rules. Table 13.4 summarizes five aspects of access control: enforcing guidelines for manual data handling, defining access privileges, enforcing access privileges, controlling incoming data, and using encryption to make data meaningless to anyone who bypasses access controls.

Guidelines for Manual Data Handling

The way people handle data manually can constitute a security risk. Consider the common practice of going home and leaving work on top of your desk. Confidential or proprietary information lying on a desk is an easy target. Consequently, organizations may require people who work with sensitive information to lock it in their desks at night or whenever they leave.

Surprisingly, the handling of garbage also can be a security risk. Many organizations are careful to shred discarded documents and manuals instead of throwing them in the trash. Failure to do this led to one of the classic stories about computer crime and security. In 1971, a 19-year-old operated an illegal business based on information he obtained from a trash bin. The trash bin belonged to a supply office of Pacific Telephone and Telegraph (PT&T). In it, he found discarded equipment, which he refurbished. He also found manuals and the detailed operating and ordering procedures used by installation

TABLE 13.4 Controlling Access to Data, Computers, and Networks

Control technique	Example
Enforce manual data handling guidelines	• Lock desks • Shred discarded documents and manuals
Define access privileges	• Give different individuals different levels of privilege for using the computer • Give different individuals different levels of access to specific data files
Enforce access privileges	
What you know	• Password • Special personal data
What you have	• ID card • Key to physical facility
Where you are	• Call-back system
Who you are	• Fingerprint or handprint • Retina pattern • Voice pattern
Control incoming data from networks and other media	• Use firewalls • Scan for viruses
Make data meaningless to anyone lacking authorization	• Data encryption

and repair crews. After posing as a freelance writer to get a plant tour, he impersonated a PT&T employee dialing orders into the PT&T computer. He drove to a PT&T facility in an old PT&T truck he had bought at an auction, picked up the equipment he had ordered, and sold it to other companies at discounted prices. Caught after stealing over $1,000,000 in inventory, he served 40 days in jail, paid an $8,500 fine, and later went to work as a security consultant.[49] If PT&T had shredded their operating procedure manuals instead of throwing them in the trash, this incident probably would not have happened. Although it is excessive to shred every document and printout that is no longer used, dumping ordering manuals, customer lists, and company plans into a trash bin invites unauthorized access to proprietary information.

Many IT users are unaware of a related fact, that deleting a document from a diskette or hard disk does not really mean that it is deleted, but rather that the directory information pointing to the document has been changed to indicate that the space is available for reuse. A product called Shredder software has been developed to permanently delete the information in deleted files.[50]

Access Privileges

Locking desks and shredding obsolete documents are security measures concerning manual data handling. Security measures for computerized systems start with defining access privileges. **Access privileges** are precise statements of which computers and data an individual can access and under what circumstances. The simplest way to define access privileges is with a list of all authorized users. Access lists are effective only if organizations enforce them strictly. Security-conscious organizations are especially concerned that all computer-related records and privileges are up to date for all employees. Such organizations ensure that all access to computers is canceled when an employee leaves.

The fact that someone can log onto a computer system doesn't mean that person should have access to all data in the system. Many systems use file access lists that grant individual users or groups of users different levels of access to specific files. Typical levels of access include: none, read only, read and copy, or read and update. For example, almost all users would have no direct access to the list of passwords. Some users would have read and copy access to a customer list. All users would have read and update access to their own personal information.

Regardless of whether the focus is physical facilities or computer networks, access lists require enforcement. We will look at ways to enforce access control based on four concepts: what you know, what you have, where you are, and who you are.

Access Control Based on What You Know

A **password** provides a simple form of protection. After logging on with an account number or user ID, the user enters a confidential password. The user can use the system only after the computer checks that this password goes with this account. Business people today may have separate passwords for electronic mail, voice mail, and several different computer networks, not to speak of PIN numbers for ATMs and credit cards.

Unfortunately, password schemes have a variety of weaknesses. People who use many different computer systems often have to remember many different passwords. Because it is hard to remember infrequently used passwords, people are tempted to use short passwords or passwords that can be guessed easily, such as the person's account number, a child's name, pet's name, or middle name. If a password is simple enough, it is easy to figure out by trial and error. This is especially true if a computer generates each trial password and tries it out automatically. Employers may forget to cancel passwords after employees leave a company. Where security is sloppy, terminated employees may be able to dial into an employer's computer months after being dismissed. Because the password list is just a file inside a computer, it may be possible to find and copy this list by working around the standard file security routines in the system. With all these shortcomings, passwords are certainly not foolproof. Nonetheless, they are useful as one part of an overall security system.

One of the most important shortcomings of passwords is that people literally give them away, such as by writing passwords on the side of a workstation or by letting other people look over their shoulders. Many computer system break-ins occur because an operator has divulged a password to someone who appears to be authorized to receive it. The impostor often telephones, pretends to be a repair person, gains the unsuspecting operator's confidence, and then asks the operator to divulge the password as part of a supposed repair process. Computer hackers cynically call this **social engineering.** This type of approach has been used to steal passwords to Internet accounts. For example, some scams have used America Online's instant message feature to send messages such as "I am with the America Online customer service department and we are experiencing difficulties with our records. I need you to verify your log-on password to me so that I can validate you as a user, and fix our records promptly." Another common message is "You are eligible to have your account promoted to an Overhead Account ... and it's totally free! All you have to do is change your password to "Overhead" and e-mail us back."[51] All users of the Internet and other networked systems should understand this threat.

Access Control Based on What You Have

ID cards provide some security by making it more difficult for people to enter a physical facility or computer system. Simple ID card systems have many problems similar to those of passwords, however. The cards may be lost. The organization may fail to insist they be returned when an employee leaves. The card may be stolen or forged, as happens often with driver's licenses and passports. The technology for ID cards is becoming more powerful, and ID cards themselves can store data other than a name, number, and picture. ID cards that can be read by scanners can be used in combination with definitive personal identification to provide more advanced security methods.

Access Control Based on Where You Are

One way to prevent unauthorized access to computer systems is to make sure that a given user can access the system only from that user's terminal. This is accomplished using a **callback system,** with which the user enters an account number and password and is then disconnected automatically. If the numbers match, the system then calls the user back at a phone number listed in an internal system directory. This prevents access by people who have stolen a password unless they are using the password from the password owner's location. Extending this idea, a device has been patented which instructs the person calling back to repeat several words over the phone. Access would be granted only if the voice matches a stored voiceprint.

Access Control Based on Who You Are

For more definitive identification than is possible with passwords and ID cards, specialized equipment can sense a person's unique physical characteristics, such as fingerprints, voice prints, blood-vessel patterns on the retina, or patterns in the iris of the eye. These are all forms of **biometric identification** because they use the individual's personal, biological characteristics. These systems are becoming competitive with magnetic card systems for restricting entrance to buildings. Hand and fingerprint identification are used to control access to high-security areas ranging from nuclear research labs to jewelry vaults and are now even available for unlocking car doors. (See Figure 13.6.) American Airlines has used a retina scanner as part of the security system for its underground computer facility. The Cook County Jail in Chicago has used retina scanners to make sure prisoners don't attempt to exchange identities by memorizing each others names, addresses, and personal information.[52]

All of the access control methods, even biometric identification, can be undermined by carelessness after the access control check is completed. For example, merely walking away from a computer terminal logged into a network can provide an opportunity for unauthorized access to data. A simple way to reduce this risk is to log off whenever you leave a terminal. To minimize unauthorized access, some computer systems apply an **automatic log off** to any terminal left unused for a fixed amount of time, such as five minutes.

Figure 13.6
Using Your Hand as a Passport

To reduce waiting time for frequent international travelers, the U.S. Immigration and Naturalization Service permits travelers at some airports to identify themselves using a hand scanner and an identification card.

Controlling Incoming Data Flowing Through Networks and Other Media

In a highly networked world, access controls that focus on identifying people need to co-exist with controls that focus on data flowing through networks. For example, a virus on a diskette might infect not only one personal computer, but also all the computers attached to the same network. A document attached to an incoming e-mail message might also bring a virus. Similarly, programs downloaded from the Internet might contain hidden code that finds, modifies, or transmits data on a hard disk without authorization.

A number of **virus protection** products are available commercially. These products automatically scan diskettes and operate at other possible sites of virus infection. They look for a wide range of known viruses and can also detect many abnormal situations that may indicate the presence of a virus whether or not the particular virus has been identified in the past. In many cases they can remove a virus and repair basic code affected by it. Virus protection software must be updated frequently because new viruses are being created all the time.

One of the basic tools for controlling incoming data is a **firewall,** a program that is like a lock on the front door. A firewall inspects incoming messages, decides whether they are legitimate, sends legitimate messages to their destinations, and keeps track of all incoming messages that were stopped. Firewalls and other filtering software are used wherever messages from the Internet or other public networks enter a private computer network. Figure 13.7 illustrates that firewalls, virus scanners, and other filters can be used at many different points within a private corporate network to make sure that only authorized access is permitted and to detect viruses before they spread. The issue here is not just detection of problems, but detection without causing excessive inefficiency. Firewall products compete on their ability to process a rapid stream of messages, to enforce a variety of controllable policies for accepting messages, and to protect against known vulnerabilities related to features of networking software.

Making the Data Meaningless to Unauthorized Users

Another way to protect data is to make data meaningless to unauthorized users. As was introduced in Chapter 8, encryption is the encoding of data to permit meaningful access only by authorized parties. Encryption applies across a wide range of applications including data stored on computers (which might be accessed illegally), e-mail messages and cellular phone conversations (that might be intercepted), and electronic transactions (that might be monitored or performed fraudulently).

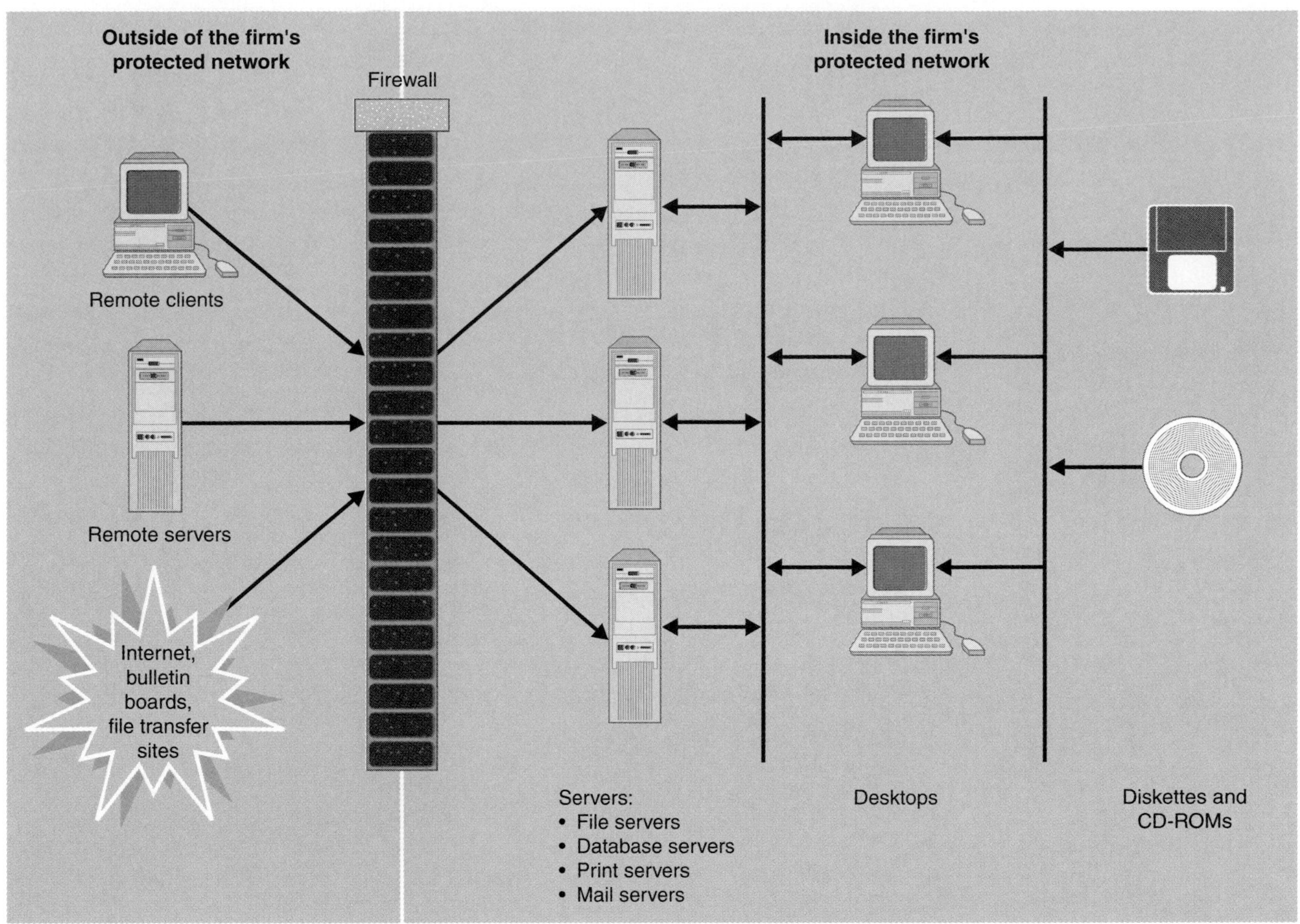

Figure 13.7
Possible locations for checking data transfers in a corporate network

Each node in the network is potentially a site for checking data transfers to avoid unauthorized access and virus propagation.

The difficult issue with encryption is to find a scheme that is difficult to break but is also practical to use. One possibility is to use an extremely long number as an encryption key, use a multiplication process to perform the encoding, and then a corresponding division process to perform the decoding. The problem with this approach is that both the sender and receiver must have the same key, leaving questions about how the receiver will obtain the key in the first place and how the key will remain private. Consider, for example, sending the same encrypted message to 500 people. It would be very difficult to keep the key secret because each individual would need a copy.

The **public key encryption** method that is currently favored involves two keys for each user, a public key that is widely available and a private key that must be kept secret. The computer sending the message uses the public key to encypt it. The computer receiving the message uses the corresponding private key to decrypt it. Figure 13.8 illustrates the basic sequence in using public key encryption. A simplified summary of the calculation technique is included in the figure to provide a general idea of how the method works even though it is based on mathematical techniques only invented in 1977. The approach is based on the idea that computerized multiplication by even a very large number is very fast on today's computers, whereas factoring a very large number (breaking the number into two very large divisors) is still slow enough that breaking a private key would take a long time. RSA Laboratories recommends that the modulus (see Figure 13.8) in a public key should be 768 bits for personal use, 1,024 bits for typical corporate use and 2,048 bits for

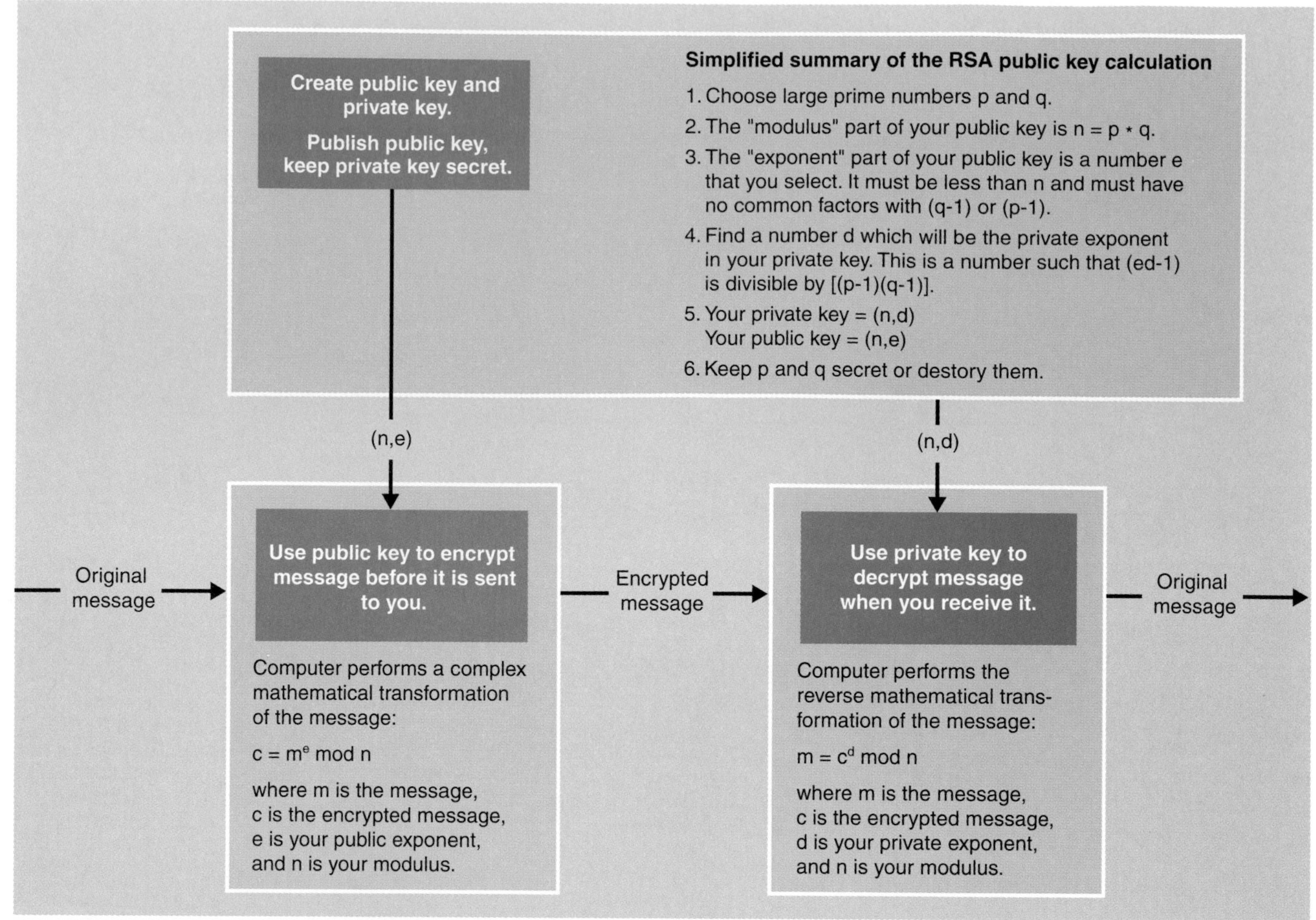

Figure 13.8
Using public key encryption

The basic idea of public key encryption may seem simple, but the mathematics summarized above involves advanced topics in number theory and is not for the faint of heart.

extremely valuable keys such as the key pair of a certification authority. It expects a 768-bit key to be secure until the year 2004, when greater computing power may mean a longer key will be required to prevent theft.[53]

Because the computations for using a public key are quite lengthy, a typical way to use public key encryption is to combine it with a secret key encryption system such as the Data Encryption Standard (DES) that was once a leading edge technique. The method is to encrypt the message using a randomly selected DES key, encrypt the DES key using the recipient's public key, and send this combined message as a "digital envelope." The recipient uses a private key to decrypt the DES key and then uses the DES key to decrypt the message. This combines the much higher speed of the DES method with the greater key-management convenience of the public key method.[54] A similar method is used to create a "digital signature" that can be used for authenticating that a message has not been changed. A mathematical procedure called "hashing" is used to create a digital signature. Both the digital signature and the message are encrypted and sent. If the message is modified later, the hashing function will not create the same digital signature.

Thus far, ways to control access to data have been described. Because insiders are responsible for most computer crime, it is clear that even people with authorized access may cause problems. The next level of control tries to make sure transactions are processed correctly.

Reality Check

CONTROLLING ACCESS TO COMPUTERS, NETWORKS, AND DATA

This section described many ways to control access to computers, networks, and data.

1. Assume you have been hired in the patent office of an extremely security-conscious company. On your second day at work you see someone across the room who appears to be copying a password written on a slip of paper taped to the side of a workstation. Do you think you have a responsibility to do anything in this situation?
2. Several weeks later the company brings in a retina scanner to check the identity of anyone entering the patent office. How would you feel about undergoing a retina scan every time you enter the office?

Controlling Transaction Processing

Control of transaction processing starts with data collection and includes the way computers process the data and the way errors are corrected. The control points we will look at include data preparation and authorization, data validation, error correction, and backup and recovery.

Data Preparation and Authorization

Data preparation and authorization creates the transaction data that will be entered into a transaction processing system. The story of Equity Funding Corporation shows the importance of controlling data preparation. Over the course of ten years, officers and computer programmers of Equity Funding colluded to make the company appear to be on a rapid growth path by issuing 60,000 fake insurance policies, accounting for about 65% of the company's total. The fake policies were sold to reinsurance companies. When the premiums were to be paid, Equity Funding generated more fake policies, sold them to reinsurers, and used the proceeds of the sale to pay premiums for policies sold earlier. In creating the fake policies, the programmers used statistical data from the company's legitimate policies to ensure that the fakes had the same profiles in coverage, premiums, policy cancellations, and benefits paid. When federal investigators asked to audit the files, the company delayed until it could forge health reports, contracts, and supporting documents. This fraud eventually cost investors $1 billion.[55]

Collusion on the scale of the Equity Funding case is extraordinary because it requires the cooperation of so many people. Crime through fraudulent transaction data is much easier to perpetrate if it can be done by one person, as is suspected in the case of the $10 million logic bomb (mentioned earlier) that erased crucial design software at Omega Engineering and disabled backup and recovery facilities. Before being fired, the suspect in that case had been the company's chief computer network designer and the company's network administrator. Consequently, he knew the details of the network and also had the supervisory privileges to make network additions, changes, and deletions.[56]

Segregation of duties is a control method that makes it more difficult to perpetrate one-person crimes and crimes of collusion. **Segregation of duties** is the division of responsibilities among two or more people to reduce the likelihood of theft or accidental misprocessing. For example, one person in an accounts payable department might write the expense voucher, another person authorizes it, and a third actually writes the check. This does not assure honesty and accuracy, but it makes dishonesty and carelessness more difficult.

Segregation of duties is used extensively in both computerized and noncomputerized systems. It is just as applicable in system development groups as it is in finance departments. Some computer frauds were possible only because an individual working in isolation from others could modify a program to put money into a particular account or perform other improper processing. IS organizations use software change control techniques (mentioned earlier) to improve software quality and avoid this problem.

Although segregation of duties has advantages for security, it has disadvantages for efficiency because it requires multiple authorizations and the involvement of many people in processes that could be handled by one person. The extent of segregation of duties is a management choice based on this tradeoff.

Data Validation

Data validation refers to checking transaction data for any errors or omissions that can be detected by looking at the data. Common computerized validation procedures include checking for missing data (such as a missing social security number), invalid data (such as an impossible ZIP code), and inconsistent data. As an example, Figure 13.9 shows a transaction screen from a hypothetical registration system at a college. Some of the validation checks are obvious, such as matching the student's name and social security number or checking that the student's financial account is current. Others require more complex processing, such as determining whether the student has taken the prerequisite courses or whether the sequence of courses will permit graduation on time.

Although it is essential to validate transaction data to keep the database accurate and avoid wasting time correcting past errors, it is impossible to validate all the data in a system. For example, transpositions such as 56 instead of 65 are often difficult to catch because there may be no reason to suspect that 65 is more likely than 56. The army clerk who made such an error on a 13-digit part number ended up ordering a 7-ton anchor instead of a $6 incandescent lamp.[57] Better information system design might have prevented this error. Instead of requiring the clerk to type a 13-digit number, an information system built today could easily permit the clerk to choose the item from a list of existing part numbers plus item descriptions.

Error Correction

Error correction is an essential component of any transaction processing system because it is impossible to assure correctness of all data in the system, regardless of how carefully the data were validated when first entered. Error correction in many TPSs is surprisingly complicated due to the possibility of fraud. If erroneous data could be corrected by editing the data values (as would be done using a word processor), correct data could also be changed using the same techniques. Embezzlement would be rampant and the validity of most databases in doubt.

To control TPSs involving data related to financial accounting, error correction is usually handled as a separate transaction that is recorded and accounted for. The transaction history from the TPS therefore includes each normal transaction that occurred, such as payment of a bill or receipt of an order, as well as each error correction transaction, such as changing a customer's account balance because a bill contained the wrong price or because the merchandise was unsatisfactory.

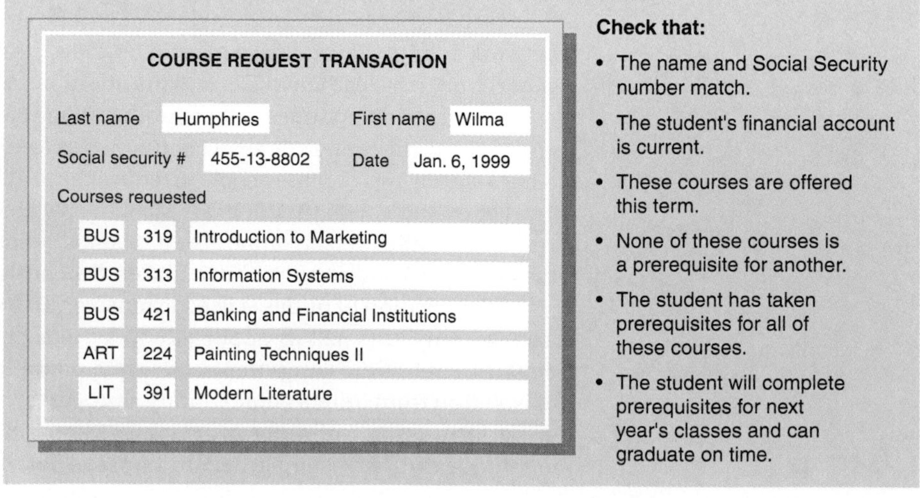

COURSE REQUEST TRANSACTION
Last name Humphries
First name Wilma
Social security # 455-13-8802
Date Jan. 6, 1999
Courses requested
BUS 319 Introduction to Marketing
BUS 313 Information Systems
BUS 421 Banking and Financial Institutions
ART 224 Painting Techniques II
LIT 391 Modern Literature
Check that:
• The name and Social Security number match.
• The student's financial account is current.
• These courses are offered this term.
• None of these courses is a prerequisite for another.
• The student has taken prerequisites for all of these courses.
• The student will complete prerequisites for next year's classes and can graduate on time.

Figure 13.9
Validation checks for a course enrollment transaction

This figure shows a transaction screen from a hypothetical registration system and a list of automatic validation checks that might be used.

Backup and Recovery

The last step in controlling transaction processing is to make sure that whenever the computer system goes down regular processing will resume with minimal pain and inconvenience. The typical method for doing this was illustrated in Figure 4.12, which shows the logic of performing periodic backups and using those backups to restore the transaction database to the point at which a disruption occurred. Because the topic of backup and recovery was explained in Chapter 4, it will not be repeated here.

Motivating Efficient and Effective Operation

Topics already discussed, such as developing the information system properly, maintaining security, and controlling transaction processing are all aspects of system management. Another side of system management is creating incentives for efficient and effective operation, especially by monitoring information system usage and by using chargeback to motivate efficiency.

Monitoring Information System Usage

Because it is difficult to manage things without measuring them, well designed information systems contain measures of performance both for the business process being supported and for the information system itself. Consider a telemarketing firm's customer service information system. It might include measures of business process results, such as sales per hour and customer waiting time before speaking to an agent. It might also contain measures of information system efficiency, such as downtime, average response time for database inquiries, and weekly operating cost. Patterns of suspicious activity might also be recognized with the help of credit card companies.

Due to the prevalence of telephone fraud, all three types of monitoring are important for PBXs. User waiting time and cost savings on outside calls routed through the PBX are measures of the business process. PBX costs and downtime describe information system performance. Peculiar patterns of using one access code for frequent calls or unusual foreign calls could be a warning that an access code has been stolen.

Regardless whether the monitoring concerns business process performance, information system performance, or unusual activity, it has little value unless users and managers are willing and able to use the information. This is one of the reasons graphs of key measurements are often posted in the corridors going into factories. Posting the indicators makes sure everyone knows they are important and that everyone recognizes how well the factory is doing.

Charging Users to Encourage Efficiency

The lack of publicized measures for many computerized systems leads users to ignore their costs, use them inefficiently, and sometimes tolerate misuse. This is one of the reasons for charging users to encourage efficiency. **Chargeback systems** try to motivate efficient usage by assigning to user departments the costs of information systems. Impacts of chargeback systems on behavior are apparent in the way offices operate. If the telephone is treated as corporate overhead and therefore appears to be free to users, people will use the phone more than if they or their departments are charged directly. Likewise, disk storage on departmental computers is filled much more quickly if the users incur no storage charges. Even if resources aren't free, the way they are charged out affects how they are used. Consider a laser printer charged at 10¢ per page and a copier charged at 5¢ per page. If you had to make 45 copies, you would probably print one copy on the laser printer and make the other copies on the copier. But if the laser printer cost 5¢ or less, you would make all the copies there. Ideally, chargeback schemes should motivate people to use resources efficiently by reflecting the organization's true costs.

The key issue in charging for using information system resources is to affect people's decisions. If, for example, total computer costs are charged to departments based only on headcount, the charges probably won't affect decisions because the charges are the same regardless of how people use the computers. Instead of using this type of broadbrush allocation, chargeback schemes should use recognizable units of output that correspond closely to business activities. Directly controllable chargeable items include pages printed, transactions performed, and amount of data stored.

Some charging schemes also reflect resource scarcity to motivate usage only when those resources are needed. For example, most computer facilities are especially busy at particular times such as late morning and midafternoon and are underutilized other times. Rate differentials are sometimes used to shift some of the work to times of low utilization, thereby making it unnecessary to buy more capacity to cope with the peaks. With rate differentials, users are charged more when resources are scarcer. Resources such as CPU cycles or telephone minutes during busy periods could cost two or more times as much as they cost during slack periods. Although some users have no choice, rate differentials succeed in shifting some of the demand to times when resources would be underutilized.

Reality Check

CHARGEBACK

Charging people for use of computer resources is one of the ways to motivate efficient usage.

1. Identify situations in your everyday life in which the way you are charged for something determines how efficiently you use it.
2. How do you think your university should encourage efficient usage of its internal telephone system and computers?

Auditing the Information System

Auditing standards and controls are designed to ensure that financial operations are neither misrepresented nor threatened due to defective procedures or accounting systems. With the advent of computer systems, the scope of auditing expanded to encompass both general controls over computer installations and application controls for assuring that the recording, processing, and reporting of data are performed properly.

Methods for verifying the phases of processing can be categorized as either "auditing around the computer" or "auditing through the computer." In **auditing around the computer,** the auditor typically selects source documents, traces associated entries through intermediate computer printouts, and examines the resultant entries in summary accounts. This approach basically treats the computer itself as a black box. Although it is useful in finding some errors, and is often cost-effective, it may not provide enough detail to catch crimes such as stealing a fraction of a penny on certain transactions. In **auditing through the computer,** the auditor attempts to understand and test the computer's processing in more detail. A common technique is to create test data and process the data through the system to observe whether the expected results occur. An important shortcoming of this approach is that only preconceived conditions are tested. Furthermore, it is impractical for the test data to represent every possible situation. If a program illegally transfers money every Thursday and the test data are processed on Tuesday, the problem will be missed.

An auditor's responsibility goes much further than just looking at how transactions are processed. Auditors must examine issues such as unauthorized access, controls on computerized data files, controls on data transmission, and procedures for recovering when the information system goes down unexpectedly.

Preparing for Disasters

You don't need to look at computer systems to understand the importance of genuine preparedness for possible disasters. Consider the oil tanker accident that polluted Prince William Sound in Alaska with 10 million gallons of oil. A large oil terminal was permitted in this area because a major accident seemed unlikely. Just in case, there was an 1,800-page contingency plan for handling a major spill. But when the accident occurred, almost nothing was done to contain and clean up the spilled oil during two days of calm seas, and almost nothing could be done after fierce winds spread the oil on the third day. Exxon, Alyeska Pipeline Service Co., and state officials blamed each other, citing reasons such as not having equipment ready or delaying authorization to use chemical dispersants. This example illustrates the necessity of genuine preparedness for disasters, not just having a plan on paper.

A **disaster plan** is a plan of action to recover from occurrences that shut down or harm major information systems. The need for such a plan is apparent from the potential impact of accidents, sabotage, and natural events such as floods and earthquakes.The nature and extent of an information systems disaster plan for a business depend on the role of information systems to the day-to-day operation of the business. Reliable online transaction processing systems are essential for banks, distributors, and airlines. For businesses such as these, any unplanned computer downtime can cut into customer service and revenues. These businesses may go to great expense maintaining redundant real time databases in different locations, with several databases updated simultaneously whenever a transaction occurs. Even businesses that use information systems primarily for accounting and management reporting still need definitive plans for recovering from unexpected downtime.

A 1997 study done by Comdisco, a company selling disaster recovery services including disaster planning and emergency processing sites, found that only 45% of the 200 major companies in its survey had a disaster plan in place. Looking back five years at the World Trade Center bombing in New York City in 1993, the operations director at Fiduciary Trust Company International said that the company would have gone out of business if a remote data processing site had not been available for an emergency situation. At that time, the company moved 450 employees to Comdisco's site in New Jersey for three weeks. In the subsequent years, Fiduciary Trust set up leased line connections to a Comdisco site so that all its transactions and databases could be replicated immediately.[58]

Having a disaster plan for temporarily transferring data processing to a backup site certainly makes sense for many businesses, but a backup site does not help if the application software itself does not work. This is why the Y2K problem creates a huge disaster planning issue that many companies have not yet faced. Regardless of how carefully they have performed their Y2K conversions, what happens if something goes wrong in mission-critical software? Prudential Insurance Company addressed this issue by creating a contingency plan for each major application area. Each plan says what will happen if the Y2K changes are not completed on time, if the application fails on January 1, if it fails after January 1, if it performs erroneous calculations that are found later, and so on. The plans will be documented, distributed, and tested.[59] Many other companies will not be as thorough, either in performing the conversions or in deciding what to do if they fail.

CHAPTER CONCLUSION

Summary

What are the main types of risks of accidents related to information systems?
The main types of risks of accidents include: operator error, hardware malfunction, software bugs, data errors, damage to physical facilities, inadequate system performance, and liability for system failure.

What are the different types of computer crime?
Computer crime is the use of computerized systems to perform illegal acts. Computer crime can be divided into theft, sabotage, and vandalism. Thefts can be perpetrated through theft of software and equipment, unauthorized use of access codes, fraudulent transaction data, modification of software, and theft or modification of data. Entering fraudulent transaction data is the simplest and most common method of computer-related theft. Even without much computer knowledge, fraudulent data can be entered by forging documents, bypassing procedures, or impersonating someone.

What issues magnify the vulnerability of information systems to accidents and crime?
This vulnerability is magnified by the nature of complex systems, human limitations, and the business environment. Complex systems have many vulnerable points that may be difficult to

identify in advance. Decentralization within systems decreases control. Human limitations such as complacency and carelessness increase opportunities for accidents and crime. Greed provides a motive for crime. Difficulty in visualizing how complex systems work makes it harder to anticipate accidents or guard against crime. The business environment creates pressures for limiting staff and attaining immediate financial results that reduce the time and effort devoted to making systems secure.

What measures can be taken to minimize accidents and computer crime?
The value chain for security starts by building the system right the first time, typically by adhering to a structured system life cycle and using software change control. The next step is training users about security issues to reduce carelessness. Once the system is in operation, maintain physical security and prevent unauthorized access to computers, networks, and data. Having controlled access, make sure transactions are performed correctly, and monitor information system usage to ensure effectiveness and find ways to improve. Even if the system seems secure, audit it to identify problems and prepare for disasters.

What are the different ways to control access to data, computers, and networks?
There are five aspects of access control: enforcing guidelines for manual data handling, defining access privileges, enforcing access privileges, controlling incoming data from networks and other media, and using encryption to make the data meaningless to anyone who bypasses access controls. Guidelines for manual data handling range from rules about leaving work on top of desks to procedures for shredding sensitive documents. Access privileges are precise statements of which computers and data an individual can access and under what circumstances. It is possible to enforce access control based on four concepts: what you know (such as passwords); what you have (such as ID cards); where you are (such as permitting access only from a particular terminal); and who you are (such as biometric identification). Control of incoming data is accomplished through firewalls and virus scanning.

Key Terms

operator error
software bug
liability
computer crime
hacker
trap door
Trojan horse
logic bomb
virus
software change control
physical access controls
access privileges
password
social engineering
call-back system
biometric identification
automatic log off
virus protection
firewall
public key encryption
segregation of duties
data validation
error correction
chargeback system
auditing around the computer
auditing through the computer
disaster plan

Review Questions

1. What are common reasons for project failure at each of the four phases of an information system project?
2. Identify the seven types of risks related to accidents rather than computer crime.
3. What factors make operator error more likely?
4. Why do software bugs occur?
5. Why does the year 2000 raise fears about problems with old computerized systems?
6. How do software vendors limit their legal liability for software they sell?
7. What are the different types of computer crime, and which is most common?
8. Describe different ways to steal through fraudulent transaction data.
9. What programming techniques have been used to commit sabotage and vandalism?

10. How is system vulnerability related to the nature of complex systems, human limitations, and pressures in the business environment?
11. Identify the steps in the value chain for system security and control.
12. How does software change control operate?
13. What techniques are used for controlling access to data, computers, and networks?
14. Explain some of the shortcomings of passwords.
15. What do computer hackers mean when they use the term social engineering?
16. How does public key encryption work?
17. Describe the main methods for controlling transaction processing.
18. How do chargeback systems encourage efficiency?
19. What is the difference between auditing around the computer and auditing through the computer?
20. Why is it important to have a disaster plan for information systems?

Discussion Topics

1. The Business Software Alliance, a software-industry trade group, announced plans to offer a bounty of up to £2,500 ($3,900) to anyone in Great Britain who informs on companies using unlicensed software. Because around half the software used in Great Britain was thought to be unlicensed, many large firms would probably be named. Information about unlicensed use would be obtained through a toll-free number dubbed the Software Crimeline. The chairman of the Computer Users of Europe complained that this was "like the old East Bloc process of informing" and that he "could not see anyone who has any desire to continue his career feeling he could turn in his boss."[60] Explain how this example is related to this chapter's ideas about computer crime and system security.
2. A 20-year-old MIT junior was indicted for managing a computerized bulletin board allegedly used for illegal distribution of copyrighted software. He was not accused of posting software to it or of profiting from the alleged illegal activities. His defense revolved around the assertion that a computerized bulletin board is just a conduit for information and is not responsible for the information posted on it.[61] What are the ethical responsibilities of a person who runs a computerized bulletin board?
3. Your friend has been given a wonderful game program and wants to show you how it operates. He has used it on his computer without problems. Under what circumstances should you allow him to run it on your computer?
4. The night before the Space Shuttle Challenger blew up, killing the astronauts aboard, several engineers at Morton-Thiokol tried to have the launch delayed. They thought that the cold weather at Cape Canaveral might affect critical joints on the body of the booster and thereby endanger the spacecraft, but they were overruled. Identify any ideas in this chapter that might help explain why the Challenger was allowed to take off.
5. You are seated on an airplane about to take off and hear the following announcement after the instructions about fastening seat belts and the location of emergency exits: "This is your pilot. I want to congratulate you as the first group of passengers to benefit from our new autopilot system, which will control the entire flight from takeoff to landing. But don't worry, I'm still here just in case." How would you react to this announcement?

A Galaxy 4 satellite operated by PanAmSat, a subsidiary of Hughes Electronics, tilted away from the earth at 6:13 P.M. on May 19, 1998, and began to spin because of a computer failure and the subsequent failure of a backup computer. This unexpected problem disabled 80% to 90% of the pager services in the United States, along with a number of credit card authorization networks, television transmissions, and other networked services. PanAmSat's efforts to realign the satellite failed, but it was able to restore service within a day by rerouting the traffic that the satellite normally handled. Of the 17 satellites PanAmSat had in orbit at the time, one was a spare. The recovery plan included rerouting signals for paging, retail-store services, and other services through its Galaxy 3R satellite and rerouting television signals through its Galaxy 6 satellite, which it was moving into roughly the same geosynchronous orbit over Kansas that the Galaxy 4 had occupied since its launch in 1993. Computer failure had transformed the Galaxy 4 from a $200 million link in the U.S. business infrastructure into a 3,700 pound piece of space junk with a 100-foot span of solar panels. The satellite was insured for $116 million.

The immediate consequences of the satellite failure demonstrated the widespread dependence on communications infrastructure. Emergency communication to police departments and physicians was disrupted for hours. Customers at 5,400 Chevron stations could no longer pay by credit card at the pump because automated credit-card authorization requests were transmitted from antennas atop gas stations through the Galaxy 4 satellite. Customers in Wal-Mart stores had similar problems. At home, the nonresponse of family members and friends when paged repeatedly led to confusion and annoyance. The cost of satellite time suddenly jumped. It had ranged from $100 to $500 for a 15-minute block depending on the satellite's location. After the failure the prices jumped to $250 to $600. Annual prices of $900,000 to $2,500,000 seemed to be increasing by up to 50%.

Although satellites have typically been extremely reliable, with a failure rate of less than 1%, the widespread impact of this event was a reminder of vulnerability to infrastructure-related weak links that affect business and society. For example, the root server for the Internet is a computer the size of a pizza box sitting in an office park in Virginia. A late-night error by a computer operator caused that root server to distribute garbled Internet address lists to the other main servers on the Internet, thereby disrupting Internet traffic for hours. (See Network Solutions case in Chapter 10.). A handful of regional air traffic control centers monitor air flights but use dangerously obsolete equipment. (See FAA case in Chapter 12.) As mentioned earlier in this chapter, automated teller machine networks rely on links to data processing centers, and many vital services depend on telephone networks that sometimes fail due to weather, human error, and other causes. For all these cases it is possible to imagine ways to reduce risks through investment in redundant capacity, but the costs are prohibitive in many situations. For example, CBS television shifted to a backup satellite when the Galaxy 4 could not carry its broadcasts as planned. CBS could afford the backup, but many paging businesses do not have the resources to keep a satellite idling in reserve.

QUESTIONS

1. It is easy to say that business and government should assess risks and take appropriate action. Thinking about IT-based systems ranging from pagers to ATMs to air traffic control, suggest general guidelines a business or government might use for deciding what failure rate to tolerate and what level of resources to devote to disaster recovery.
2. Explain how these guidelines are or are not relevant to the Y2K problem.

Sources:

Biddle, Frederic M., John Lippman, Stephanie N. Mehta. "One Satellite Fails, and the World Goes Awry," *Wall Street Journal,* May 21, 1998, p. B1.

Zuckerman, Laurence. "Satellite Failure Is Rare, and Therefore Unsettling," *New York Times*, May 21, 1998, p. C3.

King Soopers: Using Computer Access to Steal from an Employer

In March 1998 the Colorado Springs Police Department leveled charges of conspiracy, computer crime, and felony theft against three employees of Denver-based King Soopers supermarket chain, which is owned by the supermarket giant Kroger Co. The employees were a PC manager and the head clerks at two King Soopers stores. All three had been leading extravagant lifestyles even though all of them had previously filed for personal bankruptcy before 1993 and the highest of their salaries was $32,582 per year. A two-year police investigation found that one suspect had spent $691,498 between 1993 and 1996, and that two suspects had bought and sold 21 cars during this period. The estimated total loss was around $2 million. This estimate came from bank, motor vehicle, gambling, and credit card records plus the incomplete records that were available from the stores themselves.

The alleged embezzlement conspiracy may have started when King Soopers converted from outdated Data General hardware and software to IBM PCs in 1992. Few King Soopers managers were computer-savvy at the time, and they relied heavily on the PC manager and trusted him. The police investigation revealed nine different schemes for stealing money. The PC manager seemed to have modified the bar code pricing system to overcharge customers, allowing the head clerks to steal the difference during the nightly closing. The head clerks voided some customer sales and simply took the money. They rang in discount coupons and took the money themselves. The PC manager apparently modified the PC system so that sales of certain items were funneled into a fake inventory category that could later be erased from sales reports. For example, the faked records made it seem that one King Soopers store had sold no dairy products for 18 months. When internal King Soopers management seemed to become aware of the problems, the thieves changed to different methods and found other employees willing to cover for them.

A combination of King Soopers management practices and its information system procedures made it difficult to track down the fraud. The firm's accounting procedures erased backup tapes after 60 days, making it impossible to retrieve transactions more than two months old. The PC manager's boss acknowledged that he never checked on the PC manager's work or on claims that "computer problems" had been fixed at the two stores where the thefts occurred. The VP of retail sales declined to say whether audit procedures or personnel checks were being modified to avoid these problems in the future.

QUESTIONS

1. Explain how the value chain for information system security was not followed in this case.
2. Assume that you were the president of a small chain of restaurants or hardware stores and that you did not know much about computers. What do you think you might do to minimize the risk of this type of theft or of sabotage by a disgruntled employee?

Source:

Nash, Kim S. "PC Manager at Center of $2M Grocery Scam," *Computerworld*, Mar. 30, 1998, p. 1.

Notes

Chapter 1

1. "Barnes & Noble Sues Amazon.com," Book News, American Booksellers Association, www.bookweb.org/news, May 19, 1997.
2. Sliwa, Carol. "Net used to extend EDI's reach," *Computerworld*, Feb. 12, 1998, p. 1.
3. Davenport, Thomas H., and James E. Short. "The New Industrial Engineering: Information Technology and Business Process Redesign," *Sloan Management Review*, Summer 1990, pp. 11–27.
4. Bylinsky, Gene. "The Race to the Automatic Factory." *Fortune*, Feb. 21, 1983, pp. 53–64.
5. Fisher, Marshall. "What Is the Right Supply Chain for Your Product?" *Harvard Business Review*, Mar.–Apr. 1997, pp. 105–116.
6. Gartner Group, "Without Commitment, Electronic Commerce Is Doomed to Fail," advertisement, *New York Times*, Aug. 18, 1997, p. C4.
7. Davidson, William H., and Joseph F. Movizzo, "Managing the Business Transformation Process," in *Competing in the Information Age: Strategic Alignment in Practice*, ed. Jerry N. Luftman (New York: Oxford University Press, 1996), pp. 322–358.
8. Smith, Lee. "New Ideas from the Army," *Fortune*, Sept. 19, 1994, pp. 203–212.
9. Luftman, Jerry N., "Applying the Strategic Alignment Model," in Luftman, pp. 43–69. Davidson, William H., and Joseph F. Movizzo, "Managing the Business Transformation Process," in Luftman, pp. 322–358.
10. Davidson, William H., and Joseph F. Movizzo. "Managing the Business Transformation Process," in Luftman, pp. 322–358.
11. Dumaine, Brian. "Times are Good? Create a Crisis." *Fortune*, June 28, 1993, pp. 123–130.
12. Barboza, David. "On-Line Trade Fees Falling Off the Screen," *New York Times*, Mar. 1, 1998, p. B4.
13. Gelsinger, Patrick, Paolo Gargini, Gerhard Parker, and Albert Yu. "2001: A Microprocessor Odyssey," pp. 95-113 in Derek Leebaert, *Technology 2001: The Future of Computing and Communications*. Cambridge, MA: The MIT Press, 1991, p. 100.
14. Murillo, Luis Eduardo. *The International DRAM Industry from 1970 to 1993*. Ph.D. Thesis, University of California, Berkeley, 1994, p. 539.
15. Reilly, Patrick M. "The Dark Side: Warning: Portable Devices Can Be Hazardous to Your Health," *Wall Street Journal*, Nov. 16, 1992, p. R12.
16. Palfreman, Jon, and Doron Swade. *The Dream Machine.: Exploring the Computer Age*. London: BBC Books, 1991.
17. "When Machines Screw Up," *Forbes*, June 7, 1993, pp. 110–111.
18. Edmondson, Gail. "Silicon Valley on the Rhine," *Business Week*, Nov. 3, 1997, pp. 162–166.
19. Zuckerman, Laurence. "Many Reported Unready to Face Year 2000 Bug," *New York Times*, Sept. 25, 1997, p. C3.
20. Wald, Matthew L. "F.A.A. Tackles Old Air Traffic Computers," *New York Times*, Jan. 13, 1998, p. A12.
21. The Standish Group. *Chaos*, 1995 report available at www.standishgroup.com/chaos.html in June 1997.
22. Pear, Robert. "Modernization for Medicare Grinds to Halt," *New York Times*, Sept. 16, 1997, p. A1+
23. Hoffman, Thomas, and Robert L. Scheier. "Supply Chain Leaders Push for Compliance," *Computerworld*, Mar. 3, 1997, pp. 1, 16–17.
24. Ellul, Jacques. "The Technological Order," *Technology and Culture*, Fall 1962, p. 394. Quoted in Dizard, Wilson P., Jr., *The Coming Information Age*. New York: Longman, 1982.
25. de Sola Pool, Ithiel. Ed., "Bell's Electrical Toy: What's the Use." in *The Social Impact of the Telephone*, Cambridge, MA: MIT Press, 1977, pp. 19-22.
26. Ofiesh, Gabriel. "The Seamless Carpet of Knowledge and Learning," pp. 299-319 in Lambert, Steve and Suzanne Ropiequet, *CD ROM: The New Papyrus*. Redmond, WA: Microsoft Press, 1986.
27. Brand, Stewart. *The Media Lab*. New York: Viking Penguin, 1987, p. 256.
28. Smith, Douglas K., and Robert C. Alexander. *Fumbling the Future: How Xerox Invented, then Ignored the First Personal Computer.* New York: William Morrow and Company, Inc., 1988, pp. 35-36.
29. Hammer, Michael, and James Champy. *Reengineering the Corporation: A Manifesto for Business Revolution*. New York: Harpers Business, 1993, p. 85.
30. Johnstone, Bob. "Case Study: Inventing the Laser Printer." *Wired*, October 1994, p. 99.
31. Simon, H. A., and Allen Newell. "Heuristic Problem Solving: The Next Advance in Operations Research." *Operations Research*, Jan.–Feb. 1958, pp. 7-8. Cited in Crevier, Daniel. *AI: The Tumultuous History of the Search for Artificial Intelligence*. New York: Basic Books, 1993, p. 108.
32. Armstrong, J. Scott. *Long Range Forecasting*. New York: John Wiley & Sons, 1985.

33. Keegan, Paul. "The Office that Ozzie Built." *The New York Times Magazine,* Oct. 22, 1995, pp. 49-51.
34. Gartner Group. "Replace PCs with Network Computers? 'Over My Dead Body,' You Say?" *New York Times,* Aug. 27, 1997, p. C5.

Chapter 2

1. Harrington, H. J. *Business Process Improvement.* New York: McGraw-Hill, 1991.
2. Davenport, Thomas H. *Process Improvement: Reengineering Work Through Information Technology.* Boston, Mass.: Harvard Business School Press, 1993.
3. Slater, Robert. *The New GE: How Jack Welch Revived an American Institution.* Homewood, Ill: Irwin, 1993, p. 216.
4. Porter, Michael E., and Victor E. Millar. "How Information Gives You Competitive Advantage," *Harvard Business Review,* Jul.–Aug. 1985, pp. 149–160.
5. Byrne, John A. "The Horizontal Corporation," *Business Week,* Dec. 20, 1993, pp. 76–81.
6. Davenport, Thomas H., and Nitin Nohria. "Case Management and the Integration of Labor," *Sloan Management Review,* Winter 1994, pp. 11–24.
7. Salzman, Harold. "Skill-Based Design: Productivity, Learning, and Organizational Effectiveness," in *Usability: Turning Technologies into Tools,* eds. Paul S. Adler and Terry A. Winograd, New York: Oxford University Press, 1992, pp. 66–95.
8. Quinn, James Brian. *Intelligent Enterprise: A Knowledge and Service Based Paradigm for Industry.* New York: Free Press, 1992, p. 329.
9. Broadbent, Marianne, and Peter Weill. "Management by Maxim: How Business and IT Managers Can Create IT Infrastructures," *Sloan Management Review,* Spring 1997, pp. 77–92.
10. Neumann, Peter G. *Computer-Related Risks,* Reading, Mass.: Addison-Wesley Publishing Company, 1995, pp. 68–69.
11. National Research Council. *Computers at Risk: Safe Computing in the Information Age.* Washington, DC: National Academy Press, 1991.
12. Brown, John Seeley. "Reinventing the Corporation." *Harvard Business Review,* Jan.–Feb. 1991, p. 108.
13. Pfeffer, Jeffrey. *Competitive Advantage through People: Unleashing the Power of the Work Force.* Boston, Mass.: Harvard Business School Press, 1994, p. 177.
14. Darnton, Geoffrey, and Sergio Giacoletto. *Information in the Enterprise.* Digital Press, 1992, p. i.

Chapter 3

1. Harris, Catherine L. "Office Automation: Making It Pay Off," *Business Week,* Oct. 12, 1987, pp. 134–146.
2. Hammer, Michael. "Reengineering Work: Don't Automate, Obliterate," *Harvard Business Review,* Jul.–Aug. 1990, pp. 104–112.
3. Davenport, Thomas H., and James E. Short. "The New Industrial Engineering: Information Technology and Business Process Redesign," *Sloan Management Review,* Summer 1990, pp. 11–27.
4. Carroll, Paul B. "The Continuing Crisis at IBM," *Wall Street Journal,* Oct. 28, 1993, p. A18.
5. Davenport, Thomas H., and Nitin Nohria. "Case Management and the Integration of Labor," *Sloan Management Review,* Winter 1994, pp. 11–24.
6. Avishai, Bernard, and William Taylor. "Customers Drive a Technology-Driven Company: An Interview with George Fisher," *Harvard Business Review,* Nov.–Dec., 1989, pp. 107–114.
7. *The Economist.* "The Ubiquitous Machine," pp. 5–20 in an Information Technology insert, June 16, 1990.
8. Malone, T. W., and K. Crowston. "The Interdisciplinary Study of Coordination," *ACM Computing Surveys,* 1994.
9. Perrow, Charles. *Normal Accidents: Living with High-Risk Technologies.* New York: Basic Books, 1984.
10. Yang, Catherine, and Howard Gleck. "How to File: Even Accountants Don't Know for Sure," *Business Week,* Mar. 7, 1988, p. 88.
11. Hitt, Greg. "Favored Companies Get 11th-Hour Tax Breaks," *Wall Street Journal,* July 30, 1997, p. A2.
12. Herman, Tom. "A Special Summary and Forecast of Federal and State Tax Developments," *Wall Street Journal,* July 30, 1997, p. A1.
13. Tully, Shawn. "A Boom Ahead in Company Profits," *Fortune,* Apr. 6, 1992, pp. 76–84.
14. Hammer, Michael, and James Champy. *Reengineering the Corporation: A Manifesto for Business Revolution,* New York: Harper Business, 1993, p. 55
15. Carley, William M. "Jet Near-Crash Shows 747s May Be at Risk of Autopilot Failure," *Wall Street Journal,* Apr. 26, 1993, p. A1.
16. Forester, Tony, and Perry Morrison. *Computer Ethics: Cautionary Tales and Ethical Dilemmas in Computing,* Cambridge, Mass.: MIT Press, 1994, p. 108.
17. Neumann, Peter G. *Computer-Related Risks,* Reading, Mass.: Addison-Wesley, 1995, pp. 68–69.
18. Ross, Philip E. "The Day the Software Crashed," *Forbes,* Apr. 25, 1994, pp. 142–156.
19. Wald, Matthew L. "Appalled by Risk, Except in the Car," *The New York Times,* June 15, 1997, p. E4.
20. Hamblen, Matt. "Nasdaq Trades Up Network Capacity," *Computerworld,* Nov. 24, 1997, p. 3.
21. Womack, James P., and Daniel T. Jones. *Lean Thinking: Banish Waste and Create Wealth in Your Corporation,* New York: Simon & Schuster, 1996, pp. 15 and 314.
22. Roach, Stephen S. "Services Under Siege—The Restructuring Imperative," *Harvard Business Review,* Sept.–Oct., 1991, pp. 82–90.
23. Brynjolfsson, Erik. "The Productivity Paradox of Information Technology," *Communications of the ACM,* Dec. 1993, pp. 67–77.
24. Bulkeley, William M. "The Data Trap: How PC Users Waste Time," *Wall Street Journal,* Jan. 4, 1993, p. B2.
25. Heygate, Richard. "Technophobes, Don't Run Away Yet," *Wall Street Journal,* Aug. 15, 1994, p. A8.
26. Blackburn, Joseph D. "New Product Development: The New Time Wars," in ed. Joseph D. Blackburn, *Time-Based Competition: The Next Battleground in American Manufacturing,* Homewood, Ill.: Business One Irwin, 1991, pp. 121–165.
27. Hammer, op. cit.
28. Peers, Alexandra. "'Paperless' Wall Street Is Due Next June," *Wall Street Journal,* June 7, 1994, p. C1.
29. Chase, Richard B., and David A. Garvin. "The Service Factory," *Harvard Business Review,* Jul.–Aug. 1989, pp. 61–69.
30. Brody, Herbert. "Reforming the Pentagon: An Inside Job," *Technology Review,* Apr. 1994, pp. 31–36.

31. Weiner, Tim. "No One Loses C.I.A. Job in Case of Double Agent," *The New York Times*, Sept 29, 1994, p. A1.
32. Mintzberg, Henry. *The Nature of Managerial Work.* New York: Harper & Row, 1973.
33. Peters, T. J., and R. H. Waterman. Jr. *In Search of Excellence.* New York: Harper & Row, 1982.
34. Smart, Tim. "A Day of Reckoning for Bean Counters," *Business Week,* Mar. 14, 1994, pp. 75–76.
35. Keen, P.G.W. "Information Technology and the Management Difference: A Fusion Map," *IBM Systems Journal,* Vol. 32, No. 1, 1993, pp. 17–39.
36. Bulkeley, William M. "Replaced by Technology: Job Interviews," *Wall Street Journal,* Aug. 22, 1994, p. B1.

Chapter 4

1. Petroski, Henry. *Invention by Design: How Engineers Get from Thought to Thing.* Cambridge, Mass.: Harvard University Press, 1996.
2. Belden, Tom. "CATIA: The Computer Heart and Soul of Aircraft Design," *The Seattle Times,* Feb. 11, 1997.
3. Hirsch, James S. "Renting Cars Abroad Can Drive You Nuts," *Wall Street Journal,* Dec. 10, 1993, p. B1.
4. Chen, P. P. "The Entity-Relationship Model—Toward a Unified View of Data," *ACM Transactions on Database Systems,* Vol. 1, No. 1, March 1976.
5. Leonard, Dorothy, and Jeffrey F. Rayport. "Spark Innovation through Empathic Design," *Harvard Business Review,* Nov.–Dec. 1997, pp. 102–113.
6. Feld, Charles S. "Directed Decentralization: The Frito-Lay Story," *Financial Executive,* Nov./Dec. 1990, pp. 22–24.
7. Nadile, Lisa. "Databases in Step," *InformationWeek,* Dec. 9, 1996, p. 74.
8. Greising, David. "Washington's Hot Potato," *Business Week,* Dec. 16, 1996, pp. 30–33.
9. LeFauve, Richard G., and Arnoldo Hax. "Saturn—The Making of the Modern Corporation," in *Globalization, Technology, and Competition,* ed. Stephen P. Bradley, Jerry A. Hausman, and Richard L. Nolan, Boston: Harvard Business School Press, 1993, pp. 257–281.
10. Smith, Lee. "New Ideas from the Army," *Fortune,* Sept.19, 1994, pp. 203–212.
11. Geyelin, Milo. "Reynolds Sought Specifically to Lure Young Smokers Years Ago, Data Suggest," *Wall Street Journal,* Jan. 15, 1998, p. A4.
12. Kuntz, Phil, and Eva M. Rodriguez. "New Videotape Shows Clinton Thanking Donors for Contributions at Fund-Raiser," *Wall Street Journal,* Oct. 16, 1997, p. A4.
13. Hudson, Richard L. "Frankness of European Doctors Differs From One Country to Next, Survey Shows," *Wall Street Journal,* Feb. 18, 1993, p. B7D.
14. Fialka, John J. "Supersecret Complex Outside Capital Is a $310 Million Surprise to Congress," *Wall Street Journal,* Aug. 9, 1994, p. B2.
15. "The Vietnam Undead," *New Yorker,* Nov. 30, 1992, p. 41.

Chapter 5

1. Caldwell, Bruce. "Trading Size 12 for a Custom Fit," *Information Week,* Oct. 28, 1996.
2. Pounds, William. "The Process of Problem Finding," *Industrial Management Review,* 11(1), 1969, pp. 1–20.
3. Simon, Herbert. *The New Science of Management Decision,* New York: Harper & Row, 1960.
4. Tversky, Amos, and Daniel Kahneman. "The Framing of Decisions and the Psychology of Choice," *Science,* 211, Jan. 30, 1981, pp. 453–458.
5. Slovic, Paul, Baruch Fischhoff, and Sarah Lichtenstein. "Risky Assumptions," *Psychology Today,* June 1990, pp. 44–48.
6. Rubin, John. "The Dangers of Overconfidence," *Technology Review,* July 1989, pp. 11–12.
7. Janis, Irving L. *Groupthink: Psychological Studies of Policy Decisions and Fiascoes,* Boston: Houghton Mifflin, 1983.
8. Frank, Stephen E. "Eager Banks Say Walk Right In," *Wall Street Journal,* Oct. 22, 1997, p. B12.
9. Goldstein, David K. "IBM Europe Headquarters," in *Corporate Information Systems Management: Text and Cases,* 2nd ed., ed. James J. Cash, F. Warren McFarlan, James L. McKenney, and Michael R. Vitale, Homewood, Ill.: Irwin, 1988, pp. 515–534.
10. Perry, Nancy J. "Computers Come of Age in Class," *Fortune,* 121(2), Spring, 1990, pp. 72–78.
11. Johansen, Robert. *Groupware: Computer Support for Teams,* New York: Free Press, 1988.
12. Anthes, Gary H. "Learning How to Share," *Computerworld,* Feb. 23, 1998, pp. 76–79.
13. Jurvis, Jeff. "Serving Up Knowledge," *Information Week,* Nov. 17, 1997, pp. 141–157.
14. Davenport, Thomas H., and Lawrence Prusak. *Working Knowledge: How Organizations Manage What They Know,* Boston: Harvard Business School Press, 1998, p. 21.
15. Mason, Richard. "Information Systems Technology and Corporate Strategy: A Historical Overview," in *The Information Systems Research Challenge: Proceedings,* ed. F. Warren McFarlan, Boston: Harvard Business School Press, 1984, pp. 261–278.
16. Houdeshel, George, and Hugh J. Watson. "The Management Information and Decision Support (MIDS) System at Lockheed-Georgia," *MIS Quarterly,* 11(1), Mar. 1987, pp. 127–140.
17. Verity, John W. "Coaxing the Meaning Out of Data," *Business Week,* Feb. 3, 1997, pp. 134–137.
18. Stedman, Chris. "Data Mining Despite the Dangers," *Computerworld,* Dec. 29 1997/ Jan. 5, 1998, pp. 61–62.
19. Dennis, Alan R., Joey F. George, Len M. Jessup, Jay F. Nunamaker, Jr., and Douglas R. Vogel. "Information Technology to Support Meetings," *MIS Quarterly,* Dec. 1988, pp. 591–624.
20. Nunamaker, Jay, Doug Vogel, Alan Heminger, Ben Martz, Ron Brohowski, and Chris McGoff. "Experiences at IBM with Group Support Systems: A Field Study," *Decision Support Systems,* 5(2), June 1989, pp. 183–196.
21. Williamson, Miryam. "From SAP to Nuts," *Computerworld,* Nov. 10, 1997.
22. Bjerklie, David. "E-mail: The Boss Is Watching." *Technology Review.* Apr. 1993, p. 14.

Chapter 6

1. Ives, Blake, and Michael R. Vitale. "After the Sale: Leveraging Maintenance with Information Technology," *MIS Quarterly,* Mar. 1988, pp. 7–21.

2. Venkatraman, N. "IT-Enabled Business Transformation: From Automation to Business Scope Redefinition," *Sloan Management Review*, Winter, 1994, pp. 73–87.
3. Wald, Matthew L. "Reference Disks Speak Volumes, *New York Times*, Feb. 26, 1998, p. D12.
4. Lazarus, David. "Charting the Course: Global Business Sets Its Goals," Fortune, Aug. 4, 1997, p. A-41.
5. Champy, James. *Reengineering Management: The Mandate for New Leadership*, New York: HarperBusiness, 1995, p. 133.
6. Mehta, Stephanie N. "AT&T Is Seeking Cause of Big Outage in Data Network Used by Corporations," *Wall Street Journal*, Apr. 15, 1998, p. B8.
7. Sims, Calvin. "Disruption of Phone Service Laid to Computer Program," *New York Times*, Jan. 17, 1990, p. A1.
8. Pearl, Daniel. "A Power Outage Snarls Air Traffic In Chicago Region," *Wall Street Journal*, Sept. 15, 1994, p. A4.
9. Morris, Charles R., and Charles H. Ferguson. "How Architecture Wins Technology Wars," *Harvard Business Review*, Mar.–Apr. 1993, pp. 86–97.
10. Andrews, Edmund L. "Euro Transformation Will Touch Every Ledger and Purse," *New York Times*, Jan 5, 1998, p. C11.
11. Porter, Michael. *Competitive Advantage: Creating and Sustaining Superior Performance*, London: Free Press, 1985.
12. Freudenheim, Milt. "Oxford Health Drops 62% as Quarterly Loss Is Seen," *New York Times*, Oct. 28, 1997, p. C9.
13. Sparks, Debra. "Will Your Bank Live to See the Millennium?" *Business Week*, Jan. 26, 1998, p. 74.
14. Hamblen, Matt. "Y2K Shortcoming May Shutter Some Banks," *Computerworld*, Feb. 16, 1998, p. 1.
15. Clemons, Eric K., and Michael Row. "A Strategic Information System: McKesson Drug Company's Economost," *Planning Review*, Sept.–Oct. 1988, pp. 14–19.
16. Johnston, H. Russell, and Michael P. Vitale. "Creating Competitive Advantage with Interorganizational Information Systems," *MIS Quarterly*, June 1988, pp. 153–165.
17. Porter, Michael E., and Victor E. Millar. "How Information Gives You Competitive Advantage," *Harvard Business Review*, Jul.–Aug. 1985, pp. 149–160.
18. Ives, Blake, and Gerard P. Learmonth. "The Information System as a Competitive Weapon," *Communications of the ACM*, 27(12), Dec. 1984, pp. 1193–1201.
19. Brownstein, Vivian. "Business Exuberance Fades as the Economy Slows," *Fortune*, May 22, 1989, p. 22.
20. Driscoll, Lisa. "Think of It as Insurance for Insurers," *Business Week*, Jan. 8, 1990, p. 44E.
21. Diebold, John. *The Innovators*, New York: E.P. Dutton, 1990.
22. Wiseman, Charles. "Attack & Counterattack: The New Game in Information Technology," *Planning Review*, 16(15), Sept.–Oct. 1988, p. 6.
23. Froomkin, A. Michael. "The Essential Role of Trusted Third Parties in Electronic Commerce," in *Readings in Electronic Commerce*, ed. Ravi Kalakota and Andrew B. Whinston, Reading, Mass.: Addison-Wesley, 1997, pp. 119–176.
24. Violino, Bob. "The Cashless Society," *Information Week*, Oct. 11, 1993, pp. 30–40.
25. Jacob, Rahul. "Why Some Customers Are More Equal Than Others," *Fortune*, Sept. 19, 1994, pp. 215–224.
26. Blattberg, Robert C., and John Deighton. "Interactive Marketing: Exploiting the Age of Addressability," *Sloan Management Review*, Fall 1991, pp. 5-14.
27. Deighton, John, Don Peppers, and Martha Rogers. "Consumer Transaction Databases: Present Status and Prospects," in *The Marketing Information Revolution*, eds. Robert C. Blattberg, Rashi Glazer, and John D. C. Little, Boston, Mass.: Harvard Business School Press, 1994, pp. 58–79.
28. Cespedes, Frank V., and H. Jeff Smith. "Database Marketing: New Rules for Policy and Practice," *Sloan Management Review*, Summer 1993, pp. 7-22.
29. Stern, William. "Trading Celery for Oil Filters," *Forbes*, Jan. 17, 1994, p. 69.
30. Wiseman, Charles. "Attack & Counterattack: The New Game in Information Technology," *Planning Review*, 16(15), Sept.–Oct. 1988, p. 6.
31. Davis, Stanley M. "From 'Future Perfect': Mass Customizing," *Planning Review*, Mar.–Apr. 1989, pp. 16–21.
32. Canedy, Dana. "Wish You Weren't Here," *New York Times*, Nov. 20, 1997, p. C1 +.
33. Lenzner, Robert, and Heuslein, William. "The Age of Digital Capitalism," *Forbes*, Mar. 29, 1993, pp. 62–72.
34. Davis, op. cit., pp. 16–21.
35. Wilson, Linda. "The Big Stores Fight Back," *Information Week*, Apr. 26, 1994, pp. 25–32.
36. Eisenstodt, Gale. "Information Power," *Forbes*, June 21, 1993, pp. 44–45.
37. Rockart, J. F., and M. S. Scott Morton. "Implications of Changes in Information Technology for Corporate Strategy," *Interfaces*, 14(1), Jan.–Feb. 1984, pp. 84–95.
38. Schendler, Brenton R. "How Levi Strauss Did an LBO Right," *Fortune*, May 7, 1990, pp. 105–107.
39. Wilson, Linda. "One Leg at a Time," *Information Week*, Apr. 18, 1994, p. 52.
40. Jacob, op. cit. pp. 215–224.
41. Wriston, Walter. *The Twilight of Sovereignty: How the Information Revolution Is Transforming Our World*, New York: Charles Scribner's Sons, 1992.
42. LaPlante, Alice. "Shared Destinies: CEOs and CIOs," *Forbes ASAP*, Dec. 7, 1992, pp. 32–42.
43. Keen, Peter G. W., and J. Michael Cummings. *Networks in Action*, Belmont, Calif.: Wadsworth, 1994, p. 389.
44. Woolley, Scott. "E-muscle," *Forbes*, Mar. 9, 1998, p. 204.
45. Lavin, Douglas. "Chrysler's Neon Had Third Defect, U. S. Agency Says," *Wall Street Journal*, Apr. 8, 1994, p. A4.
46. Clark, Don. "High-Tech Gurus Develop Cheap Networks of Chips to Control Array of Tasks," *Wall Street Journal*, May 20, 1994.
47. Gutek, Barbara A. *The Dynamics of Service: Reflections on the Changing Nature of Customer/Provider Interactions*, San Francisco: Jossey-Bass, 1995, pp. 7–8.
48. Arnaut, Gordon. "No Frills, Just Service with a Screen," *New York Times*, Jan. 26, 1998, p. C5.
49. Leonard-Barton, Dorothy, and John J. Sviokla. "Putting Expert Systems to Work," *Harvard Business Review*, Mar.–Apr. 1988, pp. 91–98.
50. Postman, Neil. *Technopoly: The Surrender of Culture to Technology*. New York: Alfred A. Knopf, 1992, p. 120.
51. Waters, Richard. "Stock Exchange Head Quits Over Taurus," *Financial Times*, Mar. 12, 1993.
52. Whitney, Glenn. "Giant London Bourse Seeks New Identity and Focus After Costly Project Fails," *Wall Street Journal*, Apr. 22, 1993, p. A11.

53. Haeckel, Stephan H. "Managing the Information-Intensive Firm of 2001," in Blattberg, Glazer, and Little, pp. 328–354.

Chapter 7

1. Pear, Robert. "U.S. Inaugurating a Vast Database of All New Hires," *New York Times*, Sept. 22, 1997, p. A1+.
2. Betts, Michael. "Personal data more public than you think," *Computerworld*, Mar. 9, 1992, p. 1.
3. Associated Press. "Bill Would Tell I.R.S. Workers Not to Snoop," *New York Times*, Apr. 8, 1997, p. A9.
4. Ellul, Jacques. *The Technological Bluff*, Grand Rapids, Mich.: William B. Eerdmans Publishing, 1990, p. 39.
5. Perrow, Charles. *Normal Accidents: Living with High-Risk Technologies*, New York: Basic Books, 1984.
6. Norman, Donald A. *Things That Make Us Smart: Defending Human Attributes in the Age of the Machine*, Reading, Mass.: Addison-Wesley, 1993, pp. 233–236.
7. Turkle, Sherry. *The Second Self: Computers and the Human Spirit*, New York: Simon and Schuster, 1984, p. 271.
8. Sheff, David. *Game Over: How Nintendo Zapped an American Industry, Captured Your Dollars, and Enslaved Your Children*, New York: Random House, 1993, p. 10.
9. Karasek, Robert, and Tores Theorell. *Healthy Work*, New York: Basic Books, 1990.
10. "Healthy Lives: A New View of Stress," *University of California, Berkeley Wellness Letter*, June 1990, pp. 4–5.
11. Winslow, Ron. "Lack of Control Over Job Is Seen as Heart Risk," *Wall Street Journal*, July 25, 1997, p. B1.
12. Varian, Hal R. "The Information Economy: How Much Will Two Bits Be Worth in the Digital Marketplace?" *Scientific American*, Sept. 1995, pp. 200–201.
13. Schlefer, Jonathan. "Office Automation and Bureaucracy," *Technology Review*, July 1983, pp. 32–40.
14. McKay, Colin J. "Work with Visual Display Terminals: Psychosocial Aspects and Health," *Journal of Occupational Medicine*, 31(12), Dec. 1989, pp. 957–966.
15. Brody, Jane E. "Health Watch: Women Under Stress," *New York Times*, June 11, 1997, p. B10.
16. Office of Technology Assessment. *The Electronic Supervisor: New Technology, New Tensions*, Washington, DC: U.S. Congress, Office of Technology Assessment, 1987.
17. Hutheesing, Nikhil. "What Are You Doing on That Porn Site?" *Forbes*, Nov. 3, 1997, pp. 368–369.
18. Matthews, Anna Wilde. "New Gadgets Trace Truckers' Every Move," *Wall Street Journal*, July 14, 1997, p. B1.
19. Alter, Steven L. "Equitable Life: A Computer-Assisted Underwriting System," *Decision Support Systems*, Reading, Mass.: Addison-Wesley, 1980.
20. Stockton, William. "New Airliners Make Experts Ask: How Advanced Is Too Advanced?" *New York Times*, Dec. 12, 1988.
21. Dreyfus, Joel. "The Three R's on the Shop Floor," *Fortune*, 121(2), Spring 1990, pp. 86–89.
22. Zuboff, Shoshana. *In the Age of the Smart Machine: The Future of Work and Power*, New York: Basic Books, 1988, p. 135.
23. Zuboff, Shoshana. "New Worlds of Computer-Mediated Work," *Harvard Business Review*, Sept.–Oct. 1982, pp. 142–152.
24. Zuboff, Shoshana. *In the Age of the Smart Machine*.
25. Zuboff, Shoshana. "Problems of Symbolic Toil," *Dissent*, Winter 1982, pp. 51–61.
26. Bloomberg News, "Manufacturers See Lack of Basic Skills," *New York Times*, Nov. 16, 1997, p. 10.
27. Garson, Barbara. *The Electronic Sweatshop*, New York: Penguin Books, 1989.
28. Ives, Blake, and Margrethe H. Olson. "User Involvement and MIS Success: A Review of Research," *Management Science*, 30(5), May 1984, pp. 586–603.
29. Sviokla, John J. " Knowledge Workers and Radically New Technology," *Sloan Management Review*, Summer 1996, pp. 25–40.
30. Keen, Peter G. W. "Information Systems and Organizational Change," *Communications of the ACM*, 24(1), Jan. 1981, pp. 24–33.
31. Markus, M. Lynne. "Power, Politics, and MIS Implementation," *Communications of the ACM*, 26(6), June 1983, pp. 430–444.
32. Mason, Richard. "Four Ethical Issues of the Information Age," *MIS Quarterly*, 10(1), Jan. 1986.
33. Chase, Marilyn. "If the Screenplay Doesn't Shake You, the Sound Might," *Wall Street Journal*, July 21, 1997, p. B1.
34. Carnevale, Mary Lu. "Telemarketers Fight Banning of Autodialers," *Wall Street Journal*, Jan. 20, 1993, p. B1.
35. *New York Times*. "Court Blocks Caller ID," Mar. 23, 1992, p. C8.
36. Duff, Christina. "Pick Up on This: Just Don't Answer, Let Freedom Ring," *Wall Street Journal*, Jan. 14, 1998, p.A1.
37. Warren, Samuel D., and Louis D. Brandeis. "The Right to Privacy," *Harvard Law Review*, Vol. 4, Dec. 15, 1890.
38. Ito, Youichi, and Takaaki Hattori. "Mass Media Ethics in Japan," in *Communications Ethics and Global Change*, ed. Thomas W. Cooper, White Plains, NY: Longman, 1989, pp. 168–180.
39. Asenjo, Porfirio Barroso. "Spanish Media Ethics," in *Communications Ethics and Global Change*, pp. 69–84.
40. Broder, John M. "F.T.C. Opens Hearings on Computers' Threat to Americans' Right to Privacy," *New York Times*, June 11, 1997, p. A20.
41. Bernstein, Nina. "OnLine, High-Tech Sleuths Find Private Facts," *New York Times*, Sept. 15, 1997, p. A1.
42. Calandra, Thom. "'Privacy for Sale': Tales of Data Rape," *San Francisco Chronicle*, Sept. 12, 1992, p. E1.
43. Betts, Mitch. "Driver Privacy on the Way?" *Computerworld*, Feb. 28, 1994, p. 29.
44. Sandberg, Jared. "Ply and Pry: How Business Pumps Kids on the Web," *Wall Street Journal*, June 9, 1997, p. B1.
45. Hilts, Philip J. "Cigarette Makers Dispute Reports on Addictiveness," *New York Times*, Apr. 15, 1994, p. A1.
46. McGinley, Laurie. "New Labeling Doesn't Tell All About Nutrition," *Wall Street Journal*, May 6, 1994, p. B1.
47. Hilts, Philip J. "Big Flaw Cited In Federal Test On Cigarettes," *New York Times*, May 2, 1994, p. A1.
48. Knecht, G. Bruce. "Reports of Mrs. Rissmiller's Death Have Been Greatly Exaggerated," *Wall Street Journal*, Apr. 20, 1994, p. B1.
49. McMenamin, Brigid. "Invasion of the Credit Snatchers," *Forbes*, Aug. 26, 1996, p. 256.
50. Kranhold, Kathryn. "Identity Theft Bill Leaves Credit Bureaus in the Cold," *Wall Street Journal*, June 4, 1997, p. CA1.
51. Thurow, Lester C. "Needed: A New System of Intellectual Property Rights," *Harvard Business Review*, Sept.–Oct. 1997, pp. 95–103.

52. Lenzner, Robert, and Carrie Shook. "Whose Rolodex Is It, Anyway?" *Forbes*, Feb. 23, 1998, pp. 100–103.
53. Quick, Rebecca, "Framing Muddies Issue of Content Ownership," *Wall Street Journal*, Jan. 30, 1997, p. B6.
54. "Times of London in Web Dispute," *Computerworld*, Dec. 15, 1997, p. 8.
55. Betts, Mitch. "Ruling Opens Door to Software Patents," *Computerworld*, Sept. 5, 1994, p. 73.
56. DiDio, Laura, and Julia King. "Ready and Enabled," *Computerworld*, Feb. 16, 1998, pp. 69–73.
57. Coxeter, Ruth. "A Computerized Overseer for the Truck Drivin' Man," *Business Week*, Sept. 19, 1994, p. 90.
58. Betts, Mitch. "Computerized Records: An Open Book?" *Computerworld*, Aug. 9, 1993, p. 1.
59. Cespedes, Frank V., and H. Jeff Smith. "Database Marketing: New Rules for Policy and Practice," *Sloan Management Review*, Summer 1993, pp. 7–22.
60. Branscomb, Anne Wells. *Who Owns Information: From Privacy to Public Access*, New York: Basic Books, 1994.

Chapter 8

1. Lai, Jennifer, and John Vargo. "MedSpeak: Report Creation with Continuous Speech Recognition," Electronic Proceedings of CHI 97, ACM, 1997.
2. Ross, Philip E. "Hal Is Almost Here," *Forbes*, July 7, 1997, p. 256.
3. Yourdon, Edward. *Decline & Fall of the American Programmer*, Englewood Cliffs, N.J.: Yourdon Press, 1993, p. 267.
4. Nee, Eric. "Compaq Computer Corp.," *Forbes*, Jan. 12, 1998, pp. 90–94.
5. Hurwicz, Mike. "Centralized Management for Desktops," *Byte*, Jan. 1998, p. 63.
6. Sager, Ira. "A Bare-Bones Box for Business," *Business Week*, May 26, 1997, p. 136.
7. Lohr, Steve. "The Network Computer as the PC's Evil Twin," *New York Times*, Nov. 4, 1996.
8. Hayes, Mary, Tom Davey, and Bob Francis. "Intel's NC Push," *Informationweek*, Nov. 17, 1997, pp. 18–20.
9. Pollack, Andrew. "Japan Chip Maker Unveils Next-Generation Prototype," *New York Times*, Feb. 7, 1997, p. C5.
10. Port, Otis. "The Silicon Age? It's Just Dawning," *Business Week*, Dec. 9,1996, pp. 148–152.
11. Hill, G. Christian. "Bringing It Home," *Wall Street Journal*, June 16, 1997, p. R4.
12. Takahashi, Dean. "Intel's Top Chip Architect to Unveil His Latest Creation," *Wall Street Journal*, Oct. 10, 1997, p. B1.
13. Grove, Andrew. "A Revolution in Progress," Keynote speech at Comdex, Nov. 18, 1996, http: www.intel.com/pressroom/archive/speeches/ag111896.htm.
14. Pitta, Julia. "Victim of Success," *Forbes*, Dec. 10, 1990, p. 278–280.
15. Richtel, Matt. "A Single PC Chip That Almost Does It All," *New York Times*, Apr. 7, 1998, p. C2.
16. Halfhill, Tom R. "Beyond Pentium II," *Byte*, Dec. 1997, pp. 80–86.
17. Rose, Frederick. "Rockwell Is Set to Unveil Chip Created for Java," *Wall Street Journal*, Sept. 22, 1997, p. B6.
18. Gomes, Lee. "Qwerty Spells a Saga of Market Economics," *Wall Street Journal*, Feb. 25, 1998, p. B1.
19. Straub, Detmar. "The Effect of Culture on IT Diffusion: E-Mail and FAX in Japan and the U.S." *Information System Research*, 5(1), Mar. 1994, pp. 23–47.
20. Bulkeley, William M. "Computer Use by Illiterates Grows at Work." *Wall Street Journal*, June 9, 1992, p B1.
21. Thyfault, Mary. "Voice Recognition Goes Mainstream," *Information Week*, Jan. 5, 1998, pp. 90–91.
22. Carey, John. "Thinking Flat in Washington." *Business Week*, May 9, 1994, p. 36.

Chapter 9

1. Gulko, Boris. "Is Chess Finished?" *Commentary*, July 1997, pp. 45–47.
2. Byrne, Robert. "How One Champion Is Chewed Up Into Small Bits by Another," *New York Times*, May 12, 1997, p. A14.
3. Clark, Don. "'Bug Hunting' Emerges as Hot Campus Sport," *Wall Street Journal*, Mar. 14, 1997, p. B1.
4. Gleick, James. "Little Bug, Big Bang," *New York Times Sunday Magazine*, Dec. 1, 1996, pp. 38–40.
5. Rada, Roy. "Corporate Shortcut to Standardization," *Communications of the ACM*, Jan. 1998, 41(1), pp. 11–14.
6. IBM. "Is There More to Java Than Coffee Jokes?" *Forbes*, Jan. 26, 1998, pp. 74–75.
7. Hof, Robert D. "Java Can Be a Contender—If Sun Lets It," *Business Week*, Apr. 6, 1998, p. 42.
8. Shapiro, Ehud, and David D. H. Warren. "The Fifth Generation Project: Personal Perspectives," *Communications of the ACM*, March 1993, pp. 46–101.
9. Freeman, David. How to Make Spreadsheets Error-Proof, *Journal of Accountancy*, 181(5), May 1996, pp. 75–77
10. Savitz, E. J., "Magellan Loses Its Compass," *Barron's* (84:50) December 12, 1994.
11. Zachary, G. Pascal. "Agony and Ecstasy of 200 Code Writers Beget Windows NT," *Wall Street Journal*, May 26, 1993, p. A1.
12. Lohr, Steve, with John Markoff. "Why Microsoft Is Taking a Hard Line With the Government," *New York Times*, Jan. 12, 1998, p. C1.
13. Davis, Randall. "Amplifying Expertise with Expert Systems," in *The AI Business: Commercial Uses of Artificial Intelligence*, ed. Patrick H. Winston and Karen A. Prendergast, Cambridge, Mass.: MIT Press, 1984, pp. 17–39.
14. Sharda, Ramesh. "Neural Networks for the MS/OR Analyst: An Application Bibliography," *Interfaces*, Mar.–Apr. 1994, pp. 116–130.
15. Alexander, Michael. "Neural Network Bests Doctors at Diagnoses," *Computerworld*, Dec. 16, 1991, p. 22.
16. Stipp, David. "Computer Researchers Find 'Neural Networks' Help Mimic the Brain," *Wall Street Journal*, Sept. 9, 1988, p. 1.
17. Loofbourrow, T. H. "Expert Systems and Neural Networks: The Hatfields and the McCoys?" *Expert Systems*, Fall 1990.
18. McNeill, Daniel, and Paul Freiberger. *Fuzzy Logic: The Revolutionary Computer Technology That Is Changing the World*, New York: Touchstone, 1993.
19. Munakata, Toshinori, and Jani Yashvant. "Fuzzy Systems: An Overview," *Communications of the ACM*, Mar. 1994, pp. 69–76.
20. Allen, Bradley P. "Case-Based Reasoning: Business Applications," *Communications of the ACM*, Mar. 1994, pp. 40–42.
21. Minsky, Marvin. *The Society of Mind*, New York: Simon & Schuster, 1986.

22. Ross, Philip E. "The Day the Software Crashed," *Forbes*, Apr. 25, 1994, pp. 142–156.
23. Bylinsky, Gene. "Computers That Learn by Doing," *Fortune*, Sept. 6, 1993, pp. 96–102.

Chapter 10

1. Shapiro, Eileen C. *Fad Surfing in the Boardroom: Reclaiming the Courage to Manage in the Age of Instant Answers*, Reading, Mass.: Addison-Wesley, 1995, pp. 101–102.
2. Janah, Monua, and Clinton Wilder. "Networking—Special Delivery—Think FedEx Is Only About Shipping Packages? Think Again," *Information Week*, Oct. 27, 1997.
3. Schiesel, Seth. "Venture Promises Far Faster Speeds for Internet Data," *New York Times*, Jan. 20, 1998, p. A1.
4. Lemos, Robert. "Fast Phone Lines Can't Dodge Cable," *Yahoo News*, ZDNET, Jan. 21, 1998.
5. Stallings, William, and Richard van Slyke, *Business Data Communications*, 3rd ed., Upper Saddle River, N.J.: Prentice Hall, 1998, p. 85.
6. Banks, Howard. "The Law of the Photon," *Forbes*, Oct. 6, 1997, pp. 66–73.
7. Ziegler, Bart. "Building the Highway: New Obstacles, New Solutions," *Wall Street Journal*, p. B1.
8. Banks., op. cit.
9. Owens, Cynthia. "The Developing Leap," *Wall Street Journal*, Feb. 11, 1994, p. R15.
10. Lucchetti, Aaron. "New Gadget Loses Hope in Chicago," *Wall Street Journal*, Mar. 27, 1998, p. C1.
11. Hutheesing, Nikhil, and Jeffrey Young. "Curse of the Market Leader," *Forbes*, July 29, 1996, pp. 78–82.
12. Violino, Bob. "Challenges Galore," *Information Week*, Jan. 6, 1997, p. 70.
13. Davis, Beth, with Gregory Dalton. "VPNs Set to Take Off," *Information Week*, Jan. 5, 1998, pp. 85–86.
14. "Wireless Repairmen," Mobile Computing Briefs, *Computerworld*, Feb. 23, 1998, p. 65.
15. Girard, Kim. "Wireless Revolution Fizzles," *Computerworld*, Feb. 23, 1998, p. 6.
16. Sliwa, Carol. "Net Used to Extend EDI's Reach," *Computerworld*, Feb. 23, 1998, p. 1.
17. Pitta, Julia. "Format Wars," *Fortune*, July 7, 1997, p. 263.
18. Steinberg, Steve G. "Schumpeter's Lesson: What Really Happened in Digital Technology in the Last Five Years," *Wired*, Jan. 1998, pp. 80–84.
19. Schiesel, Seth. "A U.S. Judge Strikes Down Parts of the '96 Telecommunications Act," *New York Times*, Jan. 1, 1998, p. 1.
20. Huber, Peter. "The Lessons of AT&T's Cellular Move," *Wall Street Journal*, Sept. 7, 1993, p. A14.
21. Naik, Gautam. "Hurdle Cleared in Rochester, N.Y., Plan for Wide Cable-TV Phone Competition," *Wall Street Journal*, May 18, 1994, p. B5.
22. Pollack, Andrew. "Japan Considers Creating an Optical Fiber Network," *New York Times*, June 2, 1994, p. C1.
23. Pearl, Daniel. "Debate Over Universal Access Rights Will Shape Rules Governing the Future of Communications," *Wall Street Journal*, Jan. 14, 1994, p. B1.
24. Branscomb, Anne Wells. *Who Owns Information: From Privacy to Public Access*, New York: Basic Books, 1994, p. 176.
25. Betts, Mitch. "Subscriber Privacy for Sale," *Computerworld*, Oct. 10, 1994, p. 149.
26. Arnst, Catherine. "The Global Free-For-All," *Business Week*, Sept. 26, 1994, pp. 118–126.

Chapter 11

1. Steward, Thomas D. "Owens Corning: Back from the Dead," *Fortune*, May 26, 1997, pp. 118–126.
2. Koch, Christopher. "Flipping the Switch: The Big Bang Theory," *CIO*, June 15, 1996.
3. Hopper, Max D. "Rattling SABRE—New Ways to Compete on Information," *Harvard Business Review*, May–June 1990, pp. 118–125.
4. Parker, Marilyn M. *Strategic Transformation and Information Technology: Paradigms for Performing while Transforming*, Upper Saddle River, N.J.: Prentice Hall, 1996, pp. 72–74.
5. Henderson, John C., N. Venkatraman, and Scott Oldach. "Aligning Business and IT Strategies," in *Competing in the Information Age: Strategic Alignment in Practice*, ed. Jerry N. Luftman, New York: Oxford University Press, 1996, pp. 21–42.
6. Parker, p. 222.
7. Goff, Leslie, and Michael Puttre. "Business Strategies Misaligned with MIS Resources," *MIS Week*, Nov. 6, 1989, p. 38.
8. Rockart, John F. "Chief Executives Define Their Own Data Needs," *Harvard Business Review*, Mar./Apr. 1979, pp. 81–92.
9. Boynton, Andrew C., and Robert W. Zmud. "An Assessment of Critical Success Factors," *Sloan Management Review*, Summer 1984, pp. 17–27.
10. Hammer, Michael, and James Champy. *Reengineering the Corporation: A Manifesto for Business Revolution*, New York: Harper Business, 1993.
11. Hammer and Champy.
12. Stewart, Thomas A. "Reengineering: The Hot New Management Tool," *Fortune*, Aug. 23, 1993, pp. 41–48.
13. Strassmann, Paul A. "Re-engineering: An emetic in a perfume bottle?" *Computerworld*, Aug. 16, 1993, p. 33.
14. Cafasso, Rosemary. "Rethinking Re-engineering," *Computerworld*, Mar. 15, 1993, pp. 102–105.
15. Martin, Michael H. "Smart Managing: Best Practices, Careers, and Ideas," *Fortune*, Feb. 2, 1998, pp. 149–151.
16. Stein, Tom. "ERP Links to Supply Chain," *Information Week*, Jan. 5, 1998, pp. 103–104.
17. Losee, Stephanie. "Burned by Technology," *Fortune*, Sept. 9, 1996, pp. 105–112.
18. Battles, Brett E., and David Mark. "Companies That Just Don't Get IT," Wall Street Journal, Dec. 9, 1996, p. A14.
19. Broadbent, Marianne, and Peter Weill. "Management by Maxim: How Business and IT Managers Can Create IT Infrastructures," *Sloan Management Review*, Spring 1997, pp. 77–92.
20. Broadbent and Weill.
21. Ross, Jeanne. "Johnson & Johnson: Building an Infrastructure to Support Global Operations," MIT Center for Information Systems Research, CISR Working Paper #283, 1995.
22. Lacity, Mary Cecelia, and Rudy Hirschheim. *Information Systems Outsourcing: Myths, Metaphors, and Realities*. Chichester, UK: John Wiley & Sons, 1993.
23. Lacity, Mary C., Leslie P. Willcocks, and David F. Feeny. "IT Outsourcing: Maximize Flexibility and Control," *Harvard Business Review*, May–June 1995, pp. 84–93.

24. Lovelace, Herbert. "1998: Year of Conversions," *Information Week*, Jan. 5, 1998, p. 121.
25. Dalton, Gregory. "Ready to Go Global?" *Information Week*, Feb. 9, 1998, pp. 49–60.
26. Keen, Peter, *Shaping the Future: Business Design through Information Technology.* Boston: Harvard Business School Press, 1991, p. 88.
27. Hecht, Laurence, and Peter Morici. "Managing Risks in Mexico," *Harvard Business Review*, Jul.–Aug., 1993, pp. 32–40.
28. Moffett, Matt. "'Callbacks Cut Telephone Bills Of Users Abroad," *Wall Street Journal*, June 21, 1994, p. B1.
29. Andrews, Edmund L., "Europe's Cheap Phone Calls (Via U.S.) to Get Dearer," *Wall Street Journal*, Jan. 11, 1997, p. 25.
30. Cespedes, Frank V., and H. Jeff Smith. "Database Marketing: New Rules for Policy and Practice," *Sloan Management Review*, Summer 1993, pp. 7–22.
31. Davies, Simon. "Europe to U.S.: No Privacy, No Trade," *Wired*, May 1998, pp. 135+.
32. Feigenbaum, Edward, Pamela McCorduck, and Penny H. Nii. *The Rise of the Expert Company*, New York: Times Books, 1988.
33. Anthes, Gary H. "No More Creeps!" *Computerworld*, May 2, 1994, pp. 107–110.
34. Boehm, Barry W. "Improving Software Productivity," *Computer*, Sept. 1987, pp. 43–57.
35. Brooks, Frederick P., Jr. "The Mythical Man-Month," *Datamation*, Dec. 1974, pp. 44–52.
36. Yourdon, Edward. *Decline & Fall of the American Programmer*, Englewood Cliffs, N.J.: Yourdon Press, 1992, p. 162.
37. Boynton, A. C., B. Victor, and B. J. Pine, II. "New Competitive Strategies: Challenges to Organizations and Information Technology," *IBM Systems Journal*, 32(1), 1993, pp. 40–64.
38. Keen, Peter G. W. *Shaping the Future: Business Design through Information Technology*, Boston, Mass.: Harvard Business School Press, 1991, p. 141.

Chapter 12

1. Cusumano, Michael A., and Richard W. Selby. "How Microsoft Builds Software," *Communications of the ACM*, June 1997, 40(6), pp. 53–61.
2. Cringely, Robert X. "When Disaster Strikes IS," *Forbes ASAP*, Aug. 29, 1994, pp. 58–64.
3. Hersleb, James, et al. "Software Quality and the Capability Maturity Model," *Communications of the ACM*, June 1997, pp. 30–40.
4. Anthes, Gary H. "Capable and Mature?" *Computerworld*, Dec. 15, 1997, p. 76.
5. Yourdon, Ed. "Where's the Basis for Year 2000 Optimism?" *Computerworld*, Feb. 16, 1998, p. 68.
6. Frantz, Douglas. "B of A's Plans for Computer Don't Add Up," in *Computerization and Controversy: Value Conflicts and Social Choice*, 2d ed., ed. Rob Kling, San Diego: Academic Press, 1996, pp. 161–169.
7. Greenstein, Irwin. "Imaging System Snafu Snarls Calif. Banks," *MIS Week*, June 19, 1989, pp. 1+.
8. Fournier, Roger. *Practical Guide to Structured System Development and Maintenance*, Englewood Cliffs, N.J.: Yourdon Press, 1991.
9. Davidson, Elizabeth J. "An Exploratory Study of Joint Application Design (JAD) in Information Systems Delivery," in *Proceedings of the Fourteenth International Conference on Information Systems*, ed. Janice I. Degross, Robert P. Bostrom, and Daniel Robey, Orlando, Fl, 1993, pp. 271–283.
10. Dahlbom, Bo, and Lars Mathiassen. "A Scandinavian View on the ACM's Code of Ethics," *Computers and Society*, 24(2), June 1994, pp. 14–15.

Chapter 13

1. "London Ambulance Dispatch Computer," Forum on Risks to the Public in Computers and Related Systems, *ACM Committee on Computers and Public Policy*, Peter G. Neumann, moderator, 14(2), Nov. 9, 1992.
2. "Report of the Inquiry into the London Ambulance Service, February 1993," Forum on Risks to the Public in Computers and Related Systems, *ACM Committee on Computers and Public Policy*, Peter G. Neumann, moderator, 14(48), Apr. 7, 1993.
3. Oz, Effy. "When Professional Standards are Lax: The CONFIRM Failure and Its Lessons," *Communications of the ACM*, 37(10), Oct. 1994, pp. 29–36.
4. Markus, M. Lynne, and Mark Keil. "If We Build It, They Will Come: Designing Information Systems That People Want to Use," *Sloan Management Review*, Summer 1994, pp. 11–25.
5. Wald, Matthew L. "Colombians Attribute Cali Crash to Pilot Error," *New York Times*, Sept. 26, 1996, p. 12.
6. Perrow, Charles. *Normal Accidents: Living with High-Risk Technologies*, New York: Basic Books, 1984.
7. Gordon, Michael R. "Astronaut Error Adds New Anxiety on Space Station," *New York Times*, July 18, 1997, p. A1.
8. Markoff, John. "Flaw Undermines Accuracy of Pentium Chips," *New York Times*, Nov. 24, 1994, p. C1.
9. Manes, Stephen. "As Snug as a Bug in the System," *New York Times*, Oct. 15, 1996, p. B6.
10. Getler, Warren. "Errant Squirrel Causes Another Nasdaq Outage," *Wall Street Journal*, Aug. 2, 1994, p. C1.
11. Forum on Risks to the Public in Computers and Related Systems, *ACM Committee on Computers and Public Policy*, Peter G. Neumann, moderator, 18(74), Jan. 8, 1997.
12. Gleckman, Howard. "Hey, I Owe 99 Years in Back Taxes," *Business Week*, Feb. 23, 1998, pp. 119–120.
13. McGee, Suzanne. "Bank of Tokyo Blames Loss on Bad Model," *Wall Street Journal*, Mar. 28, 1997, p. A3.
14. "Postal Service Misplaces Patent Office's ZIP Code," *Wall Street Journal*, Aug. 9, 1996, p. A4.
15. Markoff, John. "Network Problem Disrupts Internet," *New York Times*, July 18, 1997, p. A1.
16. Norris, Floyd, "Salomon's Error Went Right to Floor," *New York Times*, Mar. 27, 1993.
17. Wald, Matthew L. "Peru Crash Is Attributed to Maintenance Error," *New York Times*, Nov. 16, 1996, p. 9.
18. Bulkeley, William M. "Databases Are Plagued by Reign of Error," *Wall Street Journal*, May 26, 1992, p. B6.
19. Bradsher, Keith. "How AT&T Accident Snowballed," *New York Times*, Jan. 14, 1991, p. C1.
20. Wald, Matthew L. "Dust at Center for Air Control Disrupts Travel," *New York Times*, Oct. 16, 1997, p. A1.
21. Quick, Rebecca. "Surging Volume of E-Mail Brings Blackouts at AOL," *Wall Street Journal*, Nov. 25, 1997, p. B1.
22. Ross, Philip E. "The Day the Software Crashed," *Forbes*, Apr. 25, 1994, pp. 142–156.
23. Ulrich, William. "Package Vendors Better Unbundle Year 2000 Fixes," *Computerworld*, Jan. 12, 1998, p. 37.

24. Hoffman, Thomas. "Calif. Bill Would Put Cap on Year 2000 Damages," *Computerworld*, Dec. 15, 1997, p. 1.
25. Dow Jones Newswires. "Microsoft Gear Is Stolen from Scottish Plant," *Wall Street Journal*, Nov. 19, 1997, p. B4.
26. "Computer's Theft May Cost Visa More Than $6 Million," *Wall Street Journal*, Nov. 19, 1996, p. B4.
27. Blumenthal, Ralph. "Officers Go Undercover to Battle the Computer Underworld," *New York Times*, Jan. 26, 1993, p. B 14.
28. Booker, Ellis, and Gary H. Anthes. "Toll Fraud Rings in High Cost," *Computerworld*, Oct. 10, 1994, p. 1
29. Starkman, Dean. "Russian Hacker Enters Fraud Plea in Citicorp Case," *Wall Street Journal*, Jan. 26, 1998, p. B9A.
30. Hansell, Saul. "Internet Merchants Try to Fight Fraud in Software Purchases," *New York Times*, Nov. 17, 1997, p. C1.
31. Allen, Brandt. "Embezzler's Guide to the Computer," *Harvard Business Review*, Jul.–Aug. 1975, pp. 79–89.
32. Fenyvesi, Charles. "Washington Whispers: Forging Ahead," *U.S. News & World Report*, Aug. 3, 1992, p. 20.
33. Carley, William M. "Rigging Computers for Fraud or Malice Is Often an Inside Job," *Wall Street Journal*, Aug. 27, 1992, p. A1.
34. Bulkeley, William M. "Voice Mail May Let Competitors Dial 'E' for Espionage," *Wall Street Journal*, Sept. 28, 1993, p. B1.
35. Levy, Clifford. "Founder of Renowned Store Pleads Guilty in Fraud Case," *New York Times*, July 23, 1993, p. A11.
36. Markoff, John. "How a Computer Sleuth Traced a Digital Trail," *New York Times*, Feb. 16, 1995.
37. Ziegler, Bart. "Savvy Hacker Tangles Web for Net Host," *Wall Street Journal*, Sept. 12, 1996, p. B1.
38. DiDio, Laura. "Ex-employee nabbed in $10M hack attack," *Computerworld*, Feb. 23, 1998, p. 6
39. Wildstrom, Stephen H. "Out, Out, Damned Virus," *Business Week*, July 22, 1996, p. 19.
40. National Computer Security Association. "NCSA Computer Virus Prevalence Survey," 1997.
41. Reichlin, Igor. "Many Chernobyls Just Waiting to Happen," *Business Week*, Mar. 16, 1992.
42. "The Gulf War Flu," *U.S. News & World Report*, Jan. 20, 1992, p. 50.
43. Horwitt, Elizabeth. "N.Y. Sites Unfazed by Outage," *Computerworld*, Sept. 23, 1991, p. 1+.
44. Anthes, Gary H. "FCC Blasts AT&T for New York Blowout," *Computerworld*, Nov. 18, 1991, p. 58.
45. Edwards, Tamala M. "Numbers Nightmare: A Pepsi Promotion Misfires in the Philippines," *Time*, Aug. 9, 1993, p. 53.
46. Anthes, Gary H. "GAO Finds Security Lax at U.S. Stock Exchanges," *Computerworld*, Sept. 2, 1991, p. 99.
47. Caldwell, Bruce. "Security Czars Get Locked Out," *Information Week*, June 21, 1993, p. 16.
48. Ball, Leslie D. "Computer Crime," *Technology Review*, Apr. 1982, pp. 21–30.
49. Time-Life Books. *Computer Security*, Alexandria, Va.: Time-Life Books, 1986.
50. Davies, Erin. "Great Tool for the Paranoid," *Fortune*, Feb. 16, 1998, p. 129.
51. Sandberg, Jared. "Hackers Prey on AOL Users with Array of Dirty Tricks," *Wall Street Journal*, Jan. 5, 1998, p. B1.
52. Booker, Ellis. "Retinal Scanners Eye-Identify Inmates," *Computerworld*, Mar. 23, 1992, p. 28.
53. RSA Laboratories. FAQ 3.0 on Cryptography, www.rsa.com/rsalabs/newfaq/q12.htm. 1998.
54. RSA Laboratories. FAQ 3.0 on Cryptography, www.rsa.com/rsalabs/newfaq/q16.htm. 1998.
55. Time-Life Books. *Computer Security.*
56. DiDio, Laura. "Ex-employee nabbed."
57. "A 7-Ton Clerical Fluke: Anchor Arrives Instead of Lamp," *Washington Post*, Apr. 13, 1985.
58. Hoffman, Thomas. "Denial Stalls Disaster Recovery Plans," *Computerworld*, Feb. 23, 1998, p. 10.
59. Anthes, Gary H. "When Disaster Strikes," *Computerworld*, Jan. 19, 1998, pp. 80–83.
60. Hudson, Richard L. "Know Anybody Using Pirated Software? That's Information Worth Some Money," *Wall Street Journal*, Oct. 11, 1994, p. B5.
61. Braudel, William. "Licensing Stymies Users," *Computerworld*, April 18, 1994, p. 12.

Credits

Text

Figure 7.6 Adapted from Sviokla, John J. "Knowledge Workers and Radically New Technology," *Sloan Management Review*, Summer 1996, Vol. 37, No. 4, p. 33. Reprinted by permission.

Photos

About the Author
Courtesy of Steven Alter.

Chapter 1
1.2a © Will and Deni McIntyre/Photo Researchers, Inc. 1.2b © Cindy Charles/Photo Edit. 1.2c © Jeff Mermelstein. 1.4a © Louis Psihoyos/Matrix International, Inc. 1.4b © Louis Psihoyos/Matrix International, Inc. 1.5 © Steve Firebaugh. 1.6a © The Computer Museum. 1.6b Courtesy of Intel. 1.7 © David Young Wolff/Photo Edit. 1.9 © Myrleen Ferguson MR/Photo Edit. 1.10a Courtesy of International Business Machines Corporation. Unauthorized use not permitted. 1.10b © Tom Tracy/The Stock Market. 1.11 Corbis-Bettmann.

Chapter 2
2.1a Romilly Lockyer/The Image Bank. 2.1b Courtesy of Steven Alter.

Chapter 3
3.7 Courtesy of the McKesson Corporation. 3.12 © Alan Becker/The Image Bank. 3.13 © Gamma Liaison.

Chapter 4
4.3b © Tom McCarthy/Photo Edit. 4.3c © The Image Makers/The Image Bank. 4.4 Courtesy of Steven Alter. 4.5 Courtesy of Steven Alter. 4.6 Courtesy of English Wizard. 4.8 Courtesy of MapInfo. 4.14 © Dana Hyde/Photo Researchers, Inc. 4.15 Courtesy of NASA. 4.18 © Chris Salvo/FPG International.

Chapter 5
5.2 Courtesy of NASA. 5.4a © Ulf E. Wallin/The Image Bank. 5.4b © Bruce Ayers/Tony Stone Images. 5.5 Courtesy of Oracle. 5.7 Courtesy of Steven Alter. 5.8 Courtesy of the San Francisco Police Department. 5.9 Courtesy of Ventana Corp. 5.10 © Phillip Saltonstall.

Chapter 6
6.2 © Bill Michelsen. 6.9 Courtesy of San Jose Mercury News. 6.10 © Elena Dorfman. 6.12 Courtesy of Hertz. 6.13 © Michelle Bridwell MR/Photo Edit.

Chapter 7
7.2 Courtesy of Apple Computer, Inc. 7.3 Electronic Publishing Services, Inc. 7.4 Courtesy of Boeing. 7.5 © David Graham/Black Star. 7.7a © Lebrun-Photo News/Gamma Liaison. 7.7b Courtesy of Kurzweil Educational Systems, Inc. 7.7c © Reuters/Fred Prouser/Archive Photos.

Chapter 8
8.1a Courtesy of International Business Machines Corporation. Unauthorized use not permitted. 8.1b Courtesy of Canon Computer Systems. 8.2a © Ted Horowitz/The Stock Market. 8.2b Weinberg/Clark/The Image Bank. 8.9 Courtesy of Intel. 8.10a Courtesy of International Business Machines Corporation. Unauthorized use not permitted. 8.10b Tony Freeman/Photo Edit. 8.10c David K. Crow/Photo Edit. 8.11a Courtesy of International Business Machines Corporation. Unauthorized use not permitted. 8.11b Electronic Publishing Services, Inc. 8.12 Courtesy of Intel. 8.13a Courtesy of International Business Machines Corporation. Unauthorized use not permitted. 8.13b © Frank Wing/The Image Bank. 8.13c Courtesy of International Business Machines Corporation. Unauthorized use not permitted. 8.13d © Francis Hogan/Electronic Publishing Services, Inc. 8.14a Courtesy of International Business Machines Corporation. Unauthorized use not permitted. 8.14b © Steve Firebaugh. 8.14c Ed Kashi.

Chapter 9
9.8 Courtesy of Steven Alter. 9.9a The Bettmann Archive. 9.9b Motion Picture and TV Archive.

Chapter 10
10.5 © Hank Morgan/Photo Researchers, Inc. 10.10 © T. Tracy/FPG International. 10.12 © A. Ramey/Photo Edit. 10.13 Courtesy of International Business Machines Corporation. Unauthorized use not permitted.

Chapter 11
11.2 © John Storey. 11.10 Courtesy of Steven Alter.

Chapter 12
12.6 Courtesy of Steven Alter. 12.9 Courtesy of Steven Alter.

Chapter 13
13.6 © Larry Ford.

Company Index

Author Index

Glossary/Index

C

CIM. *See* Computer integrated manufacturing
CISC Complex Instruction Set Computer. 283. *See also* RISC
Circuit switching Process of setting up a temporary circuit between the source and destination for telephone calls. 355. *See also* Packet switching
Client-server architecture Computer system architecture consisting of client devices which send requests for service and server devices which perform the requested processing. 273–276
Coaxial cable Type of cable used for local area networks and other data transmission covering less than 10 miles. 358
COBOL, 313–316
Coding data, 276–280
  binary representations of numbers, 276–277
  binary representations of text, 277–278
  data compression, 278–279
  data encryption, 279–280
  numerical representations of sounds and pictures, 278
Collaboration, 86–87
Collision Calculation of the same location for two different records while storing or retrieving data in a computer system. 125
Common sense A shared understanding of how things work in everyday life. 323–324, 327, 329
Communications. *See also* Telecommunications; Telecommunications network
  basic concepts of, 150–154
  and computing, 21, 345–347
  form and content of, 151
  improving, 152–154
  and information systems, 161–178
  social context of, 150
  time, place, and direction of, 151–152
Communication systems Information systems that help people communicate. 164–169
Compatibility The extent to which the characteristics and features of a particular technology fit with those of other technologies relevant to the situation. 263
Competing on time A business strategy of providing more value by doing things faster than competitors. 210–202
Competitive advantage Advantage of one product versus another in terms of cost, features, or other characteristics. 197–204
  and information systems, 197–203
Competitive necessity In relation to systems, the need to use or provide a particular type of system in order to remain competitive. 200
Compiler A program which translates higher-level language programs into machine language. 313
Completeness (of information) The extent to which the available information seems adequate for the task. 136
Complexity How complicated a system is, based on a combination of how many types of elements the system contains and the number and nature of their interactions. 89
Computer A programmable device that can execute previously stored instructions. 266–292
Computer aided design (CAD) Use of a computer to support a design process. 7–8, 11
Computer aided software engineering (CASE) Use of computerized systems to improve the process of analyzing, designing, developing, and maintaining information systems. 308–309, 318–320
Computer conferencing The exchange of text messages typed into computers from various locations to discuss a particular issue. 168
Computer crime The use of computerized systems to perform illegal acts. 60, 467–472
  and security risk, 467–472
Computer integrated manufacturing (CIM) Use of computers and communication technology to integrate design, manufacturing, planning, and other business functions. 10–11
Computer languages
  assembly, 311–312
  fourth generation, 316
  generations of, 311–317
  higher-level, 312–316
  machine, 311, 312
  special-purpose, 317
Computer-mediated work Work done through computers, rather than through direct physical contact with the object of the task. 237
Computer output microfilm Form of computer output that bypasses paper and shrinks pages of output to tiny images stored on film. 288
Computer performance
  approaches for increasing, 280–284
  instruction sets and, 282–283
  parallel processing, 283–284
  processors and, 280–282, 283
Computer program A set of instructions in a programming language that specifies the data processing to be performed by the computer. 303
Computer programming, 302–319
  advancements in, 307–319
  artificial intelligence (*See* Artificial intelligence)
  as a business process, 302–303
  databases, 120–121
  debugging, 306
  language generations (*See* Computer languages)
  object-oriented, 309–310
  organizing ideas for, 304–305
  testing of, 305–307, 431–432
  as a translation process, 303
Computer software. *See* Software
Computer system A system consisting of computers and computer-controlled devices that process data by executing programs. 266
  architectures of, 268–273
    centralized computing, 269–271
    distributed computing, 271–272
    network computing, 272–273
    personal computing, 271
  basic model of, 266–267
  client-server, 273–276
  and communications, 21, 345–347
  and databases, 114–122
  and data processing, 346–347
  overview of, 266–276
  and telecommunications, 349 (*See also* Telecommunications)
  types of, 267–268
Conformance to standards and regulations Degree of adherence to standards and regulations imposed by external bodies such as major customers, industry groups, or the government. 196–197
Connectivity In an organization, the ability to access and use geographically dispersed data and resources; in computerized systems, the technical ability to transmit data between devices. 20, 349
Consistency (of business processes) Applying the same techniques in the same way to obtain the same desired results. 95
Constraints Limitations that make particular changes infeasible even though they might otherwise seem beneficial. 62
Context (of a work system) The organizational, competitive, technical, and regulatory realm within which a work system operates, including external stakeholders, the organization's policies, practices, and culture, and competitive and regulatory issues that affect the system. 51
Context diagram Data flow diagram verifying the scope of a system by showing the sources and destinations of data used and generated. 76–79
Controlling The process of using information about past work performance to assure that goals are attained and plans carried out. 90–92
Convergence of computing and communications Communication capabilities become essential to many computer systems and computing capabilities become essential to communication systems. 21, 345–347
Conversion Process of converting from a previous system to a successor system. 432–434
Cost What the internal or external customer must give up in order to

D

Digitization Coding data as an equivalent or approximately equivalent set of numbers. 21–22
Digitizing The process of generating a series of numbers representing images and sounds. 278
Direct access Data access method for finding an individual item in a file by calculating its location in a computer system. 125–126
Direct marketing The process of selling through mail or other forms of communication addressed to specific individuals. 209–210
Disaster plan (for information systems) A plan of action to recover from occurrences that shut down or harm major information systems. 487
Displaying information Showing information to a user. 17
Distributed computing Computing in which individuals do their own owrk on personal computers and use a telecommunications network to link to other devices. 269, 271–272. *See also* Centralized computing, Personal computing
Distributed database Database that is spread across more than one location. 127
Documentation Formal, written explanation of how a system operates. 431
Downsizing Reduction in both total staffing and layers of management. 393–394
DSP Digital signal processor. Specialized, single-purpose microprocessor devoted to processing voice or video signals. 283
Dumb terminal Terminal that serves only as an input/output mechanism linking users with the central computer. 269
DVD Digital versatile disk. An optical disk which holds 4.7 gigabytes of data. 290

E

Ease of use Ease of learning how to use a technology, ease of setting it up, ease of becoming proficient, and ease of using it directly. 262–263
EDI. *See* Electronic data interchange
Effectiveness The extent to which a system accomplishes the right goals. 52
Efficiency The ratio between outputs and inputs for a particular task, regardless of whether the task itself is the right task to perform. 52
Electronic banking, 205–206
Electronic cash Means of transferring funds for small purchases through the use of computers. 15
Electronic commerce Using the Web and other electronic means for selling and distributing products. 12–13, 204–208
Electronic data interchange (EDI) The electronic transmission of business data such as purchase orders and invoices from one firm's computerized information system to that of another firm. 9–10, 14
Electronic mail (e-mail) The use of computers to send and retrieve text messages or documents addressed to individual people or locations. 164–167
Electronic publishing, 206
Electronic retailing, 204–205
Electronic stock trading, 205
Embedded computer A computer that is an internal component of another machine. 267
Encoding (data) Process of converting data from an original form into a form for transmission. 349. *See also* Telecommunications network
Encryption Process of coding data to make it meaningless to anyone who steals it. 138, 279–280
End-user computing (EUC) Direct, hands-on use of computer systems by end users whose jobs go beyond entering data into a computer or processing transactions. 445–449
End-user development The development of information systems by work system participants (end users) rather than information system professionals. 427–428
End-user software General-purpose tools designed for end users without assistance by programmers. 301–302
Enhancement Improvements in an existing system's function without changing its fundamental concepts or operation. 389
Enterprise information systems, 170–171
Enterprise resource planning (ERP) system Information system that uses an integrated database to support typical business processes within functional areas and consistent information access across areas. 179
Entity A specific thing about which an information system collects information. 111
Entity-relationship diagram (ERD) Diagram identifying the entity types in a situation and diagramming the relationships between those entity types. 111–112
Entity type A kind of thing an information system collects information about. 111
Environment (of a system) Everything pertinent to the system that is outside of its boundaries. 38
Ergonomics Study of the interplay of human characteristics and characteristics of machines people use. 232–233
Error correction Process of correcting incorrect data that has been entered into a computerized system. 484
Errors, in computer programs, 305–306
Ethical dilemmas Difficult choices related to ethical issues that may or may not be covered by laws. 243
Ethical theories Principles that can be used as a basis for deciding what to do in ethical dilemmas. 244–245
Ethics A branch of philosophy dealing with the principles of right and wrong behavior related to other people. 242–245
Evolutionary prototype A prototype designed to be adapted for permanent use after the ideas are clarified. 437
Executing The process of doing the work. 90–92
Execution systems Information systems that support value added work. 177–178
Executive information system (EIS) A highly interactive system providing managers and executives flexible access to information for monitoring operating results and general business conditions. 171–173
Expert systems Information system that supports work of professionals in bounded, but complex situations in which recognized experts do better than nonexperts. 178, 325–329
applicability of, 326–327
components of, 327–328
and human mimicking, 329
reasoning and, 328–329
Explanation module Part of an expert system that explains how a particular fact was inferred or why a particular question is being asked. 328
External customers People who receive and use work system outputs that go outside the firm. 45–46
External specification A document explaining the results produced by the detailed requirements analysis. 430
Extranet Private network that operates similarly to an intranet but is directed at customers or suppliers rather than at employees. 168

F

Fax The transmission of a picture of a page to create a facsimile of the page at a different location. 164–167
Feasibility study A user-oriented overview of a proposed information system's purpose and feasibility. 429
Fiber optic cable Type of cable that transmits data using a core of ultra-pure glass. 358–359
Field In a file, a group of characters that have a predefined meaning. 117–118
File A set of related records. 117–118
File server A specialized computer dedicated to retrieving data from a database. 273
Finance systems, 14–16
Firewall A program that inspects incoming messages from a network, decides whether they are legitimate, sends legitimate messages to their destinations, and keeps track of messages that were stopped. 480

Interpreter A computer program which translates and executes each successive line of a program. 313

Intranet Private communication network that uses the type of interface popularized by the Web but is accessible only by authorized employees, contractors, and customers. 168

IS. *See* Information system

ISDN (Integrated service digital network) A set of standards to handle voice and computer data in telephone networks, providing additional telephone capabilities without scrapping existing copper telephone lines. 361–362

IT. *See* Information technology

J

Joint application development (JAD) A system development strategy in which users and information systems staff members spend 2 to 4 days together in a carefully prepared meeting to come to a shared understanding of the business problem early in the project. 451

K

Key A field that uniquely identifies which person, thing, or event is described by a record in a file. 117–118

Keyboards, 284–286

Keyword Term that describes a general area of information in which a document or Web site may be classified. 131

Kilobyte, 264

Knowledge A combination of instincts, ideas, rules, and procedures that guide actions and decisions. 49

Knowledge base Part of an expert system consisting of facts and if-then rules supplied by an expert. 327

Knowledge-based system System which represents knowledge in an explicit form so that it can be used in a problem solving process. 326

Knowledge management system Communication system designed to facilitate the sharing of knowledge rather than just information. 168–169

L

LAN. *See* Local area network

Laptop computer A portable PC that fits into a briefcase. 267

Last-mile problem The question of how high speed signals will be transmitted from high capacity trunk lines into homes and small businesses. 358

Legacy system Old, and often technically obsolete, information system that still exists because it performs essential data processing such as accounting and customer billing. 395

Legal issues, and information systems, 243–244

Level of summarization A comparison between the number of individual items on which data are based and the number of items in the data presented. 138

Liability Legal responsibility fro one's actions or products. 466

Local area network (LAN) Network connecting personal computers and other equipment within a local area to help people share equipment, data, and software. 363–365

Logic bomb A type of trojan horse whose destructive actions occur based on a particular condition, such as the initiation of a particular program. 471

Logic error Bug that causes a program to perform incorrect processing even though the program is syntactically correct. 306

Logical reference Identifies the data the programmer wants but doesn't say exactly how to find the data. 126

Logical view of data View of data expressing the way the user or programmer thinks about the data. 117

Lossless compression A method of data compression for typical business data and text that does not affect data quality. 279

Lossy compression A method of data compression which causes some degradation in data quality but still suffices for some audio, video, and image applications. 279

Lower-CASE (computer aided software engineering) A set of CASE tools used by programmers to facilitate the programming process. 319

M

Machine-centered design Design of a technology or process with the primary goal of simplifying what machines must do. 227–229

Machine independence Ultimate of software portability, whereby a program written in a particular language can be executed on any brand of computer. 308

Machine language The internal programming language for a particular chip. 280, 311–312

Magnetic disks, 288–290

Magnetic ink character recognition (MICR) Data input technology based on the automatic recognition of magnetic ink. 286

Magnetic tape Sequential data storage medium that uses the magnetization and demagnetization of tiny regions on a plastic tape. 288–289

Mainframe computer Computer used to control large databases, perform high volume transaction processing, and generate reports from large databases. 267–268

Maintainability Ease with which users or technical specialists can keep the technology running and upgrade it to suit the changing needs of the situation. 263–264

Maintenance The process of modifying the information system over time after it has been implemented. 434–435

Malfunctions. *See* Accidents and malfunctions

Management
- information needed by, 102
- information sources, 102
- information systems, 171–173

Management by maxim A framework for aligning IT with business needs by identifying business maxims and defining related IT maxims, 399–400

Management information system (MIS) Information system which provides information for managing an organization. 171–173

Manipulating data Transforming data through summarizing, sorting, rearranging, reformatting, or other types of calculations. 17

Manufacturing systems, 10–11

Marketing and sales systems, 11–13

Market segmentation Process of dividing the market into different customers willing to pay different amounts for different types or levels of service. 214–215

Mass customization The use of mass production techniques to produce customized products or services. 11

Mathematical model A series of equations or graphs that describe precise relationships between variables. 140–141

Measurements of data processing
- amounts of data, 264
- internal clock speed, 265
- rate of data transfer, 265
- speed of executing instructions, 265
- time, 264–265
- transmission frequency, 265

Measures of performance, 54–55

Megabyte, 264

Megahertz, 265

Mental models The unwritten assumptions and beliefs that people use when they think about a topic. 139–140

Messaging systems, 164–166

Metadata Information defining data in the information system. 124

Micrographics, 288

Micron One millionth of a meter. 281

Microprocessor A component which integrates control logic and memory on a single chip. 280–282

Middleware Software controlling communication between clients and servers in a client server network and performing whatever translation is necessary to make a client's request understandable to a server device. 275–276

Virtual reality A simulation of reality that engages the participant's senses and intellect by permitting the participant to interact with the simulated environment. 141–142
Virus A special type of Trojan horse that can replicate itself and spread, much like a biological virus. 471
Virus protection Process of protecting against computer viruses using software which automatically scans diskettes and operates at other possible sites of virus infection. 480
Voice mail (v-mail) A computerized method for storing and forwarding spoken messages. 164–167
Voice recognition Converts from spoken words to text by matching the sound patterns of spoken words with previously stored sound patterns. 286–287
VSAT Very small aperture terminal for satellite communications. 360

W

Waste Any activity that uses resources without adding value. 96
WCA. *See* Work-centered analysis framework; Work-centered analysis method
Web page A hypertext document directly accessible via the World Wide Web. 129–130
What-if question Question posed and answered (typically using a mathematical model) to understand the effect of different assumptions or different decisions. 140–141. *See also* Sensitivity analysis
Wide area network (WAN) Telecommunications network that spans a wide geographical area such as a state or country. 366–367
Work The application of human and physical resources such as people, equipment, time, effort, and money to generate outputs used by internal or external customers. 42
Work, impacts on people, 230–238
Work-centered analysis (WCA) framework A starting point for thinking about a specific work system and information systems that support it. 44–50
Work-centered analysis (WCA) method Approach business professionals can use for analyzing systems at whatever level of depth is appropriate in the situation. 64–66
Workstation A powerful single-user computer used for computing intensive work such as complex data analysis, graphic design, and engineering. 267
Work system A system in which human participants perform a business process using information, technology, and other resources to produce products for internal or external customers. 3–4, 42–44. *See also* Business process
  architecture of, 50–53
  context of, 57–59
  customers in, 45–47
  information in, 48–49
  and information systems, 42–44
  infrastructure of, 55–57
  participants in, 48, 84–85
  and people, 227–229
  performance of, 54–55
  perspectives for viewing, 50–61, 68
  processes for, 47–48
  products in, 47
  risks of, 59–61
  technology in, 50
World Wide Web (WWW), 2–3. *See also* Internet
  copyright violations on the Internet, 250
  distribution method for bug-corrected programs, 421
  domain name registration, 377–378
  EDI systems, 368
  electronic commerce
    airline reservations and information, 204–205
    banking, 205–206
    bookstores, 2–3, 11–12, 35, 204
    credit card fraud, 468
    external customers input order data, 46
    handling transactions, 206–208
    online auctions for supplies purchases, 215
    publishing, 206
    stock brokerage, 287
    stock trading, 205
    used car auctions, 106
  growth of WWW, 27
  HTTP and, 370
  inadequate system performance of America Online (AOL), 465–466
  information purchases via, 15
  information services, 371–372
  Lexis, availability through WWW, 129
  online auctions for supplies purchases, 215
  sabotage and vandalism on, 470–471
  stock brokerage online, 16
  theft of passwords to Internet accounts, 478–479
  uniform resource locators (URLs), 129
  WebTV purchase by Microsoft, 362

Y

Year 2000 (Y2K) problem Widespread problem that may cause information system failures around January 1, 2000 due to the programming practice of using two digits to identify the year portion of a date. 24–25, 26, 339–340, 388, 463–464, 466, 487
Yield management The process of trying to maximize revenue by selling the same product (such as a seat on a flight) to different customers at different prices. 215